MASTER VISUALLY™

Adobe® Photoshop,® Illustrator,® Premiere,® and After Effects®

Visual™

by Michael Toot and Sherry Kinkoph

From

maranGraphics®

&

Hungry Minds™

Best Selling Books • Digital Downloads • e-Books • Answer Networks • e-Newsletters • Branded Web Sites • e-Learning

New York, NY • Cleveland, OH • Indianapolis, IN

Master VISUALLY™ Adobe® Photoshop,® Illustrator,® Premiere,® and After Effects®

Published by
Hungry Minds, Inc.
909 Third Avenue
New York, NY 10022

maranGraphics, Inc.

5755 Coopers Avenue

Mississauga, Ontario, Canada

L4Z 1R9

Library of Congress Control Number: 2002100177

ISBN: 0-7645-3668-0

Printed in the United States of America

10 9 8 7 6 5 4 3 2 1

1V/RX/QV/QS/IN

Distributed in the United States by Hungry Minds, Inc.

Distributed by CDG Books Canada Inc. for Canada; by Transworld Publishers Limited in the United Kingdom; by IDG Norge Books for Norway; by IDG Sweden Books for Sweden; by IDG Books Australia Publishing Corporation Pty. Ltd. for Australia and New Zealand; by TransQuest Publishers Pte Ltd. for Singapore, Malaysia, Thailand, Indonesia, and Hong Kong; by Gotop Information Inc. for Taiwan; by ICG Muse, Inc. for Japan; by Intersoft for South Africa; by Eyrolles for France; by International Thomson Publishing for Germany, Austria and Switzerland; by Distribuidora Cuspide for Argentina; by LR International for Brazil; by Galileo Libros for Chile; by Ediciones ZETA S.C.R. Ltda. for Peru; by WS Computer Publishing Corporation, Inc., for the Philippines; by Contemporanea de Ediciones for Venezuela; by Express Computer Distributors for the Caribbean and West Indies; by Micronesia Media Distributor, Inc. for Micronesia; by Chips Computadoras S.A. de C.V. for Mexico; by Editorial Norma de Panama S.A. for Panama; by American Bookshops for Finland.

For corporate orders, please call maranGraphics at 800-469-6616 or fax 905-890-9434.

For general information on Hungry Minds' products and services please contact our Customer Care Department within the U.S. at 800-762-2974, outside the U.S. at 317-572-3993 or fax 317-572-4002.

For sales inquiries and reseller information, including discounts, premium and bulk quantity sales, and foreign-language translations, please contact our Customer Care Department at 800-434-3422, fax 317-572-4002, or write to Hungry Minds, Inc., Attn: Customer Care Department, 10475 Crosspoint Boulevard, Indianapolis, IN 46256.

For information on licensing foreign or domestic rights, please contact our Sub-Rights Customer Care Department at 212-884-5000.

For information on using Hungry Minds' products and services in the classroom or for ordering examination copies, please contact our Educational Sales Department at 800-434-2086 or fax 317-572-4005.

For press review copies, author interviews, or other publicity information, please contact our Public Relations department at 317-572-3168 or fax 317-572-4168.

For authorization to photocopy items for corporate, personal, or educational use, please contact Copyright Clearance Center, 222 Rosewood Drive, Danvers, MA 01923, or fax 978-750-4470.

Screen shots displayed in this book are based on pre-released software and are subject to change.

Trademark Acknowledgments

Permissions

maranGraphics

 is a trademark of Hungry Minds, Inc.

U.S. Corporate Sales	U.S. Trade Sales
Contact maranGraphics at (800) 469-6616 or fax (905) 890-9434.	Contact Hungry Minds at (800) 434-3422 or (317) 572-4002.

Praise for Visual books...

"If you have to see it to believe it, this is the book for you!"
    –PC World

"I would like to take this time to compliment maranGraphics on creating such great books. I work for a leading manufacturer of office products, and sometimes they tend to NOT give you the meat and potatoes of certain subjects, which causes great confusion. Thank you for making it clear. Keep up the good work."
    –Kirk Santoro (Burbank, CA)

"I write to extend my thanks and appreciation for your books. They are clear, easy to follow, and straight to the point. Keep up the good work! I bought several of your books and they are just right! No regrets! I will always buy your books because they are the best."
    –Seward Kollie (Dakar, Senegal)

"What fantastic teaching books you have produced! Congratulations to you and your staff."
    –Bruno Tonon (Melbourne, Australia)

"Compliments To The Chef!! Your books are extraordinary! Or, simply put, Extra-Ordinary, meaning way above the rest! THANKYOUTHANKYOU THANKYOU! for creating these. They have saved me from serious mistakes, and showed me a right and simple way to do things. I buy them for friends, family, and colleagues."
    –Christine J. Manfrin (Castle Rock, CO)

"A master tutorial/reference — from the leaders in visual learning!"
    –Infoworld

"Your books are superior! An avid reader since childhood, I've consumed literally tens of thousands of books, a significant quantity in the learning/teaching category. Your series is the most precise, visually appealing and compelling to peruse. Kudos!"
    –Margaret Rose Chmilar (Edmonton, Alberta, Canada)

"You're marvelous! I am greatly in your debt."
    –Patrick Baird (Lacey, WA)

"Just wanted to say THANK YOU to your company for providing books which make learning fast, easy, and exciting! I learn visually so your books have helped me greatly – from Windows instruction to Web page development. I'm looking forward to using more of your Master Books series in the future as I am now a computer support specialist. Best wishes for continued success."
    –Angela J. Barker (Springfield, MO)

"A publishing concept whose time has come!"
    –The Globe and Mail

"I have over the last 10-15 years purchased $1000's worth of computer books but find your books the most easily read, best set out and most helpful and easily understood books on software and computers I have ever read. You produce the best computer books money can buy. Please keep up the good work."
    –John Gatt (Adamstown Heights, Australia)

"The Greatest. This whole series is the best computer learning tool of any kind I've ever seen."
    –Joe Orr (Brooklyn, NY)

maranGraphics is a family-run business
located near Toronto, Canada.

At maranGraphics, we believe in producing great computer books – one book at a time.

maranGraphics has been producing high-technology products for over 25 years, which enables us to offer the computer book community a unique communication process.

Our computer books use an integrated communication process, which is very different from the approach used in other computer books. Each spread is, in essence, a flow chart – the text and screen shots are totally incorporated into the layout of the spread. Introductory text

and helpful tips complete the learning experience.

maranGraphics' approach encourages the left and right sides of the brain to work together – resulting in faster orientation and greater memory retention.

Above all, we are very proud of the handcrafted nature of our books. Our carefully-chosen writers are experts in their fields, and spend countless hours researching and organizing the content for each topic. Our artists rebuild every screen shot to provide the best clarity possible, making our screen

shots the most precise and easiest to read in the industry. We strive for perfection, and believe that the time spent handcrafting each element results in the best computer books money can buy.

Thank you for purchasing this book. We hope you enjoy it!

Sincerely,

Robert Maran
President
maranGraphics

Rob@maran.com
www.maran.com
www.hungryminds.com/visual

CREDITS

Acquisitions, Editorial, and Media Development

Project Editor
Timothy J. Borek

Acquisitions Editor
Jen Dorsey

Product Development Supervisor
Lindsay Sandman

Copy Editor
Dana Lesh

Technical Editor
Dennis R. Short

Permissions Editor
Laura Moss

Media Development Specialist
Megan Decraene

Editorial Manager
Rev Mengle

Editorial Assistant
Amanda Foxworth

Production

Book Design
maranGraphics®

Project Coordinator
Maridee Ennis

Layout
Melanie DesJardins
LeAndra Johnson
Kristin McMullan
Heather Pope

Screen Artists
Mark Harris
Jill A. Proll

Illustrators
Ronda David-Burroughs
David E. Gregory
Sean Johannesen
Russ Marini
Greg Maxson
Steven Schaerer

Proofreaders
Laura L. Bowman
Andy Hollandbeck
Carl Pierce

Indexer
Johnna VanHoose

Special Help
Dana Lesh
Jill Mazurczyk
Maureen Spears

GENERAL AND ADMINISTRATIVE

Wiley Technology Publishing Group: Richard Swadley, Vice President and Executive Group Publisher; Bob Ipsen, Vice President and Executive Publisher; Barry Pruett, Vice President and Publisher; Joseph Wikert, Vice President and Publisher; Mary Bednarek, Editorial Director; Mary C. Corder, Editorial Director; Andy Cummings, Editorial Director.

Wiley Production for Branded Press: Debbie Stailey, Production Director

ABOUT THE AUTHORS

Michael Toot

Michael Toot is a Seattle-based consultant and author, writing about both desktop Web applications and middleware technology. Prior to consulting he was a senior program manager and senior product manager at Attachmate Corporation and Digital Equipment Corporation, developing enterprise middleware solutions for Fortune 2000 customers. Before working full-time in the computer industry he was a litigation defense attorney. When not writing books he can be found reading, renovating a 94-year-old home with his wife and two cats, or sailing on Puget Sound.

Sherry Willard Kinkoph

Sherry Willard Kinkoph has written more than 40 books covering a variety of computer topics ranging from hardware to software, from Microsoft Office programs to Internet topics far and wide. Her recent titles include *Teach Yourself VISUALLY Flash 5*, *Teach Yourself VISUALLY Premiere 6*, *Master VISUALLY Dreamweaver 4 and Flash 5*, and *Master VISUALLY FrontPage 2002*. Sherry's never-ending quest is to help users of all levels master the ever-changing computer technologies. No matter how many times software manufacturers and hardware conglomerates throw out a new version or upgrade, Sherry vows to be there to make sense of it all and help computer users get the most out of their machines.

AUTHORS' ACKNOWLEDGMENTS

From Michael Toot: My thanks for help on this book go to: Jen Dorsey, my acquisitions editor, who was flexible in the face of impending deadlines (emphasis on dead); Tim Borek, project editor, who kept all the balls in the air despite my attempts to create chaos out of order; Dennis Short, technical editor, who brought his considerable expertise to a complex project; Dana Lesh, who gently reminded me when I blatantly ignored style guidelines; Barry Pruett and Darlene Pitts in the front office, who managed the business side while us creative types thrashed around; the unsung heroes in Production who created the concept art, reworked the screenshots, and polished the layout; and my contributing authors, Sherry Kinkoph and Mike Wooldridge, who made my job a whole lot easier by doing all the heavy lifting in the manuscripts. A hearty round of applause to you all!

From Sherry Willard Kinkoph: Special thanks go out to acquisitions editor Jen Dorsey for allowing me to tackle such a great topic; to Tim Borek for managing the entire process with much aplomb; and to the production team at Hungry Minds for their efforts in creating such a visual masterpiece.

To Victoria, my wife, confidante, and wonderfully
funny best friend. I love you, dearest. Want
to run away with me?
— Michael

To budding digital filmmakers everywhere.
— Sherry

ADOBE® PHOTOSHOP®, ILLUSTRATOR,® PREMIERE,® AND AFTER EFFECTS®

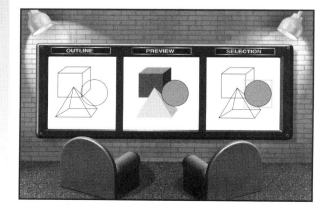

III

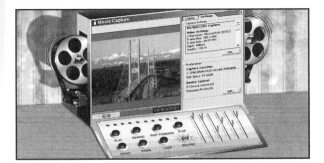

IV

1

1) GETTING STARTED WITH PHOTOSHOP

2) WORKING WITH SELECTIONS

TABLE OF CONTENTS

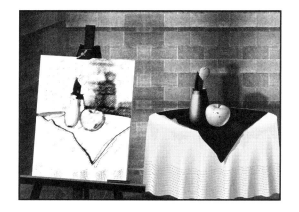

TABLE OF CONTENTS

10) WORKING WITH OBJECTS AND SYMBOLS

11) WORKING WITH TYPE

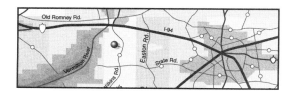

TABLE OF CONTENTS

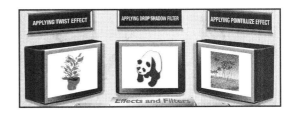

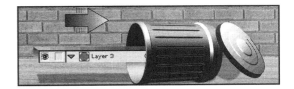

3

PREMIERE

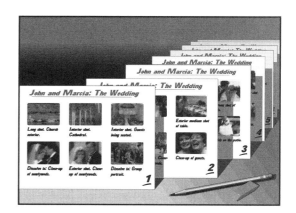

16) WORKING WITH VIDEO AND AUDIO

17) EDITING IN THE MONITOR WINDOW

TABLE OF CONTENTS

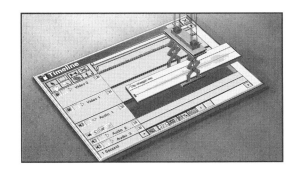

18) EDITING IN THE TIMELINE WINDOW

19) FINE-TUNING VIDEO EDITS AND TRANSITIONS

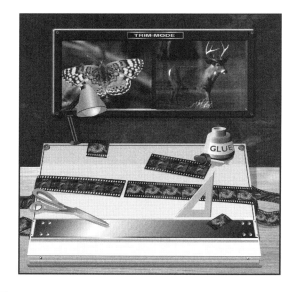

20) CREATING VIDEO AND MOTION EFFECTS

TABLE OF CONTENTS

21) EDITING AUDIO

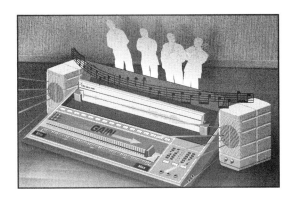

22) OUTPUTTING DIGITAL VIDEO

23) GETTING STARTED WITH AFTER EFFECTS

24) WORKING WITH VIDEO FOOTAGE

25) WORKING WITH LAYERS

TABLE OF CONTENTS

26) WORKING WITH LAYER PROPERTIES

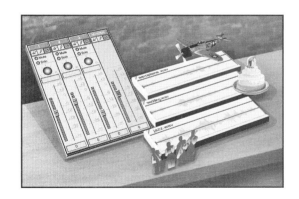

27) ADDING ANIMATION AND LAYER TECHNIQUES

28) WORKING WITH MASKS

29) CREATING VIDEO EFFECTS

TABLE OF CONTENTS

30) WORKING WITH 3D EFFECTS

31) RENDERING AND SAVING OUTPUT

APPENDIX

ADOBE® PHOTOSHOP®, ILLUSTRATOR®, PREMIERE®, AND AFTER EFFECTS®

Master VISUALLY™ Adobe® Photoshop®, Illustrator®, Premiere®, and After Effects® contains straightforward tasks to help you create and publish your own professional-quality digital videos, complete with animation, artwork, and effects. The book explains how to create graphics, manipulate digital photos, import sound and video clips, create special effects, and output your finished production to various media.

This book is designed to help a reader receive quick access to any area of question. You can simply look up a subject within the Table of Contents or Index and go immediately to the task of concern. A *task* is a self-contained unit that walks you through a computer operation step by step. That is, with rare exception, all the information you need regarding an area of interest is contained within a task.

Who This Book Is For

This book is for the beginning multimedia designer — on both Mac and Windows platforms — who wants to harness the power of the sophisticated Adobe® Digital Video Collection. It is also for the intermediate to advanced user, who knows something about computers but has never used Adobe Digital Video Collection or is just making the switch to this latest edition of Photoshop, Illustrator, Premiere, or After Effects.

What You Need To Use This Book

Below are the minimum requirements your computer needs to run Adobe Digital Video Collection. Both Macintosh and Windows systems require a CD-ROM drive, 32-bit sound card, 24-bit color display adapter, and at least 128 megabytes (MB) of RAM memory. For questions about your individual requirements, or to learn about additional requirements, see www.adobe.com/products/dvcoll/systemreqs.html.

Minimum Windows Requirements

Processor. Intel Pentium III 500 MHz or faster.

Microsoft Windows. Microsoft Windows 98, Windows Millennium Edition, Windows 2000 with Service Pack 2, or Windows XP all support Adobe Digital Video Collection.

Hard Disk. 510MB of available hard-disk space required for installation. 1GB or more hard disk or disk array space recommended for ongoing work.

Additional Windows Requirements for Premiere and After Effects:

- Dedicated large-capacity 7200 rpm UDMA 66 IDE or SCSI hard disk or disk array.
- Microsoft-certified OHCI IEEE 1394 interface.
- Premiere-certified capture card (if capturing from an analog video source).

Minimum Macintosh Requirements

Processor. PowerPC 300MHz processor G3 or faster.

HOW TO USE THIS BOOK

OS 9.1 or higher.

Hard Disk. 475MB of available hard-disk space to install all applications. For ongoing work, we recommend 1GB or more hard disk or disk array space.

Additional Macintosh Requirements for Premiere and After Effects:

- Large-capacity hard disk or disk array capable of sustaining 5MB/sec.
- QuickTime-compatible FireWire (IEEE 1394) interface.
- Apple FireWire 2.4.
- Premiere-certified capture card (if capturing from an analog video source).

The Conventions in This Book

This book uses the following conventions to describe the actions you perform when using the mouse. This book uses a number of typographic and layout styles to help distinguish different types of information:

- **Click** means that you press and release the left mouse button. You use a click to select an item on the screen.
- **Double-click** means that you quickly press and release the left mouse button twice. You use a double-click to open a document or start a program.
- **Right-click** means that you press and release the right mouse button. You use a right-click to display a shortcut menu, a list of commands specifically related to the selected item.
- **Click and Drag** means that you position the mouse pointer over an item on the screen and then press and hold down the left mouse button. Still holding down the button, move the mouse to where you want to place the item and then release the button. Dragging and dropping makes it easy to move an item to a new location.
- **Bold** represents information that you type.
- *Italics* indicate the introduction of a new term.
- **Numbered steps** indicate that you must perform these steps in order to successfully perform the task.
- **Bulleted steps** give you alternate methods, explain various options, or present what a program will do in response to the numbered steps.
- Notes are *italicized* statements beneath screen shots that give you additional information to help you complete a task.
- **Icons** indicate a program button that you must click with the mouse.

 Many tasks in this book are supplemented with a section called Master It. These are tips, hints, and tricks that extend your use of the task beyond what you learned by performing the task itself.

The Organization of Each Chapter

Each task contains an introduction, a set of screen shots, and a set of tips. The introduction tells why you want to perform the task, the advantages and disadvantages of performing the task, a general explanation of task procedures, and references to other related tasks in the book. The screens, located on the bottom half of each page, show a series of steps that you must complete to perform a given task. The tip section gives you an opportunity to further understand the task at hand, to learn about other related tasks in other areas of the book, or to apply more complicated or alternative methods. A chapter may also contain an illustrated group of pages that gives you background information that you need to understand the tasks in a chapter.

The parts of this book are organized by application. The book starts with basic Photoshop operations, shows you how to draw with Illustrator, then gets you editing video in Premiere, and finally shows you how to use After Effects to add dazzle to your finished Premiere video. The appendix explains the contents of the CD-ROM included with this book.

Part I, "Photoshop," introduces you to basic Photoshop concepts and shows you how to work with selections, color, and layers. Chapter 5 introduces the creative benefits of applying filters. You learn how to add and manipulate text in Chapter 6. Finally, in Chapter 7, you learn to save and print images for a variety of applications.

Part II, "Illustrator," shows you how to create fabulous pictures for individual display or eventual use in digital video. Chapter 8 explains Illustrator basics. Chapters 9 through 13 cover paths, objects, symbols, type, effects, filters, styles, and layers. You learn the finer points of saving and printing your Illustrator documents in Chapter 14.

Part III, "Premiere," illustrates how to create broadcast-quality videos. Chapter 16 covers audio and video basics. Chapter 17 shows you how to edit in the Monitor window, and Chapter 18 shows you how to edit in the Timeline window. Chapter 19 explains how to fine-tune your edits and transition. Chapter 20 spices things up by demonstrating the use of various video and motion effects. You learn to tweak audio in Chapter 21. Finally, in Chapter 22, you learn to output your video in different formats, and the pros and cons of each.

Part IV, "After Effects," shows you how to apply finishing touches that can give your videos true Hollywood flare. For example, Chapter 27 covers adding animation, and Chapter 30 shows how to create stunning 3D effects. Chapter 31 concludes this exciting section with a detailed discussion of rendering and saving output.

The back of the book contains supplemental material, including how to install and use the included software. You also get more detailed system requirements and troubleshooting tips.

SECTION I

3) WORKING WITH COLOR

4) WORKING WITH LAYERS

5) APPLYING FILTERS

6) ADDING AND MANIPULATING TEXT

7) SAVING AND PRINTING IMAGES

UNDERSTANDING PHOTOSHOP

Photoshop lets you create, modify, combine, and optimize digital images. As its name suggests, Photoshop excels at editing digital photographs. You can use the program to make subtle changes, such as adjusting a scanned photo's color, or you can use its elaborate filters to make your snapshots look like abstract art.

Photoshop's painting features also make it a formidable illustration tool. You can apply colors or patterns to your images with a variety of brush styles. In addition, Photoshop provides typographic tools for integrating stylized letters and words into your images.

Create a Digital Collage

You can combine different image elements, such as digital photos, scanned art, and text, in Photoshop. By putting elements in Photoshop onto separate layers, you can move, transform, and customize them independently of one another.

Organize Your Photos

Photoshop offers useful ways to keep your images organized after you have edited them. You can archive your images on contact sheets or display them in a Web photo gallery. See Chapter 7 for information on contact sheets and the Web photo gallery.

Understanding Pixels

Digital images in Photoshop are made up of tiny, solid-color squares called *pixels*. Photoshop works its magic by rearranging and recoloring these squares. If you zoom in close, you can see the pixels that make up your image.

To edit specific pixels in your image, you first have to select them by using one of Photoshop's selection tools. Photoshop also has a number of commands that help you select specific parts of your image, including commands that expand or contract your existing selection or select pixels of a specific color. See Chapter 2 to learn about selection tools.

Paint

After you have selected your pixels, you can apply color to them by using Photoshop's paintbrush, airbrush, and pencil tools. You can also fill your selections with solid or semitransparent colors. You can brighten, darken, and change the hue of colors in parts of your image with Photoshop's Dodge and Burn tools. Other commands display interactive dialog boxes that let you make wholesale color adjustments, letting you precisely correct overly dark or light digital photographs. See Chapter 3 for details.

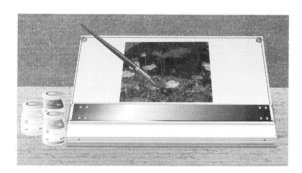

Apply Effects and Filters

Photoshop's effects let you easily add drop shadows, 3D shading, and other effects to your images. You can also perform complex color manipulations or distortions by using Photoshop filters. Filters can make your image look like an impressionist painting, blur or sharpen your image, or distort your image in various ways. Chapters 4 and 5 explain effects and filters.

Add Type

Photoshop's type tools enable you to easily apply titles and labels to your images. You can combine these tools with Photoshop's special effects commands to create warped, 3D, or wildly colored type. You can find out more about type in Chapter 6.

NAVIGATE THE PHOTOSHOP WORK AREA

Photoshop has several components for working with images, illustrations, and text.

Take some time to familiarize yourself with the on-screen elements.

Title Bar

Photoshop displays the name of the current document.

Menu Bar

Displays Photoshop menus, which when clicked show menu commands.

Options Bar

The options bar gives you quick access to the most commonly used options for the currently selected tool in the toolbox.

Toolbox

The toolbox contains shortcut buttons for common commands and tools, such as the Paintbrush tool or the Lasso tool.

Navigator Palette

The Navigator palette is used to quickly change your views of an image.

Color Palette

You use the Color palette to apply color to an object's fill and stroke, and also to edit and mix colors.

Layers Palette

The Layers palette lists all the layers in a document, starting with the front-most layer.

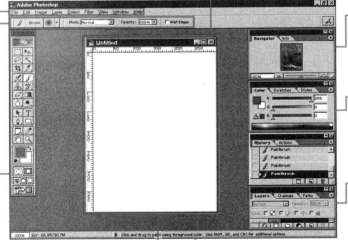

Image Window

The Image window includes the images you are working on, and is where you do most of your work.

Status Bar

The Status bar displays the current image magnification, the document size, and other information you may find useful.

Navigate Palettes

Palettes are small windows that you can quickly view or hide in Photoshop. You use palettes to change or set options for the many tools selected from the toolbox, or view artwork or object properties. If you have enough screen space, you can have all the palettes open at once.

To close an open palette on the Macintosh, click the palette's Close Button (▢). Windows users can click the Close Button (☒).

Dock a Palette

You can move palettes between the palette windows, which is called *docking* a palette. You can create the most useful combination of palettes for your artwork this way. You move a palette by clicking and dragging its tab from one palette to another and then releasing the mouse. The palette's tab appears in the new window.

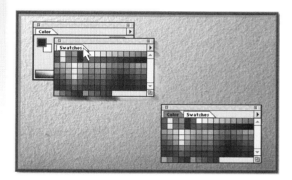

Change Palette Options

You can also change the palette viewing area and the commonly used palette options without hunting through menus. Doing this helps keep screen area available for artwork while leaving the tools still ready for use. The double arrowhead (⬍) appears only on the active tab, which is the one at the "front" of the stack. You need to click each tab to see if it has the double arrowhead on it. If no double arrowhead appears, the palette does not have other viewing modes.

SET PREFERENCES

You can use the Photoshop Preferences dialog box to let you change default settings and customize how the program looks. The Preferences dialog box also lets you adjust preferences to match the way you like to work.

Although the ability to preconfigure your software is not unique to Photoshop, it is a specialized, powerful tool, and you should take

some time and explore the Preferences to see how you can take advantage of them.

For example, you can use the Photoshop Preferences dialog box to set the file save location and format for your projects and files, set default cursors, choose your measurement units such as inches or pixels, and set scratch disk size.

Photoshop enables you to configure its look and feel in other ways. If you always have certain palettes open and certain brushes selected for digital images, you can specify which palettes should load when Photoshop starts. You select palette preferences in the Windows menu and choose whether to show or hide palettes at startup.

SET PREFERENCES

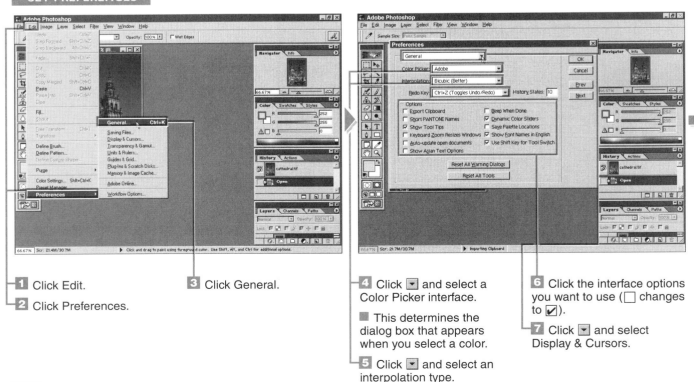

■1 Click Edit.

■2 Click Preferences.

■3 Click General.

■4 Click ▾ and select a Color Picker interface.

■ This determines the dialog box that appears when you select a color.

■5 Click ▾ and select an interpolation type.

■6 Click the interface options you want to use (☐ changes to ☑).

■7 Click ▾ and select Display & Cursors.

What type of measurement units should I use in Photoshop?

✔ Use the units most applicable to the method of output you plan to use. Pixels are best for digital imaging because computer screen dimensions are measured in pixels. Inches or picas are useful for print because those are the standards for working on paper.

Where should I save my files?

✔ You can change your file save locations depending on your project. If you are working collaboratively, you should save files on a server for your team members to access. If you are working on your own, you can save files on your own computer.

What are scratch disks?

✔ *Scratch disks* are areas on your hard drives where Photoshop can store the information it is working with. Photoshop uses these areas when it runs out of RAM on your computer. You can configure your scratch disks by clicking Edit, Preferences, and then Plug-Ins & Scratch Disks, or, if you have the Preferences dialog box already up, by selecting Plug-Ins & Scratch Disks from the Preferences type drop-down list. If possible, place your scratch disk on a separate hard drive for best performance.

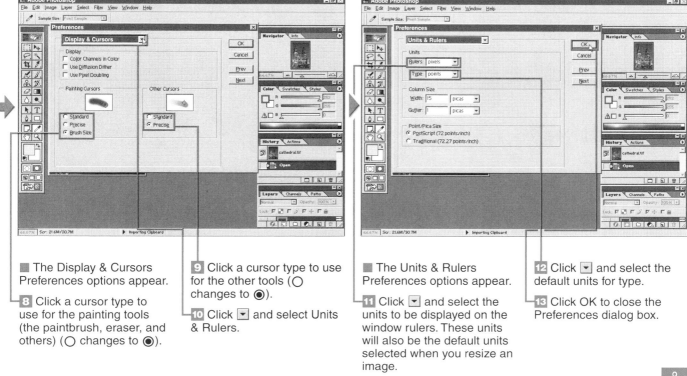

■ The Display & Cursors Preferences options appear.

8 Click a cursor type to use for the painting tools (the paintbrush, eraser, and others) (○ changes to ●).

9 Click a cursor type to use for the other tools (○ changes to ●).

10 Click ▾ and select Units & Rulers.

■ The Units & Rulers Preferences options appear.

11 Click ▾ and select the units to be displayed on the window rulers. These units will also be the default units selected when you resize an image.

12 Click ▾ and select the default units for type.

13 Click OK to close the Preferences dialog box.

CALIBRATE THE MONITOR

The three types of digital imaging devices — input (scanners and cameras), output (printers or television monitors), and your computer monitor — handle color differently. Each uses a different method of recording or outputting color images, which increases the likelihood of variance between the real world and eventual output.

Color *calibration* attempts to make adjustments on the middle link in the image chain, the computer where you are doing your digital editing. Because you are making decisions every minute regarding color, such as hue, saturation, shading, and blending, you want to make sure you are working with true colors and not ones distorted by your monitor into different areas of the color spectrum.

Photoshop gives you some basic color calibration tools that can help you calibrate your monitor to ensure that colors display accurately and reliably when you use Photoshop. An accurate color display is helpful in all applications, but is critical when working with print media. You should calibrate your monitor after you first install Photoshop, or every few months thereafter.

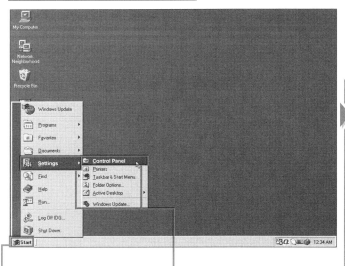

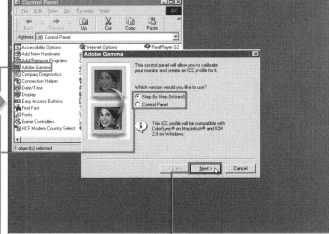

Note: For best results, let your monitor warm up for at least a half hour before calibrating. Also, make sure that your monitor is set to display thousands of colors or more.

■1 Click Start.

■2 Click Settings.

■3 Click Control Panel.

■ On a Macintosh, choose Control Panels from the Apple menu.

■4 Double-click the Adobe Gamma icon.

■5 Click an option to select an interface (○ changes to ◉).

Note: The Step By Step option provides a wizard to help calibrate your monitor. The Control Panel option lets you perform all the calibrations in a single dialog box (and is recommended only if you are a calibration expert).

■6 Click Next.

How should I calibrate my monitor if I am working collaboratively?

✔ If you are working on a Photoshop project with others — for instance, with other artists or with a printing company — it is a good idea for everyone to calibrate his or her monitor to a single standard. For instance, have everyone select the same 5000-Kelvin setting for the monitor's white point value.

What is a good gamma correction value?

✔ Macintoshes initially set gamma correction at 1.8, while PCs default to 2.5. You can set both systems to 2.2 and use that as a starting point.

Why does the same image look different on a Macintosh and a PC?

✔ PCs handle *gamma correction* differently than Macintoshes. Gamma correction is an adjustment to the difference between the monitor's pixel value and its displayed intensity, which also affects the RGB values. Macintoshes do some gamma correction on the graphics card and are more likely to display closer to the actual color than unadjusted PCs, which tend to be darker. If you work in a mixed shop, you should make sure your computer is adjusted properly.

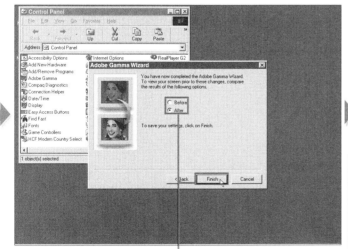

■ If you selected Step By Step, Photoshop walks you through several monitor calibration steps.

■ At the end of the Step By Step, you can toggle between your original and new calibration settings.

7 Click Finish.

8 Type a name for your profile.

9 Click Save.

Note: If you have strict color requirements for your work, you should recalibrate your monitor every few months.

11

OPEN AN IMAGE

You can open both new and saved digital images in Photoshop. When you open a new document, you must select the *document type*, which is the file format that the document will have.

Digital image files come in a wide variety of formats depending on the image's purpose and what application or device created it. Digital cameras often create images in JPEG (Joint Photographic

Experts Group) or MPEG (Moving Picture Experts Group) formats. Applications that generate images or work with images may have these formats available or have a proprietary format used only by that application.

Photoshop can open image files saved in a wide variety of formats, from the ones just mentioned to ones used by other Adobe products such as Illustrator and Acrobat.

Photoshop uses its own format (PSD, or Photoshop Document) that contains useful information about the image as well as information about layers, vector graphics, alpha channels, and other technologies that go into making up the illustration.

For information about saving files in these formats, see Chapter 7.

OPEN AN IMAGE

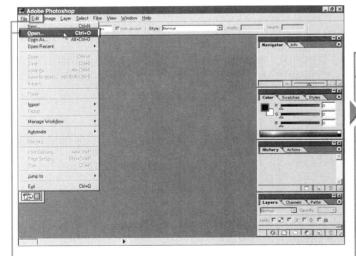

1 Click File.

2 Click Open.

■ The Open dialog box appears.

3 Click ▼ and browse to the folder that contains the image you want to open.

4 Click the filename of the image you want to open.

■ A preview of the image is displayed.

■ To limit the types of files listed, click ▼ and select a format from the Files of Type menu.

5 Click Open.

What do the file type acronyms stand for?

✔ The file type tells you what kind of file it is or what application or device created it. Here are some commonly used image file types that Photoshop can open:

Acronym	File Type
BMP (Bitmap)	A common Windows image format
PICT (Picture)	A common Macintosh image format
TIFF (Tagged Image File Format)	A popular format for printing on Windows and Macintosh
EPS (Encapsulated PostScript)	A print-oriented format containing vector information
JPEG (Joint Photographic Experts Group)	A Web image or digital camera format
GIF (Graphics Interchage Format)	A Web image format used for drawings or illustrations
PSD (Photoshop Document)	Photoshop's native file format
AI (Adobe Illustrator)	Illustrator's native format

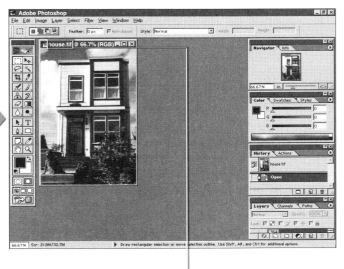

■ Photoshop opens the image in a new window.

■ The filename appears in the title bar.

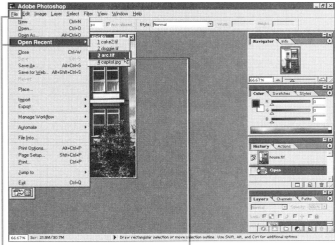

OPEN RECENTLY ACCESSED IMAGES

■1 Click File.

■2 Click Open Recent to view a list of files that you recently worked on.

■3 Click the filename of the image that you want to open.

■ Photoshop opens the image in a new window.

CREATE A NEW IMAGE

Most new Photoshop projects start with a blank image. If you are creating a new image from scratch, you can open up a new image without worrying too much about the type of image, its resolution, or its size. But if you have some ideas or size requirements for your image, you can set those parameters when you create a new image.

For instance, if you are working on a digital Web image that cannot be larger than a standard VGA screen, you have to define your new image to be 640 x 480 pixels in size. If you are working with an image that needs to be saved at different resolutions, you can set up the largest image size, create your image, and then save it in progressively smaller resolutions.

If you start small and work larger, you introduce pixelation and blurring, which must be corrected later.

This ability to define new image parameters is very helpful but requires you to plan how you will use the image ahead of time so you can avoid wasting time with editing and resizing later.

CREATE A NEW IMAGE

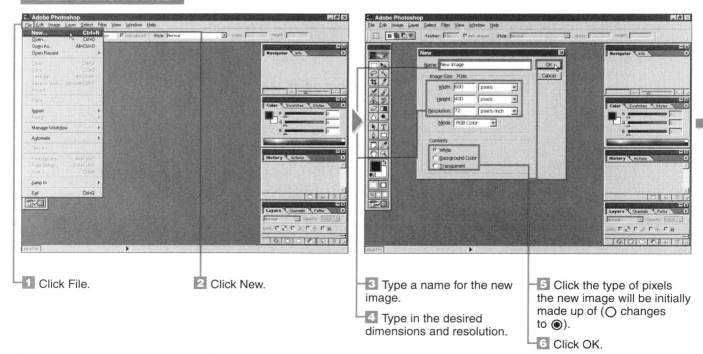

1 Click File.

2 Click New.

3 Type a name for the new image.

4 Type in the desired dimensions and resolution.

5 Click the type of pixels the new image will be initially made up of (○ changes to ◉).

6 Click OK.

What color mode should I use with digital images?

✔ You can select between the following modes: RGB Color (digital images); CMYK Color (print images); Bitmap (black-and-white images); Grayscale (print or digital images); and Lab Color (Photo CD images). For most of your digital image work, you will use RGB mode, or possibly Photo CD if you are working with images that will be saved to a photo disc.

What do the different pixel types mean?

✔ In the Contents dialog box, you can select the type of pixels to start with in your image. White generates a white background; Background Color sets the layer to the background color; and Transparent generates a single transparent layer.

How do I choose a resolution for a new image?

✔ The appropriate resolution depends on how the image will eventually be used. For Web or multimedia digital images, select 72 pixels/inch, which is the standard resolution for on-screen images. For black-and-white images to be printed on regular paper on a laser printer, 150 pixels/inch probably suffices. For full-color magazine or brochure images, you should use a higher resolution — at least 250 pixels/inch. If you work with a printing shop with specific requirements, find out what resolution works best with their equipment.

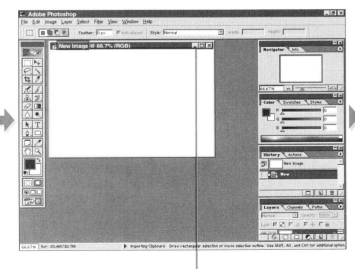

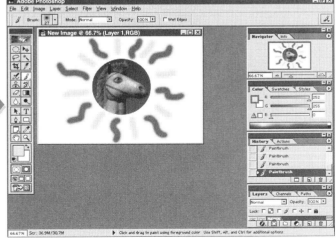

■ Photoshop creates a new image window at the specified dimensions.

■ The filename appears in the title bar.

7 Use Photoshop's tools and commands to create your image.

■ In this example, part of another image has been cut and pasted into the window, and color streaks were added with the paintbrush tool.

MAGNIFY WITH THE ZOOM TOOL

The ability to change image magnification is called *zooming*. Most applications offer some way of changing the magnification of what you see. In Photoshop, you can change the magnification of an image with the Zoom tool. The Zoom tool is one of several ways you can adjust the image magnification, either by increasing it to view a smaller area

in greater detail, or by decreasing it to view a greater area in less detail. Zooming in gives you the ability to make very small changes in images, or to apply colors, filters, or effects with a high degree of precision. Photoshop can magnify an image up to sixteen times its normal size (1600.00%), depending on the image, and down to .17%.

Depending on the type of image and its resolution, you may encounter *pixelation* at higher magnifications. Pixelation is the ability to view individual pixels in an image. You may also see image artifacts such as anti-aliased pixels used to smooth out jagged lines. You may encounter pixelation if you save an image at a size larger than its original one.

MAGNIFY WITH THE ZOOM TOOL

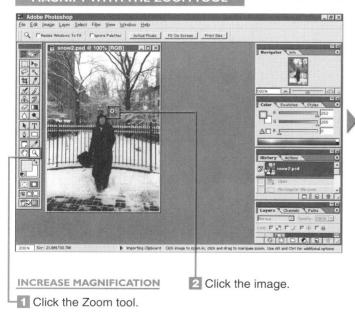

INCREASE MAGNIFICATION

1 Click the Zoom tool.

2 Click the image.

■ Photoshop increases the magnification of the image.

Note: You can also press Ctrl + + (Command - +) to increase magnification.

■ The point that was clicked in the image moves to the center of the window.

■ The current magnification is shown in the title bar and status bar.

Does the Navigator palette also have zooming tools?

✔ The Navigator palette displays an image thumbnail plus two zoom buttons, a slider bar, and zoom percentage. You can change your image magnification by pressing the buttons, moving the slider bar, or typing in a percentage in the box.

Can I type an exact percentage in the magnification box?

✔ You can type an exact percentage like 150 (as in 150%), a ratio like 3:2, or a multiplier like 1.5x, in the magnification box to change the magnification.

What do the three buttons on the options bar do?

✔ The options bar changes with the selected tool in the toolbox. When the Zoom tool is selected, you are given three buttons that provide specific zoom options. Actual Pixels sets the window zoom to 1:1, meaning each pixel in the image is matched to a pixel on your monitor. Fit On Screen adjusts the image so it is completely visible on the desktop. Print Size zooms the window to the printing resolution, which may change depending on the printer setup on your computer or the output type.

DECREASE MAGNIFICATION

1 Press and hold the Alt (Option) key and click the image.

■ The original image was clicked to reduce the magnification to 66.7%.

Note: You can also press Ctrl + – (Command - –) to decrease magnification.

MAGNIFY A DETAIL

1 Click and drag with the Zoom tool to select the detail.

■ The object appears enlarged on-screen.

USING RULERS AND GUIDES

You can turn on rulers or create guides, which help you accurately place elements in your Photoshop image. These rulers and guides help you align your text perfectly or place image elements an exact distance apart. You can also use rulers and guides to help you place repeating images on a background or to ensure that a corporate logo is accurately placed.

In most cases, digital Web-based images do not need to be precision-aligned like they do in print media. If you are working with print media, you need to use as much precision as possible. High-end printers have extremely fine resolution, and they require fine-grained control over image placement. Even on the Web, cleanly aligned images and text

show a sense of professionalism and attention to detail that will serve your Web site well.

Guides do not display in your final image, so you can use them as needed when editing images.

USING RULERS AND GUIDES

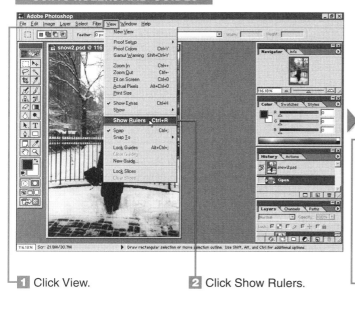

1 Click View.

2 Click Show Rulers.

■ Photoshop adds rulers to the top and left sides of the image window.

3 Click one of the rulers and drag the cursor into the window.

How do I change my ruler units?

✔ Click Preferences on the Edit menu, and then click Units & Rulers. A dialog box appears, which lets you change the units to pixels, inches, centimeters, points, picas, or percent. Pixels are useful for Web-based images, and inches or picas are useful for print-based images.

How do I snap image elements to a grid?

✔ Your elements can be aligned to a grid using the same method as for guides. Click View, Snap To, and then Grid to make your elements snap to the nearest grid lines.

Can I use multiple guides on my images?

✔ You can both set up and use multiple guides for your images, or you can use a grid. The grid is similar to a set of guides that overlays your image and helps you organize elements within your image. You turn on grids by clicking View, Show, and then Grid on menu bar.

■ A thin colored line called a guide appears.

Note: Guides help you position the different elements that make up your Photoshop image. These lines do not appear on the printed image.

4 Click the Move tool to adjust the placement of a guide.

5 Place the cursor over a guide and click and drag.

Note: To align elements moved into an image with the guides, click View and then Snap To Guides from the drop-down menu.

CHANGE THE ON-SCREEN IMAGE SIZE

When you consider what size to make your on-screen images, you can unintentionally limit your options if you choose dimensions that are not appropriate for the final product. For example, you can use a digital camera to shoot a 1600 x 1200 pixel image, and it looks great on a monitor set to display that resolution. On lower resolution monitors you will get scroll bars, or

borders, or other unintended artifacts that detract from your image.

The same can happen when you want to use the image on a Web page, and the page is set for an 800 x 600 monitor. Your image will fall far outside the Web page boundaries, or will stretch the table cell where it was included, or distort the page layout.

To avoid these unwanted consequences, Photoshop can change the size at which an image is displayed on a computer monitor so that viewers can see the entire image at the correct size. This capability enables you to set specific image sizes for the image's intended use.

CHANGE THE ON-SCREEN IMAGE SIZE

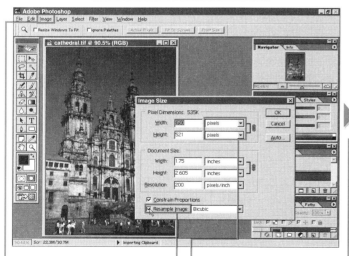

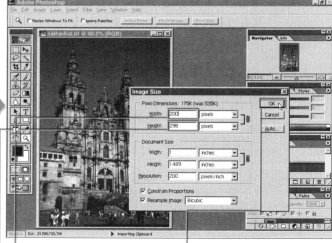

1 Click Image.

2 Click Image Size.

■ Photoshop displays the height and width of the image in pixels.

■ To resize by a certain percentage, click ▾ and change the units to percent.

3 Make sure that Resample Image is checked (☑).

Note: Resampling is the process of increasing or decreasing the number of pixels in an image.

4 Type a dimension of the size you would like.

■ Because Constrain Proportions is checked, the other dimension changes proportionally.

5 Click OK.

Note: You can restore the original dialog box settings by holding down Alt (Option) and clicking the Cancel key, which changes to Reset.

I tried enlarging my image, which made it blurry. What happened?

✔ When you enlarge an image such as a JPEG, you cannot preserve the image detail at a higher resolution. In essence, you are creating new pixels to fill a larger area, resulting in the blurred effect you see. When you resize images, you achieve better results by starting with a larger image and reducing it to the proper size, rather than enlarging an existing image.

What if I have no choice but to enlarge an existing image?

✔ You can decrease the blur by using the Unsharp Mask filter. See Chapter 5 for information about applying sharpen filters.

What does the Resample Image option do?

✔ When an image is resampled, Photoshop uses an interpolation method to assign color values to any new pixels that are created, based on the color values of nearby pixels. *Nearest neighbor* uses immediately adjacent pixels, is fast, but is much more likely to create jagged edges. *Bilinear* averages pixel values from four adjacent pixels, and generates an average image. *Bicubic* uses eight adjacent pixels and, as a result, is slower (it generates the smoothest images, however, and is the default setting).

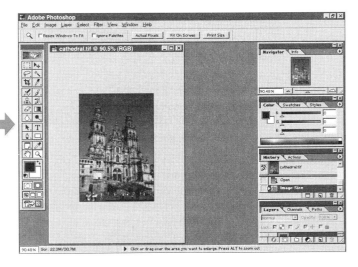

■ Photoshop resizes the image.

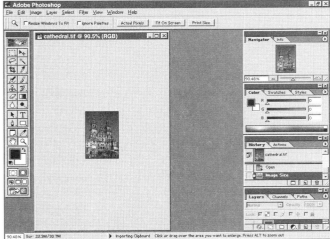

■ This image was resized by setting the units to percent and typing **25** in the Width and Height fields. Photoshop decreased the image dimensions by three quarters.

CHANGE THE PRINT SIZE OF AN IMAGE

You can adjust the size at which an image prints just as you can adjust the size at which the image displays on a monitor. The precise world of printing, where accuracy to thousandths of an inch is often required, demands this capability. You have to make sure an image fits exactly with other images in print media; otherwise, image overlaps, color bleeds, or improper registrations can result, which ruin an otherwise crisp appearance or smart design.

When creating an image for print media, you can specify image size two ways: in terms of the printed dimensions, and in terms of the image resolution. These two measurements determine the total pixel count and therefore the document size of the image. Document size also determines the size at which an image is placed into another application. You can manipulate the scale of the printed image; the changes you make affect only the printed image, however, not the document size of the image file.

CHANGE THE PRINT SIZE OF AN IMAGE

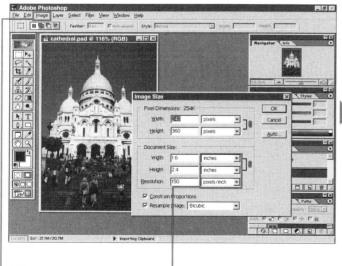

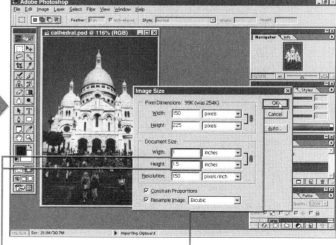

1 Click Image.

2 Click Image Size.

■ Photoshop displays the current height and width of the printed image.

■ You can click ▾ to change the unit of measurement.

3 Type a number representing the size you would like.

■ The Constrain Proportions setting changes the other dimension proportionally.

4 Click OK.

Note: You can restore the original dialog box settings by holding down Alt (Option) and clicking Reset.

What is the relationship between resolution, on-screen size, and print size?

✔ To determine the printed size of a Photoshop image, you can divide the on-screen size by the resolution. If you have an image that is 480 pixels wide (its on-screen size) with a resolution of 120 pixels per inch, the printed width will be 4 inches.

How do I preview an image's printed size?

✔ Click and hold the status bar of the application window (image window on the Macintosh). A diagram appears showing how the image will display on the printed page.

What is the difference between an image's on-screen size and its print size?

✔ On-screen size depends only on the number of pixels that make up an image. Print size depends on the number of pixels as well as the print *resolution* (which is the density of the pixels on a printed page). Windows monitors display 96 pixels per inch, while a Macintosh display is 72 pixels per inch. Higher resolutions print a smaller image, while smaller resolutions print a larger image.

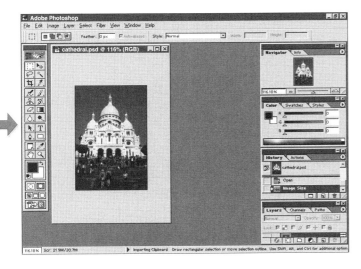

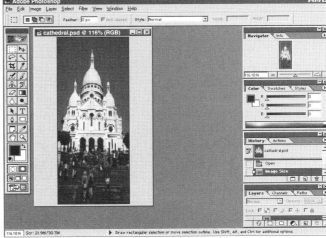

■ Photoshop resizes the image.

■ Changing the number of pixels in an image can add blur. See Chapter 5 for information about the Unsharp Mask filter.

■ This image was resized with Constrain Proportions unchecked and the width changed. Photoshop decreases the width but not the height.

CROP AN IMAGE

Cropping refers to the method of trimming off areas around an image's borders. You can use Photoshop to do in minutes what used to take hours in the darkroom, adjusting image borders and subject alignment until the photo's composition is just right.

Cropping helps image composition by centering the image's subject in

a more pleasing manner, or eliminating extraneous objects around the edges that only serve to distract viewers. This has the added benefit of reducing your image size, making it faster to download over slower Internet connections.

When you crop a digital image, you have the freedom to crop an image

as often as you like before saving your changes as a new image. Photoshop also enables you to rotate your cropping window to add artistic touches to your image, such as a "keyhole" effect or to reinforce a regular geometric pattern with the shape of the photograph.

CROP AN IMAGE

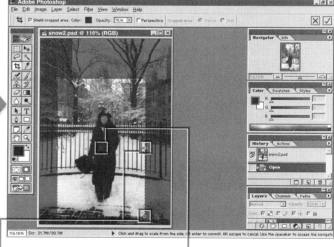

1 Click the Crop tool in the toolbox.

2 Click and drag to select the area of the image you want to keep.

Note: You can also crop an image by changing its canvas size (see the section "Change the Print Size of an Image").

3 Click and drag the side and corner handles to adjust the size of the cropping boundary.

■ You can click and drag inside the cropping boundary to move it without adjusting its size.

4 Double-click inside the cropping boundary or press the Enter key.

Note: To exit the cropping process, you can press the Esc key (Command + .).

Can I crop individual layers?

✔ Yes. You can also choose to hide the cropped area rather than delete it. The Hide option retains the pixels but does not delete them, so you can restore them later if you do not like the cropping effect.

How do I change the canvas size?

✔ The canvas is the area on which your image sits. You can change the canvas size as an alternative to cropping. To change the canvas size, click Image, Canvas Size, type the new canvas dimensions, and then click OK.

How do I increase the area of an image using the Crop tool?

✔ Enlarge the image window to add extra space around the image. Then apply the Crop tool so that the cropping boundary extends beyond the borders of the image. When you apply cropping, the image canvas enlarges.

How does changing the canvas size affect the image size and resolution?

✔ Changing the canvas size affects on-screen and print sizes but not image resolution.

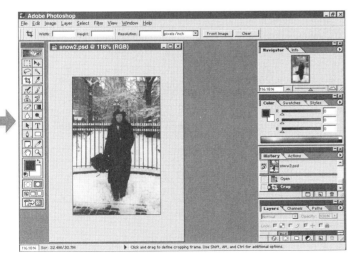

■ Photoshop crops the image, deleting the pixels outside of the cropping boundary.

ROTATE THE CROPPING AREA

1 Perform steps 1 through 3 earlier in this section.

2 Click and drag outside of the boundary lines. Photoshop rotates the cropping boundary.

3 Double-click inside the cropping boundary.

UNDO OR REVERT AN ACTION

You can undo multiple commands or revert to a previously saved state by using the Photoshop History palette. The History palette maintains a record of your previous commands and actions as you perform them, and provides a way for you to back out of any changes you have made. You can also revert to the last saved state on your image. All changes you made since you last saved will be undone, providing you with a quick way to return to a baseline image after you have altered it.

The History palette can be a lifesaving feature, especially when you commit a drastic change, such as merge layers, or apply a filter to an entire image. The History palette also gives you the freedom to try out new things: Because you can undo your commands or actions, you can try out different filters or effects, and then undo them in an instant if you do not like how the changes look.

UNDO OR REVERT AN ACTION

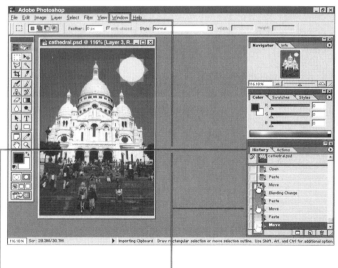

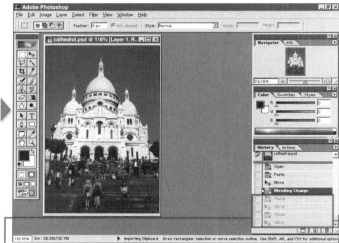

UNDO A COMMAND

■ The History palette lists recently executed commands with the most recent command at the bottom.

■ If the History palette is not visible, you can click Window and then Show History to display it.

1 Click and drag the History slider upward (or click a previous command in the history palette).

■ Photoshop undoes the previous commands.

How can I keep from overwriting any source images or files?

✔ You can keep from accidentally overwriting your original materials by either copying the files to a working directory and working on those images, or by setting Read Only permissions for source files and saving your edited ones to a different name or location. See Chapter 7 to save an image. See your operating system's online help for details on setting permissions.

Can I use document management systems with Photoshop images?

✔ Many document management systems let you check in or check out a file no matter what type it is. If you want to use document management with your Web projects, check to see that it can accept binary files in its database.

How does the History palette affect my computer's memory use?

✔ Photoshop has to store image information for each command it remembers in the History palette. The accumulation of such saved commands can sometimes cause Photoshop to run out of memory. You can limit the number of commands Photoshop saves in the History palette in the Preferences settings. (See the section "Set Preferences," earlier in this chapter, to set Photoshop preferences.) You can also free up memory by clicking Purge on the Edit menu and then Histories, which deletes the content of the History palette.

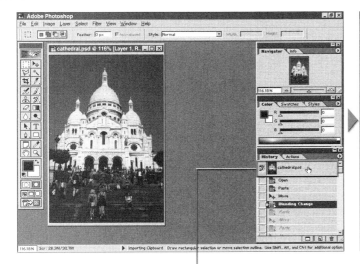

REVERT TO THE LAST SAVED STATE

Note: Photoshop stores the last saved state as a snapshot at the top of the History palette.

1 Click the snapshot image.

■ The image reverts to the last saved state.

■ You can add additional snapshots to the history palette as you work by clicking the history menu and then New Snapshot. You can then return to the previous image state by clicking the snapshot.

SELECT WITH THE MARQUEE TOOLS

Before you can work with an image, you need a way to select areas within the image. *Selection* is a way of singling out a particular area, such as a rectangular shape, so that you can then work with that area, such as copying and pasting it elsewhere, changing the color, or applying a filter or effect to it.

Some of Photoshop's tools create a boundary area that indicates your selection. This boundary area is technically called a *marquee box*, but is often called "marching ants" because the crawling dotted line resembles insects marching along in nice, neat lines. After you have selected an area, you can then use other Photoshop tools to work with that part of your image.

The most basic selection tools you can use in Photoshop are the Rectangular Marquee tool and the Elliptical Marquee tool. As the name implies, you can select a rectangular or elliptical area of your image by using the Marquee tools. Then you can move, delete, or stylize the selected area using other Photoshop commands.

SELECT WITH THE MARQUEE TOOLS

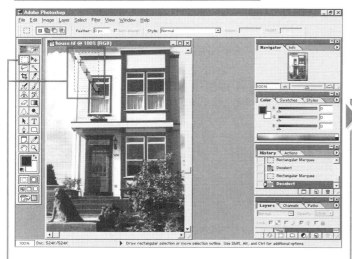

SELECT WITH THE RECTANGULAR MARQUEE

1 Click the Rectangular Marquee tool.

2 Click and drag diagonally inside the image window.

Note: You can hold down the Shift key while you click and drag to create a square selection, or hold down the Alt (Option) key to create the selection from the center out.

■ A rectangular portion of your image is selected. Now you can perform commands on the selected area.

How do I customize the Marquee tools?

✔ You can customize the Marquee tools with the boxes and menus in the options bar. Entering a Feather value softens your selection edge (which means that pixels near the edge will be partially selected). The Style drop-down list lets you define your Marquee tool as a fixed size. You define the fixed dimensions in the Width and Height boxes.

How do I select an entire image?

✔ Using the menu, click Select, then All to select your entire image. You can also press the keyboard shortcut Ctrl + A (Command - A) to select an entire image.

Is there an easy way to move my selection?

✔ You can easily move your selection to another area on your image without deselecting and reselecting. With either Marquee tool selected, click and drag the marquee box to a new area on your image.

How do I select single rows in my image?

✔ Photoshop offers two other Marquee selection tools, Single Row Marquee (⬚) and Single Column Marquee (⬚), with which you can select single-pixel horizontal or vertical lines. Click and hold the Rectangular Marquee tool, then drag the cursor to either tool. Click once to place the line; click and drag to move it.

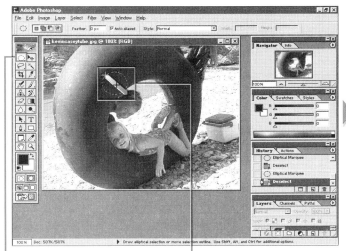

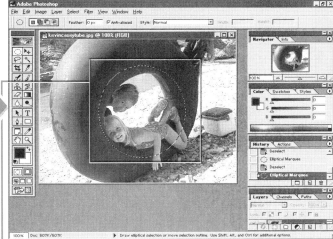

SELECT WITH THE ELLIPTICAL MARQUEE

1 Click and hold the Rectangular Marquee tool (⬚). From the box that appears, select the Elliptical Marquee tool.

2 Click and drag diagonally inside the image window.

Note: You can hold down the Shift key while you click and drag to create a circular selection, or hold down the Alt (Option) key to create the selection from the center out.

■ An elliptical portion of your image is selected. Now you can perform commands on the selected area.

SELECT WITH THE LASSO TOOLS

The Lasso and Polygonal Lasso tools are two of Photoshop's specialized selection tools. The Lasso tool is used to make irregularly shaped selections, such as tracing along an outline or along an edge of an object in your image. You need this ability when you want to extract a foreground image from the background and need to make specific choices on what is to be included or excluded in the selection.

The freehand selection ability can be somewhat unusual to use at first, as a mouse is not the most precise of tools and does not draw naturally. You can alleviate this by magnifying your selection so that you can draw with greater accuracy; you may also want to invest in a pen tablet and use it for your selections.

The Polygonal Lasso tool performs the same task as the Lasso tool, but it uses straight lines instead of freehand ones.

After you create your freehand selection with either Lasso tool, you can move, delete, or stylize the selected area using other Photoshop commands.

SELECT WITH THE LASSO TOOLS

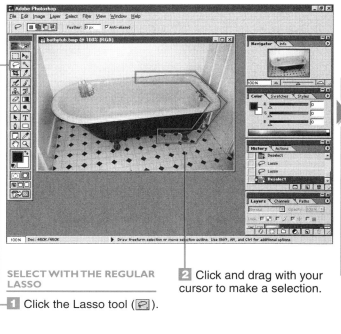

SELECT WITH THE REGULAR LASSO

1 Click the Lasso tool (🔗).

2 Click and drag with your cursor to make a selection.

3 Drag to the beginning point and release the mouse button to complete the selection.

■ The selection is now complete.

What if my Lasso selection is not as precise as I want it to be?

✔ Selecting complicated outlines with the Lasso tool can be difficult, even for the steadiest of hands. To fix an imprecise Lasso selection, you can try to fix your selection by redrawing it. Alternatively, you can switch to the Magnetic Lasso tool (see "Select with the Magnetic Lasso Tool").

How do I cancel my selection?

✔ You can deselect the area by clicking Select, then Deselect on the menu bar. You can also press Ctrl + D (Command - D) to deselect your area.

How do I create a selection that has both freehand and straight lines in it?

✔ If you need to create a mixed selection, start with the Polygonal Lasso tool. When you need to switch to a freehand line, press and hold the Alt (Option) key and keep drawing. When you want to switch back to a straight line, release the Alt (Option) key.

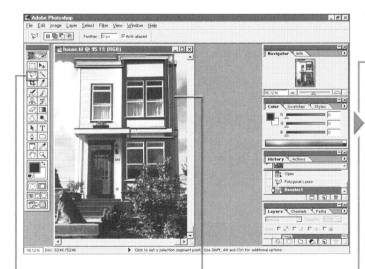

SELECT WITH THE POLYGONAL LASSO

1 Click and hold the Lasso tool in the toolbox. Then click the Polygonal Lasso tool (🔲) in the box that appears.

2 Click multiple times along the border of the area you would like to select.

3 To complete the selection, click the starting point.

Note: You can also double-click anywhere in the image and Photoshop will add a final straight line connected to the starting point.

■ The selection is now complete.

SELECT WITH THE MAGNETIC LASSO TOOL

You can take an object from one image and paste it into another with the Magnetic Lasso tool. For example, Photoshop lets you put an image of yourself in Paris, even though you have never been there.

Using one of the selection tools on a digital image, you can extract part of it, copy it, and then paste it into another picture. You could try to

use the regular Lasso tools to make your initial selection, but this often becomes a long and frustrating process.

To make this task easier, the Magnetic Lasso tool draws a selection border along a line of contrasting pixels, which helps extract one area of an image from the rest. The Magnetic Lasso tool works best along edges where

sharp differences between pixels exist. A red balloon against a blue sky is excellent; a well-camouflaged forest gecko is difficult.

For best results, you should magnify the area you are working on. If the selection is not as clean as you like, try redrawing it or adjusting the Magnetic Lasso's tool settings appropriately.

SELECT WITH THE MAGNETIC LASSO TOOL

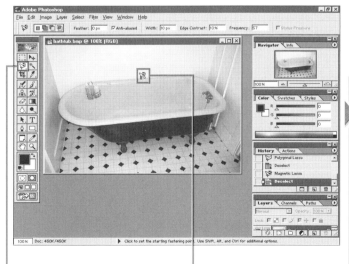

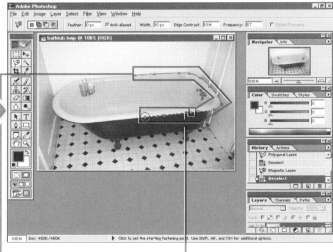

■1 Click and hold 🔲 and then select the Magnetic Lasso tool (🔲) from the box that appears.

■2 Click the edge of the element you want to select.

■ A beginning anchor point appears.

■3 Drag your cursor along the edge of the element.

■ The Magnetic Lasso snaps to the edge of the element as you drag.

■ You can click to add anchor points as you go along. This helps guide the lasso.

What do the four option buttons do?

✔ The Magnetic Lasso tool's option buttons control whether you want to add a new selection, add to an existing selection, subtract from a selection, or choose an area of intersecting selections. These buttons give you maximum flexibility when tracing with the tool so you don't have to retrace selections in order to add to them, for example. See the section "Add To or Subtract From Your Selection" for more information.

How do the Feathering and anti-aliasing options work?

✔ The Feathering option blurs the edges between a selection and its boundary; the anti-aliasing option smoothes out color transitions between edge and background pixels. You can adjust these settings to change how sharp or how smooth your edges are in your Lasso selection.

How do I adjust the Magnetic Lasso tool's precision?

✔ The options bar enables you to adjust the Magnetic Lasso tool's precision:

Width: Detects edges within the indicated number of pixels. You can set it to anywhere between 1 and 40 pixels.

Edge Contrast: Higher percentage values detect high-contrast edges; a lower percentage value sets edge detection lower.

Frequency: Determines the frequency at which anchor points are set. Higher values set points more quickly.

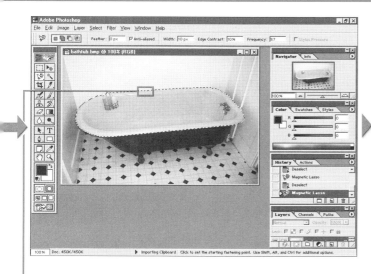

■ Click the beginning anchor point to finish your selection.

■ Alternatively, you can double-click anywhere in the image. Photoshop completes the selection for you.

■ The Magnetic Lasso is less useful for selecting areas of an image where there is little contrast.

SELECT WITH THE MAGIC WAND TOOL

You can select groups of similarly colored pixels with the Magic Wand tool. For example, instead of tracing a red balloon against a blue sky, you can select a red pixel from the balloon and tell Photoshop to select all pixels within a certain range of that color.

Working with the Magic Wand tool requires a great deal of skill. The

Magic Wand tool actually uses brightness in all three channels — red, green, and blue — not color, as its selection mode. Each channel uses a range from 0 to 255, and the Tolerance setting controls how much variance from a particular setting is applied. If you set Tolerance to 32 (the default), and a particular pixel has RGB values of 120, 132, and 240, permissible

channel values for red are 88 to 155; green, 100 to 164; and blue, 208 to 255. Try setting the Color palette to these values to see the surprisingly large color range involved.

If you are having trouble selecting a color, try adjusting the variance lower.

SELECT WITH THE MAGIC WAND TOOL

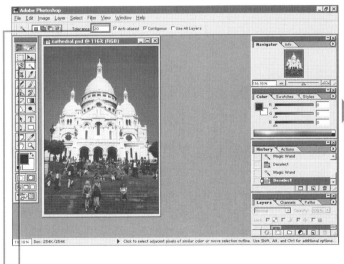

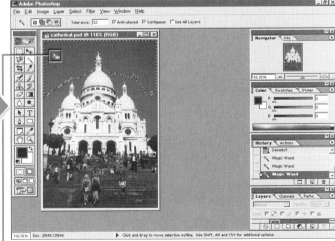

1 Click the Magic Wand (✎) tool.

2 Type a number from 0 to 255 into the Tolerance field.

■ To select a narrow range of colors, type a small number; to select a wide range of colors, type a large number.

3 Click the area you want to select inside the image.

■ Photoshop selects the pixel you clicked, plus any similarly colored pixels near it.

With what type of images does the Magic Wand work best?

✔ The Magic Wand tool works best with images that have areas of solid color. The Magic Wand tool is less helpful with images that contain subtle shifts in color or color gradients.

Why, after I have tried selecting the color, am I still not getting it all?

✔ You are probably working on an image with multiple layers that affect the color in the layer you are selecting. Click the Use All Layers check box to ensure that you are getting all the colors in your image. For more information on layers, see Chapter 4.

After adjusting the Tolerance setting, I still have problems with my selection. Should I just go back to using the Magnetic Lasso tool?

✔ Instead of trying to match pixel color ranges exactly, switch to a color channel view that contains little of the color you are isolating in it. For instance, if you want to select a red balloon against a blue sky, try changing to the Green color channel (Ctrl + 2 or Command - 2), and then use the Magic Wand tool.

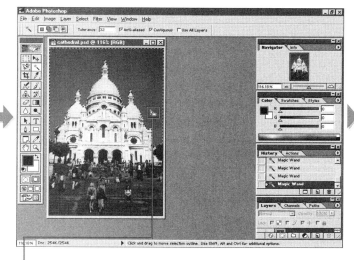

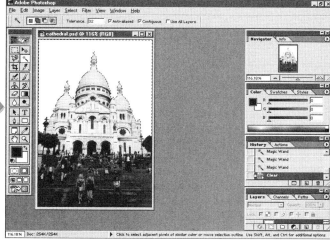

4 To add to your selection, press Shift and click elsewhere in the image.

■ Photoshop adds to your selection.

■ To delete the selected pixels, press Delete.

■ The pixels are replaced with the background color (in this case, white).

ADD TO OR SUBTRACT FROM YOUR SELECTION

You may not always get a selection correct with the first drawing. You may notice details that need to be added, or excluded, or even completely reworked to cover a new area. Rather than delete your initial selection and redraw the selection from scratch, you can add to or subtract from your selection by using various selection tools.

Photoshop provides you with three different tools to modify a selected area: the Add To Selection tool, the Subtract From Selection tool, and the Intersect With Selection tool. These tools let you add, subtract, or select intersecting areas without having to redraw or retrace a selection, which saves you time and enables you to fine-tune a selection without having to repeatedly redraw it to get it right.

The Add To and Select From tools do not need to have the selection areas intersect in order to work. For example, you can use the Elliptical tool to select a jellybean from a dish, and then use the Add To button to select a different jellybean elsewhere in the dish. Both jellybeans become part of your selection.

ADD TO A SELECTION

■1 Make a selection using one of Photoshop's selection tools.

Note: The selection in this example was made using the Lasso tool ( ).

■2 Click .

■3 Click the Add to Selection button ( ) in the options bar.

■4 Select the area to be added by using the Lasso tool.

■5 Complete the selection by closing the Lasso path.

■ The original selection is now enlarged.

■ You can enlarge the selection further by repeating steps 2 through 5.

Note: You can also add to a selection by pressing the Shift key as you make your selection with a selection tool.

What tools can I use to add to or subtract from a selection?

✓ You can use any of the Marquee tools, any of the Lasso tools, or the Magic Wand tool (🔍) to add to or subtract from a selection. All three have the Add to Selection and Subtract from Selection buttons available in the options bar when they are selected.

Is there a keyboard shortcut for the Intersect With Selection tool?

✓ Instead of pressing the options button to activate the Intersect With Selection tool, you can press and hold Alt + Shift (Option - Shift) and then drag your mouse to select using the Intersect tool.

What does the Intersect With Selection tool do?

✓ Use the Intersect With Selection tool (▣) when you want to select only areas that intersect with each other. This type of selection helps you when you have overlapping areas and want to quickly exclude the non-overlapping ones, such as when you are working with regular angles or shapes like rectangles or ellipses.

SUBTRACT FROM A SELECTION

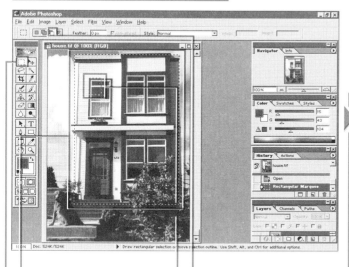

1 Make a selection using one of Photoshop's selection tools.

Note: The selection in this example was made with the Rectangular Marquee tool (▣).

2 Click ▣.

3 Click the Subtract from Selection button (▣) in the options bar.

4 Select the area to be subtracted.

■ Any part of the original selection that is part of the new selection is deselected (subtracted).

■ You can subtract other parts of the selection by repeating steps 2 through 4.

Note: You can also subtract from a selection by holding down the Alt (Option) key as you make your selection with a selection tool.

EXPAND OR CONTRACT SELECTIONS

When you are working with selections, you may not get quite the right size selection the first time around. You could spend time redrawing your selection, or trying to carefully position a new selection and use the Add To command. Both of these approaches would work, but Photoshop provides an easier way

to adjust a selection by a fixed amount.

The Expand and Contract Selections commands do just that — increase or decrease your selection by a number of pixels. For example, if you trace a stained glass window with the Rectangular Marquee selection tool and then

find you need to exclude more of the window frame, you can use the Contract Selection option to shrink your selection until the frame is no longer part of your selection.

These commands tend to work best with regular shapes such as rectangles or ellipses, rather than with freehand selections.

EXPAND A SELECTION

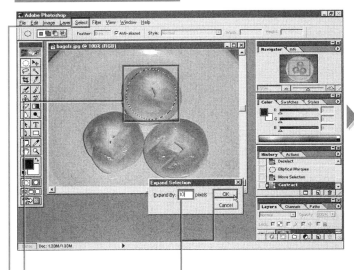

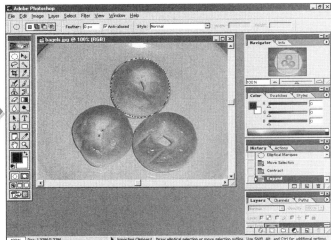

1 Make a selection using one of Photoshop's selection tools.

Note: See earlier in this chapter for more on using selection tools.

2 Click Select.

3 Click Modify.

4 Click Expand.

5 Type a value in the Expand By field.

6 Click OK.

■ Photoshop expands the selection by the specified number of pixels.

■ You can repeat steps 2 through 6 to expand a selection further.

How do I select just a border?

✔ You can draw a selection line and then select pixels on either side of your selection line using the Border command. Draw your selection line, and then click Select, Modify, and Border. Type the number of pixels to select from either side of your line, and click OK.

How can I smooth the edges of a selection?

✔ Make your selection and then click Select, Modify, and Smooth. Type a Sample Radius value. The greater the value, the more the selection is smoothed. Try setting the Radius value to the same value you used with Expand or Contract for an even, smooth selection.

How many pixels can I use as a selection value?

✔ You can specify anywhere between 1 and 100 pixels for your selection value. If you over- or underestimate your selection values and need to use a different value, you may find it easier to use the Undo command, Ctrl + Z (Command - Z), than to reapply the command using a different value. Experiment with both methods to see which works best on your image.

CONTRAST A SELECTION

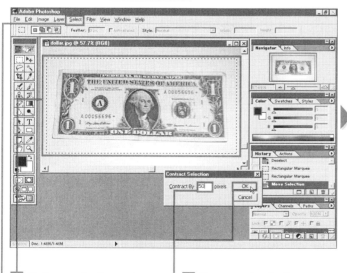

1 Make a selection using one of Photoshop's selection tools.

2 Click Select.

3 Click Modify.

4 Click Contract.

5 Type a value in the Contract By field.

6 Click OK.

■ Photoshop contracts the selection by the number of pixels specified.

■ You can repeat steps 2 through 6 to contract a selection further.

USING THE GROW OR SIMILAR COMMANDS

You can expand a selection's size by using the Grow or Similar commands. Both tools work with color, like the Magic Wand tool, instead of numerically, like the Expand or Contract commands.

You can use the Grow command to select pixels that meet two criteria: A pixel must be a neighbor to a selected pixel, and it must resemble the color of the selected pixel. Much like the Magic Wand tool, the color selection process involves all three color channels, so the color values of the red, green, and blue channels plus or minus the Tolerance value will give you the color range for your pixels.

The Similar command uses color only, without checking to see if the pixel is adjacent to your selection.

It also relies on the values for the RGB channels, plus or minus the Tolerance value.

To set the Tolerance value for use with the Grow or Similar command, switch to the Magic Wand tool and type the Tolerance value in the toolbar. Then, make a selection using a Selection tool, and use the Grow or Similar command.

USING THE GROW COMMAND

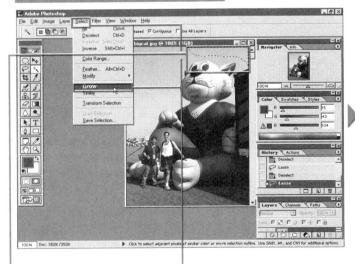

1 Make a selection using one of Photoshop's selection tools.

Note: See the preceding section of this chapter to learn about selection tools.

2 Click Select.

3 Click Grow.

■ The selection expands to include other similarly colored pixels.

How do I invert a selection?

✔ Click Select and then Invert. This deselects your selection and selects everything else.

Do the other Magic Wand options affect the Grow or Similar commands?

✔ No. Grow and Similar use only the Tolerance value; the other options — Anti-Aliased, Contiguous, and Use All Layers — are ignored.

Why am I having problems selecting pixels within a certain color range?

✔ The Similar command does not rely on just one pixel for its values, but looks at all the pixels within a selection. It also works best if a background or foreground is consistent in its coloring. If you have problems selecting all the pixels in an image, try making multiple selections of areas in your image. This gives the Similar command a greater range of pixels to use as values.

USING THE SIMILAR COMMAND

1 Make a selection using one of Photoshop's selection tools.

2 Click Select.

3 Click Similar.

■ The selection expands to include other similarly colored pixels.

Note: The Similar command expands to include pixels anywhere in the image that are of a similar color, not just pixels that are contiguous to the selection.

MOVE A SELECTION

Photoshop users spend a great deal of time moving and placing selections within the same image or within a different image. You must do this carefully in digital media, where you want to have clean, clear separations between images, such as a photo and an illustrated border, or in Web images, where you need to place objects precisely. Print media requires the most precise placement of all; if you do a lot of work with images destined for a printed page, you will spend a lot of time adjusting the size and position of elements in response to client feedback.

Moving a selection extracts, or "cuts out," the pixels from the image and moves them as a unit to another area. The pixels do not have to be moved a great distance; you can move selections one pixel width at a time if you wish. Moving a selection reveals the background color.

MOVE A SELECTION

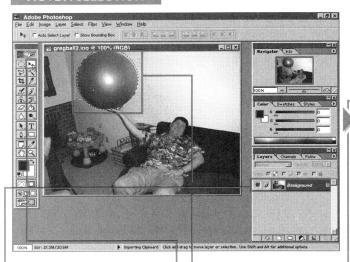

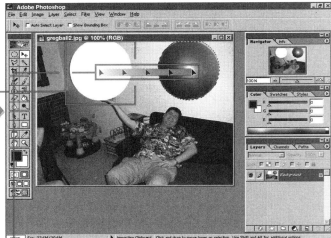

IN THE BACKGROUND

1 Click the Background layer in the Layers palette.

Note: If you are starting with a newly scanned image, the Background layer is probably your only layer.

2 Make a selection with a selection tool.

Note: See this chapter's previous sections for more on using selection tools.

3 Click the Move tool (▶⊹).

4 Click inside the selection and drag.

■ The area where the selection used to be fills with the current background color.

Note: White is the default background color.

Can I use a keyboard shortcut for the Move tool?

✔ Like most other tools in the toolbox, a single keystroke switches to that tool. Press and hold the V key to select the Move tool.

How do I move a selection in a straight line?

✔ Hold down the Shift key while you drag with the Move tool (⊞). Doing so constrains the movement of your selection horizontally, vertically, or diagonally (depending on the direction you drag).

How do I move my selection by pixels?

✔ Instead of dragging a selection with the mouse, you can "bump" a selection incrementally using the keyboard. To move a selection by 1 pixel, press an arrow key to move it in the appropriate direction. To move the selection by ten pixels, press and hold the Shift key, and then press an arrow key.

IN A LAYER

Note: You can put elements of your Photoshop image in their own layers. For more information about layers, see Chapter 4.

1 Click a layer in the Layers menu.

2 Make a selection with a selection tool.

3 Click ⊞.

4 Click inside the selection and drag.

Note: Unlike the background (Photoshop's opaque default layer), layers can be transparent. This means that you can move elements in layers, and the areas they are moved from do not uncover the background color.

COPY AND PASTE A SELECTION

You can copy a selection and make a duplicate of it somewhere else in the image, such as when you want a repeating object or motif in your image, such as a snowflake or autumn leaf. In Photoshop, the Copy and Paste commands work like the Move command, but instead of extracting pixels from an image and leaving a

void behind, it makes a copy of the pixels in the selection for placement elsewhere, leaving the original intact.

Photoshop allows for two different methods for copying and pasting images. The first, which is often called *cloning,* uses the keyboard and mouse to select and drag a

selection in order to copy it. The second method uses the menu and the Copy and Paste commands to copy an image onto the Clipboard. Either method enables you to copy the selection within the same window, between windows in Photoshop, or between applications on your computer.

COPY AND PASTE A SELECTION

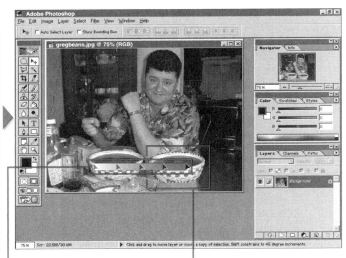

USING THE KEYBOARD AND MOUSE

■1 Make a selection with a selection tool.

Note: See earlier in this chapter for more on using selection tools.

■2 Click.

■3 Press the Alt (Option) key while you click and drag the selection.

■4 Release the mouse button to "drop" the selection.

■ A duplicate of the selection is created and appears in the new location.

44

What is the Copy Merged command?

✔ The Copy Merged command makes a merged copy of all the visible layers in the selected area. This command helps you grab all the layers, including an adjustment layer, and paste them into a new image. To use this command, select an area that contains multiple layers and then click Edit, Copy Merged from the menu.

Why does my selection appear larger or smaller in the new window?

✔ When you paste a selection or layer between images with different resolutions, the pasted data retains its pixel dimensions, which can make the pasted portion appear out of proportion to the new image. Use the Image Size command described in Chapter 1 to make the source and destination images the same resolution before copying and pasting.

Why does Photoshop not let me copy an image into another application?

✔ Photoshop usually converts its images into *raster*, or bitmap, images when moving or copying images between applications. In some cases where the image contains vector information, such as paths drawn with the Pen tool, Photoshop cannot always convert the image into a bitmap image. If this happens, try saving the copied image as its own file and then importing it into your application.

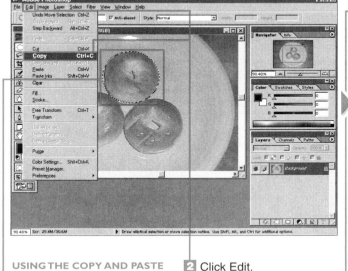

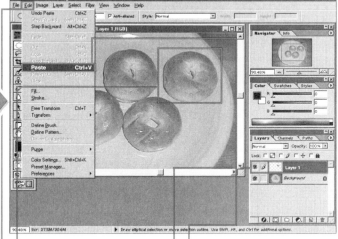

USING THE COPY AND PASTE COMMANDS

■1 Make a selection with a selection tool.

■2 Click Edit.

■3 Click Copy.

■4 Using a selection tool, select the area where you want the copied element to be pasted.

■ If you do not select an area, Photoshop pastes the copy over the original.

■5 Click Edit.

■6 Click Paste.

■ Photoshop pastes the copy into a new layer. You can now move it independently of the original image (see "Move a Selection," earlier in this chapter).

ROTATE A SELECTION

You can quickly rotate a selection to tilt or turn upside down an element in your image to make it fit with the other elements in your image.

For example, suppose that after you make a selection, you copy or paste it into a new image. Somehow it just does not fit; the beautiful

snowflake you copied would really look better if it was rotated counterclockwise a bit instead aligned north-south.

The rotation of your selection occurs with respect to the origin ◈, a point in the center of a bounding box that contains all the elements of your selection. If you want to

rotate your selection around a point located elsewhere in your image, you can move the origin by clicking and dragging it to anywhere in your image. Then continue rotating your selection using either of the following methods.

ROTATE A SELECTION

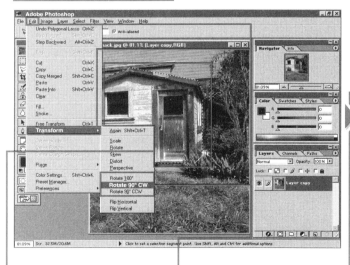

Note: You can only rotate selections made in a no background layer.

1 Make a selection with a selection tool.

Note: See this chapter's previous sections for more on using selection tools.

2 Click Edit.

3 Click Transform.

4 Click a Rotate command.

■ The selection rotates.

■ In this example, the empty space created by the rotation is transparent, and is represented by a checkerboard pattern.

Does the Transform tool let me flip the image?

✔ Yes. After you make a selection, click Edit, Transform, and then either Flip Horizontal or Flip Vertical. Photoshop swaps left for right and top for bottom, respectively.

How can I rotate my entire image?

✔ To rotate an entire image, click Image, Rotate Canvas, and then a Rotate command. If the image has multiple layers, they each rotate the same amount. Using this command lets you quickly correct a crooked scanned image without having to rescan it.

Can I rotate a selection other than 90 or 180 degrees?

✔ You can enter precise rotation amounts to control exactly how much your selection moves around the origin. After you make your selection, click Edit, Transform, and then Rotate. The Rotate options bar appears underneath the menu, and you can type a degree amount in the Rotation box, which is next to the angle bracket. Click ☑ on the toolbar to apply the rotation, or ☒ (⬜) to cancel.

ROTATE USING FREE TRANSFORM

■1 Make a selection with a selection tool.

■2 Click Edit.

■3 Click Free Transform.

■4 Click and drag outside the bounding box to rotate the selection.

■5 To apply the rotation, double-click inside the bounding box.

SCALE A SELECTION

Often, to adjust proportions of elements in an image, you need to make a selection larger or smaller. For example, imagine a baseball game image where you need to reduce the size of a ball in the foreground to give more emphasis to the batter in the background.

Scaling can be done along the horizontal axis, the vertical axis,

and along both axes independently or with *constrained proportions*. Constrained proportions means that Photoshop maintains the original proportions as you change the selection size. If you do not constrain proportions, the vertical-to-horizontal pixel proportions distort when you scale a selection. This effect can be funny if you are scaling your friend's face in a digital photograph; but your friend

is not as likely to find the newly distorted image of her face as humorous.

When you scale up a raster image selection, Photoshop behaves the same as if you were changing image size, and stretches existing pixel information to fill the gaps. This stretching results in pixelation and "jaggies" along image edges.

SCALE A SELECTION

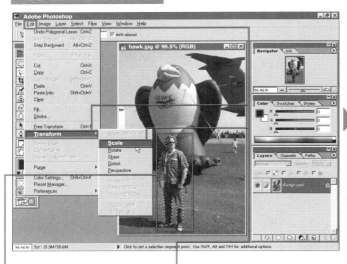

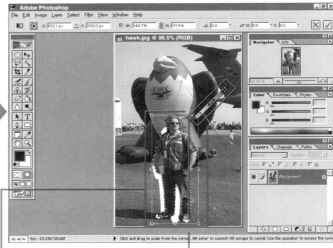

1 Make a selection with a selection tool.

Note: See this chapter's previous sections for more on using selection tools.

2 Click Edit.

3 Click Transform.

4 Click Scale.

■ A rectangular box with handles on the sides and corners surrounds the selection.

5 Click and drag a corner handle to scale both the horizontal and vertical axes.

Can I control the scaling amount precisely?

✔ When you select the Transform tool, an option bar appears directly below the menu. You can type exact scaling percentages in the Width and Height boxes; if you want to constrain proportions, click the 🔒 between the two boxes. Your selection changes immediately as a sort of preview; to accept the scaling, click ✔, or to cancel the scaling, click ✕ (🔲) on the toolbar.

How much can I scale a selection?

✔ You can scale a selection between 0.0% and 3200%, or up to 32 times the original selection size. Pixelation will appear on raster images, so after a certain point, a large amount of scaling is counterproductive.

How do I scale both dimensions proportionally without using the toolbar?

✔ Hold down the Shift key while you scale your selection. The two axes of your selection grow or shrink proportionally. Your image does not distort.

6 Click and drag a side handle to scale one axis at a time.

7 To apply the scaling, double-click inside the bounding box or press the Enter (Return) key.

■ To cancel the scaling, you can press Esc (Command + .).

■ Photoshop scales the selection to the new dimensions.

FEATHER THE BORDER OF A SELECTION

When you have a selection that has hard, crisp edges, you may want to soften the edges to give it a more flowing, graceful, or artistic look. Photoshop lets you smooth out contrasting edges between images using the Feather tool. When you feather a selection's border, you create soft edges around it.

Technically speaking, feathering blurs edges by building a transition boundary between the selection and its surrounding pixels. Feathering is an adjustable value that you can select either before or after you draw a selection area. You measure the amount of feathering in pixels in both directions from the selection.

This blurring can cause some loss of detail at the edge of the selection, so you should apply feathering to larger areas to avoid blurring all detail. Of course, this may be the effect you want, so experiment with different values. Feathering works both inwards and outwards from the selected edge. Feathering becomes apparent when you move, cut, copy, or fill the selection.

FEATHER THE BORDER OF A SELECTION

1 Make a selection with a selection tool.

Note: See earlier in this chapter for more on using selection tools.

2 Click Select.

3 Click Feather.

4 Type a pixel value to determine the softness of the edge.

5 Click OK.

6 To delete the part of the image that surrounds your selection, first click Select.

7 Click Inverse.

■ The selection is inverted (but still feathered).

Can I work with the Feather tool without using keyboard shortcuts or the menu?

✔ Feathering is one of the tools available using a context-sensitive menu. After you make a selection, right-click in Windows or Control-click on the Macintosh, then select Feathering from the menu. The Feather Selection dialog box appears, where you can select the pixel width. Click OK to feather your selection.

What happens if I feather a selection first and then apply a command to it?

✔ Photoshop applies the command only partially to pixels near the edge of the selection.

Are there shortcut keys for feathering?

✔ You can press Ctrl + Alt + D (Command - Option - D) to activate the Feather command.

How do I set the feathering amount before I have selected it?

✔ You can set the feathering amount in pixels by typing a value into the Feather box, located on the options bar for any of the Marquee or Lasso selection tools. Then, make your selection as described earlier in this chapter.

■ Press the Delete key.

■ By deleting the surrounding pixels, you can see the effect of the feathering.

■ The image in this example was feathered with a larger pixel value (20 pixels).

Note: To automate this feathering effect, see Chapter 4.

USING THE RUBBER STAMP TOOL

The Rubber Stamp tool gives you the ability to clean up small flaws or erase elements in your image by copying information from one image area to another.

This capability is invaluable for duplicating portions of an image to help cover up defects or flaws that somehow appeared in your image — for example, odd shadows or highlights that appeared when the flash attachment went off, or a dog's nose that ghosted into the lower part of the image just as you snapped the photo.

The Rubber Stamp tool is best for fixing small defects or imperfections. If you need to remove an entire object from an image, such as the whole dog and not just its nose, you are better off using regular selection tools to remove it.

USING THE RUBBER STAMP TOOL

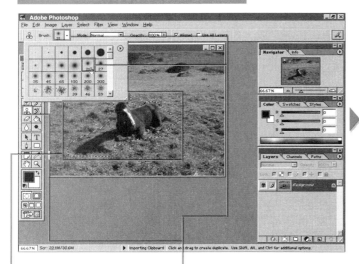

Note: Step 1 is optional. It lets you limit where the rubber stamp is applied.

■1 Make a selection with a selection tool.

Note: See earlier in the chapter for more on using selection tools.

■2 Click the Rubber Stamp tool (📇) in the toolbox.

■3 Click the Brush ▪ and select a brush size and type.

■4 Press the Alt (Option) key and click the area of the image that you would like to copy from.

■ In this example, an area of empty grass is being selected with the tool.

Note: This area does not have to be inside the current selection.

What suggestions do you have for retouching scanned photos?

✔ Photoshop excels at restoring old or historical photographs. These photos can be black and white, or color; all are probably in less-than-perfect condition, and you may want to restore them. Some ideas:

- Change your copy source often to help prevent subtle but repetitive patterns from building up.
- Switch between brush types, such as hard and soft brushes, and brush pixel sizes.
- Switch between color channels. Sometimes channels mask another channel's defects, and switching and working in a different channel may clear up the defect.
- Experiment with the Opacity setting for your clone. This lets you apply slightly darker areas over lighter ones, rather than trying to match colors exactly.

What is a good starting brush shape?

✔ When you first start working on an image that needs some help from the Rubber Stamp tool, try using a hard-edged brush with a diameter of 5 or 9 pixels. Ideally, you should start with a brush only slightly larger than the blemish you need to smudge out.

5 Click and drag inside the selection to apply the rubber stamp.

■ The area is copied to where you click and drag.

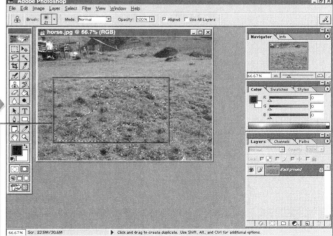

6 Click and drag repeatedly over the area to achieve the desired effect.

■ In this example, the image of the horse has been copied over by the grass selection.

USING THE ERASER TOOL

The Eraser Tool changes pixels in the image as you drag the tool through them, revealing the background layer or underlying pixels on a nontransparent layer. This action lets you remove images or parts of images to let the underlying image or effect show through — in effect, erasing the top layer. If you are working on a merged image or directly on a background layer, only the background layer shows through.

Photoshop offers four types of eraser styles you can use on a digital image: Paintbrush, Airbrush, Pencil, and Block. You can customize the first three with different brush sizes, opacity or pressure percentage, edge type, and whether the action should be saved to the History palette. The Block eraser type is a simple, 16 x 16 pixel block with no special effects of any kind.

If you need to erase large areas, you should use other tools or techniques. For instance, you can extract objects from an image using selection tools (covered earlier in this chapter) or you can create a mask layer that blocks out portions of the image without permanently erasing pixels.

USING THE ERASER TOOL

1 Click a layer.

Note: For more about layers, see Chapter 4.

■ If you want to limit where the eraser will be applied, you can make a selection with a selection tool.

2 Click the Eraser tool (⬚).

3 Click the Brush ⬚ and select a brush size and type.

Why does the eraser not remove pixels and show the layers beneath?

✔ You need to first unlock the layer on which you are using the Eraser tool. See Chapter 4 to learn how to lock and unlock layers.

What other eraser brushes are available?

✔ If you select the Paintbrush, Airbrush, or Pencil mode, click the Brush drop-down arrow. A brush palette appears with different sizes and styles. You can then load a new set of brush styles by clicking the ▶. Some of the styles include Calligraphy, Natural, and Faux Finishes.

What are some recommended start settings?

✔ Depending on the task, you may want to try the following settings:
- Use the Block as a hard-edged brush for cleaning up hard edges.
- Lower the Opacity setting to 10% for a very light eraser effect.
- Choose a small brush size and magnify your image for fine detail work.

4 Click and drag inside the selection.

■ The tool turns areas of the layer transparent.

■ The tool has no effect on the background layer.

USING THE MAGIC ERASER TOOL

You can make large portions of a layer transparent with the Magic Eraser tool. This tool acts like the Magic Wand tool in reverse: Instead of selecting pixels of a similar color, it erases pixels of a similar color.

The Magic Eraser Tool compares the brightness of the red, green,

and blue channels of the selected pixel with other pixels in the image. You adjust the tool's Tolerance setting to determine the variance from a given pixel's RGB channels; if the Tolerance setting is 20, any pixel values within 20 of the selected pixel's RGB channels get erased. This can be a significant range of color, so if you use the tool

and too much area or too little area is erased, undo the action and try again with a different Tolerance setting.

In reality, the Magic Eraser Tool does not actually erase the pixels. It instead makes them transparent to layers beneath the currently selected one.

USING THE MAGIC ERASER TOOL

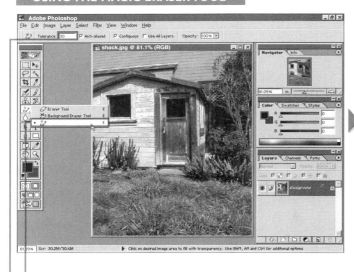

■ Click and hold ✎ and select the Magic Eraser tool (✎) from the box that appears.

■ Type a number from 0 to 255 into the Tolerance field.

■ To erase a narrow range of colors, type a small number; to erase a wide range of colors, type a large number.

■ Click inside the image.

■ The pixel you click, plus any similarly colored pixels near it, turns transparent.

■ Photoshop represents transparency with a white-and-gray-checker pattern.

What is the checkerboard pattern that appeared after I used the Magic Eraser?

✔ If you are working on an image on the background layer, it renders the layer transparent, without a default background color. The checkerboard is the default scheme for a transparent bottom layer.

What is the Background Eraser tool?

✔ The Background Eraser tool ([🖌]), accessible by clicking and holding 🖉 in the toolbox, samples the color from your image when you first click it. Then it erases similarly colored pixels as you drag it, which helps you erase the solid background around elements in your image.

What do the other Magic Eraser option settings do?

✔ The settings work similarly to the Magic Wand tool. Anti-aliased gives a hard edge when unselected, or a soft edge; Contiguous deletes only pixels that touch each other; Use All Layers uses all layers to determine if a pixel is selected; and Opacity can make the pixels translucent or even opaque instead of transparent.

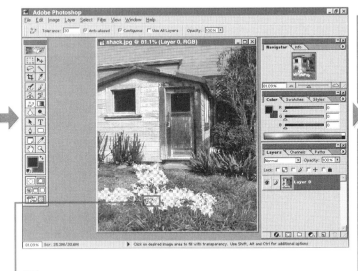

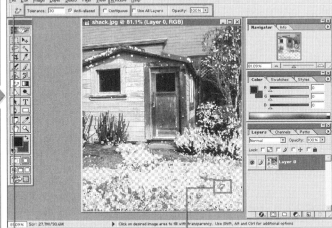

■4 Click inside the image again to delete more pixels.

Note: You can undo your eraser commands by using the Undo command (see Chapter 1).

■ You can adjust the tool by using the settings in the Options bar.

■5 Click Contiguous (☐ changes to ☑).

■6 Click inside the image.

■ Pixels of a similar color, but not necessarily contiguous, to the one being clicked are erased.

USING THE EXTRACT COMMAND

The Extract command provides you with another way of separating an object from the rest of a digital image, such as a diver from a platform. The command relies on you to provide some guidance as to what you want to keep and what you want to discard. Although it is not perfect, with some practice and fine-tuning you can get a pretty good first approximation that can be polished with other tools.

You start by drawing a highlight around the object you want to extract from an image, then filling in the area. Photoshop then extracts the image for you, placing the object on a transparent layer and discarding the rest of the image.

Like many other Photoshop tools, its accuracy depends on the image, the contrast between the object

edges and the background, and your patience and attention to detail. If your extraction object has hard, distinct edges, or a sharp contrast between it and the background, you will have a much easier time and a more successful extraction. If there is low contrast or fuzzy edges, expect to spend some time at high magnification tracing through the details.

USING THE EXTRACT COMMAND

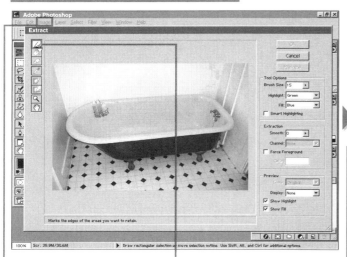

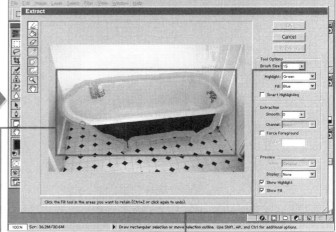

■1 Click Image.

■2 Click Extract.

■ Photoshop displays the image in the Extract dialog box.

■ If you make a selection before you perform the Extract command, only the selection will be displayed.

■3 Click the Highlighter tool (🖊).

■4 Highlight the edge of the element that you want to extract from the background.

■ The highlighting should overlay both the element and the background evenly.

■ You can change the size of the highlighter. For defined edges, use a smaller brush size; for fuzzier edges, use a larger brush size.

What does Smart Highlighting do?

✔ The Smart Highlighting option in the Extract dialog box lets Photoshop take a guess as to where the edge is. The highlighter changes to something resembling crosshairs, and as you drag it over an edge, it applies the highlighter along what it thinks is the edge. Sometimes it guesses wrong; you can turn off the Smart Highlighter while you drag by holding down the Ctrl or Command keys.

How do I create straight extraction lines?

✔ You can create straight extraction lines by holding down the Shift key while you draw with the Highlighter. This does not work if you have the Smart Highlighting option turned on.

My extraction has rough edges. What can I do?

✔ You can improve a less-than-perfect extraction by clicking the Preview button and then using either the Cleanup tool (🖌) or Edge Touchup tool (🖌). The Cleanup tool erases background traces from an image, while the Edge Touchup tool sharpens edges and adjusts opacity. When finished, click OK to finish extracting the image. You can repeatedly use the Extract Command until your image appears the way you want it.

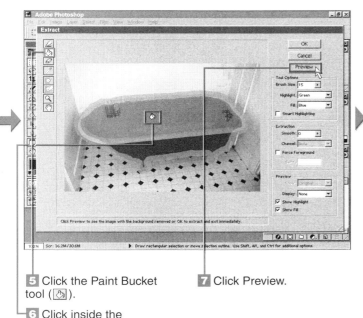

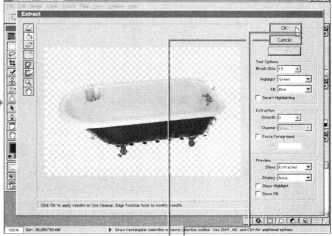

5 Click the Paint Bucket tool (🖌).

6 Click inside the highlighted element to fill it.

7 Click Preview.

■ The element is extracted from the background, and the rest of the image is erased.

8 Click OK to return to the original image window with the element extracted.

■ You can click Cancel to return without extracting.

WORK IN RGB MODE

You can work with a color digital image in RGB mode. *RGB* mode uses red, green, and blue channels that store color information. Each channel uses a brightness value between 0 and 255. With 256 levels in each of three channels, there are over 16,700,000 possible color combinations available to the digital artist. RGB is the most

common mode for working with digital color images, especially those for the Web or for digital video.

The other mode you may work with is CMYK. *CMYK* stands for cyan (blue), magenta (red), yellow, and black. This color scheme is used for print media, which often uses high-end presses that process images

using four-color separations. If you plan on using the same image with print media and digital media, you should plan on saving a version in each color mode before you start work. That way, you can work in the most appropriate color mode for each image, and your changes in one will not affect the resolution or viewability in the other mode.

WORK IN RGB MODE

■1 Click Image.

■2 Click Mode.

■3 Click RGB Color.

■ *RGB* is displayed in the image's title bar.

■ You can view the different color components of an RGB image with the Channels palette.

■4 Click Window.

■5 Click Show Channels.

■6 Click the Red channel.

■ A grayscale version of the image displays the amount of red that the image contains. Lighter areas mean lots of red; darker areas mean very little red.

What are working spaces?

✔ Working spaces are settings that apply to specific output formats, such as print or Web. To set the working space, click Edit and then Color Settings. If you have a custom monitor profile provided by your monitor manufacturer, you will probably use Custom. Otherwise, you can select U.S. Prepress Defaults from the drop-down list for a good starting point.

What color management policy should I use for broadcast video?

✔ If you will be using Photoshop to create images for broadcast video, you should select the SMPTE-C working space. This working space helps avoid color bleed and illegal colors for NTSC broadcast video, which supports fewer colors than RGB mode. From the menu, click Edit and then Color Settings. Click the Advanced check box, and then in, the RGB list, click SMPTE-C. Next, in the Conversion section, select Perceptual from the list. If you specify a color with the Color Picker that is outside the working space, a gamut warning appears in the Picker. Click the Gamut Warning to adjust the color back within the working space.

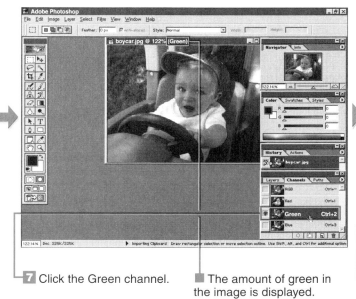

7 Click the Green channel.

■ The amount of green in the image is displayed.

8 Click the Blue channel.

■ The amount of blue in the image is displayed.

9 Click the RGB channel to return to the full-color image.

CONVERT COLOR IMAGES TO GRAYSCALE

Y ou can remove the color from your image by converting it to *grayscale* mode. Grayscale images are made up of pixels that are white, gray, and black. This mode uses up to 256 shades of gray. Every pixel of a grayscale image has a brightness value ranging from 0 (black) to 255 (white). Grayscale values can also be measured as percentages of black ink coverage (0% is equal to white, 100% to black). Digital

images produced using black-and-white or grayscale scanners typically are displayed in grayscale mode.

Although grayscale is a standard color model, the exact range of grays represented can vary. To convert a digital color image to a high-quality grayscale image, Photoshop discards all color information in the original image. The gray levels of the converted

pixels represent the luminosity of the original pixels.

Grayscale is also highly subject to the gamma setting for your monitor because the gamma correction affects pixel brightness and thus the luminosity of gray pixels. If you have not calibrated your monitor, see Chapter 1 to find out how to adjust your gamma setting.

CONVERT COLOR IMAGES TO GRAYSCALE

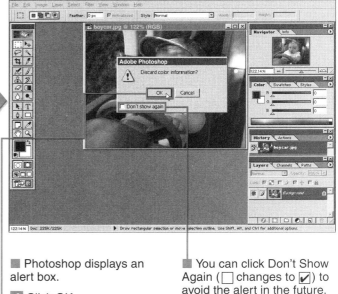

1 Click Image.

2 Click Mode.

3 Click Grayscale.

■ Photoshop displays an alert box.

4 Click OK.

■ You can click Don't Show Again (☐ changes to ✔) to avoid the alert in the future.

Should I set the Gray Color Management policy if I will be working with a lot of grayscale images?

✔ Grayscale images use only 256 shades, as opposed to 16 million or more with color images, so they are a lot more sensitive to profile conversion. Converting grayscale profiles results in off tones, which means that you will spend a lot of time correcting the gray in an image. It is best to leave the Gray Color Management setting at Off. See the section "Work in RGB Mode" for information about color policies.

How do I make just part of my image grayscale?

✔ Define the area that you would like to turn gray with a selection tool and click Image, Adjust, and then Desaturate.

Do I need to convert a grayscale image to CMYK in order to print it?

✔ You can print a grayscale image without converting it to a printer-friendly format such as CMYK. Because most offices have black and white laser or inkjet printers, you can print out grayscale images without any problems.

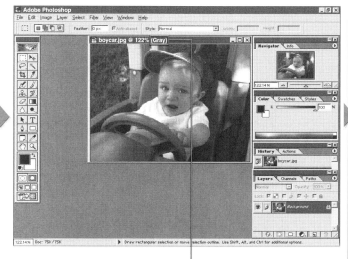

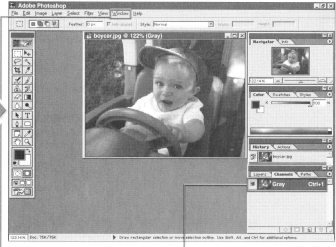

■ Every pixel in the image is converted to one of 256 shades of gray.

■ *Gray* is displayed in the image title bar.

5 Click Window.

6 Click Show Channels.

■ Grayscale images have a single channel (compared to an RGB image's three — see "Work in RGB Mode"), so grayscale image files take up less space than RGB images.

CREATE A BITMAP IMAGE

You can convert a grayscale image to a bitmap image. In Photoshop, a bitmap image is made up of only black and white pixels. The term *bitmap* is also used to describe any image made up of pixels. There is a file format called *bitmap* (abbreviated BMP) as well, so sometimes it is easy to get confused.

When you want to convert a color image to one consisting of only black and white pixels, you must convert the color image to a grayscale image first before applying the bitmap conversion. See the section "Convert Color Images to Grayscale" for instructions on how to do so.

After your image is a grayscale image, you can apply the bitmap conversion. Several options for bitmap mode change the appearance of your image, including applying custom patterns. Try working with several options to see which ones work best with your image.

CREATE A BITMAP IMAGE

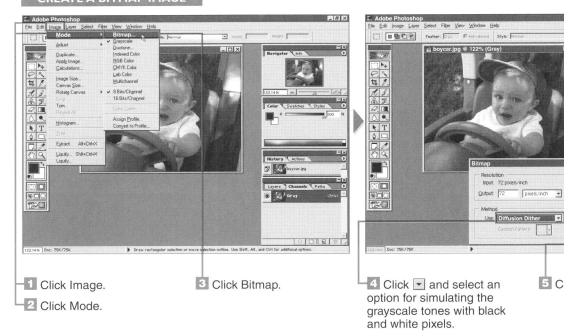

1 Click Image.

2 Click Mode.

3 Click Bitmap.

4 Click ▾ and select an option for simulating the grayscale tones with black and white pixels.

5 Click OK.

Is there a way to improve the conversion from a color image to a bitmap?

✔ Before you convert your color image to a bitmap, try looking separately at the RGB channels to see how they look as grayscale images; oftentimes you will see a less-than-suitable image in one channel that needs cleaning up before conversion. To move through the color channels, press Ctrl + 1 (Command - 1) for the Red channel, Ctrl + 2 (Command - 2) for the Green channel, or Ctrl + 3 (Command - 3) for the Blue channel. Press Ctrl + ~ (Command - ~) to return to viewing in RGB mode.

Can I edit my bitmap image after I have converted it from color or grayscale?

✔ In reality, there is very little editing that you can do; you can edit individual pixels, but you cannot return to grayscale or color mode to apply filters or different effects. Before converting your image, you should edit and then save your color image before performing a conversion.

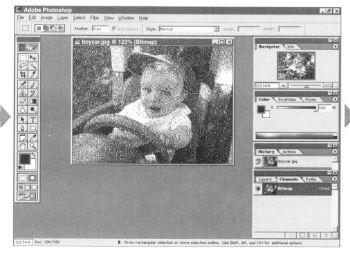

■ This figure shows the Diffusion Dither option, in which a random mixture of black and white pixels simulates the grayscale tones.

■ This figure shows the 50% Threshold option, in which pixels that are less than 50% black turn to white and pixels that are more than 50% black turn to black.

CHOOSE THE FOREGROUND AND BACKGROUND COLORS

Photoshop uses the foreground color to paint, fill, and stroke selections, and the background color to make gradient fills and fill in the erased areas of an image. Some special effects filters also use the foreground and background colors. You can select two colors to work with at a time in Photoshop and have them readily available when you switch between tools.

Painting tools such as the Paintbrush, Pencil, or Type tools apply the foreground color to selected areas. The foreground color also begins any custom gradation created with the Gradient tool.

The background color is applied when you use the Eraser tool, enlarge the image canvas, or cut

pieces out of your image. These tools remove pixels from the foreground and expose the background layer or features on layers below the currently selected one. The background color also ends any custom gradation created with the Gradient tool.

CHOOSE THE FOREGROUND AND BACKGROUND COLORS

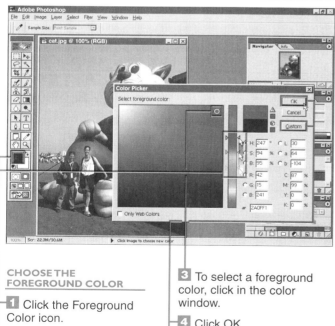

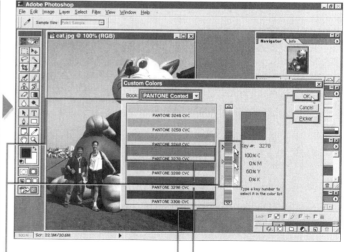

CHOOSE THE FOREGROUND COLOR

■1 Click the Foreground Color icon.

■2 To change the range of colors that appears in the window, click and drag the slider.

■3 To select a foreground color, click in the color window.

■4 Click OK.

■ Alternatively, you can click Custom to open the Custom Colors dialog box.

Note: The Custom Colors dialog box enables you to choose colors from a set of predefined color libraries.

■5 Click ▼ and choose a book.

■6 To change the range of colors, click and drag the slider.

■7 Click a color to select it.

■8 Click OK to load your selection as the foreground color.

■ You can click Picker to return to the Color Picker.

How do I reset the foreground and background colors?

✔ Click ▣ to the lower left of the Foreground and Background icons. Doing so resets the colors to black and white.

How do I switch the foreground and background colors with each other?

✔ Click ⭷ to the upper right of the Foreground and Background Color icons, or you can press the X key to switch the two colors.

How do I pick a color from another image?

✔ It is easy to "sample" a pixel color from another image and then use it as either a foreground or background color. Click either the foreground or background color; after the custom color palette appears, click the pixel in the image that you want to sample and then click OK. If you are filling an area, select 3x3 or 5x5 from the sample size list box in the options bar to get an averaged selection.

■9 Click a painting tool in the toolbox (such as ✐).

■10 Click and drag to paint with the foreground color.

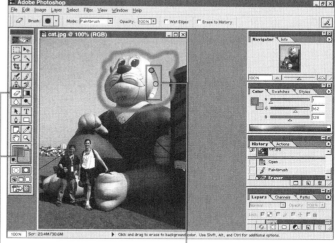

CHOOSE THE BACKGROUND COLOR

■1 Click the Background Color icon.

■2 Follow steps 2 through 8 earlier in this section to select a background color.

■3 Click ✐.

■4 Click and drag.

■ The tool "erases" by painting with the background color.

Note: This erasing occurs only in the background layer. In other layers, the eraser turns pixels transparent.

SELECT A WEB-SAFE COLOR

Back when Web pages with images were new, most computers were capable of displaying only 256 colors. This made it easier to design pictures and images because the color palette was fairly limited. However, nearly all browsers running on a specific hardware platform displayed many of the same colors differently. A digital image that would look great on a Macintosh could look bad on a PC, and both could look horrible next to a Sun.

It became necessary to create a color palette that consists only of colors that display the same — or as closely as possible — on as many platforms as possible, such as the Web-safe color palette. This type of palette ensures a consistent viewing experience no matter what platform is being used.

The Web-safe color palette has only 216 colors available out of 256 possible colors; this means that most color photographs will not be

very appealing in appearance. However, if you are heavily modifying an image for the Web, you may want to use Web-safe colors instead of a full-color palette.

If you would like more information on Web-safe colors, visit www. lynda.com/hex.html.

SELECT A WEB-SAFE COLOR

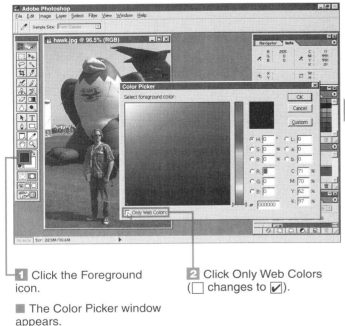

1 Click the Foreground icon.

■ The Color Picker window appears.

2 Click Only Web Colors (☐ changes to ☑).

■ Photoshop displays only Web-safe colors in the Color Picker window.

3 Click a color.

■ The hex-code value for the selected color is displayed.

4 Click OK.

What kind of images work best with Web-safe colors?

✔ While saving all your digital images destined for the Web using Web-safe colors seems like a great idea, it probably will not be the best option for every image you have. Images that have very complex patterns, or lots of subtle shading and colors, will not turn out very well; they will seem blotchy, muddy, or bizarrely shaded. The best images for the Web-safe palette are ones with large areas of single colors or ones that do not use subtle lighting effects. However, the concept of a Web-safe palette is diminishing, as most monitors are capable of displaying millions of colors. If you need to maintain backward compatibility with as many monitors as possible, use a Web-safe palette.

Why can I not enter an RGB value of 40 in the Color Picker?

✔ The Web-safe color picker uses only multiples of 51 in the color channels — 0, 51, 102, 153, 204, and 255. If you enter a different number, such as 3, the Color Picker rounds it to the nearest multiple of 51.

SELECT A WEB-SAFE COLOR WITH THE COLOR PALETTE

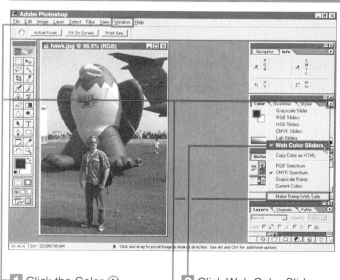

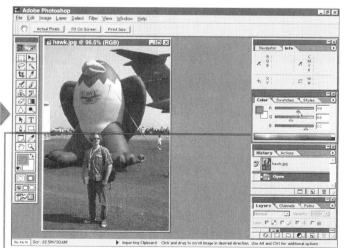

1 Click the Color ▶.

■ If the Color palette is not visible, you can click Window and then Show Color to display it.

2 Click Web Color Sliders.

3 Click the Color ▶ again.

4 Click Make Ramp Web Safe.

■ The Color palette sliders and color ramp now generate only Web-safe colors.

USING THE PAINTBRUSH TOOL

Y ou can add color to your digital images in numerous ways, but the most basic one is the Paintbrush tool. If you have worked with paintbrushes in the real world, you will appreciate using electrons and pixels to create and edit your artwork. It is a whole lot cleaner and uses no water, oil, or noxious substances, and you can quickly undo or change any of your

edits with a single keystroke on the keyboard.

The Paintbrush tool creates a colored line with slightly blurred edges, much like a regular brush does. You can change many of its options and brush types to achieve different effects on the Options toolbar. If you need to reset the Paintbrush tool options, click ✏

on the Options toolbar and then select Reset Tool from the menu.

If you want to load in different brush types, click ⊡ next to the brush size, click ⊙, and then select another set of brushes from the list. You can reload the default brushes by selecting Reset Brushes from the same menu and clicking OK.

USING THE PAINTBRUSH TOOL

1 Click the Paintbrush tool (✏).

2 Click the Foreground icon to select a color to paint with.

Note: For details, see "Choose the Foreground and Background Colors."

3 Click ⊡ and select a brush size and type.

4 Click and drag to apply the foreground color to the image.

■ To undo the most recent brush stroke, click Edit and then Undo Paintbrush.

How do I paint straight lines?

✔ If you want straight lines in your image, you do not need to use the Line tool. Use the Paintbrush tool to click once on your image, press and hold the Shift key, and then click your image again. A straight line appears between your two points. You can continue holding down Shift and clicking to keep placing straight lines in your image.

How do I paint thin lines?

✔ Use the Pencil tool, which is similar to the Paintbrush tool except that it paints only thin, hard-edged lines. You can paint straight lines or vertical or horizontal ones using the same methods as for the Paintbrush tool.

How does the Airbrush tool work?

✔ The Airbrush tool (🖊) is the only painting tool whose effects change the longer you apply it. Select the tool and then click and hold the mouse over your image. This causes a constant stream of color to come out of the tool, enlarging the painted area.

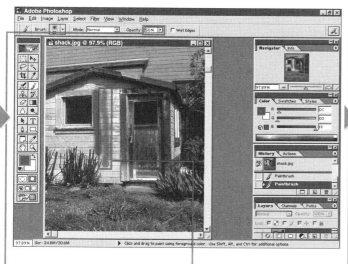

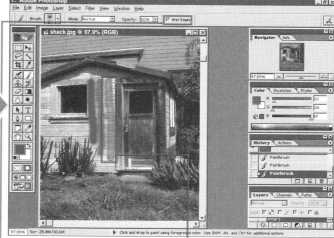

5 Type a percentage value to change the opacity of the brush strokes.

▪ Alternatively, you can click the Opacity ▸ and adjust the slider.

6 Click and drag to apply the semitransparent paintbrush.

7 Click Wet Edges to concentrate the paint at the edges (☐ changes to ☑).

8 Click and drag to apply the customized paintbrush.

USING THE PAINT BUCKET TOOL

The Paint Bucket tool is one of several fill tools in Photoshop. A *fill* is simply the addition of a color to a selection or a layer. The Paint Bucket tool is one of the more fun tools to use because you are not limited to simply filling areas with color: You can also use it to fill areas with patterns or swatches, which means that you could paint

the world tie-dye if you really wanted to.

The Paint Bucket tool does not just indiscriminately dump color into your selection; it has a lot more flexibility in how it can be applied. Like the Magic Wand tool, it uses a pixel tolerance value to select which pixels get the effect applied. You can also select the level of

opacity that your fill will have; this affects how much of the original image will show through the fill when it is applied.

Spend some time working with the Paint Bucket tool, especially with the Tolerance values and Opacity settings, to see how it works on an image.

USING THE PAINT BUCKET TOOL

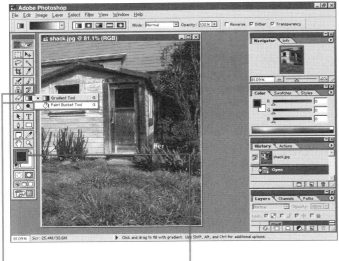

1 Click and hold the Gradient tool (▨).

2 Click the Paint Bucket tool (▨) in the window that appears.

3 Click the Foreground Color icon to select a color for painting.

Note: For details, see "Choose the Foreground and Background Colors."

4 Type a Tolerance value from 0 to 255.

5 Click inside the image.

■ Photoshop fills an area of the image with the foreground color.

Note: The Paint Bucket tool affects adjacent pixels in the image.

How do I apply a pattern instead of a color?

✔ On the Options toolbar, select Pattern from the Fill drop-down list. Click ⊡ in the Pattern list and select a pattern from the dialog box that appears. Click the image, and the pattern is applied.

Are there fast ways to apply foreground colors in a selection?

✔ To fill in the foreground color in a selection using keyboard shortcuts, press Alt + Backspace (Option - Delete).

What does the Fill menu option do?

✔ The Fill command differs from the Paint Bucket tool in that it fills the entire selected area, not just adjacent pixels based on a tolerance value.

How do I apply a "ghosted" white layer over part of an image?

✔ Use a selection tool to define the area of the image that you want to cover. Then apply the Fill command with White selected and the Opacity set to less than 50%.

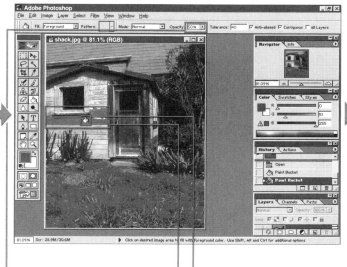

6 To fill an area with a semitransparent color, type a percentage value of less than 100 in the Opacity field.

7 Click inside the image.

■ Photoshop fills an area with see-through paint.

8 To constrain where the color is applied, make a selection before clicking.

■ In this example, the Opacity was reset to 100%.

9 Click inside the selection.

■ The fill effect stays within the boundary of the selection.

APPLY A GRADIENT

When you want colors to merge and flow into one another, you want to apply a gradient (also known as a *gradient fill*). A *gradient* is a progression of colors that blend smoothly from one to another, based on a few key colors that you select. Photoshop then generates all the intermediary colors and their positions within the gradient.

The Gradient tool works somewhat differently than the Fill or Paint Bucket tools. Instead of applying gradients with respect to a base pixel or applying colors that are within a certain tolerance of the base pixel, the Gradient tool applies colors to all the pixels within a selection.

When you apply a gradient, you begin by selecting the area where you want to apply the effect. Then you select the beginning color and ending color by dragging the Gradient tool from one end of the selection to the other. The gradient is applied in the direction that you drag the mouse.

The gradient effect can be applied over multiple selections; they do not need to be contiguous for the effect to be applied.

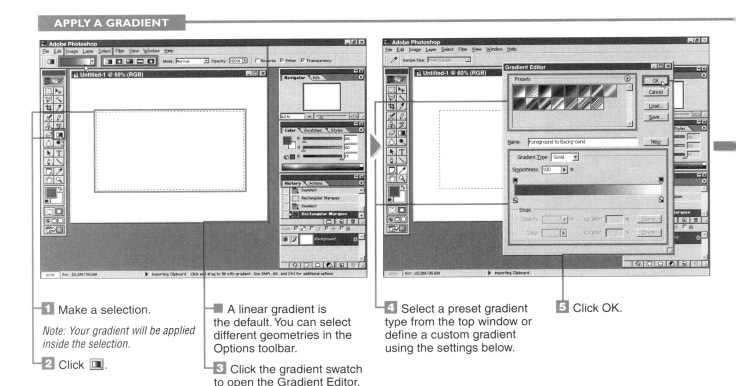

■1 Make a selection.

Note: Your gradient will be applied inside the selection.

■2 Click ▦.

■ A linear gradient is the default. You can select different geometries in the Options toolbar.

■3 Click the gradient swatch to open the Gradient Editor.

■4 Select a preset gradient type from the top window or define a custom gradient using the settings below.

■5 Click OK.

What do the gradient styles do?

✔ The gradient style buttons apply your gradient using preset styles. The five gradient styles are linear, which blends colors along a straight line; radial, which blends colors in a circular pattern; angular, which blends in a counterclockwise pattern from the starting point; reflected, which uses linear shading to either side of the starting point; and diamond, which blends outward in a diamond pattern.

How do I reverse the color order in the gradient fill?

✔ On the Options toolbar, click Reverse (☐ changes to ☑). The foreground and background colors are switched in the blend.

How can I add a rainbow gradient to my image?

✔ Click a rainbow swatch in the Gradient Editor. Doing so applies the spectrum of colors from red to violet.

How can I add a gradient in a straight line?

✔ Like other Photoshop tools, you can hold down the Shift key while dragging the mouse to create a straight line, either vertically, horizontally, or at a 45-degree angle.

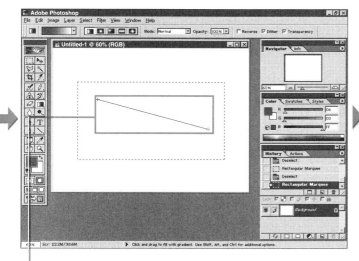

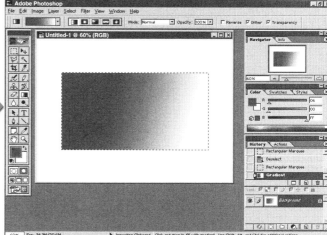

6 Click and drag inside the selection.

Note: This defines the direction and transition of the gradient. Dragging a long line with the tool produces a gradual transition. Dragging a short line with the tool produces an abrupt transition.

■ Photoshop generates a gradient inside the selection.

USING THE DODGE AND BURN TOOLS

The Dodge tool lightens specific areas of an image when you drag the tool over it. In contrast, the Burn tool darkens areas of an image when you use it. These reduce or intensify image areas, respectively. The tools work on color and grayscale digital images, but not bitmap images. If you want to edit bitmap images, you should work on a color or grayscale image first and then convert the image to a bitmap one.

The Dodge and Burn tools come to Photoshop courtesy of darkroom techniques. In order to correct images in the darkroom, photographers would hold back light to lighten an area on the print (dodging) or increase the exposure to darken areas on a print (burning).

These two tools work only on portions of an image; they are alternatives to using the Brightness/Contrast command, which affects the entire image.

USING THE DODGE TOOL

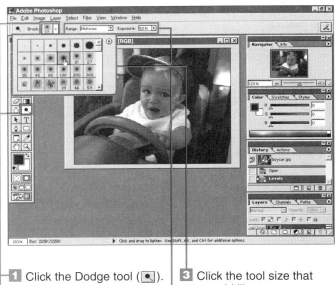

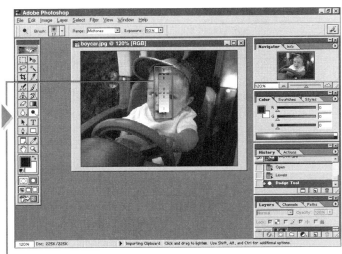

1 Click the Dodge tool (🔍).

2 Click the brush menu.

3 Click the tool size that you would like to use.

■ You can also select the range of colors that you want to affect and the tool's exposure (strength).

4 Click and drag over the area that you want to lighten.

How do I invert the bright and dark colors in an image?

✔ Click Image, Adjust, and then Invert. This makes the image look like a film negative. Bright colors become dark, and vice versa.

What does the Exposure setting do?

✔ The Exposure setting adjusts how much dodging and burning is applied by the tool. The lower the setting, the fainter or gentler the exposure; the higher the setting, the stronger the exposure.

What do the different Dodge and Burn Range modes do?

✔ The Dodge and Burn Range modes on the Options toolbar do the following: Highlights affects light pixels more dramatically than dark pixels or shades in between, Midtones affects all but the lightest and darkest pixels equally, and Shadows affects dark pixels more dramatically than light pixels or shades in between.

USING THE BURN TOOL

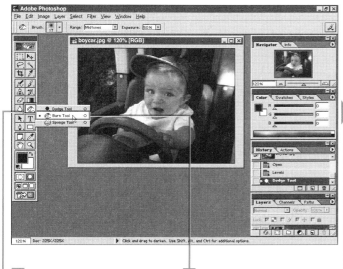

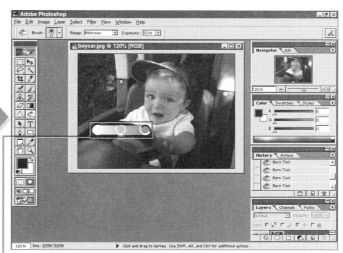

1 Click and hold 🔍.

2 Click the Burn tool (✋) in the box that appears.

3 Click and drag over the area that you want to darken.

APPLY THE BLUR AND SHARPEN TOOLS

The Blur and Sharpen tools are used to remove definition or add definition, respectively, to areas in your image. They can be used to enhance the edges of objects against a background or soften object edges to reduce the contrast. Photoshop refers to these as *focus tools,* or tools that work directly on image clarity or focus.

The Blur tool reduces the amount of color contrast between pixels in an image by averaging their values in an effort to reduce detail. The Sharpen tool focuses soft edges to increase clarity or focus by increasing the color contrast between neighboring pixels.

The Blur and Sharpen tools are used to apply an effect to specific

areas, such as highlights, shadows, or object edges. If you need to apply the effect to an entire image, you can apply a Blur or Unsharp Mask filter. See Chapter 5 for more information about these filters.

If you overuse one of the tools, such as reapplying it too many times to the same area, you increase the pixelation of the color or the area.

APPLY THE BLUR TOOL

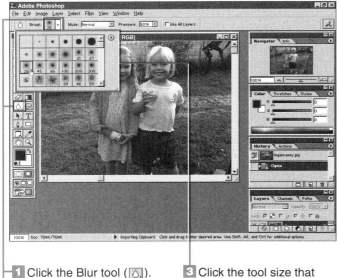

1 Click the Blur tool (⬚).

2 Click the brush menu.

3 Click the tool size that you would like to use.

4 Click and drag to blur an area of the image.

MASTER IT

What does the Pressure option do for the Blur and Sharpen tools?

✔ The Pressure value changes the color saturation or focusing for the Blur and Sharpen tools, respectively. You can change the values by dragging a slider, typing a new value in the box, or typing a new value when the tool is selected. A higher pressure means a more dramatic softening or sharpening will be applied.

What does the Shift key do with the Blur or Sharpen tools?

✔ Shift enables you to use the tool along straight lines, either horizontal or vertical ones. This is useful for working on straight edges in digital images such as buildings, sidewalks, or window frames.

What does the Smudge tool do?

✔ The Smudge tool ( ) is another option located beneath the Blur tool (click and hold to access it). It simulates dragging a finger through wet paint, shifting colors and blurring your image. Hold down Shift before you drag to smudge the starting point in addition to the rest of the smudge.

APPLY THE SHARPEN TOOL

1 Click and hold . Select the Sharpen tool ( ) from the box that appears.

2 To change the pressure (strength) of the tool, enter a value from 1% to 100%.

3 Click and drag to sharpen an area of the image.

DRAW SHAPES

Drawing shapes is normally the purview of a drawing program such as Adobe Illustrator, not an image-editing program such as Photoshop. However, there will be times when you want to add geometric shapes to your digital images before modifying them with effects or filters.

There are six different shape tools that you can use in Photoshop: the Rectangle, Rounded Rectangle,

Ellipse, Polygon, Line, and Custom Shape tools. These six tools use vectors to draw the shapes. A *vector* is a mathematical formula that describes how to create a shape. Vectors have two main advantages when used in drawings: They scale up and down without any information loss or pixelation, and they create small file sizes.

The downside to vectors is that they are not portable between most applications, so you cannot send off

a Photoshop file to someone using a non-vector-based program. Adobe does a good job of providing interoperability between vector-based and pixel-based programs such as Photoshop and Illustrator; but if you will be exchanging images with another office that is not using Photoshop, you may encounter some difficulties.

DRAW SHAPES

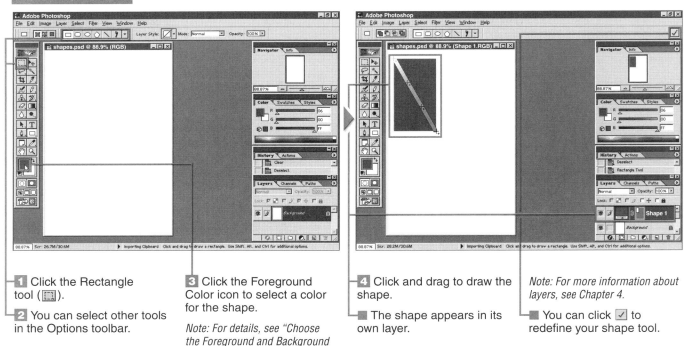

1 Click the Rectangle tool ([□]).

2 You can select other tools in the Options toolbar.

3 Click the Foreground Color icon to select a color for the shape.

Note: For details, see "Choose the Foreground and Background Colors."

4 Click and drag to draw the shape.

■ The shape appears in its own layer.

Note: For more information about layers, see Chapter 4.

■ You can click ☑ to redefine your shape tool.

How do I add arrowheads to straight lines?

✔ Click the Line tool (◻), which is one of the shape tools. Then click ▽ to the right of the shape tool buttons in the Options toolbar and select whether the arrowhead should be at the start of the line, the end, or both. Set the arrowhead width and height as a percentage of the line weight. Select the weight in pixels. Finally, click and draw your line on your image. The arrow will be filled in with the foreground color you have selected.

How do I draw squares?

✔ Hold down the Shift key as you draw with the Rectangle or Rounded Rectangle tools. You can use the same technique to draw circles with the Ellipse tool.

Do I have to redraw a shape if it is not in the right position?

✔ Hold the spacebar as you draw, and you can move the shape around the layer. When it is positioned where you want it, release the spacebar and keep drawing.

DRAW STYLED SHAPES

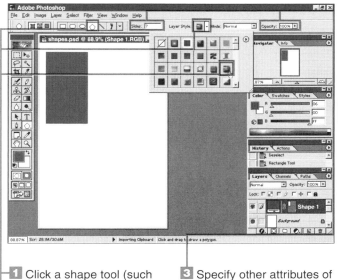

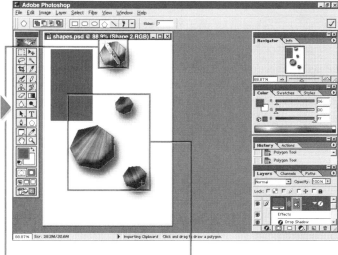

1 Click a shape tool (such as ◻).

2 Click ⊡ and select a layer style.

3 Specify other attributes of the shape.

4 Click and drag to draw the shape.

■ You can click and drag multiple times to create many shapes.

STROKE A SELECTION

Often it is helpful to create an outline of an object to make it stand out from a background or to give it some "punch." The hard way to do this is to take a tool such as the Pencil tool or Paintbrush tool, select the brush style and foreground color, and trace the object as carefully as possible.

With the Stroke command, you can automatically draw a line along the edge of a selection, using any of Photoshop's selection tools. You can use the Magnetic Lasso to quickly outline an object, and then apply a stroke to the selection to automatically generate an outline around your selection. This is a fast, easy method to add an outline to a selection.

The Stroke command is not limited to applying solid colors to your selection; you can also apply a pattern, shadow or glow effects, bevel effects, and other ways to make your object stand out. You can also change the opacity to help fade an object into or out of the background.

STROKE A SELECTION

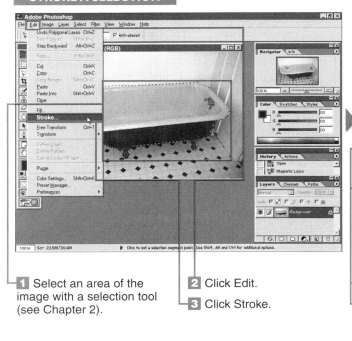

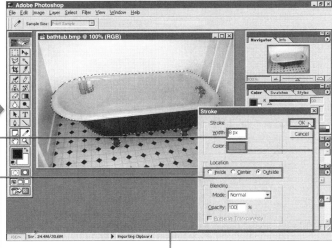

1 Select an area of the image with a selection tool (see Chapter 2).

2 Click Edit.

3 Click Stroke.

4 Type a width.

5 Click Inside to stroke a line on the inside of the selection, Center to stroke a line straddling the selection, or Outside to stroke a line on the outside of the selection (○ changes to ◉).

■ You can click the color swatch to define the color of the stroke.

6 Click OK.

How do I add a colored border to the outside of my image?

✔ Click Select and then All. Then apply the Stroke command, clicking Inside as the location. A border is added to the image.

How do I add a pattern to a selection?

✔ Select a portion of the image; then from the menu click Select, Modify, and then Border. Enter a pixel size in the dialog box and click OK. The selection expands inward and outward the pixel distance that you selected. Then from the menu choose Edit and Fill and select a pattern. Select your blending and opacity and click OK.

Where should I place the stroke: inside, outside, or center?

✔ Although this depends on the artwork and how much edge detail you want to preserve, a good default is to choose Inside. This setting lets you move the selection and the stroke together, without leaving all or part of the stroke behind.

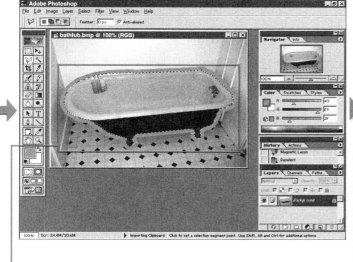

■ Photoshop strokes a line along the selection.

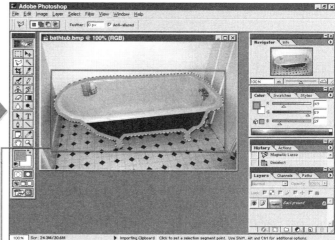

■ This stroke was applied on the inside of the selection.

CHANGE BRIGHTNESS AND CONTRAST

The Brightness/Contrast command lets you make simple adjustments to the tonal range of an image. *Brightness* refers to the color intensity of pixels in your image; *contrast* refers to the difference between the darkest pixel and the lightest pixel. Frequently, images taken with digital cameras or scanned images are too dark, too light, or

have a faded or muddy look. Adjusting the brightness and contrast can help clean up digital images that are not perfect, which can be a lifesaver if you do not have other digital images to choose from.

Unlike the Curves and Levels commands, the Brightness/Contrast command makes the same adjustment to every pixel in the image. The Brightness/Contrast

command does not work with individual channels and is not recommended for high-end output because it can result in a loss of detail in the image. But if you need a quick fix to an image and do not have the time to make more subtle or accurate adjustments, the Brightness/Contrast command gives you a fast way of sprucing up an image without a lot of work.

CHANGE BRIGHTNESS AND CONTRAST

1 Click Image.

2 Click Adjust.

3 Click Brightness/Contrast.

■ A dialog box opens with sliders set to 0.

4 To have your adjustments displayed in the image window as you make them, click Preview (☐ changes to ✔).

5 Click and drag the Brightness slider: Drag it to the right to lighten the image or drag it to the left to darken the image.

■ You can also lighten the image by typing a number from 1 to 100 or darken the image by typing a negative number from -1 to -100.

What does the Equalize command do?

✔ When you use the Equalize command (click Image, Adjust, and then Equalize), it redistributes the brightness values of the pixels in an image so that they more evenly represent the entire range of brightness levels. When you apply this command, Photoshop finds the brightest and darkest values in the composite image and remaps them so that the brightest value represents white and the darkest value represents black. Photoshop then attempts to equalize the brightness — that is, to distribute the intermediate pixel values evenly throughout the grayscale. This is useful for correcting scanned images that are too dark or too light.

How can I adjust the contrast of an image automatically?

✔ Click Image, Adjust, and then Auto Contrast. The Auto Contrast command adjusts the overall contrast and mixture of colors in an image automatically. Because it does not adjust channels individually, Auto Contrast does not introduce or remove color casts like the Auto Level command. It maps the lightest and darkest pixels in the image to white and black, which makes highlights appear lighter and shadows appear darker.

■ 6 Click and drag the Contrast slider: Drag it to the right to increase the contrast or drag it to the left to decrease the contrast.

■ You can also increase the contrast by typing a number from 1 to 100 or decrease the contrast by typing a negative number from -1 to -100.

7 Click OK.

■ The new brightness and contrast values are applied.

Note: If you make a selection before performing the Brightness/Contrast command, only the selected pixels are affected. Similarly, if your image is multilayered, only the selected layer is affected.

ADJUST LEVELS

The Levels command lets you make fine adjustments to the highlights, midtones, or shadows of an image. The Levels command offers more control over the brightness in an image than the Brightness/Contrast command does, but it is also more difficult to use.

The Levels command provides a *histogram,* which is a graphical representation of a frequency distribution. This shows how the

pixels are distributed in an image or within a selection and provides a quick way of adjusting the pixel distribution.

You can compress and expand the range of brightness values in the image and then map those values to new brightness values. Doing this balances out the composition and gives you fine-grained control over the tonal distribution.

For example, the first Input Levels box maps pixels to black depending on the value: If you type 32 in the box, all colors with a pixel value of 32 or less are set to black. The Output Levels options can lighten the darkest pixels and darken the brightest pixels by setting limits on pixel brightness.

ADJUST LEVELS

1 Click Image.

2 Click Adjust.

3 Click Levels.

■ The Input sliders let you adjust the brightness of the shadows (left), midtones (middle), and highlights (right).

4 To have your adjustments displayed in the image window as you make them, click Preview (☐ changes to ☑).

5 Click and drag the left slider to the right to darken the shadows in the image.

6 Click and drag the right slider to the left to lighten the bright areas of the image.

7 Click and drag the middle slider to adjust the midtones of the image.

Note: Performing steps 5 and 6 have the effect of boosting the contrast in an image.

How do you adjust the brightness levels of an image automatically?

✔ Click Image, Adjust, and then Auto Levels. Photoshop converts the very lightest pixels to white and the darkest pixels to black. This command is similar to the Auto Contrast command and can quickly improve the contrast of an overly gray photographic image.

How can I adjust brightness levels on part of an image?

✔ If you make a selection before performing the Levels command, only the selected pixels are affected. Similarly, if your image is multilayered, only the selected layer is affected.

How do I reset the Levels to the original values?

✔ In the Levels dialog box, press and hold Alt (Option). The Cancel button changes to Reset; click the Reset button to return the Levels values to default for the image.

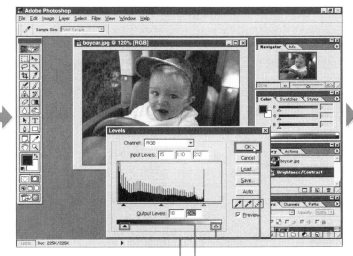

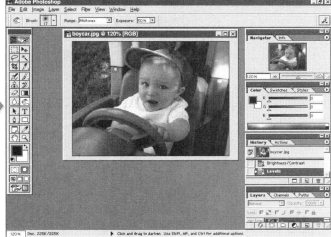

■ The Output sliders let you decrease the contrast while either lightening (using the left slider) or darkening (using the right slider) the image.

8 Click and drag the left slider to the right to darken the image.

9 Click and drag the right slider to the left to lighten the image.

10 Click OK.

■ Photoshop makes brightness and contrast adjustments to the image.

ADJUST HUE AND SATURATION

With the Hue/Saturation command, you can change an image's hue to shift the component colors, and you can change the color saturation to adjust the color intensity in an image. These functions can be applied to specific color ranges, or you can change all the colors in an image, depending on which method delivers the best results. Photoshop preserves the core brightness information from the original image, so you can change the hue and saturation without changing the image's essential brightness and contrast balance.

If you have black-and-white grayscale images, such as scanned historical photographs, you can use the Hue/Saturation command to add color to the images and turn them into "color" photographs. These commands will not work with bitmap images because they contain only black and white pixels, without any other channel information that can be manipulated by Photoshop.

If you make a selection before performing the Hue/Saturation command, only the selected pixels are affected. Similarly, if your image is multilayered, only the selected layer is affected.

ADJUST HUE AND SATURATION

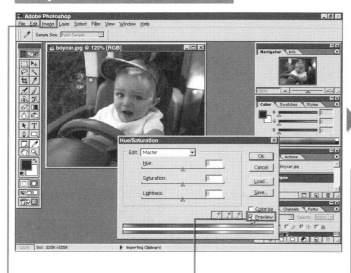

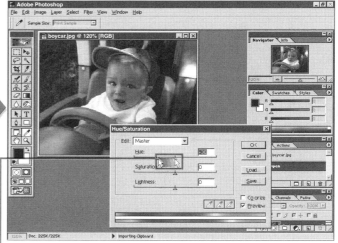

1 Click Image.

2 Click Adjust.

3 Click Hue/Saturation.

4 To have your adjustments displayed in the image window as you make them, click Preview (☐ changes to ☑).

5 Click and drag the Hue slider to shift the colors in the image. Dragging the slider left or right shifts the colors in different (and sometimes bizarre) ways.

■ In this example, adjusting the hue has changed the red to magenta and the blue to green.

How does the adjustment of an image's hues work?

✔ When you adjust an image's hues in Photoshop, its colors are shifted according to their position on the color wheel, either -180 degrees or +180 degrees.

How does the Lightness control affect the image?

✔ The Lightness setting changes all brightness levels in an image without regard to channels. Although you can change the lightness using this slider control, it is better to use the Levels command or the Brightness/Contrast command to change the image brightness.

Are all channels affected by the Hue/Saturation settings?

✔ If you have Master selected in the Edit list, all channels are affected equally. You can choose Red, Green, or Blue channels independently in the Edit list — but notice that the shortcut keys differ from the RGB shortcut keys used to view an image. You could mistakenly pick Cyan instead of Blue by hitting the wrong key.

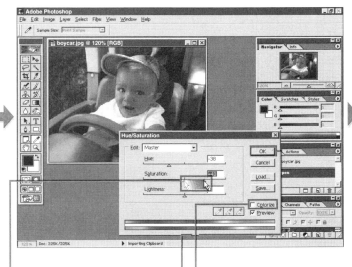

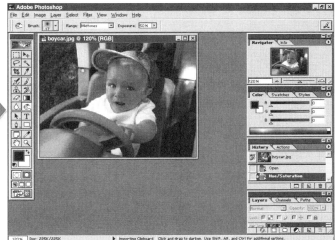

6 Click and drag the Saturation slider to the right or to the left to increase or decrease the intensity of the image's colors, respectively.

■ If you check Colorize, Photoshop turns the image — even a grayscale one — into a monotone (one-color) image. You can adjust the color with the sliders.

7 Click OK.

■ Photoshop makes the color adjustments to the image.

USING THE VARIATIONS COMMAND

The Variations command gives you a user-friendly interface with which to perform color adjustments in your image. It lets you adjust the color balance, contrast, and saturation of an image by showing you thumbnails of alternatives. You change the settings by clicking an image that more closely represents the final appearance that you want. All the images are then redrawn, and you can click again on another image to make another adjustment.

If you adjust images and dramatically different colors suddenly appear, your image is generating *gamut warnings*, or warnings that certain color ranges are exceeding the boundaries of your current color space. You can turn off clipping to disable these warnings, but you should be aware that your image will look different when you go to view it in a different color mode, such as CMYK.

The Variations command is most useful for average-key images that do not require precise color adjustments. However, it does have the distinct disadvantage of not letting you view a particular set of adjustments in full-screen mode before applying them.

USING THE VARIATIONS COMMAND

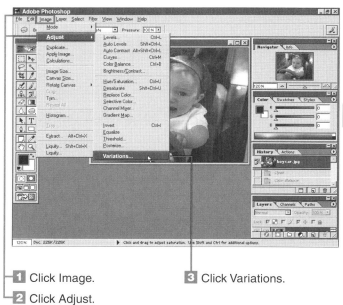

■1 Click Image.

■2 Click Adjust.

■3 Click Variations.

■4 Select a tonal range or Saturation (○ changes to ◉).

Note: Step 4 lets you apply effects to the different tones of your image. If you select Saturation, you can adjust just the image's saturation.

■5 Move the slider left to make fine (small) adjustments or right to make coarse (large) adjustments.

■6 To add a color to your image, click one of the More thumbnails.

How can I undo color adjustments when using the Variations dialog box?

✔ If you clicked one of the More thumbnail images to increase a color, you can click the More thumbnail image opposite to undo the effect. When added in equal amounts to an image, the colors opposite one another — for example, red and cyan — cancel each other out. (Clicking the Original image in the upper-left corner returns the image to the state that you started with as well.)

What does the clipping option do?

✔ Select Show Clipping if you want to display a preview of areas in the image that will be clipped by the adjustment — that is, converted to pure white or pure black. Clipping can result in undesirable color shifts because distinct colors in the original image are mapped to the same color. Clipping does not occur when you adjust midtones.

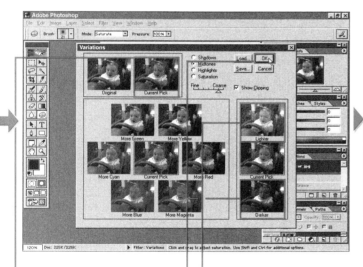

■ The result of the adjustment shows up in the Current Pick thumbnail.

■ To increase the effect, you can click the More thumbnail again.

7 To increase the brightness of the image, click Lighter.

■ You can decrease the brightness by clicking Darker.

8 Click OK.

■ Photoshop makes the color adjustments to the image.

CREATE OR ADD TO A LAYER

To keep elements in your image independent from one another, you can create separate layers and add elements to them. Layers can contain nearly anything in Photoshop — text, objects, separate color channels, effects, and even adjustment layers that modify other layers. Layers give you incredible flexibility in how you can organize all the elements in your digital images,

and can make your job of editing, arranging, and printing your modified art much simpler.

For example, you could work with all your text, images, and effects on the same layer. But suppose that you need to change your text. Now you need to edit the text, adjust the spacing and positioning with respect to other objects, reapply text effects, reapply color

adjustments, and so on. This is very labor-intensive and gets old very quickly. It is much simpler to have your text on a separate layer, edit that layer, and then make any adjustments to other objects on other layers if necessary. Start using layers, and soon you will wonder how you ever worked without them.

CREATE A LAYER

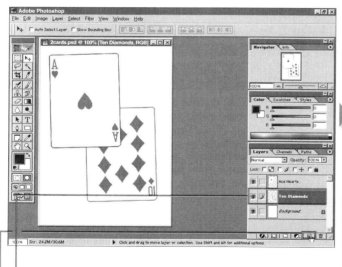

1 Select the layer above which you want to add the new layer.

2 In the Layers palette, click the New Layer button (🔲) (or click Layer, New, and then Layer).

■ If the Layers palette is not visible, you can click Window and then Show Layers to display it.

■ Photoshop creates a new, transparent layer.

■ You can rename the layer by clicking Layer and then Layer Properties.

What is the Background layer?
✔ The Background layer is the default bottom layer that appears when you create a new image or when you import an image from a scanner. You can create new layers on top of a Background layer (but not below).

Can I make the Background layer transparent?
✔ Unlike other layers, a Background layer cannot contain transparent pixels. You can, however, rename the Background layer and then move it to a different order in the stack, or convert the background to transparent pixels.

Does Photoshop always create a new layer for every object?
✔ Photoshop works with all your image elements as independent objects. However, you may want to treat similar objects as a single unit. For example, you may want to apply effects to all the flowers in an image. In that case, you will want to merge all the flowers together on a single layer. See "Merge or Flatten Layers," later in this chapter, to see how this works.

ADD TO A LAYER

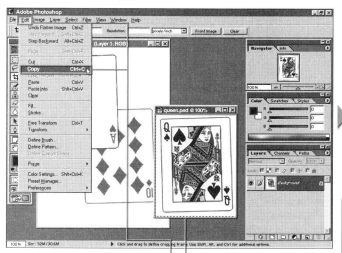

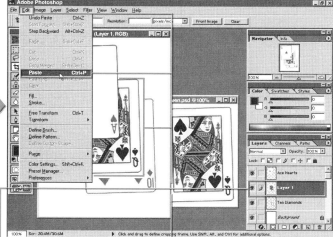

Note: This example shows adding content to the new layer by copying and pasting from another image file.

1 Open another image.

2 Using a selection tool, select the content you want to copy in the other image.

3 Click Edit.

4 Click Copy.

5 Click the image window where you created the new layer to select it.

6 Select the new layer in the Layers palette.

7 Click Edit.

8 Click Paste.

■ The content from the other image is pasted into the new layer.

DUPLICATE OR DELETE A LAYER

When you duplicate a layer, you have the freedom of being able to manipulate image elements while keeping a copy of the elements in their original state. This flexibility means that you do not have to create large numbers of hidden layers or save slightly different versions of an image to disk. Instead, you can work with different image arrangements,

image effects, and masks to see what works best for your digital image.

In addition to the method shown in this section, you can duplicate a layer using the menu. Click Layer and then Duplicate Layer, and a dialog box will appear letting you name the layer. Type the name of your new layer and click OK.

You can delete a layer when you no longer have a use for its contents. When you delete a layer, all related information is removed. If you want to remove the layer so that you can see what your image looks like without it, use the Hide Image command instead of deleting it.

DUPLICATE A LAYER

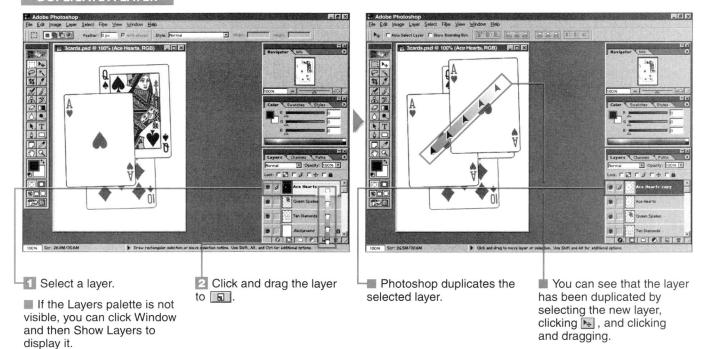

1 Select a layer.

■ If the Layers palette is not visible, you can click Window and then Show Layers to display it.

2 Click and drag the layer to 🔲 .

■ Photoshop duplicates the selected layer.

■ You can see that the layer has been duplicated by selecting the new layer, clicking 🔲 , and clicking and dragging.

How do I rename a layer?

✔ You can rename a layer in three different ways: You can press Alt (Option) and double-click the layer in the Layers palette, you can right-click (Control - click) a layer name and choose Properties, or you can click Layer and then Layer Properties. Type a new name for the layer and click OK.

How do I undelete a layer?

✔ If you accidentally delete a layer, you can press Ctrl + Z (Command - Z) to undo the Delete command. However, if you have worked on other images in Photoshop, you may need to scroll back through the History palette to restore it.

How do I hide a layer?

✔ You can hide a layer by clicking 👁 in the Layers palette. This hides a layer from view, as well as "removes" any effects or adjustments that are present on that layer. Hiding a layer lets you quickly switch components and effects in and out of your image or see how different combinations affect the final product. To redisplay a layer, click the box where 👁 was a second time.

DELETE A LAYER

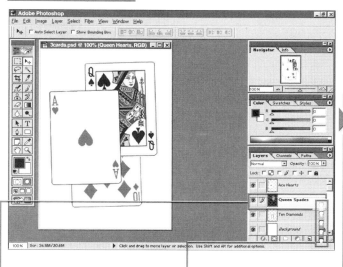

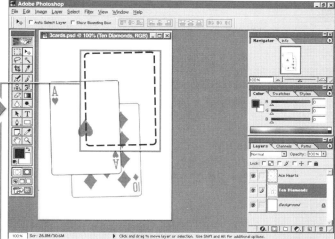

1 Select a layer.

■ If the Layers palette is not visible, you can click Window and then Show Layers to display it.

2 Click and drag the layer to 🗑.

■ Alternatively, you can click Layer and then Delete Layer, in which case a confirmation dialog box will appear.

■ Photoshop deletes the selected layer. The content in the layer disappears from the image window.

REORDER LAYERS

You can change the stacking order of layers to move elements forward or backward in your image. This is useful both for moving objects so as to change overlap order and for moving layers that contain adjustments or effects. The latter is helpful to determine the order in which effects are applied; you will find that the order in which effects are applied can have dramatically different consequences to your final image.

You can reorder layers in Photoshop two ways: by dragging layers up and down the list in the Layers palette and by using menu commands. When you drag a layer in the Layers palette, make sure that the sliding black bar is positioned between the two layers where you want to position the moving layer. When you use the menu commands, you move a layer up and down in the stack one layer at a time.

REORDER LAYERS

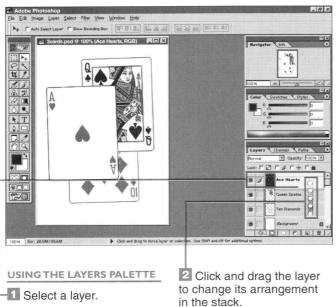

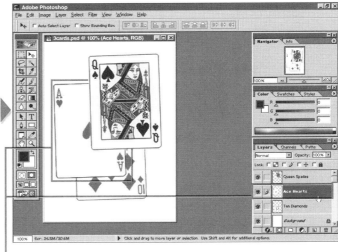

USING THE LAYERS PALETTE

1 Select a layer.

■ If the Layers palette is not visible, you can click Window and then Show Layers to display it.

2 Click and drag the layer to change its arrangement in the stack.

■ The layer assumes its new position in the stack.

Is there a shortcut for changing the order of layers?

✔ You can move a layer forward in the stack by pressing Ctrl +] (Command -]). You can move a layer backward by pressing Ctrl + [(Command - [).

Can I quickly send a layer to the front or back?

✔ You can use keyboard shortcuts. Press Ctrl + Shift +] (Command - Shift -]) to send a layer to the top of the stack; press Ctrl + Shift + [(Command - Shift - [) to send a layer to the bottom of the stack.

How do I quickly switch between layers?

✔ You can change which layer is the active, or highlighted, layer in the Layers palette using keyboard shortcuts. Press Alt +] (Option -]) to move up one layer or Alt + [(Option - [) to move down one layer. Press Shift + Alt +] (Shift - Option -]) to move to the top of the stack or Shift + Alt + [(Shift - Option - [) to move to the bottom of the stack.

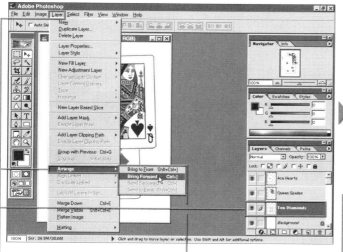

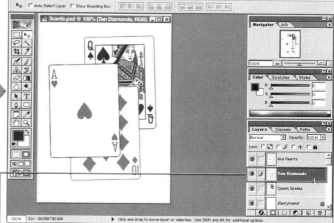

USING THE ARRANGE COMMANDS PALETTE

■1 Select a layer.

■2 Click Layer.

■3 Click Arrange.

■4 Click the command for how you would like to move the layer: Bring to Front, Bring Forward, Send Backward, or Send to Back.

■ The layer assumes its new position in the stack.

MERGE OR FLATTEN LAYERS

Layers give you maximum flexibility when working with digital imagery, enabling you to move objects around and apply or change effects. But as with anything, all that power comes with a price. Layers increase the size of your file, both in memory and on the hard drive, and eventually you will see slower performance as you edit an image with many layers.

Two techniques that you can use to reduce this performance hit are merging and flattening layers. Merging layers lets you permanently combine information from two or more separate layers. Flattening layers combines all the layers of an image into one. Both help reduce file and memory size.

Layers also have another curse: Only a few file formats preserve

layer information. The formats are PSD (Photoshop native format), PDF (Portable Document Format), and TIFF (Tagged Image File Format). If you need to work on a digital image using different programs, you need to save your file in a format that preserves layer information.

MERGE TWO LAYERS

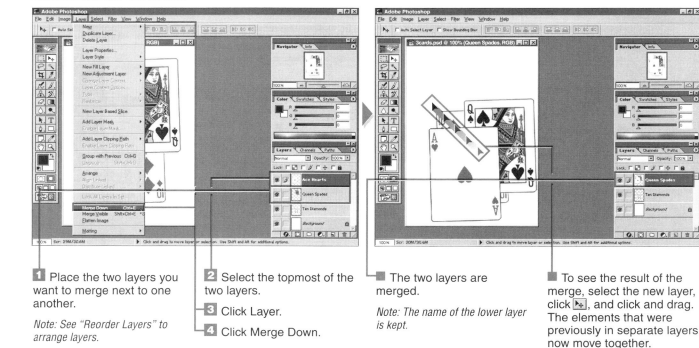

1 Place the two layers you want to merge next to one another.

Note: See "Reorder Layers" to arrange layers.

■ If the Layers palette is not visible, click Window and then Show Layers.

2 Select the topmost of the two layers.

3 Click Layer.

4 Click Merge Down.

■ The two layers are merged.

Note: The name of the lower layer is kept.

■ To see the result of the merge, select the new layer, click [move tool], and click and drag. The elements that were previously in separate layers now move together.

Why would I want to merge layers?

✔ Merging layers lets you permanently combine together elements of your image. For example, you may design a corporate letterhead that contains a picture of your building, the company name, and the corporate logo. You then merge the elements into a single layer for use elsewhere.

Should I save my final image as a flattened or a layered version?

✔ You may want to save two versions of your file — a flattened version for final use and a second version with layers intact for future edits. This gives you maximum flexibility should you need to change an image in the future, such as replace an old corporate logo with a new logo.

How does flattening layers work?

✔ In a flattened image, all visible layers are merged into the background, greatly reducing file size. Flattening an image discards all hidden layers and fills the remaining transparent areas with white. You will not want to flatten layers until you are done editing. After you flatten a file, you cannot recover the layer information.

FLATTEN AN IMAGE

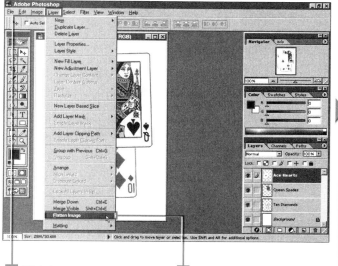

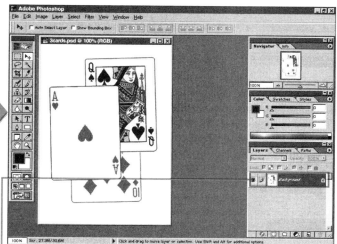

1 Click Layer.

2 Click Flatten Image.

■ All the layers are merged into one.

CHANGE LAYER OPACITY

*O*pacity refers to the ability to block light and is the opposite of *transparency*; the more opaque an object is, the less transparent it is. Adjusting the opacity of a layer lets elements in the layers below show through.

In essence, the Opacity setting combines the underlying layers with the currently active layer. For example, if you set an active layer's opacity to 10%, only 10% of the active layer's contents will be visible. This is a highly useful technique for inserting ghosted outlines or objects into digital images, or delicately painting an effect onto an underlying image.

The Opacity setting can be further modified by advanced blending

options to tweak the ways in which opacity is applied to the underlying image. Double-click the layer icon in the Layers palette to bring up the Layer Style dialog box. You can adjust the opacity and several other advanced settings, such as inner glow and bevels.

CHANGE LAYER OPACITY

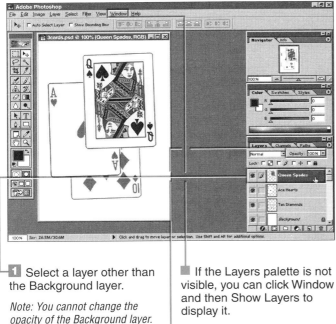

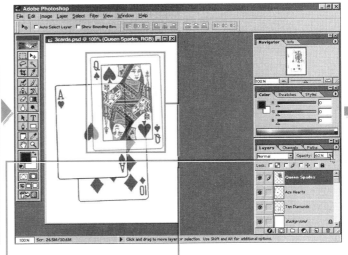

1 Select a layer other than the Background layer.

Note: You cannot change the opacity of the Background layer.

■ If the Layers palette is not visible, you can click Window and then Show Layers to display it.

■ The default opacity is 100% (completely opaque).

2 Type a new value in the Opacity field.

■ Alternatively, you can click and drag the slider.

Note: A layer's opacity can range from 1% to 100%.

■ The layer changes in opacity.

How can I use changes in opacity in my images?

✔ You can lower the opacity to add interesting type effects. For example, you can add a layer of semitransparent type over a digital image by reducing the type layer's opacity to 50%. This helps push the text into the background and keeps attention focused on the image. (For more about adding type, see Chapter 6.) You could also make a copy of an image, apply effects to it, change the opacity, and then place the edited version over the original. This creates a ghostly, surreal effect.

Why can I not change the opacity of a layer?

✔ It may be that you are trying to edit a locked layer. In order to change opacity, you must unlock the layer first.

What is the difference between the Opacity layer setting and the Opacity setting for the Paintbrush?

✔ The effects work similarly but have different scopes. The Paintbrush tool can be used to change the opacity of details or areas within a layer; changing the opacity for a layer affects all the objects on the layer.

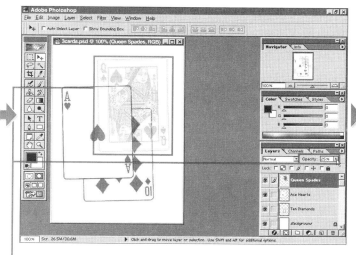

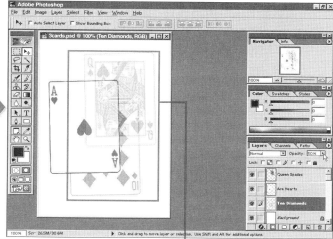

■ You can continue to adjust the opacity to suit your tastes.

■ You can make multiple layers in your image semitransparent by changing their opacities.

■ In this example, both the Queen Spades and Ten Diamonds layers are semitransparent.

CREATE AN ADJUSTMENT LAYER

Most layer commands apply to one layer at a time. A notable exception to this rule is an adjustment layer. An *adjustment layer* is a special layer that contains information that is used to correct color and tonal balance for all the layers beneath it.

You can stack adjustment layers, each of which has a separate set of adjustment information in it. For

example, you can have a separate adjustment layer for the red, green, and blue channels, and have a separate layer containing levels information. (See Chapter 3 for information on changing level settings.) Often, this is better than adjusting the pixels in a layer directly; you can alter the adjustment layer settings independently of the others, and

you still have the original image's color information intact.

You also have the flexibility of moving image layers around, so if you do not want to apply an adjustment layer to a particular layer, you can move the layer you want to protect above the adjustment layer, where it will remain unaffected.

CREATE AN ADJUSTMENT LAYER

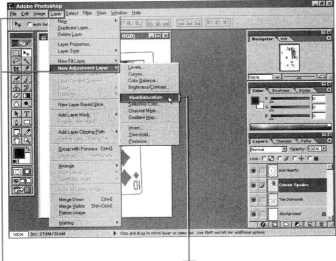

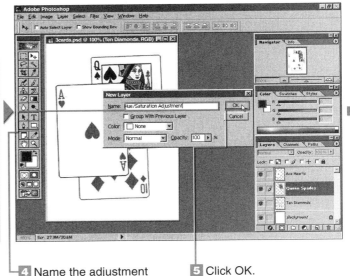

■1 Click Layer.

■2 Click New Adjustment Layer.

■3 Click an adjustment command.

■ The new adjustment layer will be placed above the currently selected layer.

■4 Name the adjustment layer.

■5 Click OK.

How do I apply an adjustment layer to only part of my image canvas?

✔ Normally, an adjustment layer applies to the entire image canvas. If you want to isolate part of the image, you can make a selection with a selection tool and then create the adjustment layer. The new layer will cover only the selected area in your image.

Do adjustment layers add to the file size?

✔ Because adjustment layers do not contain any pixels, they do not appreciably add to the file size. You can have numerous adjustment layers in a file if you want.

Can I create a new adjustment layer in the Layers palette?

✔ You can also create a new layer using the Layers palette instead of the menu. Click ⬛ at the bottom of the palette. The same layer list appears as if you had used the menu; the first three choices are dynamic fill layers, but the rest of the menu options are for creating adjustment layers. Select a layer, give it a name, and make any settings adjustments you need.

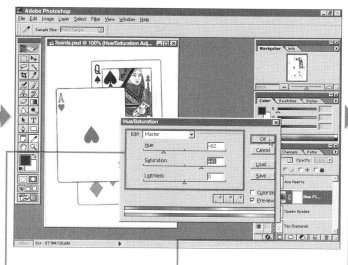

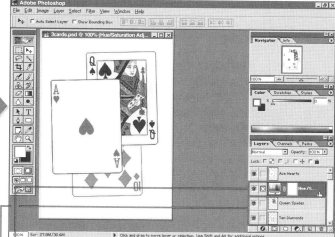

⬛ **6** Make your changes to the settings in the dialog box that appears.

⬛ In this example, an adjustment layer is created that changes the hue and saturation.

⬛ **7** Click OK.

⬛ An adjustment layer is added to the image.

⬛ Photoshop applies the effect to the layers that are below the adjustment layer.

⬛ In this example, the card layers below the adjustment layer are affected while the card layer above is not.

EDIT AN ADJUSTMENT LAYER

You can change the color and tonal changes that you defined in an adjustment layer at any time. If you have created adjustment layers for specific channels, you can change any channel information without changing the underlying image. As long as the adjustment layer is available, you can make as many or as few color and tonal adjustments as you need while editing your image.

If you double-click the adjustment layer icon, a settings dialog box will appear; its options depend on the type of adjustment layer that you created — Levels, Hue/Saturation, or a color channel mixer.

If you double-click the layer name, the Layer Style dialog box appears. In this box, you can edit specific layer style options and blending

options, set opacity, and work with advanced blending options.

When you use a regular layer with an adjustment layer, you can apply a specific adjustment layer and apply effects to that adjustment, such as outer glow or beveled edge effects. You can create very simple effects or create complex adjustment layers that can be tweaked in very small amounts.

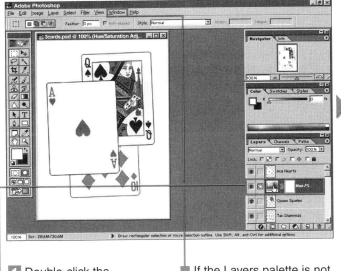

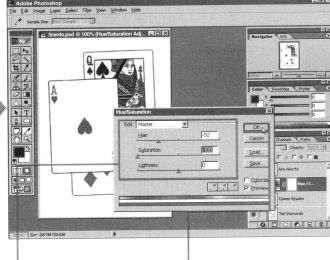

1 Double-click the adjustment layer in the Layers palette.

■ If the Layers palette is not visible, you can click Window and then Show Layers to display it.

2 Make adjustments in the dialog box that appears.

3 Click OK.

How do I merge an adjustment layer with a regular layer?

✔ Place the adjustment layer over the layer that you would like to merge it with and then click Layer and Merge Down. Merging the layers will cause the adjustment layer's effects to be applied only to the layer that it is merged with. The other layers below it will no longer be affected. After you merge the layers, however, you can no longer separate them and make new adjustments; you must create a new adjustment layer.

How do I edit an adjustment layer to apply to only part of an image?

✔ You edit your adjustment layer by painting the adjustment layer with black pixels to remove the correction from an area or with white pixels to apply the correction to an area. This is most easily seen with the Invert adjustment layer, but works with the other adjustment layers as well.

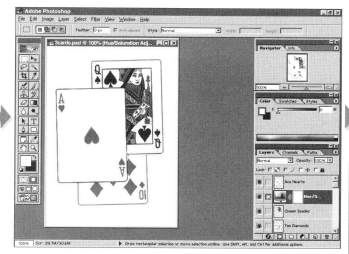

■ In this example, the saturation was reduced to the minimum, which removed the color in the layers below the adjustment layer.

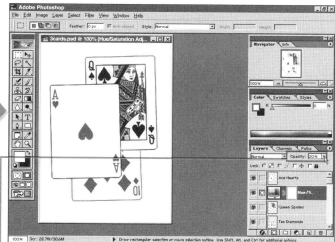

4 To lessen the effect of an adjustment layer, decrease the layer's opacity to less than 100%.

■ In this example, the opacity was decreased to 20%, which reverses the decrease in saturation. Some of the original color in the cards returns.

LINK LAYERS

If you work with many layers in an image at a time, you may need to move all the layers at once. Normally, this would cause a problem because the layers are important not only for their information and content but in their position and relation to other layers in your image. However, Photoshop lets you link layers together so that you can move them as a unit, without disturbing their order or position.

Linking causes different layers to move in unison when using the Move tool. Linking is useful when you want to keep elements of an image aligned with one another, but do not want to merge their layers (see "Merge or Flatten Layers"). Keeping layers unmerged lets you still apply effects independently to each layer.

When you press and hold Ctrl (Command) and drag and drop linked layers into another image window, the linked layers retain the link order. This lets you transfer a set of images and effects directly, without having to re-create them in the new image window.

LINK LAYERS

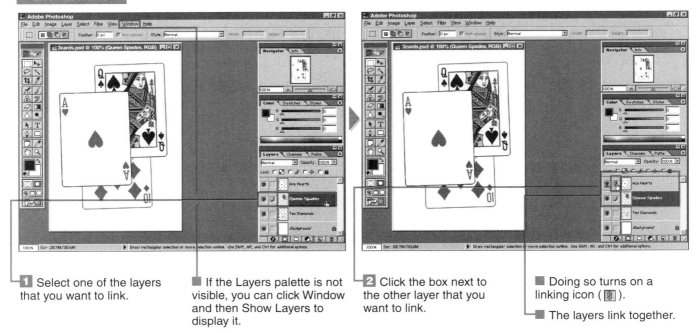

1 Select one of the layers that you want to link.

■ If the Layers palette is not visible, you can click Window and then Show Layers to display it.

2 Click the box next to the other layer that you want to link.

■ Doing so turns on a linking icon (▨).

■ The layers link together.

How can I easily align content in several layers?

✔ Link the layers that you want to align and select one of the linked layers. Create a selection using the Marquee tool. Then click Layer and Align to Selection and choose an alignment. The menu lets you align the layers six different ways along the selection outline.

Do I have to unlink a layer from a stack if I want to move it to another image?

✔ You do not need to unlink a layer in order to move it. You can just drag the image from the Layers palette into the new document window. A copy will be placed in the new window.

How do I center the linked layers in the new document?

✔ Hold down Shift while dropping your linked layers into a new document, and they will be centered in the document. If you previously selected an area in that document, the linked files will be centered within the selection.

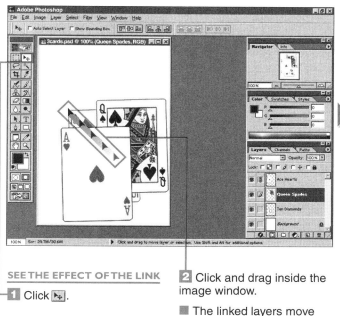

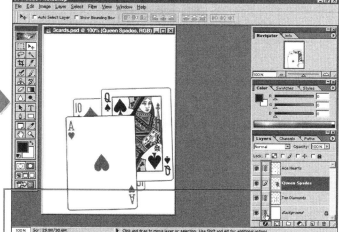

SEE THE EFFECT OF THE LINK

1 Click ▶+.

2 Click and drag inside the image window.

■ The linked layers move together.

■ You can link as many layers as you like.

■ In this example, all the layers have been linked, including the Background layer.

BLEND LAYERS

Photoshop's blend modes change pixel appearances by blending them together with every pixel in every layer below the currently selected layer, in practically a straight line, all the way to the Background layer. In essence, each pixel in the stack goes through a series of calculations to create the final appearance. Other effects perform calculations on surrounding pixels,

or nearby pixels, or change pixel values directly; blend modes adjust pixels based on the contents of other layers.

The sliders in the Blending Options dialog box let you control which pixels from the active layer and which pixels from the underlying visible layers appear in the final image. For example, you can drop dark pixels out of the active layer

or force bright pixels from the underlying layers to show through. You can also define a range of partially blended pixels to produce a smooth transition between blended and unblended areas.

Take time to experiment with the blending options on your image. It is easy to reset your image to its default values, so do not hesitate to start over.

BLEND LAYERS

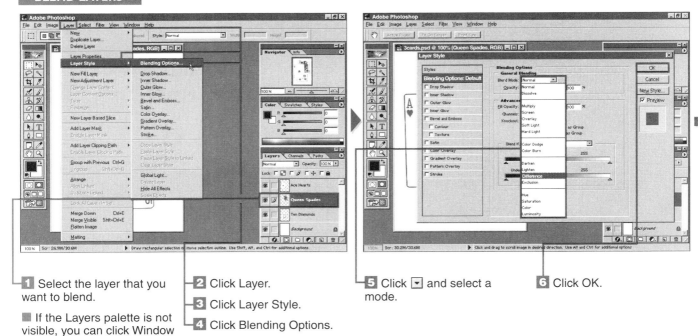

■1 Select the layer that you want to blend.

■ If the Layers palette is not visible, you can click Window and then Show Layers to display it.

■2 Click Layer.

■3 Click Layer Style.

■4 Click Blending Options.

■5 Click ▼ and select a mode.

■6 Click OK.

Can I apply a blending mode to the same layer so that all effects are included?

✔ You can choose to have the blending mode apply to all layer effects for that layer. Thus, you can choose to have a layer's blending mode apply to its own inner glow, satin, or overlay. You cannot choose to apply the layer's mode to an outer glow or outer shadow because these effects fall outside the layer's original boundaries.

How do I reset the blending options to the default values?

✔ Hold down Alt (Option); the Cancel button changes to Reset. Click Reset, and the options will return to the defaults.

What effects do some of the different blending modes have?

✔ The Multiply mode darkens the colors where the selected layer overlaps layers below it. The Screen mode is the opposite of Multiply; it lightens colors where layers overlap. Color takes the selected layer's colors and blends them with the details in the layers below it. Luminosity is the opposite of Color; it takes the selected layer's details and mixes them with the colors below it.

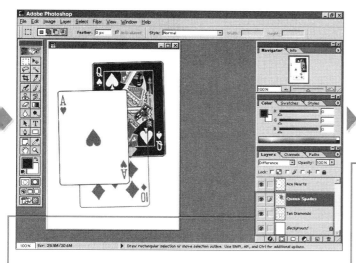

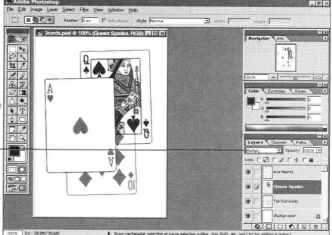

■ Photoshop blends the selected layer with the layers below it.

■ This example shows the Difference mode, which creates a photo-negative effect in which the selected layer overlaps other layers.

■ You can also adjust blending modes with the drop-down list in the Layers palette. In this example, the blend mode has been changed to Multiply.

APPLY A LAYER EFFECT

*L*ayer effects are specific transformations that are applied to layers and the objects in those layers. In the past, many of them were painstakingly applied by hand, but because they were fairly common and popular effects, Adobe developed the effects that could be automatically applied with only minor tweaking required. This saves time, energy, and makes your objects and images have a professional appearance.

Layer effects can overlay colors, add strokes to outlines, and create textures and contours to your objects. You can also control the amount of blending between an effect layer and a background layer, which makes layer effects one of the most powerful tools in the toolbox.

One popular example is a drop shadow. You can apply a drop shadow to make a layer look like it is raised off the image canvas. You specify the shadow color, opacity, position, size, and contour; Photoshop then does the hard work for you, adding a perfectly shaped drop shadow to your selected object.

APPLY A LAYER EFFECT

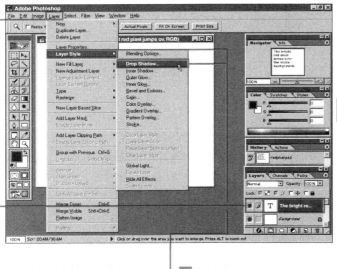

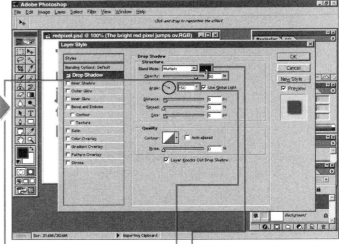

APPLY A DROP SHADOW

■1 Select the layer to which you want to add a drop shadow.

■2 Click Layer.

■3 Click Layer Style.

■4 Click Drop Shadow.

■ You can also click the Layer Effects button ( ) and select Drop Shadow.

Note: Perform steps 5 to 10 if you want to enter your own settings. If you want to use the default settings, you can skip to step 11.

■5 Type an Opacity value to specify the shadow's darkness.

■6 Click the color swatch to select a shadow color.

Note: The default shadow color is black.

■7 Type an Angle value to specify in which direction the shadow is displaced.

Here are some of the layer effects that you can apply:

Inner Shadow   Outter Glow   Inner Glow   Bevel and Emboss

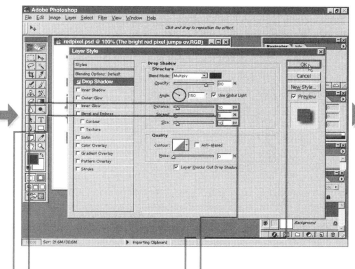

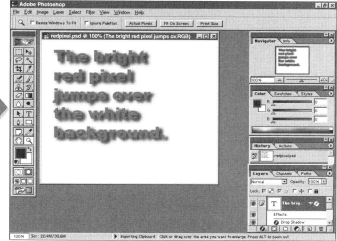

8 Type a Distance value to specify how far the shadow is displaced.

9 Type a Spread value to specify the fuzziness of the shadow's edge.

10 Type a Size value to specify the size of the shadow's edge.

11 Click OK.

■ Photoshop creates a shadow in back of the selected layer.

Note: In this example, the effect was applied to a layer of type. For more information about type, see Chapter 6.

EDIT A LAYER EFFECT

Photoshop's layer effects ship with default settings, such as pixel tolerance or opacity settings. Photoshop lets you edit layer effects that you have applied to your image. Each layer has its own settings that can be adjusted independently of the other settings. You can set different pixel distance levels for a drop shadow and an inner shadow, as well as blend modes and opacity. This fine-grained control lets you precisely determine the appearance of each effect in the layer.

For maximum control, you should consider placing each layer effect on its own layer rather than rolling up many layer effects into a single layer. Although there will be instances when you will want to have all the layer effects in the same layer (such as when working with text), when you are working with images, you can achieve greater flexibility by placing effects on separate layers, especially if you will be moving objects up and down the layers and may want to apply one effect, but not another, to an image.

EDIT A LAYER EFFECT

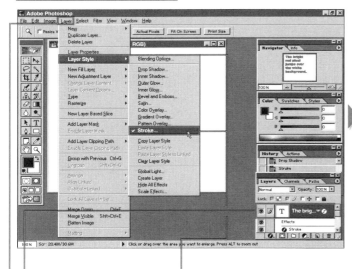

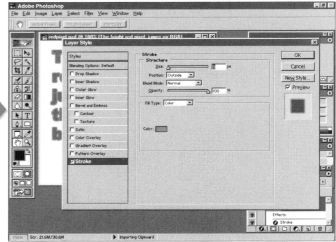

1 Select the layer whose effect you want to edit.

■ This example shows editing the color stroked around text.

2 Click Layer.

3 Click Layer Style.

4 Click Stroke.

■ You can also double-click the effect in the Layers palette.

■ Photoshop displays the current configuration values for the effect.

How do I keep a layer effect from accidentally being changed?

✔ You can lock a layer and its effects by selecting the layer and checking the 🔒 check box in the Layers palette (☐ changes to ✔).

How do I create my own custom styles?

✔ Apply one or more effects (such as Drop Shadow, Outer Glow, and others) to a layer in your image. With the layer selected in the Layers palette, click the Styles ▶ and click New Style. A dialog box appears that lets you name your custom style. Click OK in the dialog box to add an icon for your new style to the Styles palette.

How do I turn off layer effects that I have applied?

✔ When you apply an effect to a layer, the effect gets added to the Layers palette. (You may have to click ▶ to see a layer's effects [▶ changes to ▼].) You can temporarily turn off an effect by clicking 👁 in the Layers palette.

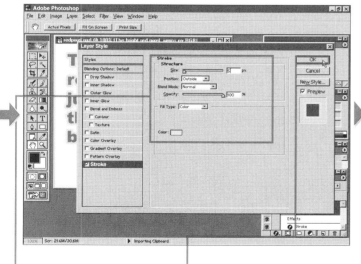

5 Edit the values in the Layer Style dialog box.

■ This example shows broadening and recoloring the stroke effect.

6 Click OK.

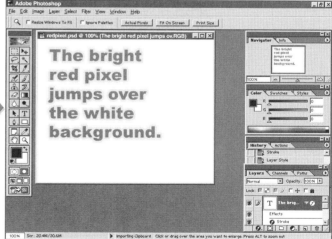

■ Photoshop applies the edited effect to the layer.

■ You can edit an effect as many times as you want.

Note: In this example, the effect was applied to a layer of type. For more about type, see Chapter 6.

CREATE A LAYER MASK

asks let you isolate and protect areas of an image as you apply color changes, filters, or other effects to the rest of the image. When you select part of an image, the area that is not selected is "masked" or protected from editing.

You can create a *layer mask* to control how different areas within a layer or layer set are hidden and revealed. By making changes to the layer mask, you can apply a variety of special effects to the layer without actually affecting the pixels on that layer. You can then apply the mask and make the changes permanent or remove the mask without applying the changes. You can save all layer masks with a layered document.

You can also use masks for complex image editing such as gradually applying color or filter effects to an image. This can be used to create "keyhole effects" or to add a gently fading object into an image.

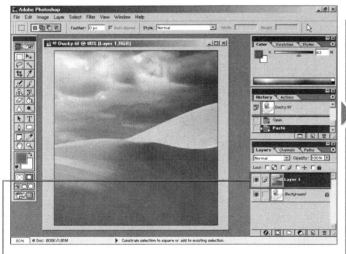

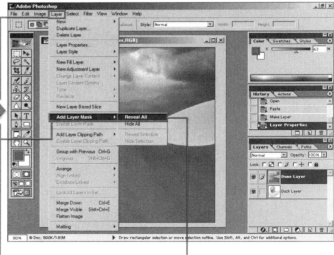

1 Select the layer to receive the mask in the Layers palette.

2 Click Layer.

3 Click Add Layer Mask.

4 Click Reveal All to create a mask that reveals the entire layer.

■ A white mask is added to the Layers palette.

What is a layer clipping path?

✔ A *layer clipping path* creates a sharp-edged mask that can be used to cover part of a layer rather than an entire layer. You can use both a layer mask and a layer clipping path on a single layer or layer set.

What is the Vignette effect?

✔ The Vignette effect creates a soft edge around a selection. It is one of Photoshop's built-in effects that is available on the Actions palette. If you need to create a soft, warm, fuzzy look, you can do it with the Vignette action rather than using layer masks.

What kind of layer mask is created with the Hide All mask?

✔ Hide All creates a mask that hides the entire masking layer, so all the underlying layers show through — in effect, the layer is initially transparent to the underlying images. To make the layer opaque and hide underlying images and layers, choose a painting tool and use white pixels to hide underlying images, gray pixels for partial transparency, and black pixels to make the mask transparent again.

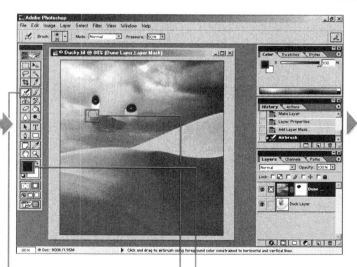

5 Select a painting tool (such as [brush]).

Note: See Chapter 3 for information about setting painting tool options.

6 Select black as the paint tool's foreground color.

7 Apply black pixels to the mask.

■ The underlying layers are revealed.

■ You can apply white pixels to re-hide the underlying layers or gray pixels to make the layer mask partially transparent.

APPLY AN ARTISTIC FILTER

Filters are effects that you can apply to your digital images in order to achieve a certain look. Many of the filters in Photoshop are designed to reproduce the look and feel of illustrations and drawings. Others are designed to enhance or reduce photographic effects in your digital images. Enhancements can sharpen edges or improve clarity; reductions can introduce noise or blur to make images seem less "perfect."

Artistic filters make your image look as though it was created with traditional artistic techniques. The Dry Brush filter, one example of an Artistic filter, applies a painted effect by converting similarly colored areas in your image to solid colors.

You can use Photoshop's effects exclusively, or you can purchase plug-ins from third-party companies that add to the number and types of effects you can add to an image. If you are going to work professionally as a graphics designer, you will probably want to acquire some additional filters and effects to round out your portfolio.

APPLY AN ARTISTIC FILTER: THE DRY BRUSH FILTER

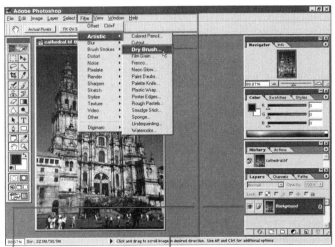

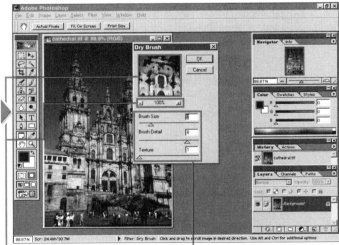

1 Select the layer to which you want to apply the filter.

Note: In this example, the image has a single background layer.

■ If you want to apply the filter to just part of your image, make the selection with a selection tool.

2 Click Filter.

3 Click Artistic.

4 Click Dry Brush.

■ A small window displays a preview of the filter's effect.

5 Click ▭ or ▭ to zoom out or in.

6 Fine-tune the filter effect by adjusting the Brush Size, Brush Detail, and Texture values.

Here are some other Artistic filters that you can apply:

Colored Pencil

Neon Glow

Palette Knife

Plastic Wrap

Poster Edges

Rough Pastels

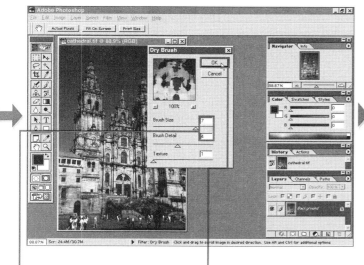

■ In this example, increasing Brush Size and decreasing Brush Detail have thickened the dry-brush effect.

7 Click OK.

■ Photoshop applies the filter.

APPLY A BLUR FILTER

Photoshop's Blur filters reduce the amount of detail in your image. Initially, you may consider this a bad thing to do to an image; most people want to see images clearly, and not as if they need a new pair of reading glasses. However, Blur filters help hide a multitude of sins that can occur in negatives, poor prints, cheap digital camera shots, or bad scans made on smudged flatbeds. Blur filters make images softer, or fuzzier, around the edges, and smooth out differences in colors across an image.

For example, sometimes an image has small imperfections or single pixels that make the image seem dirty or harsh. The Blur filter helps reduce the spottiness by diminishing the contrast between neighboring pixels — lightening dark pixels and darkening light pixels. Most of the Blur filters have settings to adjust the effect's range in pixels; the Gaussian Blur filter has advantages over the other Blur filters in that you can control the amount of blur added.

APPLY A BLUR FILTER: THE GAUSSIAN BLUR FILTER

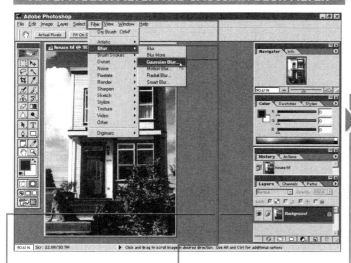

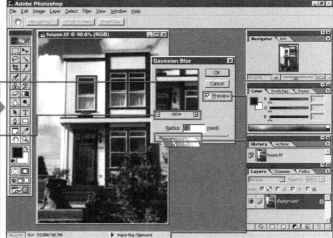

1 Select the layer to which you want to apply the filter.

Note: In this example, the image has a single background layer.

■ If you want to apply the filter to just part of your image, make the selection with a selection tool.

2 Click Filter.

3 Click Blur.

4 Click Gaussian Blur.

■ A small window displays a preview of the filter's effect.

5 Click 🔲 or ➕ to zoom out or in.

6 Click Preview to preview the effect in the main window (🔲 changes to ✔).

7 Click and drag the Radius slider to control the amount of blur added.

How does the Blur filter work?

✔ The Blur filter eliminates noise where significant color transitions occur in an image. Blur filters smooth transitions by averaging the pixels next to the hard edges of defined lines and shaded areas. The Blur More filter produces an effect three or four times stronger than that of the Blur filter.

How do I add directional blurring to an image?

✔ You can add directional blur to your image with the Motion Blur filter (click Filter, Blur, and then Motion Blur). This can add a sense of motion.

What does the Radial Blur filter do?

✔ The Radial Blur filter simulates the blur of a zooming or rotating camera to produce a soft blur. To simulate a rotating camera (to blur along concentric circular lines), select Spin and specify a degree of rotation. To simulate zooming in or out of the image, select Zoom and specify an amount from 1 to 100. Blur quality ranges from Draft, for the fastest but grainy results, to Good and Best, for smoother results, which are indistinguishable except on a large selection.

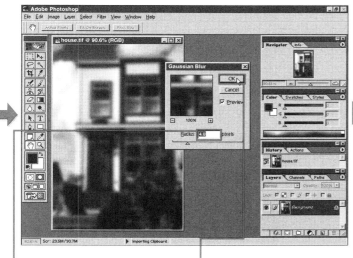

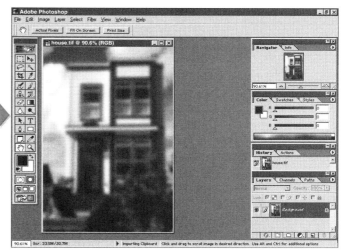

■ In this example, the amount of blur has been increased by boosting the Radius value.

8 Click OK.

■ Photoshop applies the filter.

APPLY A BRUSH STROKES FILTER

Photoshop's Brush Strokes filters are a specialized set of filters — and arguably should belong under the Artistic menu option. Much like the other Artistic filters, the Brush Strokes filters make your image look painted using various techniques, some of which you probably never used in art class. However, the Brush Strokes filter can almost instantly add a handmade look to images.

For example, the Crosshatch filter adds diagonal, overlapping brush-stroke effects to your image. Similar to the Dry Brush filter (see the section "Apply an Artistic Filter"), the Crosshatch filter converts similarly colored areas in your image to solid colors to produce its effect.

As with the Artistic filters, though, it is sometimes difficult to see how

or when you would consider using one of the Brush Strokes effects on a pure digital image. If anything, most digital images strive for a surreal effect rather than mimic a real-world appearance. But if you should need the Brush Strokes look for any of your projects, they are here for your use.

APPLY A BRUSH STROKES FILTER: THE CROSSHATCH FILTER

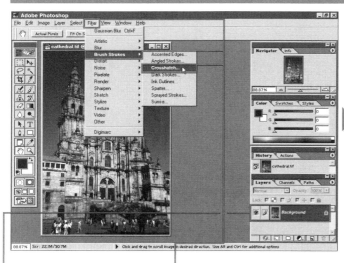

1 Select the layer to which you want to apply the filter.

Note: In this example, the image has a single background layer.

■ If you want to apply the filter to just part of your image, make the selection with a selection tool.

2 Click Filter.

3 Click Brush Strokes.

4 Click Crosshatch.

■ A small window displays a preview of the filter's effect.

5 Click ⊟ or ⊞ to zoom out or in.

6 Fine-tune the filter effect by adjusting the Stroke Length, Sharpness, and Strength values.

Here are some other Brush Strokes filters that you can apply:

Accented Edges

Ink Outlines

Angled Strokes

Splatter

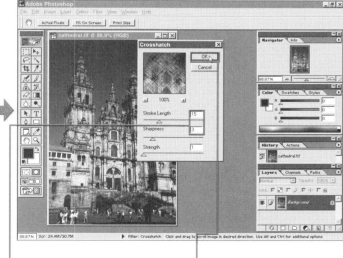

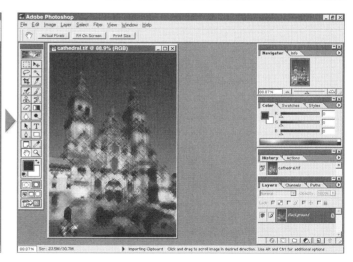

■ In this example, the brush-stroke effect has been intensified by increasing the Stroke Length value and decreasing the Sharpness value.

7 Click OK.

■ Photoshop applies the filter.

APPLY A DISTORT FILTER

Distorting images is possibly one of the most fun effects that you can apply. With one mouse click, you can apply a funhouse mirror effect or view an object through a warped piece of glass.

The main concept behind image distortion is the ability to stretch, squeeze, and morph an object's appearance. For example, the Spherize filter produces a bulbous effect, as if your image was turned into rubber and stretched over the surface of a ball.

Each distortion filter has its own group of settings that can be individually adjusted. For example, the Glass filter makes an image appear as if it is being viewed through different types of glass. You can choose a glass effect or create your own glass surface as a Photoshop file and apply it. You can adjust scaling, distortion, and smoothness settings. If you do not like the look of a filter, you can play around with the settings until you achieve the appearance that you want.

APPLY A DISTORT FILTER: THE SPHERIZE FILTER

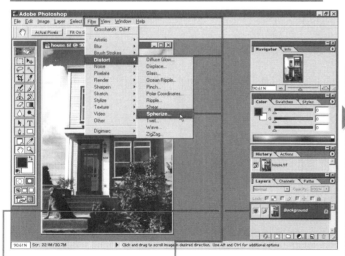 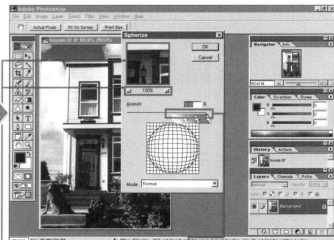

■1 Select the layer to which you want to apply the filter.

Note: In this example, the image has a single background layer.

■ If you want to apply the filter to just part of your image, make the selection with a selection tool.

■2 Click Filter.

■3 Click Distort.

■4 Click Spherize.

■ A small window displays a preview of the filter's effect.

■5 Click ■ or ■ to zoom out or in.

■6 Click and drag the Amount slider to control the amount of distortion added.

Here are some other distortion filters that you can apply:

Diffuse Glow

Glass

Pinch

Ripple

Twirl

Wave

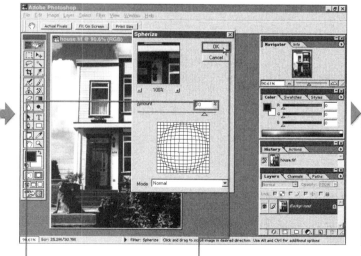

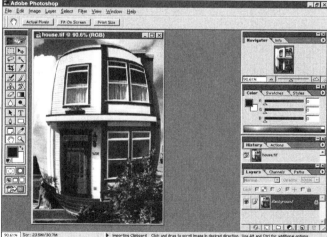

■ In this example, the intensity of the spherize effect has been decreased.

7 Click OK.

■ Photoshop applies the filter.

APPLY A NOISE FILTER

The Noise filters add or remove *noise*, or pixels with randomly distributed color levels. This helps to blend a selection into the surrounding pixels. Noise filters can also create unusual textures or remove problem areas, such as dust and scratches, from an image.

The Add Noise filter applies random pixels to an image, simulating the effect of shooting

pictures on high-speed film. The two Add Noise distribution options are Uniform, which distributes color values of noise using random numbers, and Gaussian, which distributes color values of noise along a bell-shaped curve for a speckled effect.

The other Noise filters — Despeckle, Dust & Scratches, and Median — average the values of surrounding pixels to reduce

noise. This has the effect of removing detail and blurring hard edges. These filters have various settings that you can use to adjust them, such as selecting the distance in pixels to use for value averaging.

You can make a selection with a selection tool and then apply a Noise filter. This is useful for increasing a localized speckling or blurring effect, depending on the tool being used.

APPLY A NOISE FILTER: THE ADD NOISE FILTER

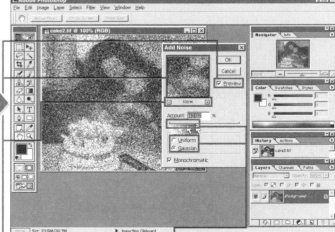

■1 Select the layer to which you want to apply the filter.

Note: In this example, the image has a single background layer.

■ If you want to apply the filter to just part of your image, make the selection with a selection tool.

■2 Click Filter.

■3 Click Noise.

■4 Click Add Noise.

■ A small window displays a preview.

■5 Click ⊟ or ⊞ to zoom.

■6 Click Preview to preview the effect in the main window (☐ changes to ☑).

■7 Click and drag the Amount slider to control the amount of noise added.

■8 Select the way you want the noise distributed (○ changes to ◉).

Note: Uniform spreads the noise more evenly than Gaussian.

What does the Monochromatic setting in the Add Noise dialog box do?

✔ If you select Monochromatic, noise will be added by lightening or darkening pixels in your image. Pixel hues will stay the same. At high settings with the Monochromatic setting on, the filter produces a television-static effect.

Can I apply noise in only one color channel?

✔ You can switch to a color channel and apply a Noise filter or make a selection and then apply a Noise filter. This has the effect of increasing the noise in only that channel; if you add noise to the Red channel, you increase the distribution of red-hued static.

Is there a way to keep the graininess, but make it not so pronounced in the image?

✔ It is fairly easy to add subtle noise effects to an image. Open the Add Noise dialog box, adjust the settings to the graininess that you like, and click OK. Then bring up the Fade dialog box by pressing Ctrl + Shift + F (Command - Shift - F), adjust the opacity, select the Lighten or Darken blend mode from the list, and click OK.

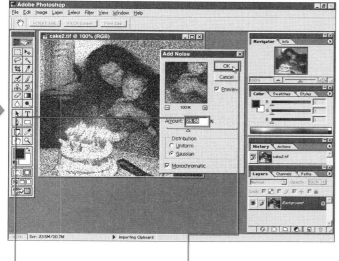

■ In this example, the Amount value has been decreased.

🔟 Click OK.

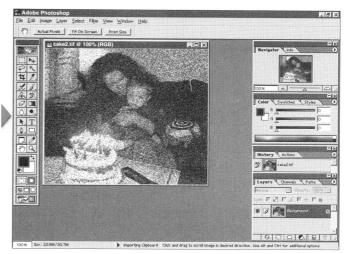

■ Photoshop applies the filter.

APPLY A PIXELATE FILTER

Pixelation is the effect that you see when you increase magnification on a digital image. The same amount of pixel information is spread over a larger area, and a single pixel is increased to a square, blocklike shape. Pixelation is an artifact of digital imaging and is not an effect that you would normally see in the real world.

The Pixelate filters divide areas of your image into solid-colored shapes, using anything from small dots to large blobs and smears. Although they are not precisely a set of digital artifacts, the Pixelate filters in Photoshop introduce artifacts commonly found in media, both print and digital.

For example, the Pointillize filter re-creates your image using colored

dots. *Pointillism* is a painting technique that was popularized by impressionist artists of the nineteenth century; one of the most famous is *A Sunday Afternoon on the Island of the Grand Jatte* by French impressionist Georges Seurat. You can apply a similar effect to any digital image to make it appear as if it was painted using tiny dots.

APPLY A PIXELATE FILTER: THE POINTILLIZE FILTER

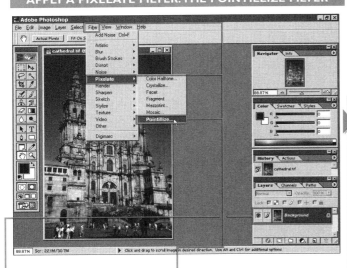

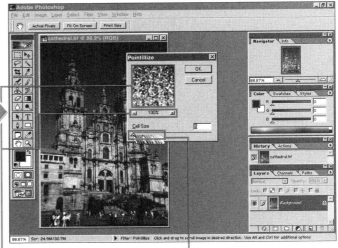

■1 Select the layer to which you want to apply the filter.

Note: In this example, the image has a single background layer.

■ If you want to apply the filter to just part of your image, make the selection with a selection tool.

■2 Click Filter.

■3 Click Pixelate.

■4 Click Pointillize.

■ A small window displays a preview of the filter's effect.

■5 Click ⊟ or ⊞ to zoom out or in.

■6 Click and drag the Cell Size slider to adjust the size of the dots.

Note: The size can range from 3 to 300.

Here are some other Pixelate filters that you can apply:

Color Halftone

Crystallize

Mezzotint

Mosaic

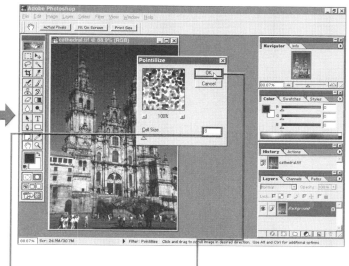

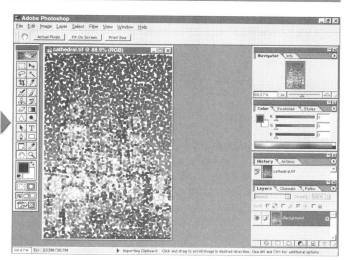

■ In this example, the Cell Size has been slightly increased.

7 Click OK.

■ Photoshop applies the filter.

APPLY A RENDER FILTER

The Render filters perform sophisticated yet simplified image manipulations. They work with digital images as if they were in a 3D image-rendering program. The filters use complex mathematical techniques to apply effects to your image. They create 3D shapes, cloud patterns, refraction patterns, and simulated light reflections. You can also manipulate objects in 3D space,

create 3D objects, and create texture fills from grayscale files to produce 3D-like effects for lighting.

The Lighting Effects filter lets you add spotlight and other lighting enhancements. For example, you can produce myriad lighting effects on RGB images by varying 17 light styles, 3 light types, and 4 sets of light properties. You can also use textures from grayscale files (called *bump maps*) to produce 3D-like

effects and save your own styles for use in other images.

The 3D capabilities in Photoshop are good for working with individual images. If you need to work with more than one image from a single source, you should consider using the 3D-rendering tools in After Effects. See Chapter 29 for more on rendering 3D images in video.

APPLY A RENDER FILTER: THE LIGHTING EFFECTS FILTER

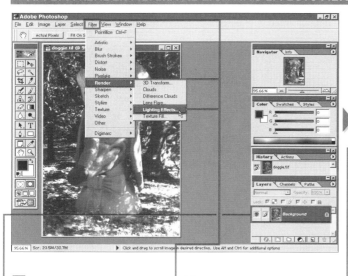

■1 Select the layer to which you want to apply the filter.

Note: In this example, the image has a single background layer.

■ If you want to apply the filter to just part of your image, make the selection with a selection tool.

■2 Click Filter.

■3 Click Render.

■4 Click Lighting Effects.

■ Photoshop displays a small preview of the effect.

■5 Click ▾ and choose a lighting style.

What is a lens flare, and how can I add it to an image?

✔ A lens flare is the extra flash of light that sometimes appears in a photo when too much light enters a camera lens. Photographers try to avoid this effect, but if you want to add it, you can use the Lens Flare filter. (The effect can make your digital image look more like an old-fashioned photograph.) Apply it by clicking Filter, Render, and then Lens Flare.

What do the cloud effects do?

✔ The Clouds filter generates a soft cloud pattern using random values that vary between the foreground and the background colors. The Difference Clouds filter uses randomly generated values that vary between the foreground and background color to produce a cloud pattern. The filter blends the cloud data with the existing pixels in the same way that the Difference mode blends colors.

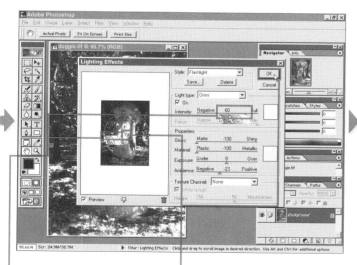

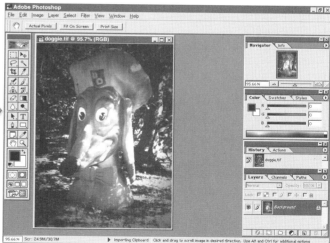

- 6 Click and drag the slider to control the light intensity.

- 7 Adjust the position and shape of the lighting by clicking and dragging the handles in the preview window.

- ■ You can click and drag the center point to change where the light is centered.

- 8 Click OK.

- ■ Photoshop applies the filter.

APPLY A SHARPEN FILTER

Photoshop's Sharpen filters intensify the detail and reduce blurring in your image. The Sharpen and Sharpen More filters focus blurry images by increasing the contrast of adjacent pixels. The Sharpen More filter applies a stronger sharpening effect than the Sharpen filter does.

The Sharpen Edges and Unsharp Mask filters find the areas in the image where significant color changes occur and sharpen them. The Sharpen Edges filter sharpens only edges while preserving the overall smoothness of the image. Use this filter to sharpen edges without specifying an amount. For professional color correction, use the Unsharp Mask filter to adjust the contrast of edge detail and produce a lighter and darker line on each side of the edge. This process emphasizes the edge and creates the illusion of a sharper image.

The Unsharp Mask filter has advantages over the other Sharpen filters in that it lets you control the amount of sharpening applied.

APPLY A SHARPEN FILTER: THE UNSHARP MASK FILTER

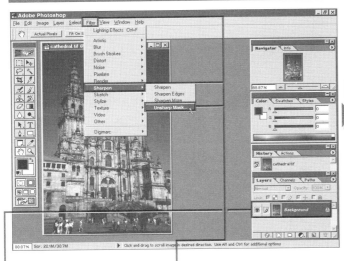

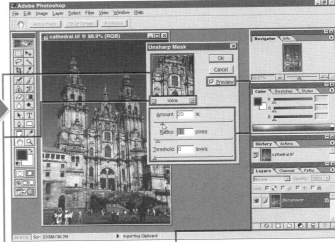

1 Select the layer to which you want to apply the filter.

Note: In this example, the image has a single background layer.

■ If you want to apply the filter to just part of your image, make the selection with a selection tool.

2 Click Filter.

3 Click Sharpen.

4 Click Unsharp Mask.

■ A small window displays a preview of the filter's effect.

5 Click ⊟ or ⊞ to zoom out or in.

6 Click Preview to preview the effect in the main window (☐ changes to ☑).

7 Click and drag the sliders to control the amount of sharpening applied to the image.

When should sharpening be applied?

✔ It is a good idea to sharpen an image after you have changed its size because changing an image's size adds blurring. For example, if you change a smaller image's resolution to a larger size, you introduce blurring and increase the visibility of anti-aliasing artifacts. Applying the Unsharp Mask filter reduces the blurring introduced this way. It can also help clarify images from low-end or inexpensive scanners and cameras.

Can I selectively apply the Sharpen filter?

✔ You can apply both the Sharpen and Sharpen More filters to selected areas in your image. The selected area can be sharpened without affecting the rest of the image. The Sharpen Edges filter affects all areas in your image where there are areas of contrast. The Unsharp Mask filter does both, allowing you to selectively sharpen an area or apply the filter to your entire image.

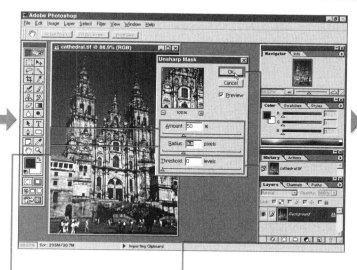

■ Amount controls the overall amount of sharpening.

■ Radius controls whether sharpening is confined to edges in the image (low Radius setting) or added across the entire image (high Radius setting).

■ Threshold controls how much contrast must be present for an edge to be recognized and sharpened.

8 Click OK.

■ Photoshop applies the filter.

APPLY A SKETCH FILTER

The Sketch filters are a collection of artistic effects that emulate a drawing technique or drawing medium that you might find in an art school. These effects can be used to make your digital image seem to have been hand-sketched or handmade rather than have the precise machine glow of a perfectly focused and sterile digital image.

Many of the Sketch filters modify your digital image by using the foreground and background colors to achieve their effects. The Charcoal filter, for example, makes an image look as if it was sketched by using charcoal on paper; the foreground color is used as the charcoal color and the background color as the paper color. So if black and white are your foreground and

background colors, you can make your image look like a black-and-white sketch.

Each Sketch filter has its own settings, so experiment with both the colors and the settings before permanently applying your filter.

APPLY A SKETCH FILTER: THE CHARCOAL FILTER

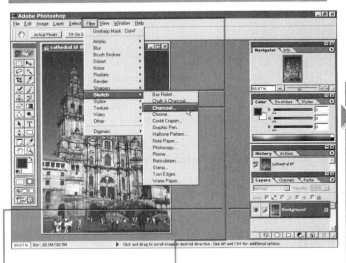

1 Select the layer to which you want to apply the filter.

■ If you want to apply the filter to just part of your image, make the selection with a selection tool.

2 Click Filter.

3 Click Sketch.

4 Click Charcoal.

■ A small window displays a preview of the filter's effect.

5 Click ⊟ or ⊞ to zoom out or in.

6 Click and drag the sliders to control the filter's effect.

Here are some other Sketch filters that you can apply:

Bas Relief

Chalk & Charcoal

Chrome

Conté Crayon

Note Paper

Water Paper

■ In this example, the thickness of the charcoal strokes has been increased. The Light/Dark Balance setting has also been increased to darken the image.

7 Click OK.

■ Photoshop applies the filter.

APPLY A STYLIZE FILTER

The Stylize filters produce a painted or impressionistic effect on a selection by displacing pixels and finding and heightening contrast in an image. The Glowing Edges filter, one example of a Stylize filter, applies a neon effect to the edges in your image. Areas between the edges are turned black. Other Stylize filters produce similarly extreme artistic effects.

Although these filters may seem to achieve cool effects, you should probably use them only once or twice in your artwork. Where they really shine is in combination with other effects or techniques to help modify or accentuate detail. For example, after using filters such as Find Edges and Trace Contour, which highlight edges, you can apply the Invert command to outline the edges of a color image with colored lines or to outline the edges of a grayscale image with white lines.

APPLY A STYLIZE FILTER: THE GLOWING EDGES FILTER

1 Select the layer to which you want to apply the filter.

Note: In this example, the image has a single background layer.

■ If you want to apply the filter to just part of your image, make the selection with a selection tool.

2 Click Filter.

3 Click Stylize.

4 Click Glowing Edges.

■ A small window displays a preview of the filter's effect.

5 Click ▬ or ⊞ to zoom out or in.

6 Click and drag the sliders to control the intensity of the glow added to the edges in the image.

Here are some other Stylize filters that you can apply:

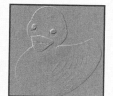

Emboss

Find Edges

Extrude

Solarize

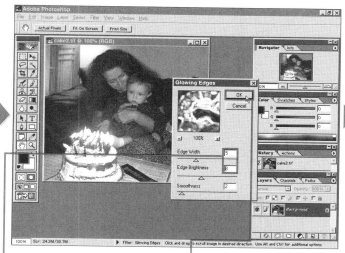

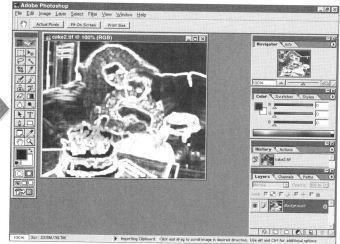

■ In this example, the Edge Width and Edge Brightness values have been increased to intensify the neon effect.

7 Click OK.

■ Photoshop applies the filter.

APPLY A TEXTURE FILTER

The Texture filters overlay different textures on your image. Actually, most of the textures look like they are surfaces underneath your image, such as burlap sacking or a tile floor. The Texture filters add three-dimensional depth to an image or to an effect, helping accentuate detail and provide the feeling that the image may pop off the page or monitor.

The Texturizer filter lets you apply other patterns besides those included with Photoshop, so you can scan and create a texture or pattern, work with it in Photoshop, save it, and then use it for adding texture to your image. To use your own texture, open the Texturizer dialog box (click Filter, Texture, and then Texturizer), and select Load Texture from the Texture drop-down list box. Browse to the Photoshop file (PSD) that you want to add as a texture, click Open, adjust your Texturizer settings, and then click OK.

APPLY A TEXTURE FILTER: THE TEXTURIZER FILTER

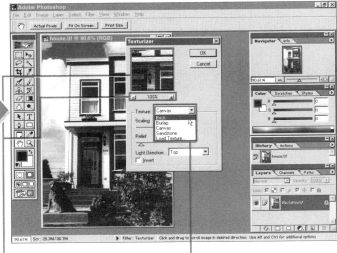

■1 Select the layer to which you want to apply the filter.

Note: In this example, the image has a single background layer.

■ If you want to apply the filter to just part of your image, make the selection with a selection tool.

■2 Click Filter.

■3 Click Texture.

■4 Click Texturizer.

■ A small window displays a preview of the filter's effect.

■5 Click ⊟ or ⊞ to zoom out or in.

■6 Click ▾ and select a texture to apply.

Here are some other Texture filters that you can apply:

Craquelure

Mosaic Tiles

Patchwork

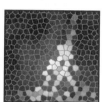

Stained Glass

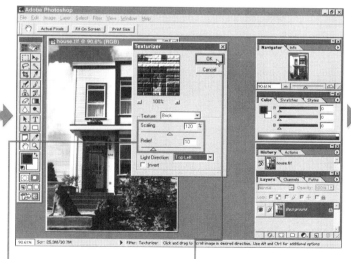

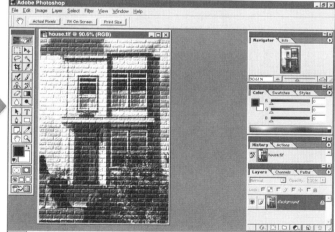

7 Adjust the sliders to control the intensity of the overlaid texture.

8 Click OK.

■ Photoshop applies the filter.

ADD TYPE TO AN IMAGE

Adding type enables you to label elements in your image or use letters and words in artistic ways. When you add type to an image, the characters are composed of pixels and have the same resolution as the image.

You can create horizontal or vertical type anywhere in an image. Depending on how you use the

Type tool, you can enter point type or paragraph type. *Point type* is useful for entering a single word or a line of characters; *paragraph type* is useful for entering and formatting the type as one or more paragraphs.

When you create type, a new type layer is added to the Layers palette. Clicking in an image with the Type

tool puts the Type tool in edit mode. You can enter and edit characters when the tool is in edit mode; however, you must commit changes to the type layer before you can perform other actions on the type, such as converting it to outlines or applying an effect.

ADD TYPE TO AN IMAGE

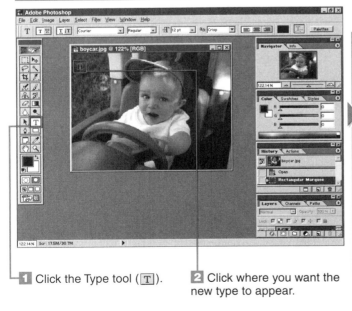

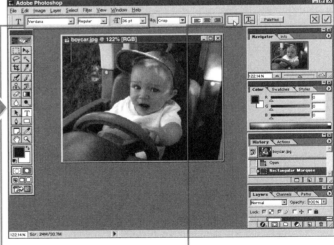

1 Click the Type tool (T).

2 Click where you want the new type to appear.

3 Click ▼ and select a font, style, and size for your type.

4 Click the color swatch to select a color for your type.

Note: The foreground color is applied by default.

How do I reposition my type?

✔ Added type is placed in its own layer. You can move the layer with the Move tool (🔍). Select the layer of type, click 🔍, and click and drag to reposition your type.

Is there a way to type a vertical line of text?

✔ You can easily add vertical text to your image. In the Type Options toolbar, click ⊞, which switches the Type tool to vertical mode, and then click and type or drag a bounding box and type. Your letters will be entered vertically.

How do I add type in a bounding box?

✔ You can add type inside a bounding box to constrain where the type appears and how it wraps. Click and drag with the Type tool; a bounding box appears. You can change the box size and shape by clicking and dragging one of the handles. When you type in the bounding box, text wraps automatically to the next line.

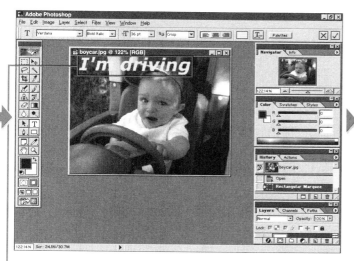

5 Type your text. To create a line break, press the Enter (Return) key.

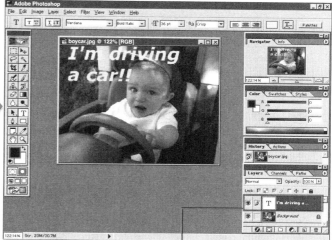

6 When you finish typing your text, press Enter on your keyboard's number pad or click a different tool in the toolbox.

■ The type is placed in its own layer.

CHANGE TYPE FORMATTING

Photoshop enables you to change the font, style, size, and other characteristics of your type.

In the world of computers, fonts come in two types: raster and vector. *Raster* fonts are optimized for screen display technology and look best on a monitor. *Vector* fonts use mathematical scaling technology so that they look the same on-screen as they do when

you print them out on paper. You should use vector fonts for most of your work unless you have specific reasons to use raster fonts, such as placing them on a Web site.

Adobe PostScript and Microsoft TrueType fonts are two kinds of vector fonts that work differently and solve different technology problems. Many design professionals use PostScript font libraries for all their work, and

most Macintosh and IBM-compatible PCs support TrueType fonts.

You are not limited to the fonts that you have available on your machine. Many free, downloadable fonts are available on the Internet, and font packages are available for purchase from Adobe and other manufacturers.

CHANGE TYPE FORMATTING

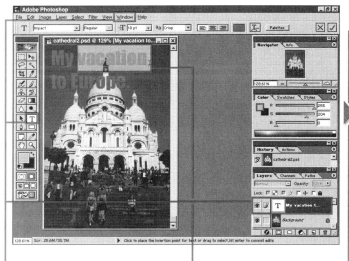

-1 Click T.

-2 Select the type layer that you would like to edit.

■ If the Layers palette is not visible, you can click Window and then Show Layers to view it.

3 Click and drag to select some text.

Note: You can press Ctrl + A (Command - A) to select all the text in a layer.

-4 Click ▼ and select a font.

-5 Click ▼ and select the type's style.

6 Click ▼ and select the type's size.

What is anti-aliasing?

✔ *Anti-aliasing* is the process of adding semitransparent pixels to edges in images to make the edges appear smoother. You can apply anti-aliasing to type to improve its appearance. (Text that is not anti-aliased often looks jagged.) You can control the presence and style of your type's anti-aliasing with the Options bar.

How do I rotate type?

✔ You can rotate type by rotating the layer that contains the type. Choose the layer in the Layers palette and click Edit and Free Transform. A bounding box appears. You can click and drag outside the box to rotate the layer. Press the Enter (Return) key to apply the rotation.

Can I change the font color?

✔ You can change the color of your type to make it blend or contrast with the rest of the image. Select the type layer and the type that you want to change, click the color swatch, and then click the Color Picker to select a color, or type the precise values in the channel boxes. Click OK, and the text changes to your new color.

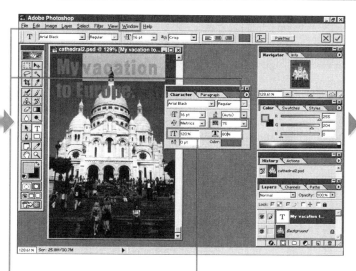

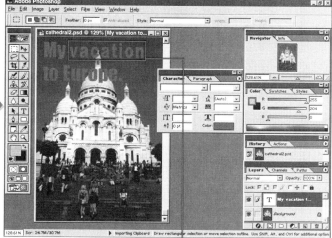

■7 To display more commands, click Window and then Show Character.

■8 Adjust the spacing between characters by specifying a value (positive or negative) in the Tracking box.

■9 Stretch the characters horizontally or vertically by typing percentage values in the scale fields.

■10 Press Enter on your keyboard's number pad or click another tool to deselect the type.

■ Photoshop applies the formatting to your type.

APPLY A FILTER TO TYPE

Many digital images have text in them, especially ones for advertising or Web-based catalogs. Some images have ordinary type, added without any effects applied. Others do have effects applied to the type, either to complement the image's theme or to make the type stand out from (or fade into) the background.

In Photoshop, type is normally added as a collection of vectors. When type is a vector, you can change the appearance of the font itself, such as stretching out the letter *T* to make it taller. But if you want to apply a filter to type, you must first rasterize it. *Rasterizing* converts your type layer to a regular Photoshop layer, so the type

is no longer a set of vectors but is instead a collection of pixels.

Rasterized type can no longer be edited using the Type tools, so if you need to change the spelling or add a few words, you need to redo the text and its effects.

APPLY A FILTER TO TYPE

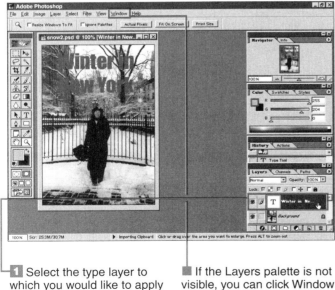

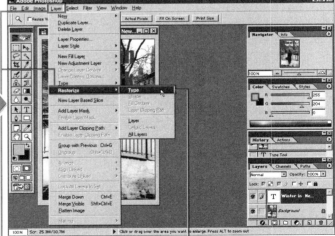

1 Select the type layer to which you would like to apply a filter.

■ If the Layers palette is not visible, you can click Window and then Show Layers to view it.

2 Click Layer.

3 Click Rasterize.

4 Click Type.

How can I create semitransparent type?

✔ Select the type layer in the Layers palette and then reduce the layer's opacity to less than 100%. This will make the type semitransparent.

Is there a simple way to save text on its own layer without rasterizing it?

✔ If you want to save your text without rasterizing it, copy the text layer to a new layer. Click Layer, New, and then Layer via Copy. Apply your effects. You can then hide the original layer by clicking 👁 in the Layers palette, hiding the vector text but making it available for future edits.

How do I edit my text as paths?

✔ You can convert your type to a work path by clicking Layer, Type, and then Create Work Path. This enables you to modify the font's appearance. After you have finished editing your font, you can rasterize it and then work with fills, gradients, and effects on your new type.

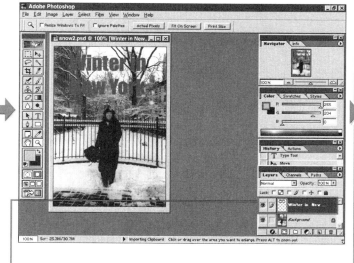

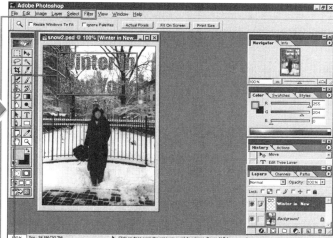

■ Photoshop converts the type layer to a regular layer.

■ Now you can apply a filter to the text.

■ In this example, noise was added to the type by clicking Filter, Noise, and then Add Noise.

Note: You can find more information about applying filters in Chapter 5.

WARP TYPE

Previous versions of Photoshop handled type in the most basic of ways. Any text entered was in a straight line, left to right. If you wanted to have the text flow along an arc, it required custom manipulation by the person editing the image.

With Photoshop 6, you can now warp text to make it conform to a shape. The Warp feature lets you

easily bend and distort layers of type into shapes such as an arc, a wave, or even a fish. The shapes all have customization settings so that you can control the amount of bend, the vertical or horizontal alignment, and other distortion effects.

As fun as the Photoshop warping effects are, they do not give you the means to have text follow a path.

Photoshop text does not have the capability to weave about in your image. If you need this ability, you should import your file into Illustrator and work with its text tools. Illustrator works almost exclusively with paths and can provide you with the ability to flow text to a path.

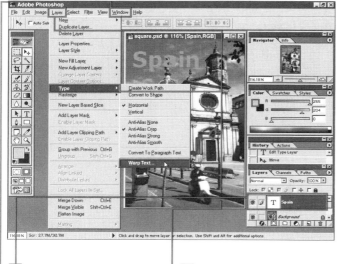

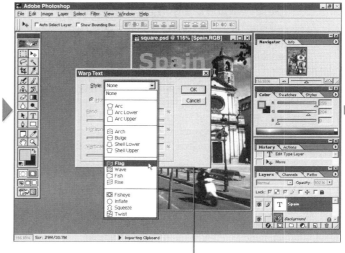

1 Select the type layer that you would like to warp.

■ If the Layers palette is not visible, you can click Window and then Show Layers to view it.

2 Click Layer.

3 Click Type.

4 Click Warp Text.

■ The Warp Text dialog box appears.

5 Click the Style ▼ and select a warp style.

How do I warp only part of my text, such as a single sentence or a word?

✔ The Warp effect applies to all text in a layer. If you want to warp only part of the text, place the text on its own layer and then apply the Warping effect.

I have tried to warp my text, but the menu option is grayed out; did I do something wrong?

✔ Photoshop warps only vector-based fonts, or fonts for which font outlines are available. The Warping effects cannot be applied if you have rasterized the font or if it is a bitmapped font.

How do I insert an image into the outline of type?

✔ First, select the image content that you would like to insert into your text and click Edit and Copy. (You can copy content from the same window or from another Photoshop window.) Convert your text layer to a regular layer by clicking Layer, Rasterize, and then Type. To insert the image into the type outline, Ctrl + click (Option - click) the layer and then click Edit and Paste Into.

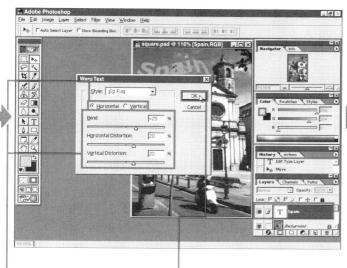

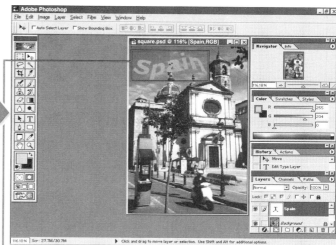

■6 Select an orientation for the warp effect (○ changes to ◉).

■7 Adjust the Bend and Distortion values.

Note: The Bend and Distortion values determine how the warp effect is applied. (At 0% for all values, no warp is applied.)

■8 Click OK.

■ Photoshop warps the text.

Note: You can still edit the style, color, and other characteristics of the type with warp applied.

SAVE A PHOTOSHOP IMAGE

In Chapter 1, you saw that Photoshop can open and work with a number of different file formats. The formats depend on the type of image and the application last used to work on it. Depending on the file, you can save your file to many of those same formats.

If you are working solely with Photoshop as your image-editing

program or you will be sharing your images with team members who are also using Photoshop, you can save your image in Photoshop's native image format (PSD). This format enables you to retain multiple layers in your image, which allows others to edit those layers to make any adjustments, corrections, or additions to the image.

If you are saving the file for use with other products in the Digital Video collection, you can save it either as a PSD file or an EPS (Encapsulated PostScript) file. Nearly every Adobe product can import native format files from another program, but with varying degrees of success. See Chapter 31 for more information about integrating your work among the other Adobe applications.

SAVE A PHOTOSHOP IMAGE

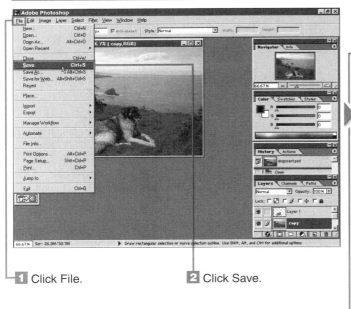

1 Click File.

2 Click Save.

■ If your file has yet to be named and saved, the Save As dialog box appears.

3 Click ▼ and choose a folder in which to save the image file.

4 Click ▼ and select the Photoshop file format.

5 Name the image file.

Note: Photoshop automatically assigns a .psd extension.

How do I choose a file format for my image?

✔ You should choose the format based on how you will want to use the image. If you want to use it in non-Adobe applications, save it as a TIFF or EPS file. If you want to use it on the Web, save it as a JPEG or GIF file. For more information on file formats, see Chapter 1.

Is there a way that I can preserve my layer information but still work in another application?

✔ You should save your file in TIFF or EPS format. These formats preserve layer information, although a non-Adobe application may not preserve other information in the file, such as color profile information.

Should I make different copies depending on how my images will be used?

✔ It is a good idea to save one copy in PSD format, preserving all your profile and layer information, and another copy in the "final" format, such as JPEG. That way, you still have the original available for future edits or modifications.

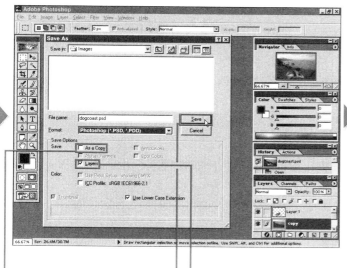

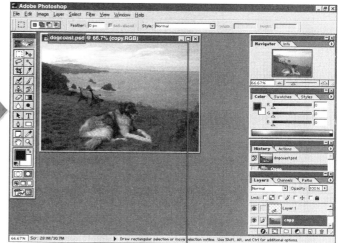

■ If you would like to save a copy of the file and keep the existing file open, click As a Copy (☐ changes to ☑).

■ If you would like to merge the multiple layers of your image into one layer, click Layers (☑ changes to ☐).

6 Click Save.

■ Photoshop saves the image file.

■ The name of the file is displayed in the image's title bar.

SAVE AN IMAGE FOR THE WEB

Web-based images come in a variety of formats. The most popular are JPEG (Joint Photographic Experts Group) and GIF (Graphics Interchange Format).

The JPEG format supports 24-bit color and preserves the broad range and subtle variations in color in an RGB image but compresses file size by selectively discarding data. Most browsers support the JPEG format.

If you plan on saving Web images that originate from digital cameras or digital scanners, you should plan on saving them in JPEG format.

The GIF format is good for saving illustrations that have a lot of solid color, such as illustrations or Web page buttons. The GIF format uses 8-bit color and efficiently compresses solid areas of color while preserving sharp detail, such

as that in line art, logos, or illustrations with type. You also use the GIF format to create animated images. Most browsers support the GIF format.

You can save your GIF images using only Web-safe colors. This ensures that the images appear the way you expect in browsers running on 256-color monitors. See Chapter 3 for information on Web-safe colors.

SAVE AN IMAGE FOR THE WEB

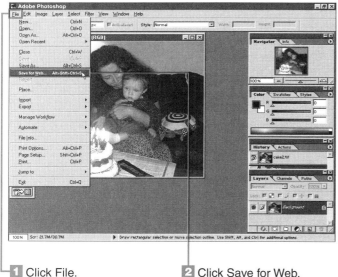

1 Click File.

2 Click Save for Web.

■ These options let you select a predefined setting or a numeric value from 0 (low quality) to 100 (high quality).

3 Select a GIF setting or the JPEG quality settings.

Note: The higher the image quality, the greater the resulting file size.

4 Check that the file quality and size are acceptable in the preview window.

5 Click OK.

What is image compression?

✔ *Image compression* involves using mathematical techniques to reduce the amount of information in an image. This results in small file sizes, which is important when transmitting information on the Web. Some compression schemes, such as JPEG, involve some loss in quality due to the compression, but the loss is usually negligible compared to the file size savings.

How do I create GIFs with small file sizes?

✔ You create small GIFs by limiting the number of colors in the final image. GIF files are limited to 256 colors or fewer; in images that have just a few solid colors, you can reduce the colors to 16 or 8 without any noticeable reduction in quality.

Should all my Web images be saved with Web-safe colors?

✔ Not necessarily. Nowadays, most people surf the Web on monitors set to thousands of colors or more, which makes Web safety less relevant. Also, it is better to save photographic Web images as non-Web-safe JPEGs because the GIF file format offers poor compression and quality when it comes to photos.

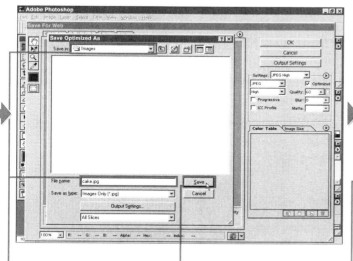

■ 6 Click ▼ and select a folder in which to save the file.

■ 7 Type in a filename.

Note: Photoshop automatically assigns a .gif or .jpg extension, depending on the format that you chose in step 3.

■ 8 Click Save.

■ The file is saved in the specified folder. You can open the folder to access the file.

■ The original image file remains open in Photoshop.

149

PRINT IN COLOR

Whether you are providing an image to a commercial printer or just sending a quick proof to a desktop printer, knowing a few basics about printing will make the print job go more smoothly and help ensure that the finished image appears as intended.

The simplest types of images, such as line art, use only one color in one level of gray. A more complex image, such as a photograph, has color tones that vary within the image. This type of image is known as a *continuous-tone image*.

To create the illusion of continuous tones when printed, images are broken down into a series of dots. This process is called *halftoning*. Varying the sizes of the dots in a halftone screen creates the optical illusion of variations of gray or continuous color in the image.

To print an image in color, you first select general printing options and then specify settings for the particular image type. You can preview how the image and selected options will appear on the printed page and adjust the position and scale of the image.

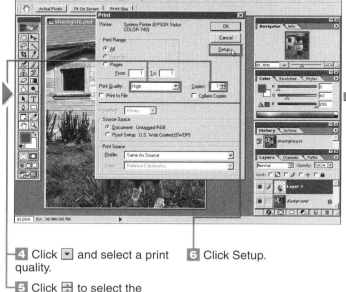

1 Make sure that the layers you would like to print are visible.

Note: An 👁 means that a layer is visible.

2 Click File.

3 Click Print.

4 Click 🔽 and select a print quality.

5 Click 🔢 to select the number of copies.

6 Click Setup.

Can I create color separations in Photoshop?

✔ Artwork that will be commercially reproduced and that contains more than a single color must be printed on separate master plates, one for each color. This process is called *color separation*. In Photoshop, you can adjust how the various plates are generated and create traps. This is normally used for print media rather than Web-based images; if you plan on doing a lot of print media, you should consult with your service bureau to see what special requirements they have for color separations.

Should I convert my RGB images to CMYK before printing?

✔ If you are printing to a consumer-grade printer, you are probably better off printing your images as RGB and not converting them to CMYK. Most printers work with RGB images better than CMYK, so you do not need to convert your images. When in doubt, print a few images in both modes and see which looks better.

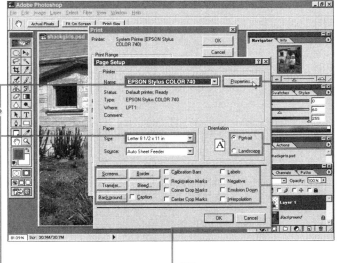

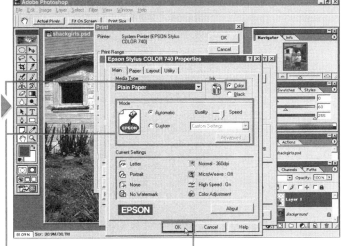

■ The Page Setup dialog box appears.

7 Click ▼ and select a color printer in the Name list.

8 Click ▼ and select a paper size.

9 Select an orientation (○ changes to ◉).

10 Click Properties.

■ The options at the bottom of the dialog box offer advanced prepress printing features.

11 Click Color (○ changes to ◉).

12 Select other properties specific to your brand of color printer.

Note: The Properties dialog box may vary depending on your printer.

13 Click OK.

14 Click OK in the Page Setup and Print dialog boxes.

■ The image is printed in color.

PRINT IN BLACK AND WHITE

Printing images in black and white seems outdated; entry-level color printers are so affordable these days that many people have them. So why would you choose to print an image in black and white?

For starters, you may be working with a scan of a black-and-white print. Unless you are trying to

colorize it, you are wasting ink by printing it on a color printer. Further, color pages cost more per page than black and white, so you would be throwing money away running a black-and-white image through a color printer. Note that you can always print in black and white on a color printer set to black and white.

There are many reasons to use a black and white printer: Many people have access to a laser printer at home or at work, which is cheaper to run; the print speed is much faster on a laser printer; and you can knock out some good basic proof sheets quickly as you make changes to your digital images.

PRINT IN BLACK AND WHITE

■1 Make sure that the layers you would like to print are visible.

Note: An 👁 means that a layer is visible.

■2 Click File.

■3 Click Print.

■ The Print dialog box appears.

■4 Click ▾ and select a print quality.

■5 Click 🖬 to select the number of copies.

■6 Click Setup.

What are duotones?

✔ A *duotone* print job uses two shades of a single color to increase the color range; while any two shades can be used, the most common duotone is composed of black and gray. Duotones increase the tonal range of a grayscale image. Although a grayscale reproduction can display up to 256 levels of gray, a printing press can reproduce only about 50 levels of gray per ink. This means that a grayscale image printed with only black ink can look significantly coarser than the same image printed with two, three, or four inks, each individual ink reproducing up to 50 levels of gray.

Should I convert an RGB image to grayscale during printing?

✔ It is best to convert an RGB image to grayscale on your computer and then print it. You can also send an RGB image to a black-and-white printer, and rely on the printer to convert the color tones into grayscale ones. This method takes far longer and is likely to introduce conversion errors that make your image muddy, coarse, or blocky.

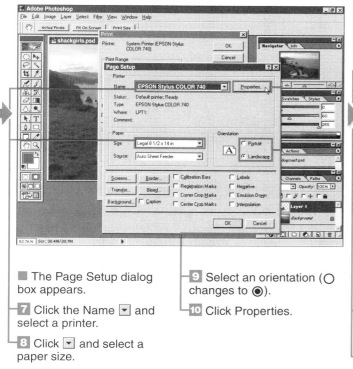

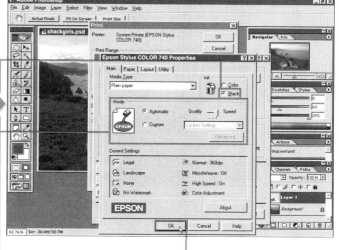

■ The Page Setup dialog box appears.

▶7 Click the Name ▼ and select a printer.

▶8 Click ▼ and select a paper size.

▶9 Select an orientation (○ changes to ◉).

▶10 Click Properties.

■ The Properties dialog box appears.

▶11 Select black ink or grayscale (○ changes to ◉).

▶12 Select other properties specific to your brand of printer.

▶13 Click OK.

▶14 Click OK in the Page Setup and Print dialog boxes.

■ The image is printed in black and white.

ADJUST PRINT OPTIONS

Photoshop provides three printing-related dialog boxes: Print Options, Page Setup, and Print. Some printing options may appear in multiple dialog boxes depending on your printer, print drivers, and operating system.

Photoshop lets you adjust the size and positioning of your printed image, and preview how the image

will be printed on the selected paper, in the Print Options dialog box. The shaded border at the edge of the paper in the preview represents the margins of the selected paper; the printable area is white.

Many printer drivers, such as AdobePS and LaserWriter, provide a scaling option in the Page Setup

dialog box. This scaling affects the size of all page marks, such as crop marks and captions, whereas the scaling percentage in the Print Options dialog box affects only the size of the printed image (and not the size of page marks). With either option, the file size does not change, only the output size.

ADJUST PRINT OPTIONS

1 Make sure that the layers you would like to print are visible.

Note: An ▣ means that a layer is visible.

2 Click File.

3 Click Print Options.

4 Type a percentage in the Scale box to shrink or expand the image.

■ Clicking Scale to Fit Media (☐ changes to ☑) scales the image to the maximum size for the current print settings.

5 Click Center Image to allow for the repositioning of the image (☑ changes to ☐).

MASTER IT

How do I quickly preview how my image will appear on a printed page in Photoshop?

✔ You can click the status bar on the lower left of the screen to bring up a pop-up window that displays how the image will print on paper at the current settings.

When I print, should I print to a file?

✔ Because Photoshop saves its files in PSD format, you really do not need to save a print job to a file. The PSD file contains all the information that you need and can always be edited.

What options are available with the Show More Options check box?

✔ A whole series of advanced options are available when this check box is active; most of them apply to print-oriented processes rather than Web-oriented ones. You can control the printer output and include registration marks or the image filename, attach a label, and even print the image over a background color. You can also adjust the color management options, including defining the color source space and the print color source space. See the online help for more details about these advanced options.

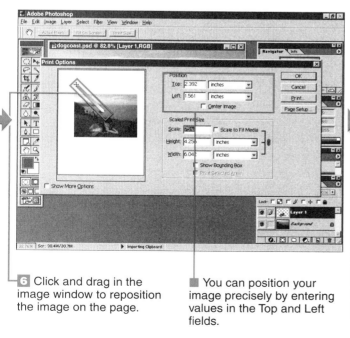

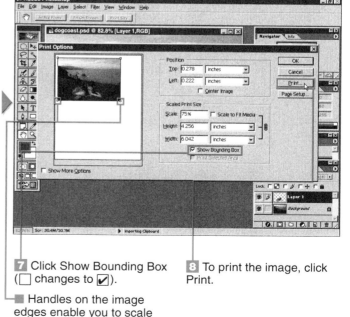

6 Click and drag in the image window to reposition the image on the page.

■ You can position your image precisely by entering values in the Top and Left fields.

7 Click Show Bounding Box (☐ changes to ☑).

■ Handles on the image edges enable you to scale the image by clicking and dragging.

8 To print the image, click Print.

CREATE AND PRINT A CONTACT SHEET

Photoshop can automatically create a digital version of a photographer's contact sheet that you can print. Contact sheets are made up of miniature versions of images and are useful for keeping a hard-copy record of your digital images. Contact sheets are most often used to create image catalogs that consist of thumbnail

images. By displaying a series of thumbnail previews on a single page, contact sheets enable you to easily preview and catalog groups of images.

One of the most common uses for the contact sheet feature is to provide a handy index for Photo CD contents. If you take a lot of

digital photographs, you can store the original images on a Photo CD as a permanent archive and then recall the images for use in other applications. A contact sheet helps you recall which images are stored on the disc — which is especially useful when the filenames are not very descriptive.

CREATE AND PRINT A CONTACT SHEET

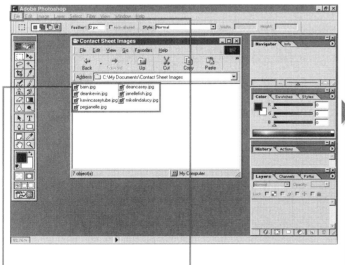

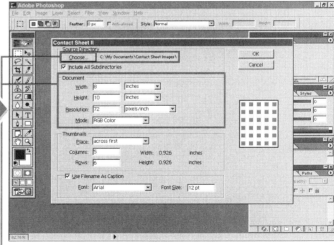

1 Place the images that you would like to put on the contact sheet in a single folder.

2 In Photoshop, click File.

3 Click Automate.

4 Click Contact Sheet II.

5 Click Choose and browse to the folder where you have stored your images.

6 Select a size and resolution for your contact sheet.

Note: Keep the size within the bounds of the paper on which you will print.

What if I want a different style for my contact sheet?

✔ If you are willing to work a little with HTML, you can create a custom Web page style for your photo gallery and save it in the WebContactSheet folder. You now have a custom style that you can use.

How do I create a picture package?

✔ Photoshop can automatically create a one-page layout with a selected image at various sizes — a *picture package*. Click File, Automate, and then Picture Package. You can choose from more than 30 picture-package layouts. This is a great option for creating pictures to send out and saves you money over using commercial photo services.

Can I create a Web page from a contact sheet?

✔ You can use the Web Photo Gallery command to generate HTML index pages with thumbnails of images. This is great for creating an HTML index for a Photo CD or for indexing images stored on a local computer. There are four simple index page formats, and you can adjust the thumbnail and image size, filenames, and other settings.

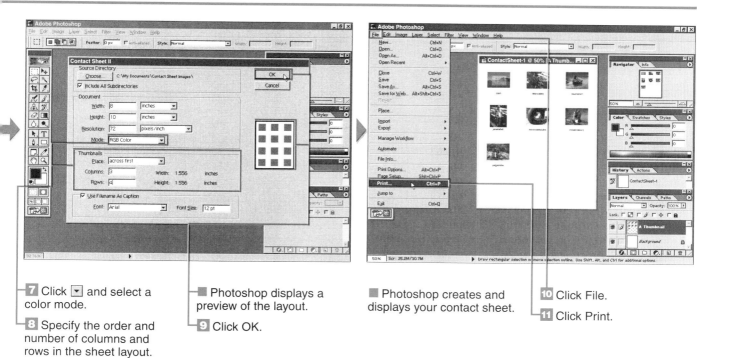

-7 Click ⏷ and select a color mode.

-8 Specify the order and number of columns and rows in the sheet layout.

■ Photoshop displays a preview of the layout.

-9 Click OK.

■ Photoshop creates and displays your contact sheet.

-10 Click File.

-11 Click Print.

SECTION II

UNDERSTANDING ILLUSTRATOR

The Illustrator tools let you create and optimize illustrations for nearly any purpose, from Web pages to print media and back again. You can easily apply colors, patterns, or recurring shapes, or apply effects to create stylized images. These advanced tools make creating complex images nearly effortless.

You can open and edit existing images in Illustrator to make necessary changes. You can make your changes as subtle as a new color shade for a corporate logo or as elaborate as a text effect for a Web page. In addition, you can use Illustrator's type tools to create and integrate stylized letters and words into images.

You can also combine different image elements in Illustrator. Your compositions can include pictures, drawings, scanned art, text, and almost anything else you can save on your computer. By placing elements on separate layers in Illustrator, you can move, transform, and customize them independent of one another.

Create Vector Graphics and Bitmap Images

Images are either *vector* graphics, which are smaller in size, or *bitmap* images, which are larger. Bitmaps display more slowly over the Internet, and vector graphics display much faster. Illustrator lets you work with either format and can save your files as either type. Vector graphics also display more clearly and look much better than bitmap graphics, especially when magnified. See Chapter 14 for more information on saving in different file formats.

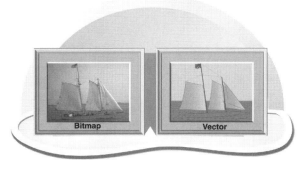

Work with Color

Illustrator lets you sample and apply color to your images by using the Eyedropper, Brush, and Fill tools. These tools fill in your selection with solid or semitransparent colors. You can also add colored textures and patterns using these tools. To find out more about color, see Chapter 3.

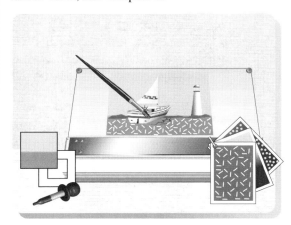

Work with Type

Illustrator's text tools enable you to easily add type and labels to your images. You can combine these tools with special effects to create warped, 3D, or wildly colored type. To learn more about type, see Chapter 11.

Create Special Effects

You can add special effects and apply filters like drop shadows, 3D shading, and other styles to your images. You can also perform complex color manipulations or distortions by using Illustrator's filters. Filters can make your images look warped, underwater, blurred, or altered in other ways. See Chapter 12 for information on filters.

Produce Web- and Print-Ready Images

Illustrator comes ready to create images in both Web-friendly and printing-press-friendly formats. Web images have different format requirements from printing press formats; these specialized requirements are available to you no matter which format you need. Learn more about Web and press file support in Chapter 14.

Integrate with Other Adobe Programs

Thanks to Illustrator's support for the most popular formats, you can share images, illustrations, and text among nearly any other illustration or editing program. If you use Adobe PageMaker, Photoshop, Premiere, or After Effects, you can freely import and export files between them, saving all your layer information and image customizations.

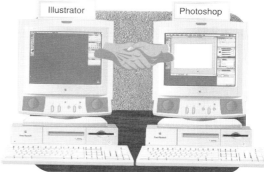

NAVIGATE THE ILLUSTRATOR WORK AREA

Illustrator provides several components for working with images, illustrations, and text.

Take some time to familiarize yourself with the on-screen elements.

Menu Bar

Displays Illustrator menus, which show menu commands when clicked.

Main Toolbox

The main toolbox contains shortcut buttons for common commands and tools, such as the Selection tool or the Type tool.

Document Window

The Document window includes the artboard and the page, and is where you do most of your work.

Page

The page is the actual printing area of your artwork, shown by dotted lines. Depending on the printer, your page may be smaller.

Artboard

The artboard is the area that includes your document and its printable area. The artboard's boundaries are shown by the solid dark lines and are usually the same physical size as the printed page.

Title Bar

Displays the name of the current document.

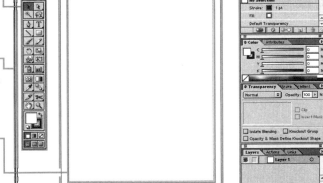

Status Bar

The status bar displays the current tool in use, the amount of available memory, or other information you may find useful.

Appearance Palette

An object's appearance attributes, such as fills, strokes, transparencies, and effects, display in the Appearance palette.

Color Palette

You use the Color palette to apply color to an object's fill and stroke, and also to edit and mix colors.

Styles Palette

The Styles palette lets you create, name, save, and apply sets of appearance attributes.

Layers Palette

The Layers palette lists all the layers in a document, beginning with the frontmost layer at the top.

Pasteboard

The pasteboard is like a giant desktop that can hold many artboards and pages. You can view areas of the pasteboard by clicking the scroll bars in the document window.

Navigate with the Mouse

Use the mouse to move around the Illustrator work area, select tools, and activate menu commands. To activate a tool or menu, move the mouse pointer over the item and click.

Navigate Palettes

Many of the Illustrator features open into separate mini-windows on screen, called *palettes*. To close an open palette on the Macintosh, click the palette's Close button (▢). Windows users can click the Close button (☒).

Navigate with the Keyboard

You can also use the keyboard to select commands. For example, Windows users can display the Text menu by pressing and holding the Alt key and then pressing the letter T. To activate a menu command, press the corresponding underlined character. You can find keyboard shortcut commands scattered throughout the menus and in Illustrator's Help files.

CREATE A NEW DOCUMENT

Most new Illustrator projects start out as blank images. If you are creating a new image from scratch, you can open up a new image without worrying too much about the type of image or its size. If, on the other hand, you have some ideas or size requirements for your illustration, you can set those parameters when you create a new image.

For instance, if you are working on an illustration that cannot be larger than a standard VGA screen, you can define your new illustration to be 640 x 480 pixels in size. If you are working with an illustration that needs to be saved at different resolutions, you can set up the largest size you need for your illustration, create your illustration, and then save it in progressively smaller resolutions.

This ability to define new illustration parameters is very helpful but requires that you plan out how you will use the image ahead of time so you can avoid wasting time with editing and resizing later.

CREATE A NEW DOCUMENT

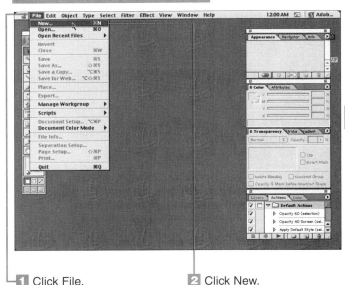

1 Click File.

2 Click New.

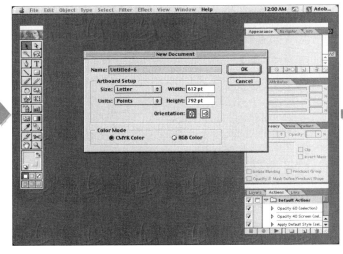

■ The New Document dialog box appears.

Where can I define my illustration size?

✔ You can set up several options for when you create a new document, including size, measuring units, and color selection. You can also change the default artboard startup size. See "Change Document Settings" for details.

How do I set the pixel size for an illustration?

✔ Illustrator assumes you are working on a print image, not a digital image, and defaults to measuring in points, not pixels. You can change the default measurement units in the Preferences dialog boxes; see "Change Preferences," later in this chapter, to learn how to switch to using pixels as a measuring unit.

How many illustrations can I have opened at once?

✔ You can open up as many illustrations as you want, within the limits of your available memory and scratch disk space. Illustrator uses quite a bit less memory than Photoshop for its illustrations, so you can have more open at one time. Practically speaking, you probably will not be actively working on more than a few illustrations at one time.

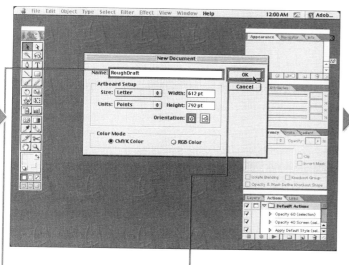

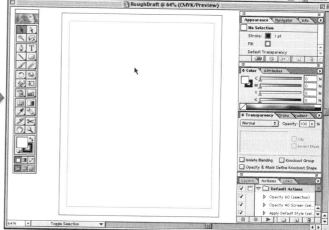

3 Type a name for your document.

■ If you are working on digital images, select RGB color.

4 Click OK.

■ Illustrator opens a new document with the name you gave it in the title bar.

CHANGE DOCUMENT SETTINGS

After you have created a document, you can set up your work area to organize your work and streamline the workflow. For example, you can change the size of the artboard, tile your workspace, or move your page boundaries. These document settings can be changed at any time. These changes affect your

artwork's size and orientation, and Illustrator applies them immediately.

You may want to change your settings if you run out of room on your artboard for scrap images. You may also need to change an imported CMYK document to RGB; Illustrator normally preserves the

format of the file you open, but you may need to change it to change the color palette available to you, and thus render a more accurate image.

With digital images, you will typically want to create RGB artwork, because it matches the color scheme used by computer monitors and video monitors.

CHANGE DOCUMENT SETTINGS

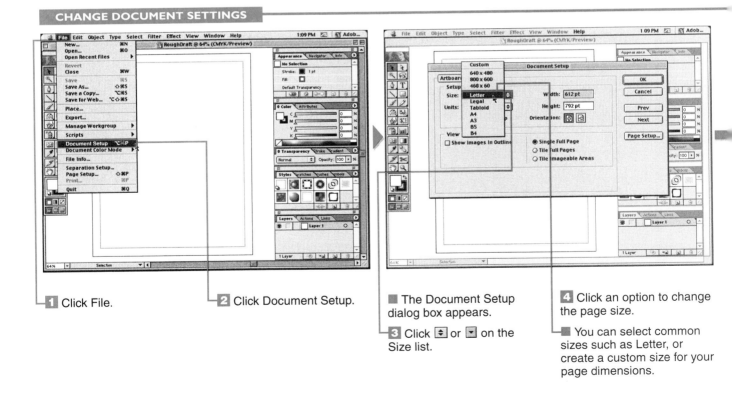

◻ Click File.

◻ Click Document Setup.

■ The Document Setup dialog box appears.

◻ Click ⬆ or ⬇ on the Size list.

◻ Click an option to change the page size.

■ You can select common sizes such as Letter, or create a custom size for your page dimensions.

Are the page tile outlines editable?
✔ You can move the page outlines with the Page tool (▭). To select the Page tool, click and hold the Hand tool (✋) until a toolbar appears, drag the mouse over to the ▭, and then click and drag in the artboard to move the page tile outlines.

When I create a new document, can I set other properties, such as printing and export properties?
✔ No. When you create a new document, you can set only the artboard dimensions, color mode, and page orientation. You can change the other settings after you open your new document in Illustrator.

What do the Page Tiling options do?
✔ The Artboard's dimensions do not necessarily match the paper sizes used by printers. As a result, when you print a file, the program divides the artboard into one or more rectangles that correspond to the page size available on your printer. Dividing the artboard to fit a printer's available page size is called tiling. Tiling is also used when you set up your file to view and print multiple pages.

You can also adjust the placement of the printable area of the page to control how artwork is printed.

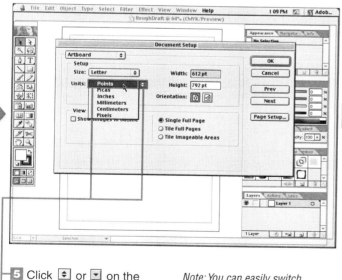

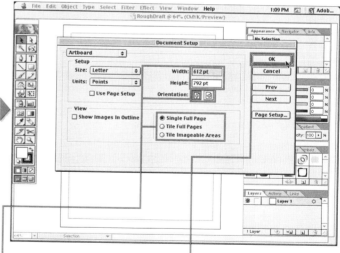

■5 Click ⬍ or ⬇ on the Units list.

■6 Click an option to change the measurement units.

Note: You can easily switch between measurement units, but it may change the accuracy of your artwork.

■7 Type the new height and width dimensions for your artwork.

■8 Click a page orientation.

■ You can click how you want the page to display (○ changes to ◉).

■9 Click OK.

■ The new settings take effect in your document.

CHANGE PREFERENCES

You can customize the Illustrator interface to better match the way you work, enabling you to more efficiently create artwork. Customized interfaces make it possible that, when you look at Illustrator on a co-worker's computer, you may barely recognize it from the version on your computer.

Illustrator provides a high degree of customization. For example, you

can use the Preferences dialog box to set the file format for your projects and files, set default cursors, choose your measurement units such as inches or pixels, and set scratch disk size.

You can configure Illustrator's look and feel in other ways. If you always have certain palettes open and certain brushes selected for digital images, you can specify which palettes load when

Illustrator starts. You select palette preferences in the Windows menu and specify whether to show or hide palettes at startup.

Illustrator offers many more preferences than those listed here. Click Help on the Illustrator menu bar for more information on how and when to use them.

CHANGE PREFERENCES

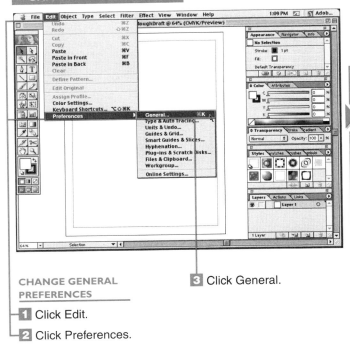

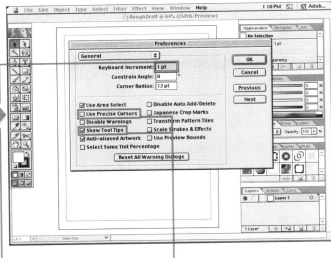

CHANGE GENERAL PREFERENCES

1 Click Edit.

2 Click Preferences.

3 Click General.

■ The Preferences dialog box appears.

■ This option sets how far an object moves when you select it and press the arrow keys (←, →, ↑, and ↓).

■ This option switches between regular cursors (✒) and precise cursors (⊹).

■ This option displays a pop-up window when you hover over a tool, showing you the tool name and shortcut keystrokes.

Where can I find the preferences files on a Macintosh?

✔ In Mac OS, the preferences file is called Adobe Illustrator 10.0 Prefs. Mac OS 9.x stores this file in the System Folder\Preferences\Adobe Illustrator 10 folder. Mac OS X stores the file in Mac OS X\Users\Home\Library\Preferences\Adobe Illustrator 10.

Where can I find the preferences files in Windows?

✔ In Windows, this file is called AI Prefs. Windows 98 and ME store it in the Windows\Application Data\Adobe\Adobe Illustrator 10 folder. Windows NT stores it in the WinNT\Profiles\username\Application Data\Adobe Illustrator 10 folder. Finally, Windows 2000 and XP store the AI Prefs file in the Documents and Settings\username\Application Data\Adobe\Adobe Illustrator 10 folder.

Why does Illustrator look different every time I start it?

✔ Illustrator saves your preferences and changes each time you quit, including window and palette position, so you do not have to readjust your settings each time you start Illustrator. These changes are stored in the files Adobe Illustrator Startup_CMYK.ai or Adobe Illustrator Startup_RGB.ai, depending on whether you use CMYK or RGB color schemes. To restore Illustrator to its defaults, simply delete these files, so Illustrator can create new ones.

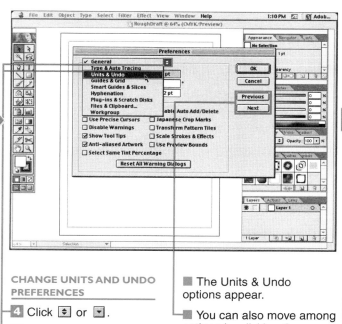

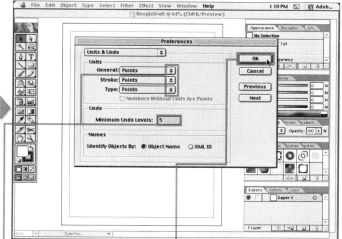

CHANGE UNITS AND UNDO PREFERENCES

■4 Click 🔽 or 🔼.

■5 Select Units & Undo from the menu.

■ The Units & Undo options appear.

■ You can also move among options by clicking the Previous and Next buttons.

■ You can set the General, Stroke or Type units by clicking 🔽 or 🔼 and then an option.

■ You can set the minimum number of undo levels in the text box.

Note: The more undo levels you set, the more memory you use, especially with complex artwork.

■6 Click OK.

■ Illustrator changes your preferences.

169

SWITCH BETWEEN VIEWS

Illustrator can switch between Preview, Outline, and Pixel Preview modes so you can work in the most convenient mode, or to see how your artwork looks before you save it.

Outline view displays only paths. Most initial work on an Illustrator object is done using *paths* (see Chapter 9), which are wireframe views of objects. Preview mode

shows you the entirety of your artwork, complete with colors, shading, gradients, and any applied effects. This view shows you exactly how your illustration should look when finished.

Pixel Preview shows you how your art looks on the Web or on a video monitor. You can preview how objects will appear when rasterized using Pixel Preview mode. Viewing

rasterized objects helps you control the precise placement, size, and anti-aliasing of objects in a rasterized graphic.

If you are working with digital images, you can create your initial drawing in Outline mode and then switch to Pixel Preview mode to see exactly how it will look on a computer monitor.

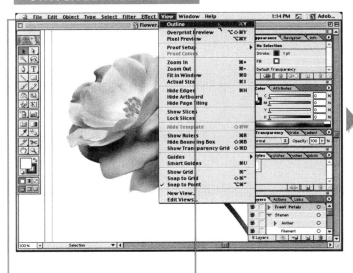

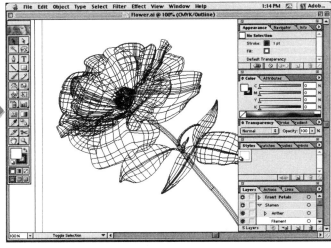

SWITCH TO OUTLINE VIEW

1 Click View.

2 Click Outline.

■ The document switches to Outline view.

■ To switch back to Preview mode, repeat steps 1 and 2.

Should I work in Outline mode or Preview mode?

✔ After you have some practice working with paths, Outline mode is much faster on your computer, especially with complex artwork. Preview mode displays your art complete with fills and color, but is much slower as the computer must calculate all the color shading and texturing that goes into a complex piece of art.

What is the difference between Preview and Pixel Preview mode?

✔ In Preview mode, Illustrator represents all paths as vectors, meaning they will scale without any loss of detail. When you use Pixel Preview, you fix the image at a certain resolution, and you lose detail at higher magnification.

Why does my digital image not look the same in Preview mode and when I print it out?

✔ A digital camera, computer monitor, and color printer each use a different technology to represent color, so what appears bright red on one may look washed out — or purple — on another. You should calibrate your monitor before doing any serious work in Illustrator. See Chapter 1 for an introduction to color calibration in Photoshop; many of the same techniques can be used in Illustrator.

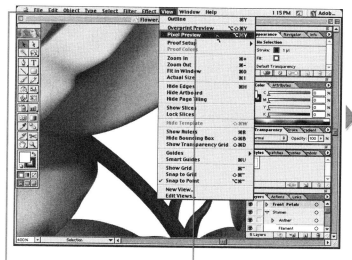

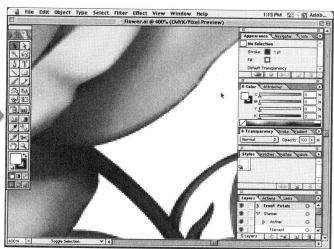

SWITCH TO PIXEL PREVIEW

1 Click View.

2 Click Pixel Preview.

■ The document switches to Pixel Preview.

■ To switch back to Preview mode, repeat steps 1 and 2.

USING THE SELECTION TOOL

As with any computer program, to work with objects you must first select them. Adobe builds selection tools into all its programs, specializing the various tools for the type of work needed by each program. The selection tools in Illustrator rely heavily on selecting paths or groups of paths, but Photoshop's selection tools rely heavily on differences in color. See Chapter 9 for information on paths, and Chapter 2 to learn about Photoshop selection tools.

In Illustrator, you use the Selection tool to select an object or an entire group of paths at one time. You can select objects by clicking them, or by dragging a *marquee box* (dotted line) around them. Unlike in Photoshop, the resulting bounding box in Illustrator is not animated, so you do not get the "marching ants" effect. Instead, the bounding box includes all your selection's paths and anchor points, and the box may expand beyond your initial selection to include paths that fall into the marquee box.

After you select an object, you can move it or resize it on the page. See Chapter 10 to reshape objects.

USING THE SELECTION TOOL

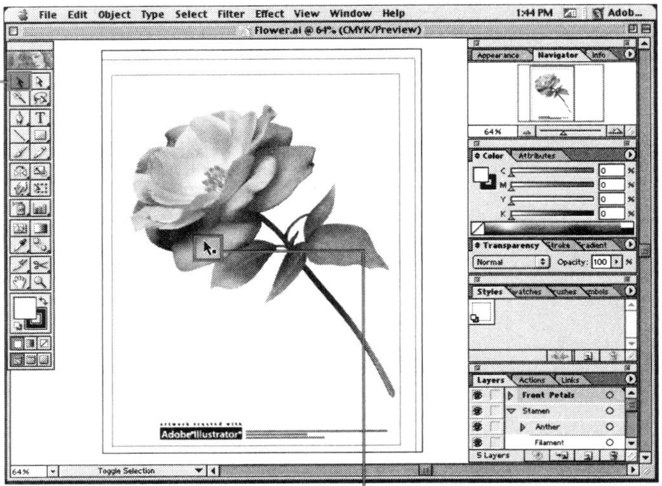

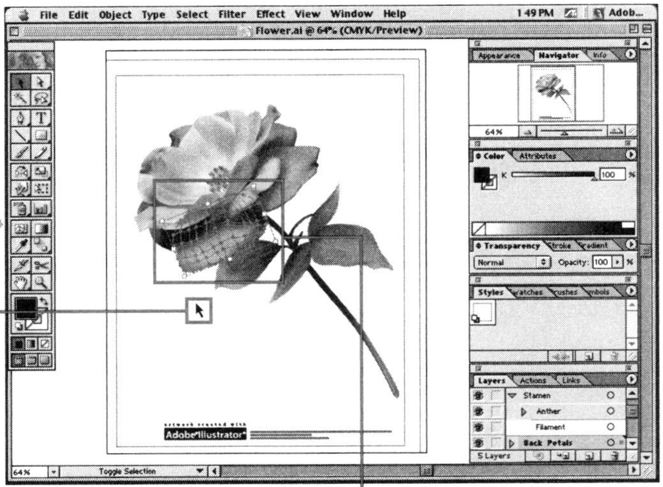

SELECT BY CLICKING AN OBJECT

1 Click the Selection tool (↖) in the toolbox.

■ You can quickly choose ↖ by pressing the V key.

2 Position the ↖ over an object.

■ The ↖ changes to a black arrow with a square ↖▪.

3 Click anywhere on the object.

■ A bounding box appears around the object, indicating the object is selected.

How do I select all objects?

✔ You can draw a bounding box around everything on the artboard you want to select. You can also use the menu and click Select, then All, which does the same thing. If you want to use a keyboard shortcut, press Ctrl + A (Command - A) to select everything on the artboard. You can deselect all the selected objects by clicking on a blank area of the artboard or in your artwork, where no other objects exist. You can also click Deselect All from the Select menu. The keyboard shortcut is Shift + Ctrl + A (Shift - Command - A).

How do I select multiple objects?

✔ If you are using the Selection tool, you select multiple objects by pressing and holding down the Shift key, then clicking with the mouse on the object you want to add. You can also deselect objects from a group the same way.

What does the Lasso tool do?

✔ The Lasso tool works similarly to Photoshop's Lasso tool. In Illustrator, it lets you draw a freehand marquee box to select entire objects or collections of paths.

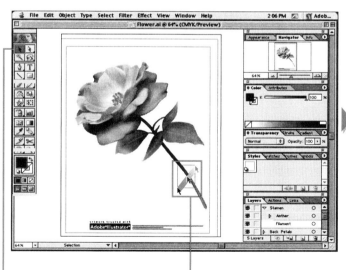

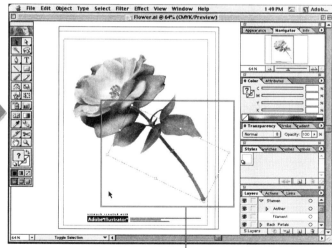

SELECT BY DRAGGING AROUND AN OBJECT

1 Click the ▶ in the toolbox.

2 Click and drag the ▶ diagonally to the opposite side of the object.

■ A box called a marquee appears.

3 Release the mouse button.

■ A bounding box appears around the selected object.

USING THE DIRECT SELECTION TOOL

If all you need to do is work on entire objects or collections of paths, the Selection tool is all you need — but that is rarely the case. In Illustrator you need to adjust single points on a path, or change a path's curve. The Selection tool does not let you work at that fine a scale; instead, you must use the Direct Selection tool.

You use the Direct Selection tool to choose only parts of an object or a path, instead of the entire object or group of paths. This capability enables you to perform detail-oriented tasks on your artwork. Suppose, for example, you need to move one corner of your triangle without moving the other two. Although the Selection tool could move the whole triangle, using the

Direct Selection tool lets you select just the one corner and move it without moving the rest of the triangle.

After you select a point, a group of points, or a path or group of paths, you can work with the points, such as moving them, changing the slope of a curve, or applying effects to them.

USING THE DIRECT SELECTION TOOL

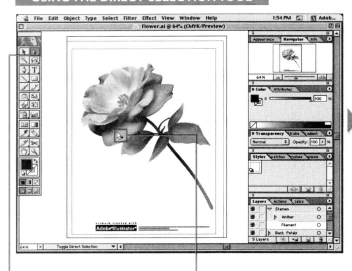

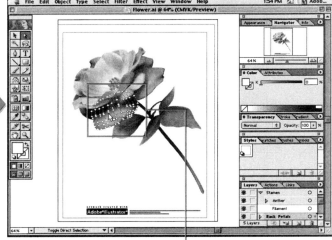

SELECT BY CLICKING AN OBJECT

1 Click the Direct Selection tool (🔲) in the toolbox.

■ You can quickly choose (🔲) by pressing the A key.

2 Position the ↖ over an object.

■ The ↖ changes to a light arrow with a dark square (↖■).

3 Click anywhere on the object.

■ All the paths on the object are selected.

MASTER IT

When I select with the Direct Selection tool, no bounding box appears. Should there be one?

✔ The Direct Selection tool selects only single paths, points, or parts of objects, rather than entire objects or grouped objects. If you need to create a bounding box so you can resize an entire object, use the Selection tool instead.

What does the Direct Lasso tool do?

✔ The Direct Lasso tool ( ) works like a freehand version of the Direct Selection tool, letting you draw freehand selections over parts of paths or objects. You access [ ] by clicking and holding [ ] until a toolbar appears, then dragging the mouse over [ ] and releasing the mouse.

What does the Group Selection tool do?

✔ The Group Selection tool ( ) lets you select an object within a group, a single group within multiple groups, or a set of groups within the artwork. Each additional click adds all objects from the next level in the group. You access [ ] by clicking and holding [ ] until a toolbar appears, then dragging the mouse over the Group Selection tool and releasing the mouse.

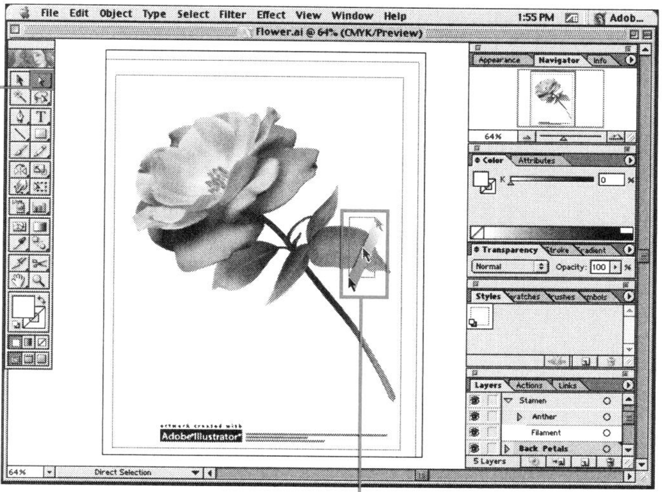

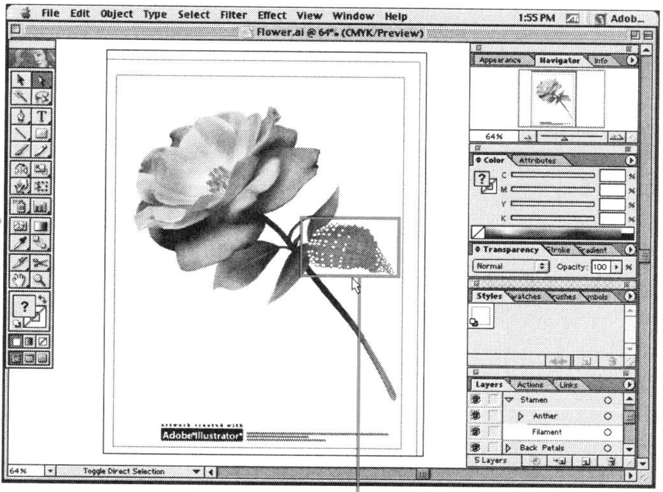

SELECT BY DRAGGING AROUND AN OBJECT

1 Click [ ] in the toolbox.

2 Click and drag the [ ] diagonally to cover part of the object.

■ A marquee box appears.

3 Release the mouse button.

■ All the paths in the object are selected.

UNDERSTANDING PATHS

Unlike other illustration programs with which you may have worked, Illustrator uses the concept of *paths* for nearly all its drawing functions. Paths look like lines, but they have some special features and function differently than lines drawn in Photoshop. For instance, in

Illustrator, a rectangle is made up of four paths, with anchor points at each corner. In Photoshop, it is four lines, without anchor points. In Illustrator, a circle is made up of four curved paths with anchor points; in Photoshop, it is a single unbroken line.

This system may seem odd at first, but there is logic behind the use of paths. If you want to work effectively in Illustrator, you must understand paths and how they function.

Paths and Bézier Curves

Illustrator paths are based on *Bézier curves*, which are mathematical formulas that describe lines. When you draw a line, you are actually "writing down" a mathematical formula on the page. Illustrator hides the math from you; all you see are the lines.

Types of Paths

Paths are made up of segments with anchor points at both ends of the segment. Paths come in three types: *open* paths, which have two distinct end points, like a straight line; *closed* paths, which are continuous with no start or end points, like a circle; and *compound* paths, which are made up of the other two types that overlap or create closed areas, such as the letter *g*. See the rest of this chapter for information on creating open, closed, and compound paths.

Visible and Invisible Paths

When working with complex projects, you may find it easier and faster to work in Outline mode, viewing only the paths. In Outline mode, all paths are visible; in Preview mode, only paths with fills and strokes applied are visible. Use Outline mode with images containing a lot of detail or when you work at high magnifications; use Preview mode for doing shading, fills, and print previews. You can make paths visible in Preview mode by selecting an object.

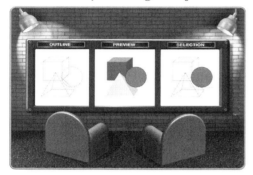

Paths and Anchor Points

Paths have *anchor points* that start and end every path, even closed ones; you can also have anchor points anywhere along a path. Anchor points can be *smooth*, meaning a path goes through them; *corner points*, meaning the path changes direction suddenly; or *combination*, which are made up of straight and curved points.

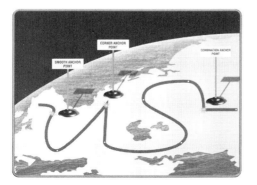

Anchor Points and Control Handles

Anchor points and control handles appear together but in different combinations depending on the type of anchor point. You use *control handles*, which extend from anchor points, to change a curve's direction. Smooth corner points or curved corner points have two handles; combination corner points have only one. Straight corner points do not have control handles. Read the rest of this chapter for information on working with anchor points and control handles on the different corner points.

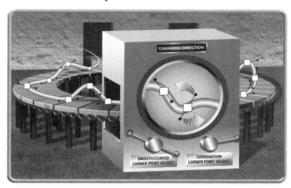

DRAW STRAIGHT LINES USING THE LINE SEGMENT TOOL

The Line Segment tool draws perfectly straight lines in your artwork, complete with anchor points for the path's start and end points. It is one of the simplest tools to use in the toolbox, but also one of the more limited ones. For instance, if you want to draw continuous line segments, you still need to click again on the last anchor point you set, and then draw your new line. The Pen tool lets you draw continuous line segments without requiring that extra click. See the section "Draw Straight Lines Using the Pen Tool," later in this chapter, for details on using the Pen tool.

When you first draw a path, it exists only as a one-point line in your drawing. It has no effects or fills. You can apply a fill to the line when you draw it by specifying an exact line segment; when the Line Segment Tool Options dialog box appears, select the Fill Line check box to apply a fill to your line. See Chapter 10 for information on line fills.

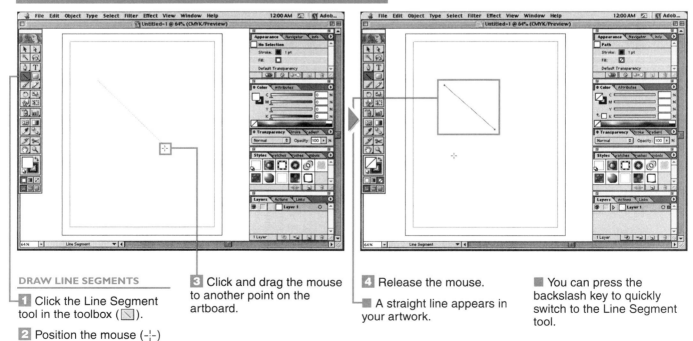

DRAW STRAIGHT LINES USING THE LINE SEGMENT TOOL

DRAW LINE SEGMENTS

1 Click the Line Segment tool in the toolbox ( ).

2 Position the mouse (-¦-) over your artwork.

3 Click and drag the mouse to another point on the artboard.

4 Release the mouse.

■ A straight line appears in your artwork.

■ You can press the backslash key to quickly switch to the Line Segment tool.

How do I draw lines at 45° angles?
✔ Hold down the Shift key as you draw. Your angles are constrained to increments of 45°.

Why do I not see any fills or effects in my line segments?
✔ You are probably viewing your artwork in Outline mode; to see your line effects, you need to be in Preview mode. From the menu click View, then Preview. You can also press Ctrl + Y (Command - Y) to switch between Preview and Outline modes.

How do I draw a radial line?
✔ A *radial line* is one that starts from a center point and radiates outward. You can draw a line outward from the initial spot in your artwork by holding the Alt (Option) key as you draw.

How do I reset the line's properties default values?
✔ When the Line Segment Tool Options dialog box is visible, hold down the Y (Option) key; the Cancel button changes to Reset. Click Reset, and the tool's default properties are restored.

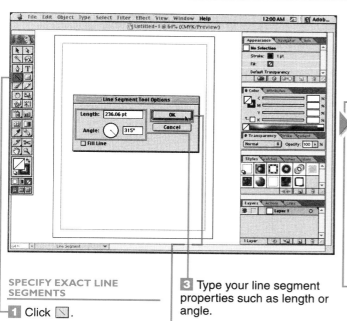

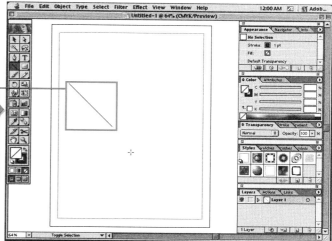

SPECIFY EXACT LINE SEGMENTS

1 Click [ ].

2 Click your artwork.

■ The Line Segment Tool Options dialog box appears.

3 Type your line segment properties such as length or angle.

4 Click OK.

■ The straight line appears in your artwork.

Note: The dialog box displays the last straight line dimensions you used.

DRAW FREEHAND LINES USING THE PENCIL TOOL

Y ou use the Pencil tool to draw freehand lines in your artwork. It behaves just like a regular pencil, following your mouse around your artwork no matter how you move it. The tool adds anchor points for you automatically as you draw, which you can change after you stop drawing. To learn more about

anchor points, see the section "Understanding Paths." The number of anchor points and line accuracy are controlled by the Pen tool's settings.

The Pencil tool is the most intuitive of Illustrator's tools, but using a mouse to draw freehand lines is often an awkward exercise. If you

plan to illustrate and draw freehand on a regular basis, you should consider investing in a tablet or pressure-sensitive pad and stylus. These devices enable you to draw using the stylus, and give you better freehand accuracy than you can get with a mouse.

DRAW FREEHAND LINES USING THE PENCIL TOOL

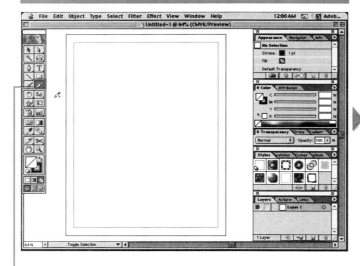

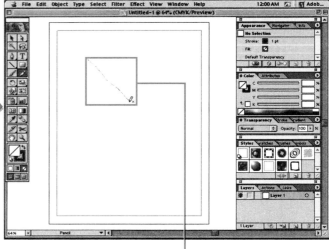

▐1 Click the Pencil tool in the toolbox (▨).

■ The ▸ changes to a pencil with a small x (✐ₓ).

▐2 Place ✐ₓ over the page.

▐3 Click and drag ✐ₓ over the page.

The paths I draw with the Pencil tool seem kind of bumpy; can I change them?

✔ Double-click the Pencil tool in the toolbox to bring up the tool's properties box. Fidelity determines how closely the final curve follows the path you drew, while Smoothness determines how angular your paths are. The higher the smoothness, the smoother the curve and the fewer anchor points. If you are just sketching an object freehand but will modify it later, you can set the Fidelity value lower and the Smoothness higher. If you need precision, set Fidelity higher and Smoothness lower.

How do I smooth out my freehand lines?

✔ You can use the Smooth Tool to reduce the number of curves on a line and thus reduce the number of anchor points. Click and hold the Pencil tool until the tear-away toolbar appears then drag the mouse to the Smooth tool 🖉 and release the mouse. Drag your mouse over a section of your freehand line; the line smooths out.

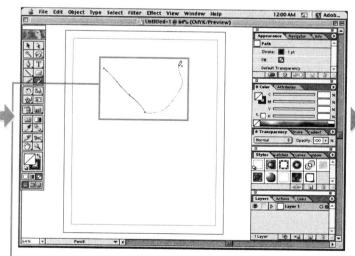

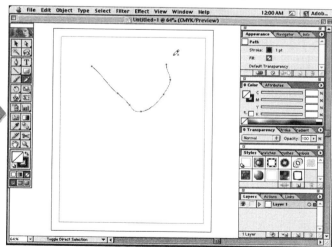

■ A freehand line is drawn on your artwork.

④ Release the mouse.

■ The line fills in with a solid color and anchor points.

DRAW CURVES USING THE ARC TOOL

The Arc tool helps you easily draw smooth curves or parts of curves. You can use it to add a curve at the end of a path or create flowing lines or borders around an illustration.

The Arc tool is almost as easy to use as the Line Segment tool. You can either draw a curve by clicking and dragging, or you can specify the exact dimensions and curvature

of the segment. If you click and drag, the curve uses the last set of properties you specified for the curve.

You can use some keyboard tricks when dragging and drawing with the Arc tool. To move the curve's position on the artboard, hold down the spacebar and move the arc into position with the mouse. If you want to flip the curve's

orientation around its origin, press the F key while drawing. Lastly, you can resize the curve using the Up and Down arrow keys.

If you need to draw a rectangle or square with rounded corners, you should use the Rounded Rectangle tool, which is discussed in Chapter 10.

DRAW CURVES USING THE ARC TOOL

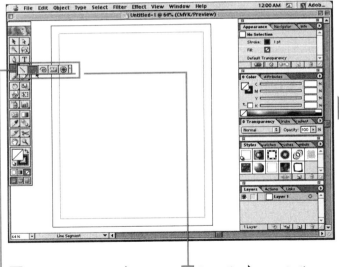

1 Click and hold the ▶ on ◻.

■ A tear-away toolbar appears with several tools on it.

2 Drag the ▶ over to the Arc tool (◻).

3 Release the mouse button.

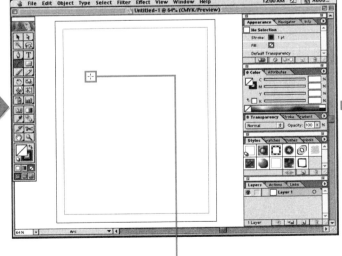

■ The ◻ changes to ◻.

4 Position the ▶ over your artwork.

■ The ▶ changes to -¦-.

What do the arc properties do?
✔ After you select the Arc tool, single-click the artboard. The Arc Properties dialog box appears with seven options.

If you set the arc values and do not like the arc, you can either select and reshape the arc or Undo the arc and try again.

Property	Effect
Length X-axis	Sets horizontal arc length
Length Y-axis	Sets vertical arc length
Origin point	Click one of the four corners to set the arc's origin point
Type	Select between open arc ("bow") or closed arc ("pie wedge")
Base Along	Select arc alignment on X or Y axes
Concave and Convex	Changes the arc's radius between the two anchor points
Fill arc	Applies line fill to arc

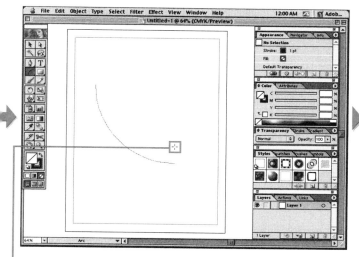

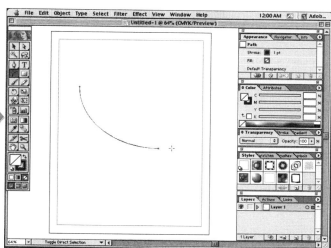

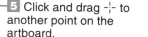
5 Click and drag ╬ to another point on the artboard.

6 Release the mouse.

■ An arc appears in your artwork.

DRAW STRAIGHT LINES USING THE PEN TOOL

The Pen tool is the most powerful drawing tool in the toolbox. You can use the Pen tool to create paths of any type, and you have the most flexibility in your drawings when you use the Pen tool. All this power brings complexity, and it takes time to get used to working with the Pen tool

for drawing curves. With a little practice, however, you will find yourself using the Pen tool more than any other tool in the toolbox, because it can do so many things so quickly.

You can draw straight lines with the greatest ease using the Pen tool. You can either click once to set the

start point and click a second time to set the end point, or you can click and drag to create a radial line that extends outward from a center point. If you draw a radial line, a center anchor point and two end anchor points are created, any of which can be further modified by the Pen tool.

DRAW STRAIGHT LINES USING THE PEN TOOL

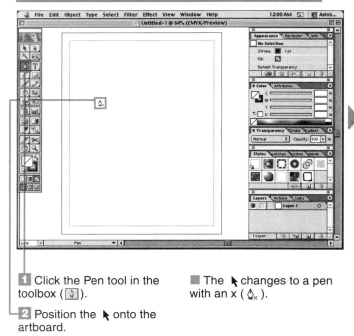

■ Click the Pen tool in the toolbox ([ ]).

■ Position the ▶ onto the artboard.

■ The ▶ changes to a pen with an x ( ).

■ Click once on the artwork.

■ An anchor point appears on the page.

How do I copy the line I just drew?

✔ Illustrator offers two ways to create a copy of the lines you draw with the Pen tool. First, after you draw your line segment, press the A key to switch to the Selection tool (▣). Press and hold the Alt (Option) key, and drag away from your new line with the mouse. Illustrator creates a copy. Second, from the menu click Edit, Copy, Edit, and then Paste. A copy appears directly on top of the new line; use ▣ to drag the copy to a new location.

Do I have to draw all my continuous straight lines one at a time?

✔ You do not have to draw one line using the steps here, then start all over again to draw the next contiguous line, and so forth. You can draw continuous straight lines by repeating steps 4 and 5 in your artwork, much like playing connect-the-dots.

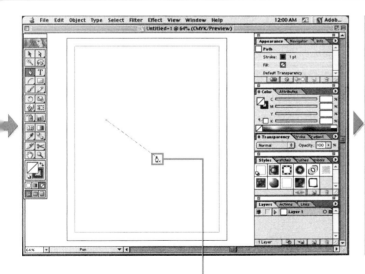

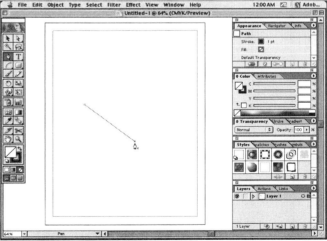

4 Position the ✒ to another area on the artboard.

Note: Do not drag the cursor.

5 Click the artwork again to create a second anchor point.

■ A line appears between your two anchor points.

■ To create a line in 45-degree increments, you can hold down the Shift key.

■ To start a new line, press Ctrl (Command) and click a blank area on the page. Then, repeat steps 1 through 5.

DRAW CURVES USING THE PEN TOOL

When you click and drag with the Pen tool on the artboard, you create an anchor point and one or two control handles for that anchor point. You use the control handles to adjust the slope and shape of the curve; you can change the effect a handle has on its nearby curve by moving the anchor point into or away from its anchor point. Likewise, you can change the curve's slope by moving

the control handle towards or away from its corresponding line. Between the two motions you can radically change the appearance of any curve drawn with the Pen tool. See the section "Reshape a Curve Using Control Handles or Anchor Points" for more information on how to do this.

You may initially find drawing curved lines with the Pen tool

counterintuitive. First, practice drawing simple arcs and then move on to more complex curves.

The Pen tool uses Bézier curves to create its paths, which you can scale to any size or shape without losing detail. For more on Bézier curves, see the section "Understanding Paths."

DRAW CURVES USING THE PEN TOOL

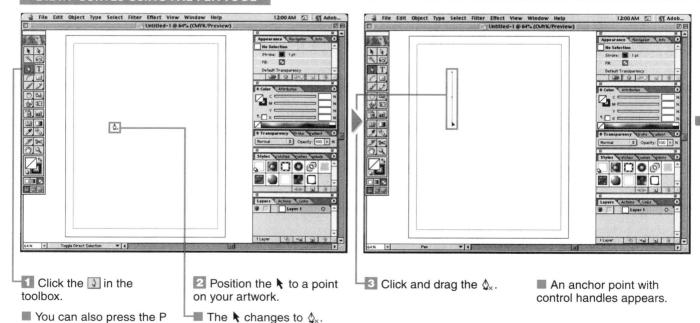

1 Click the ![pen] in the toolbox.

■ You can also press the P key to quickly switch to the Pen tool.

2 Position the ![arrow] to a point on your artwork.

■ The ![arrow] changes to ![pen].

3 Click and drag the ![pen].

■ An anchor point with control handles appears.

What techniques can I use to master drawing curves?

✔ You can practice drawing "slalom" curves as a first step to working with curves. A more advanced technique is to try to draw a "figure eight" using as few anchor points as possible. If you can do this using only two anchor points, you have mastered the Pen tool. Hint: The points will overlap, so you will need to manipulate and edit them separately.

I keep trying to stop drawing curves, but the Pen tool keeps adding points. How do I stop this?

✔ The Pen tool still thinks it is in a drawing mode, and so each time you click the mouse it thinks you want to add a new anchor point with control handles. To stop drawing curves with the Pen tool, press and hold Ctrl (Command) and click a blank area on the artboard.

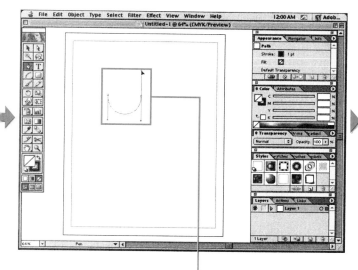

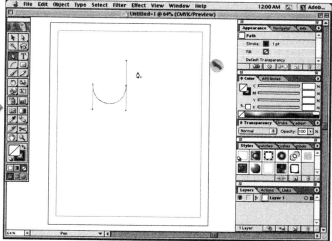

4 Release the mouse button.

5 Position the pen a short distance away.

6 Click and drag the pen in the opposite direction from step 2.

■ A curve appears between the two anchor points.

7 Release the mouse button.

■ The final curve appears on the page.

■ To continue drawing curves, repeat steps 5 through 7.

■ To start a new curve, press Ctrl (Command), click a blank area on the page, and then repeat steps 1 through 7.

RESHAPE A CURVE USING CONTROL HANDLES OR ANCHOR POINTS

You can reshape curves drawn with the Pen tool by using the control handles that appear from an anchor point. Control handles act like magnets that attract a line depending on the handle length and closeness to the line. For example, if you move the control handle farther away from the anchor point, the curve flexes and warps to follow the handle.

You can also reshape a line by moving an anchor point. Moving the anchor point changes the shape and length of the entire curve, and not just that portion affected by a control handle. When you move an anchor point, the line stretches or contracts to follow the anchor point around the artboard. After you move an anchor point, you will probably need to adjust the curve using a control handle.

Reshaping with a control handle or an anchor point is done with the Direct Selection tool.

RESHAPE A CURVE USING CONTROL HANDLES

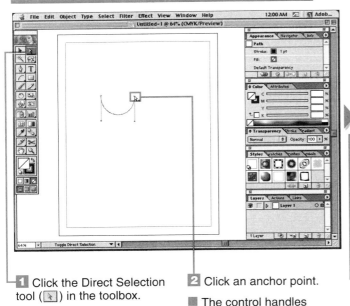

1 Click the Direct Selection tool (▶) in the toolbox.

■ You can also press the A key to switch to ▶.

2 Click an anchor point.

■ The control handles appear.

3 Click and drag a control handle.

■ The curve changes shape.

■ When the curve is the proper shape, release the control handle.

I used the control handles but cannot get my curve back to how it was?

✔ You can use the Undo command to "back out" the changes you made with the control handles. Click Edit, then Undo Move, or use the shortcut keys Ctrl + Z (Command - Z) to go back.

How long should I make my control handles?

✔ You should plan on starting with a handle size approximately one-third the size of your curve segment. This size gives you a good starting point for making future adjustments.

What happens if my control handles are too long?

✔ If you find you are drawing your control handles to extreme lengths, you should probably rethink how you are drawing your curve segments. For instance, if you are trying to draw a narrow, steep arc using two anchor points, your control handles will be very long. You should consider using three anchor points instead — two at each end of the arc, and one at the apex. Your control handles will be a more manageable size.

RESHAPE A CURVE USING ANCHOR POINTS

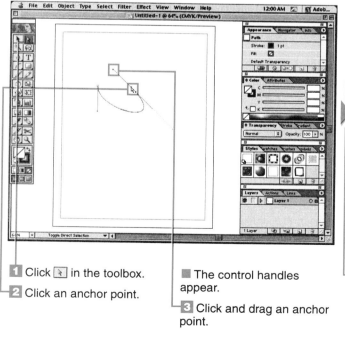

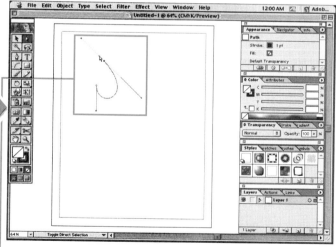

1 Click 🔣 in the toolbox.

2 Click an anchor point.

■ The control handles appear.

3 Click and drag an anchor point.

■ The curve changes shape.

■ When the curve is the proper shape, release the anchor point.

RESHAPE A LINE USING THE RESHAPE TOOL

The Reshape tool changes the look of a line by inserting an anchor point in the line. This anchor point has two effects: first, using the Reshape tool, it creates its own anchor point and set of control handles that can be used to adjust the curve; second, it shortens the existing control handles on the two nearest anchor points. This effect is the same as using the Add Anchor Point tool.

See the section "Add or Remove Anchor Points," later in this chapter, for details.

After you have used the Reshape tool to insert a new anchor point and control handles in your line, you can drag the new anchor point around the artboard to change the line's shape. This technique is one of the quickest, although not

always the most accurate, ways that you can change a line's shape.

One benefit of using the Reshape tool is that you can select multiple line segments, add new anchor points to them, and then move the collection of new points as a unit. This technique can quickly add shear or reshape numerous areas in your illustration.

RESHAPE A LINE USING THE RESHAPE TOOL

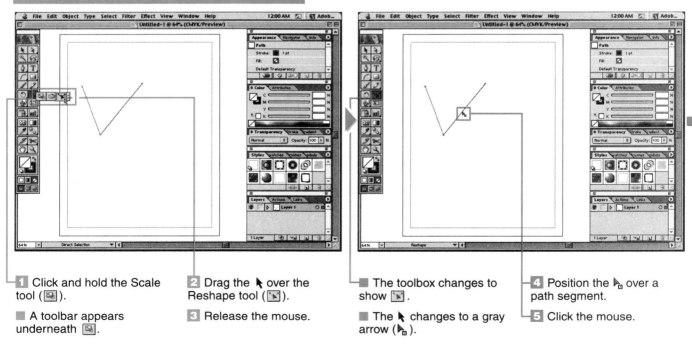

1 Click and hold the Scale tool (⬛).

■ A toolbar appears underneath ⬛.

2 Drag the ▶ over the Reshape tool (⬛).

3 Release the mouse.

■ The toolbox changes to show ⬛.

■ The ▶ changes to a gray arrow (▶).

4 Position the ▶ over a path segment.

5 Click the mouse.

What if I do not like the new look I have drawn?

✔ Switch to the 🖋× and move it over your new anchor point. When the 🖋× changes to a minus sign 🖋-, click the anchor point, and Illustrator deletes your anchor point. Your path returns to its original shape.

How do I select additional points that can be reshaped with the tool?

✔ You can add more anchor points (or select more points along a line segment) by holding down the Shift key while clicking with the mouse. The new Reshape anchor points are added.

Can I reshape an object without changing its proportions with the Reshape tool?

✔ If you want to change an object's appearance but keep the proportions the same, you need to apply shear to the object or use the Scale tool. See Chapter 10 for information on using these tools.

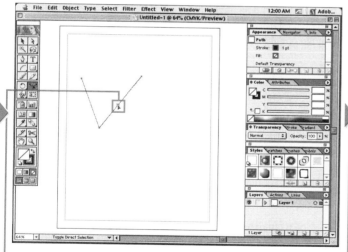

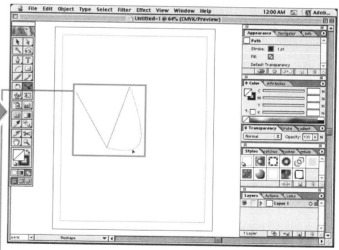

■ An anchor point with a box around it appears on the path.

Note: You must place the new anchor point within a segment; you cannot make the point an endpoint.

6 Click and drag the new anchor point.

■ The line changes shape.

CLOSE AN OPEN PATH

Open paths are ones that do not connect with other paths in your artwork. You might have whiskers on a cat that consist of single paths, for instance, or you have compound shapes that do not close off, like the letter omega. These are instances of open paths that will probably stay open.

In other cases, however, you are creating new artwork and need to close off an open area in your illustration. This is sometimes necessary, as some tools use the end of an open segment as a starting point (such as fills), which may create an effect you do not want. Closing an open path is

simple; you close an open path by connecting two anchor points together with the Pen tool.

The Pen tool gives you visual cues for when you can close off a path. The cursor changes to a pen with a small "o" next to it, indicating you can "complete the circle" and close the path.

CLOSE AN OPEN PATH

1 Click 🖊.

2 Click the artboard to create an anchor point.

■ The ▶ changes to ♦ₓ.

3 Drag the ♦ₓ to another area on the artboard.

4 Click the artboard to create a second anchor point.

When would I close an open path?

✔ Most of the time, you will want to use closed paths in your artwork, because they allow you to more easily work with paths and objects, especially for selecting them or moving them. You can apply fills to open paths, work with gradients, or apply a stroke to the object; this can, however, sometimes result in uneven or incomplete-looking objects, especially when you use fills. For artistic reasons, you may want to keep paths open, but in general, closed paths are better to work with.

How do I close a curved path and keep the anchor point smooth?

✔ If you want to make the closed anchor point a smooth anchor, you need to click and drag on the anchor point when you close the path. If you click just the anchor point, you create a combination corner point, which has only one control handle.

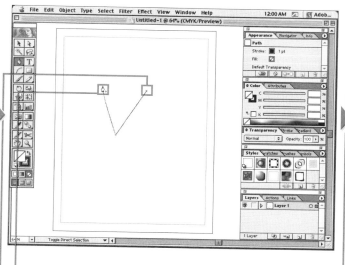

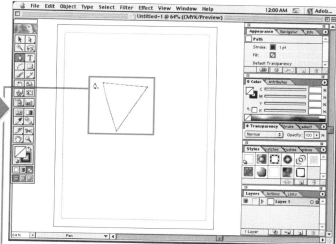

5 Click the ♧ₓ to another area on the artboard.

6 Click the artboard to create a third anchor point.

7 Click the ♧ₓ back to the first anchor point.

■ The ♧ₓ changes to a pen with a small circle (♧₀).

8 Click the first anchor point.

■ Illustrator creates a closed path.

■ This example uses straight lines; the same procedure is used with curved lines.

OPEN A CLOSED PATH

When you create objects or sets of closed paths, you may want to edit your artwork — perhaps to add a fin to a fish that you forgot to draw in. Rather than delete a line segment, or even the entire object, to add the new lines you can open a closed path. Opening a closed path is the best way to create a gap in a path so you can add to it.

You open a closed path using the Scissors tool. This tool cuts a path into two segments with overlapping anchor points at the point where you cut into the line. You can then move the two segments, delete them, or add to them. The Scissors tool does not have to be applied in the middle of a line segment; you can use it anywhere on a segment, including on an anchor point.

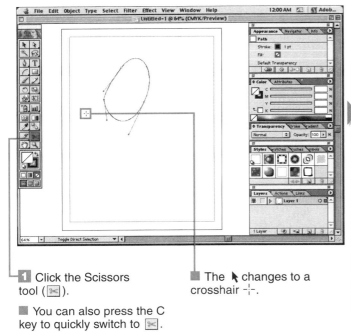

OPEN A CLOSED PATH

1 Click the Scissors tool (✂).

■ You can also press the C key to quickly switch to ✂.

■ The ▸ changes to a crosshair -¦-.

2 Position the -¦- over a path you want to cut.

3 Click the mouse button.

4 An anchor point appears on the path.

Note: There are actually two anchor points directly overlapping each other.

Can I delete a line segment if I use the Scissors tool on both ends?

✔ You can cut a line segment out of a path by using the Scissors tool (✂) to make the initial cuts, use the ▶ to select the line segment, and then press the Delete key. You create stray anchor points, however, when you do this; Illustrator deletes the line but not the anchor points. Either use ▶ to select and delete the stray anchor points, or clean up the points using the Remove Anchor Points tool (✑). See the section "Add or Remove Anchor Points," later in this chapter, for more information.

What is the difference between the Scissors tool and the Knife tool?

✔ The Scissors tool (✂) is ideal for cutting through paths. The Knife tool (◪) is best for cutting through objects or cutting around irregular areas.

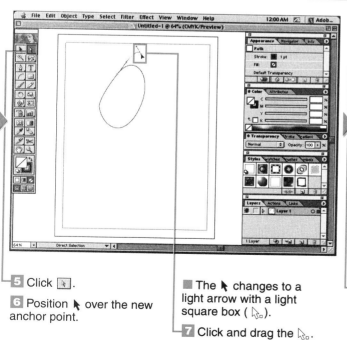

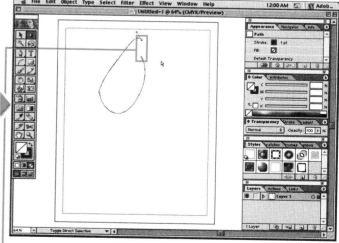

5 Click ▶.

6 Position ▶ over the new anchor point.

■ The ▶ changes to a light arrow with a light square box (▷□).

7 Click and drag the ▷□.

■ Illustrator opens the closed path.

DELETE PATHS

You may need to undo some paths, or even delete entire groups of paths, due to your illustration changing its theme mid-design. Fortunately, using paths to create illustrations makes it very easy to undo or remove parts of your illustration without disturbing other portions.

You can delete an entire path using the Selection tool, or part of a path using the Direct Selection tool. Which one you use depends on how much editing you need to do. Using the Selection tool will select an entire object, including its paths and anchor points; using the Direct

Selection tool lets you remove parts of a path.

After you select an object or a path, you delete it by pressing the Delete key.

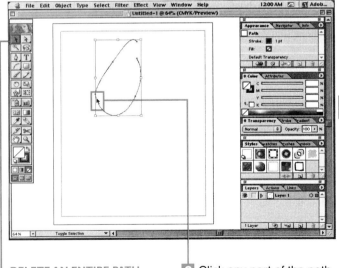

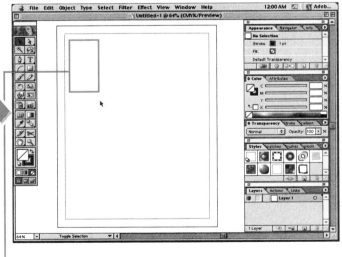

DELETE AN ENTIRE PATH

1 Click the Selection tool (▶).

■ You can also press the V key to quickly switch to ▶.

2 Click any part of the path you want to delete.

■ The path is selected and displays a bounding box.

3 Press the Delete key.

■ Illustrator deletes the path.

■ You can also drag a marquee box around all or part of a path to select it.

How can I easily select different parts of a path and delete them all at once?

✔ You can add segments or paths by clicking with either ![] or ![] while holding down the Shift key. You can then delete only the objects you selected.

I want to start over again with a blank artboard. How do I select everything?

✔ It is easy to select everything on the artboard. Using the menu, click Edit, then Select All, and then press the Delete key. Illustrator clears off the artboard.

I thought I deleted everything, but why do anchor points still appear on the artboard?

✔ If you use ![] to select a line segment, but then delete the segment without selecting the anchor points, you create stray anchor points. To avoid this, make sure that you select the anchor points for the segment; the points change from a hollow square (unselected) to a solid square (selected).

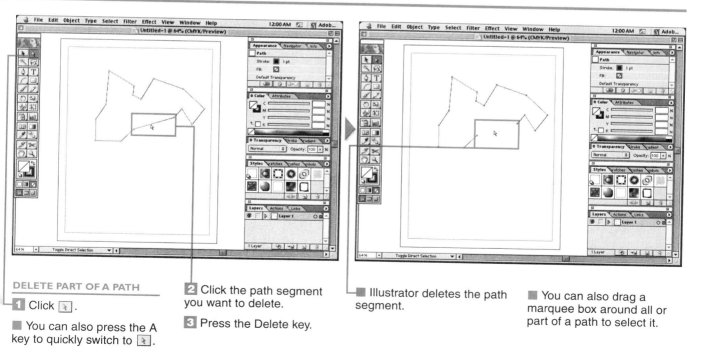

DELETE PART OF A PATH

1 Click ![].

■ You can also press the A key to quickly switch to ![].

2 Click the path segment you want to delete.

3 Press the Delete key.

■ Illustrator deletes the path segment.

■ You can also drag a marquee box around all or part of a path to select it.

ERASE PATHS USING THE ERASER TOOL

You can remove parts of a path with the Eraser tool. The Eraser tool is an unusual one in the Illustrator toolbox. You find it with the Pencil tool, and it looks like a pencil poised to erase lines. It works like a regular eraser, rubbing out as much or as little of a line segment as you want. This requires a lot of

mouse movement in order to "rub out" part of a path; even at higher magnifications, it does not seem to have any greater effect on erasing parts of a path. If you are not careful with its operation, you may erase most of a path, but leave behind a very short path segment with its own anchor points, requiring more erasing.

To make its operation interesting, it even appears to leave behind bits of eraser dust as you move the Eraser tool over a path. The bits disappear when you release the mouse, but it's an odd bit of animation. All things considered, it seems easier to delete the line and redraw it, or cut out a segment with the Scissors tool and delete it.

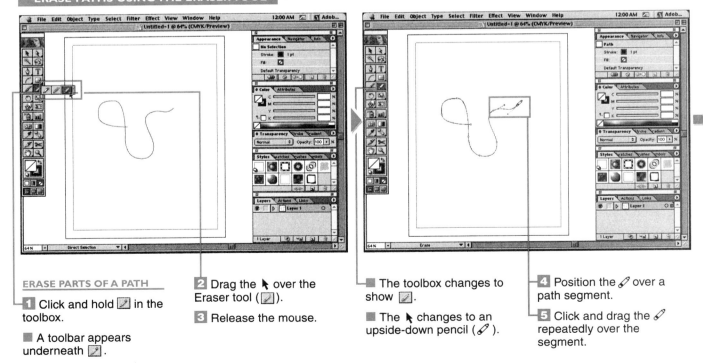

ERASE PATHS USING THE ERASER TOOL

ERASE PARTS OF A PATH

■1 Click and hold ✎ in the toolbox.

■ A toolbar appears underneath ✎.

■2 Drag the ▸ over the Eraser tool (✎).

■3 Release the mouse.

■ The toolbox changes to show ✎.

■ The ▸ changes to an upside-down pencil (✎).

■4 Position the ✎ over a path segment.

■5 Click and drag the ✎ repeatedly over the segment.

Can I use the eraser on lines drawn with the Pen tool?

✔ You can use the Eraser tool (▨) on many types of paths including ones drawn by the Pen tool (✎). However, you should probably use it to edit freeform lines drawn with the Pencil tool (▨) instead. Pen-drawn paths are best edited using the Pen tool to place new anchor points or manipulate control handles.

Is the Eraser tool good for erasing text?

✔ Unfortunately, you cannot use the Erase tool on text you have placed into your artwork with the Text tool. This would seem a natural use for it, but you must first convert your text to an outline before you can use other tools on it. See Chapter 11 for more information on working with text in Illustrator.

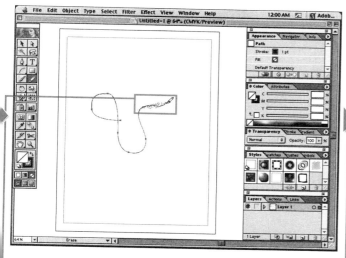

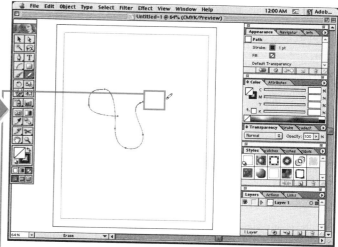

■ A dark area appears, showing where you are erasing.

6 Release the mouse.

■ The line segment you erased disappears.

■ Anchor points appear at the ends of the paths.

ADD OR REMOVE ANCHOR POINTS

You can add anchor points to give you better control over a path, or to extend an open path. For example, you may have drawn a narrow but steep curve using control handles, but the control handles are extremely long. You can shorten the handles dramatically and give you better control over the curve by placing an additional anchor point at the apex

of the curve, essentially converting the curve from a single line segment into two line segments joined at the apex. The control handles are shorter, and the new control handles allow you to reshape the curve.

Removing anchor points simplifies or changes the shape of the path. If you used the Pencil tool to draw a

path and there are more anchor points than you know what to do with, you can remove excess anchor points from the path. Illustrator will take a best guess how to recalculate the Beziér curves and draw the new line for you.

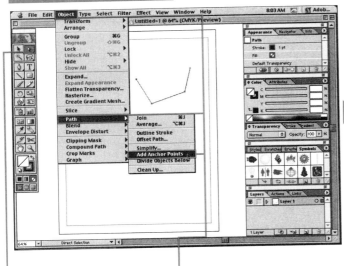

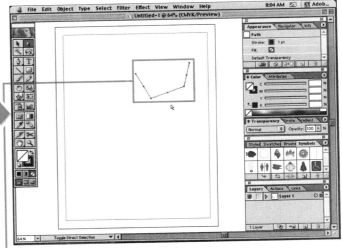

1 Select a path or group of paths with either the Direct Selection tool ( ) or Selection tool ( ).

Note: See Chapter 9 for more on selecting a path.

2 Click Object.

3 Click Path.

4 Click Add Anchor Points.

■ You can also click and hold on the Pen tool ( ), then select the Add Anchor Point tool ( ).

■ New anchor points appear equally between existing anchor points along each segment you selected.

■ If you use the Add Anchor Point tool, you can add anchor points anywhere along a path.

Which is better to use to remove excess anchor points: the Simplify tool, or the Remove Anchor Point tool?

✔ The Remove Anchor Point tool seems best for removing single anchor points, or points that were accidentally added to your paths. It often makes sudden changes to the look of your artwork. The Simplify tool has a number of adjustments that help it guess how your line should look, and seems to be better for large numbers of anchor points on your paths, such as lines drawn with the Pencil tool. When in doubt, you can make a copy of your illustration to another area of your artboard and try both techniques.

How many anchor points does the Add Anchor Point tool add?

✔ The ☒ inserts a new anchor point between every pair of existing anchor points. If you select a single segment with two anchor points, Illustrator adds one new anchor point between them. If you select a square, Illustrator adds four new anchor points in the middle of each segment.

REMOVE ANCHOR POINTS

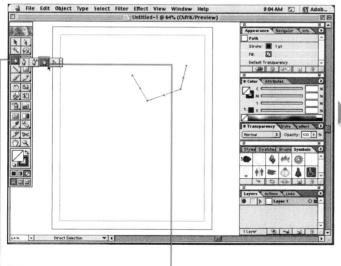

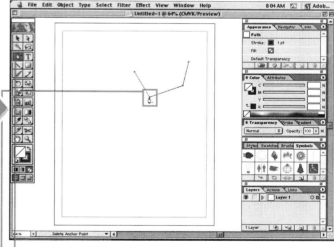

■ **1** Select a path using ☒ or ☒.

Note: See Chapter 9 for more on selecting a path.

■ **2** Click and hold on ☒ in the toolbox.

■ A toolbar appears underneath ☒.

■ **3** Drag the cursor (▶) over the Remove Anchor Point tool (☒).

■ **4** Release the mouse.

■ The ▶ changes to a ☒ with a minus sign (☒).

■ **5** Click the anchor point you want to remove.

■ The anchor point vanishes.

Note: Depending on where the anchor point is, your path changes shape.

201

CONVERT ANCHOR POINT TYPE

Drawing complex shapes with the Pen tool can be daunting. It requires that you do some planning ahead as to what your illustration will look like, how you will create its component objects and paths, and finally how the paths will interrelate. The Pen tool is used to generate many of the paths you will use, and the anchor points control each path's shape. See

"Understanding Paths," earlier in this chapter, for information on how paths work.

Depending on where you are in your drawing, you may need to convert anchor point types as your drawing changes. Doing this gives you flexibility in using existing paths without having to redraw paths just to change the anchor point type.

Converting anchor points is necessary to change how paths connect to one another, and it directly affects how your paths appear in your final illustration. You will need to become familiar with converting between the different anchor points as your use of the Pen tool improves.

CONVERT ANCHOR POINT TYPE

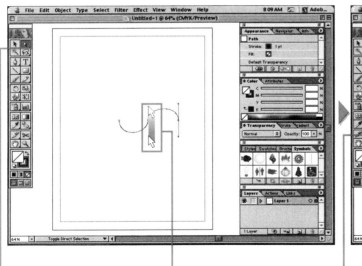

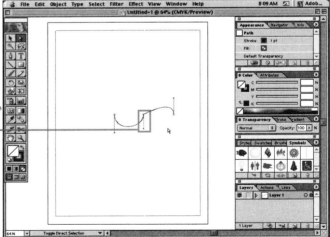

CONVERT A SMOOTH POINT TO A COMBINATION CORNER POINT

1 Click ▣.

■ The ▶ changes to a light arrow (▷).

2 Click and drag an anchor handle into the anchor point.

3 Release the mouse button.

■ A combination anchor point appears.

Note: You can also use this method to convert a curved corner point into a combination corner point.

What are the different kinds of anchor points?

✔ You can identify anchor points by the types of lines they connect and the number of control handles.

Anchor Point	Description
͙U͙ Smooth point	A curved path flowing smoothly through it. It has two linked control handles.
V Straight corner point	Two straight lines meeting; it has no control handles.
᷄C᷄ Curved corner point	Two curved lines that meet and suddenly change direction. It has two independent control handles.
͙V͙ Combination corner point	Straight and curved lines meeting. It has one independent control handle.

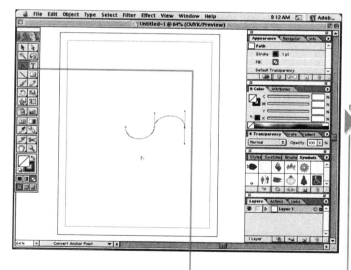

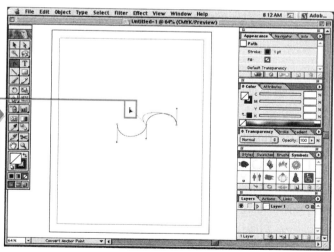

CONVERT A SMOOTH POINT TO A CURVED CORNER POINT

■1 Press Shift + C to select the Convert Anchor Point tool.

■ The ▶ changes to the Convert Anchor Point tool (∧).

■2 Click and drag a smooth anchor point control handle.

■ The smooth anchor point converts to a curved anchor point.

CONTINUED

CONVERT ANCHOR POINT TYPE (CONTINUED)

Y ou may want to convert straight or curved corner points to smooth points if you are sketching and need to smooth out sudden changes in direction.

A straight corner point has two lines that come together at an angle, without any curvature to them, and the corner point does not have any control handles

protruding from it. Straight corner points are very common and occur whenever two straight paths connect.

A curved corner point has two curves coming together into a point, and the anchor point has two control handles protruding from it. In an illustration, curved corner points often look like waves.

A smooth corner point is an anchor point that joins two curved paths, and the curves flow smoothly into one another.

The easiest way is to select the corner point and drag it with the Convert Anchor Point tool; this converts a corner point to a smooth point.

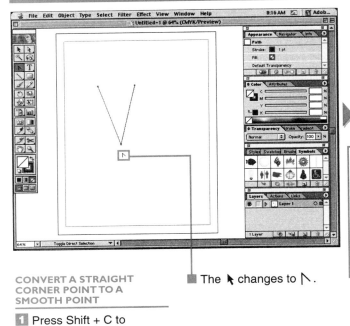

CONVERT A STRAIGHT CORNER POINT TO A SMOOTH POINT

1 Press Shift + C to select ⋀.

■ The ▶ changes to ⋀.

2 Click and drag a straight corner point.

■ The anchor point changes to a smooth corner point with linked control handles.

Note: You can also use this method to convert a curved corner point into a smooth corner point.

Where can I find all the Anchor Point tools?

✔ The Pen tool in the toolbox has all the pen tools: Pen, Add Anchor Point, Delete Anchor Point, and Convert Anchor Point. In some cases, you do not need to select them from the toolbox; Illustrator makes a best guess as to what tool you want to use and changes to that tool automatically.

How do I tell whether an anchor point is selected?

✔ Anchor points change appearance depending on whether they have been selected. A selected anchor point appears as a small filled square; if it has not been selected, it is a small hollow square.

Is there a fast way to switch between the Pen tool and the Direct Selection tool?

✔ If you are using the Pen tool or any of its variations, you can momentarily switch to the Direct Selection tool by pressing and holding the Command or Ctrl key. This lets you perform an action with the Pen tool, then work with the anchor point or its control handles immediately.

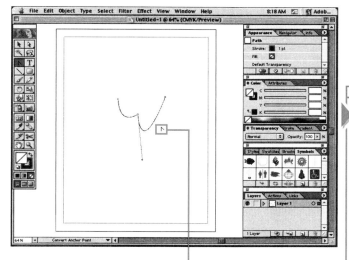

CONVERT A CURVED CORNER POINT TO A SMOOTH POINT

1 Press Shift + C to select ⌐.

■ The ⌐ changes to ⌐.

2 Click and drag a curved anchor point.

3 Release the mouse.

■ The curved corner point converts to a smooth point.

CONTINUED ▶

CONVERT ANCHOR POINT
TYPE (CONTINUED)

You may want to convert straight or curved corner points to smooth points if you are sketching and need to smooth out sudden changes in direction.

A straight corner point has two lines that come together at an angle, without any curvature to them, and the corner point does not have any control handles

protruding from it. Straight corner points are very common and occur whenever two straight paths connect.

A curved corner point has two curves coming together into a point, and the anchor point has two control handles protruding from it. In an illustration, curved corner points often look like waves.

A smooth corner point is an anchor point that joins two curved paths, and the curves flow smoothly into one another.

The easiest way is to select the corner point and drag it with the Convert Anchor Point tool; this converts a corner point to a smooth point.

CONVERT ANCHOR POINT TYPE (CONTINUED)

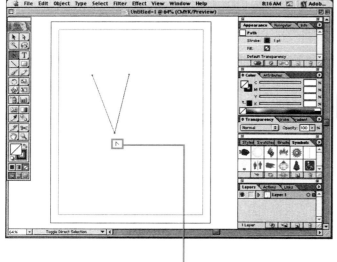

CONVERT A STRAIGHT CORNER POINT TO A SMOOTH POINT

1 Press Shift + C to select ∧.

■ The ▶ changes to ∧.

2 Click and drag a straight corner point.

■ The anchor point changes to a smooth corner point with linked control handles.

Note: You can also use this method to convert a curved corner point into a smooth corner point.

How can I more quickly switch modes with the Pen tool?

✔ You can switch Pen tool modes temporarily by using the keyboard. With one tool active, you can momentarily switch back to the other tool to continue drawing.

The status area tells you which tool is active, and you can quickly see which mode you are in or which one you are switching to by checking the tool status in the status area. Some of the tool changes you can make are:

✎× + Option or Alt + anchor point	Convert Anchor Point
✎× + Command or Ctrl + anchor point	Direct Select Mode
▨ + Command or Ctrl + anchor point	Direct Select Mode

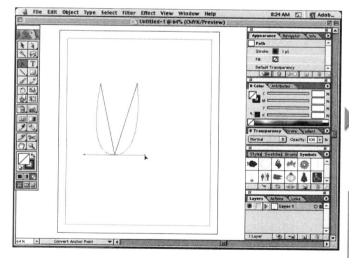

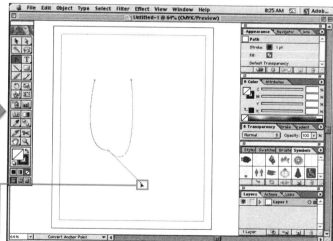

CONVERT STRAIGHT CORNER POINT TO CURVED CORNER POINT

1 Repeat steps 1 and 2 of "Convert a Straight Corner Point to a Smooth Point."

2 Click and drag one of the control handles.

■ The corner point is converted to a curved corner point.

■ You can move both control handles independently of one another.

REMOVE EXCESS ANCHOR POINTS

S ometimes your work becomes a maze of paths, anchor points, overlapping objects, and complex lines. This happens during the drafting phase while you are figuring out how all the pieces of your illustration will fit together. Often you will have far more anchor points than you need, ones which were added to help shape and manage paths but which now need to be cleaned up.

Illustrator can remove excess anchor points from a series of paths you select, which makes the paths less complex while still retaining their shapes. It does this by figuring out ways to simplify your drawing using the options you specify in the Simplify dialog box, and then showing you a preview of what your new drawing will look like.

You can also simplify your drawing by using the Remove Anchor Points tool to remove single anchors, though this does not try to recalculate the lines and keep your illustration close to its original shape.

You should always save before using the Simplify command, so you can undo your changes if the results are different than expected.

REMOVE EXCESS ANCHOR POINTS

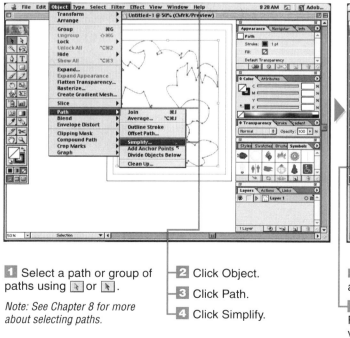

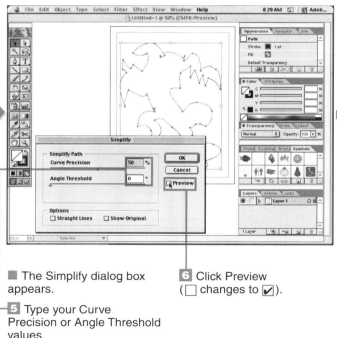

1 Select a path or group of paths using ![pointer] or ![pointer].

Note: See Chapter 8 for more about selecting paths.

2 Click Object.

3 Click Path.

4 Click Simplify.

■ The Simplify dialog box appears.

5 Type your Curve Precision or Angle Threshold values.

6 Click Preview (☐ changes to ☑).

What do the Simplify options do?

✔ The Simplify dialog box lets you change how closely Illustrator should try to match your original illustration. The options are Curve Precision, which affects how closely the new paths should match the old; Angle Threshold, which preserves angles less than the value selected; Straight lines, which converts all paths in your image to straight lines; and Show Original, which lets you compare both the original image and the new image when the Preview box is selected.

What causes excess anchor points?

✔ You can obtain excess anchor points when you use the Pencil tool to draw freehand lines; the Pencil tool creates more anchor points the more erratic the shape. You can also create a lot of anchor points when you use the Auto Trace or Streamline tools.

When I used the Simplify tool, why did I get more anchor points?

✔ Depending on the Curve Precision value, you may be increasing the number of anchor points. Try lowering the Curve Precision value and see if that reduces the point total.

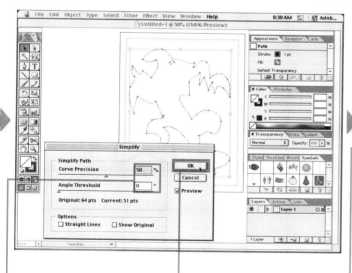

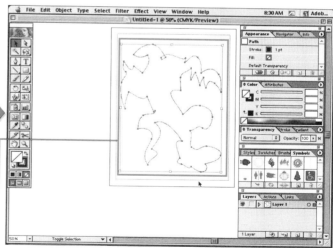

■ The dialog box displays the old and new anchor point counts.

■ You can see a preview of your paths.

-7 Click OK.

■ Excess anchor points disappear, leaving simpler paths.

AVERAGE ANCHOR POINTS

When you are drawing an illustration, you may spend a lot of time trying to get anchor points to align with an imaginary line in your art. Even at high magnification, you may be nudging anchor points using the arrow keys and scrolling around in your art trying to get the points to align. Instead of trying to manually adjust the anchor points to an imaginary line, you can use the Average command.

The Average command aligns two or more anchor points — on the same path or on different paths — vertically, horizontally, or both, to a position that is the average of their current locations. This lets you quickly overlap anchor points or align them precisely with each other.

Average does not let you select the imaginary line; instead, it adds together the location of the anchor

points, then divides by the number of points being averaged. This calculates the mean for all the points, whether vertical, horizontal, or both.

You should save your work before using this function, as you can sometimes produce unexpected results.

AVERAGE ANCHOR POINTS

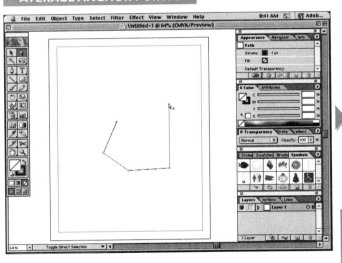

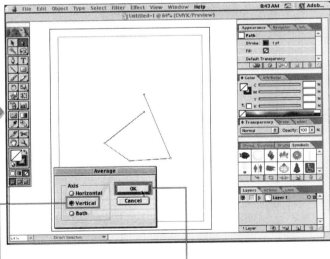

SELECT POINTS

■1 Select two points by pressing Shift and clicking.

■ You can select points on the same path or different paths.

Note: See Chapter 8 for more on selecting paths.

■2 Press Ctrl + Alt + J (Command - Option - J).

AVERAGE POINTS VERTICALLY

■ The Average dialog box appears.

■3 Click Vertical (○ changes to ●).

■4 Click OK.

■ The selected points align vertically.

Can I use the Group Selection tool to average the points?

✔ You can, but it is not recommended. If you use either the Selection or the Group Selection tool, then every point on all the paths are averaged — and it is likely that this is not what you want, especially if you average both horizontally and vertically.

How do I nudge anchor points?

✔ Anchor points can be nudged one pixel at a time using ←, →, ↑, or ↓. If you want to nudge them ten pixels at a time, hold down Shift and then press one of the arrow keys.

Do all the points have to be part of the same object?

✔ No. You can use the Direct Selection tool to select any anchor point and average it with another. This also works on grouped objects; you can select just one point from the group and average it with non-grouped anchor points.

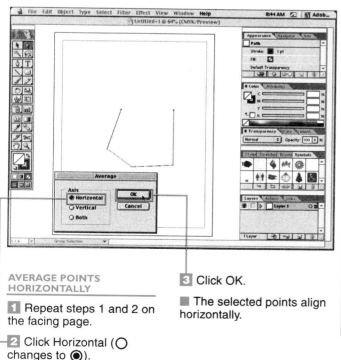

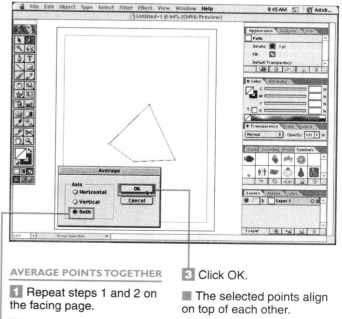

AVERAGE POINTS HORIZONTALLY

1 Repeat steps 1 and 2 on the facing page.

2 Click Horizontal (○ changes to ●).

3 Click OK.

■ The selected points align horizontally.

AVERAGE POINTS TOGETHER

1 Repeat steps 1 and 2 on the facing page.

2 Click Both (○ changes to ●).

3 Click OK.

■ The selected points align on top of each other.

JOIN ANCHOR POINTS

Other tasks have shown you how to open a closed path, which creates two new line segments with anchor points out of an existing line segment. An analogous action is the Join ability, which effectively joins two line segments together at a single anchor point. This acts both to close a path and reduce the number

of anchor points, making it easier to work with the object.

The Join command combines two points to create a single point when one point is placed directly on top of another point. The positioning and alignment can sometimes be tricky, so you will sometimes use the Average command to align the

points first before joining them with the Join command.

The Join command also lets you connect two anchor points with a single line segment, such as closing off an open arc. This offers you an alternative to using the Pen tool to add a new line segment to your illustration.

JOIN ANCHOR POINTS

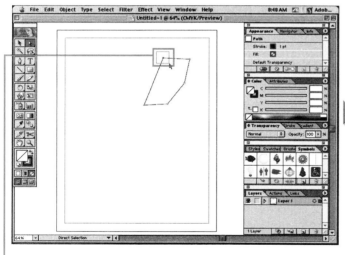

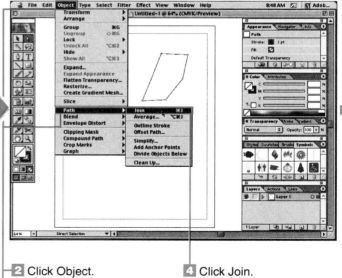

■ If you do not have overlapping points, click [cursor] to click and drag one end point over the other.

1 Click and drag a marquee box around the two end points.

Note: See Chapter 8 for information about selecting objects, paths, and anchor points.

■ The two end points are selected.

2 Click Object.

3 Click Path.

4 Click Join.

How do I join two end points with a line segment?

✔ The Join function also links two end points with a line segment. Select two end points with , then click Object, Path, and then Join to make a line segment form between the points.

Can I join more than two points into a single point?

✔ No. Illustrator will give you a warning about trying to join points that are parts of different groups. You can only join two anchor points to each other.

How do I make sure the points are directly aligned?

✔ If you are dragging anchor points over each other rather than using the Average command, you need to make sure they can align properly. From the menu, click Edit, Preferences, and then Smart Guides and Slices. Make sure the snapping tolerance value is not zero; the default value of four points is a good one to work with.

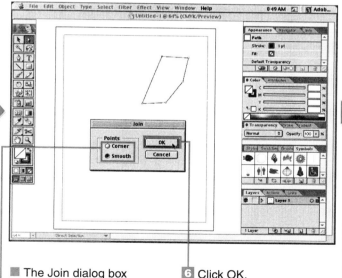

■ The Join dialog box appears.

5 Click the anchor point corner type for your joined lines (○ changes to ◉).

6 Click OK.

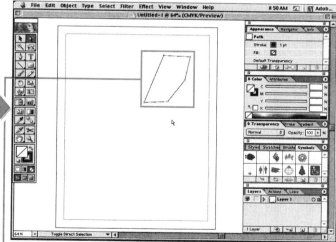

■ The lines are joined with the corner type you selected.

USING THE ADD AND SUBTRACT COMMANDS

The Pathfinder palette contains two different sets of tools that help you work with objects. The Pathfinder palette can be used to combine paths into new objects and shapes. In the Pathfinder palette, you can access filters for combining paths and you can access shape mode commands, which create and modify compound shapes.

Two of the Pathfinder's commands that are used with paths are Add and Subtract. The Add to Shape command lets you add the area of two overlapping paths so you can then work with a single joined object; this saves time so you do not have to draw a single object based on the paths of two separate objects.

The Subtract from Shape command removes the non-overlapping areas; it is a way of trimming off unneeded areas that do not intersect. Using these commands, you can easily join shapes without drawing the individual paths.

For more on different uses for the Pathfinder tool, see Chapter 10.

USING THE ADD AND SUBTRACT COMMANDS

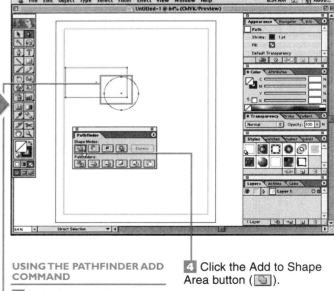

OPEN THE PATHFINDER PALETTE

1 Click Window.

2 Click Pathfinder.

■ The Pathfinder palette appears.

USING THE PATHFINDER ADD COMMAND

3 Select two overlapping paths with ▶.

4 Click the Add to Shape Area button (🔲).

Is it important which shape overlaps another?

✔ It makes a difference when determining which shape you want to add or subtract from another one. Try working with different overlapping situations to determine which areas Illustrator adds or subtracts depending on overlap. Normally the topmost selected set of paths is the "controlling" object and will have other objects joined to it (or subtracted from it).

Which fill gets applied to my joined objects?

✔ When you use the Add to Shape command, the fill of the topmost selected path and any effects are applied to the joined objects.

What happens to parts of an object that are subtracted?

✔ When you apply the Subtract from Shape command, only the visible areas are removed. The paths for the underlying shapes are still present, so you can modify the underlying objects, such as apply scaling to the remaining artwork.

How do I get rid of the unneeded paths?

✔ After you have used the Add to Shape or Subtract from Shape command, click the Expand button on the Pathfinder palette. The additional paths are removed from your artwork.

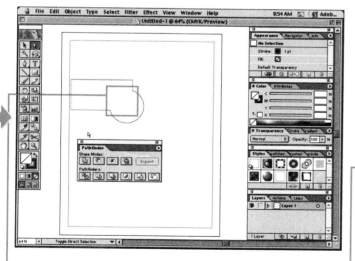

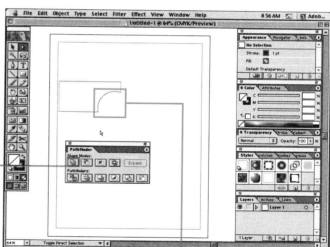

■ The overlapping area is added to the underlying area.

USING THE PATHFINDER SUBTRACT COMMAND

1 Repeat steps 1 through 3 on the previous page.

2 Click the Subtract from Shape Area button (🔳).

■ The overlapping area is subtracted from the underlying area.

USING THE INTERSECT COMMAND

The Pathfinder Intersect command removes all parts of paths that do not intersect, leaving only the intersecting paths remaining. This is a quick way to remove extraneous or overhanging areas without having to edit and redraw the paths.

For example, suppose you have two shapes that overlap, such as a letter

X and a box with a solid fill. You would like the fill to appear only in the parts of the X that overlap the box. You would create the letter X, convert it to an outline, create the box, and then place the box over the letter X. The Intersect command will pick only the parts that overlap and discard the rest, such as the serifs on the X.

You can use the Intersect command on multiple objects; however only the areas in which all the objects intersect will remain. If only two objects out of the group intersect, for instance, no paths will be selected.

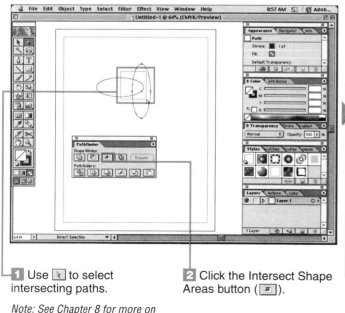

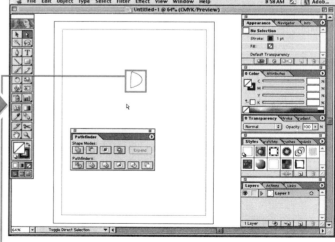

1 Use 🔲 to select intersecting paths.

Note: See Chapter 8 for more on selecting paths.

2 Click the Intersect Shape Areas button (🔲).

■ Only the intersecting areas remain.

Note: This action does not delete the other paths; you can still work with them by selecting them again.

USING THE EXCLUDE COMMAND

The Pathfinder Exclude command removes intersecting areas that have been selected. It works as the opposite of the Intersect command, and is often used to join together closed areas, such as overlapping text that has been converted to paths. In effect, it deletes the intersecting areas, leaving behind only those parts that did not have the misfortune to intersect.

You use the Exclude command to remove areas and create a "negative space" effect without having to create masks or inverse objects or elements. In the example in "Using the Intersect Command," you would create the letter and the box, then apply the effect. Depending on which object was in front, the non-overlapping areas would remain and be filled with the color from the topmost object.

If you use the Exclude command on multiple overlapping objects, you may have multiple areas of included or excluded paths; there is no requirement that all objects intersect in order for the Exclude command to apply.

USING THE EXCLUDE COMMAND

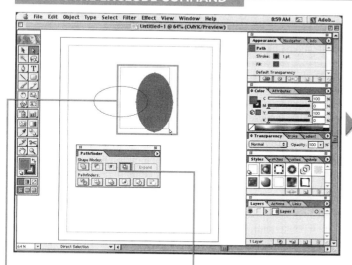

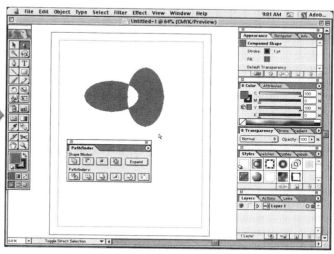

1 Use  to select intersecting paths.

Note: See Chapter 8 for more on selecting paths.

2 Click the Exclude Shape Areas button (□).

■ The selected areas remain.

CREATE A COMPOUND PATH

A compound path contains two or more open or closed paths that either intersect or create fill areas, which act as transparent pixels to layers or effects underneath the object.

The idea can be a little complicated, but it helps to think of it like rivet holes in a metal beam. The beam is made up of one set of paths, plus another set of closed paths create the rivet holes in the beam. The topmost set of paths (the rivet holes) poke holes in the underlying object or set of paths; this lets you see what lies behind the beam when you look through the rivet holes.

Compound path effects are commonly used for text, such as the capital letter O or lowercase g. They are also used for more complex masking and shadowing effects, such as stained glass window effects.

CREATE A COMPOUND PATH

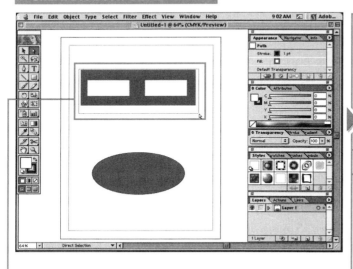

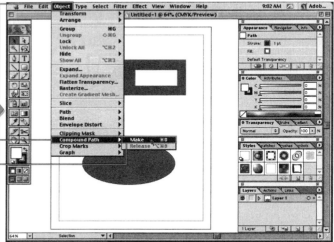

1 Select a group of paths using 🔖 or the Group Selection tool (🔖).

Note: See Chapter 8 for more on selecting objects.

2 Click Object.

3 Click Compound Path.

4 Click Make.

■ The objects become grouped as a compound path.

Note: Fill was added for clarity.

Can I create a compound path out of objects that are members of different groups?

✔ If you want to use objects that are grouped differently, you must either select all the paths in all the groups, or you must ungroup the objects, then add them to your compound path grouping.

Where can I find out more about compound paths?

✔ An excellent resource that goes into depth about compound paths is *Illustrator 10 Bible,* by Ted Alspach and Kelly Murdock, published by Hungry Minds, Inc.

What color or fill is applied to a compound path?

✔ Unlike other Illustrator commands such as Add to Shape or Remove from Shape, compound paths take on the color and fill of the bottommost object in the set of paths. If you have a fill in one object that you want applied, move the object or set of paths to the bottom of the stack.

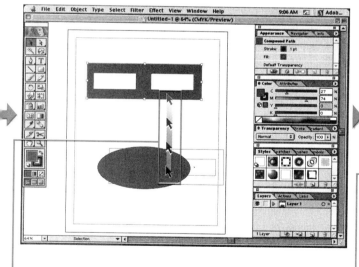

▐5 Click and drag the compound path over another object.

▐6 Release the mouse button.

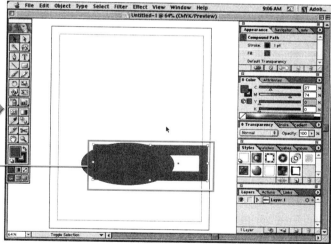

■ The compound path has holes that enable you to see the object underneath.

DRAW A RECTANGLE OR ROUNDED RECTANGLE

Rectangles are one of the most frequently used objects in artwork. Fortunately, with Illustrator they are also the easiest to draw. You can learn most of the basics of working with objects in Illustrator by practicing drawing rectangles. When you are comfortable with rectangles, you can work with other objects in a similar fashion.

A rectangle consists of four line segments connected by four straight corner anchor points. Together, the line segments and anchor points create a *path*. To learn more about paths and anchor points, see Chapter 9. After you draw a rectangle, you can reposition it anywhere in your illustration, or reshape it by selecting it and then scaling it. See

Chapter 8 to learn about selecting objects. The latter sections in this chapter cover how to scale objects.

After you have drawn a rectangle, you can fill it with color or a pattern. To learn how to fill the rectangle with color, see "Fill an Object with Color," later in this chapter.

DRAW A RECTANGLE

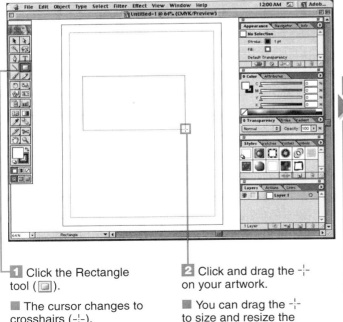

1 Click the Rectangle tool (▣).

■ The cursor changes to crosshairs (-¦-).

2 Click and drag the -¦- on your artwork.

■ You can drag the -¦- to size and resize the rectangle.

3 Release the mouse.

■ A rectangle appears.

■ To draw a square, hold the Shift key while you drag the mouse.

How do I create exact dimensions for rectangles?

✔ You can create exact dimensions for rectangles by selecting a rectangle tool, then clicking the artboard. A dialog box appears, into which you can enter exact dimensions. The ⬛ also lets you specify the rounded corner's radius.

How do I draw a line around my rectangle?

✔ Adding a line around the edge of a rectangle is called "applying a stroke to an object." A *stroke* is a line that has weight and color. Most objects have a default stroke applied to them, but you can change the weight and color as needed for your illustration. You can learn about applying strokes later in this chapter.

Why do I see only blue paths and anchor points in my rectangle?

✔ You may be in Outline mode, which shows only paths, rather than Preview mode, which shows all strokes and fills. To switch between Outline and Preview mode, click View, then Outline or Preview. Pressing Ctrl + Y (Command - Y) also enables you to switch between views.

DRAW A ROUNDED RECTANGLE

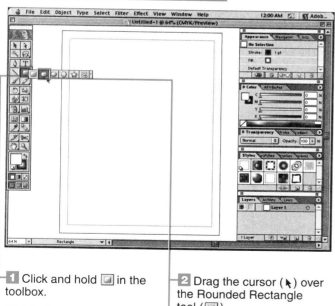

1 Click and hold ⬛ in the toolbox.

■ A toolbar appears underneath ⬛.

2 Drag the cursor (↖) over the Rounded Rectangle tool (⬛).

3 Release the mouse.

■ The ↖ changes to -¦-.

4 Click and drag the -¦- on your artwork.

■ You can drag the -¦- to size and resize the rectangle.

■ A rounded rectangle appears.

■ To draw a square, hold the Shift key while you drag the mouse.

DRAW AN ELLIPSE OR CIRCLE

Ellipses and circles are the next easiest objects to draw in Illustrator. You use the same motion of clicking and dragging diagonally as you use for rectangles and squares, with the ellipse forming from the point of origin to the point where you release the mouse. You can then reposition the ellipse or circle with

a selection tool, or draw a new circle by clicking and dragging again on the artboard.

When drawing a rectangle, one of the corners serves as the starting point so you can easily determine how to draw and position the rectangle. With an ellipse, on the other hand, the origin is a point on

the ellipse, so as you draw, the cursor's crosshairs are outside the ellipse, making it somewhat difficult to determine the ellipse's final shape and position. With practice, however, you can learn to draw and position circles and ellipses with speed and precision.

DRAW AN ELLIPSE OR CIRCLE

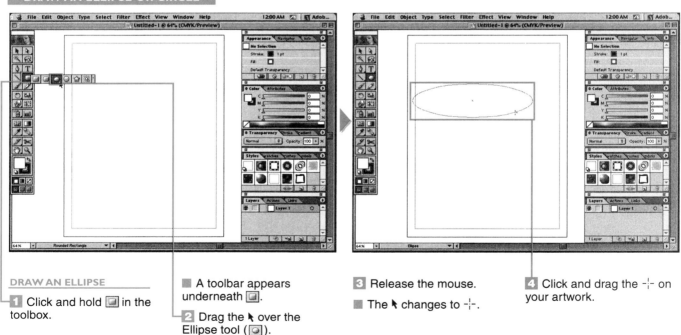

DRAW AN ELLIPSE

■1 Click and hold ◙ in the toolbox.

■ A toolbar appears underneath ◙.

■2 Drag the ▶ over the Ellipse tool (◙).

■3 Release the mouse.

■ The ▶ changes to -¦-.

■4 Click and drag the -¦- on your artwork.

How do I create exact dimensions for ellipses and circles?

✔ You can create exact dimensions for ellipses and circles by clicking 🔘 and then clicking the artboard once. A dialog box appears, into which you can enter exact dimensions for your ellipse. A circle has equal dimensions in the Height and Width boxes.

How do I draw a circle or ellipse from a center point, rather than an edge?

✔ As you click and drag the mouse, hold down the Alt (Option) key. The circle or ellipse starts from its center and grows outward as you drag.

Can I reposition the circle or ellipse as I draw?

✔ Instead of creating your circle or ellipse and then using a selection tool to reposition it, you can hold down the spacebar as you drag the mouse. Doing this lets you use the mouse to position your circle or ellipse in your drawing. To continue drawing, release the spacebar.

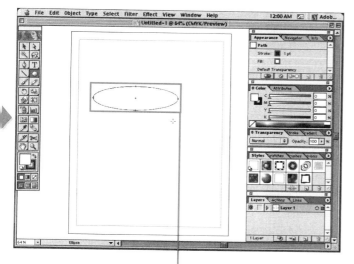

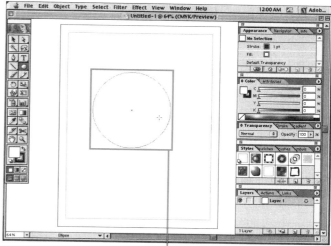

■ You can drag the -¦- to size and resize the ellipse.

5 Release the mouse.

■ An ellipse appears.

DRAW A CIRCLE

1 Repeat steps 1 through 4 from the previous page.

2 Press and hold down the Shift key while you drag the mouse.

■ A circle appears.

DRAW REGULAR POLYGONS

Y ou can draw regular polygons quickly with Illustrator. A *regular polygon* is one whose sides and angles are equal, like a pentagon or hexagon.

To create a polygon, you must specify the radius and the number of sides. A *radius* is the distance between the center and vertex; a

vertex is the point where two lines form an angle. The radius can be specified in thousandths of a unit, whether inches, picas, or pixels. You specify these dimensions in the Polygon dialog box, which you bring up by clicking the artboard. If you click and drag with the Polygon tool, you create a polygon

using the same settings you last specified in that dialog box.

If you want to draw *irregular polygons* — a shape whose sides and angles are not equal, like an isosceles triangle — use the Pen tool. To draw continuous straight lines with the Pen tool, see Chapter 9.

DRAW REGULAR POLYGONS

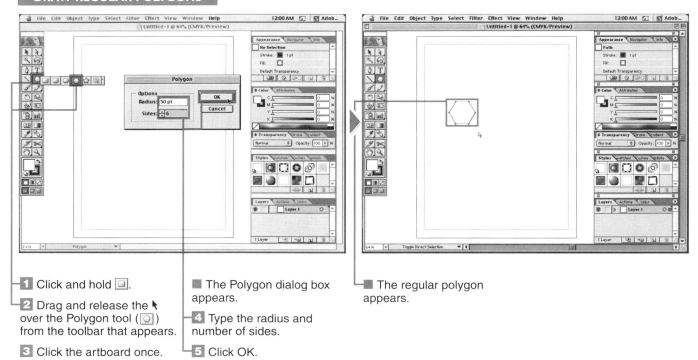

-1 Click and hold [].

-2 Drag and release the ▶ over the Polygon tool ([]) from the toolbar that appears.

-3 Click the artboard once.

■ The Polygon dialog box appears.

-4 Type the radius and number of sides.

-5 Click OK.

■ The regular polygon appears.

DRAW STARS

You can draw stars with nearly any number of points and of any size using the Star tool. Stars are fairly common design elements in artwork, and the Star tool lets you create these images quickly. If you had to create them using the Pen tool, it would take you far longer than simply clicking and dragging.

To create a star, you must specify two radii and the number of points for the star. You specify the radius values by selecting the Star tool, and then clicking the artboard to bring up the Star properties dialog box. Radius 1 is closest to the center, and radius 2 is the farthest point from center.

Illustrator has one "hidden" way to draw stars, polygons, and spirals. Hold down the tilde key (⌐) while you click and drag the mouse; this quickly repeats the star, polygon, or spiral in your artwork, creating a cascading series of images.

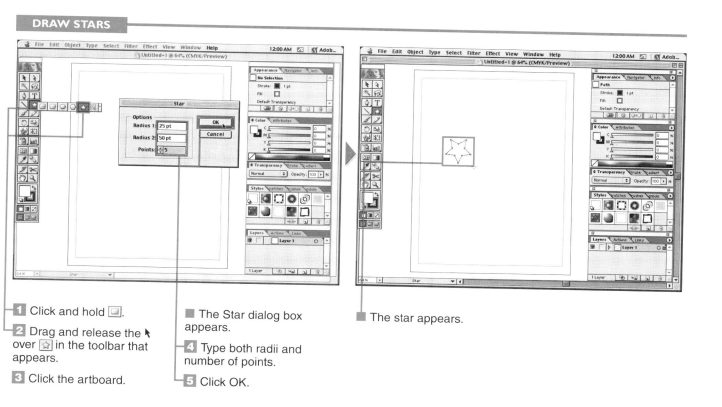

◼ Click and hold ⬜.

◻ Drag and release the ▸ over ☆ in the toolbar that appears.

◼ Click the artboard.

■ The Star dialog box appears.

◻ Type both radii and number of points.

◻ Click OK.

■ The star appears.

CREATE A RECTANGULAR GRID

The Rectangular Grid tool creates rectangular grids of a specified size with a specified number of dividers. You can quickly configure the Rectangular Grid tool for the number of rows and columns you need. Grids can help you organize other objects or elements in your artwork, such as

other illustrations, or to make sure elements are spaced equally throughout a larger image.

You can apply strokes to a rectangular grid's grid lines, apply no stroke at all, or apply fills to the cells. You can also apply a *logarithmic skew* to the grid lines,

which makes cells increase in size from one side to another, or from top to bottom, depending on the skew applied.

If you want to slant your grid, you need to apply shear or apply a free transformation. See the section "Scale an Object," later in this chapter.

CREATE A RECTANGULAR GRID

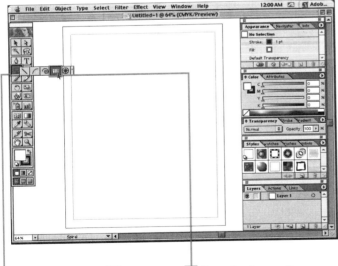

1 Click and hold ▨ in the toolbox.

■ A toolbar appears underneath ▨.

2 Drag the ▶ over the Rectangular Grid tool (▦).

3 Release the mouse.

■ The ▶ changes to ⊹.

4 Click the artboard.

■ The Rectangular Grid Tool Options dialog box appears.

Do I have to enter the new grid settings every time?

✔ Like most of the other tools in the toolbox, the 🔲 remembers the last settings you used. You can click and drag on the artboard to create a grid with the same dimensions as the previous grid.

Is it possible to reset the grid values, rather than adjust them manually?

✔ Some tools provide a hidden way to reset their dialog box's options. When the dialog box is open, press Alt (Option); the Cancel button changes to a Reset button. Click the Reset button to return the dialog box values to their defaults.

Can I draw multiple grids at once?

✔ Yes. The easiest way to draw multiple grids simultaneously is to click the artboard with the mouse where you will place each grid and then click OK. Doing this creates multiple grids each time you click. If you prefer a flashier, but arguably less useful way, hold down the tilde key and then click and drag.

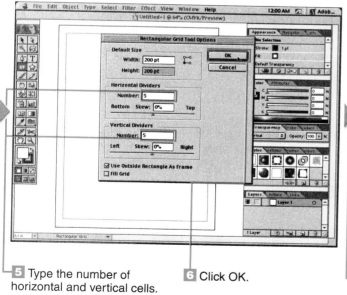

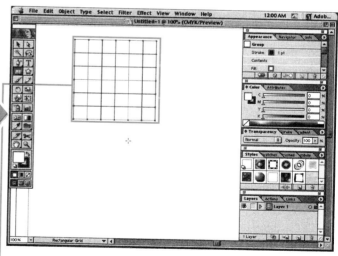

5 Type the number of horizontal and vertical cells.

■ The number of cells is one more than the number of dividers.

6 Click OK.

■ A rectangular grid appears in your artwork.

ROTATE AN OBJECT

Illustrator comes with a default alignment for many objects, and uses these constrain angle features to let you draw objects to fixed angle dimensions — typically multiples of 45 degrees. But you may need to rotate an object to another alignment, such as objects that fade to a vanishing point in your illustration. You can rotate an object with the Rotate tool to align it with other elements in your artwork or to have it follow a certain line in your art.

You can also rotate paths or grouped objects with the Rotate tool. You select the paths or grouped objects using one of the selection tools, and then apply the Rotate Object command.

The rotation will normally be applied around the center of the object, but you can move the rotation point to anywhere on the artboard, enabling you to change rotation with respect to another point in your illustration.

ROTATE AN OBJECT

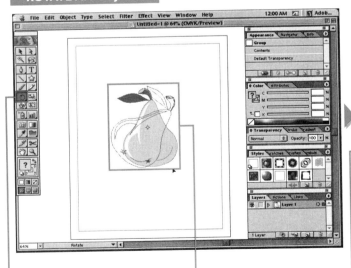

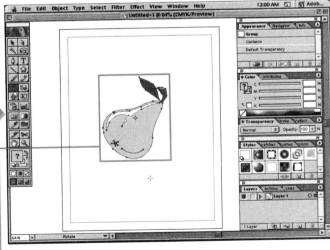

1 Draw an object with an Illustrator tool.

Note: See the previous sections in this chapter to draw shapes.

2 Click the Rotate tool ( ) in the toolbox.

3 Click and drag an object on the artboard.

■ The object rotates around its center.

4 Release the mouse.

■ The object keeps its new orientation.

■ To rotate around a different point than the object's center, first click a point on the artboard, then click and drag the object.

REFLECT AN OBJECT

You can *reflect* an object to align it with other elements in your artwork. Reflecting an object makes it flip along an imaginary axis; a left-facing person can be flipped to face right, for instance, or the sun could rise in the west instead of the east. Reflecting an object is much easier than redrawing an object as a mirror image of itself.

Illustrator reflects objects three different ways: horizontal, or left-to-right; vertical, or top-to-bottom; and to a custom angle.

The Reflect command also lets you reflect a copy, keeping the original in its starting alignment. This is an excellent way to make a duplicate and see how it looks in your

artwork; reflect it, then position it as needed in your illustration.

When you reflect a group of objects, the front-to-back alignment is preserved, and only the object's alignment with respect to itself is flipped. In other words, if one object is on top of another, it will still be on top in the reflected grouping.

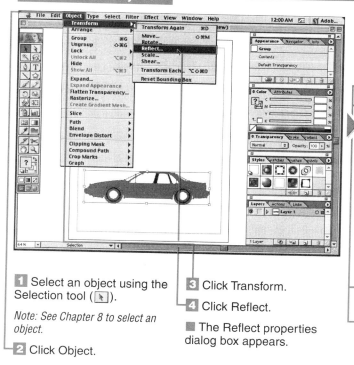

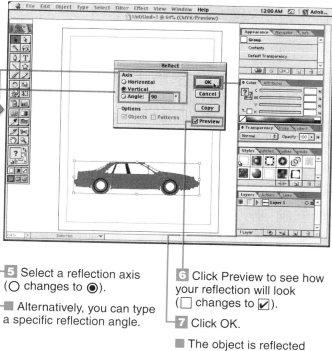

■ **1** Select an object using the Selection tool (▨).

Note: See Chapter 8 to select an object.

2 Click Object.

3 Click Transform.

4 Click Reflect.

■ The Reflect properties dialog box appears.

5 Select a reflection axis (○ changes to ◉).

■ Alternatively, you can type a specific reflection angle.

6 Click Preview to see how your reflection will look (□ changes to ☑).

7 Click OK.

■ The object is reflected along the axis you selected.

SCALE AN OBJECT

Y ou may find, after drawing an object in one size, that you need to resize the object to make it fit your artwork. You can resize objects by *scaling* them. Scaling an object enlarges or reduces it horizontally (along the x axis), vertically (along the y axis), or both horizontally and vertically. The scaling effect is relative to the point of origin you designate; the

default point of origin is the object's center point, but you can select another point in your artwork by clicking anywhere on the artboard.

In the Scale properties dialog box, you can specify to scale the object uniformly or non-uniformly. *Uniform* scaling maintains the proportions of your objects, so the

width and height are still proportional to each other. *Non-uniform* scaling lets you scale objects without respect to the proportions.

If you have a stroke or effect applied to your object, you can select the option to scale the strokes and effects along with your object.

SCALE AN OBJECT

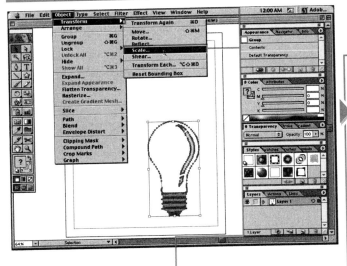

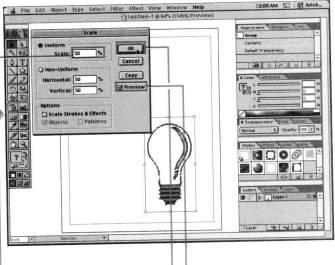

SCALE USING OBJECT PROPERTIES

■1 Select an object using ▶.

Note: See Chapter 8 to select an object.

■2 Click Object.

■3 Click Transform.

■4 Click Scale.

■ The Scale properties dialog box appears.

■5 Type the scaling percentage you want to apply to the object.

■ You can click Preview (☐ changes to ☑) to see how your scaled object will look.

■6 Click OK.

Can I use the bounding box to scale objects?

✔ The bounding box resizes but does not scale objects; dragging on a bounding box handle does not maintain a precise relationship among the component parts. If you need precision, you should uniformly scale instead of using the bounding box.

How do I apply shear?

✔ You can apply *shear* to an object to slant it in a different direction. You can do this to help force perspective or to add a feeling of motion to objects. Click and hold the Scale tool (📇) and then drag over the Shear tool (📑). You can then click and drag anywhere on an object and apply shear to it; the last Shear settings you used are applied.

How do I scale several objects at once?

✔ Select your objects using one of the selection tools. Then, click Object, Transform, and then Transform Each. After that, type your scaling percentages in the boxes or drag the sliders to set the percentage. Select the Preview option to see how your scaling looks. When you are finished, click OK.

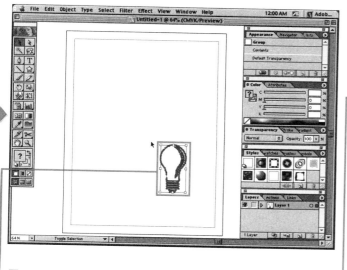

■ Your object rescales.

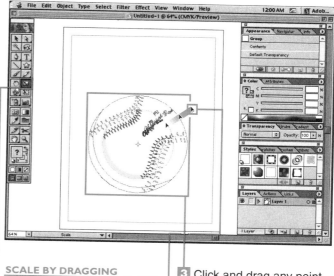

SCALE BY DRAGGING

1 Click the Scale tool (📇).

2 Click the artboard to set the scaling point.

3 Click and drag any point on the object.

4 Release the mouse.

■ Your object rescales.

MOVE OBJECTS FORWARD AND BACKWARD

When you work with overlapping objects, you work with the order in which they appear in a stack. Stacking order affects a number of other functions in Illustrator, such as which fill is applied during Intersect and Exclude commands, or how a mask is applied to other objects. Because stacking order is important in determining how the objects interrelate and how commands are applied, you need the ability to move objects forward and back in the stack.

You can use the Bring Forward and Send Back commands to move objects forward and backward to change stacking order. You can also have an object jump straight to the back or bring it all the way forward with the Send to Back or Bring to Front commands. These four commands give you the freedom to move objects without having to redraw them in a different order.

MOVE AN OBJECT FORWARD

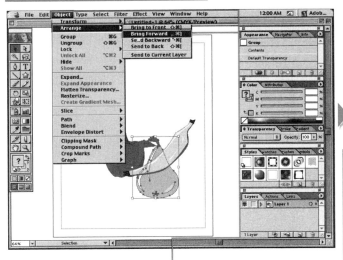

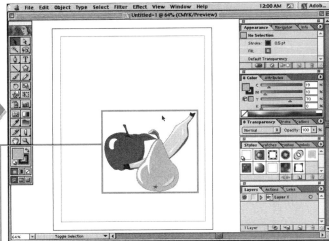

1 Select an object that is overlapped by another using ▶ or ▶.

Note: See Chapter 8 to select an object.

2 Click Object.

3 Click Arrange.

4 Click Bring Forward.

■ The selected object moves forward one position in the stack.

■ Pressing Ctrl +] (Command -]) quickly moves the object forward.

■ Pressing Ctrl + Shift +] (Command - Shift -]) quickly moves the object to the front.

Can I choose where to paste objects from the clipboard?

✔ You can paste to the front of a stack from the clipboard by pressing Ctrl + F (Command - F) or to the bottom of a stack by pressing Ctrl + B (Command - B).

When I place type in my document, how is it placed with respect to other objects?

✔ The first letter you enter in your document is on the bottom of a stack that consists only of the type. The last letter you enter is on the top. When you convert text to outlines, you can move letters in the stack. See Chapter 11 to convert text to outlines, or to modify type.

What order are my objects created in?

✔ The first object you draw is on the bottom of an imaginary stack. The last object you draw is the topmost object in the stack.

Why is my object not moving behind another object?

✔ You may have your objects on different layers, rather than overlapping in the same layer. See Chapter 13 for more information on moving objects between layers.

MOVE AN OBJECT BACKWARD

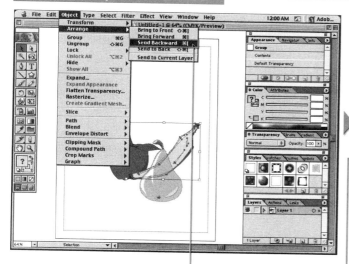

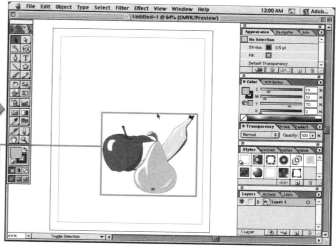

1 Repeat steps 1 through 3 on the previous page.

2 Click Send Backward.

■ The selected object moves back one position in the stack.

■ You can press Ctrl + [(Command - [ ) to quickly move the object backward.

■ You can press Ctrl + Shift + [(Command - Shift - [ ) to quickly send the object to the back.

GROUP AND UNGROUP OBJECTS

Frequently you may want to treat separate objects as a group, either for moving them around in your illustration or applying effects to them. You do this by grouping or ungrouping objects.

When you group objects together, you create a single rectangular bounding box around the set of objects. This box lets you resize the grouped objects. You can also apply

transformation commands to the group, such as Scale, Rotate, or Reflect.

You can use the Group command to add a group to another set of objects, thereby creating a hierarchy of objects. For example, you can have all the knickknacks on a table grouped together, group the objects with the table, and then group the table with the sofa. You can then treat the entire group as a

single object and move it around your drawing of the living room.

The Ungroup command separates objects out into the original components. It is also a hierarchical command; if you ungroup the sofa group, the sofa and table are now two objects, while the table and the knickknacks remain grouped together.

GROUP OBJECTS

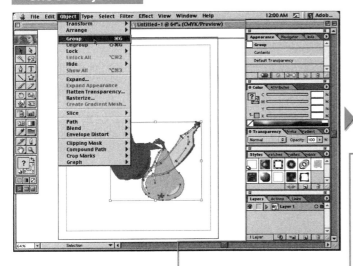

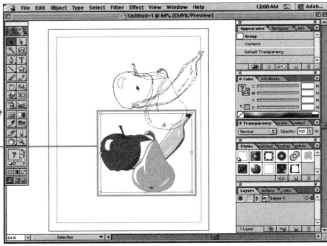

1 Select the objects you want to make part of the group using any of the selection tools.

Note: See Chapter 8 to select an object.

2 Click Object.

3 Click Group.

■ The objects are linked together as a group.

What happens when I group together objects from different layers?

✔ When you group together objects from different layers, they all move to the top layer and form a group there. The stacking order changes, and your artwork's appearance rearranges itself. You can press Command-Z if you did not intend to group objects from different layers.

How do I select objects of one type?

✔ You can select objects that are similar in appearance, such as the same fill. From the menu, click Select, Same, and then Fill Color. This method often grabs objects that are similar in appearance. If not, use the Direct Selection tool to add objects to your selection. See Chapter 8 to learn more about the Direct Selection tool.

Can I select objects within a group without ungrouping it?

✔ The Group Selection tool can be used to select one or more objects from a set of grouped objects without ungrouping it. Click and hold ▣ until a tear-away toolbar appears; drag ▸ over ▣ and release it. Then use the Group Selection tool to select an object within a group.

UNGROUP OBJECTS

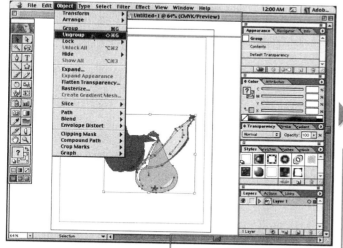

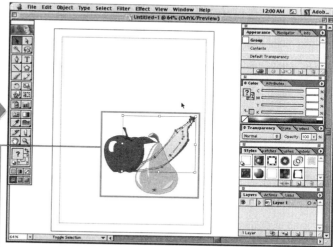

1 Select the group of objects using any of the selection tools.

Note: See Chapter 8 to select an object.

2 Click Object.

3 Click Ungroup.

■ The individual objects are ungrouped.

APPLY THE ENVELOPE DISTORT TOOL

Envelopes are objects that distort or reshape selected objects. The Envelope Distort tool enables you to create an envelope out of any path you draw. You can then use this envelope to warp text, images, or other elements with the envelope.

You can make an envelope out of objects on your artboard, or you can use a preset warp shape or a mesh object as an envelope. You can use envelopes with paths, compound paths, text objects, meshes, blends, and raster images. After you apply an envelope, you can continue to edit the original objects. At any time, you can also edit, delete, or expand an envelope.

The Envelope Distort tool is extremely useful for warping type into nonstandard shapes. Even though Illustrator ships with a number of configurable warping effects, the Envelope Distort tool allows you to reshape type using any other shape at all, such as a company logo.

APPLY THE ENVELOPE DISTORT TOOL

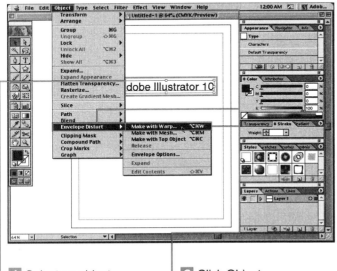

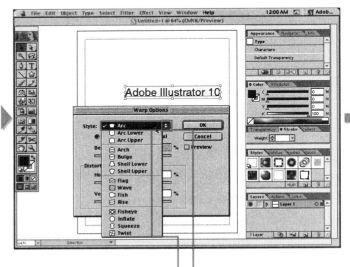

1 Select an object using ▶.

Note: For more on selecting objects, see Chapter 8.

2 Click Object.

3 Click Envelope Distort.

4 Click Make with Warp.

■ The Warp Options dialog box appears.

5 Click ⬆ or ⬇ to display warp effects.

6 Click the effect you want.

What other settings can I adjust for the Envelope Distort tool?

✔ You can change a number of other Envelope Distort settings:

Option	Action
Style	Changes the warping type
Alignment	Switches between horizontal and vertical alignment
Bend	Changes the degree of curve in your distortion
Distortion	Changes the horizontal (left-to-right) distortion effect or the vertical (top-to-bottom) alignment

✔ You can also specify a Fidelity percentage to indicate how precisely you want the object to fit the envelope mold. Increasing the Fidelity percentage can add more points to the distorted paths and increase the time it takes to distort the objects. Select Distort Linear Gradients or Distort Pattern Fills if you want to distort the respective fill type.

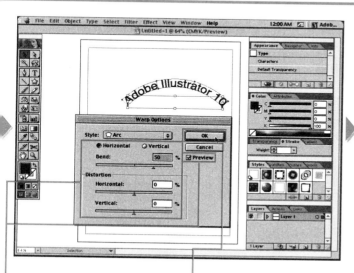

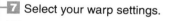

7 Select your warp settings.

8 Click Preview to see the effects of your settings (○ changes to ◉).

9 Click OK.

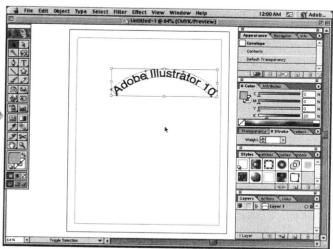

■ Your Envelope Distort settings take effect.

Note: You can edit the underlying object without having to delete and reapply the Envelope Distort effect.

USING THE LIQUEFY TOOLS

The Liquefy tools provide seven new warping effects, from twirls to crystallization or wrinkles. These effects are somewhat different than the other warping effects, in that they are area based. The other Illustrator warping tools are used to warp paths using a predefined geometric shape, such as an arc or a curve. These tools reshape your paths,

such as text or a particular digital image, to fit the predefined (but configurable) shape.

The Liquefy tools affect an area or region of your image or text. They are more freeform than the other Warp tools, enabling you to place the effect's center point anywhere in the image (the Pucker tool), or to continuously apply the effect until

you release the mouse (the Twirl tool).

Mastering the Liquefy tools may require some experimentation to discover what works best on a particular image. In many cases, the adage "less is more" applies, especially for extremely destructive warping effects like Twirl.

USING THE LIQUEFY TOOLS

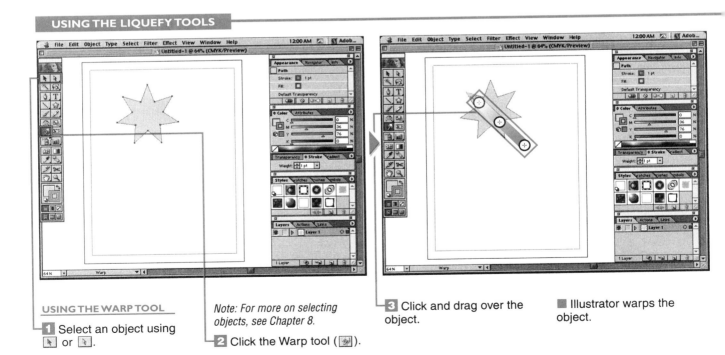

USING THE WARP TOOL

1 Select an object using ⬚ or ⬚.

Note: For more on selecting objects, see Chapter 8.

2 Click the Warp tool (⬚).

3 Click and drag over the object.

■ Illustrator warps the object.

What other Liquefy tools are available?

✔ Illustrator provides seven different warping effects:

Option	Action
Warp	Creates localized warping
Twirl	Spins an object around a point
Pucker	Distorts an image around a point
Bloat	Bulges an image out from a point
Scallop	Creates scalloped edges around an object
Crystallize	Creates shard-like object effects
Wrinkle	Adds wrinkles to objects

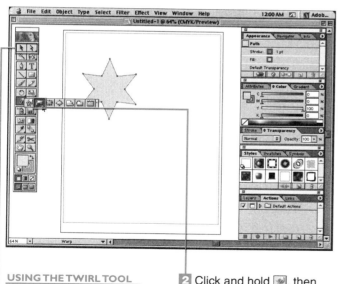

USING THE TWIRL TOOL

1 Select an object using ▶ or ▶.

Note: For more on selecting objects, see Chapter 8.

2 Click and hold 🖳, then click the Twirl tool (⊙) from the toolbar that appears.

3 Click and hold over the object.

■ Illustrator twirls the object.

■ The longer you hold the mouse button, the more the effect twirls the object.

STROKE AN OBJECT

When you create a path or object in Illustrator, you can assign a *stroke* to it. In Illustrator, a stroke is the name for the visible line that appears in Preview mode. You can stroke an object or a set of paths when you want to outline it and make it visible, when you want to highlight an object, or when an object has no fill color.

Illustrator offers several stroke properties that you can adjust in the Stroke palette, with the most common one being the stroke weight. By default, Illustrator paths have a stroke weight of 1 point, which is sufficient to make a line visible in preview mode.

You can enter a value in inches (in), millimeters (mm), centimeters

(cm), or picas (pi), and Illustrator converts it to an equal value in points. Illustrator strokes a path by centering the stroke on the path; half of the stroke appears on one side of the path, and the other half of the stroke appears on the other side of the path.

If you enter a weight of 0, Illustrator changes the stroke weight to None.

STROKE AN OBJECT

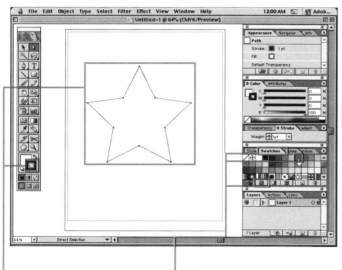

ADD A STROKE TO AN OBJECT

■1 Select the object using a selection tool.

Note: See Chapter 8 to select an object.

■2 Click the Stroke box (■).

■3 Click the Swatches palette tab.

■4 Click a color swatch.

■ You can click [🔲] to display only the color swatches, not the gradients or patterns.

■ Illustrator strokes the object with the selected color.

■ You may have to deselect the object by clicking Select, and then Deselect, to see the stroke.

■ You can remove the stroke by selecting the object and clicking ◪.

How can I customize the corners of my stroked lines?

✔ You can customize corners by adjusting the options in the Stroke palette. Clicking the Round Join button (⊞) rounds the corners of a stroke, and clicking the Bevel Join button (⊞) squares off your corners. With a Miter Limit, you can determine at what point Illustrator makes a standard corner beveled. A limit of 4 squares a corner when the corner length is at least four times the stroke width.

What are the size limits on stroked lines?

✔ You can have strokes anywhere between 1,000 points and ¹⁄₁,₀₀₀ point. Realistically speaking, the printed stroke size depends on the capabilities of your output device; a stroke with a size of .001 points displays as 1 pixel onscreen, and varies drastically in size on a desktop printer at 600 dpi or an imagesetter at 1,270 dpi. You should be very wary if you are specifying especially thin stroke weights.

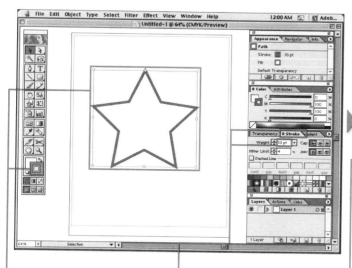

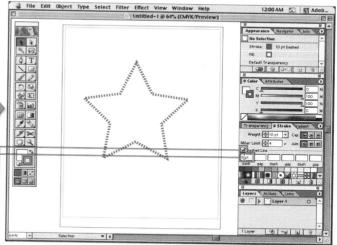

CUSTOMIZE A STROKE

1 Select the object using a selection tool.

Note: See Chapter 8 to select an object.

2 Click ▣.

3 Click the Stroke palette tab.

4 Type a Weight.

5 Press the Enter (Return) key.

■ The thickness of the stroke changes.

6 Click Dashed Line (□ changes to ☑).

7 Type a dash size.

8 Press the Enter (Return) key.

■ The stroke becomes dashed.

PAINT WITH AN ART BRUSH

An *art brush* is Illustrator's name for a brush that applies a piece of artwork to your illustration. You can make this object a simple stripe of color, or a detailed piece of artwork. The art brush stretches an object along the length of a path you have drawn in

your work, and as you paint with the brush the artwork follows the path. You can change the direction and size of objects painted along a path with an art brush and also flip the object along the path or across the path.

For example, suppose you want to use a ski pole as a border around some text. You can first create a new art brush using a ski pole and then paint with the new brush around your text. The art brush stretches your ski pole from the start point to the end point.

PAINT WITH AN ART BRUSH

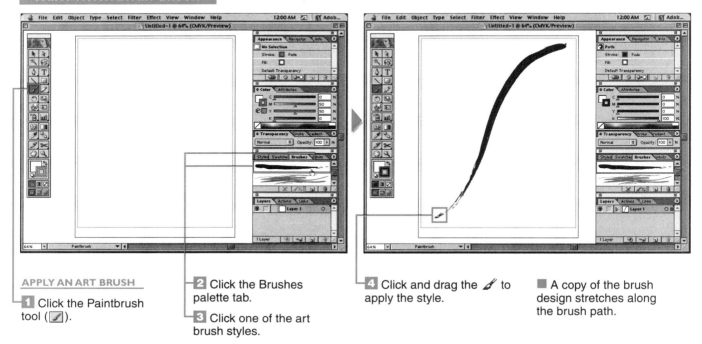

APPLY AN ART BRUSH

1 Click the Paintbrush tool (🖌).

2 Click the Brushes palette tab.

3 Click one of the art brush styles.

4 Click and drag the 🖌 to apply the style.

■ A copy of the brush design stretches along the brush path.

How can I access more brush styles?
✔ Illustrator comes with dozens of predefined brushes. Click Window, Brush Libraries, and then Brush Set in the list. The set of brushes opens in a new palette.

How do I create a new type of brush in the Brushes palette?
✔ Click ▶ in the Brushes palette and then click New Brush. Illustrator prompts you to select a brush type and then the brush options. You can also duplicate an existing brush and customize that brush. Click a brush to duplicate in the Brushes palette, then click ▶ and click Duplicate Brush.

How do I avoid filling in the curves of my painted lines?
✔ If you have a fill color defined as you paint with a brush, you may see fill color in places where your line curves, especially if the fill color is different from the background. You can avoid this by turning off the fill color. To turn off the color, click the Fill box (□) in the Toolbox and then click ⊘ in the Color palette.

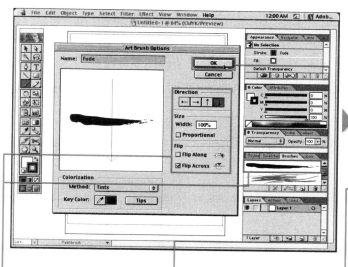

CUSTOMIZE AN ART BRUSH

1 Double-click an art brush to open its dialog box.

2 Specify the Art Brush options:

Direction buttons (←, →, ↑, ↓) set the end of the stroke.

Size specifies the art width.

Flip changes the orientation of the painted art (□ changes to ✔).

3 Click OK.

4 Click and drag the 🖌 to apply the customized art brush.

■ The art stretches along the path according to your selected options.

FILL AN OBJECT WITH COLOR

A *fill* is the name for a color or pattern that is used inside an object. Applying a fill places color within the object to create areas of solid color, as opposed to outlines. Using the Swatches palette, you can either apply an existing color or use the Color Picker to fine-tune your color choice with various tools.

If you apply a color, you can also select the transparency. After filling an object, select the Transparency palette and then type a transparency value in the Opacity box. You can then see the objects behind the one being filled, in effect making the filled object transparent. Transparency values range from completely transparent at 0% to completely opaque at 100%.

To learn more about using color in digital images, see Chapter 3. That chapter also provides specific information about using Web-safe color for images destined for the Web.

FILL AN OBJECT WITH COLOR

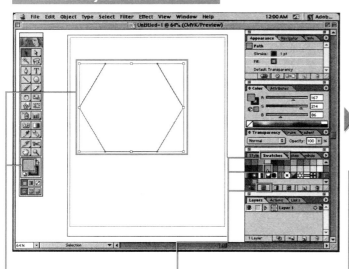

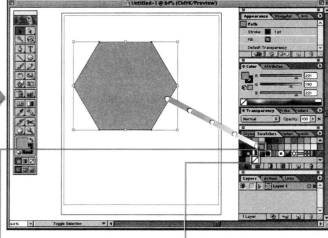

SELECT AND FILL AN OBJECT

1 Select an object using a selection tool.

Note: See Chapter 8 to select an object.

2 Click the Fill box (☐).

3 Click the Swatches palette tab.

4 Click a color swatch.

■ You can click the Show Color Swatches button (🔲) to display only the color swatches, not the gradients or patterns.

■ Illustrator fills the object with the selected color.

■ You can also apply color by clicking and dragging a color swatch onto an object.

■ You can remove an applied color by clicking the "none" swatch (⊠).

Can I apply fills only to closed paths or objects?

✔ Illustrator lets you apply fills to almost any path. If the path is open with two end points, Illustrator applies a fill between the two end anchor points, to an imaginary straight line drawn between the two points, and to the line itself.

Why do I not see the fill I just applied?

✔ You may be working in Outline mode, which shows only paths. You must use Preview mode to view fills. You can switch to Preview mode by clicking View and then Preview. You can also use the shortcut keys Ctrl + Y (Command - Y) to switch between modes.

How can I find more predefined colors with which to fill objects?

✔ Illustrator comes with dozens of predefined colors for filling objects. From the menu bar, click Window, Swatch Libraries, and then click a swatch set in the list. The set of swatches appears in a new palette.

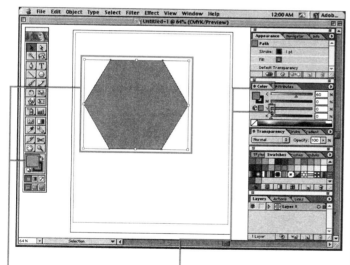

EDIT A COLOR USING THE COLOR PALETTE

1 Select an object using a Selection tool.

Note: See Chapter 8 to select an object.

2 Click □.

3 Click the Color palette tab.

4 Click and drag the ▲ to adjust the color.

■ The object's fill color changes.

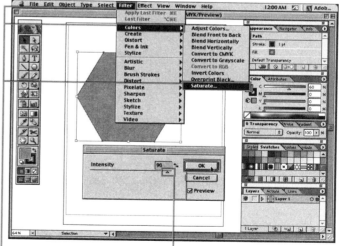

USING THE SATURATE FILTER

1 Select an object.

2 Click Filter.

3 Click Colors.

4 Click Saturate.

■ The Saturate dialog box appears.

5 Click and drag the Intensity slider.

6 Click OK.

■ The intensity of the object's color changes.

FILL AN OBJECT WITH A GRADIENT

You can fill an object with a gradient to give your artwork a shaded or 3D effect. Gradients are among the most powerful effects you can apply, smoothly blending colors across your illustration, or seamlessly integrating objects into a background around the edges. Gradients enable you to easily apply shadows or shading by applying a grayscale gradient. They also help you add contrasting color to an otherwise sedate color scheme.

You can create gradients that blend two colors, as illustrated below, or more than two colors. Illustrator supports a gradient of up to 32 colors, although for most purposes two or three gradients prove sufficient for most of your work.

Illustrator lets you apply two basic types of gradients: *linear*, in which the gradient flows from one side to another, and *radial*, in which the gradient flows from a central point outward.

As with other fills, you can change the opacity to give your gradient a more subtle and transparent feel.

FILL AN OBJECT WITH A GRADIENT

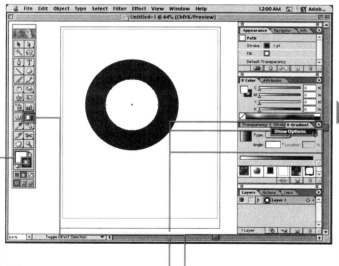

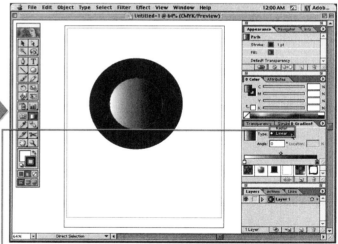

■ Select an object using a selection tool.

Note: See Chapter 8 to select an object.

■ Click ☐.

■ Click the Gradient tool (▣).

■ Click the Gradient palette tab.

■ Click ▣ in the Gradient palette and then click Show Options.

■ Click ▣ or ▣ and select a gradient Type.

■ A linear gradient blends colors along a straight line while a radial gradient blends them out from a center point.

How can I apply a predefined gradient?

✔ Illustrator provides several predefined gradients in the Swatches palette. Click to select an object, click ▢ in the toolbox, and then click a gradient in the Swatches palette. After applying a gradient fill, you can customize it using the Gradient palette.

Can I apply a gradient to a stroke?

✔ Gradients apply only to fills, not to strokes, text objects, or patterns. If you want to apply a gradient to a text object, you first need to convert it to an outline. See Chapter 11 for details.

How do I add another color to the Gradient palette?

✔ To add another color to the Gradient palette, double-click the palette. A new color stop appears, along with a gradient midpoint. The new sliders can be moved along the palette, customizing the gradient fill and its blend at midpoint. To delete a color from the palette, click and drag the color stop downward off the palette.

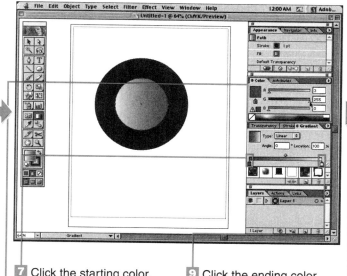

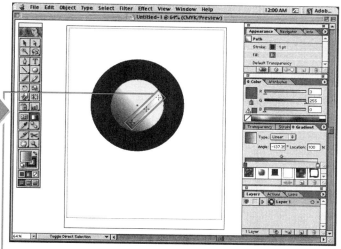

7 Click the starting color.

8 Define the starting color using the Color palette.

9 Click the ending color.

10 Define the ending color using the Color palette.

11 Click and drag the -⊢- over the selected object to specify the angle and location of the gradient.

■ Illustrator fills the gradient per your specifications.

ADJUST OBJECT OPACITY

*O*bject opacity refers to the ability for light or other objects to be seen through the object. When an object is opaque, nothing shows through it; when it is transparent, on the other hand, you can see other objects or effects through it. Sometimes opacity and transparency are often referred to together, even though

they mean the opposite of each other.

You can adjust an object's opacity to allow elements below it to show through, giving glass or liquid elements in your artwork a transparent feel. When your object is 5 percent opaque, it is 95 percent transparent. This state gives a very

light wash of color or ghostly shape in your artwork.

If you make an object semi-transparent but still cannot see other objects behind it, try moving the objects forward and back in the stacking order until you get the effect you need.

ADJUST OBJECT OPACITY

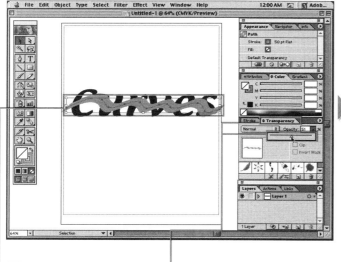

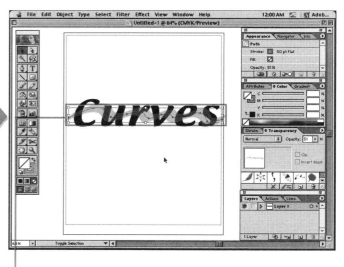

1 Select the object using a Selection tool.

Note: See Chapter 8 to select an object.

2 Click the Transparency palette tab.

3 Click and drag the Opacity slider (▲), or type a value from 0 to 100.

■ The opacity of the object changes.

ADJUST BLENDING OF AN OBJECT

You can adjust the blending of an object to control how its colors combine with elements below it. You can use blending to apply interesting overlapping effects to your art. Blending makes overlapping objects interact with each other; rather than applying a fill or placing a semitransparent object over another, you can choose how your objects' colors affect one another.

The blending mode menu has a variety of settings, with which you can experiment to create interesting effects. Some of the effects are numerical calculations based on a color's values in a channel; other effects work with hue and saturation values. See the online help for a description of what effects the options will have on various colors.

You can also adjust the opacity of your selected object, and further increase the number of effects you can have when blending objects together.

Note: See Chapter 8 to select an object.

ADJUST BLENDING OF AN OBJECT

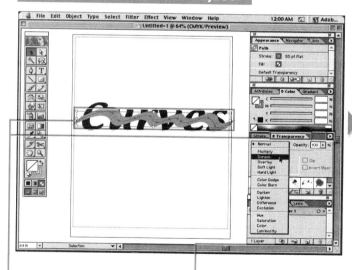

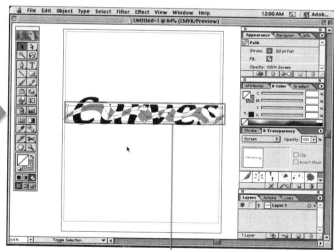

■1 Select the object using a selection tool.

Note: See Chapter 8 to select an object.

■2 Click the Transparency palette tab.

■3 Click ▶ and click a blend mode.

■ Normal, the default mode, prevents overlapping layers from blending.

■ Multiply has a darkening effect where colors overlap, but Screen has a lightening effect.

■ Exclusion creates a photonegative effect where light colors overlap.

■ The selected object blends with objects below it.

CREATE A SYMBOL

A *symbol* is an art object that you store in the Symbols palette and reuse in a document. For example, if you create a symbol from a flower, you can then add *instances* of that symbol multiple times to your artwork without actually adding the complex art multiple times. Each symbol instance is linked to the symbol in the palette. If you use

the same artwork multiple times within a document, symbols save time and greatly reduce file size.

You can create symbols from any Illustrator art object, including paths, compound paths, text, images, objects, and groups of objects.

After you create a symbol, you can edit the symbol's instances on the

artboard and, if you want, redefine the original symbol with the edits. To edit symbols in your artwork, you must first break the link between the symbol and its source in the Symbols palette. Then you can edit your symbol using any of the editing tools. If you want your changes to affect the original symbol, you can update it.

CREATE A SYMBOL

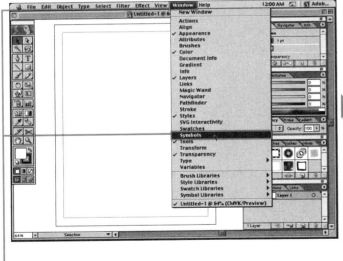

1 Click Window.

2 Click Symbols.

■ The Symbol palette appears.

■ You can also press Shift + F11 to open the Symbols palette.

3 Select an object you want to use as a symbol.

Note: See Chapter 8 to learn about selecting objects.

4 Click ▣.

■ The Options menu appears.

5 Click New Symbol.

How can I tell what the different palette symbols are?

✔ When you name your symbol, you should give it a name that is informative and short; nondescript names do not help, especially when you switch to the small or large list view. You can switch the palette view from thumbnail — the default — to a small or large list view by clicking ▣ and then clicking the appropriate view from the list. A check mark appears next to the currently selected view.

What kinds of symbols can I add to the palette?

✔ Even though you can use any kind of artwork, simpler is often better. You may even want to add artwork that you expect to reuse often as a repeating motif. You can turn a corporate logo into a symbol, for example, or use an object you spent hours tweaking and modifying but do not expect to edit again in the near future. All of these are good candidates for symbols.

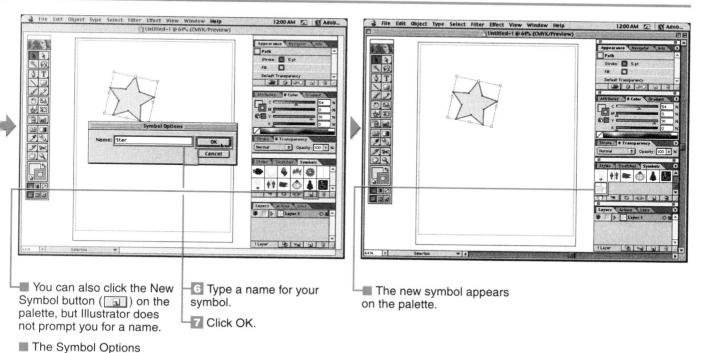

■ You can also click the New Symbol button (▣) on the palette, but Illustrator does not prompt you for a name.

■ The Symbol Options dialog box appears.

6 Type a name for your symbol.

7 Click OK.

■ The new symbol appears on the palette.

INSERT AND DELETE SYMBOLS

You can easily insert symbols into your artwork or delete unused ones from the Symbols palette. When you insert a symbol from the Symbols palette into your artwork, you create a *symbol instance* in your art. A symbol instance acts as a reference to the palette object and it inherits its appearance and effects from the master symbol. If you insert multiple symbol instances into an illustration, you do not insert the entire symbol, but a reference back to the master symbol. This way you do not insert five identical complex drawings of stars in an illustration.

When you delete a symbol from the palette, you have a choice to make.

Any existing symbol instances in your artwork can either remain in your illustration or be deleted. Without the master symbol in the palette, the symbol instances lack a reference; if you elect to keep the instances, Illustrator inserts a full copy of the symbol into your artwork.

INSERT AND DELETE SYMBOLS

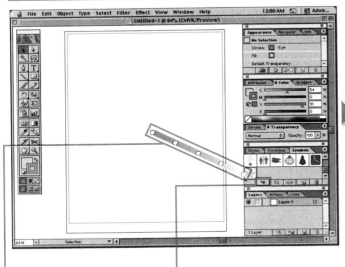

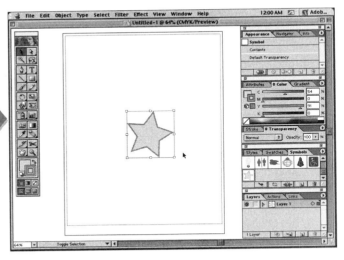

INSERT A SYMBOL

1 Click and drag a symbol from the Symbol palette onto your artwork.

2 Release the mouse button.

■ You can also click a symbol and then click the Place Symbol Instance button (□) on the palette.

■ Your symbol appears on the artwork.

■ Illustrator maintains a link between the symbol instance and the original symbol on the Symbols palette.

What should I do if symbol instances remain in my artwork after I delete a symbol from the Symbols palette?

✔ A warning dialog box displays your available options. Click Expand Instances if you want to break the symbol links and leave the symbols in your art as standalone objects, or Delete Instances if you want to get rid of the symbol instances altogether. Click Cancel if you do not want to delete the symbol from the palette. Keeping individual instances in your artwork enables you to edit or modify each one separately.

Do I have to update the original if I modify an instance?

✔ No. You do not have to update the original symbol each time you modify an instance. If you are working on a symbol that you use frequently, however, such as a company logo, you may want to create a new symbol from the modified one, so that you can switch between them easily.

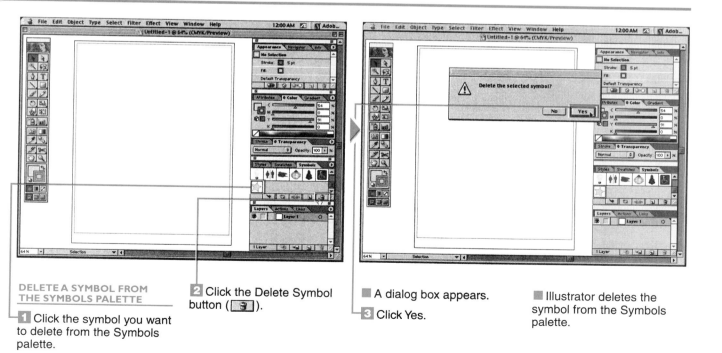

DELETE A SYMBOL FROM THE SYMBOLS PALETTE

■1 Click the symbol you want to delete from the Symbols palette.

■2 Click the Delete Symbol button (🗑).

■ A dialog box appears.

■3 Click Yes.

■ Illustrator deletes the symbol from the Symbols palette.

APPLY SYMBOL EFFECTS

Illustrator provides several symbolism tools that you can apply as symbol effects. These effects are modifications that apply solely to symbols and range from spraying symbols onto your artwork to resizing symbols on the fly.

Symbolism tools affect only the symbol or symbols selected in the Symbols palette. For example, if you create a mixed symbol instance set that represents a meadow with grass and flowers, you can change the orientation of just the grass by selecting the grass symbol in the Symbols palette and then using the symbol spinner tool. To change the size of both the grass and the flowers, select both symbols in the Symbols palette and then use the Symbol Sizer tool.

Another useful method is to apply the Symbol Sizer to a sprayed bunch of symbols, making some of the symbols larger and some smaller. Doing so saves you the time and difficulty of breaking a symbol link and editing each symbol separately.

APPLY SYMBOL EFFECTS

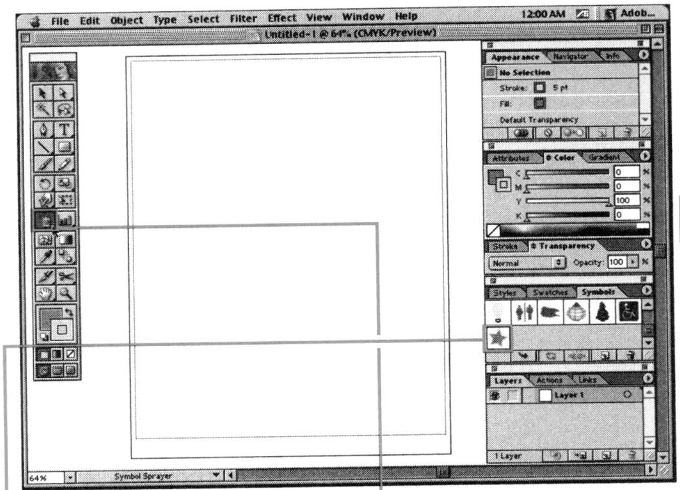

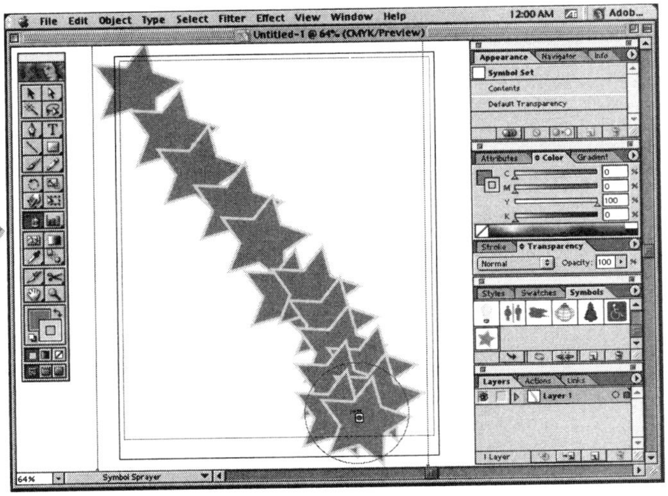

USING THE SYMBOL SPRAYER

1 Click a symbol on the Symbol palette.

2 Click the Symbol Sprayer tool ( ) in the toolbox.

3 Click and drag the mouse ( ) over your artwork.

■ The symbol sprays onto the artwork.

What symbol effects can I apply?

✔ The specialized symbol effects include:

Effect	Result
Symbol Sizer	Grows a symbol larger or smaller
Symbol Stainer	Colorizes your symbols
Symbol Screener	Adjusts symbol transparency
Symbol Styler	Applies a graphic style as a painted effect
Symbol Shifter	Moves symbol instances around
Symbol Scruncher	Pulls symbol instances together or apart
Symbol Spinner	Changes the rotation of a symbol instance

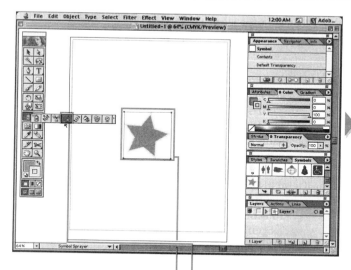

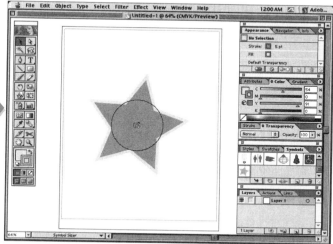

USING THE SYMBOL SIZER

1 Select a symbol on your artwork.

Note: For more on selecting objects, see Chapter 8.

2 Click and hold 📷, then drag and select 📷 from the toolbar that appears.

3 Click and hold the 📷 over the symbol.

■ The symbol grows in size.

4 Release the mouse.

■ Your symbol takes on its new size.

■ To shrink a symbol, press and hold down the Alt (Option) key before clicking the symbol.

UNDERSTANDING TYPE IN ILLUSTRATOR

Illustrator handles type differently than you might expect. Instead of employing a grafted-on word processor,

Illustrator provides sophisticated tools to meet the unique demands of using type in artwork.

Type and Text

People sometimes say "type" and "text" interchangeably, but these terms represent two different things. People use *type* to create text; type has properties such as family, font, color, case, and alignment within a document. *Text*, on the other hand, is the actual words and letters you write in a document or on your illustration.

Raster and Vector Fonts

Raster fonts are optimized for screen display technology and look best on a monitor. *Vector* fonts use mathematical scaling technology to appear the same both onscreen and printed on paper. You should use vector fonts for most of your work unless you have specific reasons to use raster fonts, such as placing them on a Web site.

PostScript and TrueType Fonts

Adobe PostScript and Microsoft TrueType fonts are vector fonts that work differently to solve different technology problems. For example, many design professionals use PostScript font libraries for all their work.

Type Outlines

Illustrator lets you create outlines from type that enable you to make ordinary letters wildly different. Because type outlines are paths, you can edit them with any of the path-editing tools in Illustrator.

Type Effects

You can apply simple type effects, like solid color. If you convert type to an outline, you can then apply wild and fanciful effects. These make your text come alive.

INSERT POINT AND AREA TYPE

I n Illustrator, you insert two different kinds of type with the Type tool. *Point type* starts from a single point in the artwork, without shape boundaries. You can insert point type into any artwork with the Type tool without having to create a path first.

Area type is type that you enter within a shape or object in your artwork that you create beforehand. Area type is often used in advertisement columns or for eye-catching newsletter design. You can use almost any shape for area type, but shapes with gentle changes of direction work better than narrow or sharp ones.

When you add type to your artwork, Illustrator creates it using paths. If you want to apply any effects to your text, such as applying a gradient, you need to convert the vector font to a raster font. See the section "Convert Type to Outlines," later in this chapter.

INSERT POINT TYPE

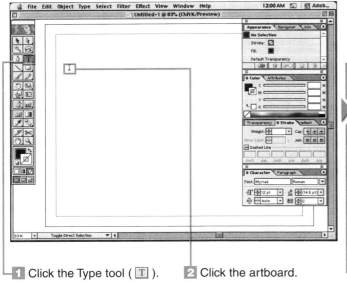

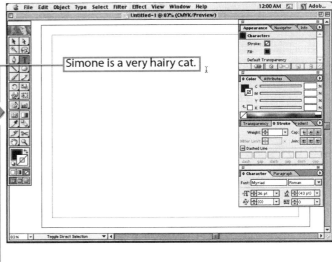

1 Click the Type tool (T).

2 Click the artboard.

3 Type your text.

■ The text appears in your artwork.

How do I change the font type or size?

✔ Open the Character palette by clicking Window, Type, and then Character. You can either change the settings before you enter text, or you can select existing text and then change the text to a new font type or font size. You can also change the font style to bold, italic, or any other style that your font supports.

How do I set paragraph indents?

✔ Open the Paragraph palette by clicking Window, Type, and then Paragraph. The lower half of the palette contains settings for paragraph indentations, hanging indents, and first-line indents. You can change the settings before you enter text, or you can select existing text and then change the paragraph indent style.

Where can I find a wider variety of fonts?

✔ You can find some fonts downloadable for free over the Internet; you can also purchase entire font libraries along with dedicated font creators and editors from several companies, including Adobe. You should be able to find a font you like — or its close approximation.

INSERT AREA TYPE

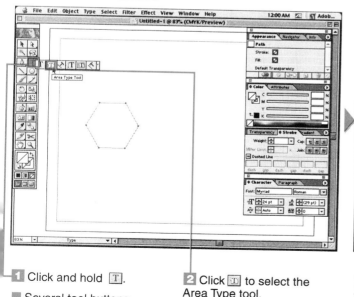

1 Click and hold T.

■ Several tool buttons appear.

2 Click T to select the Area Type tool.

3 Click an object's path where you want to place text.

4 Type your text.

■ The text appears inside your object.

TYPE TEXT ALONG A PATH

You can quickly create text that follows any path in your art, no matter how crazy. Illustrator refers to this kind of type as *Path type*. Path type enables you to easily snake type along the edge of a shape such as a circle. Illustrator provides two Path type tools: Path Type, which enters type perpendicular to the path, and

Vertical Path Type, which enters type parallel to the path. Depending on how your text flows, you may want to switch between the type tools to have the proper alignment.

Path type is a powerful feature not found in Photoshop. When you work with digital images and want

to have your type behave in creative ways, you can import your image from Photoshop, work with your type in Illustrator, and then import your image back into Photoshop. This lets you curve, swoop, or fly your text around your digital image.

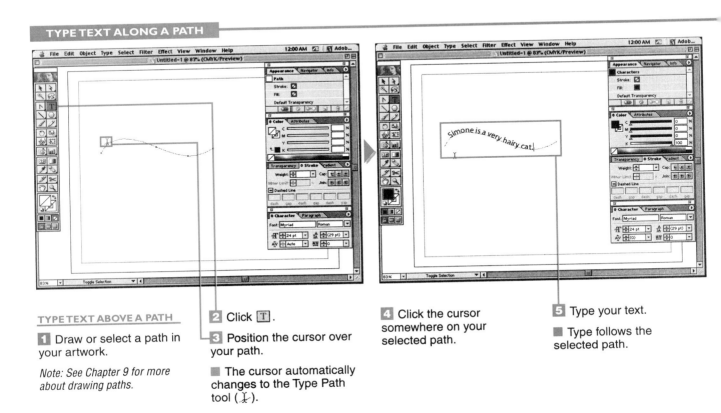

TYPE TEXT ABOVE A PATH

1 Draw or select a path in your artwork.

Note: See Chapter 9 for more about drawing paths.

2 Click T.

3 Position the cursor over your path.

■ The cursor automatically changes to the Type Path tool (I).

4 Click the cursor somewhere on your selected path.

5 Type your text.

■ Type follows the selected path.

How can I easily make type run vertically? I really do not want to rotate each letter individually.

✔ The Vertical Type tool (IT) lets you enter point text from top to bottom, but aligned normally; the Vertical Path Type tool (∖) lets you enter path text along a vertical path, also aligned normally. If you want to switch text alignment, switch to the Character palette, show all the options, and under the Direction list choose Rotate. This flips your text 90 degrees.

Can I switch between type tools without reaching back for the toolbar?

✔ Yes. Illustrator makes a smart guess as to which tool should be active and automatically switches to it. For example, if you are using the regular Type tool and pass over a closed path, it changes to the Area Type tool; if you pass it over an open path, it automatically changes to a Path Type tool.

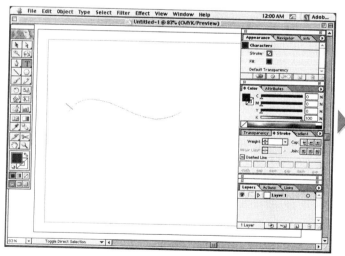

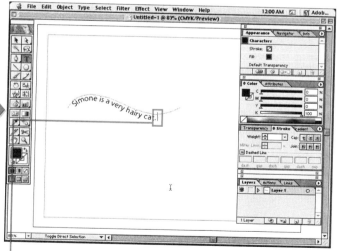

TYPE TEXT BELOW A PATH

1 Repeat steps 1 through 4 on the previous page.

2 Press Alt + Shift + Down Arrow (Option - Shift - Down Arrow).

■ The cursor moves incrementally below the path.

3 Type your text.

■ Text follows the underside of the selected path.

WRAP TYPE AROUND AN OBJECT

You can make type flow around an object, like a story flowing around a photograph in a newspaper, but with much greater creativity. You can use any object or closed path, such as a picture border or unusually shaped object, as a boundary for your text. Gentle changes in direction are better than sudden changes in direction, as the reader's eye can follow the text more easily.

When you flow type around an object's shape and want to maintain paragraph form, you must use area type; point type and path type do not automatically preserve paragraphs. You can use path type to flow type around objects, but it takes more work to make it conform to a particular shape and preserve the paragraphs.

You can make one or several type containers wrap around any

number of objects. This capability lets you design a freeform illustration with objects scattered about your image, and text flowing freely around the objects.

You can add objects to your wrapped type at any time. Place the new objects in front of your type area, and then repeat the Make Wrap process. The type now flows around the new objects.

WRAP TYPE AROUND AN OBJECT

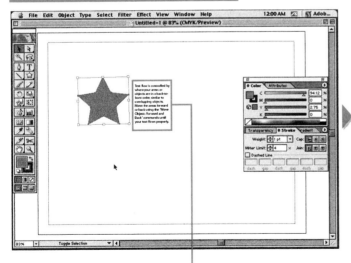

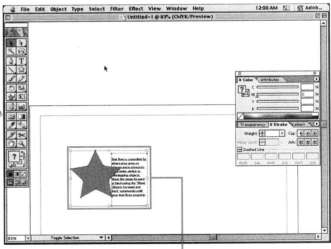

1 Create your object that you want to flow your type.

2 Create a type area and type the text that you want to flow around the object.

3 Select the object and the text using ▶.

Note: See Chapter 8 to learn more about using the Selection tool.

■ A bounding box appears around the selected object and text.

Why does my type not flow around the object?

✔ You must place your object in front of your text. Click Object, then Arrange, then Move Objects Forward or Move Objects Back until your text flows properly.

Can I wrap type around an open path?

✔ No. You cannot wrap type around an open path. You do not, however, always need to wrap text around a visible object. You can create a graphic boundary object to separate your text from other areas of your illustration, while still giving it something to wrap around.

What is a graphic boundary?

✔ A *graphic boundary* controls how closely type wraps around an object. You create a boundary to wrap type around a large type container consisting of a single piece of type, such as a large initial capital letter. You can create a boundary using an object with no fill or stroke, and then adjust and resize the unpainted boundary using a selection tool to achieve the exact kind of text wrap you want.

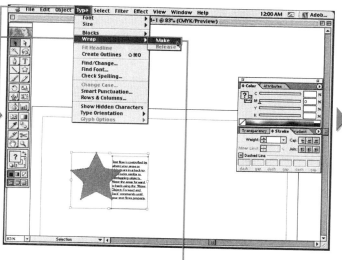

-4 Click Type.

-5 Click Wrap.

6 Click Make.

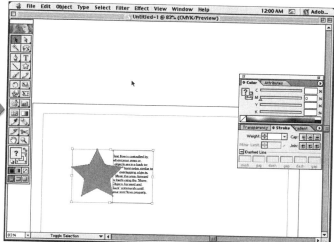

■ The text flows around the object.

■ To undo the flow, repeat steps 4 and 5, and then click Release.

CONVERT TYPE TO OUTLINES

One of the most fun things you can do is convert type to an outline. This process lets you apply many Illustrator tools, such as gradients, fills, and effects to your outlines. This lets you create custom fonts or font shapes, or to guarantee that the printer output looks exactly like the font you have chosen for the outline.

You may also want to convert type to outlines if you plan to send a project to a printer and do not want to risk the printer not having the font you are using in your image. By converting the type to an outline, you ensure that the type will print exactly as it looks onscreen, and that you do not throw off your carefully planned

design by having a different font substituted into your artwork.

Finally, outline text also allows you to create a highly customized font, such as an illustrated capital letter at the start of a chapter, much like an old illuminated manuscript from the Middle Ages.

CONVERT TYPE TO OUTLINES

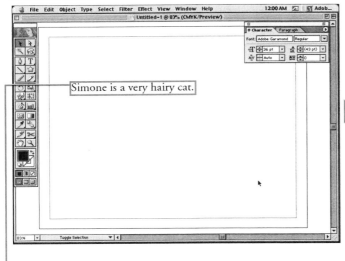

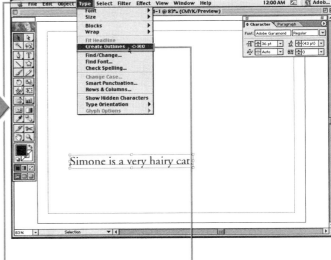

1 Create the text you want to turn into an outline.

Note: For more information, see the section "Insert Point and Area Type."

2 Select your text using a selection tool.

Note: See Chapter 8 to learn about using Selection tools.

3 Click Type.

4 Click Create Outlines.

■ You can also press Ctrl + Shift + O (Command - Shift - O) to convert outlines on the fly.

Why does my type not convert to an outline?

✔ The Create Outlines command works only with vector fonts such as Type 1 PostScript or TrueType. Bitmapped fonts, also called screen fonts, are literally pictures that resemble each letter in the font. Because they are already bitmaps, you can manipulate or apply effects to them. They cannot smoothly scale like vector fonts, and therefore are not the best fonts to use if you plan on doing complex font effects in your illustration.

Why can I not use the spell check program on my fonts?

✔ If you have converted your text to an outline, you cannot spell check the text; the conversion is irreversible, unless you immediately use the Undo command. This drawback serves as one strong argument for placing your text on a separate layer from your artwork — if you need to edit your text based on customer comments, you can edit the text and reapply any text effects without having to re-edit your entire illustration.

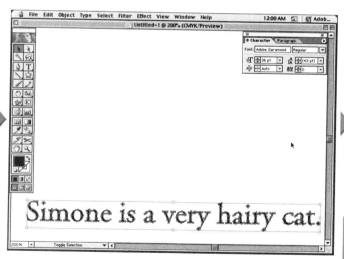

■ Illustrator converts the type to an outline.

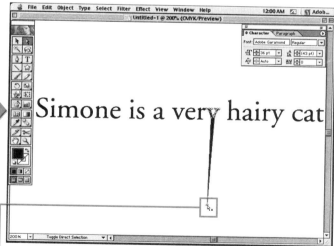

■ You can click and drag the outlines to create different effects.

APPLY A STYLIZE EFFECT

Illustrator provides several styles, filters, and effects that you can apply to objects, paths, or even entire pieces of artwork. They are ways of quickly modifying an object's appearance without modifying the underlying object. If you do not like the effect, you can undo it or remove it from your object, leaving the object and any other effects intact.

The Feather effect, for example, can soften the edges of an object. This helps fade it into a background color or object, or give a soft-focus effect to the perimeter while keeping the center in focus, much like the techniques used in Hollywood to make actresses appear all misty and sentimental. In essence, it takes an edge and, over a distance, changes the opacity from the default to transparent. Illustrator applies the effect inward from the object's outer path, gradually "fading in" to the object.

APPLY A STYLIZE EFFECT: THE FEATHER EFFECT

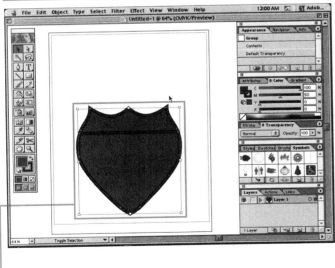

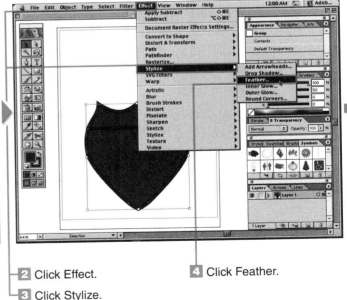

1 Select an object with a selection tool.

Note: See Chapter 8 for more information on using the selection tools.

2 Click Effect.

3 Click Stylize.

4 Click Feather.

What are the other effects available under the Stylize submenu?

✔ There are four other Stylize commands available that can enhance your objects. They are:

Tool	Effect
Add Arrowheads	Puts arrowheads on the stroke of an object
Drop Shadow	Places a blurred, offset shadow behind an object, giving it a 3D look
Outer Glow	Adds diffuse color emanating outward from the edges of an object
Inner Glow	Does the same, except the color emanates inward

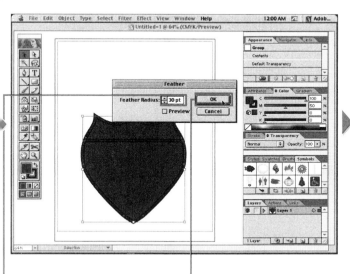

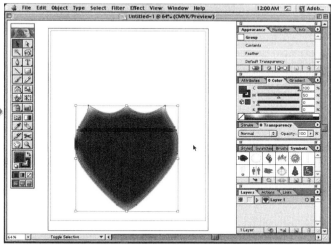

-5 Type a Feather Radius to control the amount of softness applied.

6 Click OK.

■ The settings take effect in the object.

■ You can also apply the Feather effect as a filter. Applying a filter takes less memory, but does not allow you to edit or remove the feature later.

APPLY A VECTOR-BASED FILTER

You can apply vector-based filters to paths and path-based objects in Illustrator. By using vector-based filters, you do not have to rasterize your artwork before you apply the filter. Illustrator lists the vector-based filters in the top half of the Filter menu.

Hatch Effects is a vector-based filter found under the Pen and Ink menu. This effect simulates a pen-and-ink drawing and applies random textures, such as crosshatching, to your illustration. With it, you can use existing Hatch effects or create your own.

You can apply seven types of hatching with 25 different hatching patterns for each of them, ranging from Angled Lines Gradation to Wood Grain Swirl, for a total of 175 different combinations. Illustrator lets you customize each hatching and its effect, and you are encouraged to experiment with the effects to see how your image changes.

APPLY A VECTOR-BASED FILTER: THE HATCH EFFECTS FILTER

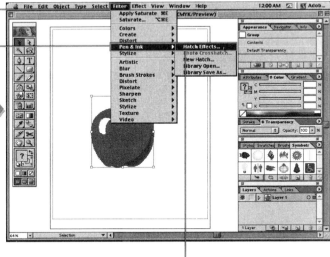

■1 Select an object with a selection tool.

Note: See Chapter 8 for more on selecting objects.

■2 Click Filter.

■3 Click Pen & Ink.

■4 Click Hatch Effects.

Can I apply hatch effects to a photographic object?

✔ Yes. You must, however, use a different command. You can apply the Photo Crosshatch filter to add hatch effects to any rasterized images on your artboard. To access the Photo Crosshatch filter, click Filter, Pen & Ink, and then Photo Crosshatch. A dialog box appears with various property settings, which you can change by clicking and dragging a specific slider ▲. Click OK to apply the effect

What do some of the hatch options do?

✔ The dispersion option controls the spacing of hatch elements; thickness controls the hatch weight; scale sets the size of the elements; and rotation sets the angle at which the hatch elements are applied. Match Object's Color changes the hatch fill to the selection's fill, and Keep Object's Fill Color applies the hatch in its original color. For more information on these options, and the range of permissible values, see the online help.

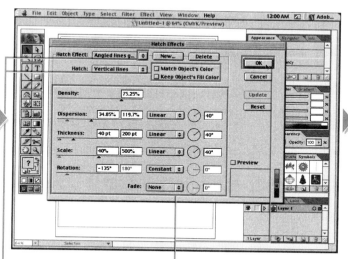

■ The Hatch Effects dialog box appears.

5 Click ▲ or ▼ to display predefined hatch effects.

6 Click the effect you want.

■ Clicking these options retains the object's current color (☐ changes to ☑).

■ You can change the hatch shape applied in the Hatch menu.

■ You can also adjust other settings to fine-tune your design.

7 Click OK.

■ The hatch effect is applied to the object.

RASTERIZE AN OBJECT

The process of changing a vector graphic to a bitmap image is called rasterization. During rasterization, Illustrator converts the graphic's paths into pixels. The rasterization options you set determine the size and other characteristics of the resulting pixels.

This is necessary if you are creating graphics for use in video production. Video equipment can only display rasterized graphics, and cannot work with any vector images. Thus, vector images must first be converted to raster images before you import them into Premiere. If you will be working with video, you should switch to a video-compatible color profile such as SMPTE-C. See Chapter 1 for more information.

After graphics are converted by either method, you can apply plug-in filters, such as those designed for Adobe Photoshop, to the image as you would with any placed image. You cannot, however, apply vector tools and commands (such as the type tools and the Pathfinder commands) to modify the bitmap image.

RASTERIZE AN OBJECT

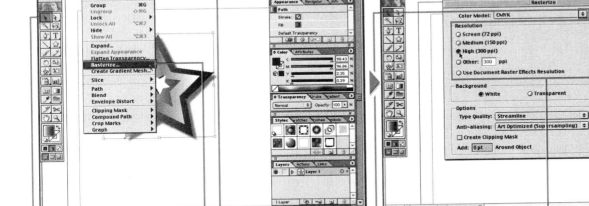

1 Click ▶.

2 Click an object.

3 Click Object.

4 Click Rasterize.

■ The Rasterize dialog box appears.

5 Click ⬆ or ⬇ and click a color mode.

Note: For more information on color modes, see Chapter 3.

6 Click a resolution (○ changes to ⬤), using a higher resolution if you want to print on a high-resolution printer.

What do the rasterization options do?

✔ The Color model option lets you choose which model to apply; for digital images, you should pick RGB. Resolution determines the pixels per inch (ppi) for the resulting image; 72 ppi is fairly common for computer monitors. Background lets you specify White or Transparent for background pixels. If you select Transparent, you create an alpha channel for the image that contains transparency information. The other options adjust type quality, anti-aliasing, and clipping mask options. These can help smooth out your image and its elements, especially if fine artwork is appearing blocky or too heavily pixilated. See the online help for details about adjusting these options.

How can I rasterize an object but still edit its fill, stroke, and other attributes?

✔ You can use the Rasterize effect. To do so, select the object, click Effect, and then click Rasterize. With an effect, the object looks pixelated, but you can still edit it.

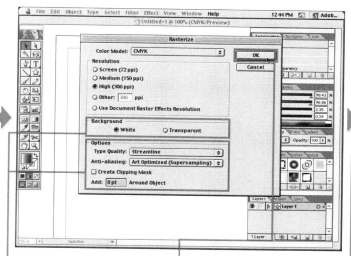

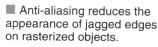

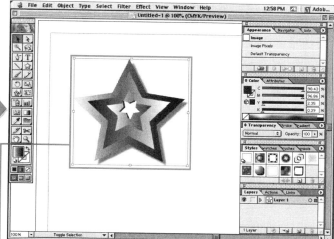

■ **7** Click an option to specify how to display background areas of the object (○ changes to ◉).

■ If you rasterize type, you can specify the quality and anti-aliasing by clicking ◆ or ▼ and clicking the appropriate settings.

■ Anti-aliasing reduces the appearance of jagged edges on rasterized objects.

■ **8** Click OK.

■ The object converts into pixels.

APPLY A STYLE

You can apply a *style* to an object to quickly and easily give it a predefined appearance. A style is a collection of appearance attributes for an object, such as fill and stroke color, pattern information, and other attributes. If you spend a lot of time working with the appearance of an object to get it just right, and you think you may want to use that same appearance again (or as a starting point for a slightly different appearance), you should save the appearance attributes as a new style. You save new styles in the Styles palette, from which they can be recalled and applied to other objects.

One example of a reusable style is with product names within a product family. Most businesses want to have a similar look and feel to products within a family, with similar fonts, stroke weights, color schemes, and so forth. If you build one style for a product, the chances are good you will be reusing that style on another product in the near future.

APPLY A STYLE

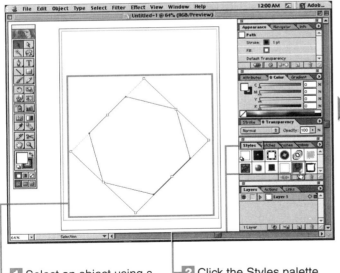

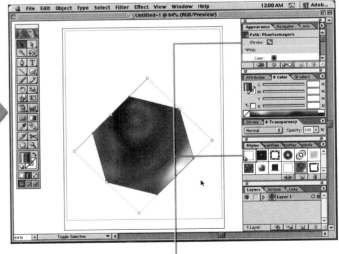

1 Select an object using a selection tool.

Note: See Chapter 8 for more on selecting objects.

2 Click the Styles palette tab.

3 Click a style.

■ Illustrator applies the style to the object.

■ This example shows a Fill style.

■ The attributes that define the style appear in the Appearance palette.

■ You can remove the style by clicking the Default style in the Styles palette.

How can I access more predefined styles?

✔ Illustrator comes with dozens of predefined styles. Click Window, click Style Libraries, and then click a style set. The set of styles opens in a new palette.

Does Illustrator provide a shortcut for creating a new style in the Styles palette?

✔ Yes. Illustrator displays the appearance attributes of a selected object in the Appearance palette. To define those attributes as a new style, you can click and drag the thumbnail at the top of the Appearance palette onto the Styles palette.

Can I re-edit a style in the Styles palette?

✔ You can re-edit a style, but be careful. Whenever you apply a style to an object, Illustrator creates a link from the object to the style. If you edit the style, Illustrator applies the new style to every object that uses the style, and you may not want this to happen. You can break the link back to the style by clicking the Break Link to Style icon on the palette.

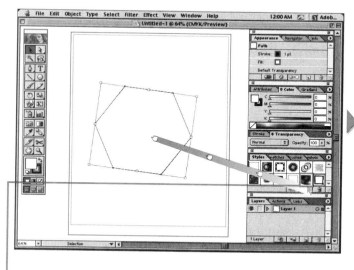

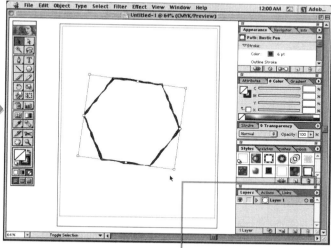

DRAG AND DROP A STYLE

1 Click a style.

2 Click and drag the style onto an object.

■ The ► changes to a 🖑 or 🖑.

■ Illustrator applies the style to the object.

■ This example shows a Stroke style.

■ To delete a style from the Styles palette, click the style and then click 🗑.

USING THE BLEND TOOL

You can create a sequence of intermediate objects between two objects with the Blend tool. Doing this can imply motion or gradual change in your artwork. Animators call this procedure a *shape blend* and use it to morph one shape into another. Color blends, also known as *gradients*, create the effect of one color changing into another. You can read more about applying a gradient in Chapter 10.

When working with shape blends, you should keep a few guidelines in mind. First, both paths must be open or closed; if open, you can only select end points between your two paths. Ideally, both paths should contain the same number of anchor points (but do not have to), and the paths should be of a roughly similar shape. For example, trying to blend a snowflake into a sea monster will probably give you some disappointing results.

You can edit blends that you created by moving, resizing, deleting, or adding objects. After you make editing changes, Illustrator automatically reblends the artwork.

USING THE BLEND TOOL

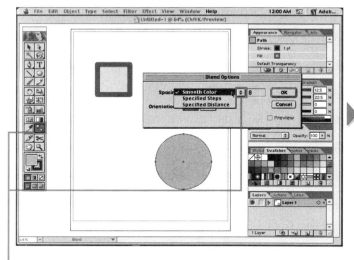

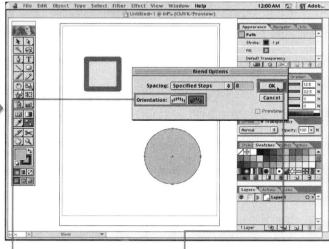

■1 Double-click the Blend tool (🖫).

■ The Blend Options dialog box appears.

■2 Click ⬍ or ⬇ to select your spacing options.

■ You can specify that intermediate steps between the objects be based on color, on a specific number of steps, or on distance.

■ Specifying a number of steps determines the number of intermediate objects that Illustrator creates.

■3 Click an option to specify whether you want the intermediate objects aligned with the enclosing page (⣿) or with the path between the objects (⣿).

■4 Click OK.

How do I change the arrangement of a blend?

✔ Select the blend, and then click Object, Blend, and Reverse Spline to reverse the order of the blended objects along the path. You can also select Reverse Front to Back under the Blend menu to switch the stacking order of the objects.

Does the Blend tool work with object attributes, like stroke weight?

✔ If you blend between objects with multiple appearance attributes (effects, fills, or strokes), Illustrator attempts to blend the options.

Can I use multiple colors for the intermediate blends?

✔ You can blend between an unlimited number of objects, colors, opacities, or gradients.

What if I do not want the blend to be along a straight line?

✔ Illustrator creates a straight path between blended objects when the blend is first applied. You can edit the blend path by dragging anchor points and path segments. Illustrator reapplies the blend along the new path.

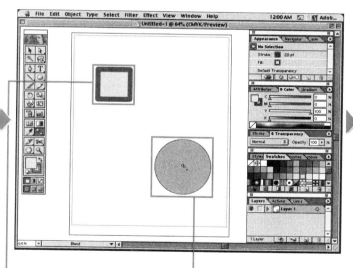

■ 5 Click a beginning object.

■ 6 Click an ending object.

■ Illustrator creates intermediate objects between the selected objects.

■ You can also select more than two objects and Illustrator creates intermediate objects between each pair of objects in the sequence.

■ To remove a blend, select the group of objects and then click Object, Blend, and then Release.

USING THE MESH TOOL

The Mesh tool transforms a path object (or a bitmap image) into a single, multicolored mesh object. When you create a mesh object, multiple lines called mesh lines crisscross the object and provide a way to easily manipulate color transitions on the object. By moving and editing points on the mesh lines, you can change the intensity of a color shift, or change the extent of

a colored area on the object, which helps create specialized color gradients or add highlights or shadows to existing objects.

At the intersection of two mesh lines is a special kind of anchor point called a mesh point. Mesh points appear as diamonds and have all of the same properties as anchor points but with the added capability of accepting color. You

can add and delete mesh points, edit the mesh points, or change the color associated with each mesh point.

Anchor points also appear in the mesh (differentiated by their square rather than diamond shape), and can be added, deleted, edited, and moved as with any anchor points in Illustrator.

USING THE MESH TOOL

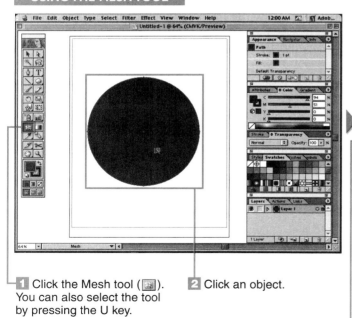

1 Click the Mesh tool (▦). You can also select the tool by pressing the U key.

2 Click an object.

■ The object converts into a mesh object, with a mesh of points laid atop it.

3 Click a point on the mesh object.

4 Click the Color palette tab.

5 Select a color.

Note: For more information about selecting colors, see Chapter 10.

How can I add or delete points on my mesh objects?

✔ You can hold down the Shift key while you click with the Mesh tool (⬚) to add a point. You can hold down Alt (Option) while you click ⬚ to delete a point.

Why does my illustration scroll on the screen so slowly?

✔ To improve performance and speed of redrawing, keep the size of mesh objects to a minimum. Because complex mesh objects can greatly reduce performance, you benefit from creating a few small, simple mesh objects instead of creating a single, complex mesh object. For additional performance gains, set the scratch disk to a disk other than the primary one. See the online help for instructions.

Why does my mesh object look bad when I print it out?

✔ Some printers have difficulty printing gradients and gradient mesh objects. For example, gradients may print with a banding effect on older PostScript Level 2 devices. In addition, gradient mesh objects may print incorrectly to some PostScript 3 devices. The Compatible Gradient and Gradient Mesh Printing option enables such printers to print your files by converting the objects to JPEG format.

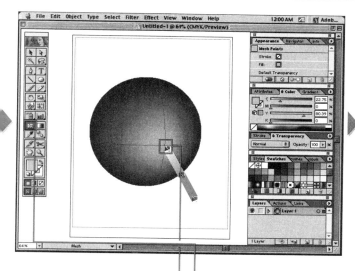

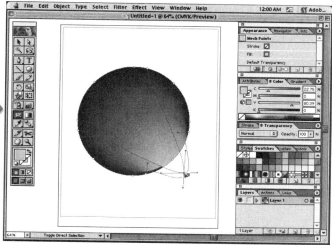

■ The color applies itself to the mesh around the selected point.

◻6 Press the U key to select the Mesh tool.

◻7 Click and drag a mesh point (⬚).

■ The mesh overlay distorts and the color gradients on the object change to reflect the distortion.

■ You can continue to add colors and adjust the mesh by repeating steps 3 to 7.

■ To create more complicated meshes, you can select an object and click Object, and then Create Gradient Mesh.

CREATE OR DELETE A LAYER

You can create artwork in Illustrator that is made up of multiple layers, with each layer containing different objects.

Illustrator layers enable you to isolate, as well as group, different parts of your artwork. Each layer can include its own collection of shapes, paths, and applied effects

that you can easily view and manipulate independently of the elements in other layers. You can also create a special type of layer that you can use as a template for creating art.

You can create, delete, and hide layers in your image using the Layers palette. The palette also lets

you combine layers or rearrange how they stack in your artwork. You can even organize layers in a nested fashion with the Layers palette by creating sublayers that exist within other layers.

Illustrator also enables you to delete a layer when you no longer need the elements it contains.

CREATE A NEW LAYER

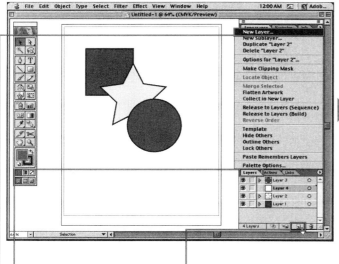

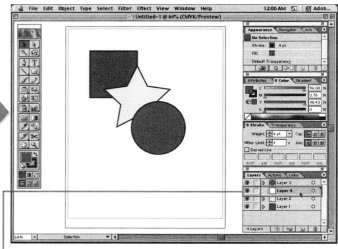

1 Click the Layers palette tab.

2 If your document already has more than one layer, select the layer below where you want to create the new layer.

3 Click the Create New Layer button (■).

■ You can also click ● from the Layers palette and click New Layer.

■ Illustrator creates and selects a new layer.

■ Illustrator adds any newly created art to the selected layer.

How do I create nesting layers?

✔ You can create *sublayers* that nest inside other layers. Sublayers enable you to arrange elements in your artwork in complex ways. To create a sublayer, click the New Sublayer button ( ) in the Layers palette. In the Layer Options dialog box, set layer options, and then click OK.

What happens to a sublayer if the layer enclosing it is hidden or locked?

✔ Illustrator locks or hides the sublayer also. A sublayer inherits these characteristics from the layer that contains it.

How do I move a layer from one level to another?

✔ In the Layers palette, simply click and drag the layer up and down the palette. A large dark line shows you where the new layer will be inserted in the hierarchy. You can move sublayers to top-level layers, or move them to be sublayers within another layer.

DELETE A LAYER

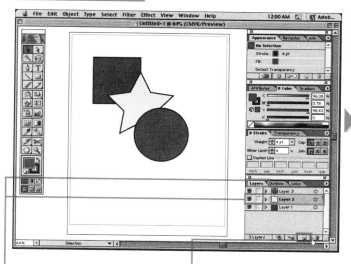

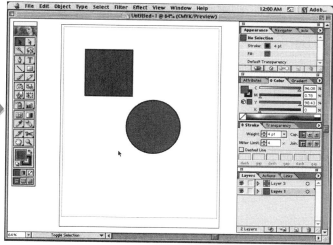

■1 Click the Layers palette tab.

■2 Click a layer.

■3 Click the Delete Selection button ( ).

■ You can also click ▣ from the Layers palette and click Delete.

■ If the selected layer contains artwork, Illustrator prompts you to confirm that you want to delete it.

■ Illustrator deletes the selected layer and all associated elements.

■ You can undo the deletion by clicking Edit, and then Undo Deletion.

EDIT LAYER OPTIONS

Just like objects, layers also have properties. The properties change how the layer behaves, how it looks, and what it is called. Properties give you the flexibility you need to design artwork using the power of layers to the fullest.

You can access a variety of layer settings, including a layer's name,

its color, and its visibility, in the Layer Options dialog box. The options change how the layer appears in the Layers palette, and how the layer is viewed, printed, and edited.

For instance, suppose a layer contains slightly different versions of a company logo. You may want

to print out your artwork with the different logo in each one for a customer's review and approval. With the Layer Options dialog box, you can select which logo version prints, and create separate versions with the appropriate logo showing.

EDIT LAYER OPTIONS

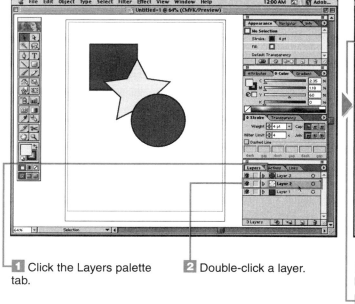

■1 Click the Layers palette tab.

■2 Double-click a layer.

■ The Layer Options dialog box appears.

■3 Type a new name for the layer.

■4 Click ⬍ or ▾ and click a selection color.

■ Illustrator highlights any selected objects from the layer with this color.

Why would I want to dim my bitmap images?

✔ Dimming your images can make tracing them with drawing tools easier. Images dimmed using the Layer Options dialog box are not dimmed when the artwork is printed; if you need to dim an object when it is printed, adjust the object's opacity. See Chapter 10 for information on adjusting object opacity.

Does the color option change the appearance of my objects in the layer?

✔ No. It only changes the selection outline color. This makes it easier to tell which object belongs to which layer.

What does a hollow eye in the Layers palette mean?

✔ A hollow eye icon (◉) in the Layers palette indicates the layer is in Outline mode. To switch back to preview mode, press Ctrl + Y (Command - Y); the icon changes back to ◉. You can also toggle between them by using the keyboard and mouse shortcut Ctrl + click (Command - click).

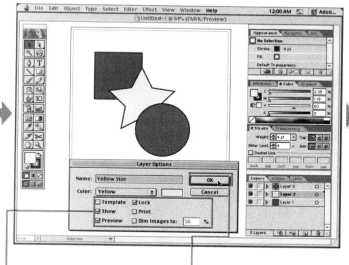

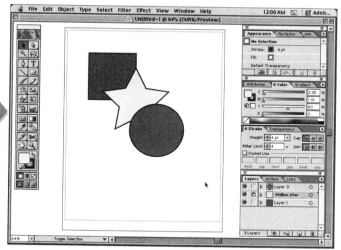

■5 Click to specify other layer options (☐ changes to ☑).

■ You can specify whether to display the layer when you print your artwork.

■ You can specify that bitmap images in your layer be dimmed.

■6 Click OK.

■ The settings take effect in the layer.

CREATE A TEMPLATE LAYER

Create a template layer whenever you want to base a new illustration on an existing piece of artwork — for example, when you want to trace over existing artwork or build an illustration from it. You can define a layer as a template that you can then use as a guide for creating artwork.

When you create a template layer, the layer contains the image you want to trace or outline. The template layer is typically under other layers, so that you can make a tracing or apply other effects without affecting the original image. Any layer can be a template layer, but only raster images can be used as templates. When you import a raster image, the image

dims by 50 percent so you can see the image without being overwhelmed by any contrast in colors or edges.

After you have finished tracing your template layer, you can delete it or hide it, depending on whether you plan on tracing any other parts of your image. You can neither print nor export a template layer.

CREATE A TEMPLATE LAYER

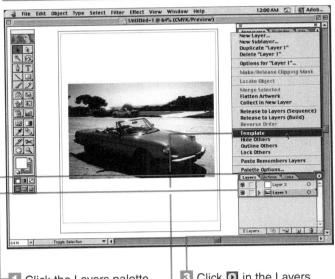

1 Click the Layers palette tab.

2 Click the layer you want to use as a template.

3 Click ▶ in the Layers palette.

4 Click Template.

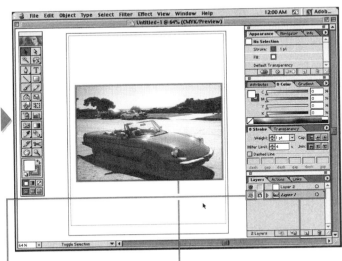

■ The layer becomes a noneditable template layer and a template icon (🖫) appears next to the layer in the Layers palette.

■ Any bitmap images in the layer dim 50 percent.

■ You can double-click the layer in the Layers palette to edit the dim setting.

How do I lock and unlock layers?

✔ If you want to protect a layer from editing, you can lock it by clicking the square box next to the eye in the Layers palette. A lock appears indicating the layer is locked. To unlock the layer, click the lock.

I cannot select objects in my template layer. Why?

✔ By default, a template layer is locked when you create it, so you cannot select or edit objects in it. If you need to edit elements in the template layer, you can unlock the layer in the Layers palette.

How do I use a vector image as a template?

✔ To use a vector-based image as a template, you need to rasterize it first. Doing this converts the paths into pixels, and renders your image as a rasterized image instead. You can rasterize the image separately (see Chapter 12) or you can add it to your layer, rasterize it, and then turn the layer into a template layer.

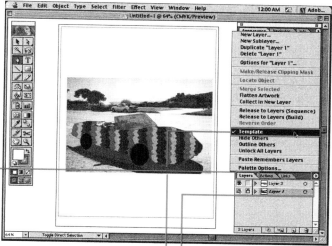

■5 Create your artwork with drawing tools in one or more layers on top of the template layer.

Note: You can learn how to create artwork in Chapters 8 through 12.

REVERT A TEMPLATE LAYER

■1 Click the Layers palette tab.

■2 Click the template layer you want to change back to a normal layer.

■3 Click ▸ in the Layers palette.

■4 Click Template to revert the layer.

■ The dimmed image in the layer reverts.

MERGE LAYERS

Y ou can merge layers to combine elements into a single layer. When you merge layers, Illustrator combines all the elements and their attributes into a single layer and deletes the other layers. Merging is a one-way process; after you merge the layers, you cannot extract the layers back out of the combined layer into their original states. The only way to go

back is to immediately use the Undo command after you merge the layers.

Objects in merged layers retain their stacking order; if one object overlaps another within a layer; it remains the overlapping object in the merged layer. In essence, one large stack is built from the merged layers, with the stack order preserved in the new layer.

Merging layers can also save memory and enable you to work faster, because it frees up memory for other tasks. You can merge layers as you go to reduce the size of your artwork. If you think you will need to edit the artwork in the future, save a version with all layers intact, and then begin merging layers.

MERGE LAYERS

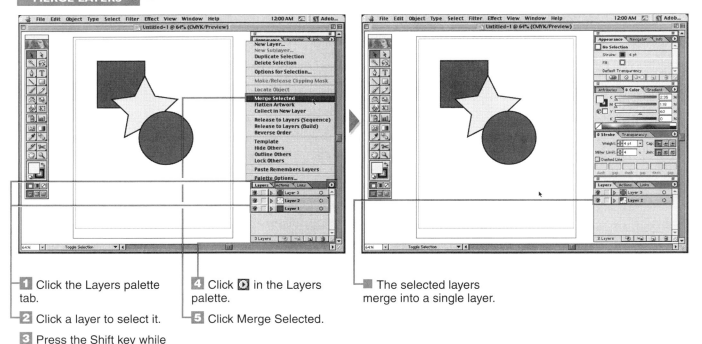

1 Click the Layers palette tab.

2 Click a layer to select it.

3 Press the Shift key while clicking to select one or more other layers.

4 Click ▣ in the Layers palette.

5 Click Merge Selected.

■ The selected layers merge into a single layer.

FLATTEN ARTWORK

You can merge all a picture's layers into one through a process called *flattening*. You may find this useful if you no longer need to work with elements in your layers individually.

Like merging, stacking order is preserved through the merger, so objects from lower layers continue to be lower in the stack than objects from higher layers. If a hidden layer contains artwork, Illustrator asks you whether to make the artwork visible so that it can be flattened into the layer, or if it should delete the artwork and the hidden layer.

You should flatten your artwork as one of the steps before posting an image to the Internet, because doing so helps reduce the file size. Always make a copy of your image and flatten the copy, so you can make changes or subsequent edits if needed.

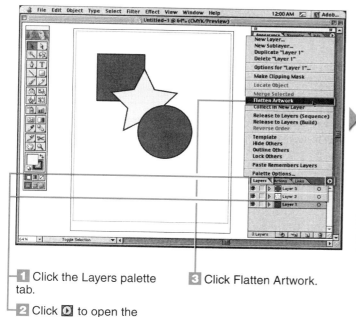

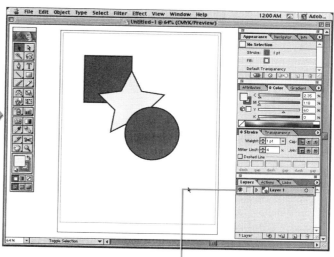

■ Click the Layers palette tab.

■ Click ◘ to open the Layers palette menu.

■ Click Flatten Artwork.

■ If any of the layers are hidden prior to flattening, Illustrator asks whether to keep or discard the hidden artwork.

■ The layers become a single layer that takes the name of the lowest layer in the original set.

UNDERSTANDING WEB ART

Y ou can create art in Illustrator and then save it in various formats for display on the Web.

Web Art Basics

Creating art for the Web involves special challenges. Because people view Web pages by connecting to remote servers around the world, Web images need to have small file sizes so that pages download quickly. For fast downloads, the majority of Web graphics are saved in one of two compressed file formats: GIF or JPEG.

GIF Images

GIF is the file format you want to use when saving flat-color illustrations for your Web pages. GIF supports only 256 or fewer colors, so it is less appropriate for photographic images. The GIF format supports transparency. See the section "Save As a GIF for the Web" for details.

JPEG Images

You want to use the JPEG format when saving photographic or other continuous-tone art for the Web. With the JPEG format, you can control the amount of compression applied to the image to balance file size with image quality. JPEG does not support transparency. See the section "Save As a JPEG for the Web" for more information.

Web-Safe Colors

If you view a Web page on a monitor that supports only 256 colors, you just see the Web-safe colors. Colors on the page that are not Web-safe are converted to ones that are, which can degrade the quality of the images on the page. Monitors with resolutions greater than 256 colors do not have this problem. Choosing Web-safe colors when creating Web art helps ensure that all viewers see your art as you intended. For more on Web-safe colors, see Chapter 3.

Slicing Artwork

Web pages often consist of many different images, such as buttons, logo art, and illustrations, each of which is optimized differently. You can create these multi-image pages as a single Illustrator document, and then slice the document to create and optimize the images.

Flash Content

Macromedia Flash movies bring motion, sound, and interactivity to your Web pages. You can use Illustrator to create a simple Flash animation, with no sound or interactivity, by building the animated frames as separate layers and then exporting the layers in the Flash file format.

COPY AN IMAGE FROM PHOTOSHOP

You can copy an image to Illustrator directly from Photoshop. This capability serves as an alternative to placing an image into Illustrator from a file, and you may find it convenient if you have both applications running at the same time.

You can use the Windows or Macintosh Clipboard to transfer selections between an Illustrator

file and other Adobe products such as Photoshop and Premiere. The Clipboard is particularly useful for importing paths because paths are copied to the Clipboard as PostScript language descriptions.

When you copy images between the two applications, you perform an action known as "round-tripping" the artwork. Your artwork gets created in one application, such as

a scanned digital image in Photoshop, where it is traced, modified, and has effects applied. Then it gets copied into Illustrator where text and text effects are added. Finally, you copy it back into Photoshop for final touch-up and sharpening object outlines. Your artwork has made a round trip between the applications.

COPY AN IMAGE FROM PHOTOSHOP

1 Open Photoshop.

2 Open an image.

3 Select all or part of the image with a selection tool.

Note: See Chapters 1 and 2 for information on opening an image in Photoshop and using its selection tools.

4 Click Edit.

5 Click Copy.

■ The selected image copies to the Clipboard.

Can I copy art from Illustrator to Photoshop?

✔ You can copy art from Illustrator to Photoshop using the clipboard as well. Just reverse the steps below.

Are my transparency and opacity settings preserved between Photoshop and Illustrator?

✔ When you share files between Illustrator and Adobe Photoshop, transparency is preserved. Opacity masks in Illustrator convert to layer masks in Photoshop, and vice versa.

Can I drag and drop art between Illustrator and Photoshop?

✔ The drag-and-drop feature lets you copy and move artwork between Illustrator and other applications. In Windows, the other application must be OLE-compliant. (See your Windows documentation.) Dragging vector artwork from Adobe Illustrator or from other applications that use the Clipboard converts the artwork to a bitmap image (also called *raster* format). In Mac OS, the application must support Macintosh Drag Manager.

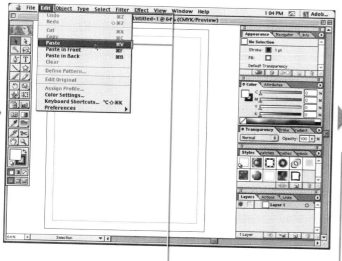

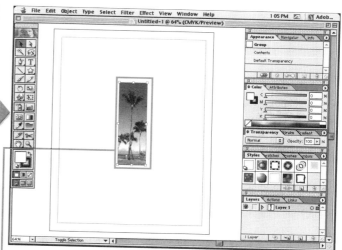

6 Switch to Illustrator.

7 If you are working with multiple layers, click the layer to which you want to paste the image.

8 Click Edit.

9 Click Paste.

■ The copied selection pastes from the Clipboard to your Illustrator document.

SAVE AS A GIF FOR THE WEB

You can optimize your artwork and save it in the Graphics Interchange Format (GIF) for displaying on the Web. The GIF format is best for flat-color art and helps ensure that the art downloads quickly.

The GIF color palette benefits you most when used for images that contain few variations in color. For example, you can save a photo of a stop sign against a blue sky as a GIF, because it has very little variation in color. Conversely, you would not save a scan of a Monet painting as a GIF because Monet's color palette most definitely used more than 256 colors. A Monet GIF would look clunky, blocky, and unattractive.

Before you save as a GIF, see if you have any Out of Web Color warnings on the Color palette. The warning looks like a cube and appears next to the Green channel in RGB mode. The color warning lets you know the color you are choosing is not a Web-safe one; click the cube to correct it to the nearest Web-safe color.

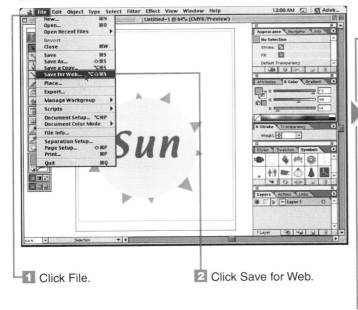

1 Click File.

2 Click Save for Web.

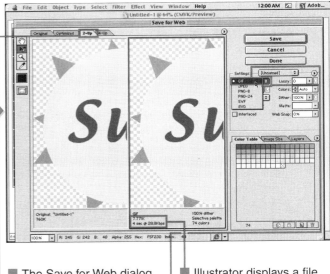

■ The Save for Web dialog box appears.

3 Click the 2-Up tab to view the original and optimized versions of your art side by side.

■ Illustrator displays a file size and download time.

4 Click ▲ or ▼.

5 Click GIF.

What is PNG?

✔ PNG (*Portable Network Graphics*) is a file-format alternative to GIF and JPEG that newer Web browsers — Microsoft Internet Explorer and Netscape Navigator versions 4 and greater — support. Like GIF, PNG excels at saving flat-color art. To save a PNG file, select PNG-8 (8-bit) or PNG-24 (24-bit) from the Save for Web file type dialog box.

When should I save a GIF image with transparency?

✔ You should save with transparency if you are creating special-purpose Web graphics such as Web page buttons or icons. Transparency lets the Web page background show through the transparent pixels.

Should I resize my image when I save it?

✔ You can enter new dimensions for your artwork in the dialog box to resize it, but you may be disappointed with the results. You should resize your image in Illustrator, make any adjustments you need to the image, and then save it without resizing it.

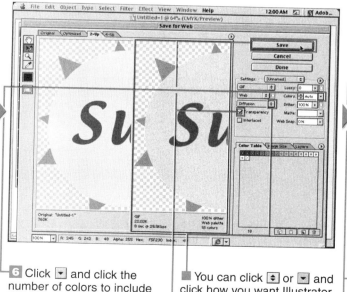

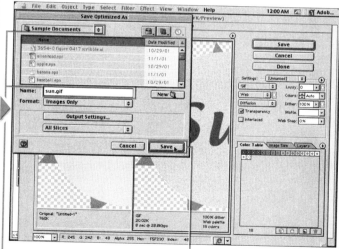

◢ **6** Click ▾ and click the number of colors to include in the saved file.

■ GIFs can include up to 256 colors.

■ You can click ▴ or ▾ and click how you want Illustrator to mix your selected number of colors.

■ You can click this option if you want to include transparency (☐ changes to ☑).

┗ **7** Click Save.

◢ **8** Click ▴ or ▾ and click the folder in which to save the file.

┗ **9** Type a name for the file.

■ GIF image files end in .gif.

◢ **10** Click Save.

■ Illustrator saves your image in GIF format.

SAVE AS A JPEG FOR THE WEB

You can optimize your artwork and save it in the Joint Photographic Experts Group (JPEG) file format for displaying on the Web. JPEG works best for photographic and other continuous-tone art. It uses compression algorithms to reduce overall image size, and you can select the amount of compression that is used when your image is

saved. JPEG supports 16.7 million colors, and many computer monitors today are configured to display 24-bit or 32-bit color by default.

When working in RGB mode (see Chapter 3), you may see an Out of Gamut warning on the Colors palette. Some colors, such as pure cyan or pure yellow, from the CMYK color space cannot display

accurately on a monitor. If your image will be printed, you can correct the color and the gamut warning by clicking the yield sign next to the Blue channel. The preview box next to the warning shows you the color it will switch to. If you do not like that new color, continue adjusting the color to remove the warning, or leave it as is.

SAVE AS A JPEG FOR THE WEB

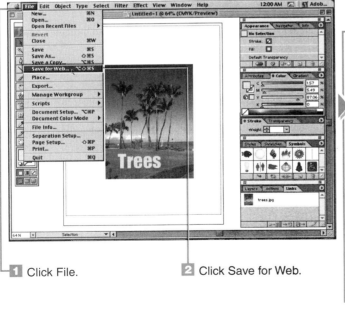

1 Click File.

2 Click Save for Web.

■ The Save for Web dialog box appears.

3 Click the 2-Up tab to view the original and optimized versions of your art side by side.

■ File size and download time are displayed.

4 Click ➕ or ➖.

5 Click JPEG.

Why does my saved image display a lot more blocky areas of color?

✓ Artifacts, such as wave-like patterns or blocky areas of banding, appear in a file each time you save it as a JPEG. You should always save JPEG files from the original image, not from a previously saved JPEG.

How do I make thumbnail JPEG images?

✓ Even though you could save each of your JPEGs as a thumbnail, doing so would take a lot of time, especially if you have a lot of images. Instead, use Photoshop's Create Web Photo Gallery command (see Chapter 7) to generate thumbnails of existing images.

What quality setting should I use for my JPEG files?

✓ It depends on your needs. Low quality produces smaller files — which download more quickly — but also introduces blurriness and pixel artifacts to your art. High quality produces larger file sizes but also results in images that are more faithful to the original. Which setting you choose depends on how much you want to sacrifice quality for download speed.

6 Type an image quality between 0 and 100.

7 Click ⬍ or ▾ and click a color with which to matte any transparency in your original image.

■ Unlike GIFs, JPEGs do not support transparency.

8 Click Save.

■ The Save Optimized As dialog box appears.

9 Click ⬍ or ▾ and click the folder in which to save the file.

10 Type a name for the file.

■ JPEG image files end in .jpeg or .jpg.

11 Click Save.

■ Illustrator saves your image in JPEG format.

EXPORT A FLASH ANIMATION

The Macromedia Flash (SWF) file format is a vector-based graphics file format for the creation of scalable, compact graphics for the Web. Because the file format is vector-based, the artwork maintains its image quality at different resolutions and is ideal for the creation of animation frames. In Illustrator, you can create individual animation frames on layers and then export the image layers into individual frames for use on a Web site. Each layer in the document turns into a frame in the animation. You can export a multi-layered Illustrator document as a Flash animation.

You can also define graphic elements called *symbols* in your Illustrator file. When exported, each symbol is defined only once in the SWF file; therefore, using symbols can greatly reduce the size of an animation. See Chapter 10 for information on creating symbols.

If you have any text in your illustrations, you should convert it to outlines before exporting your artwork to Flash format.

EXPORT A FLASH ANIMATION

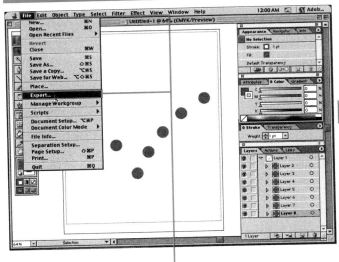

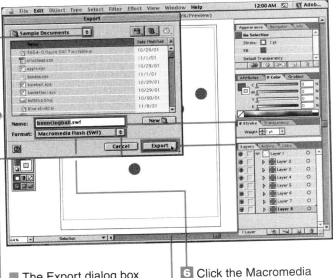

1 Create a multilayered Illustrator document with each layer including art for a frame in your animation.

Note: See Chapter 13 for details about creating layers.

2 Click File.

3 Click Export.

■ The Export dialog box appears.

4 Click ⬆ or ⬇ and click a folder in which to save your animation.

5 Click ⬆ or ⬇.

6 Click the Macromedia Flash file type.

7 Type a name for your animation ending with the extension .swf.

8 Click Export or Save.

What are the different Flash options?
✔ When you export a file and select Macromedia Flash, the Flash Format Options dialog box appears.

Option	Effect
Frame Rate	Sets how fast the illustration plays, in frames per second
Looping	Sets the animation to repeat itself
Generate HTML	Creates an HTML page that plays your animation
Read Only	Keeps others from changing your exported file
Image Format	Chooses between lossless and lossy compression
JPEG Quality	Lets you balance image quality with file size

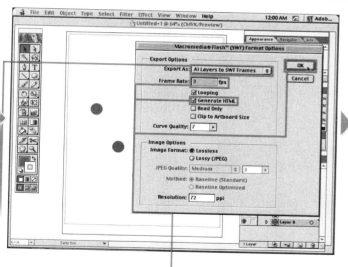

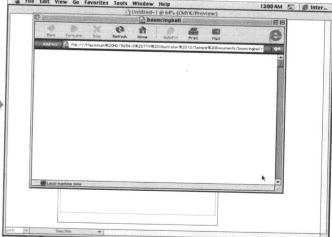

■ The Macromedia Flash Format (SWF) Options dialog box appears.

[9] Click ▲ or ▼ and click All Layers to SWF Frames in the Export As box.

[10] Type a frame rate (animation speed).

[11] Click Generate HTML to create a Web page the displays that animation.

[12] Click OK.

■ Illustrator saves the artwork as a Flash animation.

■ You can view the animation by opening the SWF file in any Flash-capable Web browser.

PRINT ARTWORK

You can print your art on a printer attached to your Macintosh, your PC, or a printer on your network to create a hardcopy version of your work.

When you print, you send an image in one color space to a device that prints in halftones (laser printer) or in CMYK (inkjet or dye-sublimation printer). If you send a color image to a laser printer, Illustrator

converts the color space into halftones. Likewise, an image created using the RGB color space and printing to a CMYK color space device (like a dye-sublimation printer) has to be converted, as there are more colors in the RGB space than in the CMYK space.

If you are working on digital images and artwork, and plan on printing out the images either for

proofing purposes or for actual inclusion in a print medium, you need to spend some time editing and printing your grayscale and color images. This kind of proofing ensures that the images appear the same — or almost the same — in print as they do on the screen.

PRINT ARTWORK

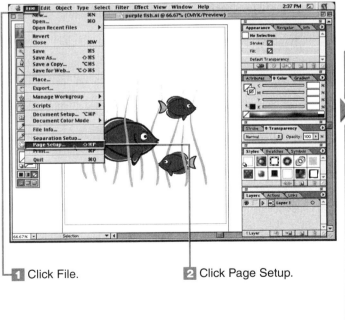

◤1 Click File.

◤2 Click Page Setup.

■ The Page Setup dialog box contains settings specific to your printer.

◤3 Click ⬦ and click a printer.

◤4 Click ⬦ and click a paper size.

◤5 Click an orientation (▯ or ▭).

■ You can type a scale value to increase or decrease the size of the illustration on the page.

◤6 Click OK.

What does the PostScript printer description file do?

✔ The file contains important information about your printer, including its resolution, available page sizes, and halftone settings. The file determines what values you can select in the Separation Setup dialog box.

How do I keep objects in my artwork from printing?

✔ You can move an object to its own layer and then hide the layer to keep the object from printing. See Chapter 13 for more information. To have the object visible onscreen but not in the printed document, double-click the object's layer to open the Layers Options dialog box and then deselect the Print option.

Where can I learn more about printing with Illustrator?

✔ We highly recommend the excellent reference, *Illustrator 10 Bible*, (Hungry Minds, Inc., 2002). It covers printing in detail, along with discussions of film transfers, CMYK color ranges, and adjustments to PPD (Photoshop Printer Description) files.

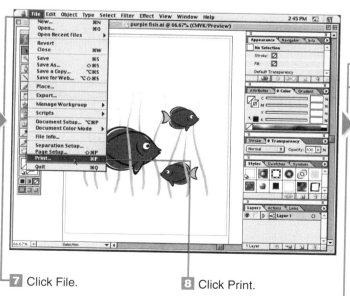

7 Click File.

8 Click Print.

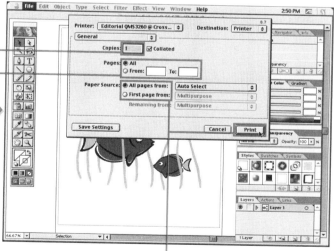

■ The print dialog box appears.

9 Type a number of copies.

10 Click to print all pages or a specific range (○ changes to ●).

■ You can select a paper source (○ changes to ●).

11 Click Print.

■ Your document prints.

SECTION III

PREMIERE

INTRODUCTION TO PREMIERE

Y ou can use Adobe Premiere to edit digital video on your computer. Whether you are using a Macintosh or a PC, Premiere can help you create dynamic movies and presentations that can be output to other sources, such as videotape or the World Wide Web.

What Can I Do with Premiere?

Premiere is a *nonlinear* editing program, which means that you can assemble a video project much like you assemble documents using other types of editing software. You can use Premiere to assemble and edit moving images.

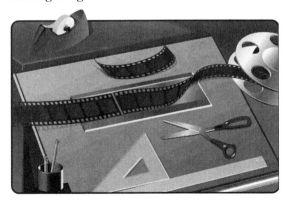

Gather Production Elements

You can import production elements, called *clips*, from other sources, such as video or audio files, and assemble them into a video project in Premiere. You can also capture digital video footage using a camcorder and bring the images into Premiere. See Chapter 16 to learn more.

Arrange the Clips

Digital editing involves arranging the clips into an actual video that you can output to another source. With Premiere, you can control where a clip starts and stops, rearrange its place on the program timeline, and preview the results to see how the project is progressing. See Chapters 17 and 18 to learn how to work with and edit clips.

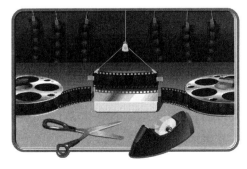

Add Video Effects

You can add *transition* effects, such as dissolves and wipes, to move from one scene to another. Premiere offers 75 customizable transition effects for you to apply. You can also create transparency effects that enable you to superimpose one clip over another. See Chapter 19 to learn more about transitions and superimposing.

Mix Audio

Using a microphone and your computer's sound card, you can record audio to use in your video. Premiere also lets you import audio files from other sources, including CDs. You can then edit the audio using the built-in audio mixer. You can create audio effects such as cross-fades and pans. See Chapter 21 to learn more about editing audio in Premiere.

Add Titles and Graphics

You can create titles with Premiere's titling feature. You can also add graphics from other programs, such as Photoshop or Illustrator, or draw simple graphic objects and text objects using the Premiere drawing tools. Premiere also provides tools for creating motion effects to make graphics or text move around the video's frames. See Chapter 20 to learn how to add titles and graphics.

Export Your Project

You can export the finished video to a variety of formats, such as Web file formats, files that can be viewed by other programs, and videotape. You can even export your project to an Edit Decision List to send off to a professional production house. See Chapter 22 to learn how to export your projects.

INTRODUCTION TO DIGITAL VIDEO

Digital video format is a high-quality imaging format. The term itself describes video signals stored in a digital form. If you are new to digital video, take a moment to familiarize yourself with the fundamentals of this format and the hardware used to create and edit digital media.

Analog versus Digital

Prior to digital media equipment, video content was analog in format. Motion picture film and audiocassette tape are two examples. Today's digital video format, called DV for short, offers higher-quality imaging. You cannot use analog media in Premiere without first digitizing it.

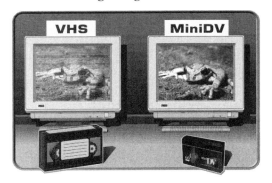

Recording Digital Media

One way to record digital media is to shoot it using a digital camcorder. MiniDV camcorders record the highest quality digital images, followed by Digital 8 (D8) camcorders. If your camcorder has IEEE 1394 output and your computer has an IEEE 1394 port, you can transfer the video directly into Premiere.

What Is IEEE 1394?

IEEE 1394 is a standard for transferring digital information between peripheral devices, such as a DV camcorder, and your computer. This standard is also referred to by the trade names *FireWire* (Apple Computer) and *i.LINK* (Sony Corp.). With an IEEE 1394 cable and port, you can also use Premiere's device control feature to control your camcorder from within Premiere.

Digitizing Analog Media

You can also use analog camcorders, such as 8mm or Hi8, if you have the necessary computer hardware, such as a capture card or capture board, for converting the analog signals to digital. Many types of analog capture cards can help you convert analog video from various sources, including VHS tapes.

Requirements for DV

To make the most of Premiere 6 and digital video, your computer system needs to meet some minimum requirements, such as processor power and an IEEE 1394 interface. For more information, see the listed system requirements at www.adobe.com/products/premiere/systemreqs.html.

Enhanced Editing Setups

For more advanced editing setups, you may include a DV deck for dedicated playback and recording, a professional-quality NTSC monitor, and a high-quality speaker system.

Editing Requirements

Digital video consumes a great deal of space. To store one hour of digital video on your computer's hard drive, you need 12.9 gigabytes (GB) of free space. Keep this in mind when storing video clips on your hard drive. The more clips you add, the more space they take up. Large-capacity, higher-speed hard drives running at 7,200 RPM or higher work best for digital video editing.

INTRODUCTION TO VIDEO EDITING

Editing video is like putting together pieces of a puzzle. As the editor, you decide where each clip goes and how long it plays. If you are new to the world of video editing, take a few moments to acquaint yourself with how editing is handled in Premiere.

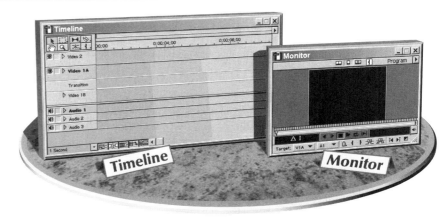

Traditional Video Editing

Traditional video editing requires expensive editing equipment and a production facility. Editors cue videotapes to edit points, copy scenes from various tapes to a master tape, and assemble a project sequentially. The process is time-consuming and tedious. If the editor decides he needs to add a new clip in the middle of the program, the entire video must be remastered.

Editing Methods

Premiere provides two main ways to edit a video. You can use the Timeline window or the Monitor window. Use the Timeline window to arrange the clips you want to appear in the video by tracks, and use the Monitor window to fine-tune the video. To learn more about editing with the Monitor and Timeline windows, see Chapters 17 and 18.

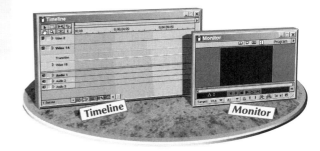

Editing Workspace

Premiere offers four workspace scenarios for you to create and edit your project: Single-Track Editing, A/B Editing, Effects, and Audio. The workspace you choose depends on what types of edits you are performing. For example, you may choose A/B editing if you want to drag clips onto the Timeline. You can learn more about the workspace later in this chapter.

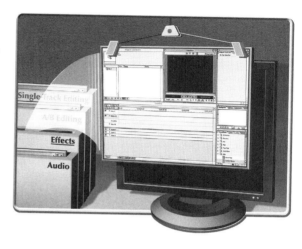

Plan Ahead with a Storyboard

Premiere also offers a storyboarding feature to help you plan out your project and the edits you want to make. With the Storyboard feature, you can visualize how your project scenes appear. When you finalize your project, you can then place the clips in the Timeline. Learn how to create a storyboard later in this chapter.

Digital Editing with Premiere

Premiere combines features commonly found in a roomful of video-editing equipment into one program you can use on your computer or laptop. Rather than deal with videotapes, you can create a project by importing or capturing clips and then assembling them in an order that best suits your project. If you need to add a clip later, you can easily insert it where it is needed.

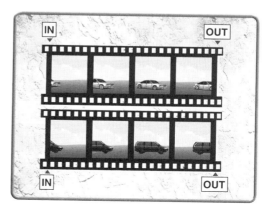

PLAN A VIDEO PROJECT

To make the best use of your time and effort editing a video project with Premiere, start by defining the process you want to use to achieve your goals. Use the tips in this task to help plan out pre-production steps and choose an editing strategy.

Pre-Production Planning

Most of your project planning occurs in pre-production. Outline, script, or storyboard your video concept. If your video includes a cast of people, plan out roles and costuming. Pre-production planning also includes establishing locations, budgets, sets, and props.

Outline

Always take time to outline your video project in some fashion, even if it is a simple paper outline of scenes, shots, or goals. An outline can help you organize your project as well as identify what items you need to complete the project.

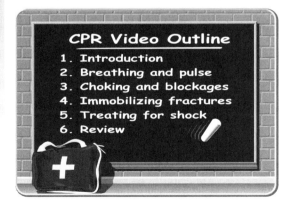

Script

If your video project includes speaking parts or narration, take time to finalize a script before shooting your video and keep the script handy as you edit clips. Formal scripts are another good tool to help you organize your project and materials needed during the shoot.

Production

Production refers to the actual shooting of your raw video footage. Things to consider during production are lighting, sound, camera angles, and *blocking* — the movement of people in the scenes.

Storyboard

To really help you visualize your video recordings, sketch out key actions needed for the project. A storyboard looks much like a comic strip, with frames showing changes in action. A storyboard may include notes about sound, camera angles, and direction.

Choose an Export Format

Decide what format you want to save your project to and make sure all the settings in Premiere comply with the specifications for that format. For example, if you are creating a project that will be broadcast on the Web, determine early on what frame size and rate you will use. Setting up your project correctly for export before you begin can save you numerous problems later.

NAVIGATE THE PROGRAM WINDOW

The Premiere interface is focused on three main areas: the Project window, the Monitor window, and the Timeline window. In addition, palettes organize commands and effects that you can apply to your project.

THE PC PROGRAM WINDOW

Monitor Window

Use this window to view and edit clips. Depending on the workspace settings you have applied, the Monitor window may show both the Source and Program monitors.

Project Window

Use this window to manage the contents of your video, including all the clips and titles.

Timeline Window

Use this window to see the tracks — the linear representations of media added to a project — that comprise your video and how they relate to other clips. You can also perform edits in the Timeline window.

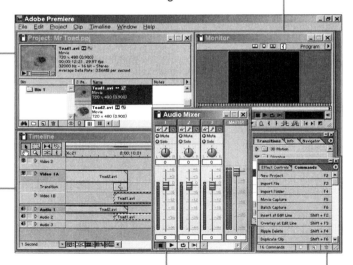

Audio Mixer

Use the Audio Mixer window to edit sounds in your video project.

Palette Windows

Premiere uses palettes to present additional commands and options you can apply to your project. Premiere provides eight palettes you can view, and some share the same palette window as others.

THE MACINTOSH PROGRAM WINDOW

Monitor Window

Use this window to view and edit clips. Depending on the workspace settings you have applied, the Monitor window may show both the Source and Program monitors.

Project Window

Use this window to manage the contents of your video, including all the clips and titles.

Timeline Window

Use this window to see the tracks — the linear representations of media added to a project — that comprise your video and how they relate to other clips. You can also perform edits in the Timeline window.

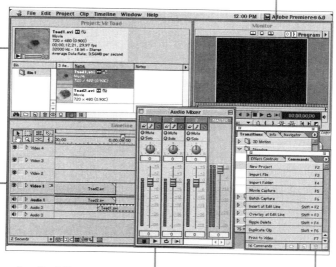

Audio Mixer

Use the Audio Mixer window to edit sounds in your video project.

Palette Windows

Premiere uses palettes to present additional commands and options you can apply to your project. Premiere provides eight palettes you can view, and some share the same palette window as others.

SET AN INITIAL WORKSPACE

Y ou can choose a workspace to use when editing in Premiere when you start the program for the very first time. A workspace determines the layout of the editing windows.

You can choose between A/B Editing or Single-Track Editing. The choice you make becomes the

default workspace for subsequent launches of the program. For most people, A/B Editing is the easiest mode to learn initially; it enables you to drag and drop clips into the Timeline, and to set In and Out points in the Clip window. You can see how the clips overlap and perform subsequent edits and fades between the clips.

Single-Track Editing lets you perform Three-Point and Four-Point edits, which involves setting three or all four In and Out points at once. Experienced Premiere users prefer working in Single-Track Editing mode. See Chapter 17 for more information on three-point edits.

SET AN INITIAL WORKSPACE

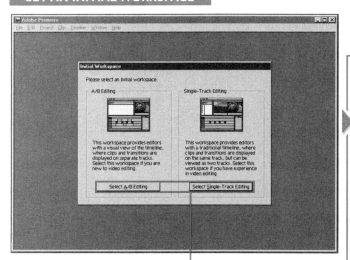

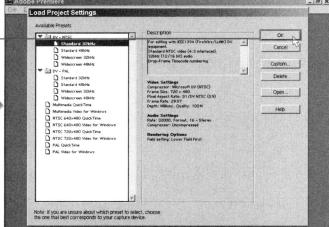

1 Open the Premiere program window.

■ The first time you launch Premiere, the Initial Workspace dialog box appears.

2 Click an editing option.

■ For basic editing, click Select A/B Editing.

■ For more complex editing tasks, click Select Single-Track Editing.

■ The Load Project Settings dialog box appears.

Note: See the section "Load Project Settings" to learn more about the various settings.

3 Click OK.

■ Premiere opens the associated editing environment.

Note: The next time you launch the program, Premiere uses the initial editing layout you chose.

CHANGE WORKSPACE SETTINGS

You may want to change workspace settings from one project to the next. If you are starting out with editing, A/B Editing mode is recommended, as it presents the most visual information to work with. Single-Track Editing mode is great for making fast edits, especially when you are familiar with the editing process.

A/B Editing mode is intended primarily for editors who wish to work by dragging clips from the Project window to the Timeline window. This mode resembles a conventional editing method called *A/B roll editing*, which uses two videotapes or rolls (A and B) and an effects switcher to provide transitions.

Single-Track Editing mode is intended for trimming and positioning clips by setting In and Out points in the Source view of the Monitor window, and inserting and overlaying the trimmed clips into the Timeline window. For basic video programs, such as a *cuts-only* (no transitions) rough cut, you may want to use Single-Track mode. All tools act on the three subtracks as a single track when they are combined in Single-Track Editing mode.

CHANGE WORKSPACE SETTINGS

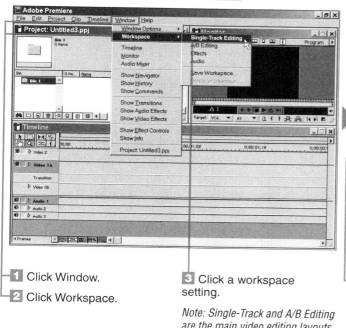

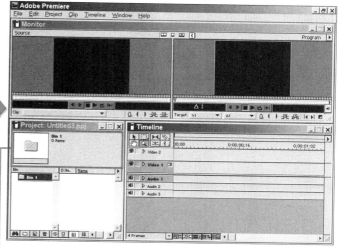

■ Click Window.

■ Click Workspace.

■ Click a workspace setting.

Note: Single-Track and A/B Editing are the main video editing layouts.

■ Premiere displays the workspace setting you specified.

■ This example shows the Single-Track Editing workspace.

Note: You can resize the various windows as needed by clicking and dragging the window borders.

START A NEW PROJECT

Y ou can start a new project at any time. A *project* is a single Premiere file that describes a video program. It stores references to all the clips in that file and contains information about how you arranged the clips. It also includes details of any transitions or effects you applied.

You can add and remove clips, organize clips into bins within the

project, and substitute low-resolution clips as placeholders for your final, high-resolution clips. All of this information is organized for you and kept in this one location, making your editing easier.

By default, Premiere opens a new project using the default presets whenever you launch the program. These defaults can be changed at the Load Project Settings screen;

you can select between NTSC (North American) and PAL (European) settings for traditional video, or between QuickTime and Video for Windows settings for content destined for the Internet.

START A NEW PROJECT

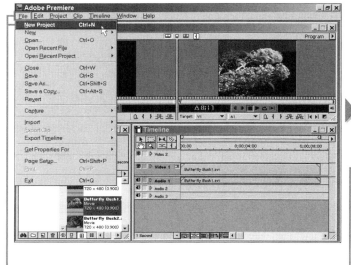

■1 Click File.

■2 Click New Project.

■ The Load Project Settings dialog box appears.

■3 Click OK to use the default settings.

■ To use another preset, click the preset from the list before clicking OK.

■ To customize the settings, click here.

■ Premiere opens a new project file onscreen.

OPEN AN EXISTING PROJECT

You can open an existing Premiere project at any time. Premiere project files end with the .ppj extension; the Open dialog box is set to look for all supported video format files. If you want to list only the project files, click the drop-down arrow (⬇) and select Premiere Project (*.ppj).

Premiere 6 can only open files created with Premiere version 4.2 or later.

A project file contains information about the project, including pointers to the files you are using in the project; it does not contain an actual copy of the files you use.

If you have renamed or moved one of the files in your project, Premiere will ask you to locate the file you were using.

Only one project is allowed to be open at a time in Premiere. Be sure to save your current project before opening another project file.

OPEN AN EXISTING PROJECT

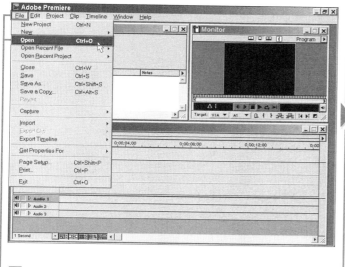

■1 Click File.

■2 Click Open.

■ The Open dialog box appears.

Note: To open a recently used project file, click File, Open Recent Project, and then the file.

■3 Click the project file you want to open.

■ You can click here to look in other folders or drives.

■4 Click Open.

■ Premiere opens the project file.

SAVE A PROJECT

Y ou can save a project file and assign it a unique name for reusing it later. Project files are much smaller in size than source files, as they include references to source files as well as all of your recent edits. Premiere will automatically save your files with a .ppj extension for you.

If you are working on a complex project, you should save your files frequently. You should also save just prior to making a complex edit, or just after making one that you are satisfied with. That way you can recover your project if your system crashes, if you do not like the edits you just completed, or to make sure your editing efforts are protected.

Premiere can also save your project file for you automatically. From the menu, select Edit, Preferences, and then Auto Save and Undo. Select the Auto Save box (□ changes to ☑) and then type the elapsed time between auto saves (default is 5 minutes).

SAVE A PROJECT

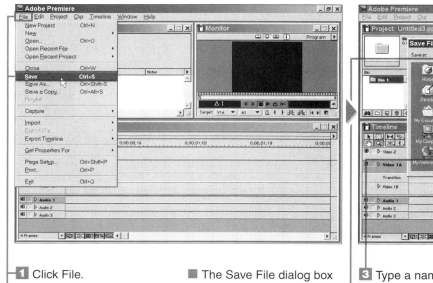

■1 Click File.

■2 Click Save.

■ The Save File dialog box appears.

■ To save an existing file under a new filename, click the Save As command.

■3 Type a name for the file.

■ Click here to locate a different folder or drive in which to save to the file.

■4 Click Save.

■ Premiere saves the project file.

Note: To save changes to an existing project, click File, and then Save.

CLOSE A PROJECT

Y ou can close a project when you want to start a new project or when you want to close the Premiere program window. Because you can have only one project open at a time in Premiere, you must close a project first before you can open a new one.

When you close a project, you do not close Premiere; in order to close Premiere, from the menu click File and then Exit. You can also use the shortcut keys Ctrl + Q (Command - Q) to exit Premiere.

If you have not saved your project, Premiere will ask you if you want to save it. Saving a project writes

out information about all the video clips, audio clips, transitions, and edits into a PPJ file. If you have not named your project — that is, you see the name "Untitled" in the title bar — you can type a name for your project at this time and click Save. Your project will be saved with the new name.

CLOSE A PROJECT

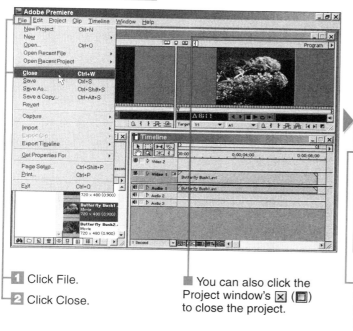

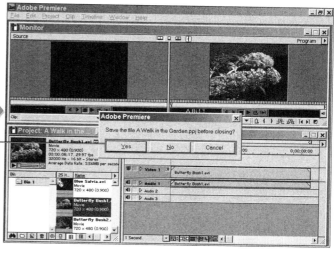

■1 Click File.

■2 Click Close.

■ You can also click the Project window's ⊠ (◻) to close the project.

■ If you have not saved your work, Premiere prompts you to do so. Click Yes to save, No to close without saving, or Cancel to abort the action.

SAVE PROJECT SETTINGS

Premiere installs with a variety of presets for different hardware configurations and video needs, but you can customize these project settings to suit your own work needs. You can save any changes you make to the project settings and reuse the settings in another project.

Project settings apply to each Premiere project and are broken

down into five categories. They include general settings, which control editing, counting time, and the time base; video settings, which control playback appearance in the Timeline; audio settings, which set audio characteristics; Keyframe and Rendering Options, which control frame characteristics when you build and play back video previews from the Timeline; and Capture

Settings, which control how Premiere transfers video and audio directly from a deck or camera.

If you want to see what your current project settings are, you can use the Project Settings Viewer to give you an overview of all your settings. See "Using the Settings Viewer," later in this chapter, for more information.

SAVE PROJECT SETTINGS

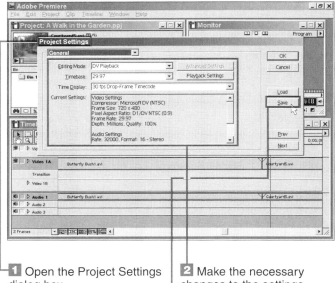

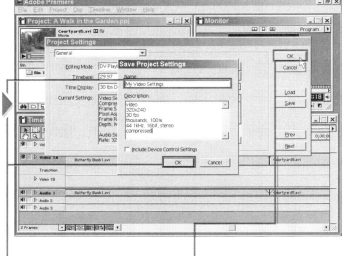

1 Open the Project Settings dialog box.

Note: See the section "Navigate the Project Window" to learn how to open the dialog box and view settings options.

2 Make the necessary changes to the settings categories.

3 Click the Save button.

■ The Save Project Settings dialog box appears.

4 Type a name for the file.

■ Optionally, you can type a description of the settings.

5 Click OK.

■ The settings are saved as a preset file.

6 Click OK again to close the Project Settings dialog box.

Note: See the section "Load Project Settings" to learn how to reuse the settings you saved.

LOAD PROJECT SETTINGS

Y ou can load your project settings and then use them with another project. Premiere stores project settings files in the Settings folder within the Premiere program folder. This central storage location enables you to easily distribute the settings file to other people you may be

working with on the same project who use the same equipment.

Preset project settings are listed in the Load Project Settings dialog box to allow you easy access to them when you begin a new project. Premiere comes equipped with settings files preset for typical programs, which you can adapt and

save for your own projects. Most certified analog video capture cards include preset settings files for Premiere. If your capture card provides a preset file, you should use it and not manually change the settings; otherwise you may get unusual output or poor-quality output in your video projects.

LOAD PROJECT SETTINGS

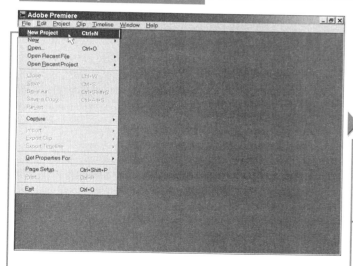

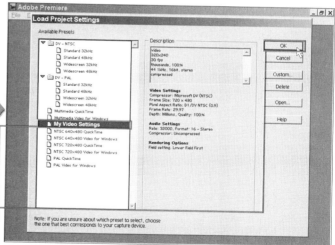

■1 Start a new project or launch Premiere.

Note: See the section "Start a New Project" to learn more.

■ The Load Project Settings dialog box appears.

■2 Click the preset you want to use.

■3 Click OK.

■ A new project opens using the presets you selected.

USING THE SETTINGS VIEWER

You can get a quick snapshot of all the settings assigned to your project using Premiere's Settings Viewer window. The Settings Viewer lets you see settings for your video capture, Premiere project, video clips, and export (that is, destination device) settings. From within the Settings Viewer you can click the

appropriate column heading to bring up the dialog box for those settings. For instance, if you need to change your Premiere settings, you can click the heading "Project Settings" and bring up the Project Settings dialog box.

You can also change your project settings while working on a project.

Clicking Project and then Project Settings gives you access to the dialog boxes for your project's five different settings categories.

For best performance when working with and rendering your project, your settings should be identical between Capture, Project, and Clip categories.

USING THE SETTINGS VIEWER

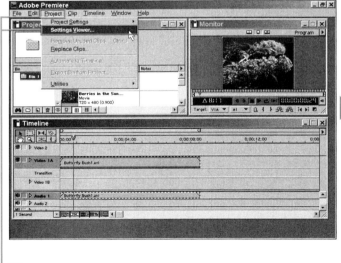

■1 Click Project.

■2 Click Settings Viewer.

■ The Settings Viewer window opens.

■ You can compare the settings for projects, capture, clips, and exports.

■ To make changes to a setting group, click here and the Project Settings dialog box appears.

■3 Click OK.

■ The Settings Viewer is closed.

NAVIGATE THE PROJECT WINDOW

You can use the Project window to manage the content of your video. The Project window lists all the clips and other production elements you plan to use in your project.

Project Window Menu

You can display a menu of commands pertaining to the Project window.

Preview Area

This area displays information about the selected clip or bin.

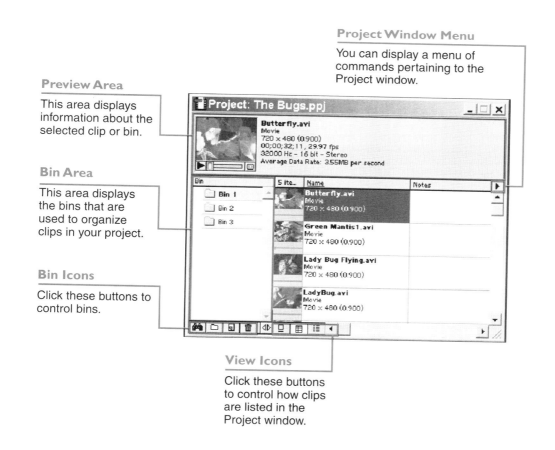

Bin Area

This area displays the bins that are used to organize clips in your project.

Bin Icons

Click these buttons to control bins.

View Icons

Click these buttons to control how clips are listed in the Project window.

CREATE A STORYBOARD

You can use a *storyboard* to help you put together a video project. In filmmaking, a storyboard is a series of drawings or illustrations that tell the story visually according to what is in the script. Storyboards typically consist of key actions within a scene, drawing it out as if it were being viewed through a camera lens. Storyboards are a crucial piece of

the filmmaking puzzle, giving you the first visual glimpse of how your scenes and sequences will come together.

In Premiere, the Storyboard window lets you arrange still images created from video clips in any order you want. This way you can position the clips in the order in which you want the final video.

You can think of the Storyboard window as a staging area or mockup area where you can quickly move elements around without worrying about any other edits, transitions, or effects.

You can save the arrangement as a storyboard file for later use in the Timeline.

CREATE A STORYBOARD

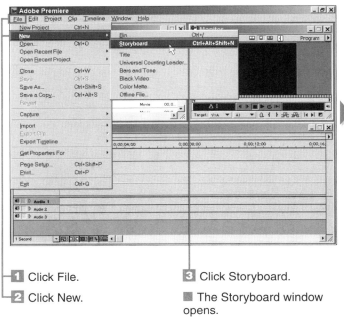

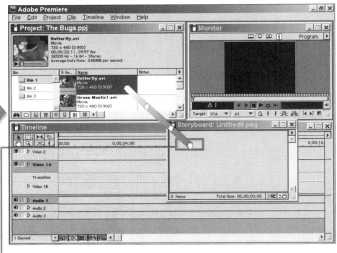

1 Click File.

2 Click New.

3 Click Storyboard.

■ The Storyboard window opens.

4 Click and drag the first clip you want to use from the Project window to the Storyboard window.

Can I create a storyboard in the Project window?

✔ Yes. Place all the clips you want to use in the same bin, switch to icon view, and arrange the clips in the order you want to place them. To automate the clips to the timeline, click Project and then Automate to Timeline.

Can I drag and drop clips directly from my desktop into the Storyboard window?

✔ No. You must first import clips into a project before you can drag them into a storyboard. If you drag a file into the Project window, it appears in a Clip window, and if you drag a file into the Timeline it is placed in both the bin and the Timeline. See Chapter 16 to import clips into the Project window.

How do I annotate the clips in the Storyboard window?

✔ You can add notes into the rectangular area below the clip information. Double-click the area and the Edit Note dialog box appears. Type your notes about the clip, the film, transitions or edits, or directorial notes, and then click OK. If you want to discard the note, click Cancel in the Edit Note box.

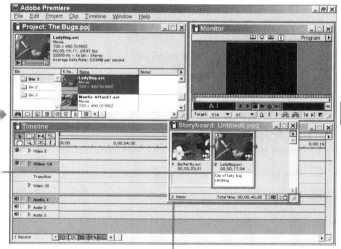

-5 Continue dragging clips to assemble the video.

■ To reorder a clip in the Storyboard window, drag a clip to a new position.

■ You can resize the window by clicking and dragging its borders.

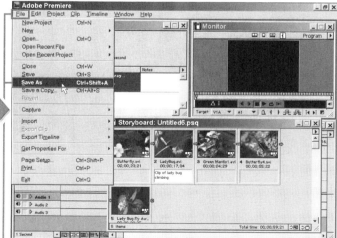

-6 Click File.

-7 Click Save As.

■ The Save File dialog box appears.

CONTINUED ▶

CREATE A STORYBOARD (CONTINUED)

The Storyboard Window is used to create a mockup of your clips in the rough order in which they are to appear. After creating your storyboard, you can have Premiere place the storyboard items into the Timeline window using the Automate to Timeline command. This handy feature enables you to make the necessary rough edits in your film within the

Storyboard window, and then import your film ready to be edited.

When the Timeline imports your storyboard, the default settings are for your video clips to be placed in a single track, with no edits, in sequential order. You can change any of these options when you automate the storyboard. A dialog box appears, enabling you to change whether you import all the

clips from the bin or just the selected ones, how much clip overlap to allow, and whether to use the default transition as separators for your clips.

After you have automated your storyboard to the Timeline, you can close the Storyboard window. If you have not saved it, you will be prompted to do so.

CREATE A STORYBOARD (CONTINUED)

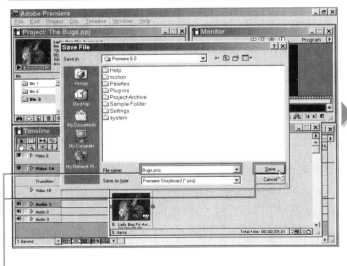

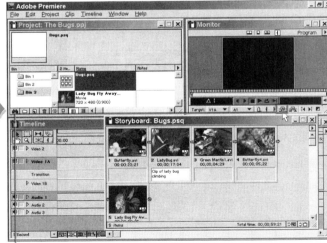

■8 Type a name for the storyboard file.

■9 Click Save.

■ Premiere saves the storyboard and adds it to the Project window.

■10 Click the Automate to Timeline button (⊞).

■ The Automate to Timeline dialog box appears.

Can I edit a clip from the storyboard window?

✔ Yes. Double-click the clip's thumbnail image to open the Clip window. See Chapters 16 and 17 to learn more about working with the Clip window and editing clips.

What should I name my storyboard files?

✔ You can give the storyboard file any name that is helpful; you can give it the same name as your film project. Storyboard files are saved with a .psq file extension. It is a good idea to save them in the same location as your project files so you can keep your Premiere files together.

Can I use a different transition than the default transition?

✔ The Storyboard uses a hard cut to transition between video clips; it does not let you specify other transitions such as a wipe or dissolve. You can add transitions to your clips in the Timeline after importing your storyboard. See Chapter 19 for information on edits and transitions for your film clips.

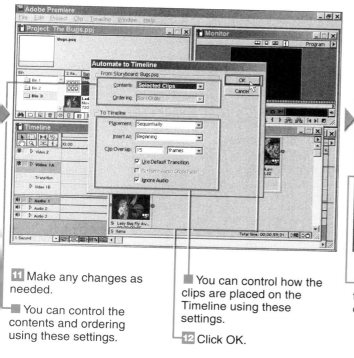

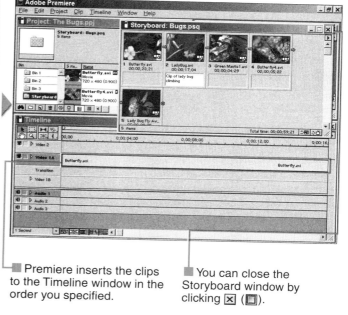

■ 11 Make any changes as needed.

■ You can control the contents and ordering using these settings.

■ You can control how the clips are placed on the Timeline using these settings.

■ 12 Click OK.

■ Premiere inserts the clips to the Timeline window in the order you specified.

■ You can close the Storyboard window by clicking ☒ (▣).

UNDERSTANDING VIDEO CAPTURE

You can transfer digital video directly from your DV camcorder to Premier as long as you have the right connection hardware. The process, called *video capture*, sends data from one source to another.

Digital Basics

Digitized video is compressed regardless of what method of capture you use. To give you some idea of why compression is necessary, consider that every frame in an uncompressed digital video consumes up to 1 megabyte (MB) of space. The DV format compresses video at a 5:1 ratio.

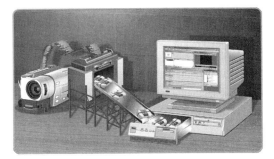

Capture Limitations

Although the Premiere Timeline can hold up to three hours of video, your computer system and capture hardware impose file size limitations. Check the appropriate hardware documentation before capturing large amounts of video.

Digital Quality

The quality of the video you capture depends on the quality of the equipment you are using. Some digital camcorders may be able to produce higher-quality footage than others. If capturing video from an analog device, try capturing from the original "master" footage, because analog copies degrade significantly with each generation.

Capture Devices

Transferring sound and video from a DV camcorder to a computer requires an *IEEE 1394*, or *FireWire*, port on your computer as well as the same output ports on your camcorder (sometimes labeled i.LINK). To capture video from analog sources, you need to use an analog-to-digital capture board. You must digitize any analog media if you want to use it in Premiere.

Timecode

Videotape uses an encoded signal called a *timecode* to identify each frame of the captured video. The timecode number includes hours, minutes, seconds, and frames. Premiere can use timecode to assist with capturing clips, particularly with capturing a batch of clips.

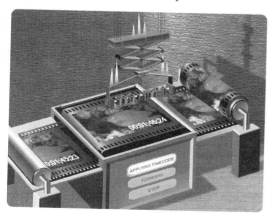

Device Control

If your camcorder and FireWire card are compatible with Premiere, you can use the device control built into Premiere to operate your camcorder or video deck from within the Premiere program window. Enabling device control lets you use the controls in the Movie Capture window to play, stop, and rewind the tape.

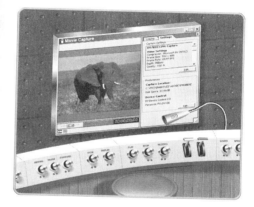

Batch Capture

If you are using device control and time-coded tape, you can capture batches of clips automatically. Premiere locates each clip you specify in a batch list and captures the clip for you.

UNDERSTANDING CLIPS

Your video project is based on *clips.* Clips are production elements you use to assemble your video. For example, in an action video, you may have a clip showing a man driving up to a building and another clip showing the same man entering the building. Yet another clip may show a close-up of the man's face. By putting the clips together, you create a scene.

Where Do I Find Clips?

Clips can be created from digital video footage shot with a camcorder, or from digital clips stored on your computer. To learn how to transfer video from a camcorder into Premiere, or to learn more about importing clips into Premiere, see subsequent sections in this chapter. Regardless of the source of your footage, all clips you use in Premiere must be digitized.

What Kinds of Clips Can I Use?

Digital video is the main type of clip you will work with in Premiere. You can also use *static clips,* such as graphics, photographs, or text, for example. You can create title clips and simple graphics in Premiere using the Title window. See Chapter 20 to learn more about the titling feature.

Viewing Clips

You can use several different methods to view a clip in Premiere. You can open the clip in a separate Clip window that has control for playing the clip, or you can play a clip directly in the Project window. You can use the Source view area in the Monitor window to view and edit a clip. To add a clip to the project, you must add the clip to the project's timeline. After you add clips to the Timeline window, you can view the video using the Program view area of the Monitor window.

Adding Clips to the Timeline

To use a clip in your video, you must add it to the Timeline window. Video, still image, and title clips appear in the timeline's video tracks. Sound clips appear in the timeline's audio tracks. To learn more about using the Timeline window, see Chapter 18.

Editing Clips

Premiere offers several routes that you can take to edit the clips you want to use in your video. You can perform a few editing techniques within the Clip window, but most editing occurs in either the Monitor or Timeline windows, or a combination of both. To learn more about editing in either window, see Chapters 17 and 18.

Setting In and Out Points

An important editing technique to master is trimming the clip by setting in and out points. The *in point* is the frame in which the clip starts. The *out point* is the frame in which the clip ends. By setting in and out points, you determine the length of the clip. You can set in and out points in the Clip window as well as the Monitor and Timeline windows.

WORK WITH THE MOVIE CAPTURE WINDOW

You can use the Movie Capture window to transfer video from a digital camcorder to your Premiere project. You can preview your video before recording it to a clip, cue the video to the segment you want to record, or set up capture settings.

The Movie Capture window includes a preview window, which displays your currently recording

video, controls for recording with and without device control, a Settings panel for viewing and editing your current capture settings, and a logging panel for entering batch capture settings. You can log clips for batch capture only when using device control. You can set the preview area to the Fit in Window mode so that the video always fills the preview area.

The Movie Capture window menu also displays options depending on the capture format you are using. For example, the QuickTime capture format includes the Video Input, Audio Input, and Advanced menu options, whereas the Video for Windows capture format does not.

WORK WITH THE MOVIE CAPTURE WINDOW

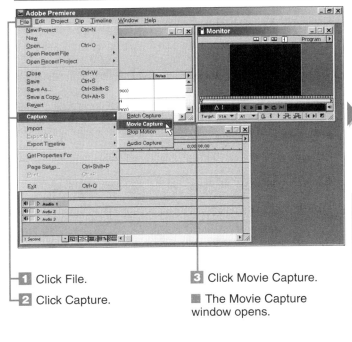

■1 Click File.

■2 Click Capture.

■3 Click Movie Capture.

■ The Movie Capture window opens.

■ You can view the video in the Preview area.

■ Use these buttons to control playback of the video.

■ If device control is enabled, you can also use these controls to control your camcorder or DV device.

■ The video's timecode appears here.

How do I capture video from a VHS camcorder or VCR?

✔ You must convert analog VHS, VHS-C, or Video8 signals to digital with a capture card in your computer or with a conversion device like those found in many electronics superstores. Refer to the capture card or converter documentation for details about configuring and using those devices.

Do I need to create a project before I can capture video?

✔ No. If you have a board that digitizes analog video signals, you can use the Movie Capture window to grab your video directly and save it onto your hard drive.

Can I have the Movie Capture window open all the time?

✔ When performing anything other than capturing in Premiere, close the Movie Capture window. Because the Movie Capture window assumes primary focus when open, leaving it open while editing or previewing video disables output to the DV device and may decrease performance.

■ These icons toggle video and audio capture on or off when not using device control.

■ On the Settings tab, you can view and specify capture settings and preferences.

■ Clicking ▶ displays the Movie Capture window menu.

■ Clicking the Logging tab lets you log clips for batch capture.

■ To close the Movie Capture window when finished, click the ⊠ (☐) button.

CHANGE CAPTURE SETTINGS

To ensure that Premiere provides the best possible support for your capture card, you can change capture settings using the Project Settings dialog box. The options available to you depend on the equipment you are using. For example, users whose computers have IEEE 1394 ports have different options than those with capture boards installed.

Most of the supported capture cards provide a settings file (preset) that you can select in Premiere's Load Project Settings dialog box. This preset automatically sets all capture settings for optimal support with your capture card. If your video capture board has a settings file, it is strongly recommended that you use that file with Premiere. Video card manufacturers

work closely with Adobe to ensure their capture cards work with Premiere, and they have spent many hours determining the optimal settings for it. You should select the settings file for projects in which you will capture clips or import clips, and you should not change the capture settings in the Settings dialog box.

CHANGE CAPTURE SETTINGS

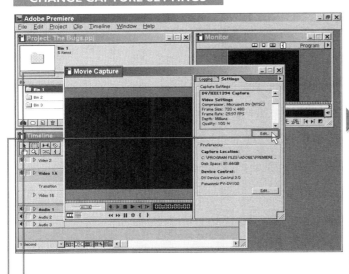

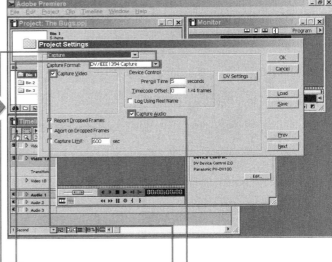

1 Open the Movie Capture window.

Note: See the section "Work with the Movie Capture Window" to open the window.

2 Click the Edit button.

■ The Project Settings dialog box appears and displays capture settings.

Note: If the capture settings are not displayed, click the Next or Prev buttons to navigate to the options.

3 Change any capture settings as needed.

Note: The options available are based on your hardware and system setup.

■ To change the capture format, click here.

■ To capture audio without video, click this option (☑ changes to ☐).

■ To capture video without audio, click this option (☑ changes to ☐).

How can I improve my capture performance?

✔ Even though the Timeline window can contain up to three hours of video, the actual working file size is determined by the amount of RAM, processor speed, disk space, and video capture card capabilities of your system. Premiere uses a designated scratch disk, like a paper scratch pad, to handle overflow files created while editing, such as previewing files and capturing clips. You can improve performance by using your fastest and least-crowded hard drive as a scratch disk. On the Settings tab, click Edit in the Preferences section. Click Select Folder from the Captured Movies drop-down list, and choose a new folder on your fastest disk.

What do the Device Control settings do?

✔ If device control is enabled, the Capture category's options are enabled; if not, the options are dimmed. The options enable you to control the playing of the source tape in a DV device, such as a DV camcorder. For example, you can set the Pre-roll Time option to specify how many seconds of tape to play to get the footage up to speed for capture.

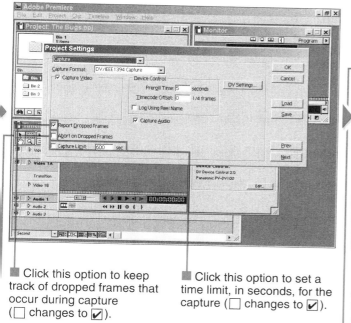

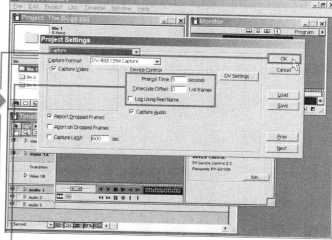

■ Click this option to keep track of dropped frames that occur during capture (☐ changes to ☑).

■ If you want to stop the capture if frames are dropped, click this option (☐ changes to ☑).

■ Click this option to set a time limit, in seconds, for the capture (☐ changes to ☑).

■ If you are using device control, you can set Device Control options.

4 Click OK.

■ The Project Settings dialog box is closed and any new settings are applied.

CAPTURE VIDEO IN THE MOVIE CAPTURE WINDOW

To import video from a camcorder, you need to capture it using your video capture card. Most cards provide the ability to digitize analog signals; this is required if you want to use analog video in Premiere. You only have the ability to work with digital video sources, so any analog signals must be converted to

digital. The capture card does this by converting variations in electrical signals (analog) into a stream of 1's and 0's (digital). You can then save the digital video onto your hard drive, and use it in Premiere.

The Movie Capture window also lets you capture video footage

directly into your project. With device control activated, you can control your digital camera from within the Premiere program window. This gives you the ability to view your footage in Premiere while you view and select footage without touching your camera.

CAPTURE VIDEO IN THE MOVIE CAPTURE WINDOW

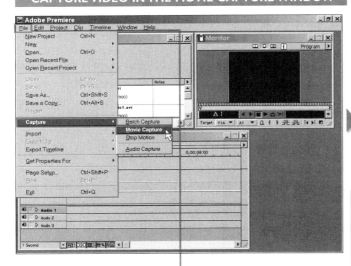

1 Turn on your camcorder and set it to VCR/VTR mode.

Note: See the section "Understanding Video Capture" to learn more about required hardware.

2 Open the project and bin you want to capture to.

3 Click File.

4 Click Capture.

5 Click Movie Capture.

■ The Movie Capture window opens.

6 Cue the video to the section you want to capture.

■ With device control, you can use the controls on the camcorder or in the Movie capture window to cue the video.

7 Click the Play button (▶).

■ If you are not using device control, click ▶ on the camcorder.

8 Click the Record button (⬛).

■ Premiere starts transferring the footage.

How do I enable device control?
✔ Turn on your DV device and start Premiere. In the Movie Capture window, click the Edit button on the Settings tab under the Preferences heading. Then, choose the device controller you are using from the Device ▼ in the Scratch Disks & Device Control category. To set additional options for the device, click the Options button.

What should I do if Premiere does not recognize my camcorder?
✔ Premiere may not show your camcorder in the the Device list in the Scratch Disks & Device Control category. If your camcorder is not listed there, visit www.adobe.com and check the DV hardware compatibility database for more information.

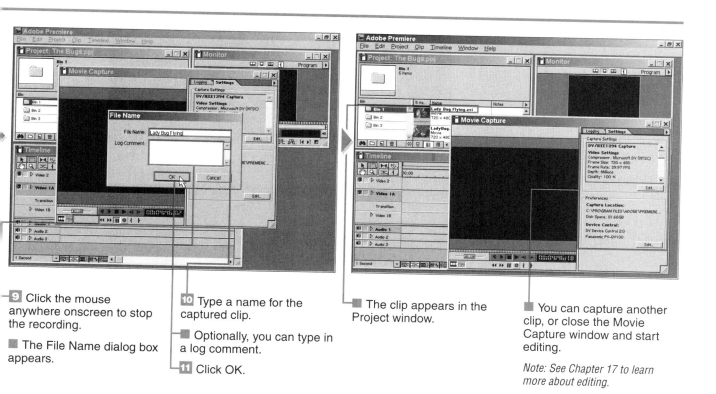

9 Click the mouse anywhere onscreen to stop the recording.

■ The File Name dialog box appears.

10 Type a name for the captured clip.

■ Optionally, you can type in a log comment.

11 Click OK.

■ The clip appears in the Project window.

■ You can capture another clip, or close the Movie Capture window and start editing.

Note: See Chapter 17 to learn more about editing.

333

PERFORM A BATCH CAPTURE

A batch capture is a process where you capture multiple video excerpts from a digital camera. If you are using device control along with time-coded tape, you can batch capture clips into Premiere. This capability lets you select which takes or scenes you want to import into Premiere all at once, rather than one at a time. It is

a very useful way of getting only the footage you want, rather than importing the entire footage and then editing it in Premiere. The batch process is automatic and unattended.

Begin by viewing your tape in Premiere using the Movie Capture window and noting the segments

along with the start and stop times for each segment. You then make a list of the segments you want to capture, and then tell Premiere to capture each clip in the list. A batch list is saved as a special batch list file type and can be reopened and edited as needed.

PERFORM A BATCH CAPTURE

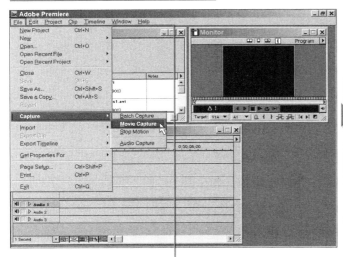

CREATE A CAPTURE LIST

1 Connect and turn on the DV device or hardware you want to use for capturing.

Note: See the section "Understanding Video Capture" to learn more about required hardware.

2 Click File.

3 Click Capture.

4 Click Movie Capture.

■ The Movie Capture window opens.

5 Click the Logging tab.

■ The Logging tab displays options for batch lists.

6 Type the name of the reel or tape you are using.

7 Cue the tape to the frame you want to start from for the first clip you want to capture.

8 Click the Set In button.

■ The current timecode is listed here.

How do I create a batch list if I am not using device control?

✔ Click File, Capture, and then Batch Control to open an untitled Batch Capture window. Click 🔲 to open the Clip Capture Parameters window, where you can specify reel name, clip name, and timecode in and out points. After manually entering information about the clip, click OK to send the information to the Batch Capture window. You can save the list and batch capture when you are ready.

I am having problems capturing the first minute of my video with batch capture. Am I not doing something right?

✔ Batch capture is not recommended for the first and last 30 seconds of your tape because of possible timecode and seeking issues. Instead, capture these sections manually. It is also a good idea, when recording with a digital camcorder, to shoot some header footage to help avoid this problem in the future.

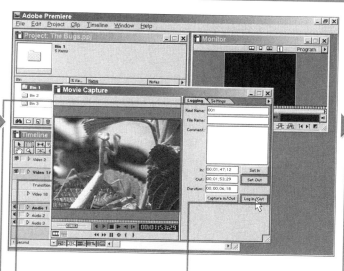

9 Cue the tape to the frame where you want to stop the capture.

10 Click the Set Out button.

■ The current timecode is listed here.

11 Click the Log In/Out button.

■ The File Name dialog box appears.

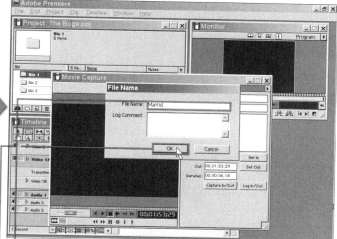

12 Type a name for the captured clip.

13 Click OK.

■ The clip appears in the batch list.

Note: The Batch Capture window appears onscreen after you create the first clip in the list.

14 Continue adding clips to your batch list by following steps 7 through 13.

■ Each clip you log is added to the batch list.

CONTINUED ▶

PERFORM A BATCH CAPTURE
(CONTINUED)

After assembling a batch list, you can start capturing the clips listed. The icons that appear next to the clips in a batch list can help tell you about the capture status. Before you begin the capturing process, be sure to make the necessary hardware connections and change any settings, such as the designated scratch disk. By

default, the settings Premiere uses to capture clips in a batch list are the settings used by the project that is open at the time you log the clips into the batch list.

When you save a batch file to disk, you create a file that contains each video clip entry and its capture settings in a file format that only

Premiere can understand. You can also export a batch list, which creates a tab-delimited ASCII text file that lists each entry but does not retain the capture settings. You may want to export a batch list as a text file to edit it in text-editing programs or in video-editing systems that can read text batch lists.

PERFORM A BATCH CAPTURE (CONTINUED)

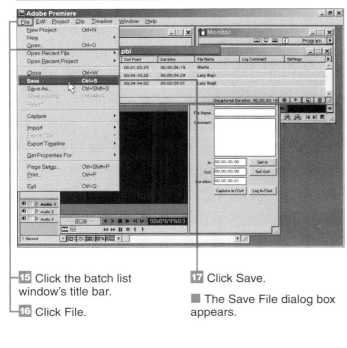

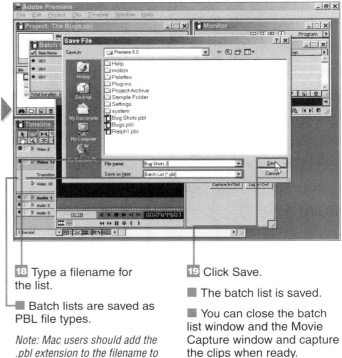

15 Click the batch list window's title bar.

16 Click File.

17 Click Save.

■ The Save File dialog box appears.

18 Type a filename for the list.

■ Batch lists are saved as PBL file types.

Note: Mac users should add the .pbl extension to the filename to keep the list cross-platform compatible.

19 Click Save.

■ The batch list is saved.

■ You can close the batch list window and the Movie Capture window and capture the clips when ready.

Why did my batch capture stop in the middle of the capture process?

✔ If the capture stops in the middle, your digital camera may be going into sleep mode in order to save battery power. Plug your camera into a wall outlet, or turn off sleep mode in your camera's settings.

I tried to stop a batch capture in the middle and Premiere gave me an error. Is this normal?

✔ If you attempt to cancel a batch capture while the device is seeking or shuttling to the next timecode, the capture will not cancel and Premiere may return an error. Wait until the device is done seeking or shuttling and then cancel the batch capture.

Why did Premiere abort my batch capture?

✔ If your tape has unrecorded areas or gaps, the broken timecode sequence can cause Premiere to abort batch capture. To work around the problem, you can log clips manually by entering in and out times. To avoid timecode gaps in the future, make sure you fully understand how your camcorder records, particularly when starting and stopping scenes.

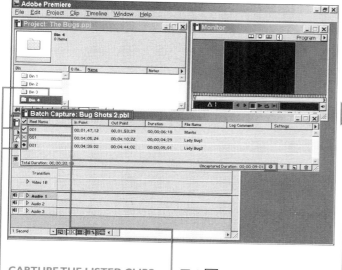

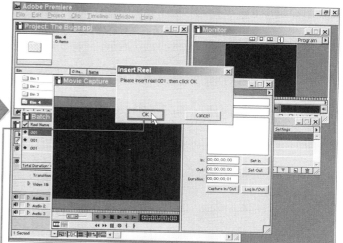

CAPTURE THE LISTED CLIPS

1 Click a bin in which to store the captured clips.

2 Open the batch list.

■ A ◆ icon indicates the clip will be captured.

■ A ✓ icon indicates the clip has been captured.

■ A ☒ icon indicates an error during capture.

3 Click the Record button ▣.

■ Premiere prompts you to insert the reel or tape.

Note: Premiere saves clips to the scratch disk that you already set. See "Set the Scratch Disk" to learn more.

4 Click OK.

■ The Movie Capture window captures the clips.

Note: To save the current status of a batch list, click File, Save while the batch list window is active.

IMPORT CLIPS

You can import video and audio clips into your Premiere project from sources other than a digital camera. Premiere can import digital video from other formats such as Microsoft Video for Windows AVI (Audio Video Interleave) files, Apple QuickTime (MOV) files, and OpenDML (Digital Media) files. Video clips cannot exceed 4,000 x 4,000 pixels

in size. Most Internet digital videos do not exceed common monitor sizes, such as 1,024 x 768 pixels, and most are less than that (AVI supports 320 x 240 pixels at 30 frames per second). If you are working with extremely large screen sizes, you should consider rendering your clip down to a smaller size.

Premiere also imports still images, including TIFF and JPEG image files. Premiere enables you to import either one clip or many, which appear in the Project window. You can then use any of these images and clips in your project.

IMPORT A SINGLE CLIP

1 Click the bin to which you want to import.

2 Click File.

3 Click Import.

4 Click File.

■ The Import dialog box appears.

5 Click the file you want to import.

■ You can click ▼ to navigate to a particular file or folder.

6 Click Open.

■ You can also double-click the filename to quickly import the file.

■ The file is imported and appears listed in the Project window.

Note: See Chapter 15 to learn more about the Project window.

Can I import Photoshop or Illustrator images?

✔ Yes. You can import images from Photoshop or Illustrator if they have been saved in the Photoshop file format (PSD). See Chapters 7 and 14, respectively, for information on saving Photoshop and Illustrator images.

What do I do if I want to import footage such as RealVideo into my project?

✔ Premiere's support for various digital formats is typically provided by plug-ins. You can attain plug-ins from the software manufacturer or from Adobe. Check the manufacturer's Web site or the Adobe Web site to find available plug-ins.

Why does Premiere call them bins and clips rather than files and folders?

✔ The terms *bins* and *clips* are taken from the world of motion picture film editing. Editors used to clip a section of processed film to a wire and let it fall into a cotton lined trash bin or basket. Any sections of the filmstrip that had to be cut out, or *clipped*, were hung in the bin until the editor was ready to cement them into place on the filmstrip.

IMPORT MULTIPLE CLIPS

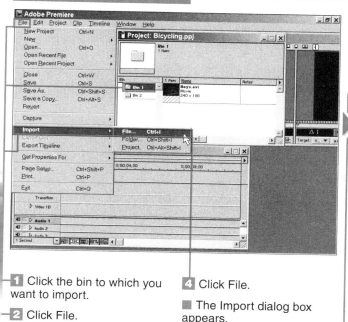

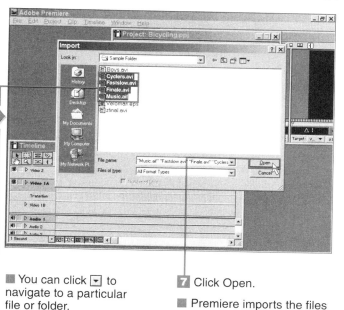

-1 Click the bin to which you want to import.

-2 Click File.

-3 Click Import.

-4 Click File.

■ The Import dialog box appears.

■ You can click ▾ to navigate to a particular file or folder.

-5 Press Ctrl (Shift).

-6 Click each filename you want to import.

-7 Click Open.

■ Premiere imports the files and lists them in the Project window.

Note: See Chapter 15 to learn more about working with clips in the Project window.

VIEW A VIDEO CLIP

When you first start a project, you may think that the Monitor window is the best place to work on video clips. You will sometimes, however, need to view different clips without moving back and forth along the Timeline, or you may want to preview some clips at full size that are in your bin but are not part of your Timeline. In those cases, you want to use a Clip window to perform basic clip viewing or editing functions.

You can open a video clip and view it in the Clip window from anywhere in Premiere. The Clip window includes controls for playing, stopping, looping, and editing a clip. When you view still images in the Clip window, no playback controls appear. Audio clips display a waveform of the audio so you can set precise in and out points.

VIEW A VIDEO CLIP

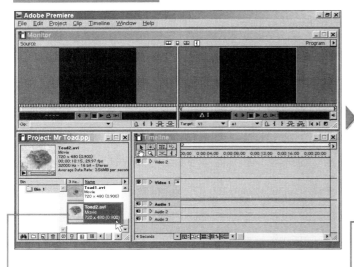

■1 With a project open, double-click the clip you want to view.

Note: See Chapter 15 to start or open a project.

■ The Clip window opens.

■2 Click ▶.

■ The clip plays.

■ You can click and drag the Set Location marker (⊽) to a particular point in the clip to play.

■ Clicking ■ stops the clip from playing.

■ Clicking ⟳ plays the clip continually.

■ Clicking ◀ and ▶ moves the Set Location marker back or forward a frame.

■3 Click ☒ (▢) to close the Clip window.

RENAME A CLIP

Organizing your clips can be an important task. Although you can sometimes easily use the same name for both the clip and the file, remembering just which clip you were planning on using becomes difficult when you have clips named after a scene and take number. To work around this

limitation, Premiere lets you create *alias names* for clips to help you identify them. The alias name can be anything you like that helps you remember the clip's purpose or usability in your project. The alias name does not affect the original clip name or reference.

When you import a clip, the project file references the clip's original location, but the clip itself is not saved until you export the video. For that reason, you should not rename a clip, but rather create an alias name.

RENAME A CLIP

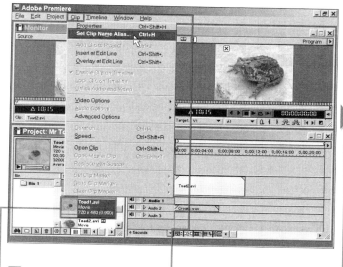

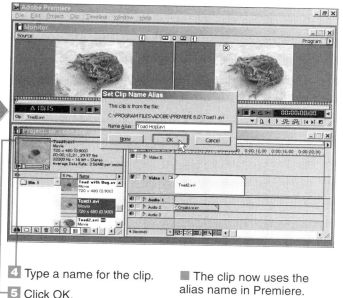

■1 Click the clip to which you want to assign an alias name.

Note: See Chapter 15 to start or open a project.

■2 Click Clip.

■3 Click Set Clip Name Alias.

■ The Set Clip Name Alias dialog box appears.

■4 Type a name for the clip.

■5 Click OK.

■ The clip now uses the alias name in Premiere.

ADD TIMECODE TO A CLIP

*T*imecode is a series of digits in hh:mm:ss:ff format that indicates exactly where you are in a clip. It is found in practically all video editing systems to give you precision in editing. Timecode enables you to select exactly which frame to set as an in or out point, or where to insert a transition.

You can add timecode to a clip to help you accurately read frames for editing. Many DV camcorders record timecode, and if you capture video using device control, the timecode is captured along with the clip. In some instances, the timecode appears on a separate track called a *window dub*. You can mark the timecode on your captured video manually.

Timecode is visible only in the tape counter on equipment that can recognize timecode, unless the timecode has been burned in, or recorded over the picture in a copy of the tape. If you do not want burned-in timecode, change the settings on your camera before you start filming on a new project.

ADD TIMECODE TO A CLIP

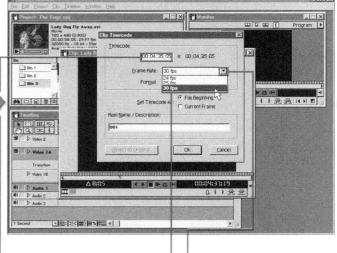

1 Open the clip to which you want to assign timecode.

Note: See "View a Video Clip," earlier in this chapter, to work with clips.

2 Click Clip.

3 Click Advanced Options.

4 Click Timecode.

■ The Clip Timecode dialog box appears.

5 Type the timecode number that matches the current frame.

6 Click ▾ to display available frame rates.

7 Click a frame rate that matches the source video.

Is timecode a part of all videotapes?

✔ Timecode is added to tapes you record to using device control. Cameras record timecode on a track that is separate from the video and audio tracks on a tape. The process is called *striping*. Tapes recorded on a home VCR, for example, do not add timecode to the tape.

My timecode seems off by several frames from my tape deck?

✔ Timecode captured with controllable devices depends on the precision of your tape deck. If your tape deck cannot read the timecode accurately, you may have to calibrate your system or manually assign the timecode to your movie by matching frames.

Why does my timecode have semicolons instead of colons?

✔ Semicolons are used to indicate you are using drop-frame timecode instead of non-drop-frame. Due to slight measuring variances, NTSC frame rate is actually 29.97 fps instead of 30 fps. If you are doing a lot of professional broadcast work on longer clip lengths, you should use drop-frame timecode in your editing.

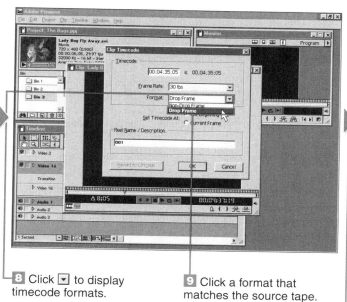

8 Click ▾ to display timecode formats.

9 Click a format that matches the source tape.

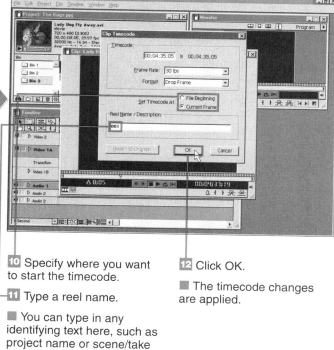

10 Specify where you want to start the timecode.

11 Type a reel name.

■ You can type in any identifying text here, such as project name or scene/take information.

12 Click OK.

■ The timecode changes are applied.

SET A FRAME DURATION FOR IMPORTED STILL IMAGES

Video projects commonly display a still image or graphic, such as those you can create in Illustrator and Photoshop, as a background against which the video plays. Newscasts and other broadcast journalism programs often use this technique. To repeat a still image for the duration of the video, you must set the frame duration in Premiere before importing the image file and

then import a still image. The image will play for a designated number of frames, even though the image itself comprises only a single frame.

You can also import an animation contained in a single file, such as an animated GIF. Premiere can import a sequence of numbered still-image files and automatically combine them into a single clip;

each numbered file represents one frame. Some programs, such as After Effects, can generate a sequential series of numbered still images. Images in a still-image sequence cannot include layers, so flatten any images that will be part of a sequence. For information on flattening layers in Photoshop and Illustrator, see Chapters 4 and 13, respectively.

SET A FRAME DURATION FOR IMPORTED STILL IMAGES

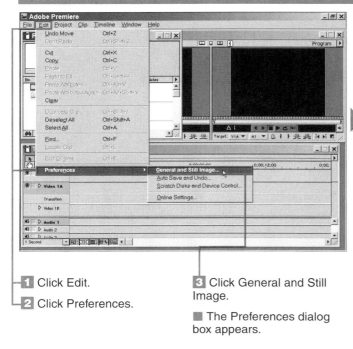

■1 Click Edit.

■2 Click Preferences.

■3 Click General and Still Image.

■ The Preferences dialog box appears.

■4 Type the number of frames you want to apply to imported still images.

Note: Still images previously imported are not affected by the new setting you type.

■5 Click OK.

■ Any new still images you import will use the frame duration specified.

Note: See the section "Import Clips" to import image files.

LOCK THE ASPECT RATIO FOR IMPORTED STILL IMAGES

By default, Premiere automatically sizes imported still images to fit the video frame size. If the image requires a different sizing ratio, you can lock the image's ratio before importing the image into Premiere. You can also scale an image to a size other than the size of the frame. If you plan to use many still images that use different aspect ratios from your project frame size, you can lock the aspect ratio of each still image before you import it.

If the image's aspect ratio differs from your project's settings, the image may appear with borders. If you import a nonsquare-pixel file that was created and saved at an odd size or a smaller frame size than used by your project, you should also select Square Pixels from the Pixel Aspect Ratio menu. Setting both of these options prevents Premiere from resizing the image to fill the screen and from resampling the file to match the pixel aspect ratio of the project.

LOCK THE ASPECT RATIO FOR IMPORTED STILL IMAGES

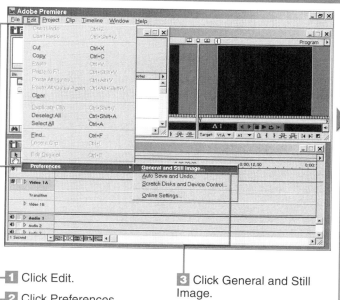

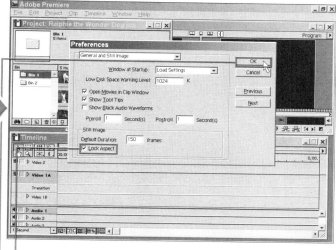

■ Click Edit.

■ Click Preferences.

■ Click General and Still Image.

■ The Preferences dialog box appears.

■ To keep the image's aspect ratio, click Lock Aspect (☐ changes to ☑).

■ Click OK.

■ The next still image you import keeps its original aspect ratio.

Note: See the section "Import Clips" to import image files.

ADD A LEADER CLIP

YYou can use Premiere source files to create *leader clips*. A leader clip appears at the beginning of a video showing a color bar and tone or a countdown that starts before the start of the actual video. You need leader clips if you plan to send your project to a production house to be finished.

Premiere lets you add three basic types of leader clips to your video. The first is bars and tone, which is used to calibrate video and audio and is 10 seconds long. The second is a *universal counting leader*. The leader is 11 seconds long and can be customized with different color and sound calibration options. The

third is a black video clip of a 640 x 480 still image with duration of 4 seconds. These three clips can be created and inserted anywhere in your project, although editors normally place the first two at the start.

ADD A LEADER CLIP

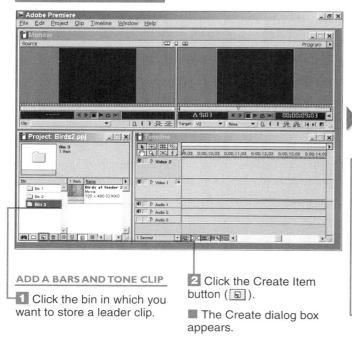

ADD A BARS AND TONE CLIP

■1 Click the bin in which you want to store a leader clip.

■2 Click the Create Item button (⬚).

■ The Create dialog box appears.

■3 Click ▾ to display object types.

■4 Click Bars and Tone.

■5 Click OK.

■ Premiere places a Bars and Tone clip in the Project window.

■ You can add the clip to your project at any time.

Note: See Chapter 18 to add a clip to the Timeline.

What custom options can I set for the universal countdown leader?

✔ You can set the Wipe Color and Background color, which specify the respective colors for the circular one-second wipe area; the Line Color, Target Color, and Numeral Color, which specify colors for those features on the counter; and the Cue Blips, which can be set to beep at the beginning of every second, at the two-second mark, and display a cue circle on the last frame of the leader.

How do I create plain black footage for a leader clip?

✔ Click the Create Item button (🖻) in the Project window, and then click Black Video in the Object Type list. Click OK, and Premiere places a new clip of plain black footage in the Project window. You can then place this black footage as a leader at the start of your project, as a spacer between footage, or anywhere else in your project.

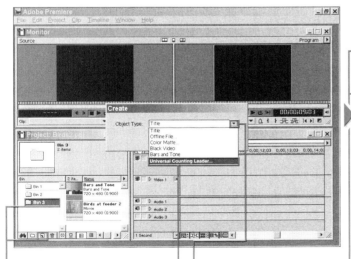

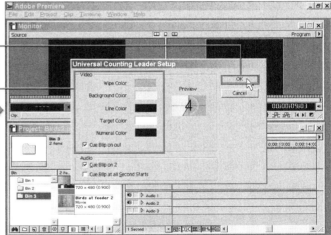

ADD A COUNTDOWN CLIP

1 Click the bin in which you want to store a leader clip.

2 Click the Create Item button (🖻).

■ The Create dialog box appears.

3 Click ▼ to display object types.

4 Click Universal Counting Leader.

5 Click OK.

■ The Universal Counting Leader Setup dialog box appears.

6 Make any changes to the settings, as needed.

7 Click OK.

■ Premiere places a Universal Counting Leader clip in the Project window.

■ You can add the clip to your project at any time.

Note: See Chapter 18 to add a clip to the Timeline.

347

UNDERSTANDING THE MONITOR WINDOW

You can use the Monitor window to view your project as well as make edits to your clips. The Monitor window offers several different views. Based on the editing mode that you use, the Monitor window shows a default view. If you use A/B editing (see Chapter 15), the window shows Single view. If you use Single-Track editing, the window shows Dual view, both a Source view area and a Program view area.

Using Dual View

In Dual view, you can view both the source clip and the program. Each side has playback controls. For many users, Dual view is the view of choice when editing because it so closely resembles traditional videotape-editing setups. Editors can see clips side-by-side, synchronize the clips, and check timing.

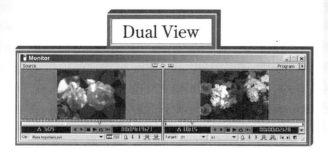

Dual View

Using Single View

Single view, the default view for A/B editing, shows just the Program view. You can use this view to play back your video. Any source clips that you view must be opened in a separate Clip window. Single view is useful when you do not need to see your source clips and want to focus only on the program. Single view also leaves screen space for you to open other features.

Single View

Using Trim Mode

Trim mode is useful when you want to make detailed adjustments in your video. Trim mode enables you to see two adjacent clips and make edits to the out and in points between the two. You can learn more about using Trim mode in Chapter 19.

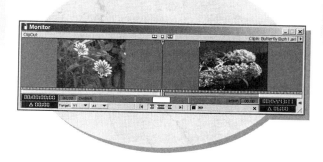

Using Playback Controls

The bottom of the Monitor window contains controls for playing the clip or program video. If you use Dual view, both the Source and Program areas have their own playback controls. Playback controls include buttons for moving back or forward one frame, stopping the clip or program, playing the clip or program, looping the play, and playing a portion of the clip or program.

Edit Controls

Below the playback controls are controls for making edits to the clip or program. Among these controls are buttons for marking in and out points, moving between edits, lifting and extracting clips, and more.

Program Details

The Monitor window gives you vital information about your project, such as listing the duration time of your video as well as the current location of the edit line in the program.

CHANGE MONITOR WINDOW VIEWS

You can edit clips in either the Monitor window or the Timeline window. The Monitor window displays individual frames of clips and the video program. Using the Single-Track Editing workspace, the Monitor window resembles the monitors in a conventional edit bay with one monitor for the *source*, or source clip, and another for the

program, or edited video in the Timeline. Controllers at the bottom of the Monitor window are like the edit controller in an edit bay.

In Dual view, the source and program are displayed side by side. You can also choose other views for the Monitor window. If you want to see only the Program view, you can select Single view. For precise

control over trimming, you can switch the Monitor window to Trim mode.

You can change how you view the Monitor window in a project regardless of which editing mode you use. For example, if you use Single-Track Editing mode, you may want to switch to Single view to focus on program playback.

1 Open a project.

Note: See Chapter 15 to start a project.

2 Click a view mode button.

Note: See "Understand the Monitor Window" to find out more about the different view modes.

■ You can click Dual View (▭) to see both a Source and Program area in the Monitor window.

How do I view my program in video safe zones?

✔ Television monitors typically cut off the outer edges of a video frame. You can tell Premiere to show video safe zones to help you determine the TV crop area. Click the Monitor window menu (▶) and click a safe margin area. See the section "Set Video Safe Zones" to find out more.

How do I change the time display options in the Monitor window?

✔ You can cycle through time display options by pressing Ctrl (Command) as you click a timecode readout. The time display options are cycled in the order that they appear in the Count menu.

How do I use the Monitor window to navigate a clip?

✔ When a controller is active for navigation, its timecode readout is green. The number at the bottom right of each controller is the current time position for that view. The number preceded by a delta symbol at the bottom left of each controller is the time difference between the in point and the out point of the currently displayed source clip or video program.

■ You can click Single View (□) to see only the program area in the Monitor window.

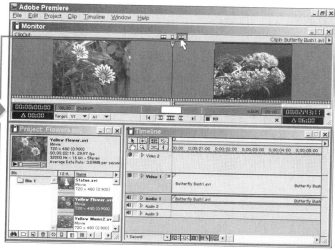

■ You can click Trim Mode View (⊞) to see adjacent clips in the video.

VIEW A CLIP IN SOURCE VIEW

In Single-Track Editing mode, you can view and edit source clips in the Source view area. When you view and edit video clips, the video clip appears in the Source view area of the Monitor window. When you view and edit audio clips, they appear as a waveform in the Source view area.

If you use Single-Track Editing mode, the Monitor window is set to Dual view by default. If you use A/B Editing mode, the Monitor window displays only the Program view area.

You can change the Monitor window's time display for both the Source and Program views. By default, the frame number of the current source clip appears in the time readout display area. You can change the count to another time display to suit your editing needs.

Click Window, Window Options, and then Monitor Window Options. You can select the time display by selecting an option from the Count drop-down list.

After viewing and editing the clip, you can choose whether to add the clip to the project outline.

VIEW A CLIP IN SOURCE VIEW

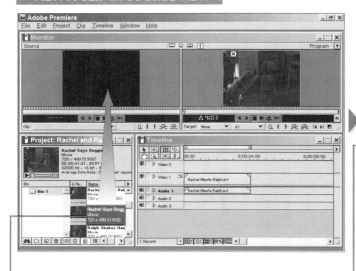

1 With a project open, click and drag the clip that you want to view to the Source view side of the Monitor window.

Note: See Chapter 16 to capture and import clips.

■ The clip appears in the Source view area.

2 Click ▶ to play the clip.

■ Clicking here displays a list of recently viewed clips; you can click the one that you want to revisit.

■ Clicking 🔁 plays the clip continuously.

■ Clicking ■ stops the clip from playing.

VIEW A CLIP IN PROGRAM VIEW

You can use the Program view area in Dual view or Single view to see the edited video play. For example, after assembling clips in the Timeline, you can preview the video project in the Program view area.

A *source clip* is a clip outside the Timeline or in the Source view of the Monitor window; a *program clip*

is a clip in the Timeline or Program view of the Monitor window. In Single-Track Editing mode, the Monitor window is set to Dual view by default, with the source clip displayed in the left window and the program clip displayed in the right window. If you use A/B editing, the Monitor window displays only the program clip.

If you are using Trim View mode, the frame to the left and the frame to the right of the edit line are in the left and right windows, respectively. This gives you exact precision for setting in and out points when you trim a clip as part of the editing process.

VIEW A CLIP IN PROGRAM VIEW

1 Open a project.

Note: See the section "Add a Source Clip to the Timeline" to assemble your project.

■ To play the video from a specific point in the project, click and drag the Set Location marker (🔽) to the frame where you want to start playing.

Note: See the section "Cue a Clip" to cue a clip.

2 Click ▶.

■ The video plays.

■ Clicking ■ stops the video from playing further.

SET VIDEO SAFE ZONES

Television sets enlarge a video image and allow some portion of its outer edges to be cut off by the edge of the screen. This is known as *overscan*. The amount of overscan is not consistent across television sets, so you should keep important parts of a video image, such as action or titles, within margins known as *safe zones*. You can change the Monitor window or the Program window to

display your video frames within video safe zones.

The two types of safe zones are title-safe zones and action-safe zones. *Title-safe zones* ensure that any titles will be displayed on National Television Standards Committee (NTSC) monitors; *action-safe zones* are larger than title-safe zones and ensure that the action will be displayed on NTSC monitors.

To ensure that all the important parts of your video are visible, switch to a video safe zone to see how the video plays. These guidelines apply only to NTSC videos; Phase Altering Line (PAL) videos can use these guidelines, but you should view them first on an appropriate monitor to see if they conform.

SET VIDEO SAFE ZONES

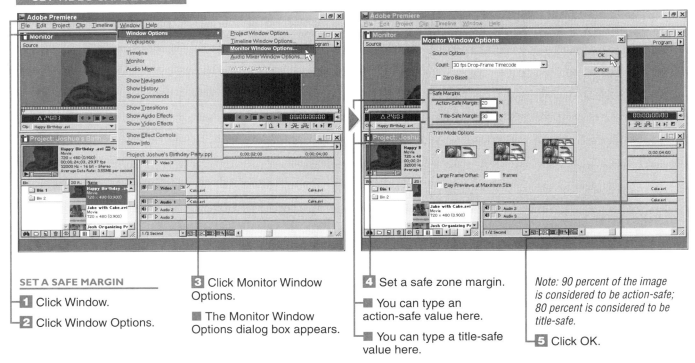

SET A SAFE MARGIN

■1 Click Window.

■2 Click Window Options.

■3 Click Monitor Window Options.

■ The Monitor Window Options dialog box appears.

■4 Set a safe zone margin.

■ You can type an action-safe value here.

■ You can type a title-safe value here.

Note: 90 percent of the image is considered to be action-safe; 80 percent is considered to be title-safe.

■5 Click OK.

What is the difference between NTSC and PAL video?

✔ NTSC is the North American standard for broadcast television. It consists of 60 half-frames (interlaced) per second, with 525 lines per frame and 16 million colors. PAL is a European broadcast standard that delivers 50 half-frames (interlaced) per second and 625 lines. A third standard is SECAM (Sequential Couleur avec Memoire), which is popular in France, the Middle East, and Eastern Europe. It uses 625 lines at 25 frames per second. SECAM is not currently supported in Premiere.

How do I know where to set title-safe zones?

✔ If you are worried that your title text exceeds the viewable area for a television monitor, check the video using the video safe margins. The standard for title text is 80 percent, which means that if the title text falls within 80 percent of the screen, the text will be viewable. If the text extends beyond 80 percent, chances are that the text will appear cut off.

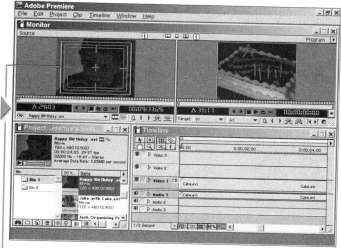

VIEW A SAFE ZONE

1 Click the Monitor window menu (▶).

2 Click a safe margin to view.

■ Click Safe Margins for Source Side to show the safe margins in the Source view.

■ Click Safe Margins for Program Side to show the safe margins in the Program view.

■ Premiere displays the safe margins.

■ This example shows safe margins in the Source view area.

CUE A CLIP

When you view clips in the Monitor window, you have a number of controls that enable you to move backward and forward through the clip. You also have controls that let you pause or stop the clip at a precise frame, with that frame visible in the Monitor window. The process of stopping at a precise point is called *cueing* a clip.

You can cue a clip in the Monitor window, either in Source view or Program view, using the Set Location marker. You can also cue a clip numerically by specifying an exact frame number, called *absolute time*, or you can add and subtract frames from the current point, called *relative time*.

After you have cued a clip, you can perform other tasks with the clip, such as set an in or out point or trim the clip. See "Set In and Out Points in the Monitor Window" in this chapter, or see Chapter 19, for more information.

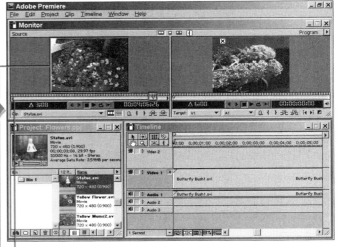

CUE A CLIP WITH THE SET LOCATION MARKER

1 With a project open, click and drag the Set Location marker (▣).

■ You can click and drag the Set Location marker in either Source view or Program view to cue the video.

2 Stop dragging when you reach the frame that you want to view.

■ The frame appears in the Source or Program view.

■ You can now play the video or perform an edit.

Note: See the section "View a Clip in Source View" or "View a Clip in Program View" to play a clip.

How do I display the same frame in Program view and Source view?

✔ To display the same frame in Program view that is displayed in Source view, make sure that the Source view is active and that the current Timeline instance of the Source view clip is displayed (the name of the clip and its in point will be in the Select Source Clip menu below the Source view), and then press T. To display the same frame in Source view that is displayed in Program view, make sure that either the Program view or Timeline is active and then press T. This displays the corresponding frame in the actual source clip, not its Timeline instance.

Can I jump ahead or back a specified number of frames?

✔ Yes. You can use the time display in either Source or Program view to cue the Set Location marker forward or backward. For example, if you type +25, Premiere moves the cue 25 frames forward. If you type −25, Premiere moves the cue 25 frames backward.

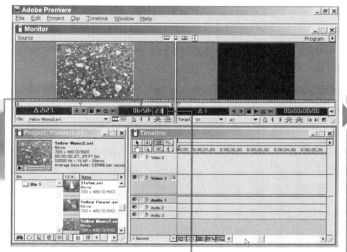

CUE A CLIP NUMERICALLY

-1 Click the time display.

■ You can cue a source clip in Source view.

■ You can cue the video program in Program view.

2 Type the frame number to which you want to cue the video.

■ You can use punctuation to type the frame number. For example, you can type 32:00, 32;00, or 32.00.

■ The Set Location marker (🔲) moves to the designated frame in Source or Program view.

SET IN AND OUT POINTS IN THE MONITOR WINDOW

Most clips are captured with extra footage at the beginning and end to allow for more precise editing later. It is common to fine-tune the beginning and end of a clip just before moving the clip into the program. You can set a clip's in and out points in the Clip window to ensure that you use only the footage that you want in the video. You define the beginning of the clip by marking an *in point* (the first frame that will appear in the video program) and the ending by marking an *out point* (the last frame that will appear in the video program).

You can also use in and out points for setting start and end points for transitions, where to trim or copy clips, or where effects should be applied. You can read more about adding edits and transitions in Chapter 19.

SET IN AND OUT POINTS IN THE MONITOR WINDOW

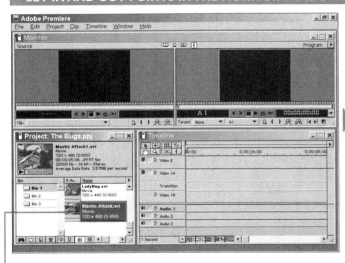

1 With a project open, double-click the clip that you want to edit.

Note: See Chapter 15 to find out how to start or open a project.

■ The Clip window opens.

2 Click and drag the Set Location marker ( ) to the frame that you want to set as the in point.

Note: See "View a Clip in Source View" or "View a Clip in Program View" to play a clip to determine edit points.

3 Click the Mark In button ( ).

■ An in point icon appears at the current frame.

■ The time readout shows the frame number.

Can I use the same technique to set audio in and out points that I use for video?

✔ Yes. Premiere handles digital video and audio in similar ways, and you can set in and out points for audio using the same technique.

How do I resize the Clip window?

✔ Move the mouse pointer over the lower-right corner of the window, and then click and drag the edge to create a new window size.

How can I trim an audio clip that was captured with the video footage?

✔ Premiere treats audio that was recorded with a video as a linked clip. If you try to set in and out points for the audio clip, the points are set for the linked video clip as well. To edit the audio separately, you must unlink the two clips. See Chapter 18 to learn how to unlink the two files.

-4 Click and drag the Set Location marker (🖸) to the frame that you want to set as the out point.

5 Click the Mark Out button (🖸).

■ An out point icon appears at the current frame.

■ The time readout shows the frame number.

6 Click the Play In to Out button (🖸) to play the clip.

■ Dragging in and out points adjusts their locations.

■ Clip duration displays here.

7 Click ⊠ (🔲) to close the Clip window.

■ You can now add the clip to the Timeline.

Note: See Chapter 18 to add clips to the Timeline window.

ADD A SOURCE CLIP TO THE TIMELINE

A clip in your project is not actually part of the final video program until you add it to the Timeline. When you do so, it appears in the Program view and in the Timeline; the first frame of the clip is the in point that you set in the Source view. You can add or remove clips by clicking and dragging clips between windows or by using Monitor window controls.

Dragging clips is a more visual method and depends heavily on using the mouse. When you add clips to the Timeline by dragging, the clip is added to the track and time position where you drop it.

Alternatively, you can use the Monitor window controls, which emphasize the keyboard and enable many edits to be performed entirely

within the Monitor window. Premiere cannot assume exactly how and where you want a clip to be added when you do this. You must specify video and audio tracks in advance and set in and out points for the clip or the program.

ADD A SOURCE CLIP TO THE TIMELINE

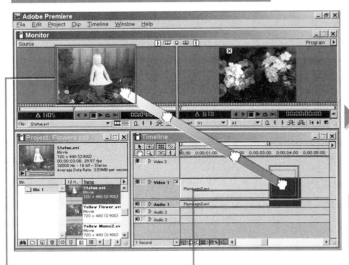

1 With a project open, edit a clip in Source view.

Note: See "Set In and Out Points in the Monitor Window" to edit a clip in Source view.

2 Click and drag the clip to the desired unused track in the Timeline (⇗ becomes ⌒).

Note: To add the video portion of the clip only, click ▥. To add only the audio portion of the clip, click ▥.

■ The clip appears in the Timeline.

Note: See Chapter 18 to find out about the Timeline.

SPECIFY A TARGET TRACK

After you edit a source clip in the Monitor window, you can add it to a specific track in the Timeline window. By targeting a track, you tell Premiere exactly where you want the clip to be inserted. In the Timeline, the Video 1A and Audio 1 Timeline tracks are the default *target*

(destination) video and audio tracks. In the Timeline, the names of the target video and audio tracks are highlighted.

If you are building a rough cut and have expanded the Video 1 track, start by dragging clips into the Video 1A track. Use the Video 1B

track as an alternate track, or B-roll, and use tracks Video 2 and higher as superimpose tracks. Avoid using the Video 1A track to insert cutaways, or alternative footage, over the Video 1B track; instead, put cutaways in the appropriate superimpose track.

SPECIFY A TARGET TRACK

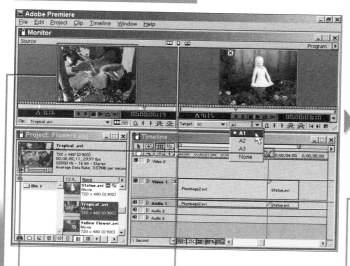

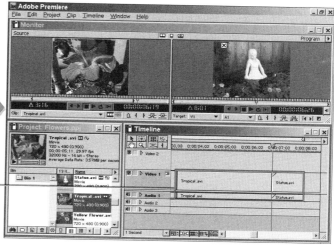

1 Click and drag the edit line (W) to where you want the clip inserted.

Note: See Chapter 18 to find out about the Timeline.

2 Edit a clip in Source view.

Note: See "Set In and Out Points in the Monitor Window" to edit a clip in Source view.

3 Click ▾.

4 Click the track to which you want to add the clip.

■ The clip appears in the Timeline.

ADD SOURCE MARKERS TO A CLIP

Markers indicate important points in time and help you position and arrange clips. You can use markers to identify points in the source clip, add numbered or unnumbered markers, or add comment text to markers. Markers are only for reference and do not alter the video program. For example, you may add a source marker to identify where a soundtrack should fade.

Premiere includes clip marker commands that you can use both to set the in and out points of a clip and to go to those points. In addition, you can also set and go to the video or audio in and out points, which is useful when you are working in a clip that includes a split edit. These commands are available only for the selected clip and do not apply to the Timeline.

In general, you add a marker to a clip for important points within an individual clip and add a marker to the Timeline for significant time points that affect multiple clips, such as when you need to synchronize video and audio on different clips.

ADD SOURCE MARKERS TO A CLIP

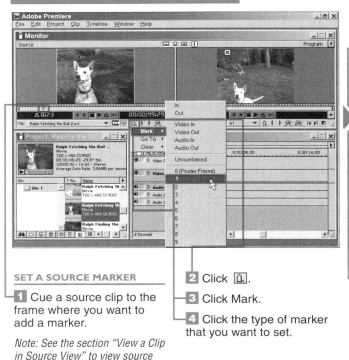

SET A SOURCE MARKER

■1 Cue a source clip to the frame where you want to add a marker.

Note: See the section "View a Clip in Source View" to view source clips.

■2 Click 🔲.

■3 Click Mark.

■4 Click the type of marker that you want to set.

■ The marker appears above the source clip.

Note: You can identify key parts of a clip with numbered and unnumbered markers. For example, you may use numbered markers to mark several possible edit points.

How do I remove markers from my source clip?

✔ Click the Marker Menu button (🔲), click Clear, and then click the marker that you want to remove. Click All Markers to remove all the markers in a clip.

How many markers can I have at once?

✔ The Timeline and each clip can individually contain its own set of up to ten markers numbered from 0 to 9. In addition, the Timeline and each clip can individually contain up to 999 unnumbered markers.

What kind of information can I put in a marker?

✔ Timeline markers can also include a comment, a Web link, or a chapter link. Comments appear in the Program view window only, Web links initiate a jump to a Web page in your browser, and chapter links initiate a jump to a chapter in a QuickTime movie or DVD.

CUE A SOURCE MARKER

1 Load a source clip containing the marker in Source view.

2 Click 🔲.

3 Click Go To.

4 Click the marker that you want to cue in Source view.

■ The Source view Set Location marker (🔲) immediately scrolls to the designated frame.

PERFORM A THREE-POINT EDIT

Y ou can create a *three-point edit* in the Monitor window that replaces a range of frames in the Program view area with a specified range of frames you designate in Source view. In a three-point edit, you mark either two in points and one out point or two out points and one in point. This type of edit is useful when one end point of source material or

program material is critical but the other is not.

When you add the source frames to the Timeline, Premiere calculates the fourth point automatically. For example, if you mark a source in point of 00:08:05, a source out point of 00:09:05, and a program out point of 18:22:15, Premiere applies the 1-second duration

between the source in and out points to the program out point and automatically sets the program in point to 18:21:15.

You can leave any single in or out point unmarked, but you must specify a total of three in and out points. You use Dual view to perform this type of edit.

PERFORM A THREE-POINT EDIT

1 Add a clip to Source view.

Note: See "View a Clip in Source View" to add source clips.

2 Choose a target track for the clip.

Note: See "Specify a Target Track" to set a target track.

3 Specify three in and out points — either two in and one out point, or two out and one in point — in both Source and Program view.

Note: See "Set In and Out Points in the Monitor Window" to add in and out points.

Do I have to specify an in or out point in Program view?

✔ No. You can cue the edit line in the Timeline window to mark where you want the clip inserted as an in or out point. See Chapter 18 to find out how to cue the edit line.

What is a four-point edit?

✔ A *four-point edit* is like a three-point edit, except that you designate all four edit points. You use the same technique as with a three-point edit, but specify the fourth point as well.

How do I check a clip's speed?

✔ You can see the speed of a clip using the Info palette. Click the clip that you want to check in the Timeline window, click Window, and then click Show Info. The Info palette appears with details about the clip, including the clip speed and duration.

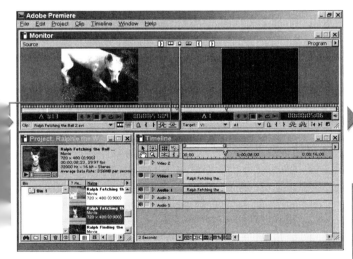

─4 Click an edit button.

■ Insert ( ) inserts the clip and shifts other clips over to accommodate the new clip.

■ Overlay ( ) overwrites any existing clips with the new clip.

Note: Make sure that the existing clips in the Timeline track are not locked. See Chapter 18 to unlock a track or a clip.

─■ The edited clip appears in the Timeline.

PREVIEW A VIDEO PROJECT

Y ou can preview all or part of a video program as you edit it without having to export the entire video program. You can display previews in the Monitor Program view, in the center of a monitor on a black background, or on any compatible NTSC or PAL monitor attached to your computer. Previewing is relatively quick for a program that simply cuts between clips. Applying transitions, effects,

or superimposition settings adds processing time to a preview.

Premiere offers several methods to preview your program; the method you choose depends on whether you want a quick preview, a preview at a precise frame rate, or a compromise between the two. The preview's appearance is controlled by the Project Settings dialog box in the Video Settings panel.

The area to be previewed, called the *work area,* is defined by a yellow bar that stretches across the top of the Timeline, or the *work area bar.* The work area bar automatically expands to encompass the whole program as you add clips to the Timeline, but it is also manually adjustable.

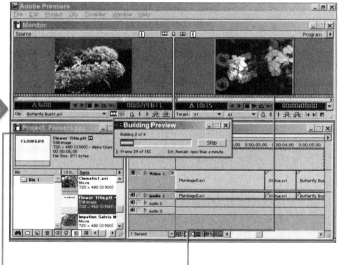

PREVIEW THE ENTIRE VIDEO

■ **1** Cue the edit line marker (🖵) to the beginning of the Timeline.

Note: See Chapter 18 to find out about the Timeline.

■ **2** Click Timeline.

■ **3** Click Preview.

■ You can also press Enter (Return).

■ Premiere builds the preview file.

■ The video program plays.

Can I create a preview file without viewing it right away?

✔ Yes. Preparing a preview file can save you time later because it will be ready to play when you want to view the project. Click Timeline and then Render Work Area. Premiere builds the preview file, which you can view at any time by pressing Enter (Return).

How long does it take for Premiere to render a video?

✔ To preview the video with edits and effects applied, Premiere must first build a copy of the video. Depending on the size of the file, the amount of RAM, and your computer's processing speed, rendering may take only a few seconds or several minutes.

Can I use my video card to help with the rendering process?

✔ When you use certain video cards, you can view in real time programs that include transitions, motion settings, and effects without the need to render a preview. To use this feature, you need a video card that supports real-time capabilities. For information on real-time capabilities, see the documentation supplied with your real-time video card.

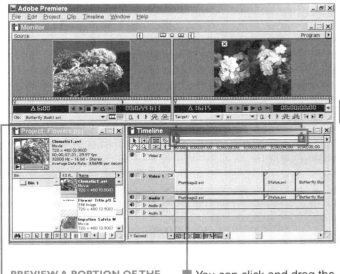

PREVIEW A PORTION OF THE VIDEO

■1 Drag ▷ and ◁ over the area that you want to preview.

■ You can click and drag the work area markers to specify where the work area begins or ends.

Note: See Chapter 18 to find out more about working with the Timeline window.

■2 Click Timeline.

■3 Click Preview.

■ You can also press Enter (Return).

■ Premiere builds the preview file.

■ The video program plays.

GANG THE SOURCE AND PROGRAM VIEWS

There may be times when you want the Source and Program views to move together. This is called *ganging* the views, and you use it to preview how a clip fits into the video program without having to actually add the clip to the program. This process synchronizes the clips so that you can see how both are playing and where you may need to further adjust the edits.

For example, if you want to compare the action in a source clip to the time available for it in the program, you can start scrubbing the program at the proposed in point for the clip, and it will move in the Source view simultaneously with the Program view. You can then use the controllers to preview where the proposed out points would fall in the source clip and existing program.

GANG THE SOURCE AND PROGRAM VIEWS

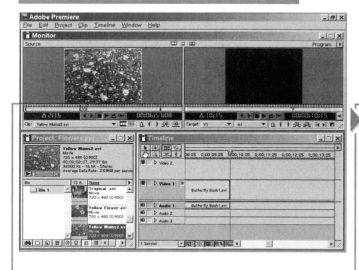

1 Cue the source clip to the frame that you want to synchronize.

Note: See the section "Cue a Clip" to cue clips.

2 Cue the Program view to the frame that you want to synchronize.

What exactly is ganging?

✔ *Ganging* is simply viewing both the source clip and the program at the same time. The term comes from traditional editing, in which an editor gangs monitors to see a clip play in one monitor while the program plays in the other. The editor can then decide whether to actually add the clip to the master video. This is often used when you have two takes from the same scene and want to see how they compare with one another.

Do I have to use the Set Location marker to view the ganged clips?

✔ No. You can use the Set Location marker, Previous Frame button, or Next Frame button on the controllers to compare frames (using other controls will turn ganging off). As you use one controller, the other controller moves the same amount of time in the same direction. There may be a slight delay as the controllers synchronize.

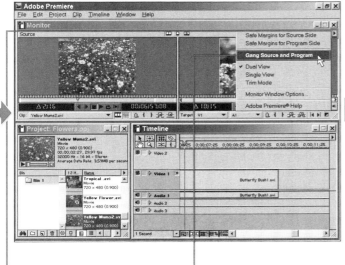

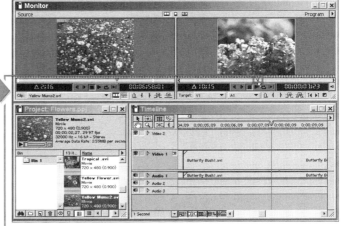

━3 Click the Monitor window ▶.

━4 Click Gang Source and Program.

━5 Click and drag the Set Location marker (𝖵) back and forth in either view to see the frames move in sync.

■ Clicking ▶ turns off the gang feature.

UNDERSTANDING THE TIMELINE

Y ou can use the Timeline window to edit and assemble clips in your video project. To better understand how the Timeline works, first take a look at some of its features.

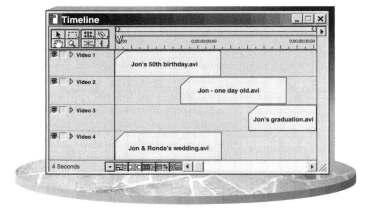

What Is the Timeline?

The Timeline window is a graphic, chronological representation of your video project. You can use the Timeline to arrange clips in the order that you want them to appear.

The Time Ruler

The top of the Timeline window shows a time ruler. Use the ruler to view in and out points of a clip as well as the length of the project. The edit line that appears on the time ruler marks the current edit point in the project.

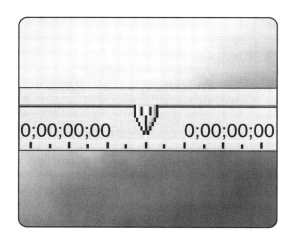

Tracks

Premiere uses tracks on the Timeline to hold your clips. You can have up to 99 video and 99 audio tracks, and you can add and remove tracks as needed. However, the tracks Video 1, Video 2, Transition, Audio 1, Audio 2, and Audio 3 cannot be deleted. These tracks are a permanent part of the Timeline window, regardless of whether you use them.

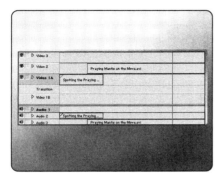

Types of Tracks

Use video tracks to hold clips, such as video, graphics, and title clips. You can add clips to a single track or use multiple tracks. Audio tracks hold audio clips for your project. The Transition track, which appears in A/B Editing mode (see Chapter 15), holds transitions that you assign to segue from one clip to another.

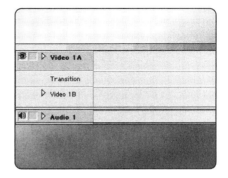

Hide and Exclude Tracks

You can expand and collapse tracks in the Timeline window. You can also create shy tracks and exclude tracks. A *shy track* is hidden from view, but still remains a part of the project. For example, you may create a shy track for a clip that you have finished editing so that you can "hide" it and concentrate on other clips. *Excluded tracks* are removed from the Timeline and are not previewed or exported with the video, but remain a part of the project.

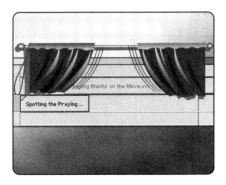

Workspace Settings

The Single-Track Editing layout displays single-track video tracks in the Timeline. This layout is useful for cuts without transitions. The A/B Editing layout turns Video Track 1 in the Timeline into two tracks, Video 1A and 1B, along with a Transition track between them. This layout is useful for creating transitions between clips.

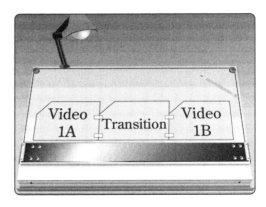

NAVIGATE THE TIMELINE

The Timeline is the backbone of your video project. Use the Timeline window to build your video, clip by clip. Take a moment and acquaint yourself with the parts of the Timeline window.

Work Area Markers

The markers can be dragged left or right to define the area onscreen that is previewed or exported.

Edit Line Marker

Marks the current edit point in the Timeline.

Toolbox

Contains tools for working with clips in the Timeline.

Video Track

Use tracks to hold clips you want to use to build your project.

Transition Track

Visible in A/B Editing mode, use the Transition track to add transitions between clips.

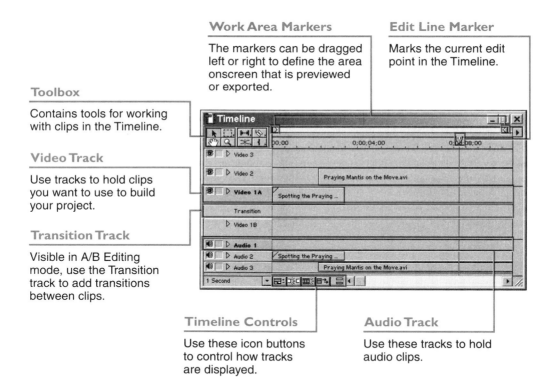

Timeline Controls

Use these icon buttons to control how tracks are displayed.

Audio Track

Use these tracks to hold audio clips.

Time Units

Use the Time Unit menu to change the way in which frames or seconds appear on the Timeline. By default, Premiere displays the Timeline in one-second intervals. You can view the Timeline in more or fewer intervals or change the intervals to frames.

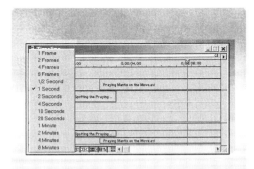

Timeline Menu

You can access commands related to the Timeline window using this menu. A check mark indicates that a feature is turned on; no check mark means that a feature is turned off.

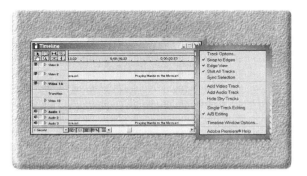

Move Around the Timeline

Premiere enables you to move around the Timeline in many ways. You can use the Selector tool from the toolbox to drag clips around the Timeline. You can also use the Timeline's scroll bars to move your view. You can move the edit line marker to the frame that you want to edit.

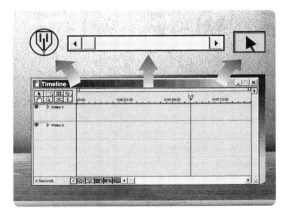

Using the Navigator Palette

Another way to navigate the Timeline is to use the Navigator palette. This palette gives you a bird's-eye view of the total Timeline for your project, and when you click an area in the palette, the Timeline immediately scrolls to that area.

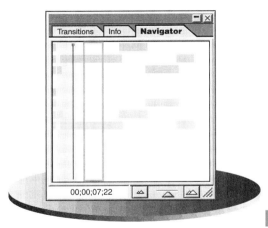

CUSTOMIZE THE TIMELINE

When you are working on a project, it helps to be able to look at an item and quickly understand what you are working with, and perhaps see some item attributes. For example, say that you have two different camera angles of the same scene — shots of two actors talking and the camera's point of view over each

actor's shoulder, watching the other speak. When you are building a scene, you need to know which camera angle you are inserting into the project.

Customizing the Timeline enables you to change how items appear in the Timeline window. For example, you may want to see a thumbnail

image of the video clip as well as the clip name, or you may prefer a larger icon size that shows more detail from the clip. If you want, you can even choose not to have an icon for the clip and just view the filename. This is the fastest option available and is best if you are very familiar with your clips.

CUSTOMIZE THE TIMELINE

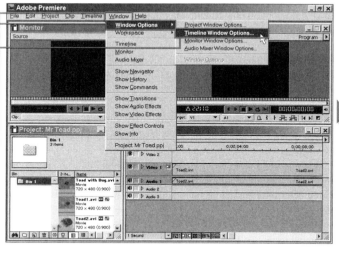

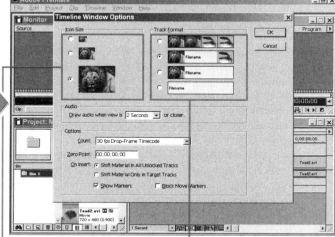

1 Click Window.

2 Click Window Options.

3 Click Timeline Window Options.

■ The Timeline Window Options dialog box appears.

Note: You can also access the dialog box by clicking the Timeline window menu and clicking Timeline Window Options.

4 Click an icon size (○ changes to ●).

Note: A larger icon size makes it easier to see clips in the Timeline window.

5 Click a track format (○ changes to ●).

Other than using the Timeline Window Options dialog box, how else can I zoom my view of the Timeline?

✔ You can click the Zoom tool (🔍) in the Timeline window's toolbox and click the Timeline to quickly change the time unit increments displayed.

What do the Track Format options do?

✔ The first displays sample frames along the clip's duration, which is useful but slows down system performance. The second displays the first and last frame plus the filename. The third displays the first frame and filename only. The last displays the clip filename only, and is the fastest.

How can I switch to a timecode view for my clips?

✔ You can have the Timeline change to a timecode view for your clips by clicking the Count 🔽 and selecting a timecode option. If you are working on shorter projects, you can use the 30 fps non-drop frame timecode option; if you are working on a longer work or are creating a video for broadcast, select the 30 fps drop frame timecode option. See Chapter 16 for more on adding timecode to clips.

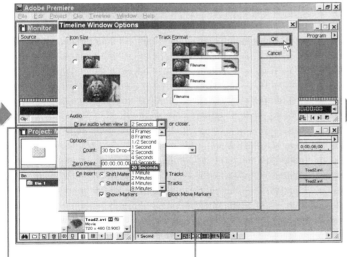

■6 Click 🔽 to display zoom level options.

■7 Click a zoom level in which to view audio waveforms.

■8 Click OK.

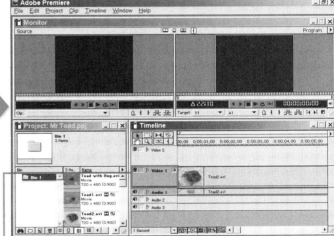

■ The Timeline changes to reflect your choices.

ADD TRACKS TO THE TIMELINE

In the Timeline, a *track* is a horizontal channel in which you can place video clips, audio clips, or still images. It functions much like a layer in Photoshop and Illustrator and gives you a way of adding organizational and editing flexibility. By having multiple tracks available, you can work with a series of clips for editing, trimming, adding or removing transitions, or combining your finished edits into a single project.

When you add tracks, you add channels for placing the different items that you want to work with. You can add tracks to the Timeline as you need them. By default, Premiere starts you off with two video tracks and three audio tracks. You may use as many as 99 of each in your project. Depending on the workspace view, you will see the tracks aligned a little differently, although they will always run horizontally, and playback will always run from left to right.

ADD TRACKS TO THE TIMELINE

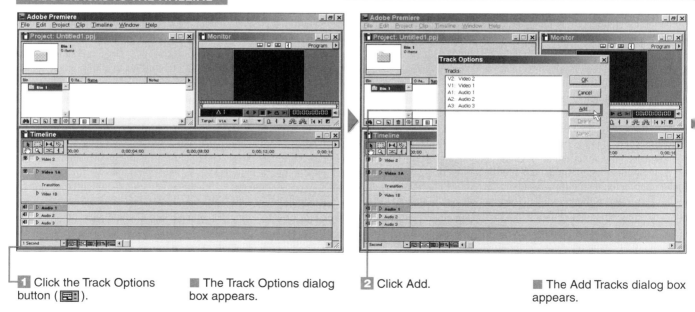

1 Click the Track Options button (▦).

■ The Track Options dialog box appears.

2 Click Add.

■ The Add Tracks dialog box appears.

Where do new tracks appear in the Timeline?

✔ New video tracks appear on top of existing video tracks, and new audio tracks appear below existing audio tracks.

I do not see my video tracks; do I need to switch modes?

✔ Depending on the workspace, the Video 1 track will display one of two ways. In A/B Editing mode, it displays as three subtracks: Video 1A, 1B, and the Transition track. In Single-Track Editing mode, the three subtracks are combined.

Does Premiere provide a way to add a single video or audio track more quickly than using the Add Tracks dialog box?

✔ You can click the Timeline menu and then click either Add Video Track or Add Audio Track to quickly insert a track. You can also click the Timeline window menu and click Add Video Track or Add Audio Track. You can even right-click over a track and click the commands from the pop-up menu.

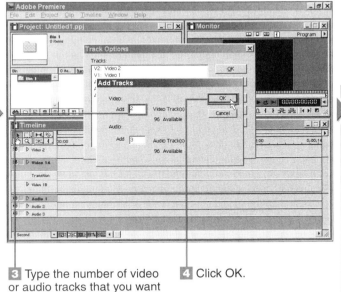

3 Type the number of video or audio tracks that you want to add.

4 Click OK.

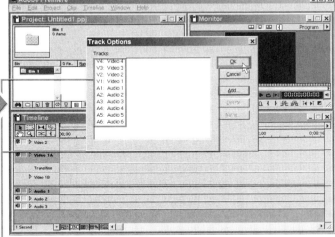

■ The tracks are listed in the Track Options dialog box.

5 Click OK again to exit the Track Options dialog box.

■ The tracks appear in the Timeline.

NAME TRACKS

When you start a new project, Premiere starts you off with tracks Video 1 and 2 and Audio 1, 2, and 3. When you add tracks, Premiere creates new tracks that use similar labels, such as Video 3 or Audio 4. Although this is workable, it may not be the most efficient system for you because the labels do not tell

you (or other editors) what the purpose of a track is.

To add usefulness and convey more information about tracks' purposes, you can rename the tracks displayed on the Timeline to help you better discern the contents of each track. For example, you can rename the Audio 2 and 3 tracks as Dialog and SFX (sound effects),

respectively. This gives you a clear idea of which audio clips can be added into which track and also gives you the added flexibility of being able to mix the respective clips, add transitions, and so on.

You can rename any track except for the Video 1B track, which is used by Premiere for A/B Editing mode.

NAME TRACKS

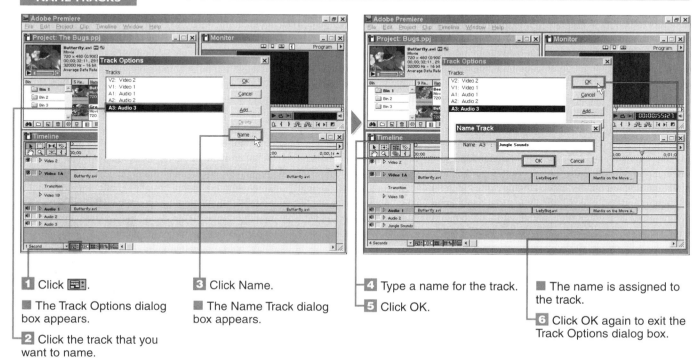

1 Click 📠.

■ The Track Options dialog box appears.

2 Click the track that you want to name.

3 Click Name.

■ The Name Track dialog box appears.

4 Type a name for the track.

5 Click OK.

6 Click OK again to exit the Track Options dialog box.

■ The name is assigned to the track.

DELETE TRACKS

Y ou may have a project in which you have numerous video and audio tracks that you use to organize your clips. For example, you may have been working on a sequence of fast cuts between three different cameras to create a single clip, which would then be placed into Video 1. After you have moved the completed

sequence, you have the leftover empty tracks in the Timeline and would like to regain screen real estate by deleting the tracks. You can delete tracks after you have finished using them or if you no longer need them.

You can delete empty tracks or ones with clips in them. Deleting a track removes all clip instances on the

track but does not affect source clips that you stored in the Project window. You cannot delete the Transition track from the Timeline, and you cannot delete the tracks Video 1 and 2 or Audio 1, 2, and 3.

If the tracks use default names, Premiere renumbers the remaining tracks for you.

DELETE TRACKS

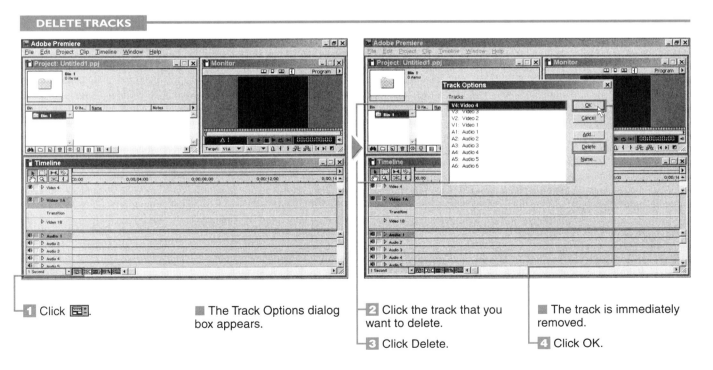

1 Click 🖳.

■ The Track Options dialog box appears.

2 Click the track that you want to delete.

3 Click Delete.

■ The track is immediately removed.

4 Click OK.

LOCK AND UNLOCK TRACKS

Locking an entire track is useful for preventing changes to any clips on that track while you work on other parts of the program. A locked track is included when you preview or export the program. If you lock the target track, it is no longer the target, so source clips cannot be

added to it until you unlock it and then target it.

A lock icon next to the track name indicates a locked track. If you position the pointer or a tool over a locked track, the pointer appears with a lock icon to remind you that the track is locked. Locked

tracks are dimmed in the Target menus below the Program view. If you want to lock both a video track and a track with corresponding audio, lock each track separately.

You cannot edit or move a locked track. To edit the track later, you can unlock it again.

LOCK AND UNLOCK TRACKS

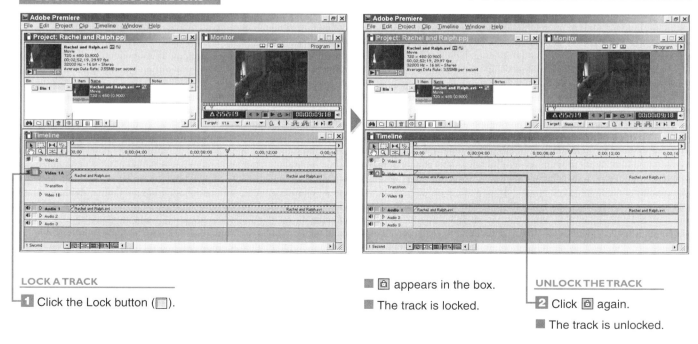

LOCK A TRACK

1 Click the Lock button (☐).

■ 🔒 appears in the box.

■ The track is locked.

UNLOCK THE TRACK

2 Click 🔒 again.

■ The track is unlocked.

EXPAND AND COLLAPSE TRACKS

You can expand tracks to view more information or additional controls. This is helpful when you have numerous tracks that are being used in your project and you need to focus on working with clips in just a few tracks at a time. Expanding tracks increases the screen area taken up in the Timeline, showing you more information and details about a

particular clip. For example, if you expand an audio track, you can see the audio clip's waveform as well as fade and pan controls. You can also see the toggle switches for the Display Keyframes and Display Opacity Rubberbands options when you expand a track.

Collapsing tracks reduces the screen area being taken up by your tracks,

although it does not completely remove the tracks from view.

If you need to increase or reduce the screen area further, you can change the clip icon size in the Timeline. See "Customize the Timeline," earlier in this chapter, for details.

EXPAND AND COLLAPSE TRACKS

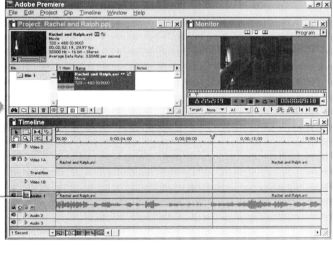

EXPAND A TRACK

1 Click the Expand icon (▷).

■ The track is expanded.

COLLAPSE THE TRACK

2 Click the Collapse icon (▽).

■ The track reverts to its collapsed state.

CREATE A SHY TRACK

You can turn a track into a shy track to conserve Timeline space, but the track still remains part of the project. Marking a track as shy does not immediately conceal it in the Timeline; you must then use the Hide Shy Tracks command to conceal all shy tracks simultaneously. Hiding tracks reduces Timeline clutter and increases scrolling or previewing performance. In the case of audio tracks, the audio is turned off. The content of shy tracks is still visible or audible, however, during playback.

Shy tracks are included in the previews and exported program even when they are not visible in the Timeline.

Shy and hidden tracks can still be edited as normal tracks. To make sure that hidden tracks are not edited, lock them before hiding them. See "Lock and Unlock Tracks," earlier in this chapter, for details.

CREATE A SHY TRACK

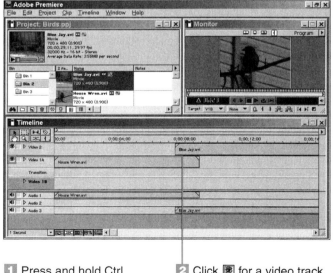

1 Press and hold Ctrl (Command).

2 Click 👁 for a video track or 🔊 for an audio track.

■ The 👁 or 🔊 turns white.

3 Click Timeline.

4 Click Hide Shy Tracks.

■ The shy tracks are hidden from view in the Timeline window.

Note: To turn the tracks on again, click Timeline and Show Shy Tracks and then click the tracks again, following steps 1 and 2.

EXCLUDE A TRACK

Y ou can exclude a track to remove it from both the Timeline and from any playbacks and exports of the project. An excluded track still appears in the Timeline but is not included either in exported video or when previewing or scrubbing the Timeline. You may use the exclude track feature to create an

export of the project without audio tracks, for example. Excluding a track also allows comparison between different versions of the program. You can create different exported versions that feature different takes from a scene. This is often used in post-production before rendering a final version.

You can still edit an excluded track as a normal track. To make sure that an excluded track is not edited, lock the track before hiding it. See "Lock and Unlock Tracks," earlier in this chapter, for details.

EXCLUDE A TRACK

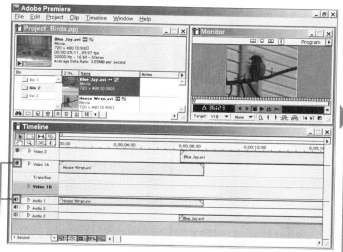

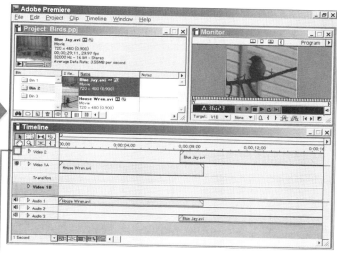

–1 Click 🎬 for a video track or 🔊 for an audio track.

■ The box appears empty, and the track is excluded.

Note: To turn the excluded track on again, repeat step 1.

USING THE NAVIGATOR PALETTE

Although you can use the horizontal scroll bars in the Timeline to move back and forth along your project, there is a quicker way in Premiere to move to particular points. The Navigator palette contains a miniature version of the Timeline, and it enables you to quickly move around the Timeline when you are working on longer video projects. It displays a

bird's-eye view of the Timeline, with video tracks in yellow, audio tracks in green, transition tracks in blue, the current work area in pale blue, and the edit line in red. It also displays a green Current View box that roughly approximates the area being viewed in the Timeline.

Moving about the Navigator palette is easy. You click and drag the

Current View box along your project, and the Timeline window scrolls along with you as you drag. When you are at the location you want to work on, release the mouse button.

The Navigator palette also lets you zoom in on the Timeline or jump to an exact time within your project.

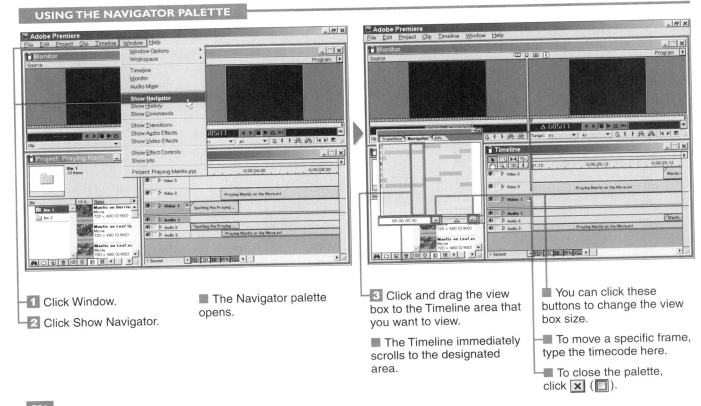

■ Click Window.

■ Click Show Navigator.

■ The Navigator palette opens.

■ Click and drag the view box to the Timeline area that you want to view.

■ The Timeline immediately scrolls to the designated area.

■ You can click these buttons to change the view box size.

■ To move a specific frame, type the timecode here.

■ To close the palette, click ✕ (□).

CHANGE THE TIME ZOOM LEVEL

By default, the Timeline uses two-second increments as its time scale. When you change the scale to a larger increment, the Timeline grows smaller, and when you select a smaller increment, the Timeline grows larger. For example, a setting of 10 seconds causes the project to shrink, and thus more of it is displayed in the Timeline

window than if you were to use a setting of 0.5 seconds, which would increase the size of the project, and thus less is visible in the Timeline.

Changing the time zoom level enables you to get as granular as you need to, down to a single frame. When you change the zoom level, you also change the

increments displayed on the Time Ruler, and thus you can view increments in frames or seconds on the Timeline.

You can change the zoom level at any time in your project. When you save your project, the zoom level is saved also.

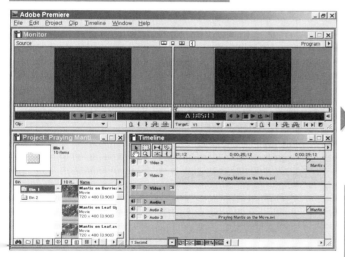

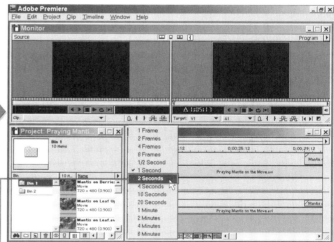

1 Click ▼ to display a menu of time units.

2 Click the unit that you want to assign to the Time Ruler.

■ The Timeline immediately reflects the new setting.

Note: You can also click 🔍 in the toolbox and click over the Timeline to change increments.

ADD OR DELETE A CLIP

In order to create a project in Premiere, you add clips to the Timeline window to assemble your video. You can use video or audio clips or insert still images created in Photoshop or Illustrator. Whether you capture clips or use existing clips, you place clips into tracks sequentially on the Timeline to build a video project.

The type of clip and type of track must match. You add video, still images, and title clips to video tracks in the Timeline. You add sound clips to audio tracks in the Timeline. See "Understanding the Timeline," earlier in this chapter, for more details on the Timeline itself.

If you add a clip to the Timeline and later decide that you do not need it for your project, you can delete the clip from the Timeline. Deleting a clip from the Timeline window does not remove the clip from the project file. The clip remains listed in the Project window.

ADD A CLIP TO THE TIMELINE

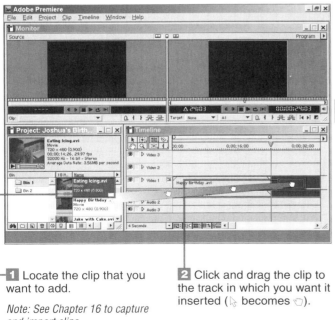

1 Locate the clip that you want to add.

Note: See Chapter 16 to capture and import clips.

2 Click and drag the clip to the track in which you want it inserted (becomes).

■ The clip appears on the Timeline.

Note: See Chapter 17 to preview a video.

Why do files remain in the Project window, even after I delete them from the Timeline?

✔ In Premiere, the original source clip is called a *master clip,* and the clip is listed in the Project window. Each time that you add the same master clip to the Timeline, you create a new instance of that master clip. This lets you work with the instance without disturbing the master clip or other instances of it in your project. To delete a file from the Project window, select it with the mouse and press Delete. All references to the file will be removed from your project.

Can I copy and paste clips?

✔ Yes. Copying a clip duplicates it on the Timeline. After you select the clip that you want to copy, click Edit and then Copy. Click the track where you want to insert the clip and then click Edit and Paste. A copy appears. If you click Paste to Fit in the Edit menu, the Fit Clip dialog box appears, and you can specify how you want the copy pasted.

DELETE A CLIP FROM THE TIMELINE

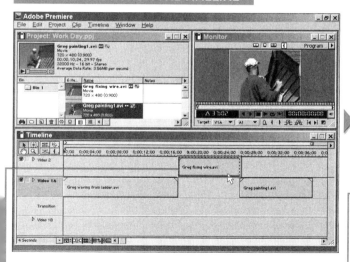

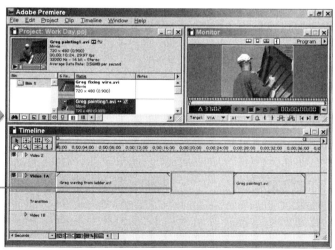

1 Click the clip that you want to remove.

2 Press Delete.

■ The clip is removed from the Timeline.

Note: See the section "Delete Gaps between Clips" to remove gaps in the Timeline.

LOCK AND UNLOCK CLIPS

You may have spent several hours working on a clip, trimming it, setting in and out points, or even resizing it. Now you want to add it to the Timeline, but you do not want anything to happen to your hours of work. You need a way of protecting that instance of your clip from willful or accidental edits.

Much as you can with tracks, you can lock a clip on the Timeline. Locking a clip prevents you from making accidental changes to the clip. When you lock a clip, it appears with a pattern of diagonal slashes on the Timeline.

You can also unlock a clip if you want to edit it or move it in the Timeline. After it is unlocked, you can delete it, move it, or edit it.

Locked clips can be copied to other areas on the Timeline. Locked clips continue to be displayed in the Monitor Program view and will appear in video files that you export. If you want to lock all clips on the same track, lock the entire track instead.

LOCK AND UNLOCK CLIPS

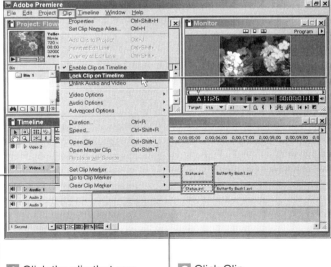

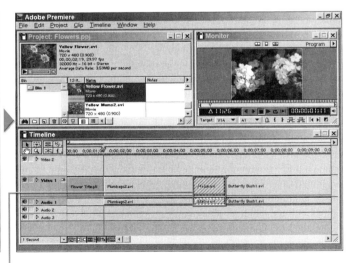

1 Click the clip that you want to lock.

Note: See the section "Add or Delete a Clip" to place clips on the Timeline.

2 Click Clip.

3 Click Lock Clip on Timeline.

■ The clip is locked.

■ Locked clips appear with slash marks on the Timeline.

■ To unlock a locked clip, repeat steps 1 to 3.

DISABLE OR ENABLE CLIPS

You can disable a clip to prevent it from playing in the video preview or from exporting when you output your project. This is useful if you want to suppress clips while you try out a different editing idea, to shorten processing time when working on a complex project, or to exclude a clip that you export. You may also

disable an audio clip so that you can concentrate on the video images. You can enable a clip in the Timeline to include it again after you have finished making your edits or working with different exported versions. Disabled clips do not appear in the Monitor Program view.

Even if you have disabled a clip, you can still make edits to it, such as trimming it, setting in and out points, or moving it in the Timeline. If you have locked a disabled clip, you must unlock it and then re-enable it. If you want to disable all clips on the same track, exclude the entire track instead.

DISABLE OR ENABLE CLIPS

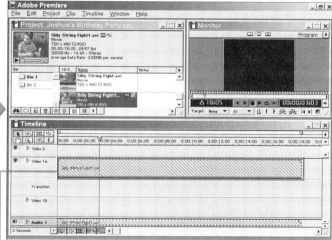

◢1 Click the clip that you want to disable.

Note: See the section "Add or Delete a Clip" to place clips on the Timeline.

◢2 Click Clip.

◢3 Click Enable Clip on Timeline.

■ A check mark next to the command name indicates that the clip is enabled. No check mark means that the clip is disabled.

■ The clip is disabled.

■ Disabled clips appear with backward slash marks on the Timeline.

■ To enable a disabled clip, repeat steps 1 to 3.

389

MOVE CLIPS IN THE TIMELINE

In general, moving a clip is as simple as dragging it to any empty track area in the Timeline. A clip can snap to the edge of another clip, to a marker, to the start and end of the Timeline, or to the edit line. Drag the clip to the left or right, position the clip by watching the in point and out

point indicator lines (if you stay on the same track) or the black rectangle that represents the clip duration (if you drag to a different track), and then release the mouse button.

You can also move multiple clips or every clip at once from one track to

another. This is useful if you have completed a series of edits on several clips, such as working on cuts from the same scene, and want to move the completed scene to another track in the Timeline.

MOVE CLIPS IN THE TIMELINE

MOVE A SINGLE CLIP

1 Click the clip you want to move.

Note: See the section "Add or Delete a Clip" to place clips on the Timeline.

2 Click and drag the clip to a new location (becomes).

■ The clip is moved.

What happens if I try to move a clip that contains both video and audio?

✔ If you have Sync mode turned on and you drag a clip containing both video and audio, Premiere attempts to keep video and audio on similar tracks. For example, if you drag a clip on track Video 3, Premiere will drag the clip's audio along on Audio 3. If you try to drag the video part of the clip to a time where the track Video 3 is empty and Audio 3 is occupied, Premiere will move the audio clip to the next empty audio track so that you can complete the drag. If there is no empty audio track at that time, Premiere will not allow the move.

Can I move just a few clips?

✔ Yes. You can move a range of clips using the Range Select tool. Click 🔲 in the toolbox and then click and drag a box around the clips that you want to move. Finally, drag the range to an unused area on the Timeline and drop it in place.

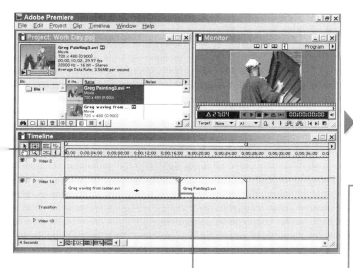

MOVE ALL THE CLIPS IN A TRACK

1 Click the Track Select tool (🔳).

2 Click the first clip in the track of clips that you want to move (▵ becomes ➡).

■ All the clips in the track are selected.

3 Click and drag the clips to a new location (▵ becomes ✋).

■ The clips are moved.

LINK AND UNLINK CLIPS

When you add a clip containing video and audio to your program and you have specified adding both the video and audio portions, the video portion appears in a video track, and the audio portion appears in an audio track. The video and audio portions of the clip are *linked* so that when you drag the video portion in the Timeline, the linked audio moves with it. If you split the clip, the video and audio are still linked within the two resulting clips. You can only link video to audio; you cannot link a video clip to another video clip.

In many situations, it is useful to link or unlink clips manually. For example, you may want to move previously unlinked audio or video clips together or edit the in or out point of the video or audio portion of a clip independently. You do not have to unlink clips if you only want to delete one clip or the other.

LINK CLIPS

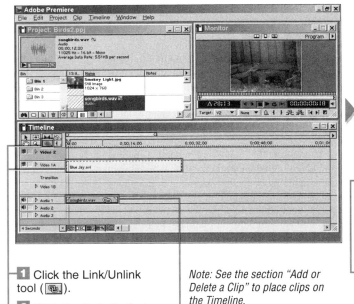

■1 Click the Link/Unlink tool (🖉).

■2 Click the first clip that you want to link.

Note: See the section "Add or Delete a Clip" to place clips on the Timeline.

■3 Click the clip that you want to link to (🖉 becomes 🖉).

■ Premiere links the clips, which you can now move at the same time.

Note: See the section "Move Clips in the Timeline" to move clips around the Timeline tracks.

How can I tell if video and audio clips are linked?
✔ The video and audio portions of linked clips are both light green so that you can easily see that they are linked.

Can I move one clip in a linked pair without moving the other?
✔ Yes, if you toggle the Sync mode. The Sync Mode button toggles on or off (⬜ to ⬜). When the mode is on, you can move the linked clips as a unit. When the mode is off, the links are ignored.

Do I need to unlink clips if I want to work on them individually?
✔ When you want to work with linked clips individually, temporarily turn off synchronized behavior by using the Sync Mode button. When the Sync mode is off, linked clips can be edited independently, as if they were not linked. Premiere keeps track of sync information, even when Sync mode is turned off. When linked clips are moved out of sync, both clips display a red triangle at the in point to indicate the out-of-sync condition.

UNLINK CLIPS

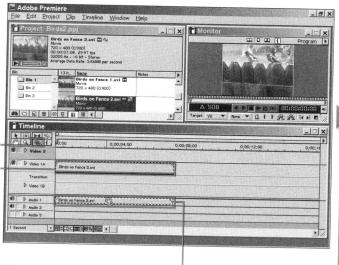

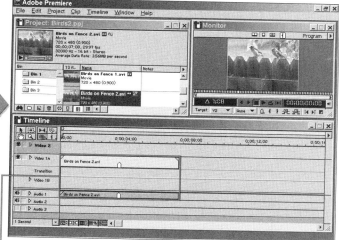

1 Click the Link/Unlink tool (⬜).

2 Click the first linked clip that you want to unlink.

3 Click the clip that you want to unlink from (▷ becomes ⬚).

■ Premiere unlinks the clips, as indicated by a white marker.

■ You can now move one clip, and the other stays in place.

SPLIT CLIPS

If you have a clip that you imported from a video camera and discover that you need to separate it into two different clips in the Timeline, you can split the clip into two by using the Razor tool. For example, you may want to split a clip to move a segment to another track in the Timeline. Splitting a clip creates a new and separate instance of the original clip, including any video and audio clips that are linked together. If Sync mode is off, Premiere splits only the audio or video portion of linked clips. (See "Link and Unlink Clips," earlier in this chapter.)

When you split a clip, Premiere creates a new instance of the clip with the same name in the Timeline. It is a good idea to create a new alias name for the two clips so as to distinguish between them during the editing process. See Chapter 16 for details.

You can also split multiple clips at the same time using the Multiple Razor tool.

SPLIT CLIPS

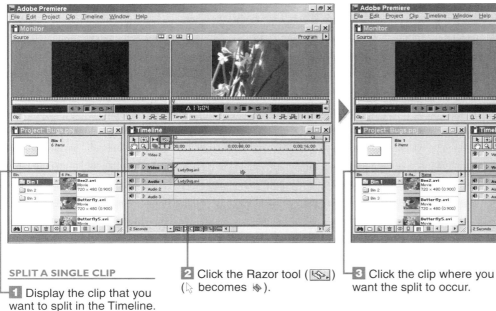

SPLIT A SINGLE CLIP

1 Display the clip that you want to split in the Timeline.

2 Click the Razor tool ( ) (becomes).

3 Click the clip where you want the split to occur.

■ The clip immediately splits into two.

I mistakenly split a clip in the wrong spot. How do I undo the split?

✔ Click Edit and then Undo immediately after performing the split; you can also use the shortcut key sequence Ctrl + Z (Command - Z) to undo a command. Premiere keeps track of your edits and lists them in the History palette. To display the palette, click Window and Show History. Click an edit in the list, and all edits performed after the selected edit, including the selected edit, are undone.

Why is it useful to split clips in the Timeline?

✔ Splitting clips can be useful when you want to use different effects that cannot both be applied to a single clip, such as different clip frame rates. However, if you want to change effect settings over time, you do not have to split the clip; you can apply keyframes to a single clip instead. See Chapter 20 for more information.

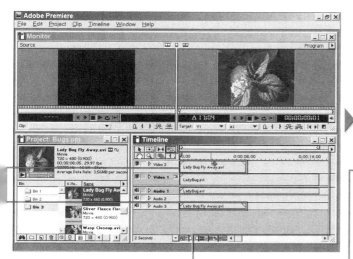

SPLIT MULTIPLE CLIPS

-1 Locate the clips that you want to split.

2 Click the Multiple Razor tool (🔲) (▷ becomes 🞩).

-3 Click at the point in the Timeline where you want the splits to occur.

■ The clips are immediately split.

DELETE GAPS BETWEEN CLIPS

Often in the course of assembling and moving clips, gaps between clips occur. This happens when you move clips between tracks, add or remove clips, or insert and remove edits and transitions, and are more likely to occur if you have Snap to Edges turned off. (See "Using Snap to Edges" for more information.) Sometimes the gaps are very small;

unless you are working at 1-frame increments in the Timeline, you are not going to see these gaps. Instead, you notice them when you render your project and preview it in the Monitor window. Then you must go back and remove the gaps in the Timeline.

You can quickly remove any gaps that appear between clips in a track by using a ripple delete edit. A

ripple delete edit "extracts" the gap between clips in a track and moves the clips together, reestablishing clip continuity.

You can also use a ripple delete to extract a clip and close the gap between other clips. See "Lift or Extract Frames," later in this chapter, to find out more about extracting a clip.

DELETE GAPS BETWEEN CLIPS

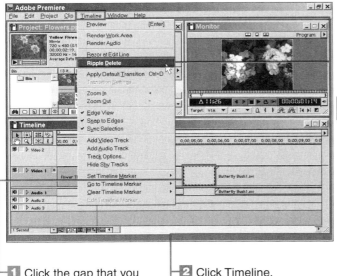

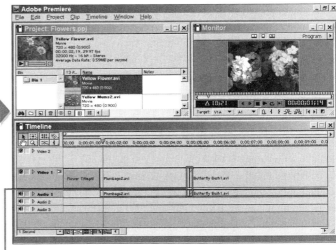

1 Click the gap that you want to remove.

Note: See the section "Add or Delete a Clip" to place clips on the Timeline.

2 Click Timeline.

3 Click Ripple Delete.

■ The gap is removed.

Note: See Chapter 19 to find out about other types of edits that you can perform.

USING SNAP TO EDGES

Unless you are working at very small time increments, such as 1-frame increments, it can be difficult to align clips in the Timeline so that they abut one another. Fortunately, there is help: You can use the Snap to Edges feature to help you move and align clips in the Timeline tracks. When this feature is activated, clips snap to the edges of other clips, much

like a magnet, when you move them.

You can toggle the Snap to Edges feature on or off as needed. If you turn the feature off, you can move clips independently, so you can position clips anywhere in a track without snapping the clip up next to an adjacent clip or transition.

The Snap to Edges feature can also be used to align a marker with a clip, another marker, or the edit line within in the Timeline. This lets you make clip edits or align your edits with markers you have placed, such as needing to align an audio effect at a precise point in a video.

USING SNAP TO EDGES

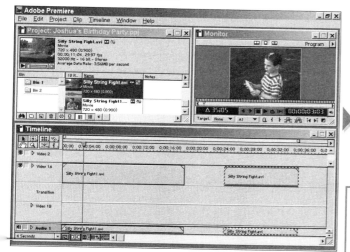

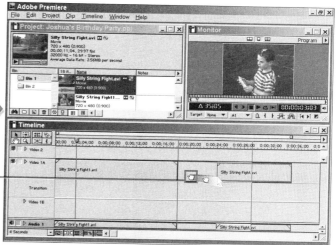

1 Click the Snap to Edges toggle button (changes to).

2 Click and drag a clip toward the edge of another clip (becomes).

■ The clip snaps to the edges of the other clip.

Note: See the section "Move Clips in the Timeline" to move clips around in the Timeline.

CHANGE CLIP SPEED AND DURATION

You can change the speed of a clip to adjust the playback rate to play faster or slower. *Clip speed* is the playback rate of the video or audio compared to the rate at which it was recorded. Clip speed is initially the same as it was when the clip was imported or captured. Changing a clip's speed alters its source frame rate and may

cause some frames to be omitted or repeated. In addition, changing the speed of a clip requires playing the same number of frames for a different length of time, which also changes the duration (moves the out point) of the clip. Changing the speed to a negative value (such as -100) causes the clip to play in reverse.

You can also change the duration of a video or audio clip. The *duration* is the length of time it plays and is the difference in time between a clip's in and out points. You can also set the duration of a clip by specifying a length of time from its current source in point.

CHANGE CLIP SPEED

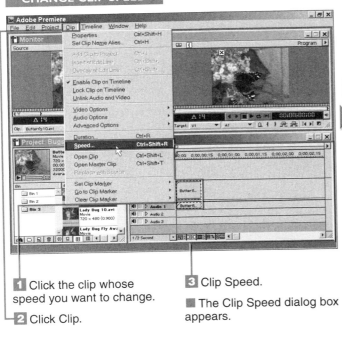

■ Click the clip whose speed you want to change.

② Click Clip.

③ Clip Speed.

■ The Clip Speed dialog box appears.

④ Click New Rate (○ changes to ◉).

⑤ Type a new speed rate based on a percentage of the normal speed.

Note: A value greater than 100% increases the clip speed; less than 100% decreases it.

Note: A value of -100% makes the clip play in reverse.

⑥ Click OK.

■ The clip plays at the new speed when previewed.

Can I increase the duration of a clip?

✔ You can only increase a clip's duration if the master clip has additional frames beyond the end of the clip. If you need a longer version of the master clip, you can try recapturing a longer segment from your camera and importing that as a new master clip. See Chapter 16 for information on capturing and importing video into Premiere.

How do I change the speed of a clip that is not yet in the Timeline?

✔ Click the clip in the Project window, click Clip, and then click Speed. The Clip Speed dialog box appears, enabling you to adjust clip speed and duration at the same time.

Is there a way to change a clip's in and out points without changing the duration?

✔ If you set a clip in the Timeline to the duration you require but you do not like where the clip begins and ends, you can use the Slip Edit tool to adjust the clip without changing the duration. See Chapter 19 to find out about creating slip edits.

CHANGE CLIP DURATION

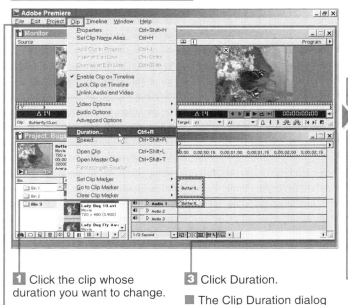

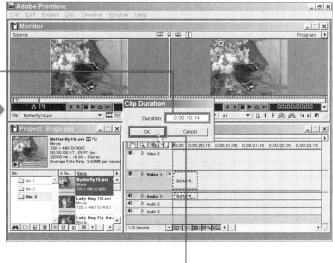

1 Click the clip whose duration you want to change.

2 Click Clip.

3 Click Duration.

■ The Clip Duration dialog box appears.

4 Type a new duration for the clip.

Note: A shorter duration increases clip speed. A longer duration decreases clip speed.

5 Click OK.

■ The new duration is assigned.

LIFT OR EXTRACT FRAMES

Before you edit a clip in the Timeline, decide how you want to affect adjacent frames and the duration of the clip and the entire program. For example, when you delete a range of frames, do you want all the following frames to stay in place or to fill the gap left by the frames that you are adjusting?

You can remove an entire clip or a range of frames from the Timeline in two ways: *Lifting* removes frames from the program and leaves a gap of the same duration as the frames that you remove; *extracting* removes frames from the program and closes the resulting gap by ripple deletion.

These methods are most useful when you want to remove frames from the middle of a clip or across multiple clips on the same track. If you just want to remove frames from one end of a clip, simply trim the end of the clip.

LIFT FRAMES

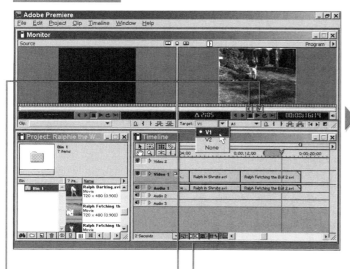

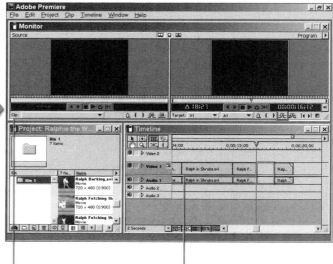

1 With a project open, set the in and out points for the portion of video that you want to remove.

2 Click ▾ to display available target tracks.

3 Click the track from which you want to remove frames.

4 Click the Lift button (⬚).

■ The frames between the designated in and out points are cleared, leaving empty frames in their place.

Is the master clip affected when I lift or extract frames from a clip in the Timeline?

✔ The master clip in the Project window never loses any of the frames that you remove from a lift or extract frames command. If you need to edit the master clip, you can do two things: make a copy of it on your computer and then import and edit the copy in Premiere or make a duplicate copy of the master clip in the Project window and then edit the master. See the online help for instructions on how to create a duplicate master clip in the Project window.

I cannot lift or extract frames. Why not?

✔ Make sure that the existing clips in the Timeline track are not locked. You cannot lift or extract frames from a locked track or clip. See "Lock and Unlock Tracks" and "Lock and Unlock Clips," in this chapter, to find out how to unlock tracks and clips, respectively.

EXTRACT FRAMES

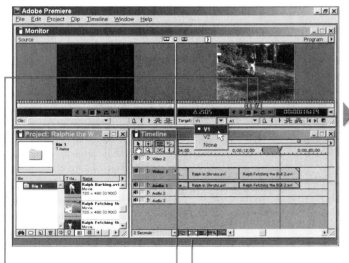

■1 With a project open, set the in and out points for the portion of video that you want to remove.

■2 Click ▾ to display available tracks.

■3 Click the track from which you want to remove frames.

■4 Click the Extract button (▦).

■ The frames between the designated in and out points are cleared, including the frames themselves.

SET IN AND OUT POINTS ON THE TIMELINE

Most clips are captured with extra footage at the beginning and end to allow for more precise editing later. It is common to fine-tune the beginning and end of a clip just before moving a clip into the program. You define the beginning of the clip by marking an *in point* (the first frame that will appear in the video program) and define the ending by marking an *out point* (the last frame that will appear in the video program).

You can set in and out points for a clip in the Timeline window. Setting in and out points enables you to trim a clip to the exact length that you want. The in point determines where the clip starts, and the out point determines where the clip ends.

You can also use in and out points to specify where transitions should begin or end, where clips should be trimmed or copied, where effects should be applied, and where still images and masks can be overlaid. See Chapter 17 for details on setting in and out points in the Monitor window.

1 Click the clip that you want to trim.

2 Click the Selection tool (🔳).

3 Move 🔖 over the left edge of the clip (🔖 becomes ⬌).

4 Click and drag the in point to a new location on the track.

Can I set different in and out points for linked video and audio clips?

✔ Linked video and audio clips can have their own set of in and out points, called *split points*. Split points are used to create split edits, such as an L-cut, in which the audio extends into the next clip. You can mark split points only when the Source view contains a linked clip. If you bring a linked clip into the Source view from the Timeline, be sure that Sync mode is selected first. For more information on Sync mode, see "Link and Unlink Clips," earlier in this chapter.

Which is the fastest method to trim a clip?

✔ You can set in and out points in the Clip window, in Source view in the Monitor window, and in the Timeline window. Most editors find it easier to see how the in and out points affect frames in the clip using the Monitor window. See Chapter 17 to find out how to trim clips in the Monitor window.

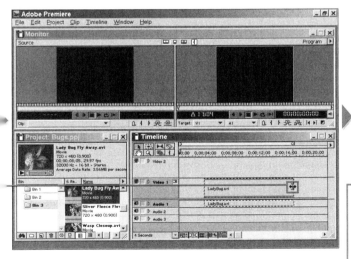

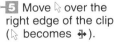

5 Move ▷ over the right edge of the clip (▷ becomes ✛).

6 Click and drag the out point to a new location on the track.

■ The new in and out points are set.

Note: You can also click the In Point and Out Point tools in the toolbox to trim a clip in the Timeline.

ADD PROGRAM MARKERS TO THE TIMELINE

You can use program markers to identify specific points in the Timeline. *Program markers* are reference points for editors that appear on the Timeline ruler but do not appear in the final video project. For example, you may add a program marker to identify where a title clip should begin or where a sound should start playing. Timeline markers can

also include a comment, a Web link, or a chapter link. Comments appear in the Program view window only, Web links initiate a jump to a Web page in your browser, and chapter links initiate a jump to a chapter in a QuickTime movie or DVD.

Program markers work the same as clip markers but apply to the

Timeline as a whole. You should add a clip marker for important points within an individual clip and add a Timeline marker for significant time points that affect multiple clips, such as when you need to synchronize video and audio on different clips. See Chapter 17 for more information on adding markers to a clip.

ADD PROGRAM MARKERS TO THE TIMELINE

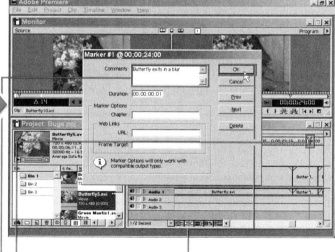

ADD A PROGRAM MARKER AND COMMENT

-1 Cue the edit line to where you want to add a marker.

Note: See "Navigate the Timeline" earlier in this chapter for details.

-2 Click Timeline.

-3 Click Set Timeline Marker.

-4 Click the type of marker that you want to set.

■ The marker appears on the Timeline ruler.

-5 Double-click the marker.

■ The Marker dialog box appears.

-6 Type comment text.

-7 Click OK.

■ The comment is added to the marker.

■ To see the comment, hover ₖ over the marker.

How do I remove a marker that I no longer need?

✔ Locate the marker using the Go to Timeline Marker command. Then, click Timeline, Clear Timeline Marker, and Current Marker. Premiere removes the marker from the Timeline. You can also use the keyboard shortcut Ctrl + Shift + G (Command - Shift - G).

How do I remove all markers?

✔ You can clear all markers by clicking Timeline, Clear Timeline Marker, and All Markers. You can also use the keyboard shortcut Ctrl + Alt + Shift + G (Command - Option - Shift - G).

Why do I see my comments appearing in my video?

✔ If you are in QuickTime Editing mode, the comments are displayed in the Monitor window as ghosted text.

How long are comments displayed in the Timeline?

✔ The default duration for marker comments is one frame (the frame where the marker appears on the Timeline), and the comment is displayed when that frame is displayed. To display the comment for longer than one frame, increase the comment duration when you create the comment.

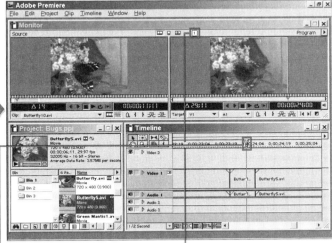

GO TO A MARKER

1 Click Timeline.

2 Click Go to Timeline Marker.

3 Click the type of marker to which you want to go.

■ Premiere immediately scrolls to the marker location in the Timeline.

■ The marker icon appears on the Timeline ruler as well as above the Program view in the Monitor window.

UNDERSTANDING TRANSITIONS

You can assign transitions to your video that help segue from one clip to another. Premiere offers more than 75 transition effects that you can apply and can customize to meet your project's needs.

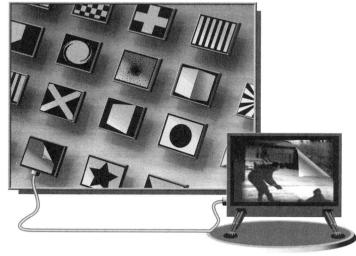

What Are Transitions?

A *transition* is simply an effect you can apply that controls how one clip visually replaces the next clip in the video. Transitions can be as simple as a wipe from left to right or as complex as a spiraling effect in which the next clip seems to spiral out from the center of the screen.

Why Use Transitions?

Transitions are great for showing the passage of time between two clips or moving from one scene to an entirely new scene. Transitions can add drama or create a bridge between clips.

Using the Transitions Palette

You can find plenty of transitions to choose from in the Transitions palette. Transitions are organized in folders. You can open a folder to display a list of associated transitions and expand or collapse folders as needed.

A/B Editing Mode

When you apply a transition in A/B Editing mode (see Chapter 15), you place the transition on the Transition track. You must have one clip in Video track 1A and another clip in Video track 1B, and both clips must overlap to create the transition effect.

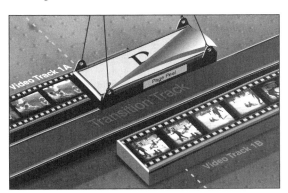

Single-Track Transitions

When you apply a transition in Single-Track Editing mode, you insert the transition between two clips on a single track. For the transition to work, there must be enough extra frames between the two clips. The first clip must have extra frames at the out point, and the second clip must have extra frames at the in point. To find out more about setting in and out points in clips, see Chapter 17.

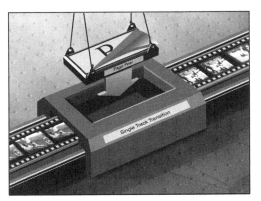

CREATE A RIPPLE EDIT

You can use a *ripple edit* to change the duration time of one clip without changing an adjacent clip. A ripple edit maintains the durations of all other clips by changing the program duration. As you click and drag to extend the out point of a clip, Premiere pushes the next clip to the right to avoid changing its in point. If you click and drag to the left to reduce the out point, Premiere does not change the in points of the following clips. Instead of manually adjusting the second clip to move over in the timeline when you change the clip duration, the ripple edit moves the remaining clips for you to make sure that no gaps occur between the clips. An empty space on one side of the edit point is treated as a clip and is adjusted by the Ripple Edit tool just as a clip would be.

Ripple edits affect the overall length of your video.

CREATE A RIPPLE EDIT

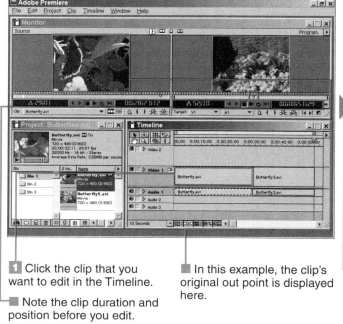

1 Click the clip that you want to edit in the Timeline.

■ Note the clip duration and position before you edit.

■ In this example, the clip's original out point is displayed here.

2 Click the Ripple Edit tool ( ) (becomes).

I cannot extend my clip's out point when I drag the end of the clip to the right. What may be the problem?

✔ When you perform any action that extends the duration of a clip, additional frames must be available in the clip's source (master) clip beyond the current in or out point. For example, if you did not trim the beginning or ending of a source clip before adding it to the Timeline, the clip is already using all frames available from its source, so its duration cannot be extended.

My clip does not adjust when I click and drag an end point. Why not?

✔ The clip is likely locked. You cannot edit locked clips or tracks in the Timeline window. See Chapter 18 to find out how to lock and unlock tracks and clips.

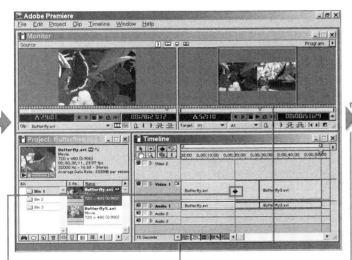

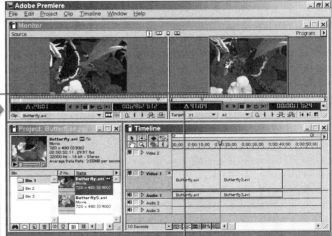

■3 Click and drag the in or out point of the clip that you want to change.

■ To ripple edit an in point, click and drag the clip's in point icon.

■ To ripple edit an out point, click and drag the clip's out point icon.

■ The Program view shows how the edit affects both clips as you drag.

Note: See Chapter 18 to find out how to work with Timeline tracks.

■ The clip is edited, and the remaining clips on the track shift over to adjust for the change.

■ In this example, the first clip's out point is shortened, so the out point shows a new frame.

■ The overall project length is changed.

Note: See Chapter 17 to preview a video project.

CREATE A ROLLING EDIT

A *rolling edit* enables you to click and drag on the edit line of one clip and simultaneously change the in or out point of the next clip on the edit line. A rolling edit enables you to shorten the current clip and make up the difference in program length by making the next clip longer. When you make a rolling edit, you adjust the edit line, and the frames

that you add to or subtract from one clip are subtracted from or added to the clip on the other side of the edit line. For example, if you add five frames to the first clip, five frames are subtracted from the next clip.

A rolling edit keeps the program duration constant and maintains

the combined duration of the two clips that you are editing.

If you are working on linked video and audio clips and want to make an L-cut, turn off Sync mode before performing a rolling edit. See "Perform a Split Edit in Trim Mode" in this chapter for information on L-cuts.

CREATE A ROLLING EDIT

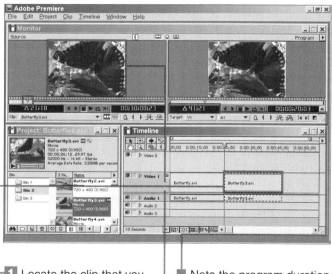

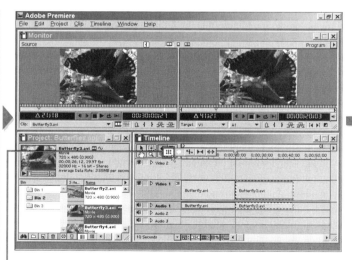

■1 Locate the clip that you want to edit.

Note: Make sure that the two clips are unlocked. See Chapter 18 to lock and unlock clips.

■ Note the program duration before you edit.

■ In this example, the clip's in point appears here.

■2 Click the Rolling Edit (⊞) tool (⌖ becomes ⇕).

I am having trouble seeing the tracks in the Timeline window. Is there any way to zoom in to better see my edits?

✔ You can make the tracks appear larger by customizing the Timeline window. Click Window, Window Options, and then Timeline Window Options to open the Timeline Window Options dialog box. Choose the largest icon size for the tracks and click OK. This should improve your view of the tracks.

How can I see the adjacent clips while making a rolling edit?

✔ You can easily view the edges of both clips in the Monitor window while making a rolling edit. In the Timeline window, click the Toggle Edge Viewing button (▦). The Monitor window splits to include both edge frames, which change as you drag the clip in the Timeline window menu. You can see how your rolling edits are affecting both clips in this manner.

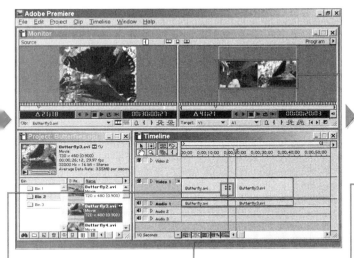

■③ Click and drag the out point of the clip that you want to change.

■ The Program view shows how the edit affects both clips as you drag.

Note: See Chapter 18 to find out how to work with Timeline tracks.

■ The out and in points are adjusted.

■ In this example, the second clip's in point was lengthened when the first clip's out point was shortened.

■ The second clip's new in point frame is displayed here.

■ No change occurred in program duration.

Note: See Chapter 17 to preview a video project.

CREATE A SLIP EDIT

Y   ou can use a *slip edit* to move
        a clip's start and end frames
        without affecting adjacent
clips. A slip edit shifts the starting
and ending frames of a clip forward
or backward without affecting
anything else in the Timeline. It
also enables you to adjust a clip's in
and out points without manually

moving both points. You drag a clip
left or right, and its source in and
out points shift accordingly. The
program duration and the source
and program in and out points of
all other clips remain unchanged.

A slip edit works only on clips that
have frames beyond its in and out

points. The Slip tool does not
require there to be a clip on either
side of the clip that you are
adjusting, but for best results you
should have the clip lie between
two other clips. The clip slips
between frames without affecting
the program length.

CREATE A SLIP EDIT

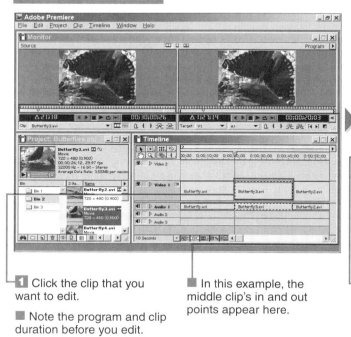

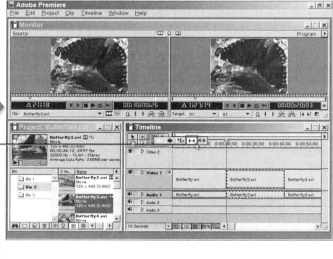

1 Click the clip that you
want to edit.

■ Note the program and clip
duration before you edit.

■ In this example, the
middle clip's in and out
points appear here.

2 Click the Slip Edit tool
(becomes).

If my clip was already trimmed pretty closely, can I still perform a slip edit?

✔ Any edit you attempt that extends past the master clip's original duration will not work. The original clip must have enough extra frames available to perform the edits. If you captured a clip as an excerpt from a video camera, you may need to go back and re-capture a longer video segment. See Chapter 16 for more information on capturing video.

Do slip edits work on linked clips?

✔ Slip edits will work on linked clips and unlinked clips. However, if you want to create an L-cut (in which the audio track extends over into the next video clip), you must unlink the video and audio clips first and then make the necessary slip edit to the video clip. See "Perform a Split Edit in Trim Mode" in this chapter to learn about L-cuts. Audio clips must then be edited separately.

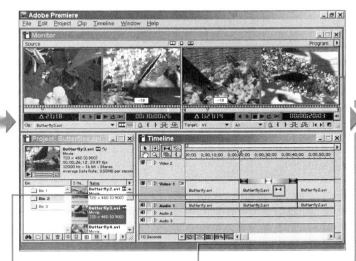

■3 Click and drag the clip right or left to slip the clip's frames.

■ The Monitor window changes to show the frames at the edit points and the number of frames that you slip or shift.

Note: See Chapter 18 to move clips on the Timeline.

■ The clip's new in and out points are set based on the number of frames that you slip.

■ In this example, the clip's new in point frame appears here.

■ No change occurred in program or clip duration.

Note: See Chapter 17 to preview a video project.

CREATE A SLIDE EDIT

You can use a *slide edit* to maintain the current clip's duration while adjusting the adjacent clips' in and out points. In essence, you keep your current clip unchanged and change the in and out points of the clips adjoining the current clip. For example, a slide edit is used when a clip is dragged

left so that it starts earlier in the program. This has the effect of shortening the preceding clip and lengthening the following clip.

When you make a slide edit, you only change the neighboring in and out points. The overall program length remains the same, and only

the adjacent clips are affected. Premiere permits slide edits only if you have three clips side-by-side. You also cannot make a slide edit past the first or last frames of the adjoining clips. If you have reached either end of a master clip, you cannot extend the edit any further.

CREATE A SLIDE EDIT

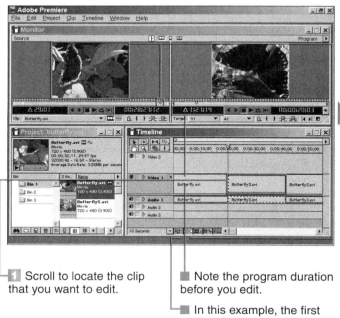

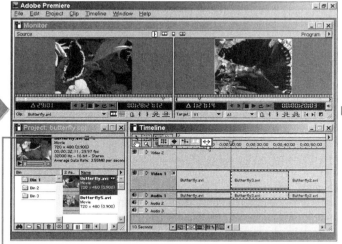

■1 Scroll to locate the clip that you want to edit.

■ Note the program duration before you edit.

■ In this example, the first clip's out point appears here.

■2 Click the Slide Edit tool (⌖ becomes ▐◀▶▌).

I do not like where I placed my slide edit. How do I undo the edit?

✔ Click Edit and then Undo immediately after performing the edit. If the edit occurred several steps back, you can use the History palette, in which Premiere keeps track of your edits. (To display the History palette, click Window and then Show History.) When you click an edit in the list, Premiere undoes all edits performed after and including the selected edit.

Can I use a slide edit to move a clip in an audio track?

✔ You cannot use the Slip and Slide tools directly on audio clips, but when you use the Slip and Slide tools on video clips, any linked audio clips will be adjusted to match the video. If you need to make other edits and adjustments to the audio clips, you need to use the Audio tools. See Chapter 21 to find out how to work with audio clips.

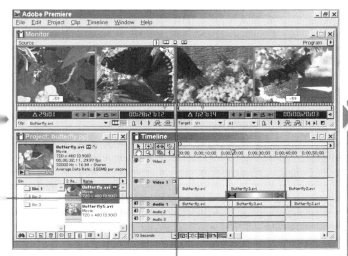

■3■ Click and drag the clip right or left to slide the adjacent clip's frames.

■ Drag the clip left to adjust the out point of the clip to the left.

■ Drag the clip right to adjust the in point of the clip to the right.

■ The Monitor window shows the frames at the edit points and the number of frames that you slide or shift.

■ The adjacent clip's in and out points are changed.

■ In this example, the first clip's new out point frame appears here.

■ No change occurred in program duration.

Note: See Chapter 17 to preview a video project.

415

EDIT IN TRIM MODE

Y ou can use the Trim mode view in the Monitor window to create detailed edits on your clips. The Monitor window's Trim view is a precise way to trim clips interactively in any video track. You can perform ripple or rolling edits at any edit along the Timeline. As you make adjustments, you see the frames on

both sides of the edit. You can also set a range of frames that you see on both sides of the edit to expand your view of the context of the edit. The Timeline updates as you perform the edit.

When you are not in Trim view, the left monitor displays source clips and the right monitor displays the

program. When you use the Trim view, both monitors represent clips in the program; the left monitor is the clip to the left of the edit line, and the right monitor is the clip to the right of the edit line.

EDIT IN TRIM MODE

1 Cue the edit line to the frame where you want to perform an edit.

■ Optionally, to trim only the clips in selected tracks, select the tracks and click the Toggle Shift Tracks button ( ).

■ Optionally, click the Toggle Sync Mode button ( ) to trim both tracks for linked tracks that you are editing.

Note: See Chapter 18 to find out how to work with the Timeline window.

Why can I not adjust a clip's out point any farther?

✔ When you perform any action that requires moving a clip's in or out point outward, such as adding frames in the Trim view, additional frames must be available in the clip's master clip beyond the current in or out point. For example, if you did not trim the beginning or ending of a source clip before adding it to the Timeline, the edit line may already be at the first or last frame available from the source, so you will not be able to move its in or out point any farther.

How do I switch back to Dual or Single view?

✔ After you finish trimming clips in Trim mode view, click the Dual View (▣) or Single View (▢) button at the top of the Monitor window to switch back. You can also click the Timeline ruler in the Timeline window to switch back to the previous view.

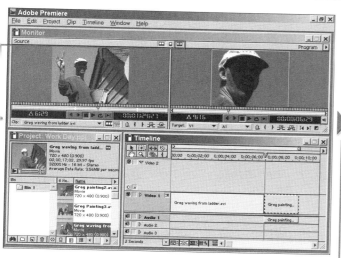

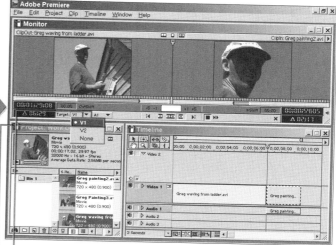

-2 Click the Trim Mode button (▣).

■ The Monitor window switches to Trim mode view.

Note: See Chapter 17 to find out how to work with Monitor window views.

3 Click ▾.

-4 Click the video track that you want to edit.

Note: To edit audio, click the ▾ labeled A1, A2, and so on, and click the audio track that you want to edit.

■ You can now edit in Trim mode and view two adjacent clips.

Note: See "Perform a Ripple Edit in Trim Mode" and "Perform a Split Edit in Trim Mode" later in this chapter to learn more about using Trim mode.

PERFORM A RIPPLE EDIT IN TRIM MODE

When you perform a ripple edit in the Timeline, you work with clips without viewing the effects of your edits. This is convenient when you need to make fast adjustments to a clip's running length or just need to rearrange clip duration especially for static images. However, if you need to see the results of your edits to the project, you can perform a

ripple edit in the Monitor window using Trim mode.

Much like a ripple edit in the Timeline, a ripple edit in Trim mode changes the duration of one clip without changing an adjacent clip. A ripple edit shifts the remaining clips over for you to make sure that no gaps form between clips. By performing the

ripple edit in Trim mode view, you can see how the clip that you are editing flows to the adjacent clip.

A ripple edit affects the overall length of your video project, so if you are trying to create a video with a precise duration, you need to keep an eye on the running time.

PERFORM A RIPPLE EDIT IN TRIM MODE

■1 Cue the edit line to where you want to perform an edit.

Note: See Chapter 18 to find out how to work with the Timeline window.

■2 Click the Trim Mode button (▦).

■ The Monitor window switches to Trim mode view.

■3 Click ▼ to specify target tracks.

Note: See the section "Edit in Trim Mode" to edit in Trim mode view.

■4 Click a clip to edit.

■ Clicking the left image lets you edit the first clip's out point.

■ Clicking the right image lets you edit the second clip's in point.

■ The active image's display appears green.

■ You can also click the Set Focus Left (▦) or Set Focus Right (▦) buttons to specify which clip to edit.

Can I perform a rolling edit in Trim mode?

✔ Yes. While in Trim mode, click the Set Focus Both button and then make your edits as you would with a ripple edit. See "Create a Rolling Edit" earlier in this chapter to find out about rolling edits.

Can I perform a ripple edit over a specific number of frames?

✔ Yes. To perform a ripple edit over a specific number of frames, type, in the space between the buttons, a negative number to move left or a positive number to move right and press Enter (Return).

Can I use a trim multiple other than 1 or 5?

✔ Yes. You can customize the Time Mode view to display another amount for trimming frames. For example, you may prefer to trim 3 frames at a time or trim some fraction of the frames per a second setting. You can find out how to customize the Trim mode view in the section "Customize Trim Mode," later in this chapter.

■ **5** Click a trim button to trim the clip by the desired number of frames.

■ Clicking the Trim Left button (-1) trims one frame to the left.

■ Clicking the Trim Right button (+1) trims one frame to the right.

■ To trim frames in multiples of 5, click -5 or +5.

■ You can also click and drag the in or out point to adjust the trim.

■ Clicking here cancels the edit and returns the clip to its previous state.

Note: See the section "Preview an Edit in Trim Mode" to preview a video.

PREVIEW AN EDIT IN TRIM MODE

One of the chief benefits of performing ripple and rolling edits in Trim mode is the ability to view your edits as you make them. When you are working in the Timeline, you see a physical representation of your clips and the edits you make, but you do not see the actual footage and the effects that your edits have on the project.

When you are in the Monitor window and performing edits in Trim mode, you can preview the results of your edits. This gives you greater control over how your finished footage will look and increased precision and flexibility in deciding how to perform your ripple and rolling edits.

You can also use all the Monitor window controls, such as looping and playing from in point to out point in the clip. When you are done with your edits, you can remain in Trim mode, or you can switch back to Dual view or Single view using the buttons at the top of the Monitor window.

PREVIEW AN EDIT IN TRIM MODE

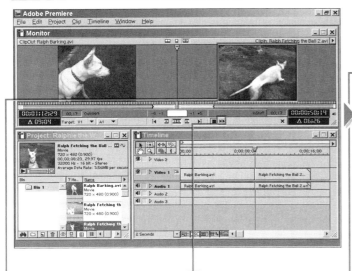

1 Perform an edit in Trim mode view.

Note: See the previous sections to edit in Trim mode view.

2 Click the Play button (▶).

■ You can also press the spacebar to preview the edit.

■ The edit plays in the right side of the Monitor window.

CUSTOMIZE TRIM MODE

The Trim mode view in the Monitor window can be customized to adjust the way that you view clips and work with ripple and rolling edits. The Trim mode defaults the Trim Right and Trim Left values to 5 frames; each time that you click the button marked 5, you move the in and out points five frames. This value can be customized to match the editing style that you commonly use.

For example, you may prefer to edit clips in whole fractions of the frames per second (fps) value; if you are working at 30 fps, you may want the Trim Right and Trim Left buttons to move in half-second increments, or 15 fps. You can change that value in the Monitor Window Options dialog box.

You can also change how frames are displayed and whether the clip previews play back at full size.

CUSTOMIZE TRIM MODE

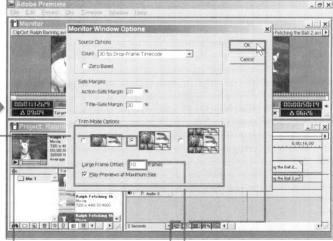

◤1 With Trim mode displayed, click Window.

Note: See Chapter 17 to find out how to use Monitor window views.

◤2 Click Window Options.

◤3 Click Monitor Window Options.

■ The Monitor Window Options dialog box appears.

◤4 Make changes among the Trim mode options.

■ Clicking display options controls how frames display (○ changes to ●).

■ You can type a number to specify a larger or smaller multiple frame option for incremental edits.

◤5 Click OK.

■ The new settings take effect.

PERFORM A SPLIT EDIT IN TRIM MODE

One of the great advantages of working with a nonlinear editing system such as Premiere is the flexibility that it gives you to work with video and audio tracks separately. Most films record video and audio separately, and it is often quite difficult to achieve some effects that have video and audio streams

overlapping. One of the most common edits in film is a *split edit,* also called an L-cut. An L-cut has the audio synchronizing and overlapping from one clip to another in an L-shape.

You can perform a split edit in Trim mode view to make a clip's audio track synchronize with another

clip. For example, you may show a clip of someone talking and then show another person but still hear the first person talking. A split edit is a great way to make a video more interesting, and it is easy to perform in Premiere.

PERFORM A SPLIT EDIT IN TRIM MODE

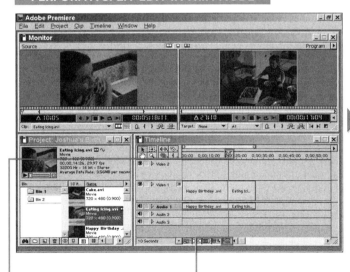

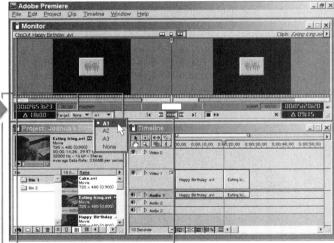

1 Cue the edit line to where you want to create a split edit.

2 Click the Toggle Sync Mode button ( ) to toggle the mode off.

■ indicates the mode is off.

3 Click the Trim Mode button ( ).

■ The Monitor window switches to Trim Mode view.

4 Click and specify target tracks.

Note: See "Edit in Trim Mode" to edit in Trim Mode view.

5 Click the Set Focus Both button ( ).

■ Both views are selected.

What is a J-cut?

✔ A *J-cut* occurs when the audio in point appears earlier than the video in point. An L-cut, on the other hand, is the reverse: An audio in point appears after the video in point.

Can I make the audio track cross-fade?

✔ Yes. A cross-fade is a good effect to apply to an audio clip that is used for a split edit. To find out how to cross-fade an audio clip and work with the audio mixer tools, see Chapter 21.

When I turn off Sync mode, do I lose all the synchronization information between the audio and video clips?

✔ No. Premiere keeps track of sync information, even when Sync mode is turned off. When linked clips are moved out of sync, both clips display a red triangle at the in point to indicate the out-of-sync condition.

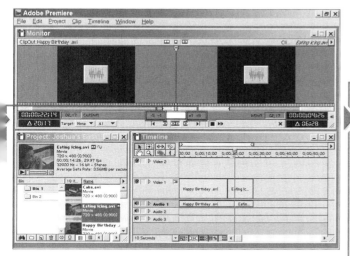

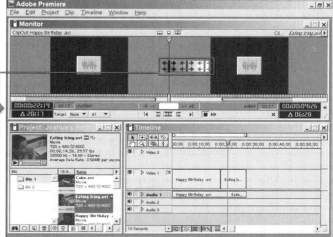

6 Click a trim button to trim the clips the desired number of frames.

■ Clicking the Trim Left button (-1) trims one frame to the left.

■ Clicking the Trim Right button (+1) trims one frame to the right.

■ To trim frames in multiples of 5, click -5 or +5 .

■ You can also click and drag the Rolling Edit pointer (becomes when the Set Focus Both button is selected) between the two clips to adjust the edit.

■ The number of trimmed frames for each clip appears here.

Note: See "Preview an Edit in Trim Mode" to preview a split edit.

APPLY A TRANSITION IN A/B EDITING MODE

Premiere provides a variety of transitions, such as wipes, zooms, and dissolves. The simplest transition is the *cut,* in which the last frame of one clip leads directly into the first frame of the next. The term comes from film editing, in which *cut* means splicing two shots together. Very often, a cut is the most effective way to move from one scene to the next. Other transitions are useful in

setting a mood or adding a creative element to your project.

The transitions included with Premiere typically involve the end of one clip and the beginning of the next. For example, the Cross Dissolve transition may dissolve the last second of one clip into the first second of the next. Some transitions, such as Inset, can

involve both clips in their entirety, depending on the desired effect.

You insert a transition in A/B Editing mode using the Transition track. As long as a clip in the Video 1A track overlaps a clip in the Video 1B track, you can position a transition between the two. The overlap determines the transition's duration.

APPLY A TRANSITION IN A/B EDITING MODE

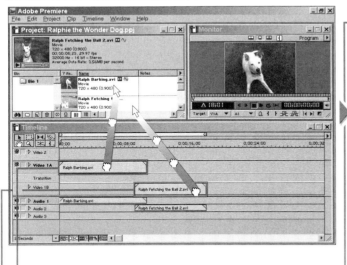

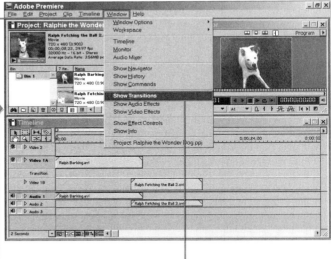

1 Drag a clip from the Project window and drop it into Video track 1A.

2 Drag another clip from the Project window and drop it into Video track 1B, overlapping a few frames.

Note: See Chapter 18 to find out more about working in the Timeline window.

3 Click Window.

4 Click Show Transitions.

■ The Transitions palette appears.

I am not familiar with video terminology; how do I tell what the different transitions do?

✔ Premiere includes over 75 transitions that you can select from the Transitions palette. Within the palette, transitions are organized by type, in folders. Each transition is represented by an icon depicting how it works, where A is the first clip and B is the second. To help you choose, you can animate these icons and view brief descriptions. See "Edit Transition Settings," later in this chapter, to find out how to edit transitions if you want to change any transition settings.

How do I adjust a transition's duration after it is in place?

✔ You can click the transition and drag it on the Transition track, or you can click and drag an edge of the transition to make it longer or shorter. If you move a transition's edge, the edge of the clip may move as well. To control this, press Ctrl (Command) while dragging an edge.

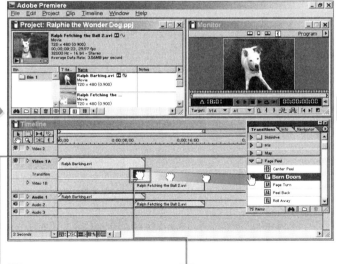

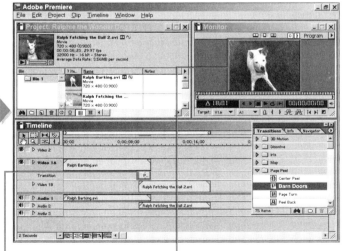

5 Locate the transition that you want to use.

Note: To preview a transition, double-click it to open its Settings dialog box and view the effect.

6 Drag the transition from the palette and drop it into the Transition track between the two overlapping clips.

▪ The transition appears on the track.

7 Save the project.

Note: See Chapter 15 to find out how to save a project.

8 Press Enter (Return).

Note: You can also click Preview from the Timeline menu to preview the video.

▪ Premiere builds a preview, and then the video plays in the Monitor window, showing any transitions assigned.

APPLY A TRANSITION IN SINGLE-TRACK MODE

You can add a transition between two clips when the Timeline is in Single-Track Editing mode. In general, this method requires more planning and is recommended for more-experienced video editors, especially those with a traditional editing background.

To create a transition in Single-Track Editing mode, Premiere either uses the extra frames available for the clips (extra frames are created by trimming a clip) or repeats frames at the beginning or ending of the clips.

The single-track method of creating a transition is similar to the one in traditional linear editing studios, in which frames that you have trimmed out of the program are used to create a transition. The frames trimmed from the beginning of a clip are called *head material;* the frames trimmed from the end of a clip are called *tail material.* If insufficient head or tail material is present when applying a transition, Premiere displays a Fix Transition dialog box in which you can choose to change the duration of the transition, change the transition's alignment, or repeat the first and last frames of the clip.

APPLY A TRANSITION IN SINGLE-TRACK MODE

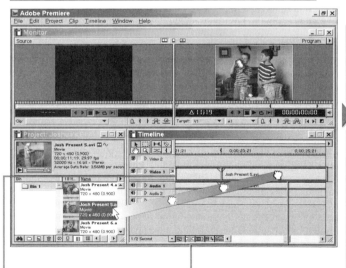

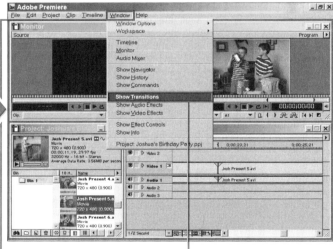

1 Drag and drop a clip onto a video track.

Note: See Chapter 18 to find out more about working in the Timeline window.

2 Drag and drop another clip to the same video track following the first clip.

Note: The first clip should have extra frames at the out point, and the second clip should have extra frames at the in point.

3 Click Window.

4 Click Show Transitions.

■ The Transitions palette appears.

Can I switch between Single-Track and A/B Editing modes while I edit transitions?

✔ Switching between Single-Track Editing and A/B Editing modes after you have begun editing in the Timeline may cause unexpected or unpredictable behavior.

What happens if I delete a transition after making adjustments with the Fix Transition command?

✔ If you delete or move a transition or a clip tied to a transition after you have made adjustments using the Fix Transition dialog box, Premiere automatically restores the in and out points of the corresponding clips. See "Fix a Transition."

How many extra frames should a clip have?

✔ A transition in Single-Track Editing mode is determined by the number of extra frames at the beginning or end of the clips. To create a 30-frame Dissolve transition between two clips, for example, each clip should have 15 extra frames. The first clip needs 15 extra frames at the out point, and the second clip needs 15 extra frames at the in point. See Chapter 17 to find out how to create in and out points in video clips.

–5 Locate the transition that you want to use.

Note: To preview a transition, double-click it to open its Settings dialog box and view the effect.

6 Drag and drop the transition in between the two clips.

Note: If there are an insufficient number of frames between the two clips to create the transition, the Fix Transition dialog box appears. See the section "Fix a Transition."

■ The transition appears on the track.

7 Save the project.

Note: See Chapter 15 to save a project.

8 Press Enter (Return).

Note: You can also click Preview from the Timeline menu to preview the video.

■ Premiere builds a preview and plays the video in the Monitor window with the transition.

■ Click here to split the track and view the Transition track separately.

427

FIX A TRANSITION

Creating transitions in Single-Track Editing mode can be tricky, and editing in this mode requires additional time and advance planning to make it work. There may be times when you miscalculate the number of head frames or tail frames available for a transition, and when you insert a transition between two clips, Premiere prompts you to fix the transition.

To fix the transition effect, you have two basic choices: You can change the clip duration so that more frames become available or repeat the last and first frames of the two clips. If you are unsure of how your transition will look with either option, you can try one transition and then undo it if you do not like the result by pressing Ctrl + Z (Command - Z).

You can take a "shortcut" when applying transitions in Single-Track Editing mode by holding down Alt (Option) when you drag a transition into place. This automatically brings up the Fix Transition dialog box, and you can make adjustments to transition duration at that time.

FIX A TRANSITION

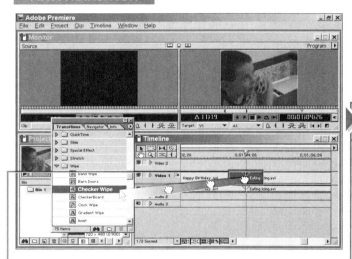

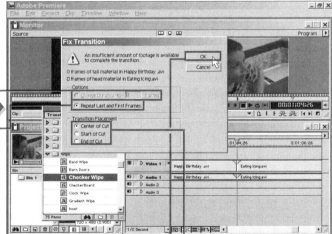

1 Add a transition between two clips in Single-Track Editing mode.

Note: See the section "Apply a Transition in Single-Track Mode."

■ If there are not enough frames to apply a transition, the Fix Transition dialog box appears.

2 Select changes to fix the transition (○ changes to ●).

■ Click here to shorten the duration of the transition effect and specify the number of frames.

■ Click here to repeat the frames to make up the difference.

■ Click one of these settings to change the transition's alignment.

3 Click OK.

■ Premiere adjusts the transition accordingly.

REPLACE OR DELETE A TRANSITION

Often when editing a film in post-production, you will insert a transition called for in the shooting script. This transition may have been storyboarded during pre-production or added while on the set as a margin note. Then, after editing the clips together and inserting the

transition, you decide the effect does not work and must be replaced with a new transition.

Instead of re-editing your clips, you can replace a transition by simply dropping a new transition on top of the old one. When you replace a transition, the original transition's

alignment and duration are preserved. However, the settings that were particular to the old transition are discarded and replaced by the default settings for the new transition or by the master transition settings if you have set them in the Transitions palette.

REPLACE OR DELETE A TRANSITION

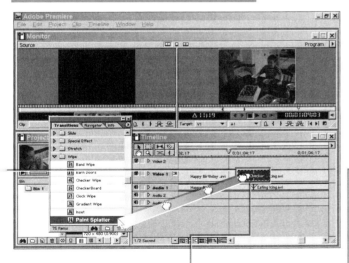

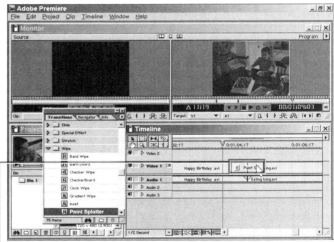

REPLACE A TRANSITION

■1 Click the transition.

Note: See the sections "Apply a Transition in A/B Editing Mode" or "Apply a Transition in Single-Track Mode" to insert transitions.

■2 Drag a new transition over the selected transition.

■ Premiere swaps the current transition with the new transition.

DELETE A TRANSITION

■1 Click the transition.

■2 Press Delete on your keyboard.

■ The transition disappears from the track.

EDIT TRANSITION SETTINGS

Premiere gives you a palette that contains many transitions that you can use to switch between clips. Many of these are common to filmmaking, and you will want to use them in your own projects. Fortunately, the transitions are not cast in stone. Each transition has settings that you can adjust to customize it in

order to match the look and feel of your project or to create a desired effect.

You can customize a transition for even greater control. You can change a number of settings for each transition, including the transition direction, the start and end values, the border, and

anti-aliasing. For example, you may change the way that a transition appears during playback or change the track direction. Depending on the transition, you may select additional options to customize the effect, such as color or point of origin.

EDIT TRANSITION SETTINGS

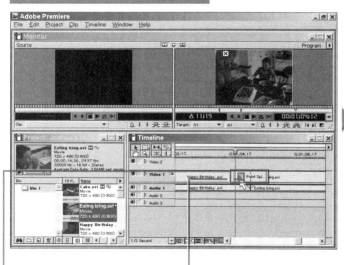

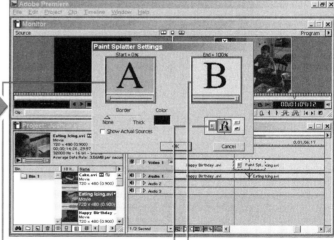

■1 Double-click the transition that you want to customize.

Note: See the sections "Apply a Transition in A/B Editing Mode" or "Apply a Transition in Single-Track Mode" to add transitions.

■ You can click here to reverse the transition direction.

■ The transition's Settings dialog box appears.

Note: The options available vary by transition.

■2 Adjust the transition settings as needed.

■ The left icon represents the transition's start point.

■ The right icon represents the transition's end point.

■ To switch the start and end points, click here. This changes the direction of the transition.

How do I create a picture-in-a-picture transition effect?

✔ If you want to create a picture-in-a-picture transition effect, use the Zoom transition and set the start and end sizes to about 30 percent; then add a border and move the center point to the desired corner.

How do I make a transition play backward?

✔ To make a transition play forward or backward, click the Forward/Reverse selector in the upper-right corner of the transition's thumbnail. For example, the Clock Wipe transition can play clockwise or counterclockwise.

I want to apply the same transition throughout my video. Can I set up a default transition?

✔ Yes. Click the transition that you want to use as the default in the Transitions palette, click the palette's menu button, and then click Set Selected as Default. The Default Effect dialog box appears. Specify a duration or alignment and then click OK. To quickly apply the default transition, click ◢ in the Monitor window.

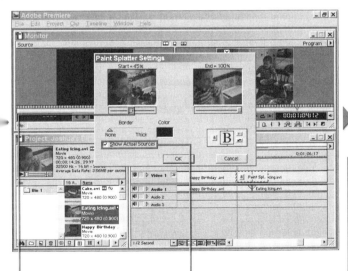

■ Clicking and dragging the slider changes where the transition effect starts.

■ Clicking here displays the actual clips involved with the transition.

3 When you have changed the settings just the way you want them, click OK.

■ Premiere applies the new settings.

UNDERSTANDING TEXT AND GRAPHIC ELEMENTS

You can use text and graphic elements in your video to convey information, create a mood, introduce a scene, and more. This section gives you an overview of the kinds of text and graphic elements you can create.

Title Clips

Adding *title clips* to a project can make your video more professional, help viewers identify key parts, and introduce important information such as names and dates. Although essentially static, title clips can be used on their own for any number of frames in your project, or you can superimpose them over other clips.

Why Add Graphics?

You can add simple graphic objects, such as shapes or lines, to a title clip to dress it up. You can also use graphic objects without text, if needed. For example, you may create a logo or graphic symbol to use at key moments in the video.

Text and Drawing Tools

You create titles and graphic objects in the Title window. The Title window provides you with simple drawing tools for creating shapes and line objects. The window also includes tools for entering and formatting text to use in your video. You can combine the text and drawing tools to make eye-catching titles. Full-featured graphics programs such as Photoshop and Illustrator enable you to create more advanced graphic objects that you can import into Premiere.

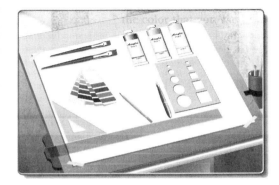

Scrolling Title Text

The Title window also offers a Rolling Title tool for creating text that moves, or *scrolls*, across the screen. You may want to use scrolling text for your video's credits, or for the opening title sequence. The Rolling Title tool enables you to control the speed of the scroll as well as which direction the text moves.

Saving Title Clips

After you create your title text or graphic objects, you must save your work before you use them in the video. Premiere saves title clip files with the .ptl extension. As soon as you save a title clip, it appears in the current video's Project window. You can also reuse the clip in other Premiere projects.

Applying Title Clips

When you are ready to use a title clip in your video, you simply place it in a track in the Timeline window. You can control exactly how long the clip plays, and whether it is superimposed over another clip or used on its own.

UNDERSTANDING VIDEO EFFECTS

Video effects add visual impact to your project. For example, you can apply an effect that makes a clip blur or shake, or assign an effect that makes a title clip glow.

What Exactly Is a Video Effect?

A *video effect* is a filter that alters the video image. You can apply video effects to any clip in your project. You can even assign multiple effects to the same clip, so that each effect cumulatively alters the image as it appears as a result of any previously applied effect.

Types of Effects

The Video Effects palette includes 14 folders, each containing one or more effects. Premiere includes effects that change the image brightness and contrast, blur and distort the image, and create waves and swirls in the image.

Fine-Tuning Effects

You can adjust effect properties to meet your particular needs. Each effect offers different options. For example, the Alpha Glow effect, located in the Stylize folder, provides sliders for you to move to adjust the glow intensity and brightness as well as a color option for changing the effect's color.

Understanding Keyframes

A *keyframe* marks a key change in the content or attributes. Every video effect includes at least two keyframes — a start keyframe and an end keyframe. Inserting a keyframe between start and end keyframes lets you adjust the effect properties to create a change in the effect.

Editing Keyframes

You can add, delete, and move keyframes on the timeline. The closer the keyframes are to one another, the faster the effect. You cannot remove the start and end keyframes. You can, however, move them to start or end the effect at a different point in the clip, but every effect must include a start and end keyframe.

Calculating In-Between Frames

Every time you add a keyframe and make a change in the effect, Premiere calculates the changes between keyframes for you. As long as you define two keyframes, Premiere interpolates all the frames in between to get from the first keyframe to the next. When you add a keyframe, Premiere duplicates the effect settings found in the previous keyframe, enabling you to adjust effect properties to change the effect.

UNDERSTANDING TRANSPARENCY

You can superimpose one clip over another by making the top clip transparent. By setting a clip's opacity, you can make video images fade in and out in your project.

What Is Superimposing?

When you superimpose a clip, you make the clip transparent to some degree. For example, you may superimpose a title clip over a video clip and make the title clip fade away after a few frames. By setting an opacity level, or *fade*, you tell Premiere how much of a transparency effect to create. You can use Premiere's alpha channel — an image layer that can be treated as different levels of transparency — to define transparency for titles or graphics.

Opacity Levels

If you set a clip to 100% opacity, the image is not transparent. If you set a clip to 0% opacity, the image becomes completely transparent. Therefore, a clip set to 50% opacity is half transparent. You can control opacity by adjusting points on a track's Opacity Rubberband or fade line.

Track Hierarchy

Clip transparency is determined by the stacking order, also known as the *track hierarchy*. You can superimpose as many as 97 tracks, but you cannot superimpose Video Track 1. Only Video Track 2 and higher can be superimposed over other tracks. By layering clips in tracks, you can create transparent overlays to create fading and keying effects in your video.

Fading

The easiest way to superimpose two clips is to place one clip in a higher track over another clip in a lower track and adjust the higher clip's fade line. Fading involves changing the higher clip's opacity level.

Keying

Another way to superimpose clips is to make particular parts of one clip transparent using a *key*. "Keying" refers to making one image peek through another, much like looking through a keyhole. The clip on the lowest track becomes the image in the keyhole while the clip on the highest track provides the shape for the keyhole.

Types of Keys

Premiere provides 15 types of keys. You can either use a clip's alpha channel as a key or key out parts of an image based on color or luminance. Matte keys turn an image into the key shape. To learn about every type of key in Premiere, consult the program's help files.

UNDERSTANDING MOTION EFFECTS

You can create dynamic animations in Premiere, called *motion effects*, which add movement to your video project. For example, you may want a still image to move from one side of the screen to the other, or you may want to make a video clip bounce across the frame.

What Clips Can I Use?

You can create motion settings using a video clip, still image clip, or text clip. For example, you may want a company logo you have saved as a GIF file to appear to glide around the screen. If you use a video clip, you can make the entire clip move around the screen.

How Do Motion Effects Work?

A motion effect is comprised of a path with at least two keyframes. A *path* determines the movement of an effect. By default, the motion path moves from left to right, but you can set the path to move in any direction you want. Whatever path you specify, the clip follows, whether up and down, zigzag, or all over the frame. Motion settings apply to the entire clip.

What are Keyframes?

A *keyframe* marks an important change in the motion path. For example, if a clip is following a zigzag path across the screen, you can use keyframes to mark a change in direction. In addition, keyframes can mark a change in the clip itself, such as size or rotation.

Save and Load Motion Settings

You can save a motion setting as a PMT file and reuse the path again for another clip or in another project. To reuse the motion setting, you load the saved PMT file.

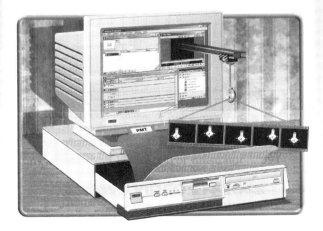

Types of Keyframe Changes

Premiere provides numerous effects settings for applying to your motion setting's keyframes. You can control a clip's Delay setting, for example, to make the clip seem to pause along the motion path, or you can use the Distortion settings to make the clip appear to distort as it travels along the path.

Using Alpha Channels

An *alpha channel* is a grayscale image layer for creating transparency effects. If you are using a still image that includes an alpha channel, you can mask out the image background and superimpose the clip over another video clip. This technique works only if you place the two clips in two different video tracks with one on top of the other.

CREATE A NEW TITLE

A mong other things, titles usually indicate time and place, introduce people, showcase graphics, provide transitions, or grant credit to those who contributed to the film. Titles add professionalism to any film or video project, and you should consider using them when appropriate.

In Premiere, the titling feature lets you create a new title and create text effects without requiring another program. For simple text and text effects, Premiere's titling feature is all you need to create and insert titles. For more complex graphics or text effects, you should use Photoshop or Illustrator to create your text, which you can then import into your Premiere

project. See Chapter 16 to learn about importing clips.

Premiere saves titles as static clips that you can add to the project timeline. You can also assign video effects to your titles as well as superimpose the title clips over other clips in your video. See the section "Apply a Video Effect" later in this chapter to learn more.

CREATE A NEW TITLE

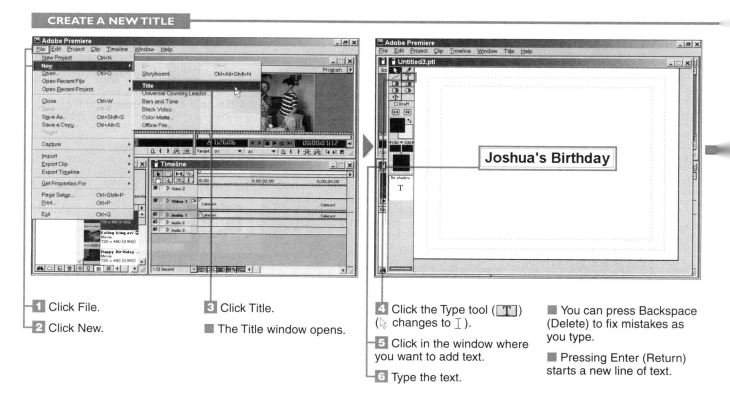

-1 Click File.
-2 Click New.

3 Click Title.
■ The Title window opens.

4 Click the Type tool ([T]) (changes to I).
5 Click in the window where you want to add text.
6 Type the text.

■ You can press Backspace (Delete) to fix mistakes as you type.

■ Pressing Enter (Return) starts a new line of text.

How do I control the size of the Title window?

✔ With the Title window open, click Window, Window Options, and then Title Window Options to open the Title Window Options dialog box. From here you can set a window size, a background color, an aspect ratio (screen width to screen height), title size for television screen, and NTSC-safe colors to ensure color compatibility with video monitors. Make your selections and click OK. You can also click and drag any window edge to resize the window.

How do I resize the text object in the Title window?

✔ Every item you add to the Title window, either text or graphics, is an object that can be moved or resized in the window. Click the text on the Title window to reveal selection handles around the text object. Click and drag a selection handle (⇲ becomes ✋) to resize the text object. To move the text object, click and drag the middle area of the text. To edit the text, double-click over the text and make your changes.

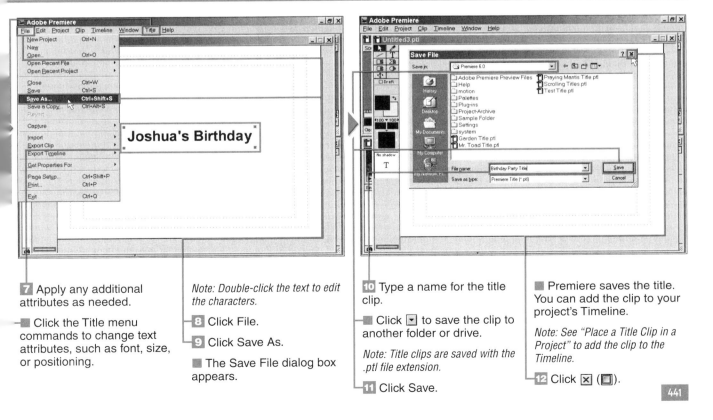

7 Apply any additional attributes as needed.

■ Click the Title menu commands to change text attributes, such as font, size, or positioning.

Note: Double-click the text to edit the characters.

8 Click File.

9 Click Save As.

■ The Save File dialog box appears.

10 Type a name for the title clip.

■ Click ▾ to save the clip to another folder or drive.

Note: Title clips are saved with the .ptl file extension.

11 Click Save.

■ Premiere saves the title. You can add the clip to your project's Timeline.

Note: See "Place a Title Clip in a Project" to add the clip to the Timeline.

12 Click ⊠ (▢).

441

APPLY A BACKGROUND FRAME

Before you begin creating titles in the Title window, you may wish to place a frame from a video clip to use as a background image. A *background frame* helps you determine attributes and placement for when you superimpose the title over a clip, such as making sure a key element in your video is not obscured by text, or by adding emphasis to a

particular area of the video. Unless you are placing text against a monochrome background, such as a black one, you should apply a background frame and check text alignment.

If a project is open on the screen, you can drag a clip from the Project window directly into the Title window. By default, Premiere uses

the first frame in the clip or the poster frame if one is defined, but you can specify which frame to use by setting marker 0 (Poster Frame) in the clip.

Premiere does not save the background frame as part of the title when you save the title file.

APPLY A BACKGROUND FRAME

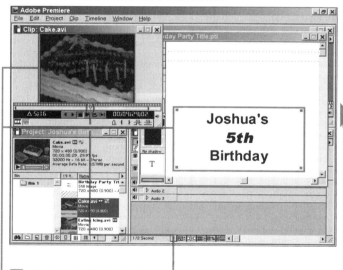

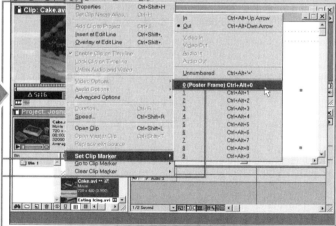

1 Display the Title window you want to edit.

Note: See the section "Create a New Title" to open the Title window.

2 Open the clip you want to use as the background.

Note: See Chapter 17 to work with clips.

3 Drag the Edit Line (🔲) to cue the clip to the frame you want to use.

4 Click Clip.

5 Click Set Clip Marker.

6 Click 0.

■ Premiere sets the current frame as the background frame for the Title window.

7 Click ✕ (🔲) to close the Clip window.

What kinds of colors should I use for my text?

✔ When designing a title to be superimposed, use colors that contrast well with the background video. You can import a sample frame to check a title against its background. If the background is complex, consider adding a shadow or a semitransparent shape behind the type. You can learn about adding additional text attributes like shadows in the online help. To create more complex text and graphics using Photoshop or Illustrator, see Parts I and II of this book.

Can I use a color as a background instead of a frame from a clip?

✔ Yes. With the Title window open, click Window, Window Options, and then Title Window Options to open the Title Window Options dialog box. Click Background to open the Color Picker dialog box, which contains a palette of colors from which you can choose. Click a color and click OK. To set an opaque background, click the Opaque check box. Click OK again to apply the color to the title clip.

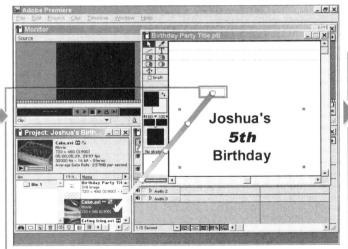

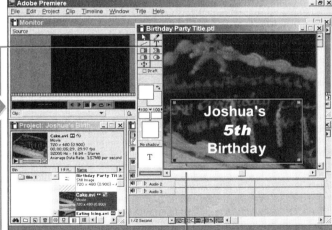

8 Click and drag the clip to the Title window (👆 becomes ✋).

Note: You may need to resize the Title window to see the Project window. Click and drag a window edge to resize the window.

■ The frame appears as the background behind the title text.

Note: To remove the frame, click Title and then Remove Background Clip.

■ You can now create or edit the title text to work with the frame background.

Note: See the section "Create a New Title" to create and save a title clip.

CREATE A SCROLLING TITLE

Y ou can create a scrolling title that makes text scroll or crawl across the screen. Scrolling titles are good for long sequences of text, such as credits at the end of a project. Using the Rolling Title tool, you can control how fast the text scrolls as well as which direction it moves. The clip length determines the speed of the scrolling motion.

When you create titles, you should follow some guidelines to improve readability.

First, use large sans-serif fonts. Avoid small type and serif fonts. The thin strokes of some small or serif characters do not display well on interlaced television sets, causing them to flicker.

Second, use semi-bold and boldface type weights, which are generally easier to read on television than regular or light type weights.

Finally, use few words in your titles. Long paragraphs of small type are difficult to read on television.

CREATE A SCROLLING TITLE

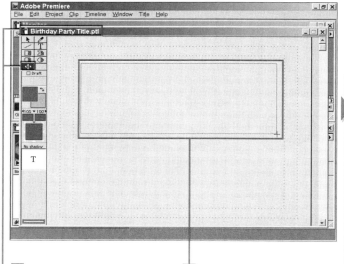

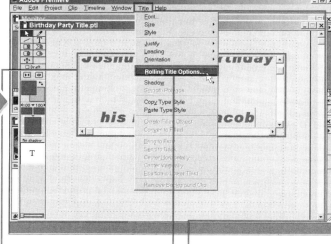

■1 Display the Title window.

Note: See the section "Create a New Title" to open the Title window.

■2 Click the Rolling Title tool ( ) (changes to +).

■3 Click and drag an area within the Title window where you want the scrolling text to appear.

■ A scrollable text box appears.

■4 Type the text you want to use as scrolling text.

■ You can click and drag a selection handle to resize the scrolling text area.

■5 Click Title.

■6 Click Rolling Title Options.

■ The Rolling Title Options dialog box appears.

I built a scrolling title, but I do not see the title when I play it back on another computer. What happened?
✔ Make sure that the fonts you use in the title file are installed on the computer with which you plan to open the title file or the project that includes it. Font names are often different between Windows and Mac OS, even when the fonts are identical. After you complete editing and record the final cut on videotape or export it to a video file, you no longer need the title fonts.

Why does the scrolling text I created seem to not scroll anywhere?
✔ You may need to readjust the size of the text object area to achieve a scrolling result. Try making the text object smaller in size. For example, shorten the depth of the text area so it only takes up half the screen. Also experiment with making the text scroll in another direction to see if the scroll effect is more noticeable.

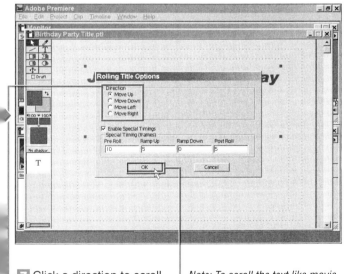

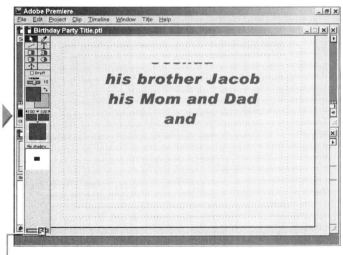

■7 Click a direction to scroll (○ changes to ◉).

Note: To scroll the text like movie credits, click Move Up.

■8 Click OK.

■9 Click and drag the scrolling slider to see the scrolling text effect.

Note: See the section "Create a New Title" to save a title clip.

EDIT A TITLE CLIP

You can reopen any title clip you create and make edits to the text or graphics. For example, you may need to edit the spelling, or add additional names of your production staff to the closing credits.

By default, a line of text displays from left to right, but if you want to,

you can change the text orientation using tools in Premiere. You can specify vertical orientation so that a line of text displays from top to bottom. This is useful for creating titles in languages such as Japanese, or as a text effect.

If you want to rotate text freely, you can apply motion settings to the

title after you add the title to the Timeline. You can also prepare the title in another application such as After Effects, which has numerous other effects you can apply to your project, including three-dimensional effects. See Part IV to learn more about visual effects that can be added to your project.

EDIT A TITLE CLIP

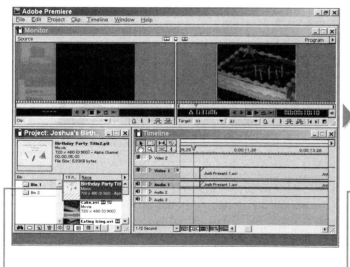

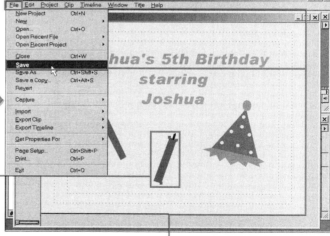

■ 1 With a project open, double-click the title clip.

Note: See the section "Create a New Title" to create and save a title.

■ Premiere opens the title in the Title window.

■ 2 Edit the title text or graphic elements as needed.

Note: See the previous sections to add text.

■ 3 Click File.

■ 4 Click Save.

■ The title changes are saved.

PLACE A TITLE CLIP IN A PROJECT

When you have completed and saved a title, Premiere automatically adds it to the open Project window. The title becomes a clip in the project, using the original title file as its source.

If you want the title to display with transparency so you can superimpose it over another clip,

add the title to a superimposition track. A superimposition track is one dedicated to superimposing clips over other clips in your project. When you add a title to a superimposition track, empty and semitransparent areas of the title are converted into an *alpha channel*, which marks transparent and semitransparent areas.

Premiere automatically applies the Alpha Channel transparency key to titles, making any mattes or clips on lower tracks visible under the title. Titles added to the Video 1A or 1B tracks appear opaque by default. See the section "Understanding Transparency," earlier in this chapter, for more information on transparency.

PLACE A TITLE CLIP IN A PROJECT

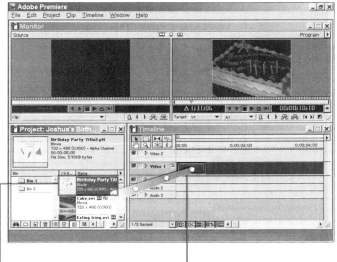

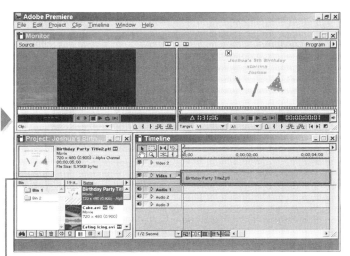

1 Click the title clip in the Project window.

Note: See the section "Create a New Title" to create and save a title.

2 Click and drag the title clip to the Timeline (⬚ changes to ✋).

■ The title is added to the project.

APPLY A VIDEO EFFECT

You can apply video effects to your project for added visual interest. Video effects, also called *filters*, alter or enhance the video image. You can add as many effects as you like to a clip. Premiere includes 74 different video effects, found in the Video Effects palette.

You can add any effect to a clip at any time. If you do not like an

effect, you can easily delete it. You can even apply the same effect multiple times to the same clip with different settings. You may create a new and unusual effect this way, or you could add too much distortion. In many cases, less is more; you should view your affected segment at full screen to see if it achieves the effect you want.

By default, when you apply an effect to a clip, the effect is active for the duration of the clip. However, you can make the effect start and stop at specific times, or make the effect more or less intense over time, by using keyframes. See "Change a Video Effect Using Keyframes," later in this chapter.

APPLY A VIDEO EFFECT

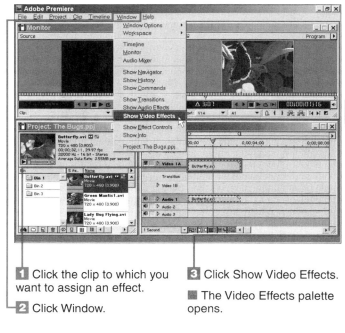

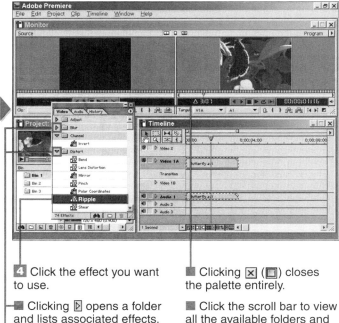

■1 Click the clip to which you want to assign an effect.

■2 Click Window.

■3 Click Show Video Effects.

■ The Video Effects palette opens.

■4 Click the effect you want to use.

■ Clicking ▷ opens a folder and lists associated effects.

■ Clicking ▽ closes a folder list.

■ Clicking ⌧ (▣) closes the palette entirely.

■ Click the scroll bar to view all the available folders and effects.

Where can I apply a video effect?

✔ You can apply a video effect to a video clip in the Video 1 track and in any superimposed track. You can also apply an audio effect to any audio clip in the Timeline window. Clips that have effects applied to them appear with a blue border at the top in the Timeline window.

You can apply or remove an effect at any time. See the section "Disable or Remove Effects" for more information.

What are the icons that appear in front of the effect names?

✔ The 📧 icons denote effects original to Premiere. The 📧 icons denote effects borrowed from Adobe's After Effects plug-in program, a program for designing visual effects. Effects with the 📧 icons can be viewed in both Premiere and After Effects. See Part IV of this book to learn more about the effects you can produce using that program.

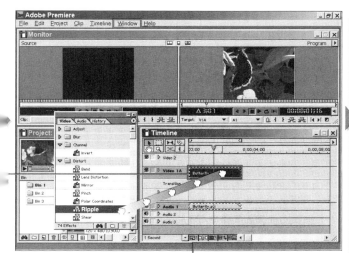

5 Drag the effect from the palette and drop it onto the clip (🖐 changes to ⟨⟩).

■ Premiere applies the effect to the clip, and the Effect Controls palette appears, enabling you to fine-tune the effect, if needed.

Note: Each effect you assign is added to the Effect Controls palette list.

6 Click Timeline.

7 Click Preview.

Note: You can also press Enter (Return) to begin the preview process.

■ Premiere builds a preview, which plays in the Monitor window and shows any video effects assigned.

Note: See "Adjust Effect Settings" to fine-tune the effect.

ADJUST EFFECT SETTINGS

Premiere gives you many effects that you can use to switch between clips. Each effect has customizable settings that you can adjust to match the look and feel of your project, or to create a desired custom effect.

Premiere stores all effects in the Video Effects palette, which you can customize to best suit your working style. This palette groups

effects by type; for example, all video effects that create a blur appear in a Blurs folder in the Video Effects palette. You can hide effects that you do not use and create new folders containing special groups of commonly used effects or rarely used effects.

Depending on the video effect you are using, you can use additional controls to fine-tune the

performance of the effect. Property values for an effect reside in the Effect Controls palette. The palette lists all the effects assigned to a clip. The number and type of values you can adjust vary from controlling color and opacity to positioning.

ADJUST EFFECT SETTINGS

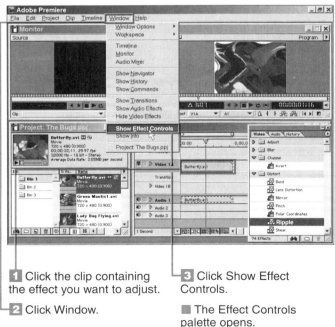

1 Click the clip containing the effect you want to adjust.

2 Click Window.

3 Click Show Effect Controls.

■ The Effect Controls palette opens.

4 Use any of the available controls to adjust the effect's property values.

■ Clicking and dragging △ decreases or increases the value.

■ Clicking ▾ displays a menu of options.

■ Clicking an underlined value displays an additional dialog box of options.

How do I create a new effects folder?

✔ To create a new folder in the Video or Audio Effects palette, you open the palette and then select New Folder from the Effects palette menu, or click the New Folder button. Type a name for the new folder, and then click OK.

How do I delete a custom folder?

✔ To delete a folder, select the folder and then click the Delete button. When you delete a custom folder, the folder is deleted and all its effects are restored to their original folders.

What happened to the video effects included with Premiere 5?

✔ For backward compatibility, Premiere 6 offers several effects found in earlier versions. This is helpful if you created projects in Premiere 5 but need to edit them in Premiere 6. To find them, click the Video Effects menu button and click Show Hidden. This command displays the Obsolete folder in the palette, and you can choose from the effects you may be used to using from previous versions of Premiere.

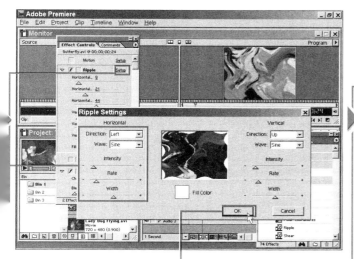

5 Click Setup.

■ The effect's Settings dialog box appears.

6 Make changes to the settings as needed.

■ The settings available vary based on the type of effect. This example shows the settings for the Ripple effect.

7 Click OK.

■ To preview the adjustments, press Enter (Return).

■ The preview plays in the Monitor window, showing any video effects assigned.

■ Clicking here closes the Effect Controls palette.

DISABLE OR REMOVE EFFECTS

When editing clips in post-production, you combine clips, transitions, and effects in the Timeline window to create a finished video. During this process, you add and remove effects to see how the transitions work when you render the video. Premiere gives you two methods for editing transitions out of the

timeline: disabling an effect, or removing it entirely.

When you disable an effect in the Timeline window, the effect retains its settings but is excluded from any previewing or exporting actions. This behavior serves as a good way of trying out different effects and combinations of effects

without repeatedly dragging effects into the Timeline.

If you decide not to use a particular effect in your project, you can remove it. When you remove an effect, you delete it from the clip so that it is no longer part of your project.

DISABLE A VIDEO EFFECT

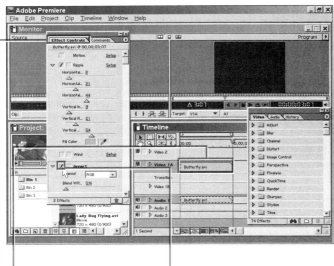

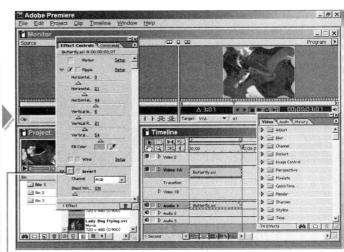

1 Click the clip containing the effect you want to disable.

2 Display the Effect Controls palette.

Note: See the section "Adjust Effect Settings" to open the Effect Controls palette.

3 Click the Enable Effect box.

■ The 🗹 icon disappears and the effect is disabled.

Note: Click the Enable Effect box again to toggle the effect back on.

What happens to an effect's keyframes when I disable it?

✔ Disabling an effect does not delete the keyframes created for any of the effect's settings; all keyframes remain until the effect is deleted from the clip.

How do I remove all the effects from a clip at once?

✔ In the Timeline window, select the clip from which you wish to have all the effects removed. Click the Effect Controls palette, click ☐, and then click Remove all effects from clip. Premiere removes all effects.

Can I change the order in which effects are listed in the Effect Controls palette?

✔ Yes. Premiere plays the effects in the order listed in the Effect Controls palette. To change the order, click an effect name and then drag the effect up or down in the list. This lets you recombine effects without removing them from the timeline.

REMOVE A VIDEO EFFECT

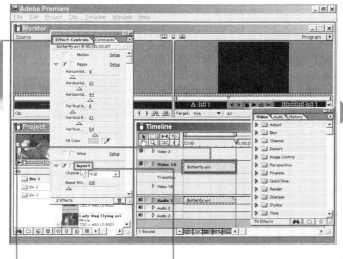

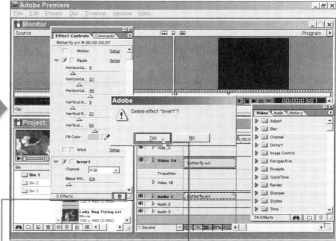

1 Click the clip containing the effect you want to remove.

2 Display the Effect Controls palette.

Note: See the section "Adjust Effect Settings" to open the Effect Controls palette.

3 Click the name of the effect you want to remove.

4 Click the Delete (🗑) button.

■ Premiere displays a warning box.

5 Click Yes to remove the effect.

CHANGE A VIDEO EFFECT USING KEYFRAMES

Premiere uses *keyframes* to change an effect over time. A keyframe contains the values for all the controls in the effect and applies those values to the clip at the specified time. By default, when you apply an effect to a clip, Premiere creates a beginning and ending keyframe with the same values, but by applying different values to keyframes, you can change an effect as the clip plays.

Premiere automatically interpolates the values of the controls between the keyframes using linear progression; you do not have to create a keyframe for every frame in the clip.

For example, suppose that you wanted to use the Crystallize effect and have it increase and then decrease over time. In this case, you would need to set three keyframes — the first with light crystallization, the second with more significant crystallization, and the third with light crystallization. Because Premiere automatically interpolates the distortion between each keyframe as the clip plays, the crystallization gradually increases between the first and second keyframes and then gradually decreases between the second and third keyframes.

CHANGE A VIDEO EFFECT USING KEYFRAMES

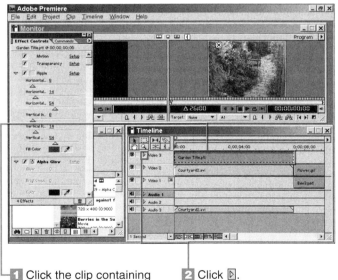

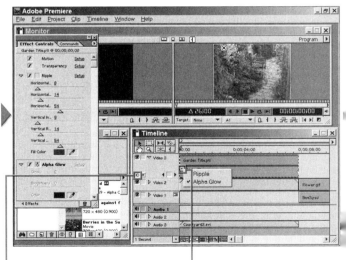

1 Click the clip containing the effect you want to adjust.

2 Click ▶.

Note: See Chapter 18 to learn more about working with tracks in the Timeline window.

3 If the clip is on Video Track 2 or higher, click ◌ to display the keyframe line.

■ If the clip has more than one effect assigned, click here and click the effect you want to adjust.

How do I tell what the different keyframe types look like on the Timeline?

✔ Keyframe icon appearance depends on where it is on the track. The default keyframes are white rectangles that rest at the edges of the clip. After you add additional keyframes, the initial keyframes become white half-diamonds. After you move the keyframes from the edges, they become full diamonds. The first keyframe is gray on the left half, and the last keyframe is gray on the right half.

How can I easily move between keyframes within a clip?

✔ After you set the initial keyframe for a clip and the keyframe button is pressed, Premiere displays the keyframe navigator, which you can use to move from keyframe to keyframe or to set or remove keyframes. A check mark in the keyframe navigator box indicates that the edit line lies precisely at a keyframe for that clip. When the box contains no check mark, the edit line lies between keyframes.

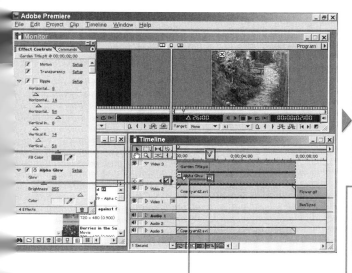

▪ Click and drag the edit line to where you want to change the effect.

▪ Click ☑.

■ Premiere adds a keyframe to the Timeline.

─ 6 In the Effect Controls palette, change the desired property values.

Note: See the section "Adjust Effect Settings" to open the Effect Controls palette.

■ You can continue adding keyframes as needed.

7 Press Enter (Return) to preview the effect.

■ Premiere builds a preview and the video plays in the Monitor window.

EDIT VIDEO EFFECT KEYFRAMES

A video effect keyframe has properties that change the effect's default behavior over time, using a process called *interpolation*. Premiere uses interpolation to make incremental changes between one keyframe's properties and the next, which results in a smooth change to the effect between the keyframes.

For example, you have an effect that lasts 4 seconds at 30 frames per second. You want to have the effect grow brighter and then dimmer again. With a keyframe set at the 2-second mark, Premiere now has 60 frames to apply the brightness effect evenly, and 60 frames to dim out evenly.

You can edit keyframes in the Timeline window to change the speed of, or make additional changes to the effect. For example, you can move two keyframes closer together to speed up the effect, or you may need to remove a keyframe to extend an effect's duration.

EDIT VIDEO EFFECT KEYFRAMES

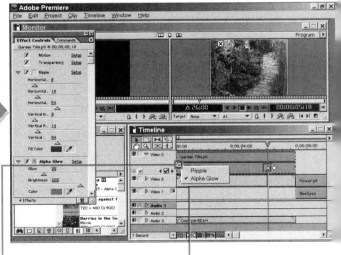

MOVE A KEYFRAME

1 Click the clip containing the effect you want to adjust.

2 Click ▼.

Note: See Chapter 18 to learn more about working with tracks.

3 If the clip is on Video track 2 or higher, click ◈ to display the keyframe line.

■ If the clip has more than one effect assigned, you can click here and then click the effect you want to adjust.

4 Click and drag the keyframe to a new position.

How do I remove all the keyframes I added?

✔ To remove all keyframes except the start and end keyframe, which all effects must include, click 🔯 for the effect in the Effect Controls palette. Premiere displays a warning box; click Yes to delete all extra keyframes and return your video effect to its default behavior. If you want to disable an effect rather than delete all keyframes, see the section "Disable or Remove Effects" earlier in this chapter.

How can I quickly edit the start or end keyframe?

✔ You can drag the first and last keyframes to reset the time at which the effect begins or ends. A black keyframe line appears when you drag either of these two keyframes, indicating that no effect will be applied in that area. You can reposition keyframes only for effects with adjustable controls. To more easily drag the default keyframes, deselect the clip by clicking in an empty area in the Timeline window.

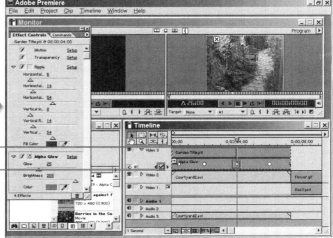

REMOVE A KEYFRAME

-1 Click the clip containing the effect you want to adjust.

-2 Click ▶.

Note: See Chapter 18 to learn more about working with tracks.

-3 If the clip is on Video track 2 or higher, click 🔯 to display the keyframe line.

-4 Click the keyframe you want to remove.

-5 Click ✔.

■ Premiere removes the keyframe from the Timeline.

Note: See the section "Change a Video Effect Using Keyframes" to add keyframes to the Timeline.

FADE A TRACK

You can *fade* a track over another track to superimpose the images. Fading a track changes the opacity of the clip. For example, you can fade a title clip over a video clip. You can fade in a clip to be gradually visible or fade out to be gradually not visible. Fading is one of the most common

effects you can apply to title clips, as well as a versatile way to introduce new images into a video.

You can also control a fade effect's opacity at a given point in the timeline with the Opacity Rubberband feature. By default, a superimposed clip includes two

fade handles, one at the beginning and one at the end.

You can superimpose any track except Video track 1. By default, each new project includes one superimpose track, called Video 2. You can add up to 97 superimpose tracks.

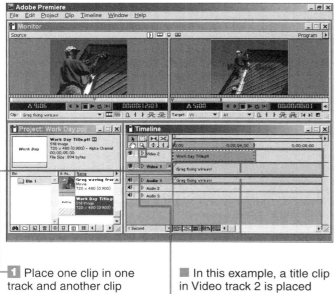

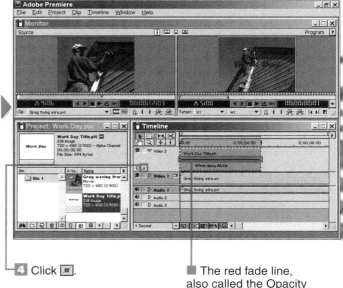

1 Place one clip in one track and another clip directly above the first clip.

Note: See Chapter 18 to add and move clips in the Timeline.

■ In this example, a title clip in Video track 2 is placed over a video clip in Video track 1.

2 Click the top clip.

3 Click ▷.

■ Premiere expands the track in the Timeline.

4 Click ▥.

■ The red fade line, also called the Opacity rubberband, is revealed.

How can I check a fade handle's opacity levels?

✔ Click a fade handle, Window, and then Show Info to display the Info palette, where you can quickly see the opacity setting for that particular point on the fade line. The opacity level appears at the bottom of the palette.

Can I use the Fade effect to fade in one clip and fade out another simultaneously?

✔ If you want to fade in one clip and simultaneously fade out another clip, use a Dissolve effect instead of applying two separate fade effects.

Can I use tools in the Timeline toolbox to edit the fade line?

✔ Yes. You can use the Fade Scissors tool (⬛) to cut the Opacity Rubberband and create two handles for you to move separately. You can then use the Fade Adjustment tool (⬛) to move sections of the segmented fade line. See Chapter 18 to learn more about using the Timeline window's editing tools.

5 Click and drag the left or right fade handle up or down to increase or decrease the fade opacity (↓ changes to ☜).

■ The higher you drag the handle, the more solid the image. The lower you drag, the more faded the image becomes.

■ To gradually fade the top clip, move the right end of the fade line down at the end of the clip.

6 Press Enter (Return).

■ Premiere previews the effect in the Monitor window.

Note: See Chapter 15 to save your project file.

459

APPLY A KEY

Certain parts of clips can be made transparent using tools called *keys*. A key finds pixels in an image that match a specified color or brightness and makes those pixels transparent or semitransparent, depending on the type of key. This process is called "keying," or "keying out," the color. When you apply a key to a clip

superimposed over another clip, you determine what areas of the lower clip show through. Keys can also use a clip's alpha channel to create transparency.

Premiere provides 15 keys that you can apply to a clip to create transparency in many different ways. You can use color-based keys for superimposing, brightness keys

for adding texture or special effects, alpha channel keys for clips or images already containing an alpha channel, and matte keys for adding traveling mattes or creative superimpositions.

To learn more about keys, see "Understanding Transparency" earlier in this chapter.

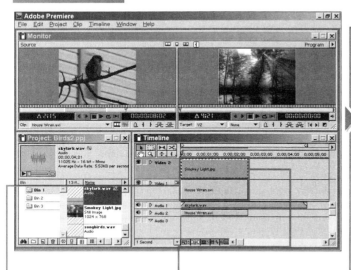

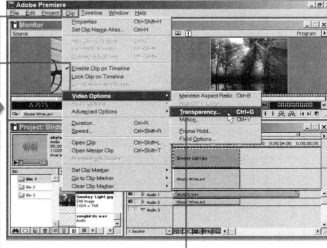

1 Place one clip directly above another clip in the Timeline window tracks.

■ In this example, a still image clip in Video track 2 is placed over a video clip in Video track 1.

Note: See Chapter 18 to add and move clips in the Timeline.

2 Click the top clip.

3 Click Clip.

4 Click Video Options.

5 Click Transparency.

■ The Transparency Settings dialog box appears.

What is an alpha channel?

✔ An *alpha channel* is a fourth channel in an RGB image that defines what parts of the image are transparent or semitransparent. Many graphics programs, such as Illustrator and Photoshop, use alpha channels so that you can specify transparent regions in an image. Use the alpha channel key on clips that contain a straight alpha channel, such as images created in Photoshop, Illustrator, and After Effects.

I am using A/B edit mode and Premiere will not let me apply a key. Why not?

✔ You cannot superimpose Video track 1 in the Timeline window. If you are using A/B edit mode, the track is split into Video track 1A and Video track 1B. Both tracks still act as Video track 1 and cannot be superimposed. Switch to Single-Track editing mode, or move the superimposed clips to higher tracks in the timeline such as Video 2.

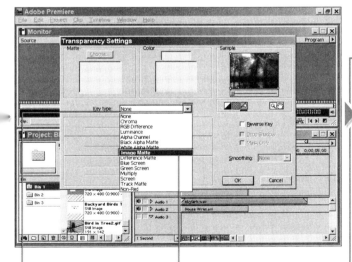

6 Click ▼ to display available key types.

7 Click a key type you want to apply.

■ Make any changes to the available key options, as needed.

■ You can preview the key here.

Note: See "Edit Key Settings," later in this chapter, to learn more about previewing a key.

8 Click OK.

■ The key is applied.

■ Pressing Enter (Return) previews the superimpose effect in the Monitor window.

EDIT KEY SETTINGS

You can edit a key to fine-tune the way in which the clip superimposes another clip. For example, you can adjust the available parameters for a key and preview how the effect looks before applying it to a clip. The Transparency Settings dialog box offers several controls to help you analyze the key effect.

For example, you can toggle between a black or white background behind the keyed-out image; display a checkerboard pattern to help you view transparency in areas that may be difficult to see against a solid background, or against the actual underlying image; and display the actual underlying image in your project.

These help you see how the key settings work in conjunction with the transparency settings, and make a better determination as to how your key will look in the final product. Working with the different key settings enables you to see how they work together.

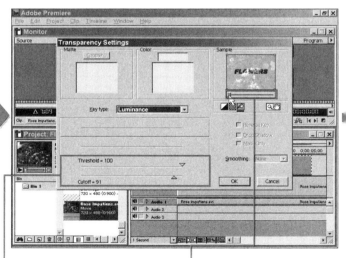

1 Click the clip containing the key you want to adjust.

Note: See the section "Apply a Key" to set a key.

2 Click Clip.

3 Click Video Options.

4 Click Transparency.

■ The Transparency Settings dialog box appears.

5 Make any changes to the available key parameters as needed.

■ Clicking and dragging ▲ adjusts a key parameter.

6 Clicking and dragging ■ previews the effect.

What does the Drop Shadow option do?

✔ The Drop Shadow option is available only for certain keys and adds a 50% gray, 50% opaque shadow to opaque areas. The shadow is placed four pixels below and to the right of any contiguous opaque region. Drop Shadow is most effective for titles or simple graphics. If you need to create more complex shadow or glow effects for an image, you should work with that image in Photoshop or Illustrator. For video clips, use After Effects.

What do the three check boxes below the Sample area do?

✔ The three check box options are only available for particular keys. Clicking the Reverse Key option inverts the opaque and transparent areas of the effect. Clicking the Drop Shadow option adds a gray or opaque shadow to opaque areas of the key. Clicking the Mask Only option creates a key that displays only the alpha channel matte of the clip.

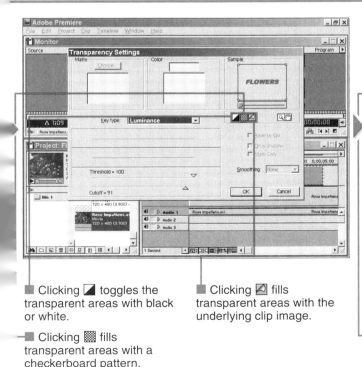

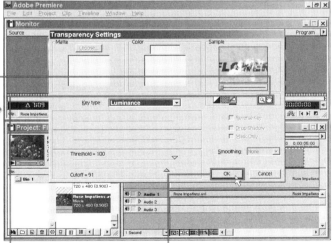

■ Clicking 🔲 toggles the transparent areas with black or white.

■ Clicking 🔲 fills transparent areas with the underlying clip image.

■ Clicking ▦ fills transparent areas with a checkerboard pattern.

■ You can click 🔍 and then click the sample area to zoom your view of the effect.

■ To view different areas of a zoomed sample, click 🖑 and then click and drag the sample area.

■ Mac users can click 🔽 to view the effect in the Monitor window.

7 Click OK.

■ Any changes are applied to the superimpose effect.

APPLY A GARBAGE MATTE KEY

Sometimes the subject of a scene is properly keyed except for undesired objects. You can use a *garbage matte key* to key out areas of the clip frame that you do not want to appear in the final key. You can then place the keyed subject in another scene for simple effects.

For example, if your clip includes an unwanted object in the clip

frame, referred to as "garbage" in video-editing lingo, you can mask it out so that it does not appear in the final superimpose effect.

A garbage matte is a very rough matte as opposed to an articulate matte. It is generally used to isolate the subject from unwanted background elements. In a bluescreen operation, for example, you can stack the keying operations in

this order: Apply a garbage matte to remove the garbage outside the blue screen area in the shot (such as lights or rigging), then use a chroma key to finish isolating the subject.

Garbage mattes are also sometimes called rough or hold-out mattes.

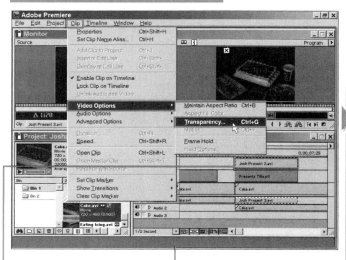 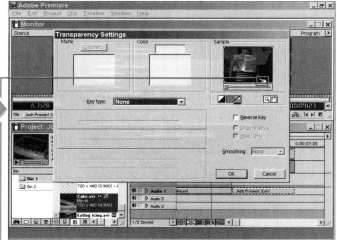

1 Click the clip to which you want to assign a key.

Note: See the section "Apply a Key" to prepare clips for a key effect.

2 Click Clip.

3 Click Video Options.

4 Click Transparency.

■ The Transparency Settings dialog box appears.

5 Click and drag the image handles in the Sample area to mask out the unwanted portion of the frame (⌖ becomes ✋).

■ You can drag all four handles, or just one or two.

What is a chroma key?

✔ A *chroma* key selects a color or a range of colors in the clip to be transparent. You can use this key when you have shot a scene against a screen that contains a range of one color, such as a shadowy blue screen. Select a key color by clicking the color swatch or by using the Eyedropper tool to choose a color from the thumbnail beneath the color swatch; click and drag the slider bars in the dialog box to adjust the color that you want to key out.

How do I smooth out the edges of a garbage matte?

✔ If you use the garbage matte with the RGB Difference key, you can select a smoothing option from the Smoothing list rather than assign a color. The Smoothing control sets anti-aliasing that blends the pixel colors to create a smoother edge.

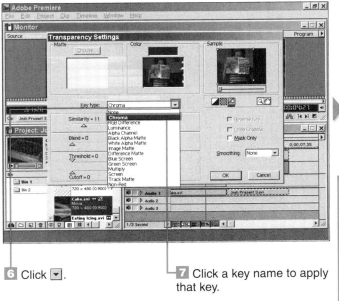

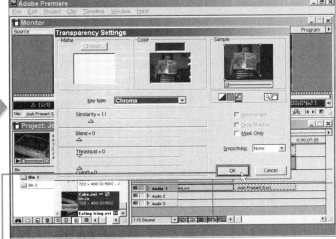

6 Click ▾.

7 Click a key name to apply that key.

■ If needed, make changes to the available key parameters.

8 Click OK.

■ Premiere applies the key to the clip.

■ Pressing Enter (Return) previews the superimpose effect.

CREATE A SPLIT-SCREEN EFFECT

Split screens enable you to simultaneously present two different information streams. In old movies, it was commonly used to show two halves of a telephone conversation. In today's fast-paced world, split screens often show a lecturer presenting information in one half of the screen and a slideshow or

multimedia presentation in the other.

You can easily create split screens in Premiere by using two clips and setting a transparency effect on the uppermost video clip. Premiere presents a dialog box that lets you split the screen and preview the appearance before applying the

transparency effect. Your clips can be either video clips or still image clips.

While you can use a clip in either the A or B tracks in A/B Editing mode, you must use one of the other superimpose video tracks such as Video 2 for your clip.

CREATE A SPLIT-SCREEN EFFECT

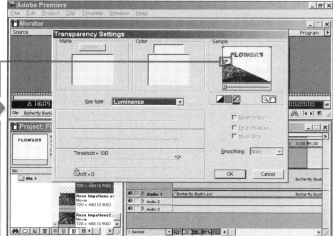

1 Click the clip to which you want to assign a split screen key.

Note: See the section "Apply a Key" to prepare clips for a key effect.

2 Click Clip.

3 Click Video Options.

4 Click Transparency.

■ The Transparency Settings dialog box appears.

5 Click and drag a top image handle in the Sample area to the area where you want the screen to split

■ ⬚ becomes ✋.

How are the clips placed in the split screen?

✔ When you select a clip in the first step, you set a transparency effect on that clip. In other words, when you adjust the sliders, you are making parts of the selected clip transparent so the other clip can show through. Because the sliders are adjustable, you can choose which part of the screen becomes transparent, so if you want the selected clip to appear on the left, move the right sliders to the left, revealing the clip.

Can I split the screen in any direction and size?

✔ Yes. You can split a screen horizontally, vertically, or even diagonally. Premiere determines the size of the split by where you drag an image handle in the Transparency Settings dialog box's Sample area. The alignment does not need to be even; you can have one corner of the split start low on the left side, and have the other corner of the split be in the center of the upper edge.

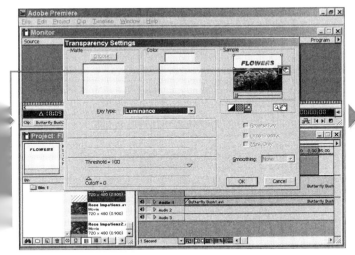

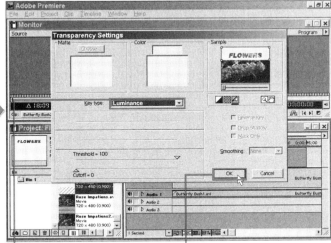

-6 Click and drag a bottom image handle in the Sample area to match the same position as the top image handle.

7 Click ▾.

8 Click the key you want to assign.

■ Make any changes to the available key parameters, as needed.

9 Click OK.

■ Premiere applies the key to the clip.

■ Pressing Enter (Return) previews the superimpose effect.

ADD A MOTION PATH TO A CLIP

You can add a motion path to a clip to make the clip move around the frame. You can control the path of movement as well as rotate the clip and zoom in and out to make the clip larger or smaller.

A motion path is based on *keyframes* — key points of change along the path — that mark key changes along the path. By adding and moving keyframes, you tell Premiere exactly how you want a clip to move around the screen in a motion setting. By default, the motion path is set to move from left to right across the screen. When you add keyframes, you can make the path go in any direction, including off screen.

To learn more about keyframes, see the "Understanding Motion Effects" section earlier in this chapter.

You can also use After Effects to create motion settings in your video. See Chapter 27 to learn how to use After Effects to create motion paths.

ADD A MOTION PATH TO A CLIP

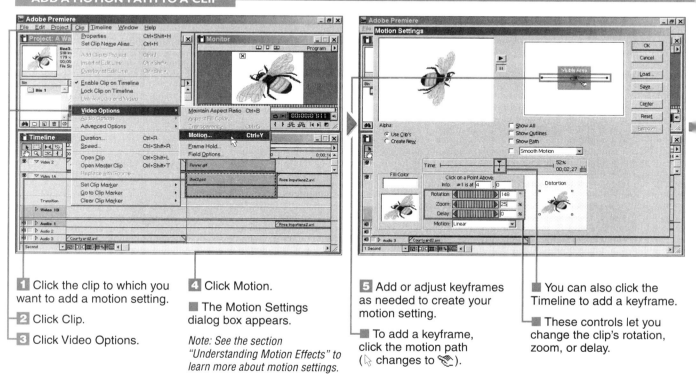

■1 Click the clip to which you want to add a motion setting.

■2 Click Clip.

■3 Click Video Options.

■4 Click Motion.

■ The Motion Settings dialog box appears.

Note: See the section "Understanding Motion Effects" to learn more about motion settings.

■5 Add or adjust keyframes as needed to create your motion setting.

■ To add a keyframe, click the motion path (↳ changes to ✋).

■ You can also click the Timeline to add a keyframe.

■ These controls let you change the clip's rotation, zoom, or delay.

How can I make the motion setting pause at a keyframe?

✔ Use the Delay attribute in the Motion Settings dialog box to pause the clip for a specific amount of time. The delay amount is a percentage of the clip's total time duration and is based on keyframes. Simply put, you cannot set the delay to 2 seconds if the next keyframe is only 1 second away. You can also control motion speed by the placement of keyframes. See the section "Change Motion Speed" to learn more.

What does the Smooth Motion option do?

✔ Click the ▼ next to the Smooth Motion listing in the Motion Settings dialog box to display a menu of smoothing options. These options make the clip follow a smoother course as it moves along the keyframe points. The Smooth Motion setting offers the least amount of smoothing, and Averaging-High offers the most amount of smoothing.

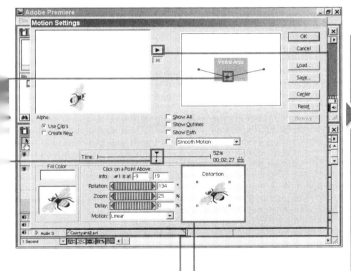

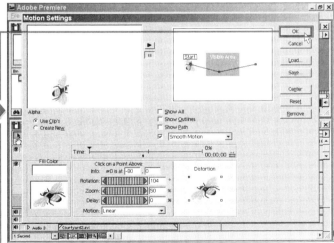

■ Clicking and dragging a keyframe point changes the motion path.

■ You can also click and drag keyframe points on the Timeline to change the speed of the motion setting.

■ You can create distortion effects by clicking and dragging points.

-6 Click ▶ to preview the motion setting.

-7 Click OK.

■ The clip adopts the motions settings.

Note: Clips with motion settings are marked with a red bar in the Timeline window.

■ Clicking Save saves the motion path as a motion settings file to reuse later.

■ Clicking Load loads a path you already saved.

■ Clicking Reset restores the default settings.

CHANGE MOTION SPEED

When you create a motion path, the placement of keyframes along the path determines the animation's speed. You can make the effect appear to speed up or slow down at key points along the path without changing the path itself. Use the motion timeline in the Motion Settings dialog box to change keyframe distances.

The motion timeline also includes a control for specifying the view of time. Clicking the two red arrows to the right of the timeline toggles between the source clip's time display and the Timeline window's time display. Use this control to synchronize motion or specify motion at an exact point in time.

To synchronize motion with other events in your video program, or to specify an exact time for motion, use the time display next to the motion timeline. The time display shows the time of the selected motion keyframe, as measured from either the beginning of the clip, or from the beginning of the entire video program.

CHANGE MOTION SPEED

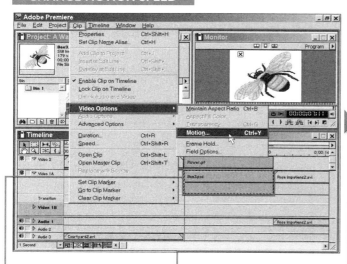

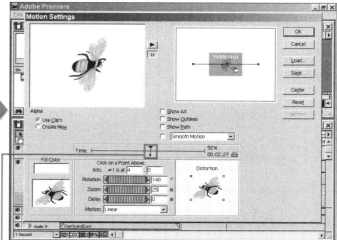

1 Click the clip containing the motion setting you want to adjust.

Note: See the section "Add a Motion Path to a Clip" to add a motion setting.

2 Click Clip.

3 Click Video Options.

4 Click Motion.

■ The Motion Settings dialog box appears.

5 Click and drag the keyframe markers on the Timeline.

Note: To add more keyframe markers to the Timeline, simply click the Timeline.

■ To increase the speed between two keyframes, click and drag one keyframe closer to the other.

How do I make my animation speed up at the end?

✔ By default, Premiere plays the motion setting at a constant rate, called Linear, proceeding from one keyframe to the next. You can, however, make the animation appear to speed up or slow down using the Motion option in the Motion Settings dialog box. Select Accelerate or Decelerate from the Motion list. The Accelerate setting makes the animation appear to play more quickly, and Decelerate makes the animation appear to slow down.

I built a clip that has other objects within it. Can I add motion to those objects?

✔ No. You can add motion only to the clip itself, as a whole; you cannot add motion to elements within the clip. If you need to animate elements within the clip, use the motion path process on the individual clips to create motion. Alternatively, remove the object from within the clip and treat it as a separate object to be animated.

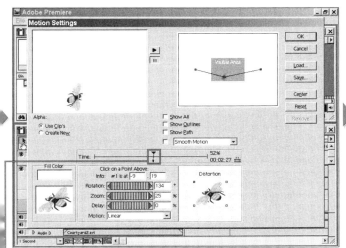

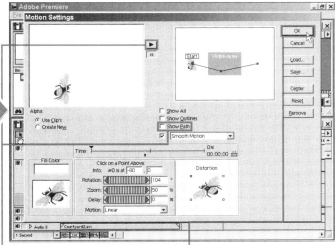

Note: To delete a keyframe marker, click the marker and press the Delete key.

Note: You can also drag a keyframe point on the motion path to move a keyframe.

■ To decrease the speed between two keyframes, click and drag one keyframe farther away from the other.

⬛ 6 Click ► to preview the changes.

■ Clicking here shows the speed between keyframes as dotted lines. The closer the dots appear, the faster the speed.

⬛ 7 Click OK.

■ The motion setting is applied to the clip.

SAVE A MOTION SETTING

If you are making a series of videos that require a common look and feel, you want to be able to save common elements and reuse them in other videos. For example, you may want to have a corporate logo "fly in" using the same motion path every time. Rather than recreating the path

every time — and risk creating inconsistent paths — you can save a motion setting to reuse again later in another video project. That way you can maintain consistency across all your videos without requiring extra work.

Motion settings default to saving as PMT file types, in the same

directory as your project file. You can change the directory to another one when you save, but you should leave the file extension alone.

When you save a motion setting, you save only the path and any assigned characteristics, such as zoom and rotation settings.

SAVE A MOTION SETTING

1 Create the motion setting using the Motion Setting dialog box.

Note: See the section "Add a Motion Path to a Clip" to create a motion setting.

2 Click Save.

■ The Save Motion Settings dialog box appears.

3 Type a name for the file.

■ You can click ▼ to save the file to another folder or drive.

4 Click Save.

■ The motion setting is saved.

Note: See the section "Load a Motion Setting" to reuse the file.

5 Click OK to exit the Motion Settings dialog box.

LOAD A MOTION SETTING

A team member has created a motion setting for your corporate logo and you want to use it in a training video you are creating. Instead of watching the motion setting in action and trying to recreate it from memory, you can load the motion setting from a file.

In this manner, you can reuse motion settings that have been saved from other projects.

For example, you may want to reuse the motion path with another clip in your project, or reuse it in another project file. You can either browse across a network to the motion settings file, or you can have the file sent to you or copied onto a disk for your use.

Motion settings files have the .pmt extension and normally share the same folder with your project files.

LOAD A MOTION SETTING

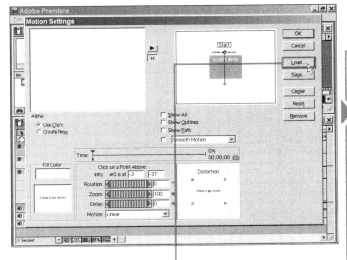

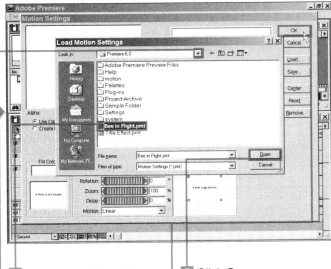

1 Click the clip in the Timeline to which you want to assign the motion setting file.

2 Open the Motion Settings dialog box.

Note: See the section "Add a Motion Path to a Clip" to open the Motion Settings dialog box.

3 Click Load.

■ The Load Motion Settings dialog box appears.

4 Click the motion setting file you want to assign.

■ You can click ▼ to locate the file in another folder or drive.

5 Click Open.

■ The motion setting is applied to the current clip.

6 Click OK to exit the Motion Settings dialog box.

PREVIEW A MOTION SETTING

When you add a motion setting to your project, you need to see how it will behave in the final product. Simply pressing Play does not work; you see only the clip and not the motion setting.

After you assign a motion setting, you can preview how the setting looks during playback. When previewing a motion setting, Premiere must build the preview file for playback in the Monitor window. Depending on the size of the clip, this process takes a few seconds to several minutes to complete.

When the rendering process is complete, you can view the clip, along with its motion settings, transitions, and effects, in the Monitor window.

If you need to view only the section of your clip with the motion setting, you can cue up the clip to view only that portion. See Chapter 17 for details.

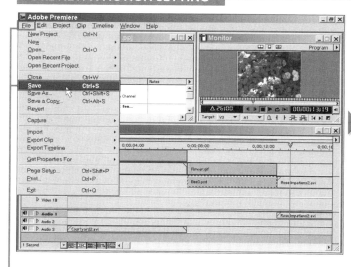

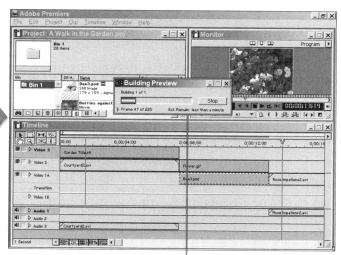

-1 Click File.

-2 Click Save.

■ Premiere saves the changes you have made to the project.

3 Press Enter (Return).

Note: You can also click Timeline, then Preview.

■ Premiere builds the preview and plays the video in the Monitor window.

Note: To preview the motion setting within the Motion Settings dialog box, click ▶.

REMOVE A MOTION SETTING

Y ou may need to remove a motion setting from a clip and return the clip to its original state, such as if you decide that you do not like the motion setting, or if you plan on creating a motion setting in After Effects instead.

You can easily remove a motion setting from a clip and return the

clip to its original state. Removing a motion setting does not affect a saved motion setting file, but simply detaches any applied PMT file from the clip. If you need to reload the motion setting file, you can do so and place it back into your clip.

If you want to remove the motion setting for purposes of seeing how

it plays, you can disable the motion effect instead in the Effect Controls panel by clicking the Enable Effect button. You can then preview your project without the motion setting to see which version you prefer. You can also save two different versions of your project, one with the motion setting and one without.

REMOVE A MOTION SETTING

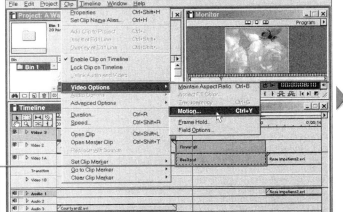

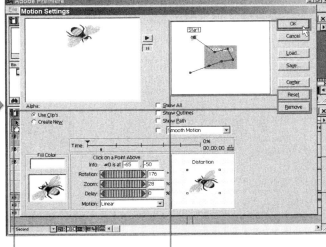

■1 Click the clip containing the motion setting you want to remove.

Note: See the section "Add a Motion Setting to a Clip" to create a motion setting.

■2 Click Clip.

■3 Click Video Options.

■4 Click Motion.

■ The Motion Settings dialog box appears.

■5 Click Remove.

■ The motion setting is removed from the clip.

■6 Click OK to close the Motion Settings dialog box.

■ To reset the default motion setting, click here.

UNDERSTANDING AUDIO

S ound, or audio, is an important part of any project. It can help set the mood of your project and enhance the impact of your video images. You may use up to 99 audio tracks in your Premiere video project. You can adjust the *audio level* (volume) of each sound to get just the right overall mix.

Where Can I Find Sound Clips?

All sounds you incorporate into Premiere must be digitized. You can import sound clips, such as Audio Interchange Format (AIF), MP3, and WAV file types. See Chapter 16 to learn how to import clips. You can also use the sounds recorded along with video footage shot with a recording device, such as a MiniDV camcorder.

Working with Sound Clips

Sound clips work in much the same way as video clips. You can open a sound clip in a Clip window, but rather than viewing a visual image, you see the sound's waveform pattern. From within the Clip window, you can play the clip, determine where a clip starts and ends, and more.

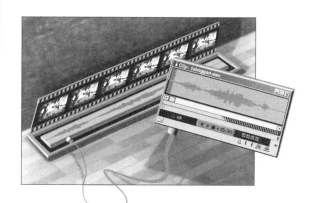

Audio Tracks

You can use audio tracks, which are located directly below the video tracks in the Timeline window, to contain sound clips or sounds recorded along with the video footage. By default, Premiere provides three audio tracks to every new project. You can add additional audio tracks as needed.

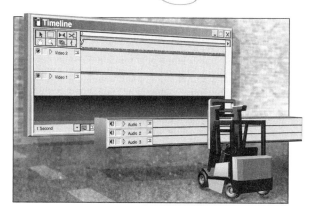

Mixing Audio

You can open the Audio Mixer window to mix sound for one or several clips at once. The Audio Mixer looks very much like a traditional mixing board with stylized controls, such as pan knobs and faders, for mixing sounds on tracks.

Balancing Volume

You can control the balance of sound between the left and right speakers by using panning controls. For example, if your video image shows a truck driving by from left to right, you can make the truck's sound correspond to its motion by panning it from the left speaker to the right speaker.

Using Audio Effects

Premiere provides audio effects that you can apply to correct and enhance your video's sounds. The Audio Effects palette contains 20 audio effects, such as Chorus, Echo, and Reverb. After you apply an audio effect, you can adjust the effect to suit your needs.

Gaining and Fading Sound

The most popular ways to edit sound are to control the *gain,* or volume, or to fade sound in and out. The Gain command enables you to adjust an entire audio clip's volume. Premiere's fade controls enable you to gradually fade sound in or out for a particular clip.

VIEW AUDIO CONTROLS

When you add video clips to the Timeline that contain sound, you also add an audio clip to one of the audio tracks at the same time. The audio track is represented by a light green bar and has a squiggle on it representing an audio waveform. If you do not see the squiggle, you can change the Timeline window display options to show the graphic representation. See Chapter 18 for details.

You can view the audio controls for an individual audio track in the Timeline window to quickly access pan and fade lines for making adjustments to the clip volume. All tracks in the Timeline expand or collapse. Audio controls appear only in the expanded state.

The *pan line* controls the balance of audio between the left and right speakers. The *fade line* controls the volume level.

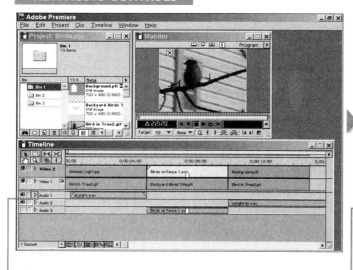

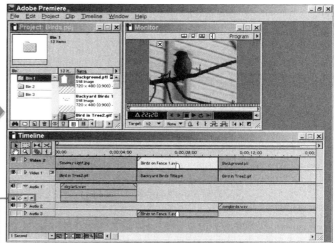

1 Click the audio track's Expand (▷) icon.

■ Premiere expands the track.

Note: See Chapter 18 to learn more about working with tracks in the Timeline.

2 Click a control.

■ Clicking ▣ toggles a visible and hidden waveform in the track.

■ Clicking ◈ toggles visible and hidden keyframes for assigned audio effects.

■ Clicking ▣ toggles between a visible and hidden fade line.

■ Clicking ▣ toggles between a visible and hidden pan line.

PLAY AN AUDIO CLIP

When you add a video clip that contains sound to the Timeline, you also add an audio clip. If you are working with audio clips, you can play audio from the video clip without playing the video, or you can play audio clips that you have added separately, such as music or sound effects.

Much like you can with video clips, you can open a Clip window to play an audio clip. The Clip window has controls for playing, looping, setting in and out points that determine where a clip starts and ends, and more. The Clip window is the best way to work with clips individually for common tasks; when you are finished

working with your clip; you can close the Clip window. Your changes happen dynamically, so any edits you make in the Clip window automatically affect the clip in the Timeline.

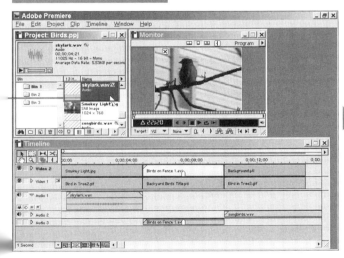
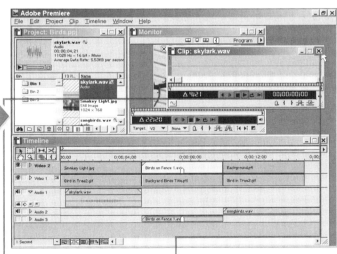

1 With a project open, double-click the audio clip in the Project window.

■ The Clip window opens.

Note: You can also play a sound clip in the Project window by clicking the Play button (▶).

2 Click ▶ to play the clip.

■ Clicking ◀ and ▶ moves the Set Location Line back and forth a frame.

■ Clicking ■ stops the play.

■ Clicking ⟳ causes the clip to loop during play.

3 Click ✕ (☐) to close the Clip window.

Note: See Chapter 17 to learn how to set in and out points.

ADD AN AUDIO CLIP TO THE TIMELINE

If you add a video clip that contains audio, you automatically add an audio track to the Timeline. But if you want to add separate audio tracks, such as theme music or sound effects, you do not need to use a video clip with the audio tracks attached; instead, you can add audio clips to the audio tracks in the Timeline window in the same way in which video clips are added.

First, import an audio file, such as a WAV file, into your project. Next, click and drag your file from the project window into an audio track in the Timeline window. The track then appears in the Timeline, and you can move the audio clip anywhere in the audio track, work with audio settings, or link the audio to a video clip. See Chapter 18 for more information on linking video and audio clips in the Timeline window.

ADD AN AUDIO CLIP TO THE TIMELINE

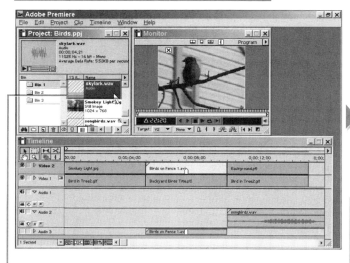

1 Locate the sound clip you want to add to the Timeline.

Note: See Chapter 16 to learn how to import production elements into Premiere.

2 Drag and drop the clip onto an audio track (↕ becomes ☜).

■ The clip appears in the track.

Note: See Chapter 18 to learn more about working with Timeline tracks.

■ To play the video in the Monitor window, save the project and then press the Enter (Return) key.

Note: See Chapter 15 to save a project, and Chapter 17 to set in and out points.

CHANGE VOLUME WITH THE GAIN COMMAND

When you assemble audio for your video project, you will find that there is a disparity in the quality and audio level between the different audio clips. For instance, dialog recorded on the set may be soft, while a musical soundtrack is loud and brash. To balance out the sound levels, you can adjust the volume for an entire audio clip using the Gain command.

The Gain command works like a volume control for the clip. You can raise or lower the volume, depending on the original audio's level and the final level you want to achieve.

The Gain command works equally on all parts of an audio clip. If you have audio defects such as skips or background noise in your clip, those will be amplified along with the sounds you wish to preserve. If you need to work with mixing different audio levels, you need to work with the clip in the Audio Mixer. See "Using the Audio Mixer," later in this chapter, for details.

CHANGE VOLUME WITH THE GAIN COMMAND

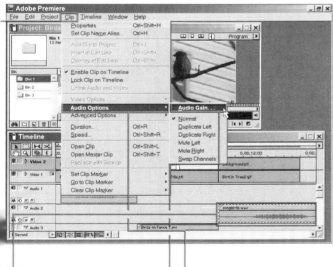

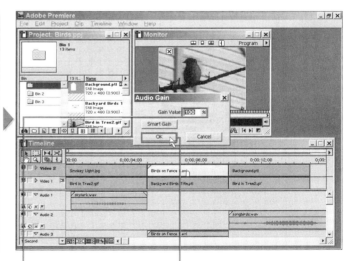

■1 Click the audio clip you want to adjust.

■2 Click Clip.

■3 Click Audio Options.

■4 Click Audio Gain.

■ The Audio Gain dialog box appears.

■5 Type a value based on percentage of volume.

■ Type a number greater than 100% to increase volume.

■ Type a number less than 100% to decrease volume.

■6 Click OK.

■ To hear the sound clip, press the Enter (Return) key.

FADE A SOUND

Y ou can use a track's *fade line*, also called the rubberband option, to raise or lower sound levels within a clip. For example, you may want a sound to gradually increase in volume or to fade out at the end of the clip. Using the fade line, which appears red in the audio track, you can control the clip's audio level.

You can also use the Fade Scissors tool to help you make further adjustments to a clip's fade line. The Fade Scissors tool enables you to "cut" the fade line by inserting two adjustable side-by-side fade handles. This lets you adjust the sound in a specific area of the audio clip without affecting the rest of the clip. For example, you would do this to "punch" part of a sound effect or bit of dialogue, or to momentarily reduce the sound to cover some audio glitches.

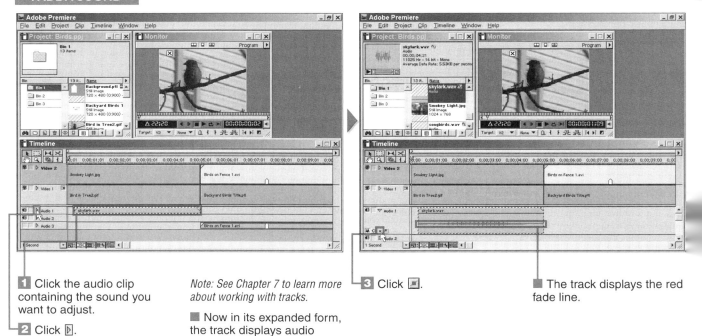

1 Click the audio clip containing the sound you want to adjust.

2 Click ▷.

Note: See Chapter 7 to learn more about working with tracks.

■ Now in its expanded form, the track displays audio controls.

3 Click 🔲.

■ The track displays the red fade line.

What are the limits to the audio level I can fade?

✔ By default, Premiere starts a sound clip at 100%. You can drag the fade line up to 200%, which is twice the volume, or drag the fade line to 0%, which is no sound.

How do I use the Fade Adjustment tool to edit the audio fade line?

✔ When you use the Fade Adjustment tool (▣), you can click and drag the fade line to move it at a constant percentage. In other words, any handles on the fade line move as a single line.

How do I adjust the fade numerically?

✔ Position the pointer over the volume handle you want to adjust so that the pointer changes into a pointing finger with red arrows. Press and hold Shift as you drag the volume handle up or down. A numeric display appears over the audio track to indicate the current volume level as you drag.

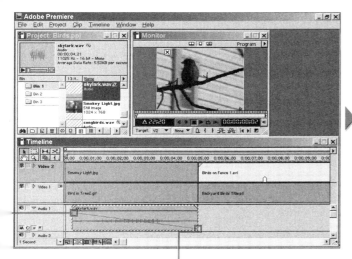

■4 Click and drag the left or right fade handle up or down to increase or decrease the audio level.

■ The volume increases as you drag the handle higher.

■ To gradually fade the sound out, move the right end of the fade line down at the end of the clip.

■5 Press Enter (Return).

■ Premiere previews the sound in the Monitor window.

■ Click the fade line to add another fade handle that you can move or adjust.

■ *To remove a fade handle, click and drag it outside the audio track.*

CREATE A CROSS-FADE

Premiere enables you to create a *cross-fade*, the process of one sound clip fading out while another sound clip fades in. To perform a cross-fade, the two sound clips must overlap in the Timeline window.

Often a cross-fade is added to an L-cut, where the audio from one video clip overlaps into the video of another clip and gradually fades out. For example, a conversation from one scene continues as a voice-over into another scene. See Chapter 19 for details on L-cuts and J-cuts.

When audio clips are linked to video clips that do not overlap, cross-fading the audio clips is more complex than an audio-only cross-fade. The audio clips linked to video clips cannot be dragged to overlap if the video clips are on the same track. You can solve this problem by moving the clips onto different tracks. First turn off Sync mode, so that you can move or trim a clip independently of its linked video or audio.

CREATE A CROSS-FADE

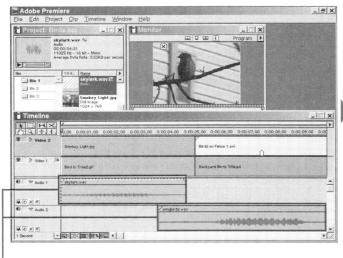

1 Place two overlapping sound clips in the Timeline.

Note: See "Add an Audio Clip to the Timeline" to learn how to add sound clips to audio tracks.

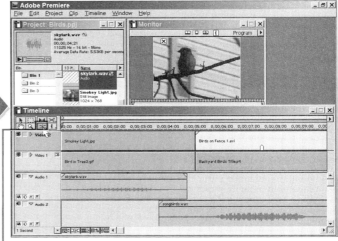

2 Click the Cross Fade tool (⊠).

Note: If the Cross Fade tool is not showing, click ⊡ and then press the U key on the keyboard to cycle through the buttons until you see ⊠.

How do I create a cross-fade effect for a sound recorded with my video footage?

✔ To turn the audio portion of the recording into a separate sound clip, click the clip in the Timeline, click Clip, and then click Unlink Audio and Video. Premiere immediately unlinks the two clips and marks both clips with a white link icon. You can now move and edit the audio as a separate sound clip.

Why can I not cross-fade two audio tracks?

✔ Cross-fading existing clips in the Timeline usually requires extending the duration of one or more audio clips. Whenever you extend the duration of a clip, additional frames must be available in the clip's source (master) clip beyond the current in or out point. For example, if you did not trim the beginning or ending of a source clip before adding it to the Timeline, the clip is already using all frames available from its source, so its duration cannot be extended.

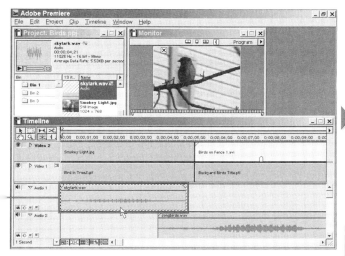

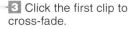
3 Click the first clip to cross-fade.

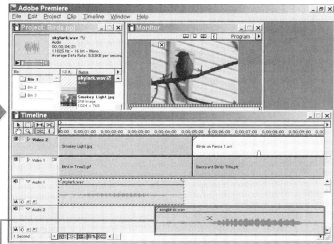

4 Click the second clip to cross-fade (⃗ changes to ▷◁).

■ A standard cross-fade effect is created.

5 Press the Enter (Return) key.

■ Premiere previews the sound in the Monitor window.

PAN A CLIP

You can control the balance of sound in an audio clip by *panning* the clip. Panning enables you to position an audio clip's sound between the left and right speakers. For example, your video may show a person walking along a sidewalk. With panning, you can make the footstep sounds seem to follow the person based on

the direction they enter and exit the frame.

You can also pan a monophonic audio clip to set its position between the left and right stereo channels. For example, if an audio clip contains one person's dialogue, you can pan the audio to match the person's position in the frame.

As with volume adjustments, you can pan or balance a clip in either the Timeline or Audio Mixer window. The Pan rubberbands in the Timeline correspond to the pan/balance controls in the Audio Mixer window and serve the same purpose.

PAN A CLIP

1 Click the audio clip containing the sound you want to adjust.

2 Click ▶.

Note: See Chapter 18 to learn more about working with tracks.

■ The track displays additional controls.

3 Click ▣.

■ The track displays a blue line, also called the pan line.

Note: By default, Premiere sets the pan line so that both left and right speaker sounds are audible.

Can I use the Fade Adjustment and Fade Scissors tools on keyframes on the pan line?

✔ Yes. The tools are interchangeable with the video fade line as well as the audio fade and pan lines.

Can I pan a stereo clip to indicate a person's position like I can with a monaural clip?

✔ You cannot pan a stereo audio clip because both channels already contain audio information. When you work with a stereo audio clip, the pan control adjusts the balance of the stereo channels within the clip.

How do I adjust the pan numerically?

✔ Press and hold Shift as you drag the pan/balance handle. A numeric display appears over the audio track to indicate the current pan or balance level as you drag. As long as you hold the Shift key, you can drag beyond the top and bottom of the audio track. The larger drag area lets you pan or balance in 1% increments to the left or right with the center at 0%, as indicated by the numeric display.

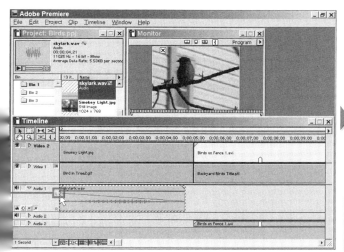

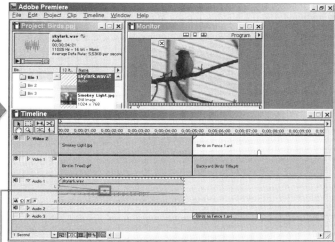

■ Click and drag the left or right pan handle up or down to designate sound direction.

■ Move the pan line up to make audio play through the left speaker.

■ Move the pan line down to make audio play through the right speaker.

■ To make adjustments to sound direction along the pan line, click the line to add additional handles to control.

■ Press the Enter (Return) key.

■ Premiere previews the sound in the Monitor window.

■ *To remove a handle, click and drag it outside the audio track.*

USING THE AUDIO MIXER

In the Audio Mixer window, you can adjust the volume level and pan/balance of multiple audio tracks while listening to them and viewing the video tracks. Premiere uses automation to record these adjustments and then to apply them as the clip plays back. The Audio Mixer window, like an audio mixing console, contains a set of controls for each audio track, which is numbered according to the

corresponding audio track in the Timeline.

Click and drag a track's volume fader to adjust its volume over time. As you make adjustments using the Audio Mixer window, Premiere creates handles in the audio clip's volume rubberband in the Timeline and applies your changes. A segmented VU meter to the left of the volume fader

represents audio level graphically. The small indicator at the top of the VU meter turns red when the level causes *clipping*, or distortion.

Each of the mixer's tracks also contains a pan/balance control, so that you can pan a monophonic clip from left to right or balance a stereo clip.

USING THE AUDIO MIXER

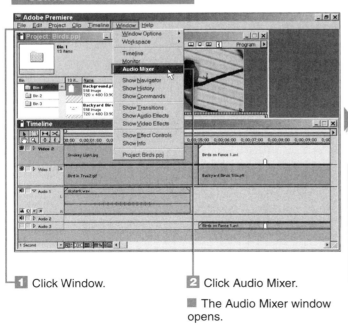

1 Click Window.

2 Click Audio Mixer.

■ The Audio Mixer window opens.

3 Cue the edit line in the Timeline window to the spot where you want to start mixing.

Note: See Chapter 17 to learn how to cue the edit line.

4 Click ▶ or ↻.

■ Premiere plays the audio

Is there a way to adjust several tracks simultaneously?

✔ You can gang tracks to make volume changes to several tracks at once, but because you have only one mouse and pointer, you cannot operate each volume fader independently. To make different changes to multiple tracks, play the program a number of times, recording changes for one track at a time. Right-click (Control-click) the Volume fader you want to assign to a gang and choose a gang number from the context menu. Repeat this process for the other channels you want to gang, assigning each the same gang number. When a Volume fader control is assigned to a gang, its handle changes color to indicate its gang assignment.

My program window is pretty crowded. Is there a better way to edit audio in my current workspace?

✔ Premiere has a preconfigured editing workspace you can use to help you edit audio content in your project. Click Window, Workspace, and then Audio to optimize the workspace for mixing audio.

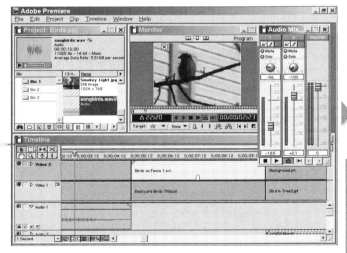

5 Adjust the Audio Mixer controls as needed.

■ Click and drag the Volume fader (≣) to fade a track's audio.

■ Click the Pan/Balance knob (◔) to pan the track's audio.

Note: You can also type a value in the Pan/Balance or Volume fader fields.

6 Click ■ to stop mixing.

■ Any adjustments you make are added to the audio tracks.

APPLY AN AUDIO EFFECT

You can apply audio effects, also called *filters*, to your project to enhance or correct audio. You can add as many effects as you like to a sound clip. Premiere provides 20 different audio effects in the Audio Effects palette, which include Echo, Reverb, Flanger, and Chorus.

The Echo effect repeats the sounds in the audio clip after a specified

amount of time. This simulates sound bouncing off a surface, such as a wall some distance away. The Reverb effect simulates the effect of a spacious or acoustically live interior.

The Flanger effect can add interest to a sound by inverting the phase of the audio signal at its center frequency. The effect can sound similar to the Chorus effect, and

often adds a wavy whooshing sound to the audio.

The Chorus effect applies a copy of the sound that is *detuned*, or played at a frequency slightly offset from the original. Chorus is commonly used to add depth and character to a clip that contains a single instrument or voice.

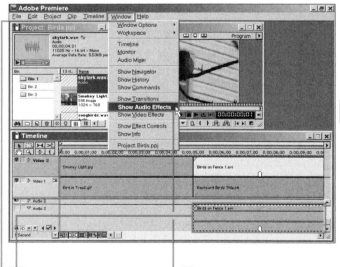

■ Click the sound clip to which you want to assign an effect.

■ Click Window.

■ Click Show Audio Effects.

■ The Audio Effects palette opens.

■ Locate the effect you want to use.

■ Clicking ▷ opens a folder and lists associated effects.

■ Clicking ▽ closes a folder list.

■ Clicking ✕ (□) closes the palette entirely.

■ Click the scroll bar to view all the available folders and effects.

How are audio effects processed?

✔ When you preview, play, or export a video, Premiere first converts its audio using the settings you specify in the Audio Settings dialog box. If you selected stereo as one of the audio settings, additional stereo commands such as Duplicate Left or Mute Right are then processed. Audio effects you have applied are processed next, followed by any pan/balance or volume adjustments in the Timeline audio track for the clip. Finally, Premiere processes any gain adjustments you applied. If your audio is muddled after you have adjusted it, try working with the effects in the order they are processed.

How can I edit audio effects?

✔ You can edit audio effects listed in the Effect Controls palette, or you can open an effect's Settings dialog box and make adjustments to the effect's parameters. To open the Effect Controls palette, click Window, and then click Show Effect Controls. To learn more about editing effects with this palette, see Chapter 20.

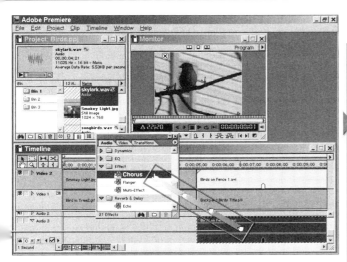

5 Drag the effect from the palette and drop it on the clip (👆 becomes 👋).

■ The effect is added to the clip and the Effect Controls palette appears.

Note: Each effect you assign is added to the Effect Controls palette list.

■ To preview the effect, press the Enter (Return) key.

■ You can use the Effect Controls panel to adjust the effect's parameters.

Note: See Chapter 20 to fine-tune effects.

UNDERSTANDING PREMIERE OUTPUT

You can output your video projects into a variety of formats. The output method you choose determines what options are available.

Project Settings·

When you selected your project's settings at the beginning of your video's production, you determined characteristics such as frame size and compression. Premiere applies these same settings during output unless you specify otherwise. To learn more about the different project settings available, see Chapter 15.

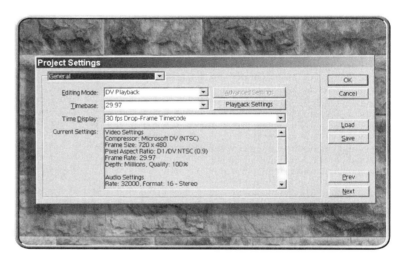

Output Options

You can output your project from either the Timeline or from a clip. When outputting from the Timeline window, you can export either the entire project or a portion of the work area. When outputting from a clip, you can export the entire clip or just the portion between the in and out points. For more information on in and out points, see Chapter 17.

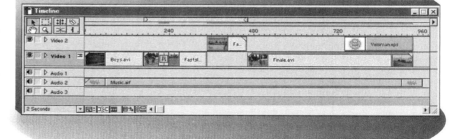

Output to Videotape

You can use either the Print to Video or the Export to Tape commands to output to videotape. The method you choose depends on your hardware configuration. You can record directly onto a tape recorder device, such as a DV camcorder or a DV deck. Premiere lets you use device control or operate the recording device manually.

Output to Other File Formats

You can output your project to movie file formats, such as QuickTime or Windows AVI, or to formats used by other programs, such as After Effects. You can even output a single frame in your video to an image file.

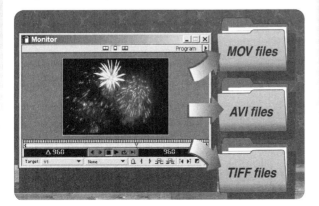

Output for the Web

You can export your video to the Web with a little help from three plug-in programs that come with Premiere 6 — Media Cleaner EZ, RealMedia Export, and Windows Media. Each plug-in follows a different procedure, so be sure to check each plug-in's documentation to learn about the available features.

Output to a CD-ROM

When outputting to a CD-ROM, you must consider the type of CD-ROM drive the intended audience is using, compatibility issues, file size, and playback. For older CD-ROM drives, set the exported file to play at a lower frame rate.

EXPORT TO A MOVIE FILE

You can prepare variations of one program or clip for several uses. For example, you can prepare low- and high-resolution versions of a program or clip, or create separate versions for broadcast television, CD distribution, and Web viewing.

When you export your video, or a part of your video, to a movie file

format, you are creating a file that a movie player program can display. For example, exporting your project as a QuickTime movie or a Windows AVI movie allows people who have QuickTime or Windows Media Player installed to play back your movie on their computers.

You do not need to have QuickTime or Windows Media Player on the

computer generating the file; Premiere contains the plug-ins necessary to generate the file in the correct format. All you need to do is create your project with the appropriate settings and then export the movie. See Chapter 15 for more on project settings and how they affect your movie.

EXPORT TO A MOVIE FILE

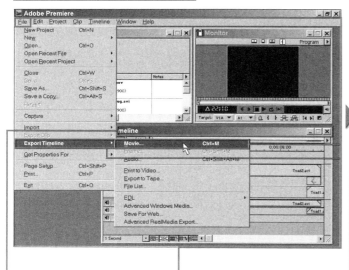

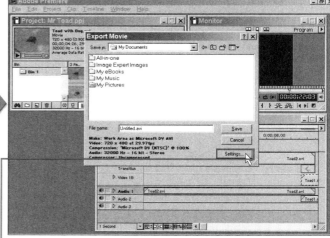

■1 Select the Timeline or Monitor window.

■ To export a portion of your video, set the work area over the range in the Timeline window.

Note: See Chapter 18 to learn more about using the Timeline window.

■2 Click File.

■3 Click Export Timeline.

■4 Click Movie.

■ The Export Movie dialog box appears.

■5 Click Settings.

■ The Export Movie Settings dialog box appears.

Note: See Chapter 15 to learn more about project settings.

I want to make several versions of my movie for different players; is there a quick way to change the project settings?

✔ Yes. You can use the Save and Load buttons in the Export Movie Settings dialog box to save and later quickly load export settings that you use frequently. Loading saved settings is particularly useful when you create several types of video files (for example, NTSC and Web video) from the same project. See Chapter 15 for more information on project settings.

Can I export a clip instead of my edited video?

✔ Yes. Open the clip from the Project window and set the in and out points, if needed. You can also trim the clip, but this step is not necessary. Finally, follow the steps shown below to export the clip as a movie file. To learn more about working with the Clip window, see Chapter 17.

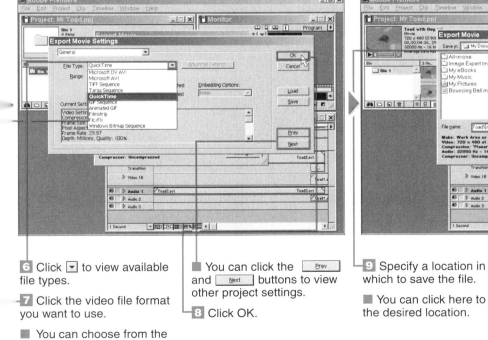

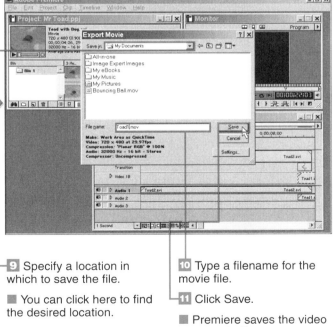

6 Click ▼ to view available file types.

7 Click the video file format you want to use.

■ You can choose from the other available options as needed.

■ You can click the ⬚Prev⬚ and ⬚Next⬚ buttons to view other project settings.

8 Click OK.

9 Specify a location in which to save the file.

■ You can click here to find the desired location.

10 Type a filename for the movie file.

11 Click Save.

■ Premiere saves the video as a movie file.

EXPORT A SINGLE FRAME

You can export a single frame or still image from your video project as an image file type that another program can display. Exporting stills is useful when you want to create promotional materials for your movie, or when you want to include certain screen shots in hard copy documentation, such as training

materials or instructional videos. Export a single frame if you want to import the frame for use in Photoshop or Illustrator.

You can also export a clip or program as a sequence of still images, with each frame in a separate still-image file. Doing this can be useful to move a clip to

animation and three-dimensional applications that do not import video file formats, or for use in animation programs that require a still-image sequence. When you export a still-image sequence, Premiere numbers the files automatically. See the online help for instructions on how to export a sequence of still images.

EXPORT A SINGLE FRAME

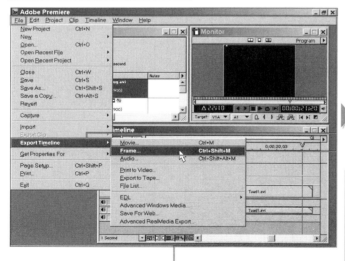

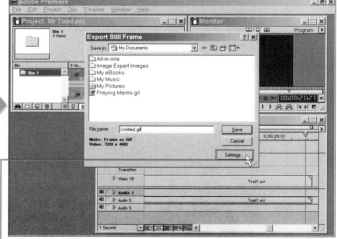

1 Cue the Timeline's edit line to the frame you want to export.

Note: See Chapter 18 to learn more about working with the Timeline.

2 Click File.

3 Click Export Timeline.

4 Click Frame.

■ The Export Still Frame dialog box appears.

5 Click Settings.

■ The Export Still Frame Settings dialog box appears.

Why do the export settings look different than the project settings?

✔ Although the Export Settings dialog box is similar to the Project Settings dialog box, important differences exist. For example, the Special Processing panel is included so that you can apply certain changes to all clips in the Timeline window at export time, such as resizing, cropping, and noise reduction. Also, some capture card software and plug-in software provide their own dialog boxes with specific options. If the options you see are different that those described in Premiere's online Help, refer to the documentation for your capture card or plug-in.

How do I set a frame size for the exported image file?

✔ In the Export Still Frame Settings dialog box, click [Next] or [Prev] to move back and forth between the General, Video Settings, Keyframe and Rendering Options, and Special Processing panels. The Video Settings panel has options for setting frame size. To learn more about project settings, see Chapter 15.

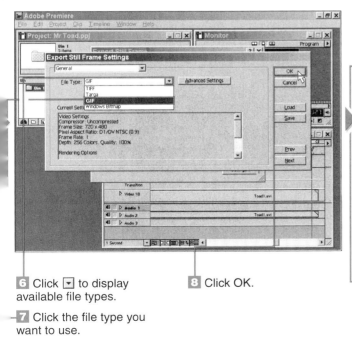

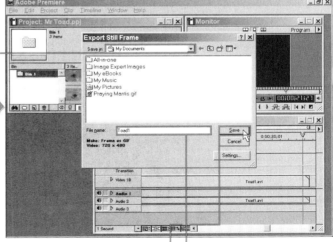

6 Click ☑ to display available file types.

7 Click the file type you want to use.

Note: Premiere supports TIFF, Targa, GIF, and Windows Bitmap image file formats.

8 Click OK.

9 Specify a location in which to save the file.

■ You can click the Save In ☑ to locate the folder or drive in which you want to save.

10 Type a filename for the still image.

11 Click Save.

■ Premiere saves the file for later use.

EXPORT TO VIDEOTAPE

You can record your edited program onto videotape directly from your computer. This can be as simple as playing the Timeline and recording on a connected DV camcorder or analog VCR. Use the Export to Tape command to play video on a black background for recording on videotape.

When recording directly from the Timeline, Premiere uses settings

from the Project Settings dialog box. Many video capture cards include Premiere-compatible plug-in software that provides a menu command for recording to videotape. Consequently, if the options you see differ from those described here, refer to your capture card or plug-in documentation for instructions on the most efficient way to export to tape.

If you will play the video program from the Timeline while recording directly to videotape, make sure that the project is using compression settings that preserve the highest picture quality without dropping any frames. Tune the settings for the computer on which you will play the program during videotape recording.

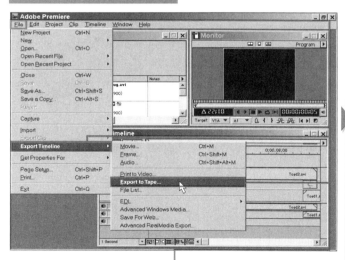

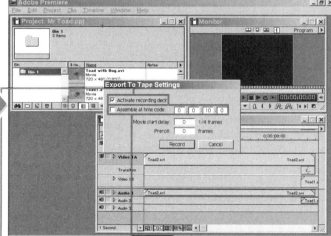

1 Connect the DV device you want to record to, making sure the device is powered on with a tape inserted.

Note: Most tape recorder devices use a black, coded cassette tape that has a black video signal and timecode.

2 Click File.

3 Click Export Timeline.

4 Click Export to Tape.

■ The Export to Tape Settings dialog box appears.

Note: The options in the dialog box may vary based on the hardware you are using.

5 Click Activate recording deck.

■ The record mode for the DV deck or camera is activated.

■ Click here if you want to enter a timecode number to start the recording and type the number.

What does the Print to Video command do?

✔ Use the Print to Video command when you want to operate the recording device manually. Make sure the tape you are recording to is cued and ready to go, and click File, Export Timeline, and then Print to Video. The Print to Video dialog box appears, and you can specify color bar or playback options. When you are ready to record, click OK and start the recording device.

How do I record my digital video onto an analog recorder?

✔ If you plan to record DV audio and video to an analog format, you need a device capable of converting DV audio and video to analog using the connectors supported by your analog video recorder. Most DV camcorders and all DV videotape recorders can perform this conversion; some DV cameras require you to record the video to DV tape, and then dub the DV tape to the analog video recorder.

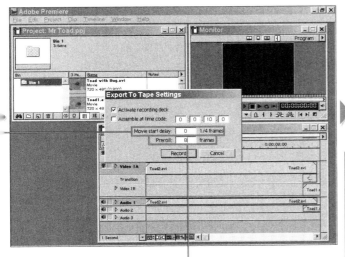

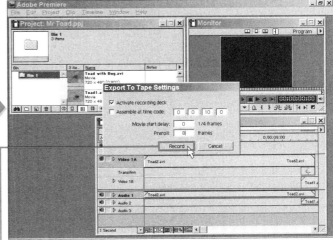

■ Use this option to delay the playback a specified number of quarter-frames.

■ Use this option to specify a number of frames to rewind from the start time to get the tape up to speed.

⬛6 Click Record.

■ Playback begins.

■ If you are controlling the recorder device manually, push the Record button on the device.

Note: To stop recording, push the Stop button on the recorder device.

EXPORT FOR THE WEB WITH CLEANER EZ

You can output your video for the Web or an intranet by saving your project as a streaming video file using one of three plug-in programs that come with Premiere. Streaming video is one of the most popular video formats on the Web because it lets users watch the video as it downloads rather than wait for the entire file to download.

Cleaner EZ is an accessory program that is available when you install Premiere. When you export a Timeline, a new option, "Save for Web," appears in the dialog box. This option launches the Cleaner EZ program, which can create a streaming video program from your Timeline file for you.

With Cleaner EZ, you can create streaming files in a number of

different formats, including QuickTime, Windows Media Player, and RealMedia, as well as CD-ROM and still image formats. Each of the streaming formats enables you to select a download speed, to optimize your file for users with fast or slow Internet connections.

EXPORT FOR THE WEB WITH CLEANER EZ

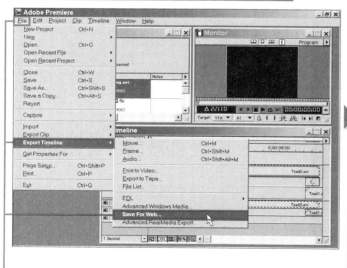

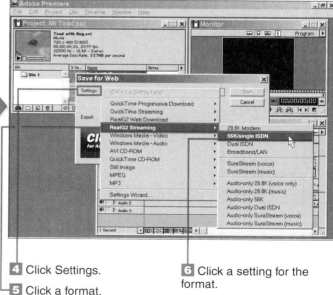

1 Click File.

2 Click Export Timeline.

3 Click Save for Web.

■ The Cleaner EZ plug-in dialog box appears.

Note: Cleaner EZ must be installed for this feature to be available.

4 Click Settings.

5 Click a format.

6 Click a setting for the format.

Which download speed should I use when I export my movie?

✔ Your choice of download speed will depend on how your movie will be used and where your viewers will be. If you are creating an internal training video that will be viewed over your internal network only, you can use a faster speed such as Broadband/LAN (local area network). If you are creating a movie that will be viewed over the Internet, you should choose a slower speed such as 28 or 56 kilobits per second (Kbps). When you optimize a file for slower speeds, you reduce the frame size and image quality, so you should view your movies after you export them to see how they look at those download speeds.

How do I know which plug-in to use?

✔ All three plug-ins will optimize your video for the Web. Use the RealNetworks plug-in to create RealVideo formats. Use the Advanced Windows Media plug-in to output in WMV format for Windows Media Player version 7 and higher. The Cleaner EZ plug-in can create QuickTime or Windows streaming media.

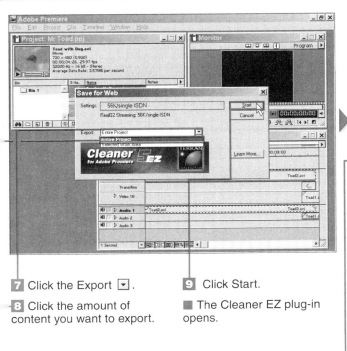

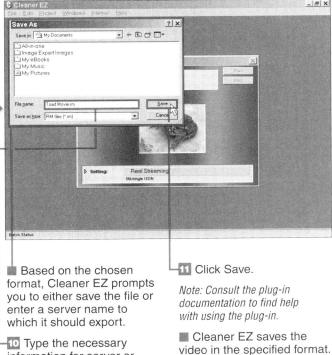

7 Click the Export ▾.

8 Click the amount of content you want to export.

9 Click Start.

■ The Cleaner EZ plug-in opens.

■ Based on the chosen format, Cleaner EZ prompts you to either save the file or enter a server name to which it should export.

10 Type the necessary information for server or filename.

11 Click Save.

Note: Consult the plug-in documentation to find help with using the plug-in.

■ Cleaner EZ saves the video in the specified format.

INTRODUCING AFTER EFFECTS

Y ou can use Adobe After Effects to create myriad special effects for moving images. Whether you have a Mac or a PC, After Effects can help you add dynamic effects to digital images, text, audio, and even 3D animation.

You can export the finished effects to other sources, such as videotape, CD-ROM, or the Web.

After Effects borrows features from both Photoshop and Premiere and expands on their capabilities,

allowing you to add enhancing special effects that you cannot achieve in the other programs in the digital video collection.

Import Source Material

Files you create in After Effects are called *projects*. You can import a variety of source material into After Effects to use with a project. The source material you import into After Effects is called *footage*. For example, you can import digital video and audio files, bitmapped still images, vector-based images, and 3D file formats. Imported items are listed in the Project window. After Effects cannot capture such source material directly; however, you can use other programs to do so and then import the files into After Effects.

The files you import are merely references to the original source material. For that reason, it is important not to move or delete the original files or After Effects can no longer locate the files for use in the project.

Build a Composition

You can take the footage you import into After Effects and arrange it in a composition. The Composition window allows you to work with layers, arrange the footage in the order you want it to appear, and assign effect attributes. You control layers in space and time in the composition. You can also control the frame size, frame rate, and duration for the composition.

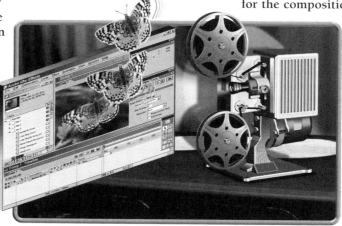

Creating Output

When your project is just the way you want it, you can export the results to a number of file formats. You can output your animation for presentation on the Web, for example, or to video format for CD-ROM or DVD. Learn more about exporting your project in Chapter 30.

Assigning Effects

By changing the attributes of layers over time you can create animated effects. For example, you can control the intensity of effects, and make layers appear and disappear, create masks, and much more. You can use the program's preview feature to check the animation at any time and make changes accordingly.

NAVIGATE THE AFTER EFFECTS WORK AREA

You can use After Effects to create all kinds of digital special effects for moving images. The program works hand-in-hand with Photoshop, Illustrator, and Premiere.

The After Effects interface focuses on three main areas: the Project window, the Composition window, and the Timeline window. In addition, After Effects uses palettes to present commands and effects you can apply to your project.

Whether you are using a PC or a Mac, the program window features the same elements.

Composition Window

Visually shows the layers of a composition for a single frame.

Project Window

Manages the content of your project, including audio, graphic, and video files.

Timeline Window

Shows the linear representation of time in your project.

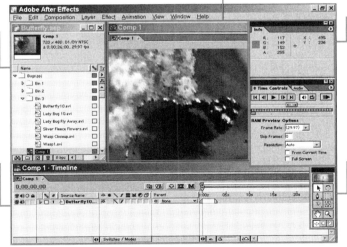

Palette Windows

Present additional commands and options that you can apply to your project.

Toolbox Tools

Apply an assortment of tasks pertaining to effects, such as changing camera view or effect rotation.

WORK WITH PALETTES

You can use the After Effects palettes to access commands and other features as well as to help you edit your project.

Palettes are mini-windows that you can move around the screen, minimize, maximize, and close. Palettes always appear on top of the other After Effects window elements so you can quickly access the controls you need.

To save space, After Effects groups some palettes into a single window. You display each palette by clicking the tabs at the top of the palette window.

If you install third-party plug-ins to work with After Effects, additional palettes are available.

Can I dock a palette window?
✔ No. Palette windows always float. To move a palette out of the way, drag the palette by its top bar to the desired position. You can also collapse a palette to display only the palette's top bar. To collapse an open palette, double-click the palette's top bar. To display the full palette window again, double-click the top bar.

Can I hide a palette and still keep it open?
✔ Yes. Press the Tab key to quickly hide all open palette windows. Press Tab again to bring the palettes back.

WORK WITH PALETTES

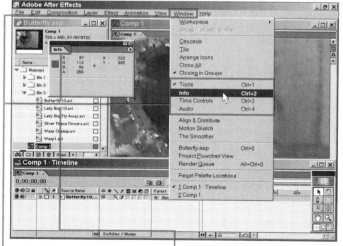

OPEN A PALETTE

1 Click Window.

2 Click the name of the palette you want to display.

■ After Effects opens the palette.

■ If a palette containing the features you want to use is already open, you can simply click the tab you want to display.

CLOSE A PALETTE

1 Click the top bar of the palette window you want to close.

2 Click the palette's ☒ (▣).

■ The palette vanishes from the screen.

■ You can also click the Window menu and click the palette name to close an open palette.

SET A TIME DISPLAY

Before you create a project, you can specify how you want to display time in the project. The Display Style options allow you to specify the unit of measure used to describe time in your project.

By default, After Effect uses Society of Motion Picture and Television Engineers (SMPTE) timecode, which displays time in hours, minutes, seconds, and frames. You can choose other formats, if

you find this necessary. The Frames option counts frames of footage rather than time. The Feet and Frames option counts frame numbers based on 16mm or 35mm film, and counts fractions of feet; 16mm film uses 40 frames per foot while 35mm film uses 16 frames per foot.

If you choose to use the SMPTE timecode base, you can also opt whether to use drop-frame timecode or non-drop-frame timecode.

What is the difference between drop-frame and non-drop-frame timecode?

✔ The true frame rate for NTSC video — the video standard for North America and Japan — is 29.97 frames per second. SMPTE timecode rounds off to 30 frames per second. To compensate between the two, the drop-frame timecode skips two frame numbers, not actual frames, at the end of every minute of video (except for every tenth minute). Non-drop-frame timecode counts 30 frames per second without dropping frame numbers. Non-drop-frame timecode uses colons between the hours, minutes, seconds, and frames in the timecode display while drop-frame timecode displays a semicolon between increments.

SET A TIME DISPLAY

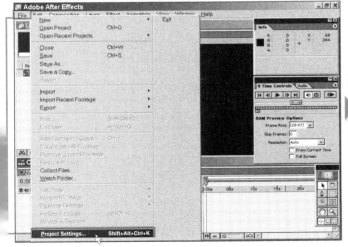

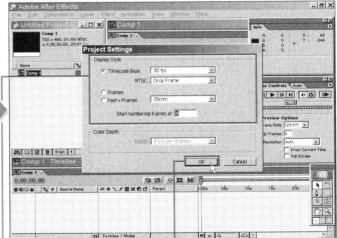

■1 Click File.

■2 Click Project Settings.

■ The Project Settings dialog box opens.

■3 Click a Display Style option (○ changes to ◉).

■ Timecode Base applies timecode to number frames.

■ Frames numbers frames sequentially.

■ Feet + Frames numbers frames based on 16mm or 35mm film frames.

■4 Click OK.

■ The time display takes effect.

CREATE OR OPEN A PROJECT

You can create a new project in After Effects to begin working on, or open an existing project to continue working on a file you already started. After Effects limits you to having only one project open at a time.

When you first open After Effects, a new untitled project appears in the Project window by default. You can start adding project elements to the default project, or you can open

another new project or an existing project.

When you open a project, the Project window opens automatically. The Project window is the heart of your project, listing all the elements referenced for the project, such as video and audio files.

Before you begin any project, determine any output settings first. For example, if you are using After

Effects to create an enhanced video effect, be sure to determine frame size, frame rate, and which file format you want to export the project to after you create the effect in After Effects. To change settings, open the Project Settings dialog box. See the section "Set a Time Display" to learn more.

See the section "Save or Close a Project" to learn how to name a project file and save it for future use.

CREATE A NEW PROJECT

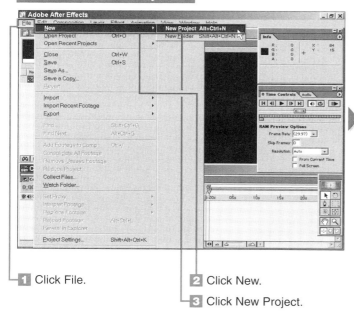

1 Click File.

2 Click New.

3 Click New Project.

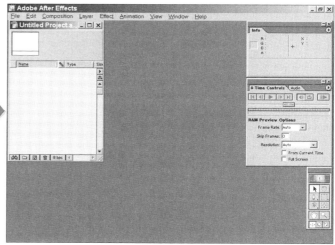

■ An untitled project opens onscreen, displaying an empty Project window.

Why do some of my projects open with lots of windows displayed and others do not?

✔ By default, when you create a new project, the Project window opens along with a few palette windows and the toolbox. The other main windows, such as the Composition window and the Timeline window open later as you add and edit footage. After Effects keeps track of which windows you leave open when you exit a particular project file and redisplays those same windows when you reopen the file.

After Effects displays a warning box when I try to open a project. Why?

✔ If you moved or deleted a file referenced in an After Effects project, a warning box appears when you try to reopen the project. This simply means that the program cannot find the source file you referenced and considers it missing. You can click OK to keep working, and After Effects italicizes the missing file in the Project window. To correct the problem, return the footage file to it's original location, or import the file again to create a new link. You can then remove the unreferenced footage item from the Project window.

OPEN A PROJECT

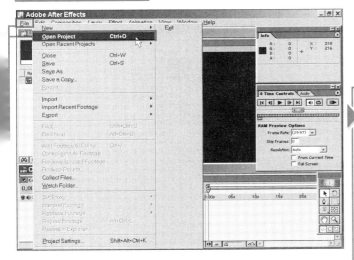

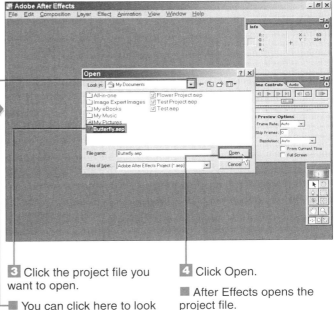

■1 Click File.

■2 Click Open Project.

■ The Open dialog box appears.

■ To open a recently used project file, you can click File, Open Recent Projects, and then the file.

■3 Click the project file you want to open.

■ You can click here to look in other folders or drives.

■4 Click Open.

■ After Effects opens the project file.

SAVE OR CLOSE A PROJECT

Y ou can save a project file and assign it a unique name for reusing it later. After Effects saves project files in the AEP file format.

You can also save the file to another format if the project is finished. See Chapter 31 to export an After Effects movie.

When you save a project, After Effects saves the references to source files imported into the Project window as well as the composition and effects you create. Because the AEP file saves references only, project files are much smaller in size than if you saved the original source files with the project.

After Effects does not offer an autosave feature, so be sure to save your work often in case of a power outage or computer glitch.

You can close a project when you want to start a new project or when you want to close the After Effects program window. You can only have one project file open at a time in After Effects.

SAVE A PROJECT

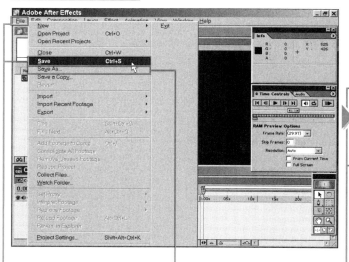

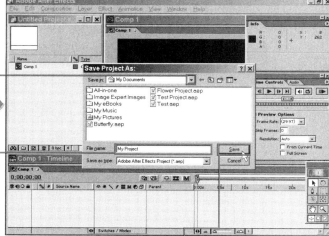

■ Click File.

■ Click Save.

Note: The Save command is inactive unless you create a new composition or import a file. See the section "Import a File" to learn more.

■ To save an existing file under a new filename, you can click Save As.

■ The Save Project As dialog box appears.

■ Type a name for the file.

■ Click here to locate a different folder or drive in which to save to the file.

■ Click Save.

■ After Effects saves the project file.

How do I save a file to be cross-platform compatible?

✔ Add the .aep file extension to the project filename to make the file cross-platform compatible on both Windows and Mac systems. Only Mac users need to add the extension to filenames. If you are using Windows, After Effects automatically adds the extension.

How do I save my project to another file format?

✔ When you complete a project, you can output the composition to a variety of audio and video file formats, such as SWF (Macromedia Shockwave/Flash). To do so, you must render your composition. See Chapter 31 to learn more about designating a specific output form for a project.

How do I close the Project window to get it out of the way, yet continue working on the project?

✔ You can minimize the Project window if you need to free up more on-screen workspace. To do so, simply click the Project window's Minimize button (▢). This reduces the Project window to a bar at the bottom of the program window. To redisplay the window again, click the Restore button (▣).

CLOSE A PROJECT

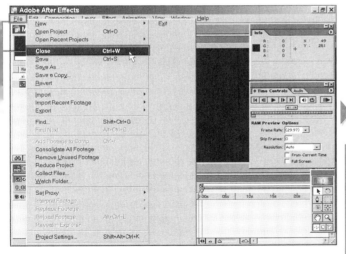

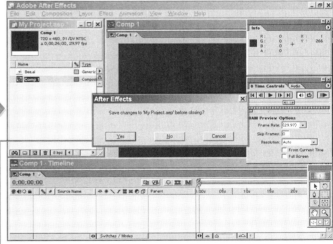

█1 Click File.

█2 Click Close.

■ You can also click the Project window's ✕ (▢) to close the project.

■ If you have not saved your work, After Effects prompts you to do so. Click Yes to save, No to close without saving and to lose your current work, or Cancel to abort the action.

Note: To close the program window entirely, click File, and then Exit.

IMPORT A FILE

You can import source material — called *footage* items — into After Effects and then assign special effects to that material. You can import a variety of file types into After Effects, including movie files, still images, and audio files.

After Effects supports the following file formats: QuickTime (MOV), AVI, WAV, JPEG, GIF, TIFF, Targa (TGA), PICT, Cineon (CIN/DPX), SGI, FLS/FLI, RLA, Electric Image (IMG/EI), Filmstrip (FLM), Softimage (PIC), EPS, PDF, and files from the other Adobe Digital Collection programs.

When you import a file, you actually create a reference link to the original source file. You cannot alter the original file by making changes to the After Effects project. By using references instead of actual source material, After Effects saves file space. If you move or delete the source file, however, you break the reference link, which you must reestablish in order for After Effects to include the item again. For that reason, you should store your project's source files in a single folder and then use subfolders within that folder to organize the material.

If you break a footage item's link, you can return the item to it's original location to re-establish the link or import the item again to establish a new link.

You can import a single file or multiple files. You can also import an item once and use it repeatedly throughout your project. Depending on the file type, you can choose to import a file in composition format or as footage. For more information on these options, see the section "Introducing After Effects."

IMPORT A FILE

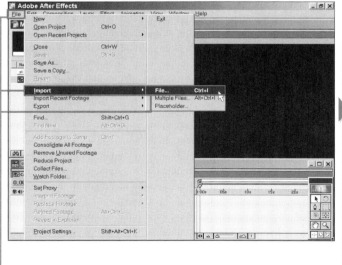

IMPORT A SINGLE FILE

1 Click File.

2 Click Import.

3 Click File.

■ The Import File dialog box opens.

Note: See the section "Import Other Adobe Files" to learn more about importing files from Photoshop, Illustrator, and Premiere.

4 Click the file you want to import.

■ Click here to locate a different folder or drive in which to locate the file.

■ Click here to import either a composition or footage item.

5 Click Open.

■ After Effect imports and adds the file to the Project window.

How can I view an item I imported?

✔ You can view the imported footage in a Footage window. Simply double-click the item listed in the Project window. Within the Footage window, you can trim the footage and then insert the item into the Timeline window. Learn more about working with footage in Chapter 24.

Can I select multiple files to import?

✔ Yes. You can import multiple files in one fell swoop without importing them one at a time. To do so, press Ctrl (Command) while clicking files in the Import Multiple Files dialog box. Then click Open to import them all at the same time. To import a sequence of files, such as a sequence of animated GIF files for example, open the Import File dialog box, click a file in the sequence, and then click the Sequence check box. Click Open to import all the files in the sequence.

After Effects does not recognize the file type I want to import. How can I import the file?

✔ After Effects does not list unrecognizable file types in the Import Files dialog box, not even if you choose All Acceptable Files from the File Type list. You can manually import the file by clicking All Files from the File Type list. A warning box appears; click OK. Click the file and then click the Import As ▼ to choose an import format. Click Open to import the file. You can also try saving the file in another program as a recognizable file type.

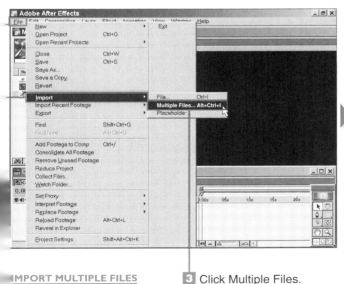

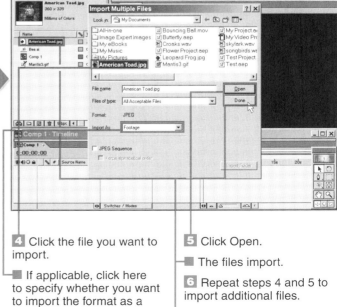

IMPORT MULTIPLE FILES

1 Click File.

2 Click Import.

3 Click Multiple Files.

■ The Import Multiple Files dialog box opens.

4 Click the file you want to import.

■ If applicable, click here to specify whether you want to import the format as a composition or as footage.

5 Click Open.

■ The files import.

6 Repeat steps 4 and 5 to import additional files.

7 Click Done to close the dialog box.

IMPORT OTHER ADOBE FILES

You can import files from the other Adobe Digital Collection programs to which you can assign special effects using the After Effects controls. After Effects readily recognizes the other Adobe file types and transfers the data seamlessly.

You can import a single layer from a Photoshop or Illustrator file, or import the entire file as a composition to manipulate in After Effects. For example, you can import a Photoshop file as a single-layer file type, a merged layer, or as a layered composition.

If you import an Illustrator file, After Effects converts any empty areas into a transparent alpha channel and any text into a path

that you can easily edit for special effects.

If you import a Premiere project, After Effects immediately recognizes the Premiere file type and imports the file in composition format, treating each clip as a layer. After Effects maintains clip order, duration, and in and out points.

IMPORT OTHER ADOBE FILES

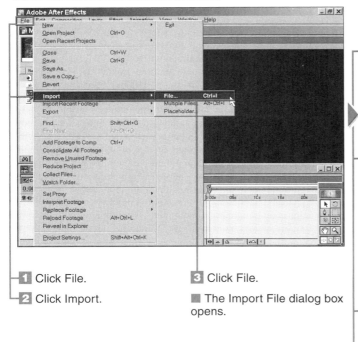

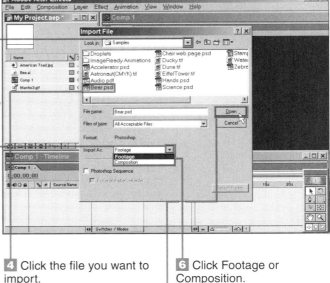

1 Click File.

2 Click Import.

3 Click File.

■ The Import File dialog box opens.

4 Click the file you want to import.

■ Click here to locate a different folder or drive in which to locate the file.

5 Click the Import As ▼.

6 Click Footage or Composition.

Note: If you want to import a Photoshop or Illustrator layer as a single item, be sure to select Footage as the format.

7 Click Open.

Can I import motion footage into After Effects?

✔ Film plays at 24 frames per second (fps), while NTSC video plays at 29.97. When transferring film to video, the *3:2 pulldown* process makes up for the difference in frame rates. As long as you have digitized footage, you can import footage from sources such as Hi8, scanned Cineon files, and digital video. However, After Effects may interpret the file types differently. In these circumstances, use the Interpret Footage command to help you determine frame rate, field order, 3:2 pulldown, and pixel aspect ratio. Click File, click Interpret Footage, and then click Main. This command opens the Interpret Footage dialog box where you can specify film-related options.

Can I import another After Effects project into my current project?

✔ Yes. Simply select the project file in the Import File dialog box and After Effects immediately identifies the file as an After Effects project, displaying Project in the Import As field.

Can I import an effect I created in another project?

✔ Yes, but you must import the entire After Effects file in which you have saved the effect, then replace the source footage with the new footage to which you want to apply the effect.

How can I view my imported footage?

✔ Double-click the footage item listed in the Project window to open a Footage window displaying the item.

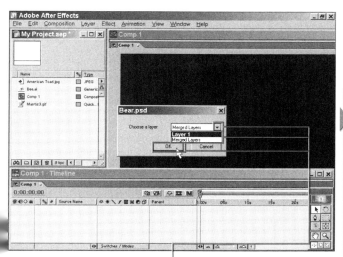

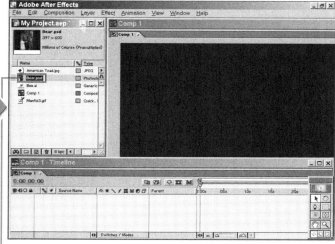

■ If you choose to import a Photoshop or Illustrator layer as a single footage item, a prompt box opens.

8 Click the Choose a Layer ▾.

9 Click the layer you want to import.

10 Click OK.

■ After Effects imports the file and lists it in the Project window.

■ You can undo an import, by clicking the Edit menu, and then clicking Undo Import.

SET FOOTAGE OPTIONS

When you import source material, also called *footage*, you can adjust a number of options to control frame rate, alpha channel settings, fields and pulldowns for motion picture footage, and more. You access these controls through the Interpret Footage dialog box.

For example, if you import a sequence of images to use in an animation, you can change the

frame rate in After Effects to create a specific effect. Frame rate is the number of frames that play per second. In most instances it is best to match the frame rate of the source material, however, in the case of a still image sequence; you can change the frame rate to control the playback speed. If you intend to output your project to the Web, you may need to slow the frame rate to 10–15 frames per second.

Another option in the Interpret Footage dialog box is the Loop setting. If you plan to use the same item in a composition over and over again, you can use the Loop setting to make the image repeat. Setting a loop number is much easier than copying the item repeatedly in the Composition window.

SET FOOTAGE OPTIONS

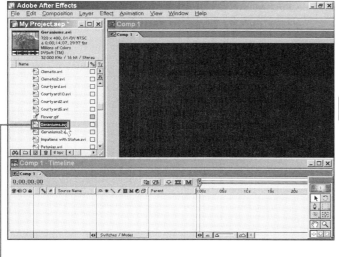

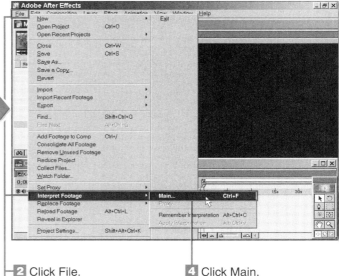

1 Click the footage item to which you want to set options.

Note: See the sections "Import a File" and "Import Other Adobe Files" to import footage items into the Project window.

2 Click File.

3 Click Interpret Footage.

4 Click Main.

■ The Interpret Footage dialog box opens.

How do I know what frame rate to use?

✔ The standard frame rate for film is 24 frames per second, and the standard for video is 30 frames per second. Video with higher frame rates appears more fluid. Slower frame rates, however, download more quickly from the Web. Consider your project's output when determining frame rate.

What values can I enter for a loop setting?

✔ You can only use integers for looping, not fractions or decimals. When you set a loop number, the footage item loops for the specified number of cycles. The Loop setting merely loops the content of the footage. It does not loop the movement of a layer in the composition.

What does the Pixel Aspect Ratio do?

✔ Computers typically display pixels as square, using a 1:1 pixel aspect ratio. Some formats, such as NTSC DV, use non-square pixels. After Effects interprets the footage to correct for the unusual pixel aspect. To make sure the aspect is just the way you want it, however, consider opening the Interpret Footage dialog box and checking the setting.

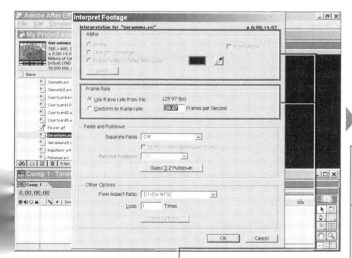

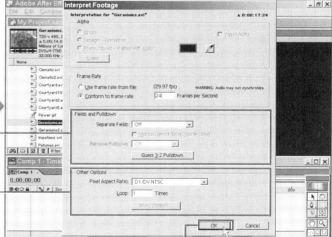

■5 Change any footage options as needed.

Note: Depending on the type of footage item you select, only certain options may be available.

■ The Alpha options allow you to choose how an item's alpha channel is handled in After Effects.

■ The Frame Rate options allow you to set a frame rate for the item.

■ The Fields and Pulldown options allow you to set options for motion picture footage items.

■ The Other Options area allows you to control pixel aspect ratio and looping for an item.

■6 Click OK.

■ After Effects applies any changes you make.

CREATE AND NAME A COMPOSITION

Before you can start working with footage items — source files you import into After Effects — and creating special effects, you must first create a composition. A *composition* is the arrangement of footage items as you want them to appear in the effect. After Effects arranges and stores items in layers, which you can manipulate to create the illusion of time and space.

The composition appears in the Composition window. By default, when you create a new composition, After Effects uses the same settings assigned from the previously created composition. You can change the settings to tailor the composition to the new project. See the section "Change Composition Settings" to learn more.

When you create a new composition, the Timeline window opens as well. After Effects also adds the composition to the list of items in the Project window. See the section "Add Composition Footage" to learn how to add items to the Composition window.

After Effects uses default names for new compositions, *Comp 1*, *Comp 2*, and so on. You can rename the composition to distinguish it from other compositions in the project.

You do not need to name your compositions, but it helps if you want to quickly identify your Project window content, especially if you use several compositions in one file. After Effects saves your compositions when you save the project file. See Chapter 23 for more on project files.

CREATE AND NAME A COMPOSITION

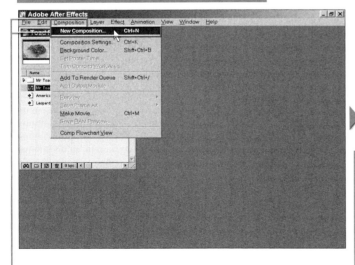

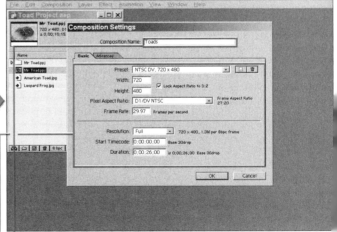

1 Click Composition.

2 Click New Composition.

■ The Composition Settings dialog box appears.

Note: In this figure, the default palettes and toolbox are closed. See Chapter 23 to learn more about working with palettes.

3 Type a name for the composition.

4 Make any changes to the composition settings, as needed.

Note: See the section "Change Composition Settings" to learn more about changing compositio settings.

My Composition window is huge. How do I resize it?

✔ A new Composition window opens to a default size, which often fills the screen and obscures the view of other open windows, when active. As you work with the composition, the larger window size makes it easier to move items around. You can resize any of the windows in After Effects just as you resize windows in other programs. Drag a window border to resize the window.

Can I place one composition within another?

✔ Yes. This technique is called *nesting*, and you can create compositions that nest within other compositions. For example, you may prefer to organize a group of layers in one composition and then add the group to another composition. You can quickly nest one composition into an open composition by simply dragging the composition you want to nest from the Project window and dropping it into the open composition window in which you want it nested.

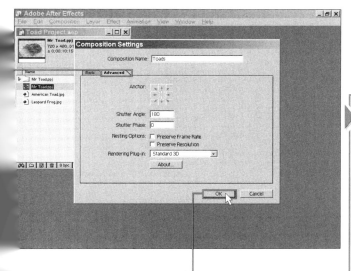

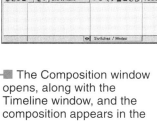

■ Clicking the Advanced tab displays more advanced settings for the composition, such as nesting options.

5 Click OK.

■ The Composition window opens, along with the Timeline window, and the composition appears in the Project window.

Note: See Chapter 23 to learn more about the project window and saving files.

■ To close a Composition window, click ☒ (☐).

■ To open another composition, double-click the composition in the Project window.

NAVIGATE THE COMPOSITION WINDOW

You can use the Composition window to assemble layers of footage for your project. You can assign masks, special effects, keyframes and motion paths, and much more. See Chapter 23 to learn more about adding footage to a project.

You can have numerous compositions in a project. If you open two or more compositions, each appears as a tab in the Composition window.

Take a moment and familiarize yourself with the elements of the Composition window before you begin adding footage.

Rulers

Help you align layers and footage items. Pixels are the default measurement. Rulers are not displayed by default.

Timeline Button

Displays the composition's Timeline window.

Magnification Ratio Menu

Changes the magnification view for the window.

Title Action Safe Button

Allows you to toggle between viewing title-safe and action-safe zones. This helps to ensure that you have not cut off important text and content when a user views it on a television screen.

Current Time

Displays the current time or frame in timecode for the composition.

Take and View Snapshot Buttons

Allow you to capture a screen image of the Composition window to view and compare with another window.

Channel Buttons

Display only the red, green, blue, or alpha channel for a composition.

Region of Interest Button

Limits the area of an image you want to include in the preview or playback. This feature helps to free up RAM for rendering the image or movie.

NAVIGATE THE TIMELINE WINDOW

You can use the Timeline window to see a graphical representation of your composition layers as they relate to time and space. Each layer in the composition appears as a row in the Timeline. Layers hold footage items and effects. After Effects only allows one layer per row. If you open two or more compositions, each appears as a tab in the Timeline.

The stacking order determines how After Effects arranges the layers with layers at the top of the Timeline appearing at the front of the composition. You can use the Timeline window to assign attributes to layers and change the order in which they appear.

The Timeline controls for working with layers are arranged in panels and a time graph at the end of the window shows the overall project length and the duration of each layer.

Timeline Tools

Control the way in which content displays in the Timeline.

Time Marker

Indicates the current frame in the Composition window.

Current Time

Displays the current time or frame in timecode for the composition.

Layers

Each layer in a composition comprises one row in the Timeline. Use layers to place footage items and effects in a composition.

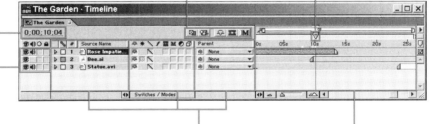

Panels

Four panels, or columns, appear by default: Audio/Video Features, Layer Outline, Switches, and Parenting. Each panel includes controls for working with layers. You can resize each panel to show more or less information in the window.

Time Graph

Shows an overview of layer duration and when each layer starts and stops.

CHANGE COMPOSITION SETTINGS

Before you add footage to a composition, you can define the composition's settings. For example, you can specify spatial attributes for controlling frame size and pixel aspect ratio, as well as temporal attributes, such as composition duration and frame rate. Assigning composition settings at the beginning of a project saves you time and effort later.

While you can certainly customize the settings for any given project, After Effects includes a list of presets you can assign to save some effort. The presets are a list of the most common settings for projects based on the type of output you expect to produce. If you do require customized settings, you can specify them in the Composition Settings dialog box and save them for reuse with another project.

By default, the Composition Settings dialog box appears when you first create a new composition. You can revisit the dialog box to make changes to the settings. See the section "Create and Name a Composition" to learn how to start a new composition.

CHANGE COMPOSITION SETTINGS

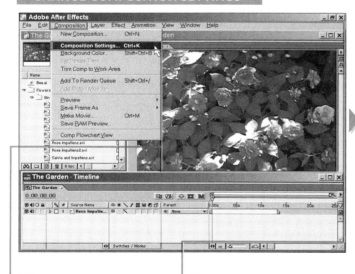

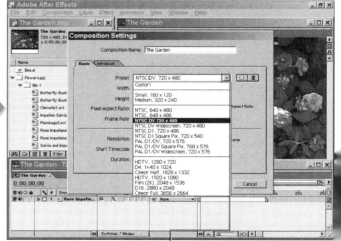

1 Click the composition in the Project window or open the Composition window.

Note: See the section "Create and Name a Composition" to start a new composition.

2 Click Composition.

3 Click Composition Settings.

■ The Composition Settings dialog box appears.

Note: See the section "Add Composition Footage" to add items to the Composition window.

4 Make the necessary changes to the composition settings.

■ Click here to display a list of common presets.

How do I save my composition settings as a preset?

✔ Make the necessary adjustments to the settings in the Composition Settings dialog box, then click the Save button (⬚). The Choose Name dialog box appears. Type a unique name for the preset, then click OK. After Effects adds the settings to the list of presets. To see the list, click the Preset ▾.

Which presets are the most common?

✔ You commonly use NTSC, which has a frame size of 640 x 480, for full screen, full motion video. NTSC DV, is the digital video standard for North America and Japan, while NTSC D1 is the broadcast standard.

How do I know which pixel aspect ratio to use?

✔ Computers typically use square pixels, but professional video equipment often uses non-square pixels to display the image. If you view a computer image using professional video equipment, the image may appear distorted. After Effects can readily compensate for these differences if you make sure the composition's pixel aspect ratio, called PAR for short, matches the final output's PAR. For example, if you plan to export your project for broadcast, use the NTSC D1 preset setting (PAR of .09).

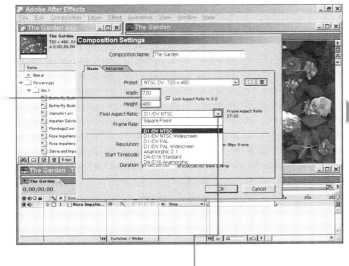

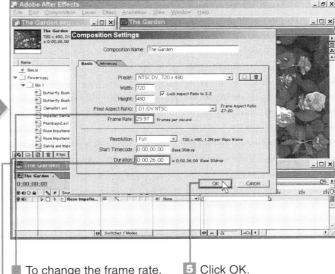

■ To change the frame size, type a new width and height, in pixels, here.

■ To change the pixel aspect ratio, click here.

■ To change the frame rate, type a new value here.

■ To change the composition's duration, type a new timecode value here.

5 Click OK.

■ After Effects applies the new settings.

SET A BACKGROUND COLOR

You can set a background color for the Composition window. By default, After Effects assigns the color black, but you can choose from a palette of other colors more suitable to your project. You can even set the background color to a checkerboard pattern.

Background color automatically becomes the alpha channel for a composition if you export the project as a still image sequence or movie. If you use the composition as a nested layer in another composition, the background becomes transparent. If you prefer the nested composition's background to remain solid, you must assign a solid color to the layer.

Where do I find the checkerboard background setting?

✔ The Checkerboard Background command is not located on the Composition menu. You must click the Comp Window Options button ([▶]) located in the top right corner of the Composition window to display a menu of related commands. Click Checkerboard Background to apply the checkerboard feature to the composition background. To turn the feature off again, reopen the menu and click Checkerboard Background again.

SET A BACKGROUND COLOR

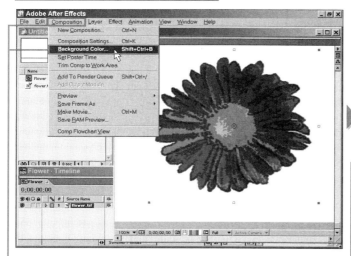

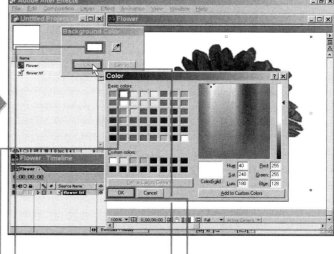

1 With a composition open, click Composition.

2 Click Background Color.

■ The Background Color dialog box appears.

Note: See the section "Add Composition Footage" to learn how to add items to the Composition window.

3 Click the color swatch.

■ The Color dialog box appears.

4 Click a color.

5 Click OK.

6 Click OK again.

■ After Effects assigns the new color.

CUE THE CURRENT TIME MARKER

Before you add footage to a composition, you can specify where you want the layer to begin in the Timeline. By default, After Effects adds a new footage layer to the Timeline at the current Time marker. The Time marker indicates the current frame in the composition.

You can set the start time in one of two ways: Using the buttons on the Time

Controls palette, or cueing the Time marker manually.

The Time Controls palette includes several playback controls that enable you to adjust the layer placement as well as play and preview the layer. You may want to leave the Time Controls palette open as you add footage to your composition for easy access to the playback controls.

How do I move the Time marker to a specific frame in my composition?

✔ Click the time display area in the Timeline or Composition window to open the Go To Time dialog box. Type a specific frame you want to move to, then click OK. You can also type an absolute time, or a relative time preceded by a plus or minus sign. For example, type +40 to jump 40 frames beyond the current Time marker position.

CUE THE CURRENT TIME MARKER

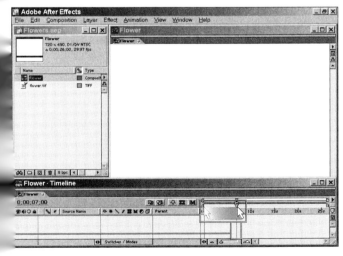

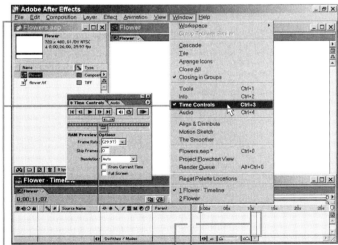

CUE THE TIME MARKER MANUALLY

1 Click and drag the Time marker (▽) to a new position in the Time graph.

2 Release the mouse button.

■ The Time marker moves.

Note: See the section "Navigate the Timeline Window" to learn more about the parts of the Timeline.

USING THE TIME CONTROLS PALETTE

1 Click Window.

2 Click Time Controls.

■ The Time Controls palette opens.

3 Click and drag the slider (▭) to a specific frame.

■ The Time marker immediately repositions in the Time graph.

Note: See Chapter 23 to learn how to use palettes.

ADD COMPOSITION FOOTAGE

After you create a new composition, you can begin adding *footage*. Footage items are files you import into After Effects. Footage can also consist of another composition or a solid layer that you created in After Effects. To learn how to import files, see Chapter 23.

After Effect treats each item you add to the Composition window as a layer. You can add different items or use the same item multiple times.

You can add a footage item either to the Composition window or to the Timeline window. Regardless of which location you use to add footage, the item appears in both places. The image, itself, displays in the Composition window while a graphical representation of the footage item appears as a bar in the Timeline window.

Because each footage item you add acts as a separate layer, the placement of the item dictates the order in which it displays. For

example, if you add three footage items to a composition, each item appears as a layer bar on the Timeline. The top layer in the Timeline window displays in the front of the Composition window, while the bottom layer in the Timeline displays as the back layer in the Composition window. You can learn more about arranging layers in Chapter 25.

ADD COMPOSITION FOOTAGE

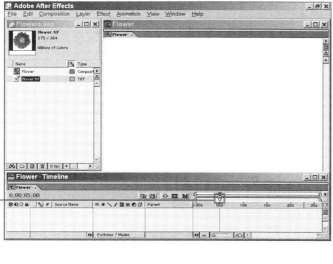

ADD AN ITEM TO THE TIMELINE

1 Set the Time marker to the frame in which you want to start the new item in the Timeline.

Note: See the previous section, "Cue the Current Time Marker," to learn how to set the Time marker.

2 Click the footage item you want to add.

3 Click and drag the item over the Timeline.

■ After Effects adds the item as a new layer in the Timeline window and it appears in the Composition window.

Can I add more than one item at a time?

✔ Yes. You can drag as many footage items as you want over to the Composition or Timeline windows. The items are ordered in the same order in which they appear in the Project window. To add several footage items at once, press Ctrl (Command) while clicking footage items in the Project window. You can then drag and drop them all in one fell swoop.

How do I remove a previously added item from the composition?

✔ Click Edit, Undo immediately after adding the item to remove the addition. You can also click the item in the Timeline window, then press Delete.

How do I add another item in the middle of the existing items?

✔ The easiest way to see the placement of items is to view them in the Timeline window. To add another item, click and drag it in the Timeline between the existing items. As you drag the new item over the existing layers, a black bar appears between the existing item names indicating where After Effects will insert the new item. When you release the mouse button, the existing items shift to make room for the new item.

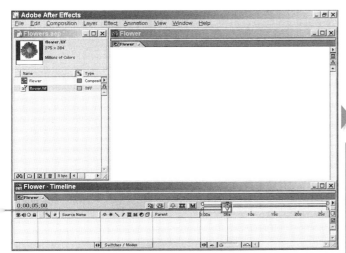

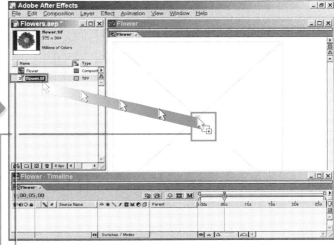

ADD AN ITEM TO THE COMPOSITION WINDOW

1 Set the Time marker to the frame in which you want to start the new item in the Timeline.

Note: See the previous section, "Cue the Current Time Marker," to learn how to set the Time marker.

2 Click the footage item you want to add.

3 Drag and drop the item over the Composition window.

■ The item is added as a new layer in the Timeline window and appears in the Composition window.

ORGANIZE FOOTAGE IN FOLDERS

A s you work with the various footage items you import into After Effects, you can organize them into folders. The more items you add, the more important it is to organize them so you can easily keep track of their location and how they relate to other items.

For example, you may decide to keep still image files separate from video footage, or group related footage items into folders. The After Effects folder system works the same way as your computer's hard disk folders. You can add and rename folders. You can also move items between folders. After Effects lists folder names alphabetically in the Project window.

You can add as many items as you like to a folder. When you close or collapse the folder, After Effects does not list the items. You can open or expand a folder to display its contents. You can also sort the items by type, name, date, and more.

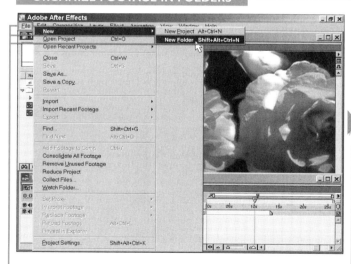

CREATE A NEW FOLDER

1 Click File.

2 Click New.

3 Click New Folder.

■ A new folder appears at the bottom of the Project window.

■ You can also click the Create a New Folder button ( ) to open a new folder in the Project window.

4 Type a name for the folder.

5 Press Enter (Return).

■ After Effects names the folder.

■ Double-click the folder to open it.

■ You can also click the Expand icon ( ) in front of the folder name to expand the folder.

How do I rename a folder?

✔ Click the folder to select it, then press Enter (Return). The folder name highlights and you can type a new name or edit the existing name. Press Enter (Return) again to save the new name.

Is there an easy way to remove footage items that I did not intend to import?

✔ Yes. Click the File menu, and then click Remove Unused Footage. After Effects removes anything that you are not currently using in the project from the Project window.

How do I remove an item from a folder?

✔ Expand or open the folder and click the item you want to remove. You can select more than one item by pressing Ctrl (Command) while clicking the footage items you want to remove. Then press Delete or click the Delete button (🗑) at the bottom of the Project window. After Effect removes the item, or items, from the Project file.

How do I sort folder items?

✔ Click the heading you want to sort at the top of the Project window. If you cannot see all the headings, resize the Project window by dragging the window's border.

MOVE AN ITEM TO A FOLDER

1 Click the footage item you want to move.

Note: See Chapter 23 to learn how to import footage.

2 Click and drag the item over the folder to which you want to move the item.

■ After Effects adds the item to the folder.

VIEW FOOTAGE

You can view a footage item at any time to check its contents before or after you add it to a composition. When you view footage, a separate Footage window opens. Depending on the type of footage, the Footage window may display controls for playing the footage, changing the magnification view, or cueing to a specific frame.

For example, if you open a still image file, the Footage window displays the image. If you open an audio file, the Footage window displays playback controls for listening to the audio.

See Chapter 23 to learn how to import footage. See the section "Add Composition Footage" to learn how to add footage to the composition.

MASTER IT

When I open a footage item, I do not see any controls for viewing or playing the item. Why not?

✔ With some items, the player window associated with the file opens instead of the After Effects Footage window. To open the item in the Footage window, press Alt (Option) while double-clicking the item in the Project window. This ensures that the item opens in the After Effects Footage window.

VIEW FOOTAGE

VIEW VIDEO FOOTAGE

1 Double-click the footage item you want to view.

■ The Footage window opens.

2 Click the Play button (▶) to play the footage.

■ The video plays.

■ You can also drag the Time marker to the frame where you want to start playing.

3 Click ☒ (☐) to close the window.

VIEW STILL IMAGE FOOTAGE

1 Double-click the footage item you want to view.

■ The Footage window opens.

Note: In the case of audio files, the Footage window opens without an image.

■ Click here to change the magnification.

2 Click ☒ (☐) to close the window.

TAKE A SNAPSHOT

You can use the Snapshot tool to take a snapshot of a Composition or Footage window to compare frames. This feature also works with the Layer window.

For example, to compare a frame at the beginning of the movie with a frame at its end, you take a snapshot of the first frame, then move the window view to the last frame. When you activate the Show Last Snapshot command, the current view replaces the snapshot. You can then toggle between the two views to compare both images.

You can view the most recent snapshot in any Composition, Footage, or Layer window. For example, you can view a Composition window snapshot in the Footage window.

Can I take multiple snapshots?

✔ Yes. Hold down the Shift key and press the F5, F6, F7, or F8 key to take multiple snapshots, then press and hold the F5, F6, F7, or F8 key to view the corresponding snapshots. For example, if you took a snapshot of the first frame and assigned it to F5, press and hold the F5 key to view the frame. To quickly purge your snapshots, press and hold Ctrl + Shift (Command - Shift) while pressing the F5, F6, F7, or F8 key.

TAKE A SNAPSHOT

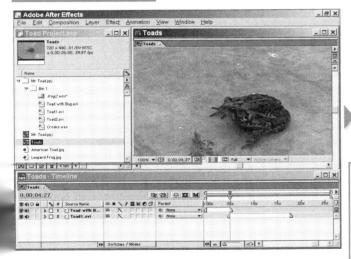

1 Click the Take Snapshot button (□).

■ After Effects takes a snapshot of the current frame.

2 Activate the window or frame to which you want to compare the snapshot.

Note: See "Cue the Current Time Marker" to learn how to cue a composition to another frame.

3 Click and hold the Show Last Snapshot button (□).

■ The current view in the active window replaces the most recent snapshot.

■ You can release the mouse button to return to the current view.

DISPLAY RULERS AND GUIDES

You can use rulers and guides in the Composition window to help you place and align footage items. By default, After Effects hides the rulers.

You can display rulers along the top and left side of the Composition window to help you arrange and position items. By default, the zero point marks where the

measurement for both rulers starts. You can change the zero point to start a new position from which to measure. For example, you may need to measure spacing from the center of the window rather than the upper-left corner.

You can also show rulers in the Footage window, if needed. The rulers toggle on or off.

Guides are another tool you can use to help with placement. A guide is simply a vertical or horizontal line you place onscreen. You can then use the guide to help you align items in the composition. You can also lock the guide lines in place to prevent any accidental movement.

DISPLAY RULERS AND GUIDES

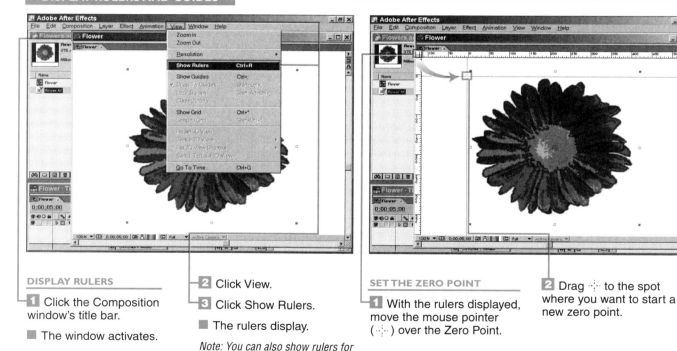

DISPLAY RULERS

1 Click the Composition window's title bar.

■ The window activates.

2 Click View.

3 Click Show Rulers.

■ The rulers display.

Note: You can also show rulers for a Footage window.

SET THE ZERO POINT

1 With the rulers displayed, move the mouse pointer (⊹) over the Zero Point.

2 Drag ⊹ to the spot where you want to start a new zero point.

How do I reset the zero point?

✔ To move the zero point back to its original location — the upper-left corner of the window — double-click the Zero Point area where the two rulers meet at the upper-left corner of the window.

Can I display a grid in After Effects to help with positioning?

✔ Absolutely. You can turn on the grid by clicking the View menu and then Show Grid. To hide the grid later, click View, and then Hide Grid.

How do I clear my screen of guide lines?

✔ Click the View menu and then click Clear Guides. This removes all the guide lines.

Can I customize the grid or guide color?

✔ Yes. Click Edit, then Preferences, then Grids & Guides. This opens the Preferences dialog box and displays the Grids & Guides options. You can use these options to change the color, spacing, and line style of grid lines, or change the color and line style of guide lines. Make your changes and click OK to apply them.

How do I lock a guide line?

✔ Click the View menu and then click Lock Guides. This locks all the guide lines. To unlock the guides, click View, Unlock Guides.

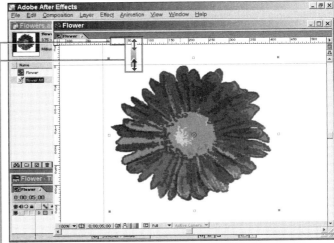

■3 Release the mouse button and the zero point is set.

■ To turn the rulers off again, you can click View, Hide Rulers.

SET A GUIDE LINE

■1 With the rulers displayed, move the mouse pointer (↕) over the vertical or horizontal ruler.

■2 Drag the guide to the window area.

■3 Release the mouse button.

■ The guide line positions.

■ A vertical guide already appears in this example.

■ To move a guide line, you can drag it to a new position onscreen.

TRIM FOOTAGE IN THE TIMELINE

You can trim the in and out points of a footage item in the After Effects Timeline window. The in and out points specify where a clip starts and stops. For example, you can trim a video clip to change the clip's duration or to edit out frames you do not want to appear in the project. You can also trim a still image clip or audio clip in the Timeline window.

Clips appear as layers in the Timeline window. You can employ several methods to trim a clip. You can manually adjust a clip's in and out points in the Time Graph area, or you can open the In and Out panel.

You can use the In and Out panel to edit a layer's in and out points. By default, After Effects hides the In and Out panel. Once you reveal the panel, however, it displays four related panels: In, Out, Duration, and Stretch. You can manually adjust the times for a clip by entering new values in these panels.

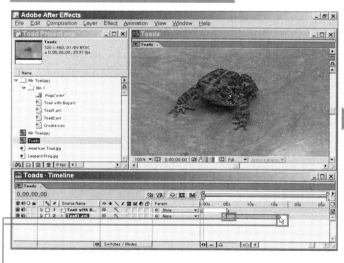

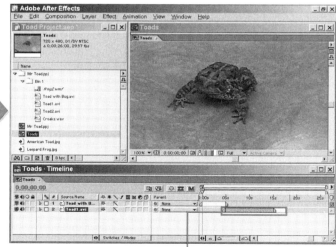

MANUALLY TRIM A CLIP

1 Click the layer you want to trim.

2 Drag the in or out point you want to trim.

Note: Trimming the layer's in point changes the layer's starting point in the composition.

Note: See Chapter 25 to learn how to trim footage in the Layer window.

3 Release the mouse button.

■ After Effects trims the clip.

What do the Duration and Stretch panels do?

✔ The Duration panel changes the clip's speed, thus its duration, but does not change the clip's out point. The Stretch panel change's the clip's speed to match the duration you set, either speeding up or slowing down the playback to match.

Can I move an entire layer in the Timeline without changing in and out points?

✔ Yes. Simply click and drag the layer to move it, then release the mouse button and the layer moves.

Can I customize which panels appear in the Timeline window?

✔ Yes. You can display and hide panels to reveal only the panels you work with the most. In addition to the default panels, you can find several optional panels, such as Comment, Mode, and Keys. To switch panels, right-click (Control-click) over a panel heading in the Timeline window to reveal a menu. Click Panels, and then click the panel you want to display or hide. A check mark next to the panel name means the panel is already displayed. No check mark means the panel is hidden.

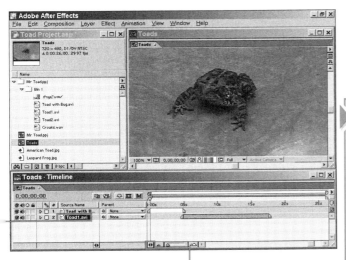

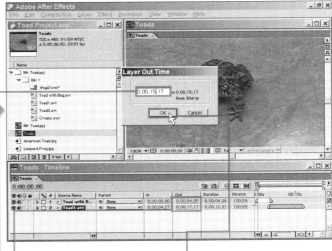

TRIM FOOTAGE USING THE IN AND OUT PANEL

■1 Click the layer you want to trim.

■2 Click the Optional Panel button (⬥).

■ The In and Out panel displays.

■3 Click the panel you want to edit.

■ The Layer In Time or Layer Out Time dialog box appears.

■4 Type a new in or out point setting.

■5 Click OK.

■ The clip layer moves to its new position in the Timeline.

■ To hide the panel again, click the Optional Panel button (⬥).

USING PROXIES AND PLACEHOLDERS

Y ou can use proxies and placeholders in your project to help speed up the time you spend assembling the project. In After Effects terminology, a *proxy* is simply a low-resolution version of the actual footage, while a *placeholder* is a stand-in for footage you plan to add later.

For example, you may need to start assembling the project while waiting on footage from another department or coworker. After

Effects allows you to substitute generic still images to use as temporary placeholders. When you create a placeholder, its name appears in italics in the Project window and the image is a standard color bar test pattern. You can reuse the placeholder as often as you want. Just be sure to assign the image the same dimensions and duration as the footage item with which you eventually intend to replace it.

Proxies, on the other hand, can help you speed up previewing tasks as you work on your composition. Previewing and rendering your composition consumes quite a bit of your computer's RAM. If your system has less than ideal RAM for processing video, you can choose to preview and render a lower resolution of the file, thus consuming less RAM.

USING PROXIES AND PLACEHOLDERS

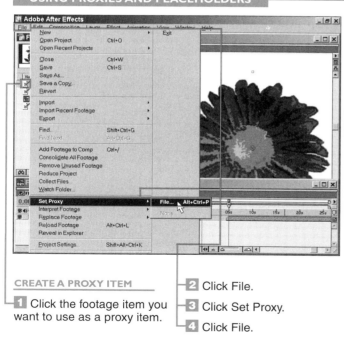

CREATE A PROXY ITEM

1 Click the footage item you want to use as a proxy item.

2 Click File.

3 Click Set Proxy.

4 Click File.

■ The Set Proxy File dialog box appears.

5 Click the file you want to use as a proxy file.

6 Click Open.

■ A black box (■) appears in front of the footage item name indicating the item is in use as a proxy.

Note: See Chapter 31 to preview and render a project.

How do I stop using the proxy and return to high resolution?

✔ Click the proxy item in the Project window, then click the File menu and click Set Proxy, None. This removes the proxy icon in front of the footage item name.

Is there a way to switch back and forth between proxy status and actual footage?

✔ Yes. You can click the black proxy icon in front of the footage item name in the Project window to toggle between high-resolution and low-resolution status.

How do I replace a placeholder with the actual footage item?

✔ Double-click the placeholder item in the Project window to open the Replace Footage dialog box. Click the actual source file you want to use, and then click Open. Every instance of the placeholder item is replaced with the source footage.

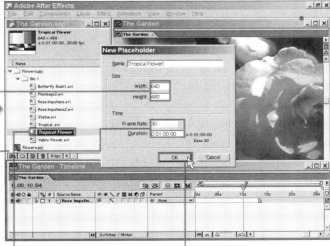

CREATE A PLACEHOLDER

1 Click File.

2 Click Import.

3 Click Placeholder.

■ The New Placeholder dialog box appears.

4 Type a name for the placeholder.

5 Type the size of the placeholder in pixels.

6 Type the duration for the placeholder.

7 Click OK.

■ The placeholder now appears in italics in the Project window, and you can insert it in place of actual footage.

SELECT LAYERS

You can select a layer in either the Timeline window or the Composition window. Each footage item you add to a composition appears as a layer in the Timeline as well as in the composition. You can select a layer to assign an effect, arrange it in another stacking order, or perform another editing technique.

When selecting a layer in the Composition window, you must remember that layers are stacked from front to back, where the topmost one is considered the front and the one on the bottom is considered the back. The topmost layer is easy to select, but selecting a layer at the back of the stack requires more effort. For that reason, you can more easily select

back layers using the Timeline window. After you select a layer in the Timeline window, its name appears highlighted.

When a layer is selected, selection or *layer handles* — tiny black squares — appear around the item in the Composition window. You can also select more than one layer at a time.

SELECT LAYERS

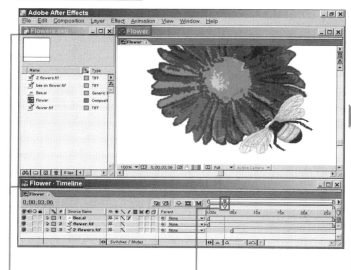

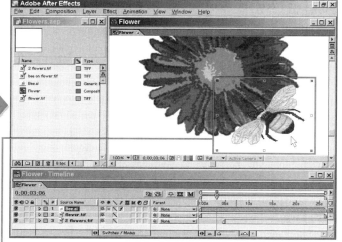

SELECT A LAYER IN THE COMPOSITION WINDOW

■ Open the composition containing the layer you want to work with.

Note: See Chapter 24 to create a composition.

■ Cue the Time marker to the frame to which you want to select a layer.

Note: See Chapter 24 to cue the Time marker.

■ Click the layer you want to select.

■ The layer is surrounded by layer handles and highlighted in the Timeline.

■ To select multiple layers, press and hold the Shift key while clicking layers.

■ To move a layer, drag it to a new position in the Timeline.

Can I select a layer by layer number?

✔ Yes. Layer numbers determine stacking order; Layer 1 represents the topmost layer. To select a layer, first click the Timeline window's title bar to make the window active and then type the layer number you want to select.

How do I select all the layers at once?

✔ Click the Edit menu and then click the Select All command. This immediately selects every layer in the composition. To deselect the layers, click an empty area in the Composition or Timeline window, or click the Edit menu and click Deselect All.

How do I select multiple layers without selecting all the layers?

✔ You can press and hold the Ctrl (Command) key down while clicking layer names in the Timeline window. To select adjacent layers, press and hold the Shift key while clicking layers. You can also drag a marquee box around the layers you want to select; simply drag around the layer names and a dotted line box — called a marquee — appears as you drag. Layer names inside the dotted lines are selected.

SELECT A LAYER IN THE TIMELINE WINDOW

1 Open the composition containing the layer you want to work with.

Note: See Chapter 24 to create a composition.

2 Cue the Time marker to the frame to which you want to select a layer.

Note: See Chapter 24 to cue the Time marker.

3 Click the layer you want to select.

■ The layer is highlighted in the Timeline and surrounded by layer handles in the composition.

■ To select multiple layers, press and hold the Shift key while clicking layers.

■ To move a layer, drag it to a new position in the Timeline.

NAVIGATE THE TIME GRAPH

You can use the time graph in the Timeline window to see a graphical representation of your composition layers as they relate to time and space. Each layer in the composition appears as a duration bar in the time graph, one layer per row. The vertical arrangement shows the layer stacking order, from top to bottom.

By default, the time graph shows the measurement of time in timecode, which displays frames per second. Zoom in closer to see the time frame by frame, or zoom out to view increments in seconds. See Chapter 23 to learn how to set another time display measurement.

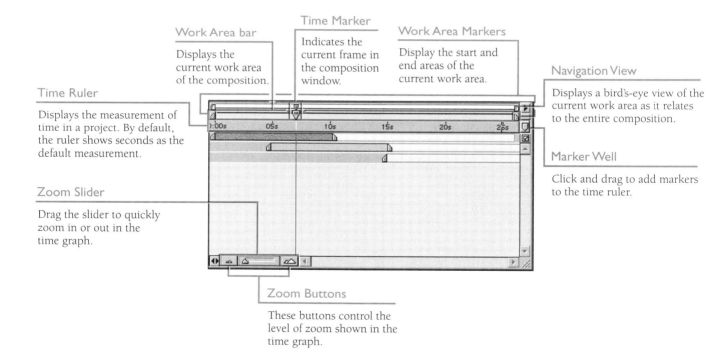

Work Area bar

Displays the current work area of the composition.

Time Marker

Indicates the current frame in the composition window.

Work Area Markers

Display the start and end areas of the current work area.

Navigation View

Displays a bird's-eye view of the current work area as it relates to the entire composition.

Time Ruler

Displays the measurement of time in a project. By default, the ruler shows seconds as the default measurement.

Marker Well

Click and drag to add markers to the time ruler.

Zoom Slider

Drag the slider to quickly zoom in or out in the time graph.

Zoom Buttons

These buttons control the level of zoom shown in the time graph.

VIEW FOOTAGE IN THE LAYER WINDOW

You can view a layer item in the Layer window to check its contents apart from the rest of the composition. When you open a layer through the Composition or Timeline window, a separate Layer window appears showing the footage. The Layer window includes controls for setting in and out points, cueing the footage to a specific frame, viewing specific color channels, and more.

For example, you can use the Layer window to edit a clip's in and out points in the same way you edit clips in Premiere. Trimming a clip in the Layer window enables you to see exactly where the clip starts and stops and to control the clip's duration. See Section III to learn more about editing video in Premiere.

The Layer window includes a time ruler as well as time displays for in and out points. If you open the Layer window for still image footage, the same editing controls appear.

Is it better to trim footage in the Layer window or the Footage window?

✔ You can trim footage in either window, or you can trim footage in the Timeline window. The method you choose is entirely up to you. To learn how to trim footage in the Timeline, see Chapter 24. To trim footage in the Layer window, see the section "Trim Footage in the Layer Window."

VIEW FOOTAGE IN THE LAYER WINDOW

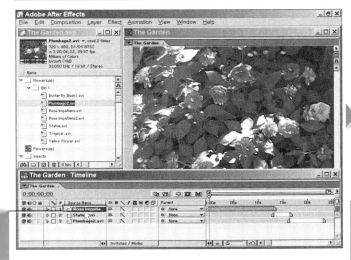

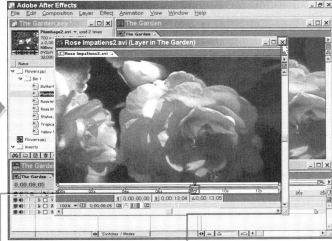

1 Double-click the layer you want to view.

Note: See Chapter 24 to create a composition.

■ The Layer window opens.

■ You can drag the Time marker, also called scrubbing, to play the footage; drag the marker left and right on the Timeline.

2 Click ✕ (☐) to close the window.

Note: See the next section, "Trim Footage in the Layer Window," to work with the Layer window.

TRIM FOOTAGE IN THE LAYER WINDOW

You can trim the in and out points of a footage item, also called a *clip*, in the After Effects Layer window. The in and out points specify where a clip starts and stops. For example, you can trim a video clip to change the clip's duration or to remove unwanted frames. You can also trim a still image clip or audio clip in the Layer window.

The Layer window shows three time displays: In Point, Out Point,

and Duration. You can use the Set In Point and Set Out Point buttons to edit a layer's in and out points. These editing functions work similarly to the way they do in Adobe Premiere, but the key to using them in After Effects is to cue the Time marker to the frame you want to trim first.

Can I manually trim a clip in the Layer window?

✔ Yes. Move the mouse pointer over the clip's in or out point on the ruler, then drag the point to a new location on the ruler to trim the clip.

TRIM FOOTAGE IN THE LAYER WINDOW

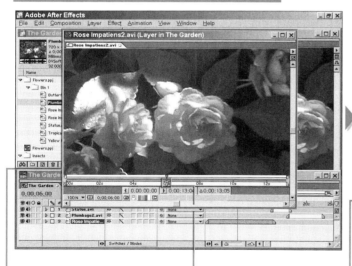

1 Open the Layer window for the layer you want to trim.

Note: See the section "View Footage in the Layer Window" to open the window.

2 Cue the Time marker to the spot where you want to set a new in or out point.

Note: See Chapter 24 to cue a Time marker.

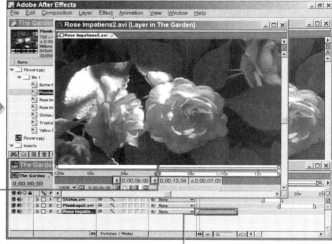

3 Click either the Set In Point (◄) or Set Out Point (►) button.

Note: Trimming the layer's in point changes the layer's starting point in the composition.

■ The new in or out point is assigned and the in or out point changes in the Timeline window.

SWITCH AUDIO/VIDEO ON OR OFF

You can turn a layer's audio and video on or off during previewing and rendering. This can save you RAM and processing power, particularly for elaborate projects you create in After Effects. Also, you may prefer to preview the composition without the audio playing, or hear the audio without the video.

The A/V Features panel appears at the far left end of the Timeline window. The A/V Features panel

includes switches for video and audio and a Solo button, which lets you to play a single layer, excluding all the other layers in the composition.

The A/V Features panel also includes a switch for hiding layers. Learn how to hide layers in the section "Create and Hide Shy Layers."

How do I hide the A/V Features panel?

✔ Click the Timeline Options Menu button (▶), located in the upper-right corner of the Timeline window. Click Panels and then click A/V Features to hide the panel. A check mark next to the panel name in the menu means the panel is in view; no check mark indicates that the panel is hidden.

SWITCH AUDIO/VIDEO ON OR OFF

■1 Click the layer you want to adjust.

Note: See Chapter 24 to add footage items to a composition.

■2 Click a switch.

■ Clicking here turns the video or image off.

■ Clicking here turns the audio off.

■ Clicking here makes the layer solo.

Note: See the section "Lock or Unlock Layers" to use the Lock switch.

■ The Composition window reflects the appropriate A/V switch.

Note: See Chapter 31 to preview and render a composition.

■ In this layer, the video is off.

■ In this layer, the audio is off.

CREATE AND HIDE SHY LAYERS

You can hide a layer from view by assigning it shy status. Shy layers do not appear in the Timeline window, enabling you to concentrate on only the layers with which you want to work.

Shy layers do appear in the Composition window, but in the Timeline window, where space is often tight, assigning shy layers makes it easier to scroll through the layers in your project because you can conceal shy layers and see only the layers you want to view.

After marking a layer as a shy layer, you must activate the Hide Shy Layers command to conceal the layers in the Timeline window. You can bring the layers back again when you want to view them.

How do I hide a layer in the Composition window?

✔ You can use the Video switch in the A/V Features panel of the Timeline window to hide a layer in the Composition window. Click the Video column for the layer you want to hide (☐ becomes ◉). To display the layer again, click the Video column again (◉ becomes ☐).

CREATE AND HIDE SHY LAYERS

CREATE A SHY LAYER

1 Click the layer to which you want to assign shy status.

Note: See the section "Select Layers" to make a layer active.

2 Click the Shy switch.

■ After Effects assigns the layer shy status (☐ becomes ◻).

Note: To unmark a shy layer, simply click ◻ again.

HIDE SHY LAYERS

1 Click the Hide Shy Layers button (◻).

■ All shy layers are immediately hidden from view in the Timeline.

Note: To view shy layers again, click ◻ again.

LOCK OR UNLOCK LAYERS

You can lock a layer in the Timeline window to prevent accidental edits. For example, you might lock a layer to keep it from moving in the layer stacking order.

You can lock and unlock layers using the Lock switch, one of the switches found in the A/V Features panel. See the section "Switch Audio/Video On or Off" to learn more about the A/V Features panel. See Chapter 24 to learn more about panels in the Timeline window.

If you lock a layer and then attempt to select it, the layer name blinks for a moment to indicate its locked status. In order to edit the layer again, you must unlock the layer.

MASTER IT

Can I unlock all the locked layers in my Timeline at once?

✔ Yes. You can use the Unlock All Layers command to quickly unlock all the locked layers in the Timeline window. With the Timeline window active, click Layer, Switches, and then click Unlock All Layers from the menu bar.

LOCK OR UNLOCK LAYERS

1 Click the layer you want to lock.

Note: See the section "Select Layers" to select a layer.

Note: See Chapter 24 to add footage items to a composition.

2 Click the Lock switch (☐ becomes 🔒).

■ The layer is now locked.

3 Click the locked layer's Lock switch (🔒 becomes ☐).

■ The layer is now unlocked.

INSERT OR OVERLAY A LAYER

When working with video footage, you can add a layer to the Timeline window using the Ripple Insert or Overlay commands found in the Footage window. The *ripple insert* technique enables you to insert the new layer by making the existing layers shift over to accommodate the new layer. The *overlay* technique adds the layer over existing layers and no shifting occurs.

For example, if the new footage item you want to add is 10 seconds long in duration and you use a ripple insert to add the layer to the top of the Timeline, all the other layers move over 10 seconds in the composition length. If you add the new layer to appear in the middle of another layer, the existing layer splits to make room for the 10 second footage.

The Timeline window's Time Graph shows exactly how the new layer affects existing layers around it. To learn more about using the Timeline window, see Chapter 24.

INSERT A LAYER

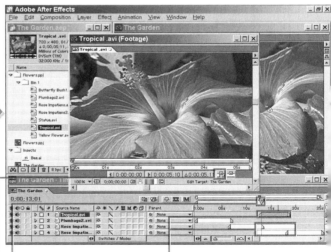

1 Open the composition to which you want to insert a layer.

Note: See Chapter 24 to create a composition.

2 Open the footage item you want to add in the Footage window.

Note: See Chapter 24 to view footage.

3 Cue the Time marker to where you want to insert a new layer.

Note: See Chapter 24 to cue the Time marker.

4 Click the Ripple Insert Edit button ( ).

■ The layer appears in the Timeline.

■ In this example, the new layer's addition splits an existing layer below, creating two new layers.

How do I set in and out points in the Footage window?

✔ Click the Set In Point button (🔳) to create an in point. To create an out point for the footage, click the Set Out Point button (🔳).

How do I display the Ripple Insert and Overlay buttons in my Footage window?

✔ Press and hold the Alt (Option) key and double-click over the footage item in the Project window. Doing this opens the footage in the After Effects Footage window, where you can now see the editing controls.

Can I perform a slip edit in After Effects?

✔ Yes. With After Effects 5.0, you can now perform a *slip edit*, a common nonlinear editing technique that moves a clip's start and end frames without affecting adjacent clips. Click the Pan Behind tool (🔳) in the toolbox, move the mouse over the layer (🔖 becomes 🔳), and then drag the clip left or right.

OVERLAY A LAYER

▐▌ Open the composition to which you want to overlay a layer.

Note: See Chapter 24 to create a composition.

▐▌ Open the footage item you want to add in the Footage window.

Note: See Chapter 24 to view footage.

▐▌ Cue the Time marker to the spot in which you want to overlay a new layer.

Note: See Chapter 24 to cue the Time marker.

▐▌ Click the Overlay Edit button (🔳).

▐▌ The layer appears in the Timeline.

RENAME A LAYER

You can name the layers you add to the Timeline window. By default, After Effects assigns the footage item name for the layer, but you can rename the layer to something else. For example, you may have a footage item you want to use more than once in a composition. You can use the layer as many times as you like and give each instance a unique name to help you identify it in the Timeline window.

By default, each layer includes a number and color label in the Timeline window. The layer number indicates the stacking order of the layer. Color labels represent another way to uniquely identify layers. Learn more about setting layer properties in Chapter 26.

Can I assign a different color label to a layer in the Timeline window?

✔ Yes. Select the layer, click the Edit menu, click Label, and then click the color you want to assign. Color labels are handy if you want to categorize related footage items in a composition.

RENAME A LAYER

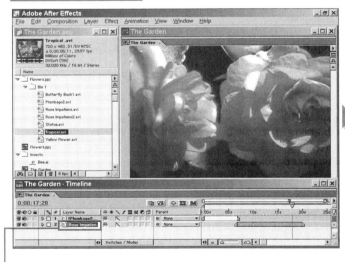

1 Click the layer you want to select.

Note: See Chapter 24 to add footage to a composition.

2 Press the Enter (Return) key.

■ After Effects highlights the layer name.

3 Type a new name for the layer.

4 Press the Enter (Return) key.

■ The new name takes effect.

CHANGE LAYER STACKING ORDER

You can rearrange the order of layers in the Timeline window to affect the stacking order of the layers in the Composition window. Every footage item you add to a composition appears as a layer in the Timeline window. The order in which you add the items and their placement in the Timeline determines the stacking order. After Effects assigns a number to each layer. Layer 1 appears at the top of the stack.

You can move the layers up or down to change the stacking order,

or you can move the layers left or right to change their arrangement in time. For example, if you move a layer to the bottom of the Timeline, the layer appears as the bottom layer in the composition.

Although you can move layers in the Composition window, the Timeline window lets you more quickly ascertain their order.

Can I change stacking order of layers in the Composition window?

✔ Yes. Select the layer in the Composition window, click the Layer menu, and then click Bring Layer to Front, Bring Layer Forward, Send Layer Backward, or Send Layer to Back. Although you can certainly rearrange the stacking order of smaller items in the Composition window either manually or using the Layer menu, larger layers that take up the window's on-screen space may be difficult to select to move. For that reason, you may want to manually move the layers in the Timeline window.

CHANGE LAYER STACKING ORDER

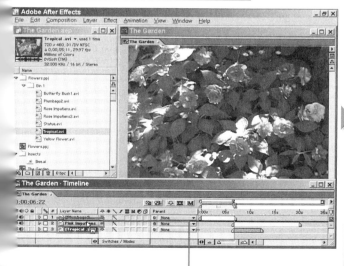

■ Click the layer you want ■ move.

Note: See the section "Select layers" to select a layer.

2 Drag the layer name up or down.

■ A thick, black line indicates the layer's current position.

3 Release the mouse button to place the layer.

Note: To undo your last edit, click Undo from the Edit menu.

CREATE A SOLID LAYER

You can create a solid layer to use as a background or as a simple four-sided graphic element in your composition. You can treat solid layers just like other layers in After Effects, assigning properties, effects, and masks.

You can assign a specific size and color to a solid layer. For example, you may decide to add a green

square behind a still image, or use a rectangle shape as a mask. Using the Solid Settings dialog box, you can control the dimensions of the solid layer as well as the units used to define the layer. By default, After Effects assigns pixels as the unit measurement, but you can specify inches, millimeters, or a percentage instead.

To assign a color to the solid layer, you must open the Color dialog box, which displays a palette of colors from which to choose. After you create a solid layer, you can return to the Solid Settings and Color dialog boxes to edit the dimensions and color at any time.

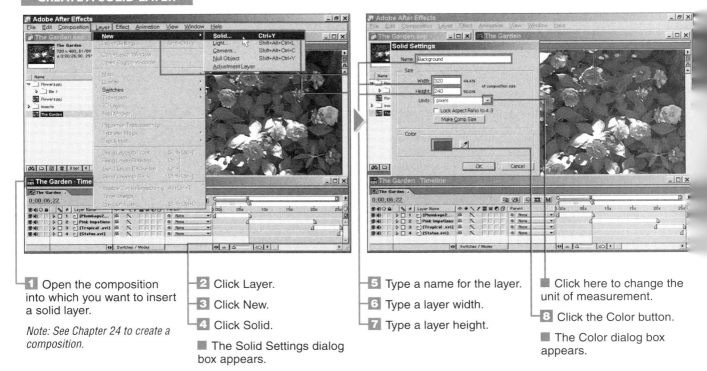

1 Open the composition into which you want to insert a solid layer.

Note: See Chapter 24 to create a composition.

2 Click Layer.

3 Click New.

4 Click Solid.

■ The Solid Settings dialog box appears.

5 Type a name for the layer.

6 Type a layer width.

7 Type a layer height.

■ Click here to change the unit of measurement.

8 Click the Color button.

■ The Color dialog box appears.

How do I create an adjustment layer instead of a solid layer?

✔ An *adjustment layer* contains only effects, with no footage or solid color. You can use adjustment layers to assign effects to all layers below the adjustment layer in the Timeline. You can also import adjustment layers created in Photoshop to use in After Effects. To create an adjustment layer, open the composition to which you want to add the layer, and click the Layer menu, New, and then Adjustment Layer. To learn more about adjustment layers, see Chapter 4 in the Photoshop section of this book.

Is there an easy way to make the new layer the same size as my composition?

✔ Yes. Click the Make Comp Size button in the Solid Settings dialog box to make the new layer the same size as the composition itself.

How do I assign a color that already appears in my composition?

✔ You can click the Eyedropper button (⬚) in the Solid Settings dialog box and then click the on-screen color you want to assign to the solid layer.

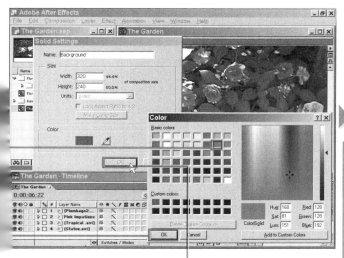

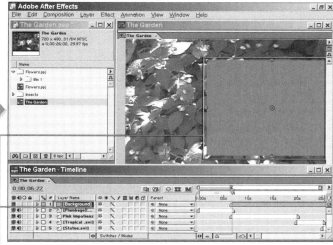

9 Click a color.

0 Click OK.

11 Click OK again to close the Solid Settings dialog box.

■ After Effects places the layer in the composition.

CREATE MARKERS

You can add markers to your project to mark important points, such as a particular frame you want to synchronize or a point in the project where a musical beat occurs. After Effects uses two kinds of markers: composition-time and layer-time.

Composition-time markers can help you with the arrangement of your composition by identifying key areas for editing. Composition markers are numbered. You can create up to ten composition-time markers to the Timeline window's time ruler or within a composition. Markers are numbered in the order in which you add them.

Layer-time markers are tiny triangle icons that appear on the layer duration bar. You can add comment text to layer-time markers. The text label appears when you hover your mouse pointer over the triangle icon. Because markers are only used for editing, they do not appear in previews or the export file.

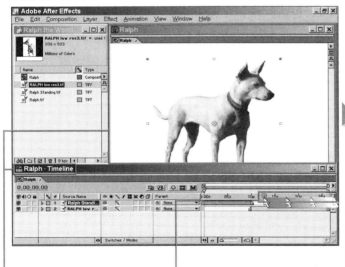

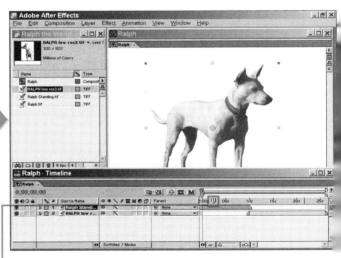

1 Open the composition to which you want to add a marker.

Note: See Chapter 24 to create a composition.

2 Drag a marker from the Composition Marker Well.

3 Drop it on the Timeline.

■ A numbered marker appears.

Can I move a marker?

✔ Yes. Simply click and drag the marker to place it in a new location on the Timeline. You can drag both composition-time and layer-time markers to move them to a new position.

How do I remove a marker?

✔ To remove a composition-time marker, click and drag it off the Timeline window. To remove a layer-time marker, press and hold the Ctrl (Command) key and move the mouse pointer over the marker. The becomes ✂. Click the marker to remove it.

How do I move the Time marker to a specific marker?

✔ Simply type the number of the marker you want to jump to in the Timeline window using the number keys on the main keyboard. This technique does not work, however, with numbers pressed on the numeric keypad.

My project shows markers I did not add. Where did they come from?

✔ If you imported a video project from Premiere, the markers you assigned in Premiere copy over when you import the file into After Effects.

CREATE A LAYER-TIME MARKER

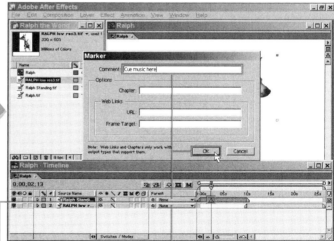

1 Click the layer to which you want to add a marker.

2 Click Layer.

3 Click Add Marker.

■ A marker appears on the layer's duration bar.

4 Double-click the marker.

■ The Marker dialog box appears.

5 Type any comment text you want to assign to the marker.

6 Click OK.

■ The text label appears with the marker on the layer's duration bar.

ARRANGE LAYERS IN A SEQUENCE

You can use the Sequence Layers keyframe assistant to help you arrange layers in a *sequence* for your project. A sequence simply places layers one right after the other in the Timeline. Where one layer ends, another begins. In the time graph area, the layers appear stair-stepped across time.

You can also specify an overlap, if you wish, so that each layer overlaps another by a set number of frames. With overlapping layers, you can also specify how you want each layer to transition into the other using a cut or crossfade effect.

To sequence a layer, the layer's duration must be less than the

composition's duration so that room exists in the program length to sequence other layers. You may need to trim your layers before using the Sequence Layers feature. See the section "Trim Footage in the Layer Window" to learn more.

ARRANGE LAYERS IN A SEQUENCE

1 Select the layers you want to sequence.

Note: See the section "Select Layers" to select layers in the Timeline window.

2 Click Animation.

3 Click Keyframe Assistant.

4 Click Sequence Layers.

■ The Sequence Layers dialog box appears.

What do the crossfade options do?

✔ The crossfade options in the Sequence Layers dialog box are only available if you choose to overlap layers in your sequence. The options listed in the Crossfade list control how layers transition. If you choose Front Layer Only, the end of each layer fades out. If you choose Front and Back Layers, a fade out is added at both ends of each layer.

How do I set a duration for a still image in my sequence?

✔ If the file is already imported, you can double-click it in the Timeline window to open the image in the Layer window. You can then set in and out points to set a duration time for the image. See the section "Trim Footage in the Layer Window" to learn how.

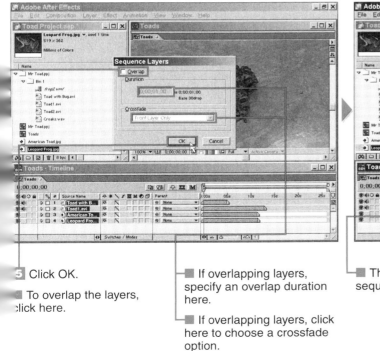

5 Click OK.

■ To overlap the layers, click here.

■ If overlapping layers, specify an overlap duration here.

■ If overlapping layers, click here to choose a crossfade option.

■ The selected layers are sequenced in the Timeline.

UNDERSTANDING LAYER PROPERTIES

You can assign a variety of values to your project layers. Layer properties control visual and audio characteristics. After Effects groups layer properties into three main types: masks, effects, and transform. If your project features audio, audio properties is an additional property type to which you can assign values. By assigning different values to these property types, you can create different looks and effects for a layer.

You can animate a layer by changing its layer properties in either the Composition or Layer window. You can access property controls through the switches in the Timeline window, or through the Layer menu.

Listed in an expandable/collapsible format in the Timeline window, you directly enter values into the property settings. Alternatively, you can drag or scrub a value. *Scrubbable hot text* is a new feature that enables you to change a setting value by dragging the mouse

pointer directly over the value setting. Drag right to increase the value setting or drag left to decrease the value. You can also enter values using dialog boxes.

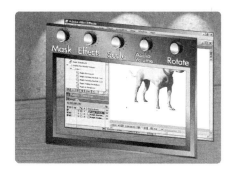

Masks

A *mask layer* enables you to view or conceal portions of underlying layers or apply effects to only certain areas on layers. You create masks with paths built from line segments and control points. Control points define where path segments start and stop. You can apply multiple masks to a layer. You can also animate masks over time. Learn more about working with masks in Chapter 28.

Effects

You can use *effect properties* to make minor adjustments to a layer, such as color correction, or you can use them to create more complex changes, such as distorting the image. You can assign keying effects to build composite images or transition effects to specify how layers blend into each other. Learn more about working with effects in Chapter 29.

Transform

Transform properties include such basics as rotating, scaling, and opacity. In previous versions of After Effects, these properties were known as geometrics, but in After Effects 5, they are called transform properties. You can assign transform properties regardless of whether you plan to assign masks or effect properties to the layer later. Each layer you add starts with default transform properties. You can change the properties to control the appearance of the layer in the composition. Learn more about assigning these properties to layers in the remainder of this chapter.

Audio Properties

If a layer contains audio, or the layer is audio-only, you can view and alter the audio properties. *Audio properties* include settings for volume and the display of the audio waveform — a graphical representation of the sound in the Timeline window. Learn more about setting audio properties later in this chapter.

VIEW LAYER PROPERTIES

You can quickly view layer properties in the Timeline window. Much like an outline or folder list, you can expand layer properties to view various settings and collapse the list to close the view.

For example, if you expand the layer outline and expand the Transform properties, you find and change the anchor point, position, scale, rotation, and opacity properties. New to After Effects 5, the values are *scrubbable hot-text*,

denoted with a dotted line, which means you can drag the value setting to reset it.

You can set a property value for the entire duration of the layer, or you can set different values at different points using keyframes. After Effects marks *Global values*, which remain unchanged, with an I-beam icon in the time graph area, and *animated values*, which change at key points, with a diamond icon and a stopwatch icon next to the property name.

I do not see the audio property. Why not?

✔ You can only see a listing for the audio property if the layer includes audio or is an audio-only footage item. The audio property is not available for still-image footage items.

VIEW LAYER PROPERTIES

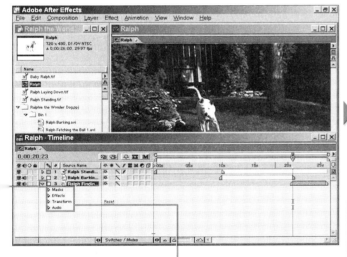

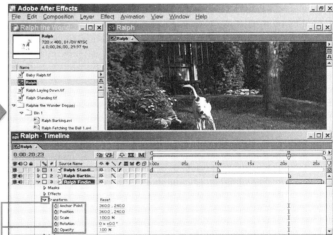

1 Click the Expand arrow (▷) for the layer in which you want to view properties (▷ changes to ▽).

Note: See Chapter 25 to learn how to work with layers.

■ The layer expands to reveal layer property types.

2 Click the property type Expand arrow (▷) for the layer in which you want to view property settings.

■ The layer expands to reveal layer properties.

Note: See the remaining sections to learn how to set various property values.

■ You can click the property type Collapse arrow (▽) to collapse the layer level.

VIEW SPATIAL CONTROLS

A s you work with layers in the Composition window, you can use controls to handle spatial properties of any given layer. Spatial controls include layer handles, keyframes, paths, and more.

You can display different layer controls based on the task at hand. For example, to edit the position of a layer as it changes over time, you can view only the Layer Paths controls and toggle the other controls off.

You access spatial controls via the Comp Window Options menu, which you can find on the Composition window. You can quickly assess which controls to toggle on or off; active controls are checked while inactive controls are not.

The Layer Handles control surrounds a selected layer, and when dragged, scales the layer in size. The Layer Paths control helps you to see how a layer changes position over time when you use it in a motion path. The Layer Keyframes control shows keyframe positions for a layer. The Layer Tangent control allows you to edit the curve of a layer's motion path. The Layer Masks control enables you to crop out parts of a layer. The Effect Controls display the spatial controls of assigned effects.

VIEW SPATIAL CONTROLS

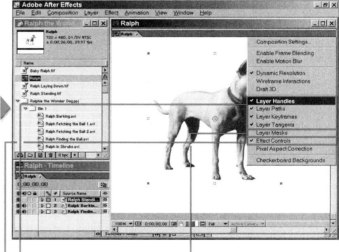

■1 Click the Comp Window Options button (▶).

Note: See Chapter 24 to learn how to create a composition.

■ The Comp Window Options menu appears.

■2 Click the spatial control you want to toggle off or on.

■ A check mark (☑) next to a control name indicates the control is active.

■ No check mark next to a control name indicates the control is not active.

CHANGE THE LAYER ANCHOR POINT

You can use an anchor point as a base to change the position, scale, or orientation of a layer in the Composition window. The anchor point appears as a tiny circle icon with an X in the middle.

By default, After Effects assigns the very center of the layer as the anchor point. You can change the

anchor point to scale the layer to a new size or to move the anchor point in order to animate the layer from one end. For example, to animate a magic wand so it looks like it is shaking on one end only, you must move the layer's anchor point to appear at the end of the wand instead of the middle of the image.

How do I scrub the anchor point value setting?

✔ You can change a layer's anchor point by displaying the Anchor Point property in the Timeline window. Expand the layer properties until you see the Anchor Point property. Then drag the x-axis (left) or y-axis (right) value to a new setting. As you drag, the anchor point moves, in increments of pixels, in the Composition window. See the section "View Layer Properties" to learn how to expand layer properties.

CHANGE THE LAYER ANCHOR POINT

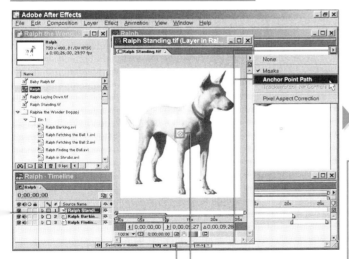

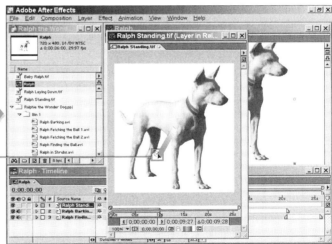

■1 Double-click the layer you want to edit.

Note: You can double-click the layer name in the Timeline window, or double-click the layer in the Composition window.

■ The Layer window opens.

■ The anchor point (⊗) appears here.

Note: See Chapter 25 to learn more about working with the Layer window.

■2 Click the Layer Window Options button (▶).

■3 Click Anchor Point Path.

■4 Drag the anchor point to the desired location (⊗ changes to ▶).

■ The anchor point resets.

CHANGE LAYER POSITION

You can reposition a layer to move it up or down in the composition, to better adjust it in a mask, or to create an interesting effect. After Effects references layer position, expressed in x, y coordinates, by where you first placed the footage item in the composition. If you drag the item to the Timeline window, the layer centers in the composition. If you drag the item to the Composition window, the layer inserts where you drop it.

You can move a layer around in the composition window as well as position it outside the composition — in the pasteboard, or work space, area. For example, you may place the layer half in and half out of the composition window and apply an animation effect that moves it into the window and out the other side.

Can I use the Position property value to move a layer?

✔ Yes. You can expand the layer's properties and drag the Position property's x or y coordinate to reposition the layer. New to After Effects, you can use this technique, called *scrubbing*, to quickly change values for all the layer properties in the Timeline window.

CHANGE LAYER POSITION

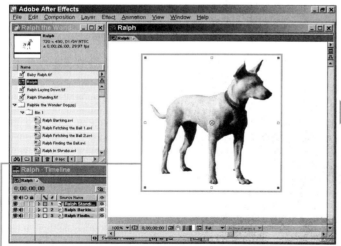

1 Click the layer you want to edit.

■ Handles surround the layer.

Note: See Chapter 25 to learn more about selecting layers.

2 Drag the layer to a new location on the composition (☐ becomes ▶).

■ The layer repositions.

CHANGE THE LAYER SCALE

You can resize a layer to make it larger or smaller than its original size. By default, After Effects keeps all layers at 100 percent of the original, imported size. You can resize the layer to fit your project's needs. For example, you might make a still image smaller to animate it across a motion path.

As you scale a layer, it resizes around its anchor point. See the section "Change the Layer

Anchor Point" to learn how to move the anchor point to another position in the layer.

When working with a layer, keep in mind that scaling a bitmap image more than 100 percent of its original size can cause the image to look as if it has jagged edges. If you scale a path-based image, such as a file created in Illustrator, you can use the Continuously Rasterize switch to keep its quality.

How do I use the Continuously Rasterize switch?

✔ After Effects *rasterizes*, or converts, vector-based files into bitmaps, which are pixel-based. If you plan to scale the image, turn on the Collapse Transformations/ Continuously Rasterize switch (🔆) in the Timeline window to keep rasterizing the image and maintain image quality (🔲 becomes 🔆).

CHANGE THE LAYER SCALE

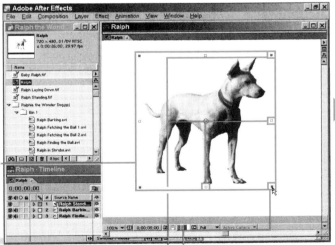

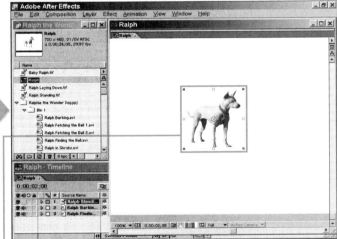

■1 Click the layer you want to edit.

■ Handles surround the layer.

Note: See Chapter 25 to learn more about selecting layers.

■2 Drag a layer handle to scale the layer.

■ Drag a corner handle to scale both horizontally and vertically.

■ Drag a middle handle to scale horizontally or vertically only.

■ The layer resizes.

Note: To access the Scale dialog box where you can type scaling values manually, click the Layer menu, click Transform, then click Scale.

ROTATE A LAYER

You can rotate a layer in a two-dimensional space. For example, you might rotate an image upside down to use in an animation path.

After Effects bases rotation on absolute positioning and measures it in degrees. Positive values rotate the layer in a clockwise direction while negative values rotate the layer counterclockwise. By default, After Effects sets the rotation value for a layer to 0. If you change the value to 180, the layer appears upside down.

Layer rotation pivots an image based on its anchor point. See the section "Change the Layer Anchor Point" to learn how to move the anchor point to another position in the layer.

The easiest way to rotate a layer is to use the scrubbable hot text feature. With this feature, you can drag the layer property values in the Timeline window to new settings. You can see the value changes immediately in the Composition window.

Can I open a rotation dialog box?

✔ Yes. Click the layer you want to edit, then click the Layer menu, click Transform, and click Z Rotation. This opens the Rotate dialog box where you can type in values for Revolutions and Degrees.

ROTATE A LAYER

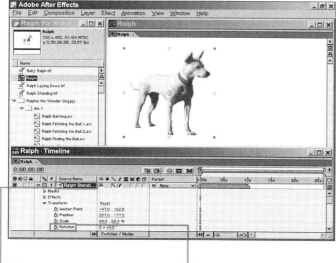

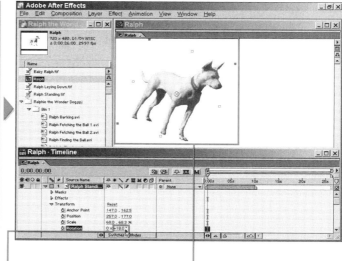

1 Click the layer you want to edit.

■ Handles surround the layer.

2 Expand the layer's properties to view the Rotation property.

Note: See the section "View Layer Properties" to learn how to display layer properties in the Timeline.

3 Drag the Rotation property to a new value setting.

■ The layer rotates.

CHANGE LAYER OPACITY

You can change the *opacity*, or degree of transparency, of a layer. By default, After Effects makes all layers 100 percent opaque, which means the layer is completely visible. You can reset this value to make the layer appear transparent or completely invisible.

Changing a layer's opacity property affects the overall layer. This differs from creating a matte or keying effect to make areas of a layer transparent. You can learn more

about masking and keying in Chapters 27 and 28.

The easiest way to change opacity is to use the scrubbable hot text feature. With this feature, you can drag the layer property values in the Timeline window to new settings. You can see the value changes immediately in the Composition window.

Can I manually set opacity in the Composition window?

✔ No. Opacity is the one property that you cannot control with the handles in the Composition window or with a toolbox tool. You can, however, click the Layer, click Transform, and then click Opacity to open the Opacity dialog box, where you can type a value for opacity.

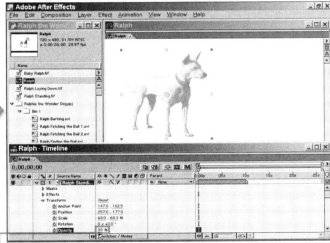

1 Click the layer you want to edit.

■ Handles surround the layer.

2 Expand the layer's properties to view the Opacity property.

Note: See the section "View Layer Properties" to learn how to display layer properties in the Timeline.

3 Drag the Opacity property to a new value setting.

Note: You cannot scrub the value to a setting beyond 100 percent.

■ After Effects applies the new setting.

VIEW AUDIO WAVEFORMS

You can view audio waveforms for a footage clip that contains audio or for an audio-only footage item. Waveforms, graphical representations of a sound, display in the time graph located in the Timeline window. Waveforms include both a left and right audio channel. The left channel appears above the right channel. You may find it helpful to view waveforms to note where key music beats occur or where a sound synchronizes with another layer.

The amount of detail in your view of waveforms depends on the zoom level in effect for the time graph. Zooming in displays a closer look at the waveform detail, for example. You can also view more of the waveform's details by resizing the waveform track border to increase the size of the waveform display. Changing the track size does not affect the sound level in any way.

See the next section, "Set Audio Properties," to learn how to set audio layer properties.

Is there a way to emphasize or de-emphasize sounds in an audio layer?

✔ After Effects includes several audio effects, including the Stereo Mixer, which you can use to control sound levels and pan channels. See Chapter 29 to learn more about adding audio effects to your project.

VIEW AUDIO WAVEFORMS

■1 Click the layer you want to edit.

■2 Expand the layer's properties to view the Audio property.

■3 Expand the Audio property.

Note: See the section "View Layer Properties" to learn how to display layer properties in the Timeline.

■4 Expand the Waveform property to view the waveforms.

■ Left and right channel waveforms appear in the Timeline.

■ To better view the waveform track, drag the track's bottom border down to increase the size of the track display.

■ You can also click the time graph zoom buttons to zoom your view of the waveforms.

SET AUDIO PROPERTIES

You can set properties for audio you add to your project. Whether the audio is part of a footage item or an audio-only file you imported, you can control channel decibel levels for left or right channels, or both at the same time. For example, you may need to lower the volume for a layer.

You can use the Audio palette to quickly set audio levels for a layer. The palette works much like a traditional audio mixing board in that you can drag sliders up or down to adjust sound level. The Audio palette shares space with the Time Controls palette.

You can also view the audio as a waveform in the Timeline window. The waveform shows both left and right channels. See the previous section to learn how to view the audio's waveforms.

How do I change the VU meter scale to percentage instead of decibels?

✓ With the Audio palette open, click the Options button ( ). This opens the Audio Options dialog box. Click the Percentage unit and click OK.

SET AUDIO PROPERTIES

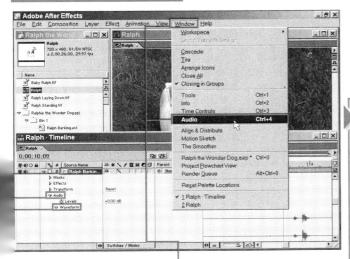

1 Click the layer you want to edit.

2 Expand the layer's properties to view the Audio and Waveform property.

Note: See "View Layer Properties" to display layer properties in the Timeline.

3 Click Window.

4 Click Audio.

■ The Audio palette opens.

5 Drag a channel slider to set the audio level.

■ Drag the left slider ( ) to change the left channel audio level.

■ Drag the center slider ( ) to change both left and right channel audio levels.

■ Drag the right slider ( ) to change the right channel audio level.

6 Click × ( ).

■ The palette closes and your audio properties change to your specifications.

ADD KEYFRAMES

You can use *keyframes* in After Effects to animate a layer in a composition. Keyframes mark key changes in the layer properties. Suppose, for example, that you want to make the layer image appear to move across the screen. To do so, you add keyframes to every spot in the Timeline where you want a movement to occur, and then change the layer position properties for each keyframe.

Keyframing is an essential technique for animating. With the

addition of keyframes, you can create animation effects such as making an image rotate, grow larger or smaller, change color or shape, and more.

The placement of keyframes in the Timeline determines the amount of time that occurs before the layer changes. If you add a keyframe to the beginning of the layer duration and another at the end, the layer makes only one change during the time the layer plays in your video. If you add numerous keyframes between the layer's start and end

times, you can animate numerous changes at a faster pace.

You can view keyframes in both the Timeline and Composition windows. After adding keyframes, you can move them to new positions in the Timeline or select them to change properties. If you move a keyframe in the Composition window, After Effects automatically moves it in the Timeline window as well, and vice versa.

ADD KEYFRAMES

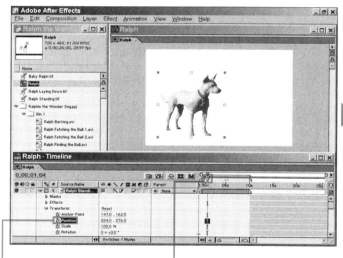

1 With the Composition window open, expand the property you want to change and animate.

Note: See Chapter 26 to view layer properties.

2 Cue the Time marker to the spot where you want to create a keyframe change.

3 Click the Stopwatch icon (🕑) in front of the property you want to change.

Note: See Chapter 26 to set layer properties.

■ A keyframe icon (◆) appears on the Timeline.

4 Change the property value.

How do I remove a keyframe?

✔ Click the keyframe in the time graph and then press Delete. Make sure the keyframe you plan to delete is no longer needed in the animation sequence. To check the keyframe's appearance in the composition, cue the Time marker to the keyframe to view the layer image in the Composition window.

Why do I see circle icons instead of keyframe icons on the Timeline?

✔ If you collapse the property to which you have assigned keyframes, the keyframes appear as circle icons in the Timeline. Expand the property again to view the diamond-shaped keyframe icons. If all the layer properties are collapsed, you cannot see keyframe icons.

Is there another way to view keyframe icons?

✔ You can toggle between viewing keyframe icons as diamond shapes or as numbered indices. Click the Timeline window's Timeline Options Menu button (▶) and click either Use Keyframe Icons or Use Keyframe Indices.

How do I move a keyframe?

✔ Click and drag the keyframe icon (◆) left or right in the time graph to change its position in the Timeline.

5 Cue the Time marker to where you want to create a keyframe change.

6 Change the property value again.

■ A keyframe icon is added to the Timeline to mark the change.

7 Continue adding keyframes to complete the animation for the layer.

■ You can now play the footage to see the animation in action.

Note: To see the keyframe changes, play the composition footage. See Chapter 31 to preview movies.

EDIT A KEYFRAME

As you add keyframes to a composition property to create animation effects, you can perform edits on individual keyframes. For example, you may need to remove a keyframe you no longer need or move a keyframe's position in the Timeline.

You can edit keyframes directly in the Timeline window, or you can view and edit keyframes in the Composition window. The method

you use is a matter of personal preference and the type of animation you assigned. If you created an animated motion path for the layer, for example, you may find it easier to edit the keyframes on the path directly in the Composition window because After Effects displays the path onscreen. For other types of keyframe effects, you may find selecting and editing keyframes in the Timeline window easier.

If you do prefer editing keyframes in the Composition window, you may need to turn some of the other spatial controls off in the Composition window to view the keyframes more easily. See Chapter 26 to learn more about viewing spatial properties in the Composition window.

EDIT A KEYFRAME

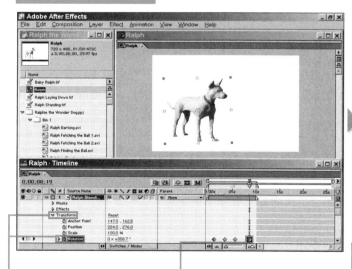

EDIT A KEYFRAME IN THE TIMELINE WINDOW

1 Click ▶ to expand the property containing the keyframe you want to edit.

Note: See the previous section to add keyframes.

2 Click the keyframe.

Note: To adjust multiple keyframes, press the Shift key while clicking keyframes.

3 Edit the keyframe.

■ Drag the keyframe to a new position to move the keyframe.

■ Press Delete to remove the keyframe.

■ If needed, change the property settings.

Note: See Chapter 16 to learn more about changing layer properties.

I want to move my layer in time. Will the assigned keyframes move with the layer?

✔ Yes. Anytime you move the layer in the Timeline, either to a different stacking order or to a new position in time, any keyframes assigned to the layer automatically move with the layer.

If I changed the wrong keyframe, how do I return the keyframe properties?

✔ Click Undo from the Edit menu to immediately undo any changes you made to the selected keyframe.

I trimmed a layer clip that had keyframes assigned. Are the keyframes trimmed, too?

✔ No. Any keyframes that extend beyond the in or out point of a footage item are not trimmed when you trim the item. If the keyframe shows a key change beyond the in or out point, however, you cannot see it during playback or rendering. Starting or ending a keyframe outside the frame, however, can help you create smooth motions for an animated effect.

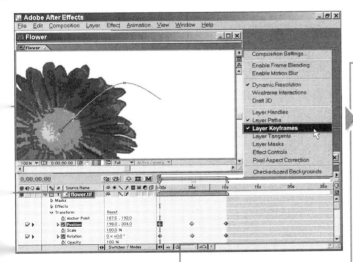

EDIT A KEYFRAME IN THE COMPOSITION WINDOW

1 Click the layer containing the keyframes you want to edit.

Note: See the previous section to add keyframes.

2 Click the Comp Window Options button (▶).

3 Make sure that the Layer Keyframes control is selected.

Note: Turn off other spatial controls to better see the keyframes.

■ Keyframes appear as x's on the layer.

4 Edit the keyframe.

■ Drag the keyframe to a new position to move the keyframe.

■ Press the Delete key to remove the keyframe.

UNDERSTANDING KEYFRAME INTERPOLATION

To understand more about how keyframes work in animating your composition layers, you need to know about *interpolation*. When you assign two or more keyframes to a layer property and change the property over time, After Effects calculates the changes for you. This process is called interpolation in After Effects. You may recognize it by another name, *tweening*, in other animation programs.

With interpolation, After Effects makes and performs all the calculations necessary to cause the layer image to change from one keyframe to the next keyframe, ensuring that all the in-between phases occur to morph or change the property. If no change occurs from one keyframe to the next, the value you assigned in the first keyframe repeats.

Spatial Interpolation

After Effects refers to changes that are calculated when a layer changes position in space as *spatial interpolation*. Those changes may take a direct path from point A to point B, or they may follow a curved path.

When you edit an animated layer's motion path, After Effects applies spatial interpolation. Only the path itself is calculated, not the speed of the animation. After Effects enables spatial controls changing the following properties: position, anchor point, effect point, and 3D orientation.

Temporal Interpolation

Rate of change values that occur between two keyframes over time are referred to as *temporal interpolation* in After Effects. Instead of calculating a path, temporal interpolation calculates whether change occurs at a constant rate or an accelerated or decelerated rate. You can control temporal interpolation for all layer properties.

Interpolation Graphs

You can view how spatial and temporal interpolation occurs over the space of time by viewing the property's graph. For example, if you assign keyframes to the position property of a layer and change the layer's position over time, you can expand the position property to view a graph of the changes.

Interpolation graphs give you a quick picture of how the changes occur from keyframe to keyframe. The next section shows you how to view property graphs.

VIEW PROPERTY GRAPHS

You can view a graph of interpolation changes over time for any property to which you have assigned keyframes. The interpolation graphs appear in the Timeline window incorporated into the time graph area.

As a property changes from one keyframe to the next, After Effects graphs the change with lines marking ups and downs in the value setting. Larger values create peaks

on the graph, while smaller values create valleys. You can even drag a point on the charted property to change the value setting.

Property graphs are expandable and collapsible. You can also view more than one property graph at a time. To learn more about expanding and collapsing properties in the Timeline window and changing property values, see Chapter 26.

How do I change a property value in the graph?

✔ Click the Selection tool button (![]) in the toolbox and then drag a keyframe up or down to change the value. If the toolbox is not displayed, click Window, then Tools to open the tools.

Can I add keyframes to a property graph?

✔ Yes. With the property value graph displayed, click the Pen tool (![]) in the toolbox. Move the Pen tool over the line where you want to insert a new keyframe and click. To turn off the Pen tool, click the Selection tool button (![]).

VIEW PROPERTY GRAPHS

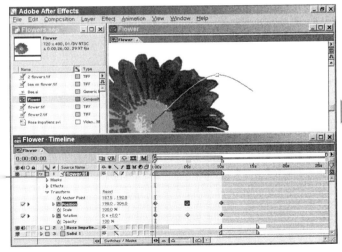

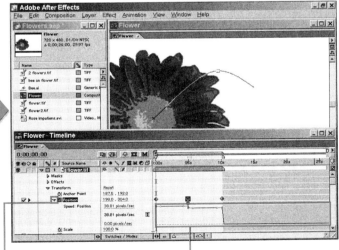

1 Expand the layer containing the property you assigned keyframes to.

Note: See Chapter 26 to learn more about expanding and collapsing layer properties.

2 Expand the property containing keyframes.

■ The property graph is displayed.

DRAW A MOTION PATH

Although you can certainly plot out a path to animate a layer keyframe by keyframe, you may find it easier to draw the path in the Composition window. You can do so using the Motion Sketch feature.

A *motion path* defines the direction in which a layer is moved, creating an animation effect. You draw the

path you want the layer to animate to, and After Effects takes care of the rest by adding keyframes for you. The path can be straight or curvy and can go in any direction you like. The Motion Sketch path does not interfere with other keyframes assigned to other layer properties. Rather, the motion path you establish affects only the position layer.

Before you start drawing a path, you can specify a few settings in the Motion Sketch palette. You can set a capture speed based on how fast you draw. You can also choose to view a wireframe of the layer as you sketch the path or keep the background in view so you can direct the path based on other layers in the composition.

DRAW A MOTION PATH

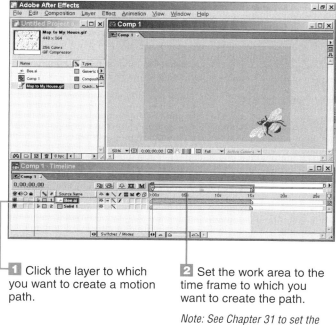

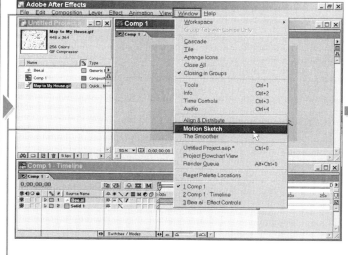

1 Click the layer to which you want to create a motion path.

2 Set the work area to the time frame to which you want to create the path.

Note: See Chapter 31 to set the work area.

3 Click Window.

4 Click Motion Sketch.

■ The Motion Sketch palette opens.

Can I edit keyframes in a drawn motion path?

✔ Yes, but you need to zoom your view of the time graph so that you can see the individual keyframes that make up the path. To edit a keyframe, first click the keyframe and then change the properties.

How do I undo a path I just drew?

✔ Immediately after you draw the path, click Edit and then Undo. After Effects removes the path.

What capture speed should I set?

✔ If you type a capture speed value greater than 100%, it sets the playback faster than the sketching speed. A value less than 100% sets the playback speed slower than the sketching speed.

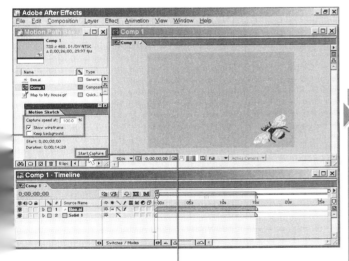

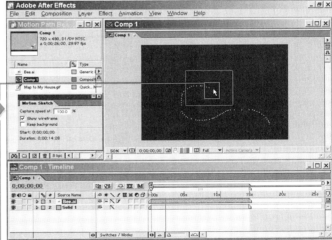

5 Set any options you want to assign to the path.

■ Type in a percentage value to define the capture and playback speed.

■ Click the top check box if you want to see wireframes of the layer image as you draw (☐ changes to ☑).

■ Click the bottom check box if you want to see the background layers as you draw (☐ changes to ☑).

6 Click Start Capture.

7 Draw the path in the Composition window by holding down the mouse button and dragging the mouse pointer.

■ When you release the mouse, the path is set.

Note: To see the layer follow the path, click the ▶ in the Time Controls palette. Learn more about previewing and playback in Chapter 31.

ORIENT A LAYER ALONG A MOTION PATH

You can use the Auto-Orient feature to orient layers along a motion path in your composition. By default, a layer image follows a motion path always maintaining its original orientation. For example, perhaps you have a layer image of a bee and a motion path that makes the bee seem to fly around the screen in different directions. No matter which

direction the path takes, however, the bee always maintains its original orientation, with its bee head and wings always facing the same way.

To make the animation more realistic, you can make the bee align itself with the path. In other words, the bee head and wings rotate to follow the path. This is

accomplished with the Auto-Orient command. With the feature activated, the layer object remains perpendicular to the motion path.

Although you can create the same animation effect keyframe by keyframe yourself, you can save time and effort by employing the Auto-Orient command instead.

ORIENT A LAYER ALONG A MOTION PATH

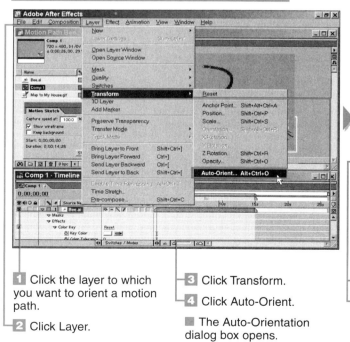

1 Click the layer to which you want to orient a motion path.

2 Click Layer.

3 Click Transform.

4 Click Auto-Orient.

■ The Auto-Orientation dialog box opens.

5 Click Orient Along Path.

6 Click OK.

■ The layer now orients itself to the motion path during playback.

Note: See Chapter 31 to play and preview compositions.

CHANGE ANIMATION SPEED WITH A KEYFRAME ASSISTANT

You can change the animation speed for a keyframe animation to make the layer seem to speed up or slow down at the beginning or end of the layer. Called *easing* in After Effects, you can use three keyframe assistants to change the speed.

The Easy Ease keyframe assistant adjusts both the beginning and ending speed for the layer. The Easy Ease In keyframe assistant starts the animation out slow and then reaches the assigned speed. The Easy Ease Out keyframe assistant slows the animation speed at the end of the animation sequence.

How can I make jumpy animation flow more smoothly?

✓ You can use the Smoother feature to smooth out a motion path or curves. The Smoother removes or adds keyframes to make the effect flow better. First save your file, then to apply the Smoother, select the keyframes you want to apply the feature to, then click Window, The Smoother. The Smoother palette opens. Make any settings adjustments, then click Apply.

CHANGE ANIMATION SPEED WITH A KEYFRAME ASSISTANT

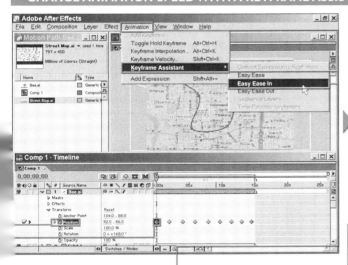

■1 Expand the layer property containing the keyframes you want to adjust.

■2 Click the keyframe you want to speed up or slow down.

Note: Press the Shift key while clicking keyframes to select multiple keyframes.

■3 Click Animation.

■4 Click Keyframe Assistant.

■5 Click an ease command.

■ The ease speed is assigned. The keyframe icon changes to indicate that an ease setting is applied.

Note: See Chapter 31 to play back and preview compositions to see the new speed in action.

CREATE A MOTION BLUR

You can give an animated layer the appearance of movement by activating the layer's motion blur status. Motion blur makes the layer object seem to blur as it moves in the composition. By default, After Effects displays sharp images for animated keyframes, but you can make them appear more realistic with a motion blur.

After you activate a layer's motion blur status, you must also activate

the Enable Motion Blur button to view the blur in playback and previews. You can also set the shutter angle for the blur before you preview the animation. The shutter angle setting determines the amount of blur that occurs when the frames are played back. The shutter angle control simulates a real camera shutter, controlling exposure time.

When you assign a motion blur to a layer, you increase the time needed to render and preview the composition. For that reason, you may wish to assign the blur state, but delay enabling it until you render the composition. See Chapter 31 to learn more about previewing and rendering compositions.

CREATE A MOTION BLUR

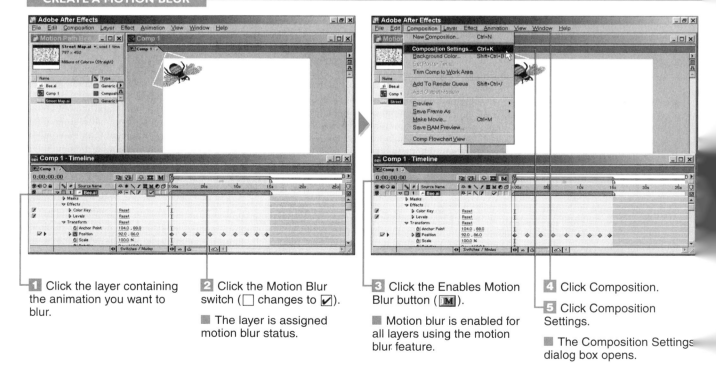

1 Click the layer containing the animation you want to blur.

2 Click the Motion Blur switch (☐ changes to ☑).

■ The layer is assigned motion blur status.

3 Click the Enables Motion Blur button (M).

■ Motion blur is enabled for all layers using the motion blur feature.

4 Click Composition.

5 Click Composition Settings.

■ The Composition Settings dialog box opens.

How do I disable a motion blur?

✔ Deselect the Motion Blur switch to turn off the layer's motion blur status. To disable motion blurs for all the layers, click the Enables Motion Blur button (M) at the top of the Timeline window.

I do not see the Switches panel. How do I find the Motion Blur switch?

✔ To turn the panel on, click the Timeline Options Menu button (▶), click Panels, and then click Switches.

What does the Frame Blending switch do?

✔ If you imported footage that used a different frame rate than the one set for your composition, the footage may appear jerky in its movement. You can use the Frame Blending switch to compensate for lower or faster frame rates. Click the Frame Blending switch (▦) to turn the feature on (☐ becomes ✓). Then, click the Enables Frame Blending button (▦).

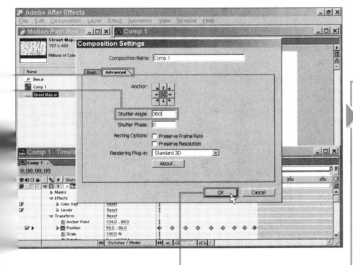

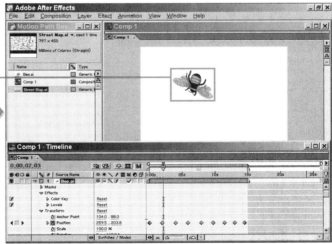

6 Click the Advanced tab.

7 Type a shutter angle in degrees.

■ A higher degree creates more blur.

■ A lower degree creates less blur.

8 Click OK.

■ When you preview or play back the composition, the animated layer appears blurred.

Note: See Chapter 31 to learn more about using playback and preview features.

ASSIGN LAYER MODES

Y ou can use layer modes to combine layers in a composition to create a variety of visual effects. For example, you can blend two layers so that the top layer swaps hues with the underlying layer, or the top layer becomes a stencil pattern that shows through to the underlying layer.

Layer modes work by blending or combining underlying layers with

the current layer. The After Effects layer modes work the same way as Photoshop layer modes. See Part I to learn more about using Photoshop.

After Effects provides 21 different layer modes. You may need to experiment with each one to see the type of effects you can create. The blended layers you create rely totally on the color characteristics of the layer images. Some images

are better suited for blending than others.

As you choose from the various layer modes, you may notice that some of the modes are grouped together in the layer modes menu. Grouped modes share similar values, but different results.

ASSIGN LAYER MODES

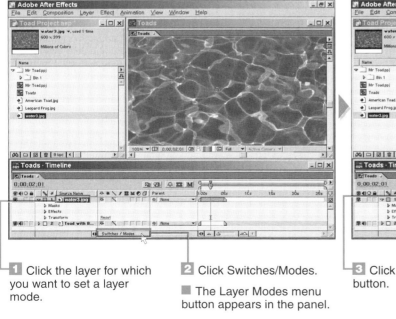

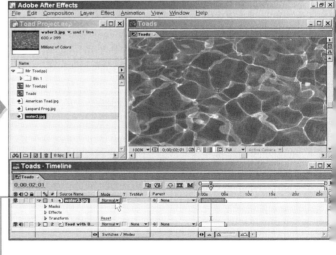

1 Click the layer for which you want to set a layer mode.

2 Click Switches/Modes.

■ The Layer Modes menu button appears in the panel.

3 Click the Layer Modes button.

■ The Layer Modes menu opens.

How do I get rid of a mode I applied if I do not like it?

✔ Click the Edit menu and then click Undo to remove the effect. You can also reopen the Layer Modes menu and click Normal or any other mode.

What does the T switch do?

✔ The T switch in the Switches/Modes panel is the Preserve Underlying Transparency switch. It enables you to make opaque areas of a layer display the opaque areas of the underlying layers. Artists frequently use this effect to create reflected light effects. Click the T switch for the layer you want to blend with the layer below.

What is the difference between the Stencil and Silhouette modes?

✔ Both modes use either the alpha channel or luminance values to change the same for the underlying layer. Stencil mode cuts a hole through the current layer to view the layer beneath, and the Silhouette mode does the exact opposite.

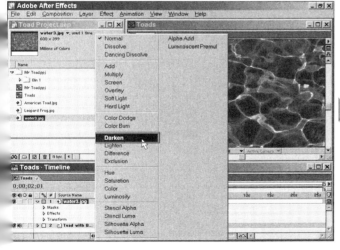

4 Click a layer mode.

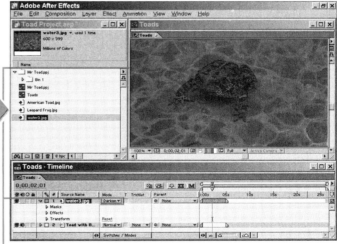

■ The mode is applied.

CREATE A TRACK MATTE

When you create a track matte, one layer acts as a mask to the layer directly below. The layer on top is called the *track matte*, while the underlying layer is called a *fill* layer. You can use a track matte when you want one layer to peek through another. For example, you may want the image on the top layer to act as a window to the image on the bottom layer.

You can use the Modes panel in the Timeline window to set a track matte. After Effects offers several transparency options to set for the layer acting as the fill image for the mask layer. Use the Alpha Matte option to set the alpha channel pixel value to 100%, which means the underlying layer is completely visible through the top layer's mask or window. Applying the Alpha Inverted Matte option does the

opposite of the Alpha Matte option; the two layers are inverted.

The Luma Matte option uses luminance values to define the transparency. The layer is opaque when the luminance value is 100%. The Luma Inverted Matte option does the exact opposite; the layer is opaque when the luminance value is 0%.

1 Arrange the layer you want to use as a mask to appear above the layer you want to use as a fill.

Note: See Chapter 25 to add and move layers in the Timeline window.

2 Click Switches/Modes to display the Modes panel.

■ The Track Matte menu button appears in the panel.

3 Click the Track Matte button.

■ The Track Matte menu opens.

How do I reset my track matte layer back to normal?

✔ Click the Track Matte menu button in the Timeline and click None. Doing this sets the track matte layer above to normal, and the underlying layer no longer has fill status.

How do I adjust the fill layer's transparency setting?

✔ Click the layer acting as a fill and, using the Transform properties, adjust the layer's Opaque property. See Chapter 26 to learn more about setting layer properties in the Timeline window.

If I move the fill layer, is the track matte disabled?

✔ No. The assigned track matte status remains with the layer, no matter where the layer is moved in the stacking order. However, any layer that appears above it takes on the track matte masking effect. To turn off the track matte feature, click the layer's Track Matte button and click None.

Can I animate a track matte?

✔ Yes. You can add keyframes and animate either the track matte layer or the fill layer. Animated track mattes are called *traveling mattes*.

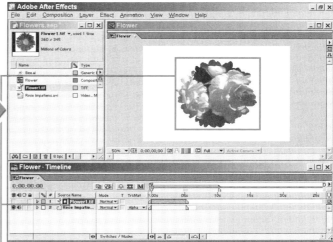

4 Click a track matte option.

■ After Effects applies the matte effect.

■ A track matte icon (⬛) appears next to the mask layer's name, indicating the layer is defining transparency.

Note: The Video switch for the top or mask layer is turned off by default when a track matte is applied to the underlying layer.

UNDERSTANDING MASKS

You can use *masks* in your composition's layers to control the visibility of layers underneath. You can assign multiple masks — up to 127 — to a single layer to create a variety of visual effects. For example, you might create a mask that acts as a keyhole that peeks into the layer below. You can also create animated masks by animating control points along the mask shape.

Although you can certainly create matte effects in Premiere, you can create more sophisticated matte effects using masks in After Effects, including masks that are animated over time in your project. For example, you can import an entire Premiere project into After Effects and then create a mask to isolate a specific area of the video clip so only a part of the clip is visible during playback.

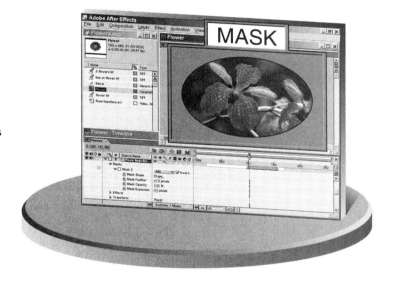

Types of Masks

You can create a mask by defining a mask shape, drawing a path using the After Effects tools, or importing a mask from Photoshop or Illustrator.

You can use the drawing tools found in the After Effects toolbox to draw simple mask shapes, such as rectangles, squares, circles, and ovals. You can also create freehand shapes using the Pen tool, such as open or closed Bezier curves.

Masks come in handy when you want to block out an area on an underlying layer. By combining masks with other effects, you can add pizzazz to your video projects.

Viewing Masks

You can view and change mask properties in the expandable layer properties outline in the Timeline window, and you can view and work with masks in both the Layer and Composition windows. You can also hide masks from view to work on other composition elements.

Mask Paths

You can create mask paths in After Effects using path segments and connecting control points. *Control points* define key positions and changes in the path.

You can create both open and closed paths. For example, a straight line is considered an open path because the shape you create is not enclosed by any sides, and a square is considered a closed path because the four line segments (sides) meet in its four corners. A circle is also a closed path because it, too, forms an enclosed area. When creating a transparent mask for a layer, you must use a closed-path mask.

VIEW OR HIDE MASK PATHS

You can turn mask paths on and off in the Composition window. For example, you may want to turn a mask path off in the Composition window to work with other composition elements. You can turn the mask path back on again when you want to work with the mask.

The steps to hiding a mask path differ from those performed to hide a layer. To learn how to hide entire layers, including any masks assigned to the layers, see Chapter 26.

By default, After Effects makes all new masks viewable for a

selected layer. Mask paths appear as yellow so you can easily identify them. If you create another new mask for the layer, After Effects reveals all existing masks.

You add masks to your project in three ways: drawing the mask manually with a toolbox tool, specifying mask dimensions using the Mask Shape dialog box, or importing a mask from another program.

The Layer Masks spatial control turns mask paths on or off. You can learn more about working with spatial controls in Chapter 26.

How do I hide a mask layer in the Layer window?

✔ Click the Layer Window Options button (▶) in the upper-right corner of the Layer window, and then click None. Doing this turns off any masks assigned to the layer. To view the masks again, click ▶ and then Masks.

How do I view mask properties?

✔ In the Timeline window, click ▷ to expand the layer's properties and expand the Mask property to view property settings pertaining to masks.

VIEW OR HIDE MASK PATHS

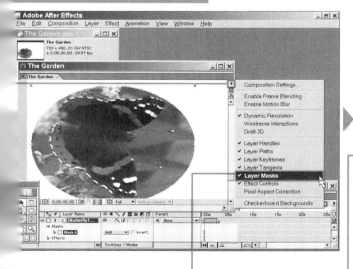

■ With the Composition window open, click the Comp Window Options button (▶).

Note: See the section "Draw a Mask Shape" to learn how to create a mask.

2 Click Layer Masks.

■ The mask path is hidden from view, but the mask itself remains in view.

Note: See Chapter 24 to learn more about working with the Composition window.

DRAW A MASK SHAPE

Y ou can easily create a mask by drawing a shape using the toolbox tools. A mask shape enables the underlying image or layers to peek through the shape while the area outside the shape is hidden from view. You can use a mask shape to view only a portion of the layers below.

You can use the Rectangle tool to create rectangle and square shapes,

or the Oval tool to create oval or circle shapes. If the After Effects toolbox is hidden, you must first display the toolbox in order to use the tools. The Rectangle and Oval tools share space in the toolbox. Your drawing a mask shape using either of these tools produces a closed path mask. To create an open path mask, use the Pen tool. See the next section, "Draw a

Freeform Mask Shape," to learn how.

You can draw a mask shape in the Composition window or in the Layer window. Masks remain visible in the selected layer unless you turn off the mask view. The previous section, "View or Hide Mask Paths," shows you how to hide a mask.

DRAW A MASK SHAPE

DRAW A RECTANGLE MASK

■1 Click the layer to which you want to add a mask.

■2 Click the Rectangle tool (▢).

■ If the Rectangle tool is not visible, click and hold the ▢ to display both tools, and then move the mouse pointer over ▢ to select it.

Note: If the toolbox is not visible, click Tools from the Window menu.

■3 Click and drag to create a mask shape.

■ To keep the size proportional, press and hold the Shift key while dragging.

■ After creating the shape the mask appears as a pat with control points. Areas within the mask shape are visible and areas outside t shape are hidden.

Note: See "View or Hide Mask Paths" to hide a mask path.

How do I edit a mask shape?

✔ Click the Selection tool (⬚) in the toolbox, and then either click the mask shape to display control points along the mask path or double-click the mask. You can then drag a control point to change the line segment, thus changing the mask shape. To remove a control point, click the control point and press the Delete key.

How do I move a mask shape?

✔ With the mask shape selected, click Layer, Mask, and then Free Transform Points. You can now reposition the mask over another area of the layer. Double-click outside of the mask to exit the Free Transform Points mode.

Can I invert the mask?

✔ Yes. Inverting makes the mask shape obscure the image within the mask shape while the areas outside the shape are viewable. To invert a mask, click the Invert check box in the Timeline window's Mask Layer property. See Chapter 26 to view layer properties.

DRAW AN OVAL MASK

1 Click the layer to which you want to add a mask.

2 Click the Oval tool (⬚).

■ If ⬚ is not visible, click and hold ⬚ to display both tools, and then click ⬚ to select it.

Note: If the toolbox is not displayed, click Tools from the Window menu.

3 Click and drag a mask shape.

■ To keep the size proportional, press and hold the Shift key while dragging.

■ The mask appears as a path with control points. Areas within the mask shape are visible.

Note: See the section "View or Hide Mask Paths" to hide a mask path.

DRAW A FREEFORM MASK SHAPE

A *freeform* shape follows a path you specify rather than a regular rectangle or oval shape. You can draw a freeform mask shape using the Pen tool.

If the After Effects toolbox is hidden, you must first display it to use the Pen tool. You can draw both open path and closed path masks with the Pen tool. You create a path by building it segment by segment. At the end of each segment you draw, a control point appears. You drag a control point to create a curve in the path.

You can draw a mask shape in the Composition window or in the Layer window. Masks remain visible in the selected layer until you turn off the mask view. See the section "View or Hide Mask Paths" to learn how to hide a mask from view.

DRAW A FREEFORM MASK SHAPE

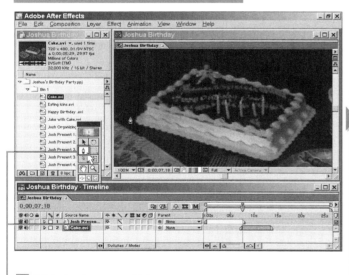

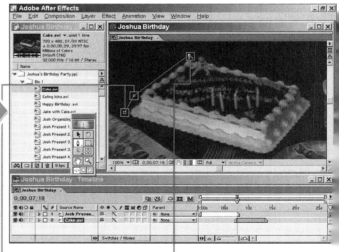

1 Click the layer to which you want to add a mask.

2 Click the Pen tool (✎).

Note: If the toolbox is not displayed, click Tools from the Window menu.

3 Click to create an anchor point to start the freeform path.

4 Click the next point where you want to end the line segment and start another.

■ To create a smooth path, drag the ✎.

5 Continue clicking to create more line segments to create the shape you want.

How do I close an open mask path?

✔ Mask paths can be open or closed; an open path is a line rather than an enclosed shape, while a closed path is an enclosed shape, such as a circle. You can turn an open path, such as a curved line, into a closed path using the Closed command. Open the path Layer window, hold down the Shift key, and click the control points at each end of the line. Click the Layer menu, Mask, and then Closed. After Effects connects the two end points with another line to close the path. You can use the same technique to open a closed path.

How do I remove a mask shape?

✔ Click Layer, Masks, and then Remove Mask to remove a mask shape.

Can I rotate or scale a mask?

✔ Yes. With the mask selected, click Layer, Mask, and then Free Transform Points. You can now move, scale, or rotate the mask. See Chapter 26 to learn more about changing scale and rotation properties.

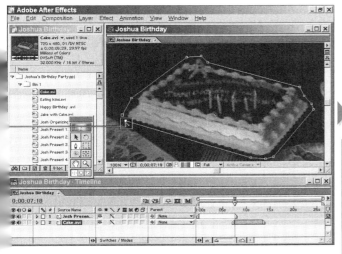

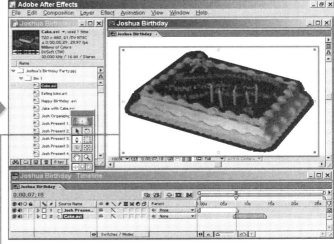

▇ Double-click to end the mask path.

■ After Effects joins the anchor point with the last control point in the path to create a closed path shape.

■ The mask is complete.

■ You can drag control points along the selected mask path to change the mask shape.

Note: Double-click the mask shape to edit control points.

LOCK AND UNLOCK MASKS

You can lock a mask to prevent accidental edits. For example, if a layer contains more than one mask, you can lock the other masks to edit just one of the masks. Locking masks can also help you better select only the mask you want.

You can use the Lock switch in the Timeline window to lock and unlock masks. To see the individual masks for a layer, you must expand the layer properties in the Timeline window. To learn more about expanding and collapsing properties, see Chapter 26.

How do I hide a locked mask?

✓ First, click the layer containing the locked mask in the Timeline window. Next, click Layer, Mask, and then Hide Locked Masks. Doing this toggles the mask view off. To display the mask again, click Layer, Mask, and then Show Locked Masks. This command removes the check mark next to the command name and makes the mask viewable again.

LOCK AND UNLOCK MASKS

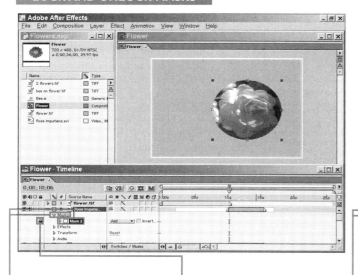

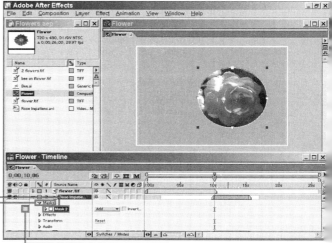

LOCK A MASK

1 Expand the layer outline in the Timeline window to display the Mask property.

2 Click the mask you want to lock.

Note: See Chapter 26 to view layer properties.

3 Click the box under the Lock category next to the mask name (☐ becomes 🔒).

■ After Effects locks the mask.

UNLOCK A MASK

1 Expand the layer outline in the Timeline window to display the Mask property.

2 Click the mask you want to unlock.

Note: See Chapter 26 to view layer properties.

3 Click the Lock icon (🔒 becomes ☐).

■ After Effects unlocks the mask.

SET A MASK MODE

You can specify how you want multiple masks to interact for a layer. By selecting a mask mode, you can create a variety of masking effects. For example, you can make two circular masks act as a binocular mask to view the image or layers below. Remember, masks are layered when you add more than one mask to a layer.

After Effects offers seven different mask modes. Using the None mode

makes After Effects ignore the mask. The Add mode enables you to join other masks to the selected mask, creating one big mask. The Subtract mode subtracts all the masks layered above the mask. Use this type of mask to create a hole in the middle of another mask, for example.

The Intersect mode compiles the masks into one big mask, but only where the mask areas intersect. The

Lighten mode combines the mask with masks layered above it, but opacity remains the same even where the masks overlap. The Darken mode does the opposite of the Lighten mode, allowing the opaque areas where masks overlap to appear as the mask.

The Difference mode displays only areas where two or more masks do not intersect.

SET A MASK MODE

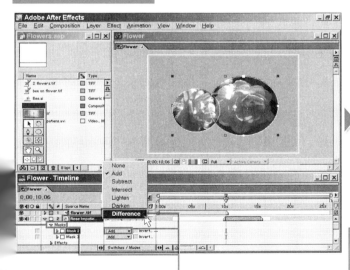

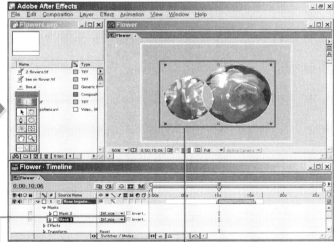

■1 Click the layer containing the masks.

■2 Display the mask layer properties.

Note: See Chapter 26 to view layer properties in the Timeline window.

■3 Click the mask you want to change.

■4 Click the Mode box.

■5 Click a mask mode.

■ After Effects assigns the mode.

■6 Repeat steps 3 through 5 to set the mode for other masks on the layer.

■ In this example, the Difference mode is assigned to two masks and only the intersecting area is not included in the mask.

FEATHER MASK EDGES

You can adjust the edges, or *feather*, a mask to either blur or sharpen it. By setting a Mask Feather value, you control how sharp or fuzzy the edges of a mask appear. The Mask Feather value can make the mask edge more or less opaque.

Feathering is most often used to soften the edges of a mask. By default, the width of the feathering effects half of the mask edge and half of the area

outside the mask edge. By adjusting the values, you can reset the feathered area. For example, if you set the feather value to 20, the feathering effect extends 10 pixels inside the mask edge and 10 pixels outside the mask edge.

The quickest way to feather a mask is to use the scrubbable hot text value in the mask properties. To learn more about setting layer properties, see Chapter 26.

How can I set a precise value for the feathered edges?

✔ With the mask selected, click Layer, Mask, and then Mask Feather. Doing this opens the Mask Feather dialog box. You can type a horizontal and vertical value for the effect.

FEATHER MASK EDGES

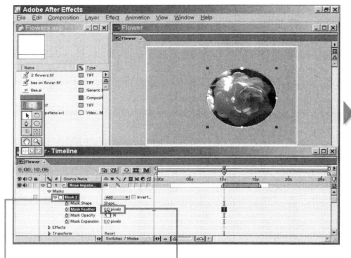

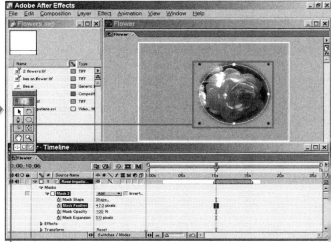

1 Expand the mask you want to edit to display Mask properties.

Note: See Chapter 26 to view layer properties in the Timeline window.

2 Drag the Mask Feather value.

■ After Effects applies the feathering.

Note: Be sure to experiment with mask properties, such as feathering, to create different effects for your masks.

COPY A MASK FROM PHOTOSHOP OR ILLUSTRATOR

You can copy masks created in Adobe Photoshop or Adobe Illustrator to use as masks in your After Effects project. You can copy just the Photoshop or Illustrator path rather than the entire image file.

For example, you can copy the path used to create an image outline of a star to use as a mask in a layer of your After Effects composition.

To employ this technique, copy and paste the image path into the After Effects Layer window. If you paste the path into the Composition window, After Effects displays the image as a motion path instead of a mask.

I imported a mask path from Photoshop, but I want it to mask the area within the path, not the area outside the path. How do I do this?

✔ You can invert the imported mask. Click the mask in the Timeline window, then click the Layer menu and click Mask, Invert.

COPY A MASK FROM PHOTOSHOP OR ILLUSTRATOR

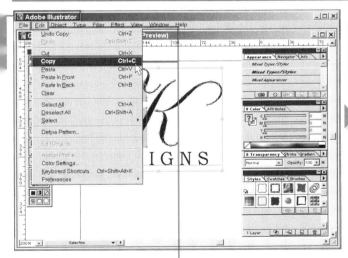

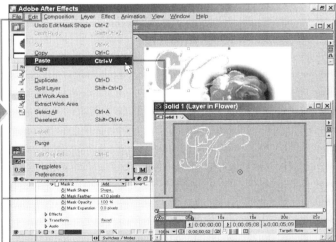

1 Open the file containing the path you want to copy in Photoshop or Illustrator.

Note: See Parts I and II to learn how to work with Photoshop and Illustrator.

2 Click Edit.

3 Click Copy.

4 Switch to the open Layer window to which you want to copy After Effects.

5 Click Edit.

6 Click Paste.

■ After Effects turns the path into a mask.

APPLY AN ADJUST EFFECT

You can use Adjust effects to change a layer's color or brightness. Adjust effects include Brightness and Contrast, Color Balance, Hue/Saturation, and Levels, among others.

For example, the Levels effect lets you edit either a layer image's brightness or its contrast, enabling you to change the range of input color levels. People most commonly use the Levels effect to adjust image quality for photographs. If you import a black-and-white photograph that seems a bit dull, you can adjust the brightness levels using the Levels effect to give the image more contrast.

The Levels effect, when applied to a layer, includes the Histogram property — a map of input levels of the image that resembles a graph of peaks and valleys. Adjusting levels on the graph modifies the effect. Photoshop includes a similar Levels adjustment setting; to learn more about it, see Chapter 3.

To adjust the contrast of the image, you can move the Input Black and Input White sliders in the graph. Or, to adjust midtone or gray values, move the middle slider, called the Gamma slider.

Although the steps below focus on applying the Levels effect, you access all effects in the Adjust category through the same menu commands.

APPLY AN ADJUST EFFECT: THE LEVELS EFFECT

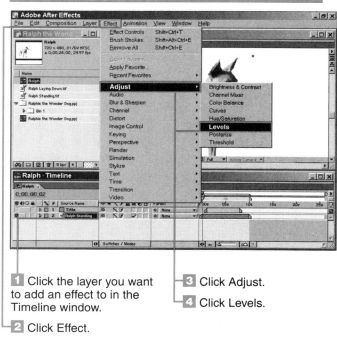

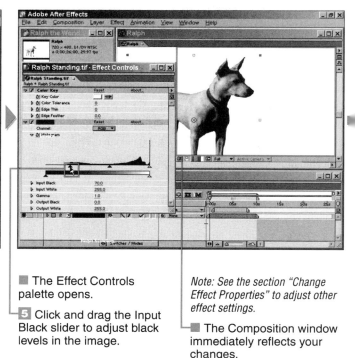

1 Click the layer you want to add an effect to in the Timeline window.

2 Click Effect.

3 Click Adjust.

4 Click Levels.

■ The Effect Controls palette opens.

5 Click and drag the Input Black slider to adjust black levels in the image.

Note: See the section "Change Effect Properties" to adjust other effect settings.

■ The Composition window immediately reflects your changes.

I cannot see the entire histogram in my palette. What do I do?

✔ You can resize the palette window to see more of the graph. Move the mouse pointer over the right edge of the palette window, and then drag the window border to the right to increase the window size.

Is it easier to adjust the level values by dragging the scrubbable hot text properties?

✔ The method you use depends entirely on you and what you want to adjust for the image layer. You can certainly accomplish the same thing using either method.

I do not like the changes I made. How do I restore the original settings?

✔ Click the Reset property next to the effect name in the Effect Controls palette to restore the effect to its default settings.

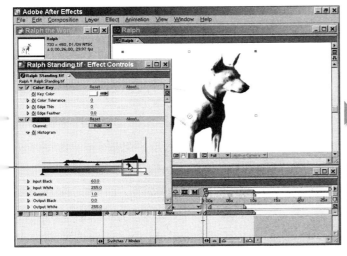

■6 Click and drag the Input White slider to adjust white levels in the image.

■ The Composition window immediately reflects your changes.

■7 Click and drag the Gamma slider to adjust midtone levels in the image.

■ The Composition window immediately reflects your changes.

Note: You can click the Effect Controls palette's ✕ (□) *to close the palette.*

APPLY BLUR & SHARPEN EFFECTS

After Effects provides Blur effects to soften image focus and Sharpen effects to make images crisper. The Blur & Sharpen effects category offers eight effects you can apply, including six Blur effects. Each Blur effect creates a different type of blurred image. For example, the Radial Blur blurs the image starting with a particular point in the image, and the Compound Blur uses two layer images to create a blur that makes parts of one layer blurred by using the other layer as the blurring source.

The following example shows how to apply a Directional Blur, which blurs the image in a specified direction. You may apply a Directional Blur to give an image the feeling of motion without actually assigning motion keyframes.

You access all effects in the Blur & Sharpen category through the same menu commands.

Is a Blur effect the same as a motion blur?

✔ Chapter 27 describes how to use the motion blur layer technique to make a layer seem blurred to enhance motion. The motion blur technique is very similar to the Blur effects, but adds the blur to the moving image. The Blur effect applies the blur to the entire image regardless of whether it is animated.

APPLY A BLUR & SHARPEN EFFECT: THE DIRECTIONAL BLUR EFFECT

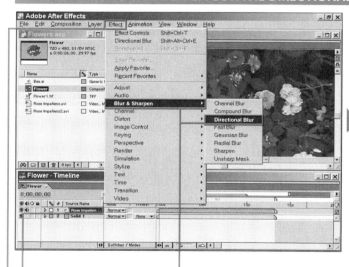

1 Click the layer you want to add the Directional Blur effect to in the Timeline window.

2 Click Effect.

3 Click Blur & Sharpen.

4 Click Directional Blur.

■ The Effect Controls palette opens.

5 Drag the Direction angle control to specify a direction for the blur.

■ The greater the value, the more blurred the image becomes.

6 Drag the Blur Length property to set a length for the blurring.

■ The Composition window immediately reflects your changes.

Note: See "Change Effect Properties" to adjust properties.

APPLY A KEYING EFFECT

Keying effects enable you to key out color and luminance values for a layer image. Key effects can turn all the pixels of a particular color transparent. The color you choose to key out is called the *key color*. There are only two Keying effects in Adobe After Effects: Color and Luma. Use the Luma key to key out regions of a layer and the Color key to key out colors.

For example, you may use a color key to key out a background around a subject. Color keys are frequently used with footage shot against a blue or green screen background. You can also use a color key to key out a solid color background, such as white surrounding a graphic image you import into After Effects. Normally, if you place the graphic image layer on top of a solid layer of color, the graphic image's surrounding border of white obscures parts of the color layer, depending on the size of the graphic image. You can key out the surrounding white around the graphic so that the image appears as part of the color layer.

APPLY A KEYING EFFECT: THE COLOR EFFECT

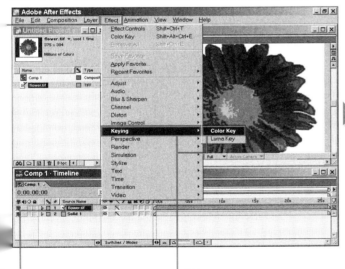

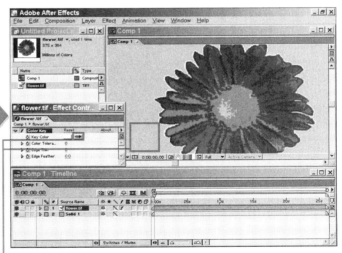

1 Click the layer to which you want to add a color key.

2 Click Effect.

3 Click Keying.

4 Click Color Key.

■ The Effect Controls palette opens.

5 Click the Eyedropper button (⬛).

6 Click a color to key out in the image layer.

■ The Composition window immediately reflects your changes.

■ In this example, the white background is made transparent to the solid green layer beneath.

Note: See "Change Effect Properties" to learn more about adjusting properties.

APPLY A CHANNEL EFFECT

Use Channel effects to alter individual layer channels: red, green, blue, or alpha. Color information for an image is stored in the three color channels, while the fourth, *alpha*, stores transparency information. Alpha channels are an important part of creating mattes, which make a layer transparent or opaque to another layer.

The Channel effects category offers ten effects including Blend, Invert,

and Remove Color Matting. You can use the Blend effect, for example, to combine two layers much like a cross-dissolve transition. You can also use the layer modes to create similar effects. See Chapter 27 to learn more about assigning layer modes.

The Blend effect is a compound effect because it combines two layers in the composition to create the effect. It does so by combining the layers in one of five modes

assigned by you: Crossfade, Color Only, Tint, Darken, or Lighten. The mode you assign determines how the layers blend together.

Although the example below focuses on the Blend effect, you can access all effects in the Channel category through the same menu commands.

APPLY A CHANNEL EFFECT: THE BLEND EFFECT

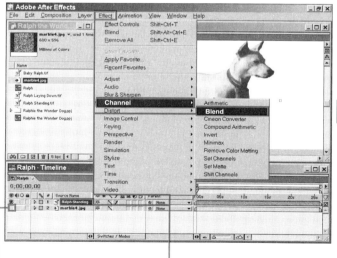

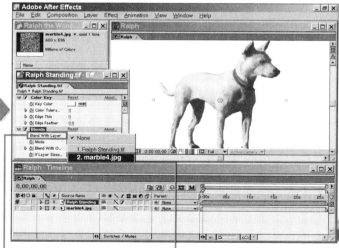

1 Add the two layers you want to blend to the composition.

2 Hide the source layer.

Note: See Chapter 25 to learn how to hide layers.

3 Click the layer you want to blend.

4 Click Effect.

5 Click Channel.

6 Click Blend.

■ The Effect Controls palette opens.

7 Click the Blend With Layer ▾.

8 Click the name of the source layer to which you want to blend.

What does the If Layer Sizes Differ property do?

✔ You can use this property to make the target layer size center within the source layer or stretch to fit the size of the source layer.

When combining layers, which is easier — to create a blend with the Blend effect or use the Layer Modes?

✔ While using layer modes to combine two layers is much faster, you cannot animate layer modes as you can with the blend effect. To learn more about applying layer modes, see Chapter 27.

What does each Blend Mode do?

✔ The Crossfade mode creates a fade effect between the two layers, while the Color Only and Tint Only modes colorize or tint the target layer according to corresponding color pixels in the source layer. The Darken Only and Lighten Only modes darken or lighten pixels in the target layer based on corresponding pixels in the source layer.

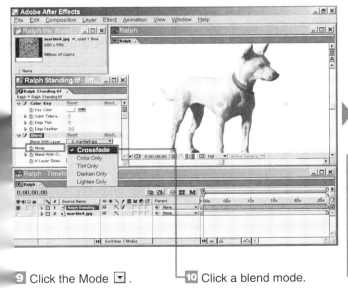

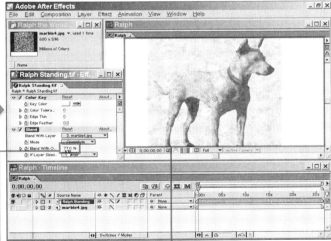

9 Click the Mode ▾ .

10 Click a blend mode.

11 Adjust the Blend With Original value.

Note: See "Change Effect Properties" to adjust properties.

■ The Composition window immediately reflects your changes.

Note: The Blend effect works very well when animated over time. See Chapter 27 to learn more about animating in After Effects.

APPLY A DISTORT EFFECT

You can use Distort effects to literally distort your layer images by adjusting pixels. After Effects offers 12 different Distort effects for you to create unusual morphed and distorted images. The Mirror effect, for example, splits an image and makes one side seem to reflect onto the other, just like a mirror.

The Mirror effect includes two properties: Reflection Center and Reflection Angle. Adjust the Reflection Center property to move the area that After Effects

uses as the center or dividing line for the mirror image.

Adjust the Reflection Angle property to control the angle of the reflection measured in degrees. For example, a setting of 90 degrees makes the top part of the image reflect onto the bottom part of the image. To set the Reflection Angle value, you can use the scrubbable hot text or the angle dial.

You can access all Distort effects through the same menu commands.

What does the Offset effect do?

✔ The Offset effect pans the image to make it offset. The result is a partial view of the image layer. You might use the Offset effect to create a layer that resembles a slot machine or odometer readout.

APPLY A DISTORT EFFECT: THE MIRROR EFFECT

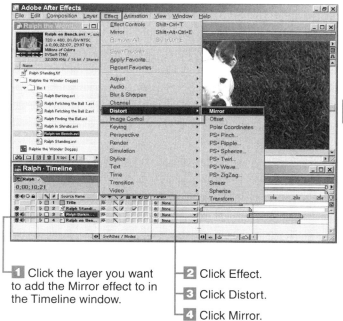

1 Click the layer you want to add the Mirror effect to in the Timeline window.

2 Click Effect.

3 Click Distort.

4 Click Mirror.

■ The Effect Controls palette opens.

5 Drag the Reflection Center property to change the dividing line for the mirror image.

6 Drag the Reflection Angle property to set an angle of reflection for the image.

■ The Composition window immediately reflects your changes.

APPLY A PERSPECTIVE EFFECT

 ou can assign a Perspective effect to give a layer the illusion of depth. You can choose from four different Perspective effects: Basic 3D, Bevel Alpha, Bevel Edges, and Drop Shadow.

For example, the Bevel Alpha effect can give a layer image the appearance of embossing, while the Drop Shadow effect adds a shadow to the layer image. Each Perspective effect includes properties for

controlling various aspects of the effect, such as angle and distance.

You can access all Perspective effects through the same menu commands.

MASTER IT

Here are some other Perspective effects that you can apply:

Basic 3D

Bevel Alpha

Bevel Edges

APPLY A PERSPECTIVE EFFECT: THE DROP SHADOW EFFECT

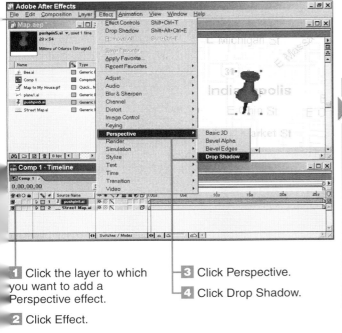

■1 Click the layer to which you want to add a Perspective effect.

■2 Click Effect.

■3 Click Perspective.

■4 Click Drop Shadow.

■ The Effect Controls palette opens.

■ After Effects adds a shadow to the layer image.

■ Drag the Direction property setting to change the direction of the shadow.

■ Drag the Distance property to control the distance of the shadow from the image.

APPLY A TRANSITION EFFECT

You can use Transition effects to enhance the transition between layers in the Timeline. Transition effects act just like transition effects found in nonlinear editing programs, such as Premiere.

After Effects offers six types of transition effects: Block Dissolve, Gradient Wipe, Iris Wipe, Linear Wipe, Radial Wipe, and Venetian

Blinds. For example, the Iris Wipe transition gradually reveals the underlying layer using the shape of a camera iris, while the Venetian Blinds transition reveals the underlying layer in strips, much like a blind. With all transitions, you can control properties such as direction or level of completeness.

Transition effects require at least two layers in the composition. You

can assign a Transition effect to the top layer you want to transition from and use keyframes to define the progress of the transition across time in the composition. The result is that the layer below the transition layer is slowly revealed. See Chapter 27 to learn more about animating with keyframes.

You can access all Transition effects through the same menu commands.

APPLY A TRANSITION EFFECT: THE VENETIAN BLINDS EFFECT

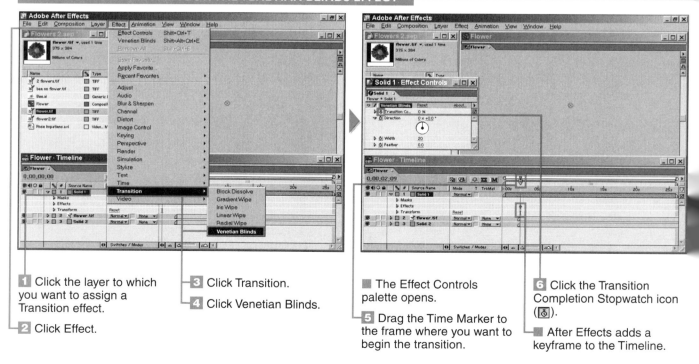

■1 Click the layer to which you want to assign a Transition effect.

■2 Click Effect.

■3 Click Transition.

■4 Click Venetian Blinds.

■ The Effect Controls palette opens.

■5 Drag the Time Marker to the frame where you want to begin the transition.

■6 Click the Transition Completion Stopwatch icon ().

■ After Effects adds a keyframe to the Timeline.

Here are some other Transition effects that you can apply:

Block Dissolve

Gradient Wipe

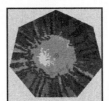

Iris Wipe

Linear Wipe

Radial Wipe

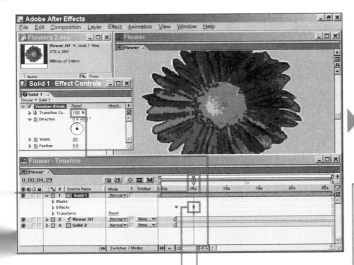

7 Drag the Time Marker to the frame where you want to end the transition.

8 Set the Transition Completion value to 100%.

■ After Effects adds a keyframe to the Timeline.

■ You can preview the transition by dragging the Time marker to see the effect.

Note: See Chapter 31 to learn more about previewing compositions.

APPLY A TEXT EFFECT

Text effects enable you to add text to your project and manipulate it across a layer. For example, you can make the text seem to wrap around a circle or a Bezier shape. You can also utilize a custom path from another program, such as Illustrator (see Part II of this book) or Photoshop (see Part I). Path Text is just one of three Text effects you can apply to your After Effects layers.

You can use text in your project as titles, labels, captions, or to suit any other text-related issue. When assigning text effects, you can choose from any of the fonts available on your computer system, including specialized fonts that feature graphic shapes and designs, such as Wingdings.

After assigning a text effect, you can access myriad text properties.

For example, you can align, kern, and track text. You can change text color, fill colors and patterns, sizing, and more.

You access all three Text effects through the same menu commands.

APPLY A TEXT EFFECT: THE PATH TEXT EFFECT

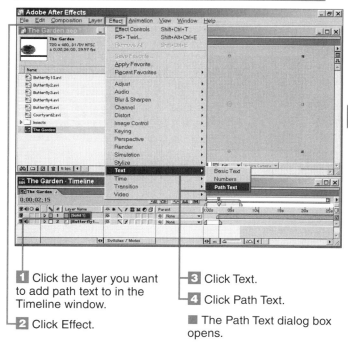

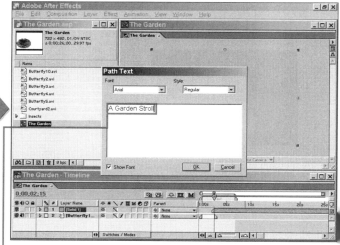

1 Click the layer you want to add path text to in the Timeline window.

2 Click Effect.

3 Click Text.

4 Click Path Text.

■ The Path Text dialog box opens.

5 Type the path text you want to use.

How do I add regular text to a layer?
✔ You can add text to any layer by applying the Basic Text effect. When applied, this effect works similarly to the Path Text effect, but you do not specify a path for the text. Just type the text and specify a font and style. You can alter text properties, such as fill color or alignment, as needed.

How do I animate path text?
✔ You can add keyframes to the layer containing the path text to animate the text. Create the illusion of movement by changing each keyframe's path text position. See Chapter 27 to learn about basic animating principles.

What does the Numbers effect do?
✔ The Numbers effect adds numbers to your layers. Unlike the Basic Text and Path Text effects, you enter numerical values using the Value/Offset/Random Max property rather than in a dialog box when you first assign the effect. You can also let After Effects generate the numbers randomly. Like other text effects, a variety of properties enable you to control the look and placement of the numbers.

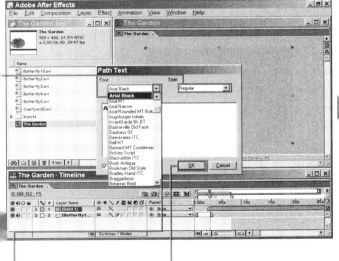

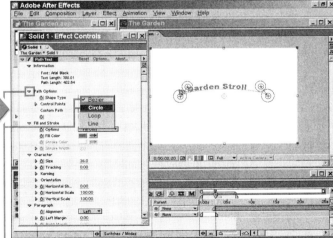

6 Click ▼ to display available fonts.

7 Click a font.

■ Optionally, you can use the Style list to specify a style.

8 Click OK.

■ After Effects places the text in the layer.

9 Expand the Path Options property.

10 Click the Shape Type menu button.

11 Click a shape type.

■ The text takes on the shape you specified.

■ You can adjust the other text properties to change text color, alignment, and more.

APPLY A STYLIZE EFFECT

You can use all 13 Stylize effects to create abstract looks for your layers, or to create a stylized appearance, such as embossing or mosaic tiles. For example, applying the Brush Strokes effect makes your layer image look as if it was painted with a paintbrush.

The Brush Strokes effect includes eight different properties you can

set. Those that impact the layer image the most are the Stroke Angle, Brush Size, and Stroke Density properties. Experimenting with these properties can give the layer image quite a few different looks. For example, the larger the brush size you set, the larger the brush strokes appear on the layer. The Stroke Angle property controls the direction of the brush strokes.

In the illustrated effect below, the brush strokes are applied to the edges of any masks assigned to the layer.

You access all effects in the Stylize category through the same menu commands.

APPLY A STYLIZE EFFECT: THE BRUSH STROKES EFFECT

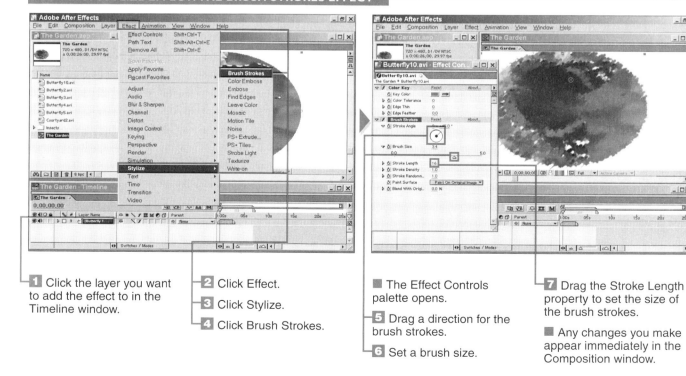

1 Click the layer you want to add the effect to in the Timeline window.

2 Click Effect.
3 Click Stylize.
4 Click Brush Strokes.

■ The Effect Controls palette opens.

5 Drag a direction for the brush strokes.

6 Set a brush size.

7 Drag the Stroke Length property to set the size of the brush strokes.

■ Any changes you make appear immediately in the Composition window.

APPLY A RENDER EFFECT

Render effects enable you to manipulate pixels and turn them into graphical shapes and lines. The Beam effect, for example, creates the illusion of a beam of light or a laser beam. When combined with other effects, you can create a variety of beam styles.

A Beam effect offers properties for controlling the beam's length, thickness at either end, color, and positioning, just to name a few. Most of the

properties are adjustable by scrubbable hot text settings, or you can expand the property to reveal a slider.

Be sure to turn on the Composite on Original property to make the beam appear on the layer, and enable the 3D Perspective property to give the beam depth.

You can access all effects in the Render category through the same menu commands.

How do I set the Starting Point and Ending Point properties?

✔ Click the crosshair button (⊞) for either property and After Effects pinpoints the start or end point in the Composition window. Click and drag the point to a new location on the layer, and then click in place. The start or end point moves.

APPLY A RENDER EFFECT: THE BEAM EFFECT

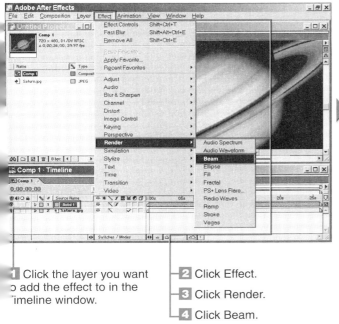

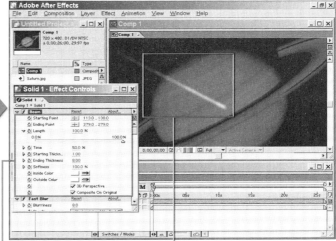

1 Click the layer you want to add the effect to in the Timeline window.

2 Click Effect.

3 Click Render.

4 Click Beam.

■ The Effect Controls palette opens.

5 Make any changes to the beam properties as needed.

Note: See the section "Change Effect Properties" to alter effect properties.

■ In this example, notice a Fast Blur effect gives the beam a soft edge.

APPLY AN AUDIO EFFECT

You can enhance sound used in your project with the Audio effects, the most versatile of which is the Stereo Mixer effect. Whether you import separate sound files, such as MP3 or WAV files, or use sound recorded with digital video footage, you can mix the sound to create just the right audio experience.

The Stereo Mixer effect enables you to set audio levels and panning levels for sounds that play with your video footage. You can create fades, for example, that make the sound slowly increase or decrease in percentage values rather than decibel values.

You can set left and right level values to control audio levels, or

you can use the left and right panning controls to distribute sound between speakers. When setting pan values, a negative value pans the channel to the left and a positive value pans the channel to the right.

You access all Audio effects through the same menu commands.

APPLY AN AUDIO EFFECT: THE STEREO MIXER EFFECT

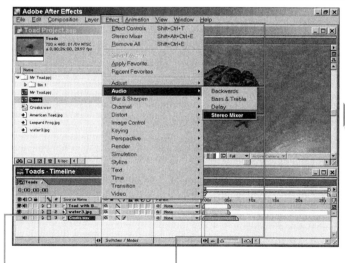

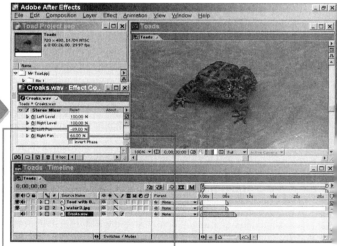

1 Click the layer you want to add an audio effect to in the Timeline window.

Note: See Chapter 25 to learn more about working with layers in the Timeline.

2 Click Effect.

3 Click Audio.

4 Click Stereo Mixer.

■ The Effect Controls palette opens.

5 Click and drag the Left Pan property to pan sound to the left speaker.

Note: See the section "Change Effect Properties" to learn more about adjusting properties.

6 Click and drag the Right Pan property to pan sound to the right speaker.

What exactly do the other Audio effects do?

✔ The Backwards audio effect plays the audio footage item in reverse. The Bass and Treble effect lets you boost or cut audio frequencies. The Delay effect repeats sound much like an echo.

Why should I pan channels?

✔ Audio channels can give listeners a feeling of depth and space when sounds are divided between left and right speakers. With mono sounds, the audio is equally distributed between speakers, but with stereo sound, the audio is mixed. Although stereo and mono sounds share a layer, you can view waveforms for each and you can mix the sounds.

Why would I want to invert a phase?

✔ When you pan one channel to another, you are creating two waves of the same frequency. The two waveforms you create in this procedure are synchronized, or in phase. If the two waves are out of phase, the sounds cancel each other out. You can apply the Invert Phase property to prevent the two waves from canceling each other out.

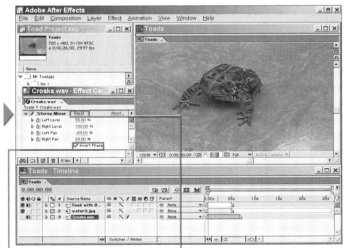

■ Click and drag the Left level to set a sound level for the left channel.

Note: A level value of 100% is the default, normal value. Lower percentages reduce the level, and higher percentages boost the level.

8 Click and drag the Right Level to set a sound level for the right channel.

■ Click here to invert the audio phase to prevent sounds from canceling each other out (☐ changes to ☑).

Note: You can click the Effect Controls palette's ☒ (☐) to close the palette.

■ If you do not like the new settings, click here to reset them to the default settings.

CHANGE EFFECT PROPERTIES

After you assign an effect to a layer in your composition, you can adjust that effect's properties. For example, you may need to change an angle or hue to get just the right look for the layer image. You can change effect properties through the expanded property list in the Timeline window, or in the Effect Controls palette.

Like the Timeline window, the Effect Controls palette list can be expanded and collapsed to reveal effect properties. Each tab in the palette lists the effects assigned to that particular layer. The more layers you assign effects to, the more tabs appear at the top of the palette window. As you add multiple effects to a layer, the list of effects and properties expands.

The properties you see listed for each effect are tailored to that particular effect. For example, the Color Key effect includes properties for controlling color tolerance and feathered edging, and the Brush Stroke effect lists properties for stroke length and brush size.

CHANGE EFFECT PROPERTIES

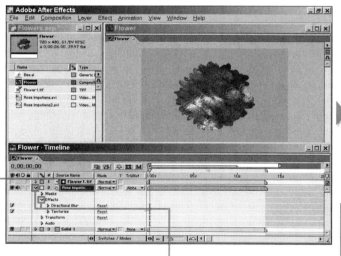

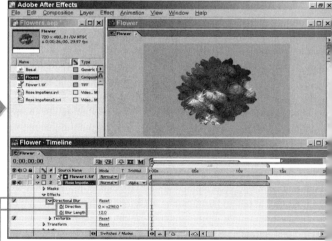

CHANGE EFFECTS IN THE TIMELINE WINDOW

1 Click the layer containing the effect.

Note: See Chapter 25 to learn more about working with layers in the Timeline window.

2 Expand the layer to view layer properties.

Note: See Chapter 26 to expand and collapse layer properties.

3 Expand the Effects property.

■ A list of effects appears.

4 Expand the effect you want to edit.

■ A list of associated properties appears.

■ You can now change a property value to modify the effect.

Note: See Chapter 26 to set layer properties.

Can I move the Effect Controls palette out of the way?

✔ Yes. You can drag the palette's top bar to move the palette, or you can minimize the palette. If you close the palette, you can quickly reopen it again by clicking the effect name in the Timeline window, or by clicking Effect Controls from the Effect menu.

How can I quickly expand all the effects for a layer?

✔ Select the layer in the Timeline window, and then press the E key. Doing this expands the layer properties to reveal all the assigned effects.

How do I change the angle property for an effect?

✔ Depending on the effect, you may see an effect property setting that looks like a dial. You can adjust the property by dragging the dial or by adjusting the scrubbable hot text for the property. To learn more about the scrubbable hot text feature, see Chapter 26.

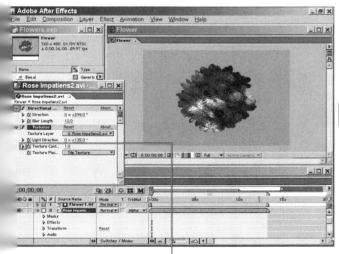

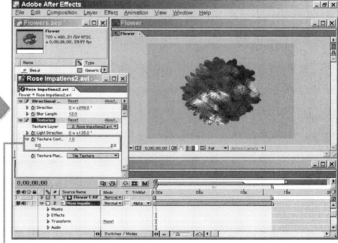

CHANGE EFFECTS IN THE EFFECT CONTROLS PALETTE

■ In the Effect Controls palette, expand the effect you want to edit.

Note: If the Effect Controls palette is closed, click the effect listed in the Timeline window to open the palette.

2 Expand the property you want to change.

■ You can now change the property value to modify the effect.

Note: See Chapter 26 to set layer properties.

SAVE AN EFFECT

Y ou can save an effect you have modified to reuse it again on another layer or in another project entirely. For example, you may have labored for quite some time to make the settings just right for a particular layer effect, and do not want to repeat the process again to create

the same effect again later. You can save the settings as a favorite effect.

You can save a single effect and its related settings, or you can save multiple effects. Favorite effects are saved as cross-platform FFX files and can be used with other After Effects projects. As a separate file,

saved effects enable you to easily share and swap them with other After Effects users.

You can easily apply favorite effect files when you want to use them. After Effects keeps a list of recently saved favorite effects and lists them on the Effect menu.

SAVE AN EFFECT

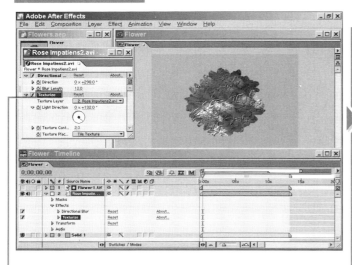

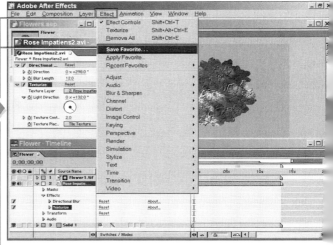

1 With the Effect Controls palette open, click the effect or effects you want to save.

Note: To select multiple effects, press and hold the Shift key while clicking the effect names.

2 Click Effect.

3 Click Save Favorite.

■ The Save Favorite Effect Settings As dialog box appears.

How do I apply a favorite effect to another project?

✔ In the new project file, select the layer to which you want to assign a favorite effect. Click Effect and then click Apply Favorite. The Open dialog box appears. Click the effect file you want to assign and then click Open. After Effects applies the effect.

Can I copy and paste effects in my composition?

✔ Yes. You can use the Edit menu's and Paste commands to copy effects from one layer to another. You cannot, however, copy keyframes along with the effect settings. You can copy and paste keyframes as a separate task.

Can I reorder my effects?

✔ Yes. You can drag an effect and drop it elsewhere in the Timeline window or the Effect Controls palette to reorder the effect. After Effects renders effects in the composition from top to bottom.

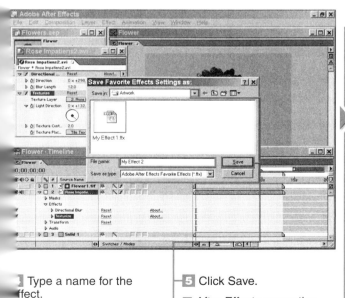

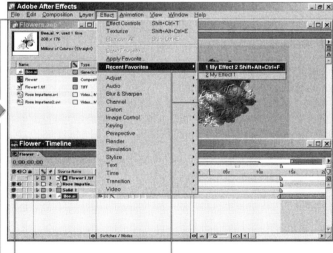

1 Type a name for the effect.

■ Click here to save the effect file to another folder or drive.

5 Click Save.

■ After Effects saves the effect.

6 Click the next layer to which you want to assign the same effect.

7 Click Effect.

8 Click Recent Favorites.

9 Click the effect.

■ After Effects applies the favorite effect.

DISABLE AN EFFECT

You can disable a layer's effect to temporarily turn it off. For example, you may need to disable one effect so that you can view another effect assigned to the same layer. You may also need to disable an effect to speed up the composition preview.

After you disable an effect, you can easily enable it again when you are ready to view the effect.

You can activate the Effect switch in the Timeline window to disable and enable a single effect listed in the expanded layer properties. Also, you can activate the layer's Effect switch to disable or enable effects for the entire layer.

Can I disable an effect in the Effect Controls palette?

✔ Yes. Clicking the Effect switch next to the effect name in the Effect Controls palette also disables the effect in both the palette and the Timeline window.

What does the About setting do for an effect?

✔ Click About to view a description. The About setting option appears only if the Switches/Mode panel is widened. To widen the panel, move the mouse pointer to the panel border at the top of the panel column until ▶ becomes ↕ and then drag the panel border left or right.

DISABLE AN EFFECT

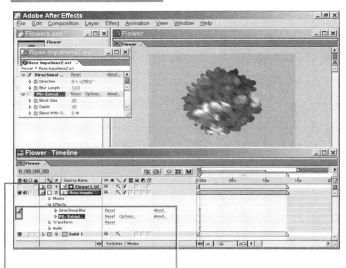

DISABLE A SINGLE EFFECT

1 Click the layer containing the effect.

2 Expand the layer to view layer and effect properties.

Note: See Chapter 26 to expand and collapse layer properties.

3 Click the Effect switch for the effect you want to disable (▣ becomes ▢).

■ After Effects disables the effect.

Note: To enable the effects, click the Effect switch.

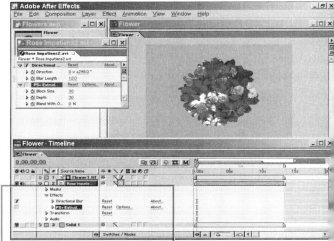

DISABLE ALL LAYER EFFECTS

1 Click the layer containing the effect.

Note: See Chapter 25 to learn more about working with layers in the Timeline window.

2 Click the Effect switch ([becomes ▢).

■ After Effects disables the layer's effects.

Note: To enable the effects, click the Effect switch.

REMOVE AN EFFECT

You can easily remove an effect you no longer need. If you made modifications to the effect properties, you can also reset the properties to their default settings.

For example, perhaps you experimented with adding several different effects, and decided to keep just one. You can remove the effects you no

longer want assigned to the layer.

When you remove an effect, it no longer appears in the Effect Controls palette or Timeline window. After Effects removes any properties you changed when setting the effect.

Can I just use the Undo command to remove an effect?

✔ Yes, but only if you employ the command immediately after assigning the effect. If this is the case, click Edit and then Undo. If you change your mind about the effect removal, you can quickly restore the effect again by first clicking Edit and then clicking Redo.

REMOVE AN EFFECT

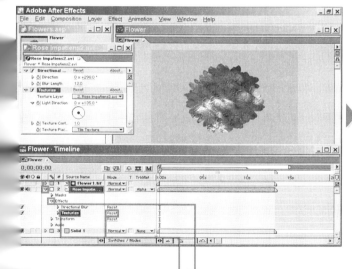

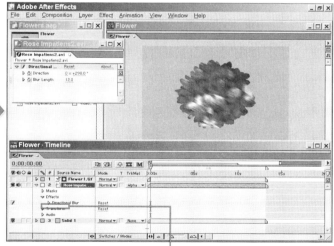

■ Click the layer containing the effect.

■ Expand the layer to view layer properties.

note: See Chapter 26 to expand and collapse layer properties.

3 Expand the effects properties to view effects assigned to the layer.

4 Click the effect you want to remove.

■ To reset the effect's default values, click here.

5 Press the Delete key.

■ After Effects removes the effect.

UNDERSTANDING 3D LAYERS AND EFFECTS

After Effects 5.0 enables you to create 3D compositions to give your video projects added dimensionality. Three-dimensional layers provide additional properties for increased flexibility. For example, you can control how a layer image responds to an imaginary light source.

2D versus 3D layers

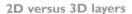

By default, all layers you add to a composition are 2D, which means you can position the images along horizontal (x) and vertical (y) axes. When you assign 3D status to a layer, an additional axis, z, establishes depth. By assigning depth, you can create realistic shadows and light, and the image seems to move through space.

A positive z coordinate moves the image closer to the viewer, and a negative one sends the image farther away from the viewer. You can assign z-axis values manually in the Composition window, or you can enter values for the property in the Timeline window.

3D layers can be placed behind or in front of each other in the Composition window without affecting the order of layers in the Timeline window. To create shadow effects with lighting, however, you must turn shadow-casting options on and adjust the z axis.

Axes

Axes are color-coded in After Effects. As soon as you assign 3D status to a layer, the axes appear as arrows emanating from the center of the layer image. A red arrow indicates the x axis, a green arrow represents the y axis, and a blue arrow represents the z axis. You can drag an arrow to change the layer's position in the 3D space. Axes colors are the same for camera and light layers used with 3D effects.

As you position items in 3D layers, you can change axes modes to determine which set of axes is transformed. After Effects offers three axes modes you can assign: Local Axes, World Axes, and View Axes. The Local Axes mode aligns the axes to the surface of the 3D layer. The World Axes mode aligns the axes to absolute coordinates, and the View Axes mode aligns the axes to the selected view. You can quickly change axes modes using the buttons found at the bottom of the toolbox.

Lights

You can use light layers to create simulated lights that shine on your 3D layer image. Light layers appear at the top of the Timeline window in the order in which you add them. You can control exactly what kind of light to use, such as a spot or point, and where the light shines. You can assign more than one light to a light layer. You can also control angle, shadows, and intensity of the lights.

Cameras

You can use simulated cameras with your 3D layers to set a particular angle or distance for a view. You determine the distance from the subject, which in After Effects is the layer image, and the angle of the camera view. When you assign a camera view, it defines how you look at your compositions' layers.

Like the lights feature, cameras occupy layers in your project. Multiple camera views enable you to view your project in different ways.

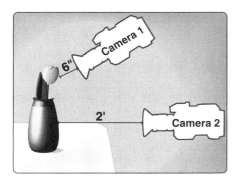

Point of Interest

The Point of Interest property works with camera and light layers to define the point of focus on a 3D layer object. By default, After Effects assigns the point of interest for a new camera or light layer at the center of the composition.

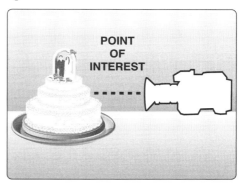

3D Views

Three-dimensional status entails additional viewing options for your layers. You can choose from a variety of 3D views in the Composition window to help you as you edit and move a 3D image. You can utilize three view categories: Orthogonal, Custom, and Camera. Orthogonal views include front, back, top, bottom, left, and right. You can switch views using the Composition window's 3D View pop-up menu.

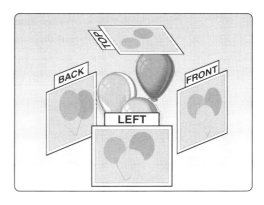

CHAPTER 5

CREATE A 3D LAYER

You can turn a 2D layer into a 3D layer in After Effects and utilize additional effects. By default, all layers are 2D unless you switch a layer to 3D mode.

3D mode adds a z axis to the layer, and you can assign 3D transform and material properties. Axis coordinates appear color coded in a 3D layer. A red arrow represents the x axis, a green arrow represents the y axis, and a blue arrow represents the z axis.

By changing a 2D layer to 3D, you can create the illusion of depth, including shadows, light, angles, and distance.

You cannot make an adjustment layer a 3D layer.

How do I move an axis?

✔ Click and drag an axis point to move it. You may need to switch 3D views to better see the axis point you want to change. See the section "Switch Between 3D Views" to learn more about view modes.

Does it matter where I place a 3D layer in the Timeline's layer order?

✔ Yes. If you want the layer to cast shadows on the layer or layers below, be sure to place the 3D layer above the other layers.

CREATE A 3D LAYER

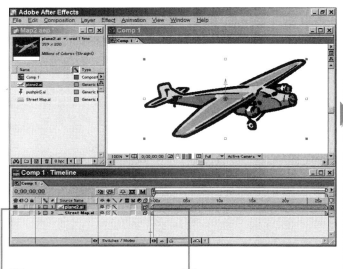

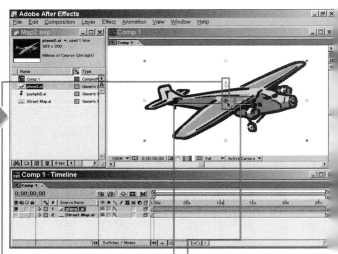

1 Click the layer you want to make 3D.

Note: See Chapter 26 to learn more about working with layers in the Timeline window.

2 Click the 3D Layer switch (☐ becomes ⊡).

■ After Effects assigns the layer 3D status.

■ The layer image shows three axes, along with the image anchor point.

Note: Zoom your view of the Composition window to better see the axis points.

■ The y axis controls vertical placement.

■ The x axis controls horizontal placement.

■ The z axis controls depth and may be difficult to see the Active Camera view.

Note: See the next section to switch views.

SWITCH BETWEEN 3D VIEWS

As you work with 3D layers in your project, you can change the way you view the layer in the Composition window. For example, you can view a layer without perspective, such as front or back, or you can view the layer as if looking through a camera lens.

You can use the orthogonal views to see the composition from one of six sides: front, left, right, back, top, and bottom. Use the custom and camera views to see the composition using a 3D perspective.

You can find the view options for 3D layers both under the View menu and as a pop-up menu in the Composition window.

How do I view 3D layer properties?

✔ You view 3D layer properties just as you view other layer properties: by expanding and collapsing the property lists in the Timeline window. See Chapter 26 to learn more about viewing properties in the Timeline window.

How can I more quickly switch views?

✔ You can use shortcut keys to quickly switch between views. For example, pressing F10 switches to Front view, F11 switches to custom view, and pressing F12 switches back to Active Camera view.

SWITCH BETWEEN 3D VIEWS

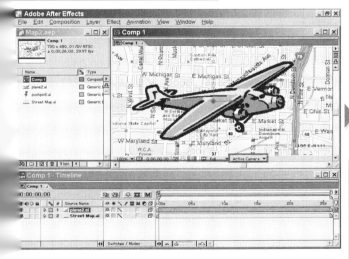

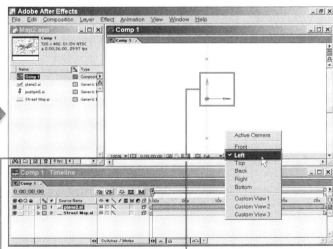

■ With the Composition window open, click the 3D Views pop-up ▼.

-2 Click a view.

■ The Composition switches to the view you selected.

■ This figure shows the Left view, which gives you a better view of the z axis.

Note: You may need to switch to an orthogonal view, such as Left, to more easily drag the position of the z axis.

SET 3D LAYER PROPERTIES

Y ou can set a variety of properties for 3D layers in addition to regular layer properties. When you create a 3D layer, a new property category, called Materials, is immediately added to the list of properties in the Timeline window.

The Materials property includes settings for lighting effects, shadows, and more. For example, if you add a light layer and want to illuminate a 3D layer, you can turn on the 3D

layer's Accepts Lights or Casts Shadows property. 3D layer properties are available for light and camera layers as well as layers you turn into 3D layers.

In addition, a z axis rotation property is added to the Transform property category, which enables you to rotate an object's z axis.

See Chapter 26 to learn more about setting other layer properties, such as position and rotation.

How else can I access 3D layer properties?

✔ You can access the layer's z rotation property by clicking the layer, the Layer menu, Transform, and then Z Rotation. You must use the expand/collapse buttons in the Timeline window to view 3D layer properties.

SET 3D LAYER PROPERTIES

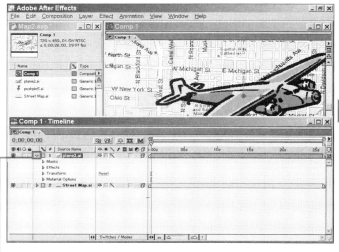

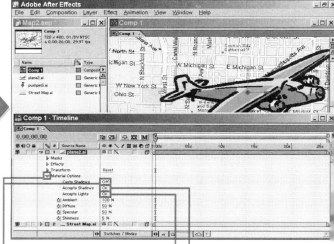

1 Expand the 3D layer whose properties you want to view.

Note: See Chapter 26 to expand and collapse layer properties.

2 Expand the Materials properties.

■ The 3D properties appear in a list.

■ Click here to make the layer image cast a shadow when a lighting effect is applied.

■ Activate this property to accept lighting effects.

■ If the layer is used as a background layer to other 3D images, activate this property to accept shadow effects.

CHANGE AXIS MODES

You can use axis modes to designate a set of axes you want to transform. By specifying a set before making changes to the 3D layer properties, you can more easily make needed changes to the layer properties.

After Effects offers three axes modes: Local Axes, World Axes, and View Axes. Each axis mode uses a Spatial

Transform property that defines how the x, y, and z axes of a 3D layer interact.

The Local Axes mode aligns the three axes to the layer's surface in the composition. The World Axes mode aligns the axes to coordinates in the 3D world. The View Axes mode aligns axes to a designated view, such as front, back, or camera.

How do I move a single axis?

✔ First select an axes mode, and then click the Selection button (▸) in the toolbox. Move the mouse pointer over the axis you want to layer. When you hover the mouse pointer over the x axis, for example, the pointer is labeled X. If you move the mouse pointer over the z axis, however, the pointer is labeled Z, and so on. Now click and drag the axis to edit the axis point.

CHANGE AXIS MODES

■ Click the 3D layer you want to transform.

Note: See Chapter 25 to select layers in the Timeline window.

■ Click an axis mode on the toolbox.

Note: If the toolbox is not displayed, click Tools from the Window menu.

■ This figure shows Local Axes mode.

■ Click the Local Axes button (⊞) to align axes to the layer surface.

■ Click the World Axes button (◻) to align axes to the 3D world.

■ Click the View Axes button (▦) to align axes to the current 3D view.

■ This figure shows View Axes mode.

CREATE LIGHTS

You can create a variety of illumination effects on your 3D layers by assigning lights. Lights are simulated lighting you can direct toward a 3D layer that is set up to accept lights. The Accept Lights property is available only on 3D layers.

You can add lights to a 3D layer by creating a light layer directly above the layer you want to affect. You can choose from four light effects: Parallel, Spot, Point, and Ambient. Parallel light resembles sunlight, and illuminates in one direction from a seemingly far-away source. A spotlight is similar to lighting you see on a theatrical stage, and radiates from a cone shape which you can adjust in angle and direction. Point light radiates omnidirectional lighting from a source area such as a light bulb.

Ambient light does not emanate from a source, but lights up the entire scene.

To cast shadows on objects in the light's path, the light layer's Cast Shadows property must be turned on. You may also need to reposition the object's z axis to create the shadow effect.

CREATE LIGHTS

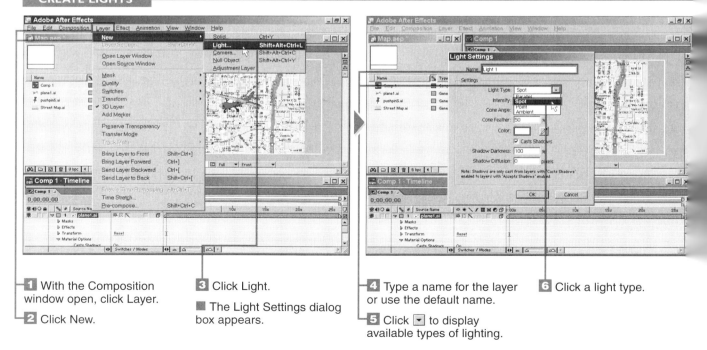

1 With the Composition window open, click Layer.

2 Click New.

3 Click Light.

■ The Light Settings dialog box appears.

4 Type a name for the layer or use the default name.

5 Click ▾ to display available types of lighting.

6 Click a light type.

How do I move a light?

✔ First, click the light layer in the Timeline. Next, click and drag the light cone to adjust the light perspective; you can do this only with spot and point light types. You may need to zoom your view of the Composition window to better see the light effect and the axes.

How do I edit the light settings?

✔ Double-click the light layer to quickly launch the Light Settings dialog box where you can change the settings as needed.

How do I control the shadow created by the light?

✔ Use the Shadow Darkness and Shadow Diffusion settings in the Light Settings dialog box to set shadow darkness levels or make the shadows appear softer or harder. For example, if you type a larger value in the Shadow Diffusion box, you can make the shadow appear lighter as if a greater distance from the object image.

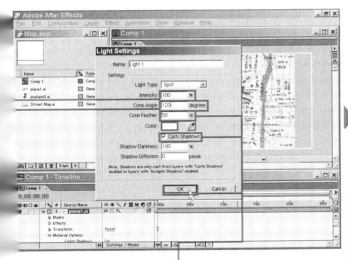

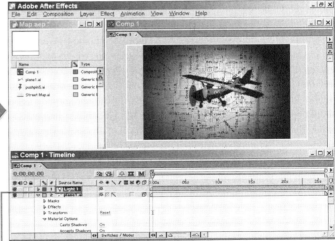

■ 7 Change any other light settings as needed.

■ Type a new value here to change the intensity.

■ Type a new value here to change cone width.

■ Type a new value here to adjust sharpness or softness of the light's edges.

■ Select this option to make the light cast shadows beneath layer images.

■ 8 Click OK.

■ After Effects adds the light layer to the Timeline and the light effect appears in the Composition window.

■ This figure shows a spotlight added.

Note: Make sure the layer you are lighting has the Casts Shadows and Accepts Shadows properties turned on.

CREATE A 3D CAMERA

Y ou can create a camera layer and employ it to view your 3D composition using a variety of camera angles and distances. Simulating a real camera, a camera layer enables you to move around within the space of a 3D layer and examine different perspectives and angles.

When you create a camera layer, you can specify exactly what camera settings to use, such as

focal depth, film size, aperture, and more. The layer itself is added to the top of the Timeline window. Like the other 3D layer types, the camera layer includes additional properties.

You can find a selection of preset camera types you can use. The presets are named for focal lengths. For example, if you prefer the camera layer to see the composition much like human sight, you can

choose the 35mm or 50mm preset. Each preset includes default camera settings. You can also change the camera settings to create a custom camera view.

You can add multiple camera layers to any composition. After you add a layer, you can move the camera object around to view different perspectives.

CREATE A 3D CAMERA

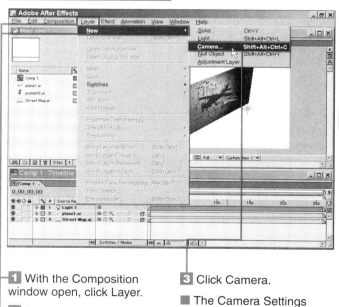

■1 With the Composition window open, click Layer.

■2 Click New.

■3 Click Camera.

■ The Camera Settings dialog box appears.

■4 Type a name for the layer or use the default name.

■5 Click here to display available presets.

■6 Click a camera lens.

I have several cameras assigned. How do I switch camera views?

✔ Click the 3D View pop-up menu in the Composition window and then click the camera view you want to apply. By default, After Effects applies the Active Camera view unless otherwise specified.

How do I edit the camera settings?

✔ Double-click the camera layer to quickly open the Camera Settings dialog box where you can change the settings as needed.

Is there an easier way to move the camera?

✔ You can utilize the camera tools in the Toolbox to change the camera position and view. With the camera layer selected, click the Orbit Camera tool (⊙) and drag it on the Composition window to rotate the view around the current point of interest. Use the Track XY Camera tool (⊕) to move the view horizontally and vertically, or use the Track Z Camera tool (⬦)to move the view along the point of interest.

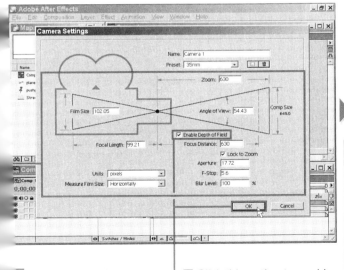

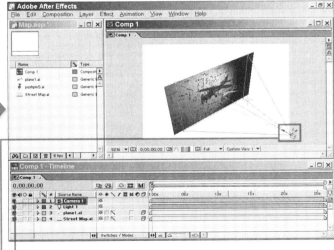

7 Change any other camera settings as needed.

■ Click this option to enable settings for focus distance, aperture, f-stop, and blur level.

8 Click OK.

■ The camera layer appears in the Timeline.

■ You can now manipulate the view by dragging the camera.

Note: You can drag the camera in any view, but it may be easier to see the camera in other 3D view modes, such as Custom View.

UNDERSTANDING PREVIEW AND RENDER OPTIONS

Y ou can utilize playback controls to preview your project as you assemble it. You can then *render,* or output, it to a file for sharing with others.

If you are new to using After Effects, take a moment and acquaint yourself with the various ways you can view and export your project.

Playback versus Preview

In After Effects, *playback* refers to the standard controls for viewing frames, while *previewing* refers to playing a project to check it at various stages of assembly. After Effects renders an approximation of the composition during a preview.

Playback controls appear in both the Time Controls palette and the Footage window. Playback controls include the typical Play and Stop buttons in addition to buttons for advancing or going back one frame at a time.

You can always *scrub* the Time marker in any window to see how the composition, layer, or footage item looks. Scrubbing refers to dragging the Time marker left or right to see frames play.

Preview controls, on the other hand, enable you to actually play a part of the composition, including effects and edits. The Time Controls palette also features preview controls.

Preview Options

The more elaborate your composition, the more slowly it may preview. You can specify how much detail you want to preview by changing magnification, resolution, and preview quality. You can also utilize caching and dynamic resolution to create faster previews as well as Composition window updates. The RAM preview options let you preview video and audio frames at the same frame rate assigned to the composition, or as fast as your computer system and available RAM allow. After Effects loads a number of frames into RAM before it starts playing the preview. You define the work area you want to view, and then After Effects displays the total number of frames you specified in the work area. With Wireframe previews, After Effects renders transformations in the composition as wireframe outlines instead of the full effect, which frees up RAM processing power.

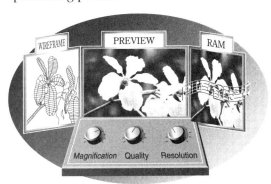

Render

When your project is just the way you want it, you can output, or *render,* the composition to a movie or other file format. Rendering is the process of applying all the editing, masks, and effects you assigned to a composition and then transfering the settings to a final movie.

Export

You may want to export your project to another file type. For example, if you plan to use the video on the Web, you can export the project as a Macromedia Flash file. Users whose Web browsers support the Flash Player plug-in can view the video. The movie's audio is encoded in MP3 format and streamed with the video. Based on what your system supports, additional export modules, including QuickTime and Video for Windows components, appear on the File, Export submenu.

USING PLAYBACK CONTROLS

The Time Controls palette lets you control playback of footage with any active After Effects window. The playback controls include buttons for moving backward and forward one frame at a time, a jog track for scrubbing footage, loop options, and RAM preview options.

As you view footage using the Time Controls palette, the Timeline window's Time marker corresponds with the playback.

You can use the playback buttons to start and stop playback, or you can scrub the slider on the jog track to view the frames. *Scrubbing* refers to clicking and dragging the slider or Time marker left and right to view frames.

You can keep the Time Controls palette open to use with any window, or you can close the palette and summon it only when you need it.

What does the Audio tab do?
✔ Click the Audio tab to see a VU meter that displays audio levels as they play.

What does the Loop button do?
✔ Click the Loop button (⟳) to continuously play the footage. Clicking the button once loops the footage once (⟳ becomes ▶). Clicking the button a second time (▶ becomes ⟷) activates the Palindrome feature, which first plays the footage forward and then backward without stopping.

USING PLAYBACK CONTROLS

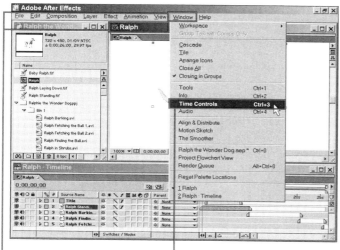

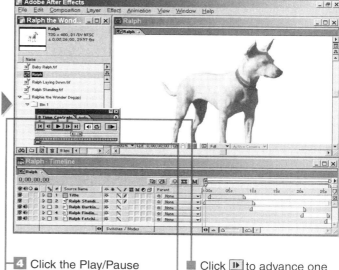

1 Click the window in which you want to view footage.

Note: Use the Time Controls palette to play footage in the Composition, Layer, Footage, and Timeline windows.

2 Click Window.

3 Click Time Controls.

■ The Time Controls palette appears.

Note: To better view on-screen elements, simply click and drag the palette's top bar to move the palette.

4 Click the Play/Pause button (▶) to play the footage.

■ The footage plays.

■ Click ◀ to move back to the first frame.

■ Click ▶ to advance one frame.

■ You can also drag the slider to move back and forth along the footage Timeline.

■ Click the Play/Pause button again to stop playback.

SET THE WORK AREA

Y ou can specify the work area you want to include in a preview. A work area is a range of Timeline frames. Setting helps you when you want to use the RAM preview without previewing the entire composition.

The work area appears in the Timeline window, just above the Time graph area. Two handles define the work area. When you adjust these left and right handles, After Effects shades the area between the two handles differently in the time graph area, showing you exactly which layers are included in the work area and which are viewable in the preview.

How do I make the time graph area appear larger?

✔ You can close the other panels in the Timeline window to free up room to view more of the time graph. To do so, click the Timeline Options Menu button (▶), click Panels, and then click a panel to close. You can also zoom your view of the time graph using the Zoom buttons and Zoom slider at the bottom of the time graph area.

SET THE WORK AREA

1 Open the composition you want to preview.

2 Click and drag the left work area handle to the frame where you want to start the work area.

Note: See Chapter 24 to learn more about the Timeline window, and Chapter 25 to learn more about the time graph area.

3 Drag the right work area handle to the frame where you want to end the work area.

■ The work area is defined.

■ You can now execute a RAM preview and view only the layers that fall between the work area handles.

Note: See the section "Create a RAM Preview" to preview the composition.

CREATE A RAM PREVIEW

You can preview how your composition looks using the After Effects RAM preview option. The standard RAM preview plays your entire composition, or just the specified frames. You can find the RAM preview controls in the Time Controls palette. You can preview in the Composition, Footage, or Layer windows.

You can assign preview options, such as frame rate and resolution. For example, you may want to see how the composition plays at a lower frame rate or a higher resolution. You can also specify the number of times the RAM preview plays back the composition.

Can I prevent a layer from previewing?

✔ Yes. You can use the Audio/Video switches in the Timeline window to turn off the display for audio or video in a preview. Learn more about the Audio/Video switches in Chapter 25.

How do I set RAM preview options?

✔ In the Time Controls palette, click the RAM Preview Options button (▶), then click which preview type you want to use: Show RAM Preview Options or Show Shift+RAM Preview Options. The preview options appear listed in the bottom of the Time Controls palette. Set any options and then click ▶ to see the preview.

■1 Display the Time Controls palette.

Note: See the section "Using Playback Controls" to use the Time Controls palette.

■2 Click the window you want to preview, set the work area, or cue the Time marker to the frame you want to preview.

■3 Click the RAM Preview button (▶).

■ The footage plays, and a green line appears over cached frames in the Timeline.

■ To stop the preview, press the spacebar.

SAVE A RAM PREVIEW

You can save a RAM preview and use it as a draft version of the composition. For example, you may need to share the preview file with another department or client for review before completing the final project.

RAM previews save the current composition frame size and resolution settings. Unlike a rendered movie,

RAM previews cannot include interlaced fields.

When preparing to save a RAM preview, first establish the work area and create a RAM preview. To set a work area, see the section "Set the Work Area." To create a RAM preview, see the previous section, "Create a RAM Preview."

I do not have much RAM to work with. Can I purge RAM for previews?

✔ You can manually clear the cache frames of any rendered frames. To do so, click Edit, Purge, and then Image Caches.

Can I optimize my cache size?

✔ Yes. Click Edit, Preferences, and then Cache to open the Preferences dialog box and display cache options. You can set a maximum amount of RAM and memory usage (Windows) or set a memory mode or cache size (Mac).

SAVE A RAM PREVIEW

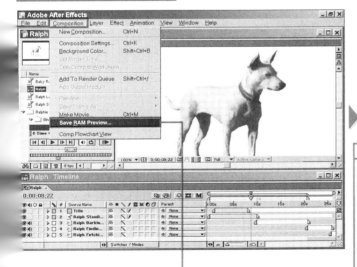

1 Click Composition.

Note: See the section "Create a RAM Preview" to preview a composition.

2 Click Save RAM Preview.

■ The Output Movie To dialog box appears.

3 Type a name for the preview file or use the default name.

■ Click ⏷ to change the folder or drive.

■ Click ⏷ to save the preview file as another file type.

4 Click Save.

■ The Render Queue window appears briefly and renders the project.

629

SET THE REGION OF INTEREST

Y ou can specify a portion of an image to play during playback or previews. By playing only a portion of the image, After Effects requires less RAM and creates a faster preview.

Video frames you play in After Effects are cached into memory, your computer's RAM, which means they are temporarily loaded. Whenever you move the Time marker to an unrendered frame, After Effects caches the frame. Once cached, the frame plays back

more quickly. As you render more and more frames for a preview, After Effects removes the older cached frames from RAM to make room for new frames.

To help speed up the process and save on the amount of RAM required, specify which part of the screen, or region, is your focus. Define a rectangular area in the Composition window to include in playback. The preview omits areas outside the rectangle you draw.

Can I stop After Effects from continually updating changes I make to the Composition window?

✔ Yes. You can suppress window updates to save preview rendering time. Pressing the Caps Lock key suppresses updates. Pressing it again toggles the feature off.

SET THE REGION OF INTEREST

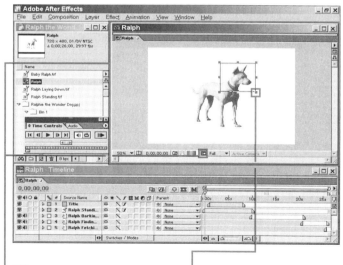

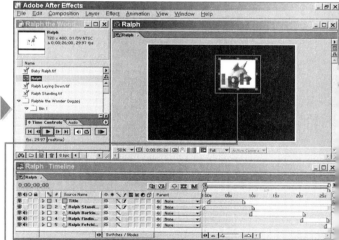

1 Open the composition you want to preview.

2 Click the Region of Interest button (🔲).

3 Drag a square or rectangle, referred to as a marquee, around the area you want to include in the preview.

■ To resize the area, click and drag a corner handle.

4 Preview the composition.

Note: See the previous section to use the Time Controls palette.

■ Only the region of interest area previews.

Note: To return to the full image, click 🔲 again to toggle it off.

CREATE A WIREFRAME PREVIEW

You can use a wireframe preview to view the motion path for an animated composition. Rather than use up valuable RAM to create a rendered preview, you can save your computer some work and preview only the outlines of moving layers.

Wireframe preview shows not only the motion a layer takes in the

composition, but also any scaling, change in position, or rotation. Every frame appears in the wireframe motion path and, depending on the layer movement, the wireframe may show subtle movement or a multiple number of outline images.

How do I preview audio instead of video or wireframes?

✔ First, cue the Time marker where you want to start previewing audio in the Timeline window. Next, click the Composition window. Finally, click Preview and then Audio Preview (Here Forward). The audio plays without the video. Pressing the spacebar stops the audio from playing.

CREATE A WIREFRAME PREVIEW

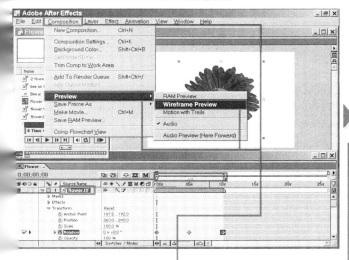

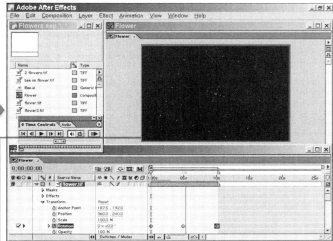

■ From the Timeline window, click the layers you want to preview using the wireframe preview feature.

■ Set the work area.

Note: See the section, "Set the Work Area" to set the work area over the time graph.

3 Click Composition.

4 Click Preview.

5 Click Wireframe Preview.

■ After Effects creates a preview of the layers in wireframe form.

■ To stop the preview, press the spacebar.

RENDER A MOVIE

You can turn a project into a movie using the Render Queue window. From the Render Queue window, you can specify the order in which items are rendered and any specific settings for each item.

As a composition is rendered, you can check its progress and remaining rendering time in the Render Queue window. Depending on the size and amount of detail the composition entails, the rendering process may take a few minutes or hours.

Within the Render Queue window you can set specific rendering settings to determine how frames are calculated for output, resolution and layer quality, and more. By default, After Effects renders the movie using the same settings assigned when you started the project. If you need to change the settings for your output goal, you can do so in the Render Queue window.

The Render Queue also enables you to set output-module settings, which determine how the project is saved to disk.

RENDER A MOVIE

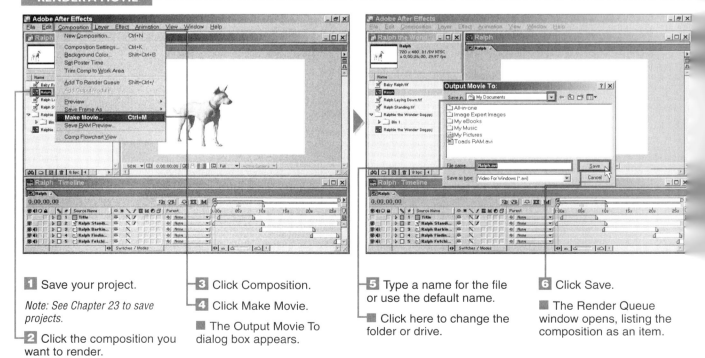

1 Save your project.

Note: See Chapter 23 to save projects.

2 Click the composition you want to render.

3 Click Composition.

4 Click Make Movie.

■ The Output Movie To dialog box appears.

5 Type a name for the file or use the default name.

■ Click here to change the folder or drive.

6 Click Save.

■ The Render Queue window opens, listing the composition as an item.

How do I change render settings?
✔ The Render Queue window offers a variety of settings you can select from before starting a rendering process. Click Current Settings to display the Render Settings dialog box, which displays various settings you can change. To learn more about project settings, see Chapter 23.

How do I change output settings?
✔ Output settings determine how the rendered movie frames are saved. Called *output modules*, the options enable you to choose file format, compression settings, and more. To view output settings, click Lossless. The Output Module Settings dialog box appears, where you can make any changes to the output settings.

Can I create multiple versions of my movie?
✔ Yes. Add the composition to the Render Queue window, select the item in the window, click the Composition menu, and then click Add Output Module. Another copy of the item, for which you can set different output settings, appears in the queue.

How do I stop rendering?
✔ Click the Stop button. To pause rendering, click the Pause button.

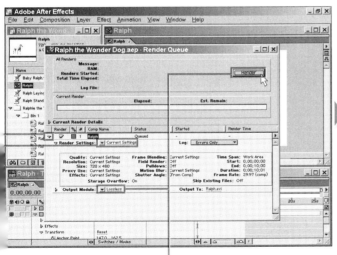

7 Click here to view current settings (▷ becomes ▽).

■ Click here to specify any render settings you want to change.

■ Click here to specify any output options, if needed.

8 Click the Render button.

■ After Effects renders the composition, displaying a progress bar.

EXPORT A MOVIE

You can export your project to a variety of file formats. For example, if you create a movie to use on a Web page, you can output the project to Macromedia Flash format (SWF), one of the most popular formats for Web movies. You can also export your movie as a QuickTime (MOV) or Video for Windows (AVI) file.

When exporting a movie, you can set compression options. Compression schemes, called *codecs*, are essential to saving video files. Video files contain large amounts of data, and without compression, would prohibit viewing because of file size. With compression, however, you can

reduce the file size and still maintain quality playback.

The After Effects output modules include compression settings that you can adjust. For example, if you choose to export the movie in QuickTime format, you can specify which QuickTime codecs to assign.

EXPORT A MOVIE

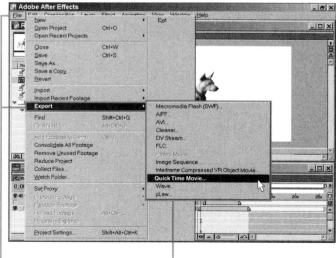

1 Save your project.

Note: See Chapter 23 to save a project.

2 Click File.

3 Click Export.

4 Click an export format.

■ The Save As dialog box appears.

5 Type a name for the file.

■ Click ▼ to change the folder or drive to which you want to save.

6 Click Save.

■ Based on the format you chose in step 4, an additional dialog box appears.

■ If you chose QuickTime Movie, the Movie Settings dialog box appears and you can change compression settings.

Can I set compression settings for my composition before exporting?

✔ Compression enables you to store large amounts of data in smaller increments. The end goal of your output determines your compression choices. You can find compression options in the Compression Settings dialog box. To access the dialog box through the Render Queue window, click the Output Module's underlined name to open the Output Module Settings dialog box, choose a format, then click the Format Options button to open the Compression Settings dialog box. From this box you can choose a *codec* (compression/decompression preset), set bit depth, quality, and more.

Can I export a single frame from my composition?

✔ Yes. First cue the Time marker in the Timeline window to the frame you want to save. Click Composition, Save Frame As, and then File. The Save As dialog box appears. Type a name for the file and change the destination drive or folder if needed. Click Save. After Effects adds the item to the Render Queue window. To render the frame, select it and then click the Render button.

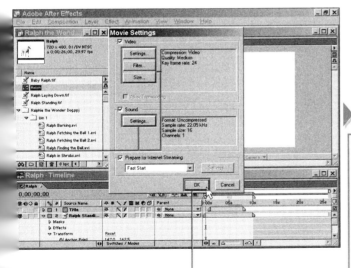

7 Specify any additional output settings you want to assign or use the current settings.

8 Click OK.

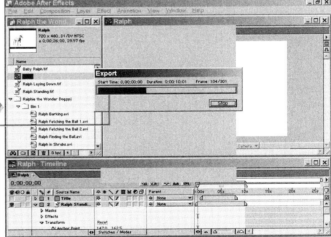

■ After Effects begins exporting the file and displays a progress bar.

Note: Depending on the size and detail of the project, the export may take several minutes or hours.

WHAT'S ON THE CD-ROM

The CD-ROM included in this book contains tryout versions of all the programs described in this book, and some plug-ins you can use to enhance the software. Before installing any of the programs or plug-ins on the disc, make sure that a newer version of the program is not already installed on your computer.

For information on installing different versions of the same program, contact Adobe Systems, Inc. or the plug-in's manufacturer.

System Requirements

To use the contents of the CD-ROM, your computer must be equipped with the following hardware and software:

Windows Requirements

- Intel Pentium III 500 MHz or faster (700 MHz recommended).
- Microsoft Windows 98, Windows Millennium Edition, Windows 2000 with Service Pack 2, or Windows XP.
- 128MB of RAM to run any one application (256MB of RAM or more recommended). Additional RAM is recommended if you want to run two or more applications simultaneously.
- 510MB of available hard-disk space required for installation. 1GB or more hard disk or disk array space recommended for ongoing work.
- A CD-ROM drive.
- A 16-bit sound card.
- A 24-bit color display adapter and monitor.
- For Adobe PostScript printing: a printer with PostScript Level 2 or PostScript 3 support.
- Apple QuickTime 5.0 recommended.
- Microsoft DirectX 8.1 recommended.

Additional Windows Requirements for Premiere and After Effects:

- Dedicated large-capacity 7200 rpm UDMA 66 IDE or SCSI hard disk or disk array.
- Microsoft-certified OHCI IEEE 1394 interface.
- Premiere-certified capture card (if capturing from an analog video source).

Macintosh Requirements

- PowerPC 300MHz processor G3 or faster (G4 or G4 dual processor recommended).
- Mac OS 9.1 or higher.

- 128MB of RAM to run any one application (256MB of RAM or more recommended). Additional RAM is recommended if you want to run two or more applications simultaneously.
- 475MB of available hard-disk space to install all applications. For ongoing work, we recommend 1GB or more hard disk or disk array space.
- A CD-ROM drive.
- A Sound card.
- A 24-bit color display adapter.
- For Adobe PostScript printing, we recommend a printer with PostScript Level 2 or PostScript 3 support.
- Apple QuickTime 5.0.

Additional Macintosh Requirements for Premiere and After Effects:

- Large-capacity hard disk or disk array capable of sustaining 5 MB/sec.
- QuickTime-compatible FireWire (IEEE 1394) interface.
- Apple FireWire 2.4.
- Premiere-certified capture card (if capturing from an analog video source).

  Note: The following Adobe products support Mac OS X version 10.1: Adobe Illustrator 10 and Adobe After Effects 5.5.

Installing and Using the Software

Program Versions

Shareware programs are fully functional, free trial versions of copyrighted programs. If you like a particular program, you can register with its author for a nominal fee and receive licenses, enhanced versions, and technical support.

Freeware programs are free, copyrighted games, applications, and utilities. You can copy them to as many computers as you like, but they have no technical support.

GNU software is governed by its own license, which is included inside the folder of the GNU software. There are no restrictions on distribution of this software. See the GNU license for more details.

Trial, demo, and evaluation versions are usually limited either by time or functionality. For example, you may not be able to save projects using these versions.

For your convenience, the software titles appearing on the CD-ROM are listed alphabetically.

aeFlame

For Windows 98, ME, 2000, or XP, and Mac OS 9.1 or later. GNU. An After Effects plug-in that enables you to create frame fractals you can animate to simulate the appearance of flames. Using the After Effects motion controls, you can create stunning fire effects, ranging from wisps of smoke to full-out burning pyres.

After Effects 5.5, from Adobe Systems, Inc.

For Windows 98, ME, 2000, or XP, and Mac OS 9.1 or later. Tryout version. After Effects 5.5 software delivers a comprehensive set of tools to efficiently produce motion graphics and visual effects for film, video, multimedia, and the Web. You can explore unlimited creative possibilities with precise control while working in a 2D or 3D compositing environment. After Effects offers unparalleled integration with Premiere, Photoshop, and Illustrator to produce professional results. *Note: You cannot save or export files with the tryout version.*

Flash Player 5, from Macromedia, Inc.

For Windows 98, ME, 2000, or XP, and Macintosh. The Flash Player is a free Web player application for viewing Flash content on the Web. For more information, visit www.macromedia.com/software/flashplayer.

Illustrator 10, from Adobe Systems, Inc.

For Windows 98, ME, 2000, or XP, and Mac OS 9.1 or later. Tryout version. Illustrator 10 lets you create graphics for the Web and digital video using both vector and bitmap images. It expands your creative options, introducing powerful new vector-based Web design tools, symbols, and the most versatile transparency capabilities available in any vector program. It's packed with dozens of other innovative features that help you work faster and with more creative control. *Note: You cannot save, print, or export files with the tryout version.*

Photoshop 6, from Adobe Systems, Inc.

For Windows 98, ME, 2000, or XP, and Mac OS 9.1. Tryout version. Photoshop is the industry standard photo-editing suite. With it, you can correct digital images, apply effects, adjust color balance, and generate brilliant effects and dynamic objects for use in digital video or Internet applications. It is capable of both bitmap and vector graphic manipulation, and has dozens of features and filters that make ordinary images sparkle and come to life. *Note: You cannot save, print, or export files with the tryout version.*

Premiere 6, from Adobe Systems, Inc.

For Windows 98, ME, 2000, or XP, and Mac OS 9.1. Thirty-day evaluation version. Premiere is a stunningly simple and powerful professional video nonlinear editing tool. It supports digital video on both Windows and Macintosh platforms, and has cross-platform support for all of the leading Web video formats. Premiere also integrates a variety of features and functions into its long-held marketplace position as simply the best video-editing application for the PC and Macintosh. *Note: The software is fully functional, but expires 30 days after installation.*

Troubleshooting

We have tried our best to provide programs that work on most computers with the minimum system requirements. Your computer, however, may differ, and some programs may not work properly for some reason.

The two most likely problems are that you do not have enough memory (RAM) for the programs you want to use, or you have other programs running that are affecting installation or running of a program. If you get error messages like "Not enough memory" or "Setup cannot continue," try one or more of these methods and then try using the software again:

- Turn off any anti-virus software.
- Close all running programs.
- In Windows, close the CD-ROM interface and run demos or installations directly from Windows Explorer.
- Have your local computer store add more RAM to your computer.

If you still have trouble installing the items from the CD-ROM, please call the Hungry Minds Worldwide Customer Service phone number: 800-762-2974 (outside the U.S.: 317-572-3994).

APPENDIX

HUNGRY MINDS, INC.
END-USER LICENSE AGREEMENT

READ THIS. You should carefully read these terms and conditions before opening the software packet(s) included with this book ("Book"). This is a license agreement ("Agreement") between you and Hungry Minds, Inc. ("HMI"). By opening the accompanying software packet(s), you acknowledge that you have read and accept the following terms and conditions. If you do not agree and do not want to be bound by such terms and conditions, promptly return the Book and the unopened software packet(s) to the place you obtained them for a full refund.

1. **License Grant.** HMI grants to you (either an individual or entity) a nonexclusive license to use one copy of the enclosed software program(s) (collectively, the "Software") solely for your own personal or business purposes on a single computer (whether a standard computer or a workstation component of a multi-user network). The Software is in use on a computer when it is loaded into temporary memory (RAM) or installed into permanent memory (hard disk, CD-ROM, or other storage device). HMI reserves all rights not expressly granted herein.

2. **Ownership.** HMI is the owner of all right, title, and interest, including copyright, in and to the compilation of the Software recorded on the disk(s) or CD-ROM ("Software Media"). Copyright to the individual programs recorded on the Software Media is owned by the author or other authorized copyright owner of each program. Ownership of the Software and all proprietary rights relating thereto remain with HMI and its licensers.

3. **Restrictions on Use and Transfer.**

    (a) You may only (i) make one copy of the Software for backup or archival purposes, or (ii) transfer the Software to a single hard disk, provided that you keep the original for backup or archival purposes. You may not (i) rent or lease the Software, (ii) copy or reproduce the Software through a LAN or other network system or through any computer subscriber system or bulletin-board system, or (iii) modify, adapt, or create derivative works based on the Software.

    (b) You may not reverse engineer, decompile, or disassemble the Software. You may transfer the Software and user documentation on a permanent basis, provided that the transferee agrees to accept the terms and conditions of this Agreement and you retain no copies. If the Software is an update or has been updated, any transfer must include the most recent update and all prior versions.

4. **Restrictions on Use of Individual Programs.** You must follow the individual requirements and restrictions detailed for each individual program in the "What's on the CD-ROM" appendix of this Book. These limitations are also contained in the individual license agreements recorded on the Software Media. These limitations may include a requirement that after using the program for a specified period of time, the user must pay a registration fee or discontinue use. By opening the Software packet(s), you will be agreeing to abide by the licenses and restrictions for these individual programs that are detailed in the "What's on the CD-ROM" appendix and on the Software Media. None of the material on this Software Media or listed in this Book may ever be redistributed, in original or modified form, for commercial purposes

5. **Limited Warranty.**

    (a) HMI warrants that the Software and Software Media are free from defects in materials and workmanship under normal use for a period of sixty (60) days from the date of purchase of this Book. If HMI receives notification within the warranty period of defects in materials or workmanship, HMI will replace the defective Software Media.

APPENDIX

GNU General Public License

Version 2, June 1991

Copyright © 1989, 1991 Free Software Foundation, Inc.

675 Mass Ave, Cambridge, MA 02139, USA

Everyone is permitted to copy and distribute verbatim copies of this license document, but changing it is not allowed.

Preamble

The licenses for most software are designed to take away your freedom to share and change it. By contrast, the GNU General Public License is intended to guarantee your freedom to share and change free software—to make sure the software is free for all its users. This General Public License applies to most of the Free Software Foundation's software and to any other program whose authors commit to using it. (Some other Free Software Foundation software is covered by the GNU Library General Public License instead.) You can apply it to your programs, too.

When we speak of free software, we are referring to freedom, not price. Our General Public Licenses are designed to make sure that you have the freedom to distribute copies of free software (and charge for this service if you wish), that you receive source code or can get it if you want it, that you can change the software or use pieces of it in new free programs; and that you know you can do these things.

To protect your rights, we need to make restrictions that forbid anyone to deny you these rights or to ask you to surrender the rights. These restrictions translate to certain responsibilities for you if you distribute copies of the software, or if you modify it.

For example, if you distribute copies of such a program, whether gratis or for a fee, you must give the recipients all the rights that you have. You must make sure that they, too, receive or can get the source code. And you must show them these terms so they know their rights.

We protect your rights with two steps: (1) copyright the software, and (2) offer you this license which gives you legal permission to copy, distribute and/or modify the software.

Also, for each author's protection and ours, we want to make certain that everyone understands that there is no warranty for this free software. If the software is modified by someone else and passed on, we want its recipients to know that what they have is not the original, so that any problems introduced by others will not reflect on the original authors' reputations.

Finally, any free program is threatened constantly by software patents. We wish to avoid the danger that redistributors of a free program will individually obtain patent licenses, in effect making the program proprietary. To prevent this, we have made it clear that any patent must be licensed for everyone's free use or not licensed at all.

The precise terms and conditions for copying, distribution and modification follow.

GNU GENERAL PUBLIC LICENSE

TERMS AND CONDITIONS FOR COPYING, DISTRIBUTION AND MODIFICATION

0. This License applies to any program or other work which contains a notice placed by the copyright holder saying it may be distributed under the terms of this General Public License. The "Program", below, refers to any such program or work, and a "work based on the Program" means either the Program or any derivative work under copyright law: that is to say, a work containing the Program or a portion of it, either verbatim or with modifications and/or translated into another language. (Hereinafter, translation is included without limitation in the term "modification".) Each licensee is addressed as "you".

Activities other than copying, distribution and modification are not covered by this License; they are outside its scope. The act of running the Program is not restricted, and the output from the Program is covered only if its contents constitute a work based on the Program (independent of having been made by running the Program). Whether that is true depends on what the Program does.

1. You may copy and distribute verbatim copies of the Program's source code as you receive it, in any medium, provided that you conspicuously and appropriately publish on each copy an appropriate copyright notice and disclaimer of warranty; keep intact all the notices that refer to this License and to the absence of any warranty; and give any other recipients of the Program a copy of this License along with the Program.

You may charge a fee for the physical act of transferring copy, and you may at your option offer warranty protectic in exchange for a fee.

2. You may modify your copy or copies of the Program or any portion of it, thus forming a work based on the Program, and copy and distribute such modifications or work under the terms of Section 1 above, provided that you also meet all of these conditions:

a) You must cause the modified files to carry prominent notices stating that you changed the files and the date of any change.

b) You must cause any work that you distribute or publish, that in whole or in part contains or is derived from the Program or any part thereof, to be licensed as a whole at no charge to all third parties under the terms of this License.

c) If the modified program normally reads commands interactively when run, you must cause it, when started running for such interactive use in the most ordinary way, to print or display an announcement including an appropriate copyright notice and a notice that there is no warranty (or else, saying that you provide a warranty) and that users may redistribute the program under these conditions, and telling the user how to view a copy of this License. (Exception: if the Program itself is interactive but does not normally print such an announcement, your work based on the Program is not required to print an announcement.)

These requirements apply to the modified work as a whole. If identifiable sections of that work are not derived from the Program, and can be reasonably considered independent and separate works in themselves, then this License, and its terms, do not apply to those sections when you distribute them as separate works. But when you distribute the same sections as part of a whole which is a work based on the Program, the distribution of the whole must be on the terms of this License, whose permissions for other licensees extend to the entire whole, and thus to each and every part regardless of who wrote it.

Thus, it is not the intent of this section to claim rights or contest your rights to work written entirely by you; rather, the intent is to exercise the right to control the distribution of derivative or collective works based on the Program.

In addition, mere aggregation of another work not based on the Program with the Program (or with a work based on the Program) on a volume of a storage or distribution medium does not bring the other work under the scope of this License.

3. You may copy and distribute the Program (or a work based on it, under Section 2) in object code or executable form under the terms of Sections 1 and 2 above provided that you also do one of the following:

a) Accompany it with the complete corresponding machine-readable source code, which must be distributed under the terms of Sections 1 and 2 above on a medium customarily used for software interchange; or,

b) Accompany it with a written offer, valid for at least three years, to give any third party, for a charge no more than your cost of physically performing source distribution, a complete machine-readable copy of the corresponding source code, to be distributed under the terms of Sections 1 and 2 above on a medium customarily used for software interchange; or,

c) Accompany it with the information you received as to the offer to distribute corresponding source code. (This alternative is allowed only for noncommercial distribution and only if you received the program in object code or executable form with such an offer, in accord with Subsection b above.)

The source code for a work means the preferred form of the work for making modifications to it. For an executable work, complete source code means all the source code for all modules it contains, plus any associated interface definition files, plus the scripts used to control compilation and installation of the executable. However, as a special exception, the source code distributed need not include anything that is normally distributed (in either source or binary form) with the major components (compiler, kernel, and so on) of the operating system on which the executable runs, unless that component itself accompanies the executable.

If distribution of executable or object code is made by offering access to copy from a designated place, then offering equivalent access to copy the source code from the same place counts as distribution of the source code, even though third parties are not compelled to copy the source along with the object code.

4. You may not copy, modify, sublicense, or distribute the Program except as expressly provided under this License. Any attempt otherwise to copy, modify, sublicense or distribute the Program is void, and will automatically terminate your rights under this License. However, parties who have received copies, or rights, from you under this License will not have their licenses terminated so long as such parties remain in full compliance.

APPENDIX

GNU General Public License (continued)

5. You are not required to accept this License, since you have not signed it. However, nothing else grants you permission to modify or distribute the Program or its derivative works. These actions are prohibited by law if you do not accept this License. Therefore, by modifying or distributing the Program (or any work based on the Program), you indicate your acceptance of this License to do so, and all its terms and conditions for copying, distributing or modifying the Program or works based on it.

6. Each time you redistribute the Program (or any work based on the Program), the recipient automatically receives a license from the original licensor to copy, distribute or modify the Program subject to these terms and conditions. You may not impose any further restrictions on the recipients' exercise of the rights granted herein. You are not responsible for enforcing compliance by third parties to this License.

7. If, as a consequence of a court judgment or allegation of patent infringement or for any other reason (not limited to patent issues), conditions are imposed on you (whether by court order, agreement or otherwise) that contradict the conditions of this License, they do not excuse you from the conditions of this License. If you cannot distribute so as to satisfy simultaneously your obligations under this License and any other pertinent obligations, then as a consequence you may not distribute the Program at all. For example, if a patent license would not permit royalty-free redistribution of the Program by all those who receive copies directly or indirectly through you, then the only way you could satisfy both it and this License would be to refrain entirely from distribution of the Program.

If any portion of this section is held invalid or unenforceable under any particular circumstance, the balance of the section is intended to apply and the section as a whole is intended to apply in other circumstances.

It is not the purpose of this section to induce you to infringe any patents or other property right claims or to contest validity of any such claims; this section has the sole purpose of protecting the integrity of the free software distribution system, which is implemented by public license practices. Many people have made generous contributions to the wide range of software distributed through that system in reliance on consistent application of that system; it is up to the author/donor to decide if he or she is willing to distribute software through any other system and a licensee cannot impose that choice.

This section is intended to make thoroughly clear what is believed to be a consequence of the rest of this License.

8. If the distribution and/or use of the Program is restricted in certain countries either by patents or by copyrighted interfaces, the original copyright holder who places the Program under this License may add an explicit geographical distribution limitation excluding those countries, so that distribution is permitted only in or among countries not thus excluded. In such case, this License incorporates the limitation as if written in the body of this License.

9. The Free Software Foundation may publish revised and/or new versions of the General Public License from time to time. Such new versions will be similar in spirit to the present version, but may differ in detail to address new problems or concerns.

Each version is given a distinguishing version number. If the Program specifies a version number of this License which applies to it and "any later version", you have the option of following the terms and conditions either of that version or of any later version published by the Free Software Foundation. If the Program does not specify a version number of this License, you may choose any version ever published by the Free Software Foundation.

10. If you wish to incorporate parts of the Program into other free programs whose distribution conditions are different, write to the author to ask for permission. For software which is copyrighted by the Free Software Foundation, write to the Free Software Foundation; we sometimes make exceptions for this. Our decision will be guided by the two goals of preserving the free status of all derivatives of our free software and of promoting the sharing and reuse of software generally.

NO WARRANTY

11. BECAUSE THE PROGRAM IS LICENSED FREE OF CHARGE, THERE IS NO WARRANTY FOR THE PROGRAM, TO THE EXTENT PERMITTED BY APPLICABLE LAW. EXCEPT WHEN OTHERWISE STATED IN WRITING THE COPYRIGHT HOLDERS AND/OR OTHER PARTIES PROVIDE THE PROGRAM

"AS IS" WITHOUT WARRANTY OF ANY KIND, EITHER EXPRESSED OR IMPLIED, INCLUDING, BUT NOT LIMITED TO, THE IMPLIED WARRANTIES OF MERCHANTABILITY AND FITNESS FOR A PARTICULAR PURPOSE. THE ENTIRE RISK AS TO THE QUALITY AND PERFORMANCE OF THE PROGRAM IS WITH YOU. SHOULD THE PROGRAM PROVE DEFECTIVE, YOU ASSUME THE COST OF ALL NECESSARY SERVICING, REPAIR OR CORRECTION.

12. IN NO EVENT UNLESS REQUIRED BY APPLICABLE LAW OR AGREED TO IN WRITING WILL ANY COPYRIGHT HOLDER, OR ANY OTHER PARTY WHO MAY MODIFY AND/OR REDISTRIBUTE THE PROGRAM AS PERMITTED ABOVE, BE LIABLE TO YOU FOR DAMAGES, INCLUDING ANY GENERAL, SPECIAL, INCIDENTAL OR CONSEQUENTIAL DAMAGES ARISING OUT OF THE USE OR INABILITY TO USE THE PROGRAM (INCLUDING BUT NOT LIMITED TO LOSS OF DATA OR DATA BEING RENDERED INACCURATE OR LOSSES SUSTAINED BY YOU OR THIRD PARTIES OR A FAILURE OF THE PROGRAM TO OPERATE WITH ANY OTHER PROGRAMS), EVEN IF SUCH HOLDER OR OTHER PARTY HAS BEEN ADVISED OF THE POSSIBILITY OF SUCH DAMAGES.

END OF TERMS AND CONDITIONS

Appendix: How to Apply These Terms to Your New Programs

If you develop a new program, and you want it to be of the greatest possible use to the public, the best way to achieve this is to make it free software which everyone can redistribute and change under these terms.

To do so, attach the following notices to the program. It is safest to attach them to the start of each source file to most effectively convey the exclusion of warranty; and each file should have at least the "copyright" line and a pointer to where the full notice is found:

<one line to give the program's name and a brief idea of what it does.>

Copyright © 19yy <name of author>

This program is free software; you can redistribute it and/or modify it under the terms of the GNU General Public License as published by the Free Software Foundation; either version 2 of the License, or (at your option) any later version.

This program is distributed in the hope that it will be useful, but WITHOUT ANY WARRANTY; without even the implied warranty of MERCHANTABILITY or FITNESS FOR A PARTICULAR PURPOSE. See the GNU General Public License for more details.

You should have received a copy of the GNU General Public License along with this program; if not, write to the Free Software Foundation, Inc., 675 Mass Ave, Cambridge, MA 02139, USA.

Also add information on how to contact you by electronic and paper mail.

If the program is interactive, make it output a short notice like this when it starts in an interactive mode:

Gnomovision version 69, Copyright © 19yy name of author

Gnomovision comes with ABSOLUTELY NO WARRANTY; for details type 'show w'. This is free software, and you are welcome to redistribute it under certain conditions; type 'show c' for details.

The hypothetical commands 'show w' and 'show c' should show the appropriate parts of the General Public License. Of course, the commands you use may be called something other than 'show w' and 'show c'; they could even be mouse-clicks or menu items—whatever suits your program.

You should also get your employer (if you work as a programmer) or your school, if any, to sign a "copyright disclaimer" for the program, if necessary. Here is a sample; alter the names:

Yoyodyne, Inc., hereby disclaims all copyright interest in the program 'Gnomovision' (which makes passes at compilers) written by James Hacker.

<signature of Ty Coon>, 1 April 1989

Ty Coon, President of Vice

This General Public License does not permit incorporating your program into proprietary programs. If your program is a subroutine library, you may consider it more useful to permit linking proprietary applications with the library. If this is what you want to do, use the GNU Library General Public License instead of this License.

<Picture: ASbutton>   GNU General Public License

INDEX

INDEX

INDEX

INDEX

INDEX

(continued)

INDEX

Read Less – Learn More

Visual

with these two-color Visual™ guides

 "Master It" tips provide additional topic coverage.

Title	ISBN	Price
Master Active Directory™ VISUALLY™	0-7645-3425-4	$39.99
Master Microsoft® Access 2000 VISUALLY™	0-7645-6048-4	$39.99
Master Microsoft® Office 2000 VISUALLY™	0-7645-6050-6	$39.99
Master Microsoft® Word 2000 VISUALLY™	0-7645-6046-8	$39.99
Master Office 97 VISUALLY™	0-7645-6036-0	$39.99
Master Photoshop® 5.5 VISUALLY™	0-7645-6045-X	$39.99
Master Red Hat® Linux® VISUALLY™	0-7645-3436-X	$39.99
Master VISALLY™ Adobe® Illustrator®, Premiere®, After Effects®, and Photoshop®	0-7645-3668-0	$39.99
Master VISUALLY™ HTML 4 & XHTML™ 1	0-7645-3454-8	$39.99
Master VISUALLY™ Microsoft® Windows® Me Millennium Edition	0-7645-3496-3	$39.99
Master VISUALLY™ Photoshop® 6	0-7645-3541-2	$39.99
Master VISUALLY™ Web Design	0-7645-3610-9	$39.99
Master VISUALLY™ Windows® 2000 Server	0-7645-3426-2	$39.99
Master VISUALLY ™ Windows® XP	0-7645-3621-4	$39.99
Master Windows® 95 VISUALLY™	0-7645-6024-7	$39.99
Master Windows® 98 VISUALLY™	0-7645-6034-4	$39.99
Master Windows® 2000 Professional VISUALLY™	0-7645-3421-1	$39.99

TRADE & INDIVIDUAL ORDERS

Phone: **(800) 762-2974**
or **(317) 572-3993**
FAX : **(800) 550-2747**
or **(317) 572-4002**

EDUCATIONAL ORDERS & DISCOUNTS

Phone: **(800) 434-2086**
FAX : **(317) 572-4005**

CORPORATE ORDERS FOR VISUAL™ SERIES

Phone: **(800) 469-6616**
FAX : **(905) 890-9434**

Qty	ISBN	Title	Price	Total

Shipping & Handling Charges

	Description	First book	Each add'l. book	Total
Domestic	Normal	$4.50	$1.50	$
	Two Day Air	$8.50	$2.50	$
	Overnight	$18.00	$3.00	$
International	Surface	$8.00	$8.00	$
	Airmail	$16.00	$16.00	$
	DHL Air	$17.00	$17.00	$

Subtotal _____

CA residents add applicable sales tax _____

IN, MA and MD residents add 5% sales tax _____

IL residents add 6.25% sales tax _____

RI residents add 7% sales tax _____

TX residents add 8.25% sales tax _____

Shipping _____

Total _____

Ship to:

Name _____

Address _____

Company _____

City/State/Zip _____

Daytime Phone _____

Payment: □ Check to Hungry Minds (US Funds Only)
□ Visa   □ Mastercard   □ American Express

Card # _____ Exp. _____ Signature _____

Hungry Minds™

maranGraphics